Schumpeter's Venture Money

Schumpeter's Venture Money

MICHAEL PENEDER, ANDREAS RESCH

OXFORD
UNIVERSITY PRESS

OXFORD
UNIVERSITY PRESS

Great Clarendon Street, Oxford, OX2 6DP,
United Kingdom

Oxford University Press is a department of the University of Oxford.
It furthers the University's objective of excellence in research, scholarship,
and education by publishing worldwide. Oxford is a registered trade mark of
Oxford University Press in the UK and in certain other countries

First Edition published in 2021

Impression: 1

Published in the United States of America by Oxford University Press

198 Madison Avenue, New York, NY 10016, United States of America

British Library Cataloguing in Publication Data
Data available

Library of Congress Control Number: 2020944055

ISBN 978–0–19–880438–3

DOI: 10.1093/oso/9780198804383.001.0001

Printed and bound in Great Britain by
Clays Ltd, Elcograf S.p.A.

Acknowledgments

We are grateful for the access and support provided by the Austrian State Archives, the Municipal and Provincial Archives of Vienna, the Harvard University Archives, and the Georges F. Doriot Collection at the Harvard Business School. Ulrich Hedtke provided valuable hints and generously gave us access to numerous documents from his private archive in Berlin. Georg Herrnstadt supplied documents from the estate of his mother, Gundl Steinmetz-Herrnstadt. In 1999, Wolfgang Stolper provided valuable comments on early preliminary results.

We are especially indebted to the probing questions, constructive comments, and suggestions provided during conversations on our research, for example, by Felix Butschek, Tom McCraw, Kurt Dopfer, Caroline Gerschlager, Christian Glocker, Takeo Hoshi, William Janeway, Dale Jorgenson, Martin Kenney, Heinz D. Kurz, Richard Nelson, Tom Nicholas, Atanas Pekanov, Bill Sahlman, Frederic M. Scherer, Andrei Shleifer, and Gunther Tichy. We also thank Astrid Nolte for her invaluable support in proofreading the text. As a matter of course, only the authors bear responsibility for any remaining omissions, errors, or imprecisions.

The idea for this book arose from repeated meetings of the two authors at Kurt Dopfer's Vienna Seminar on Evolutionary Economics. Each chapter benefitted from numerous suggestions and critical comments freely shared between both authors. It may be worth mentioning that Andreas wrote Chapters 8 to 10, while Michael bears the principal responsibility for the remainder of the monograph.

Finally, we want to thank our families, friends, and colleagues for their enduring patience and support. Michael dedicates the work especially to his wife Beate and their children, Jonas and Theresa.

Contents

List of Figures

List of Tables

1
Introduction—Schumpeter's life and vision

Ever-newer waters flow on those who step into the same rivers.
(Heraclitus, ca. 535–475 BCE)

In many economic disciplines—ranging from entrepreneurship, innovation research, and industrial organization to growth theory, business cycles, business history, and public choice—various ideas of Josef Schumpeter have become widely accepted or even commonplace. Yet this is not the case in the study of money and finance, which in fact consumed a disproportionally high portion of his time, effort, and attention. This neglect partly has to do with difficulties in dealing with his dedicated focus on innovation and the financing of new ventures. Seeking to dispel mysteries and misunderstandings, the book will follow Schumpeter's distinctive angle to grasp the originality of his "venture theory" of money and economic development.

This introductory chapter begins with a brief prologue on the logos of "perpetual change"—arguably the single most characteristic attribute of Schumpeter's theoretical vision. Perpetual change also characterized his turbulent personal vita. Next we therefore offer a brief synopsis of his life and work, referring to a number of excellent biographical studies for further reading. The final section explains the aim, scope, and plan of the book, laying out the individual threads that will intertwine to tell its story.

1.1 *Panta rhei*—a prologue

Panta rhei, everything flows, or "all entities move and nothing remains still."[1] This notion, which *Heraclitus* proclaimed to be the major *logos* or principle of universal order, is arguably also the most distinctive characteristic of Schumpeter's vision of the economy—one that Stanley Metcalfe described as "restless capitalism."[2] Beyond merely acknowledging that objects continuously change, it considers change a basic category of existence, in which hardly anything remains constant except change itself.

[1] As quoted in Plato, Cratylus Paragraph Crat. 401 section d line 5.

[2] Metcalfe (1998).

Schumpeter's Venture Money. Michael Peneder and Andreas Resch, Oxford University Press (2021). © Michael Peneder and Andreas Resch.
DOI: 10.1093/oso/9780198804383.003.0001

Championing an ontology of "becoming" instead of "being," Heraclitus encountered strong opposition. For example, Plato resented the implication that something cannot exist if it does not change. Relatedly, early Christian scholars opposed the logos of Heraclitus, because of its presumed denial of a pure and perfect, and therefore immutable, eternal being behind nature. In turn, for instance, in *History of Economic Analysis* (*HEA*), Schumpeter expressed doubts about Plato's rigidly "stationary ideal."[3]

From a contemporary perspective, however, the proclaimed irreversibility of all natural states stands in striking accordance with the *laws of thermodynamics*, which arose by the middle of the nineteenth century and provided a "general account of the time asymmetry of ordinary physical processes."[4] In short, the first law states that in a closed system the total quantity of energy is always conserved, and that energy can neither be created nor destroyed, but only flow and change its form. The second law states that in a closed system entropy, which is a measure of molecular disorder or randomness, increases over time. Hence, energy degrades in an irreversible process toward increasing disorder until none is available for useful work. According to the third law, entropy approaches its constant maximum value in the final state of thermodynamic equilibrium, where there can be no further spontaneous change and the system "is completely identified with its environment."[5] In other words, the system ceases to exist.

In contrast, open systems maintain their internal structure by absorbing low-entropy energy from the environment. Moreover, they allow for novel and complex structures to emerge, typically implying a more effective use of free energy.[6] Living organisms can evolve because they are such open systems. By the middle of the nineteenth century, *Charles Darwin* (1809–82) had established a set of general principles of evolutionary change in natural history. His concept of "natural selection" was a process of local adaptation, which allowed an increasing variety of organisms to exploit ever more ecological niches, thus effectively supporting their means of subsistence. It is foremost a theory of speciation and functional differentiation under the conditions of a perpetual struggle for existence in the natural environment. Natural history is therefore a process driven by the interplay of genetic *variation*, *selection* in favor of better adapted varieties, and the *accumulation* of successful traits by means of genetic inheritance.

Josef Alois Schumpeter (1883–1950) was a progeny of the nineteenth century and its scientific advances. In economics, this applies foremost to the so-called "marginalist revolution," which he thoroughly absorbed from the founders of the Austrian School of economics at his *alma mater* in Vienna. This came with a strong awareness that the analytical tools of perfect equilibria can be useful, but are invalid as descriptions of reality. Unlike many of his peers, he never discarded the

[3] *HEA* (1954, p. 556). [4] Drake (2018b). [5] Nicolis and Prigogine (1989, p. 55).
[6] Georgescu-Roegen (1971); Ayres (1994).

historical approach, thereby maintaining a strong preoccupation with perpetual change and development in all social affairs. Innovation thus became his pivotal focus, further elaborated in a series of general principles thought to govern economic development. Distinguishing between *adaptive* and *creative* response, his aim was to open the doors to a comprehensive analysis of dynamic systems:

> Whenever an economy or a sector of an economy adapts itself to a change in its data in the way that traditional theory describes [...] we may speak of the development as adaptive response. And whenever the economy or an industry or some firms in an industry do something else, something that is outside of the range of existing practice, we may speak of creative response. [The latter] can always be understood *ex post*; but it can practically never be understood ex ante, [while it still] shapes the whole course of subsequent events and their "long-run" outcome. ("The Creative Response in Economic History" (CRH), 1947, p. 150)

There is a deep connection between Schumpeter and the above strands of thought. For instance, from 1934 to 1936 he mentored a young Romanian mathematician and statistician named *Nicholas Georgescu-Roegen* (1906–94), who is best known for *The Entropy Law and the Economic Process* (1971), which became a foundational work of ecological economics. Sharing his dedicated interest in economic structure and dynamics,[7] Schumpeter offered him a position at the economics faculty at Harvard and planned to work on a joint treatise.[8] The plans failed when Georgescu-Roegen returned to Romania. However, Schumpeter apparently had a lasting impact. In Georgescu-Roegen's own words: "Every single one of his distinctive remarks were seeds that inspired my later works. In this way, Schumpeter turned me into an economist."[9] Among other aspects, both were apparently influenced by the fact that the laws of thermodynamics command irreversibility and perpetual qualitative change.[10]

More widely known, however, are Schumpeter's struggles with the Darwinian principles of evolutionary change.[11] At a younger age, he was highly critical of "all kinds of evolutionary thought that centre in Darwin—at least if this means no more than reasoning by analogy." Associating it with the mistaken notion of a "uniform unilinear development," he proclaimed that "the evolutionary idea is now discredited in our field" and that "with all the hasty generalisations in which the word 'evolution' plays a part, many of us have lost patience."[12] When he later wrote the *History of Economic Analysis* (henceforth *HEA*) Schumpeter drew a sharper

[7] "The paramount importance of time for economics comes from the fact that it envelops every human action, actually, all actions of every life bearing structure" (Georgescu-Roegen, 1994, p. 235).
[8] Samuelson (1966); Heinzel (2013). [9] Georgescu-Roegen (1992, p. 130).
[10] Heinzel (2013, p. 263). [11] Nelson and Winter (1982); Metcalfe (1998).
[12] *Theorie der wirtschaftlichen Entwicklung* (*TED*; 1911/34, p. 57).

distinction. Yet he still forcefully denounced Social Darwinism and its infamous proponent Herbert Spencer:

> No other word but "silly" will fit the man who failed to see that, by carrying laissez-faire liberalism to the extent of disapproving of sanitary regulations, public education, public postal service, and the like, he made his ideal ridiculous and that in fact he wrote what would have served very well as a satire on the policy he advocated. Neither his economics nor his ethics [...] are worth our while. What is worth our while to note is the argument that any policy aiming at social betterment stands condemned on the ground that it interferes with natural selection and therefore with the progress of humanity. The reader should observe, however, that the almost pathetic nonsense could have been avoided and that the sound element in his argument could have been partly salvaged by adding "unless methods more humane and more scientific than natural selection can be found."
>
> (*HEA*, 1954, p. 773f)

Conversely, in HEA Schumpeter acknowledged Darwin's importance in no fewer than seven independent entries, reserving for him some of his most generous accolades. He praised the *Origin of Species* as "one of the most important pieces of scientific history ever written" and its author as "a living and walking compliment to himself and also to the economic and cultural system that produced him."[13] Essentially, Schumpeter appreciated Darwin's principles of evolutionary change, as applied to natural history, while himself claiming a distinct faculty for the study of economic development.

1.2 Under the *skin*, not the *veil* of money

Panta rhei, or the "continuous stream of ever new waters," may also be an apt characterization of monetary history. In short, money has transformed from being simple symbols of account to precious items that facilitate exchange, and from there to plain social conventions increasingly cast into mere digital data. *Milton Friedman* (1912–2006) and *Anna J. Schwartz* (1915–2012), two influential proponents of monetarism, explained their fascination with the fact that money "is so full of mystery and paradox." Owing to "fiction" and "myth," people accept pieces of paper as means of payment, because they are confident that others will do the same: "The pieces of green paper have value because everybody thinks they have value, and everybody thinks they have value because in his experience they have had value".[14] Monetarism is best known for its revitalization of the

[13] *HEA* (1954, p. 444).

[14] Friedman and Schwartz (1963, p. 695).

classical quantity theory. It portrays money as a *veil* that is detached from and has no systematic direct impact on real production and income in the long-term. In his influential synthesis of the classical orthodoxy, *John Stuart Mill* (1806–73) expressed it as follows:

> There cannot, in short, be intrinsically a more insignificant thing, in the economy of society, than money; [...] The relations of commodities to one another remain unaltered by money: the only new relation introduced is [...] how the exchange value of money itself is determined. (Mill, 1848/71, p. 351)

In other words, money only matters in determining the average price level, which must vary in exact proportion to its overall quantity. As a consequence, the latter has no systematic impact on production or real income, that is, the amount and type of goods people will actually consume. But there is one exception: since this "fiction" is neither fragile nor indestructible,[15] over expansion or contraction of the money base can tear the veil and cause an economic crisis. Thus, the nexus between finance and growth mainly exists in the negative and is to be contained by sound monetary policy.

Schumpeter dissented from the classical orthodoxy in many respects. Characteristically, he liked to contrast the image of money as a veil with that of money as a *skin*, that is, an organ which is invariably and intimately connected to the living organism.[16] The skin carries out indispensable functions, such as enabling the sensation of touch and heat or helping to regulate body temperature, and at the same time it reflects the overall health of an organism. Similarly, the condition of a monetary system simultaneously has an impact on, responds to, and mirrors the performance of the economy at large. In short, Schumpeter treated money as endogenous to the economic system.

Having experienced the times of hyperinflation in Austria and therein lost a fortune, Schumpeter clearly acknowledged the dangers of a mismanaged currency. However, in contrast to the classical orthodoxy, along with monetarism and other followers of the quantity theory, he refused to throw the baby out with the bath water. Instead, he deliberately embraced the historical evolution and growing speciation of money and finance into increasingly complex social institutions that are malleable to the various needs of entrepreneurial finance. He absorbed it into a deliberately monetary theory of development, in which "credit"—defined broadly as any form of pre-financing of new ventures—is the indispensable *alter ego* of entrepreneurial initiative, jointly fostering innovation, structural change, and the growth of real income.

[15] Friedman and Schwartz (1963, p. 696).

[16] *Das Wesen des Geldes* (*WDG*; 1970, p. 2).

However, before we turn to these core themes of the monograph, we would like to briefly summarize selected biographical facts in order to plot the personal background of Schumpeter's diverse monetary ventures.

1.3 Schumpeter's life and work

Finally, *panta rhei*, the principle of perpetual change, offers a succinct description of Schumpeter's eventful life story. Living during a time of great political and social transformation, two world wars, and deep economic crisis, his path was one of professional struggles, alternating triumphs and defeats, personal drama, and exceptional endurance (Tables 1.1 and 1.2). Having grown up as a half-orphan, he would marry three times and even be accused of bigamy. In addition to his numerous travels, he resided in Moravia, Graz, Vienna, Chernivtsi, Cairo, and Bonn before finally settling down in Cambridge, Massachusetts, at Harvard University. Among his many professional activities, he worked as a lawyer, state secretary for finance, bank president, and "proto-venture capitalist." Yet despite these temporary distractions from his main calling to pursue an academic career, his scientific output was exuberant. It comprised various extensive monographs in addition to innumerable articles and speeches. It is no wonder that his life and work has been the subject of numerous biographies and treatises which have regularly found new angles to explore. Given the wealth of existing monographs

Table 1.1 Selected milestones of Schumpeter's life and work Pt. 1

Year	Milestones
	Adolescence
1883	Born in Třešt
1887	Death of his father (a textile manufacturer)
1888	Relocation to Graz
1893–901	Education at an elite highschool in Vienna
1901–6	Studies and PhD at the University of Vienna
1902–5	Management studies at the Export Academy
1906–7	Study trips (Berlin, London, Cambridge, etc.)
1907–20	First Marriage with *Gladys Ricarde Seaver*
1907	Practice of law in Cairo
	Science prodigy
1908	*Das Wesen und der Hauptinhalt der theoretischen Nationalökonomie* (*WHN*)
1909–11	Professor at the University of Czernowitz
1911	*Theory of Economic Development* (*TED*)
1911–21	Professor at the University of Graz
1913	Visiting professor at Columbia University
1917–18	*Money and the Social Product* (MSP)
1918	*Die Krise des Steuerstaates* (*KSS*)

Table 1.2 Selected milestones of Schumpeter's life and work Pt. 2

Year	Milestones
	The "great waste"
1919	State secretary for finance (March to August)
1921–24	President of the Biedermann Bank
1921–25	"Proto-Venture Capitalist"
1925–32	Professor at the University of Bonn
1925	Second marriage with *Annie Reisinger*
1926	Within a short period of time his mother dies, then his wife and son in childbirth
	Harvard
1927/30	Visiting professor at Harvard University
1930	Co-founder of the *Econometric Society*
1931	Visiting professor in Tokyo
1932–50	Professor at Harvard University
1937	Third marriage with *Elizabeth Boody Firuski*
1939	US citizenship; *Business Cycles* (*BC*)
1942	*Capitalism, Socialism and Democracy* (*CSD*)
1947	*Creative Response in Economic History* (CRH)
1948	President of the American Economic Association
1950	Dies on January the 8th
1954	*History of Economic Analysis* (*HEA*)
1970	*Das Wesen des Geldes* (*WDG*)

and shorter articles on Schumpeter,[17] in this introduction a brief biographical sketch should be sufficient to provide a context for our later analyses.

Education and early career

Schumpeter was born in 1883 in the Moravian town of Třešt, which at the time belonged to the Habsburg Empire and is now part of the Czech Republic. His mother came from a town near Vienna, while his father was a local textile manufacturer who belonged to the German-speaking minority of the region. His father died as a result of a hunting accident when Josef was only 4 years old. Taking her son and moving to Graz, his mother then married a retired army officer and member of the Austrian nobility. Her marriage enabled Schumpeter to attend the Theresianum, an elite secondary school in Vienna. There, he received a rigorous education, not only in mathematics, science, and history, but also in Latin, Greek, English, Italian, and French. His knowledge of many languages was clearly instrumental to his later career. It not only compelled him to practice his

[17] See, for instance, März (1983/91); Allen (1991); Swedberg (1991); Stolper (1994); Shionoya (1997); Hanusch (1999); McCraw (2007); Andersen (2011); Cantner and Dopfer (2015); or Sturn (2016).

skills by reading, but enabled him to directly source literatures from exceptionally varied historical and geographical origins.

In 1901 he enrolled at the University of Vienna to study jurisprudence (economics was not yet an independent branch of study). There, he attended the classes of Eugen Böhm-Bawerk, Friedrich Wieser, and other proponents of the Austrian School of economics. Furthermore, he had to take a substantial number of courses in philosophy, a field in which the positivist legacy of the physicist and philosopher of science Ernst Mach still exerted a strong influence. According to Andersen, Schumpeter additionally "designed for himself an extensive and fairly advanced programme of mathematics courses."[18] This rendered Schumpeter distinctly capable of absorbing modern developments in economic theory and embracing an open perspective on methodology—especially when compared to his peers from the Austrian and German Schools, who displayed little inclination for and often hostility toward the use of mathematical tools in economics.

Schumpeter also signed up to study management at the Export Academy, the precursor of today's Vienna University of Economics and Business. Between 1902 and 1905 he took classes that included economic geography, commercial law, and accounting, as well as the handling of business correspondence in German, English, and French. Yet, according to our findings and judging from the quite poor grading, he seems not to have taken these studies very seriously. For example, on a scale ranging from one ("excellent") to five ("failed") he barely passed his introductory courses in business accounting and bookkeeping with a grade of four ("sufficient") in his first semester, and then failed both in the subsequent courses.[19] In retrospect, one could consider these poor grades a bad omen for his business ventures during the 1920s.

After earning his PhD at the University of Vienna in 1906, Schumpeter set out on educational journeys to Berlin, Paris, London, Oxford, and Cambridge. In 1907, he married his first wife, *Gladys Ricarde Seaver* (1871-1932). The couple moved to Cairo, where Schumpeter represented clients at the International Mixed Tribunal and made a certain fortune. Simultaneously, he managed to write his habilitation thesis: *Das Wesen und der Hauptinhalt der theoretischen Nationalökonomie* (henceforth *WHN*, 1908).[20]

Habilitation made Schumpeter eligible to hold a chair at a university. He initially became an associate professor at the University of Cernivtsi,[21] where he

[18] Andersen (2011, p. 22f). Andersen estimated that mathematics "covered nearly 30 per cent of the half of Schumpeter's syllabus that was not dedicated to jurisprudence."

[19] Schumpeter's studies at the Export Academy went largely unnoticed by his biographers, but was pointed out by Hedtke and Swedberg (2000, p. 5). Our recent findings on his grading originate from the *Archive of the Vienna University of Economics and Business*, Report Cards of Josef Schumpeter, 1902/3 to 1904/5, and First Main Catalogue, First Volume, Colloquia (from 1901 to 1908/9).

[20] The title translates as "The Nature and Content of Theoretical Economics."

[21] Then called Czernowitz, located in the Habsburg Empire's eastern provinces (now western Ukraine).

authored what is arguably his most original and important work:[22] the *Theory of Economic Development* (henceforth *TED*; translated to English in 1934). In 1911, Schumpeter became a full professor at the University of Graz. When in 1913 he left for Columbia University to work as visiting professor for a year, his wife Gladys chose to return to England. After Schumpeter came back to Graz, the outbreak of the First World War made her return unlikely and the communication between them increasingly difficult. According to McCraw, by 1920 he considered himself unmarried, without ever having bothered to get a formal divorce.[23] More recently, however, new evidence confirmed that the spouses were formally divorced on December 24, 1920, at the district court "Innere Stadt" in Vienna.

The "great waste"

During the First World War Schumpeter was a pronounced pacifist opposing attempts at a custom union with Germany, since he feared this would be the first step toward a further consolidation of the German-speaking territories.[24] In private communication, he advocated a separate peace treaty of the Austro-Hungarian Empire with the Allied forces, anticipating that the Habsburg monarchy would in the end suffer the greatest losses among any war participants. According to McCraw, his political vision at the time was to save the empire through a gradual transformation toward constitutional monarchy, similar to the British example.[25]

Yet with the end of the First World War the political order in which Schumpeter had grown up inevitably fell apart. Immersing himself first in politics and then business, in the war's aftermath he also found his private life shattered by a series of spectacular failures. Schumpeter later referred to this period as the *gran rifiuto* or "great waste" of his life.[26] It began quite innocuously with an economic text on the crisis of public finance (*Die Krise des Steuerstaates*; henceforth *KSS*, 1918), in which Schumpeter addressed the challenges of economic reconstruction. On recommendation of Rudolf Hilferding[27] he became state secretary for finance in

[22] Hanusch and Pyka (2007). [23] McCraw (2007, p. 87f).

[24] A letter written in 1916 to his former teacher and member of parliament Heinrich Lammasch, demonstrates his alertness to the prospect of unification: "Consider what all this means [...] A Prussian-Lutheran-militaristic Central Europe ('Mitteleuropa') would from now on confront the rest of the world like a predatory animal. [...] *that* Austria which we know and love would cease to exist" (quoted from McCraw, 2007, p. 91).

[25] McCraw, (2007, p. 92ff). Hedtke (2004a,b) offers the most comprehensive analysis of Schumpeter's political memoranda.

[26] McCraw (2007, p. 104).

[27] And with the consent of Emil Lederer and Otto Bauer, both former classmates of Schumpeter in the famous seminar held by Böhm-Bawerk at the University of Vienna.

the coalition government headed by the socialist Karl Renner in March 1919. However, lacking any party affiliation, independent power base, political experience or skills, he was forced to resign by August of the same year when the cabinet refused to support his first financial plan.

To make a brief story[28] even shorter, within five months Schumpeter had managed to alienate the socialist members of the cabinet (in particular the foreign minister Otto Bauer) by openly opposing unification with Germany, advocating the complete repayment of the state's debts, and impeding nationalization by supporting the sale of industrial shares to foreign investors. At the same time, he lost the support of the conservative party by demanding a capital levy on all liquid assets of companies and private citizens in order to curb the post-war inflation. While the economics behind his proposals seem reasonable, Schumpeter lacked the awareness and skills with which to form political alliances and antagonized the cabinet with his solitary, know-it-all demeanor, which bordered on disloyalty. In light of these shortcomings, few people appreciated his economic principles. Of those who did, one was his former teacher at the University of Vienna, Friedrich Wieser. In his diaries he acknowledged that Schumpeter was "not misled by prevalent sentiment" and "has courage, an asset which cannot be over-praised."[29]

After Schumpeter dropped out of the cabinet he had no inclination to return to his academic position at the University of Graz. Instead, he was keen to live out his theoretical vision by actively participating in the post-war reconstruction effort, both as president of the Biedermann Bank and as the co-founder of an industrial group investing in new, mostly technology-oriented start-up companies. Both ventures, however, failed, leaving Schumpeter with a large personal debt to pay off throughout many years to come. Still, he was fortunate to be cleared of any legal accusations.

In 1925, Schumpeter escaped his inevitable social decline in Vienna by accepting an appointment to hold a chair at the University of Bonn. With the prospect of another prestigious social position and regular income, he rushed to propose marriage to *Anna Josefina Reisinger* (1903–26).[30] Yet, according to Austrian law, Schumpeter's earlier divorce was considered an obstacle to (re-)marriage and required formal special permission.[31] In Catholic Austria this permission was

[28] See, for instance, März (1983/91) and Stolper (1991).

[29] Quotation from McCraw (2007, p. 101).

[30] Anna Reisinger was twenty years younger than him and the daughter of the concierge of the apartment building, where Schumpeter's mother lived in Vienna. Despite their parents' disapproval, neither the age difference, nor different social rank, nor the fact that Anna had had an abortion from a previous relationship seem to have mattered much. Their diaries and letters provide ample evidence of the genuine affection between the two. See, for example, McCraw (2007, p. 113ff).

[31] From 1922 on, a very vague law provided for the possibility of granting special permission for marriage despite such an obstacle. That same year, Vienna was separated from Lower Austria and became governed as an independent province by a Social Democrat majority. The provincial governor of Vienna, Albert Sever, unlike his conservative colleagues in the other provinces, made generous use of this possibility.

generally denied by the conservative authorities, but at the time afforded liberally in "Red Vienna." Josef and Annie had to leave the Catholic church so that Schumpeter could apply for the indulgence of the "marriage obstacle of marriage," which was given without delay. He and his fiancée then joined the Evangelical Church of the Augsburg Confession and married on November 5, 1925 in the Protestant city parish church. Neither set of parents attended the ceremony, but *Hans Kelsen* (1881–1973), a famous Jewish legal scholar and "architect" of the Austrian republican constitution was his best man.[32]

His private happiness with Anna greatly helped Schumpeter cope with his acute financial distress and new professional start. Their life indeed took a very positive turn, as both Anna and Josef were well received in Bonn and excitedly expecting a baby. However, personal tragedy would soon impede their return to a stable life. In 1926, Josef's mother passed away. Six weeks later, Anna and the couple's new-born son died in childbirth. Having effectively lost at once the three most important people in his life, Schumpeter never fully recovered. The break is apparent in both his personality and his scientific output, which changed from the almost frivolous optimism and self-confidence of his early years to a darker and more pessimistic, sometimes cynical mindset. In a letter to Gustav Stolper, Schumpeter clearly articulated what he needed to keep his mind together: "[e]verything now hangs on my ability to work."[33]

Monetary analysis

In the following years, the major focus of Schumpeter's intellectual effort was an attempted general treatise on money. However, as he did not rapidly recover from the above catastrophes, his capacity for focused and productive work was diminished. Serious writing on the book probably began in 1926, but he was never able to consolidate his ideas into his aspired general theory of money. Despite repeated announcements, the *money book* never materialized into a cohesive work which he would have considered worthy of publication.

Though his monetary writings remained scattered and fragmented, his general vision was formed early on and his ideas appear strikingly consistent from the first to the last, even unfinished posthumous publications.[34] Characteristic elements already appeared in his comprehensive survey of the received doctrine in *WHN* (1908). Therein, Schumpeter announced planned extensions, which he realized a few years later in *TED* (1911/34). There, the major elements of his monetary theory were in place, though its broader foundations often remained implicit and little-developed. In *Money and the Social Product* (henceforth MSP, 1917–18/56;

[32] Budischowsky (2014).

[33] From a letter to Gustav Stolper, quotation from McCraw (2007, p. 140).

[34] See also Marget (1951) or Naderer (1990).

translated to English in 1956) he set out to expand on the general role of money as a social technology for the settling of accounts. Influenced by Wieser, he thereby elaborated an income-expenditure approach with endogenous money that stood in contrast with the traditional quantity theory. It is mostly based on this theme of a social clearing mechanism that he envisaged delivering a general treatise within which he would integrate monetary theory and his dynamic vision of the economy.

During the years in Bonn, Schumpeter expanded on the previous text of *MSP*, adding new chapters on such diverse aspects as the history of monetary thought and the sociology of money or index numbers, and drafting detailed financial flows between households, firms, banks, and the central bank. Yet progress was slow. In addition to being drained by unsettling personal tragedy, he poured much time and attention into public speeches and shorter articles, which he pursued in order to pay off the debts from his failed financial adventures.

Then, Keynes' *Treatise on Money* appeared in 1930. According to some reports, Schumpeter believed that Keynes had appropriated some of his ideas without attribution.[35] If this was the case, he did not indicate it in public. On the contrary, he acknowledged Keynes' treatise as a "splendid achievement" and "spoke admiringly" of it in his Bonn lectures.[36] In any case, Keynes had raised the bar for another endogenous theory of money to strike the profession as profoundly novel. Despite several premature announcements of its publication, Schumpeter practically ceased work on his "money book" in the early 1930s.[37] Finally, an unfinished and incomplete German version of the manuscript was posthumously published in 1970 as *Das Wesen des Geldes* (henceforth *WDG*), while three further draft chapters remained in the Harvard University Archives.[38]

Despite the enormous effort he had invested, Schumpeter considered the book a failure.[39] As did Rothschild (1973), when commanding respect for his "heroic" decision not to publish it. In contrast, Tichy (1984) appreciated the originality and relevance of Schumpeter's contribution, but considered its generalization into a genuine dynamic theory a vain endeavor. He pointed at Schumpeter's unlimited ambition and striving for perfection as the source of failure. And indeed, the attempted general theory of money and banking often strays into long-winded and detailed discussions, which many readers will find tedious. While it demonstrates much intellect and effort, the book adds little new thought compared to his more radical earlier presentations. Its central contribution is the analysis of the manifold

[35] McCraw (2007, p. 155).

[36] See Letter to Walter Eucken, April 19, 1932, reproduced in Stolper (1994, p. 48) or Dathe and Hedtke (2018, p. 19).

[37] Schumpeter, however, refused to let the "money book" go for good. In a letter written two months before his death, he expressed his intention of finishing it within "a year or two" (Hedtke and Swedberg, 2000, p. 391).

[38] See Messori (1997) for an excellent discussion.

[39] McCraw (2007, p. 155) reports that Schumpeter himself "judged the whole effort 'a thoroughly bad performance,'" even though he had "poured endless hours into the book."

interactions through which the credit market coordinates entrepreneurial activity during the business cycle, which received a much more thorough account than it had in his previous work. First unknown and then published at a time when monetary analysis had long shifted to other topics, its appearance had little impact on the discipline. Among the notable exceptions, Messori acknowledges its enduring value and considers it "the peak of that stream of analysis," which is comprised of Marx, Wicksell, A. Hahn, Robertson, and Keynes.[40] Contrasting Schumpeter's attempt to specify the sequential structure of interactions with the later methods of optimization. Hellwig points out that "Schumpeter was ahead of his time in many ways and many unsolved problems still are. You could say that today we are confused at a higher level."[41]

Settling at Harvard

Schumpeter's turbulent life finally culminated in an industrious late career at Harvard University. On the initiative of his mentor and friend *Frank Taussig* (1859–1940), he first arrived there as a visiting professor in autumn 1927 (his initial course was on "Money and Banking")[42] and then again in 1930. In 1931 he lectured in Tokyo, before being appointed to a permanent chair at Harvard in 1932. There, his ardent support of a mathematical approach to economics stood in stark contrast with the lack of any formal modeling in his own work. To the facile observer this may appear a vain masquerade. However, Andersen's careful examination reveals the intriguing inner struggle of a responsible instructor and creative scientist.[43]

Together with *Ragnar Frisch* (1895–1973) and *Jan Tinbergen* (1903–94), Schumpeter was one of the co-founders of the *Econometric Society* and chaired its initial meeting in 1930. After joining the faculty at Harvard, he also became committed to advancing the use of mathematical tools in the economics curriculum. As nobody volunteered to do this, he taught the first classes, but soon handed them over to a more gifted younger generation (in particular, his protégé Wassily Leontief).[44] Still, he remained alert and attentive to the work of his more mathematically inclined colleagues. Richard Goodwin, for instance, remembered that Schumpeter patiently listened to his lectures but found no way to apply the deterministic models to his own analytical problems. Aware that his theories were too "refractory to mathematical formulations," Schumpeter increasingly turned his attention

[40] Messori (2014, p. 56).

[41] Quotation from an oral presentation of Martin Hellwig on *Das Wesen des Geldes* at a Schumpeter Colloquium of the University of Vienna, Ocober 14, 2016.

[42] McCraw (2007, p. 187). [43] Andersen (2011).

[44] W.L. Crum invited him to co-author the second edition of his textbook on *Rudimentary Mathematics for Economics and Statisticians* (Crum and Schumpeter, 1947), after Schumpeter had provided detailed comments and various amendments to it.

toward the study of history. However, the fact that he failed to produce a formal representation of his theory never prompted him to discard the promise of precise analytical tools. In a letter to Gottfried Haberler he admitted to feeling "like Moses must have felt when he beheld the Promised Land and knew that he himself would not be allowed to enter it."[45]

Schumpeter's thorough theoretical foundations and undogmatic but principled approach to methodology certainly contributed to the rise and fame of the economics department at Harvard University. Among the many distinctive scholars and disciples who worked with or studied under Schumpeter one finds, for instance, Wassily Leontief, Paul Samuelson, James Tobin, Richard Musgrave, Richard Goodwin, Hyman Minsky, Paul Sweezy, or John Kenneth Galbraith.

Schumpeter's private life also took a much needed positive turn when he became acquainted with *Romaine Elizabeth Boody* (1898-1953), herself an accomplished economist, fifteen years younger and also divorced. They married in 1937. Her letters and correspondence at the University Archives in Harvard reveal an emancipated, confident, and unassuming companion, who must have greatly helped to stabilize his precarious mental condition. Later, her dedication and support would render possible the posthumous publication of his final and unfinished monograph, which she pursued with much skill and endurance. Nevertheless, Schumpeter's solitary immersion into his ambitious academic endeavors appears to have made him increasingly detached from the world around him. Though many students described him as an exceptionally attentive and flamboyant teacher, sarcastic statements and ill temper caused tensions within the faculty. Furthermore, at a time when Keynes' (1936) *General Theory* proved extremely popular among his younger disciples, his own repudiation of the *New Deal* politics contributed to his alienation.

Compared to Keynes, his approach and attitude toward policy generally placed him outside the limelight when it came to practical relevance and public attention. While Keynes was never shy to spell out clear political priorities and concrete policy prescriptions, Schumpeter's main interest always lay in the essential theoretical aspects, even when asked to comment on policy. He attempted to contribute by helping authorities and the public better understand a situation, but provided no solutions for the considerable complexity and uncertainty involved in real-life decisions. We may say that he tried to educate rather than give prescriptions, pointing at the historical and institutional specificity of a policy, but leaving the concrete choices (and, accordingly, responsibility) to the policy makers.[46] For example, in the introduction to *Business Cycles* (henceforth *BC*) Schumpeter frankly declared: "I recommend no policy and propose no plan. [...] What our

[45] Reproduced in Hedtke and Swedberg (2000, p. 240).

[46] Consequently, the Schumpeterian approach does not lend itself easily to a systematic analysis of economic policy. See, for example, Hanusch (1999, p. lvi).

time needs most and lacks most is the understanding of the process which people are passionately resolved to control" (*BC*, 1939, p. vi).

Finally, and consistently with his earlier pacifism during the First World War, he favored appeasement with the Nazi regime. He naively hoped that the Germans would themselves get rid of the tyranny and instead worried more about the rise of Stalin's power.[47] Another reason for his restraint in public statements was that he still had friends there, whom he cared about, and for whom he feared retaliation.[48] All these matters taken together, he must have increasingly appeared to be a hopeless reactionary. In contrast, his enduring support of European migrant economists, most of whom were either Jewish and/or socialists, in receiving fellowships and jobs in the US probably went rather unnoticed, except among his close friends.[49]

By any measure, Schumpeter's years at Harvard are characterized by an enormous academic output. After he moved there, his attention to the money book soon gave way to *BC* (1939), in which he produced a comprehensive elaboration of the emergence of capitalism with more than 1,000 pages and plenty of historical and empirical detail. Yet, despite this being the most ambitious project he ever completed, *BC* had little enduring impact on the profession. Though reviewers were generally respectful, they struggled with what to make of the work. One reason for its lukewarm reception was that Schumpeter considered it a treatise on business cycles, though it was more an extension and attempted empirical validation of *TED*. Thereby, he portrayed the economy as evolving through the continuous stream of recurrent fluctuations caused by multiple and overlapping waves of different length. This rendered their statistical identification extremely difficult and called for detailed historical analysis. Another reason for its failure was the unfortunate timing of *BC*. Published three years after Keynes' *General Theory*, toward the end of the great recession and at the beginning of the Second World

[47] In the words of McCraw (2007, p. 316): "Schumpeter radically underestimated the Nazi's strength and capacity for evil; but at the same time he anticipated with great insight the situation that led to the Soviet-American Cold War of 1945–89."

[48] Schumpeter continued to support the family of Anna Reisinger and in particular Mia Stöckel, his former secretary and later companion after the death of his second wife. The two maintained a lively correspondence, which they were aware could be monitored by the German authorities. Schumpeter regularly sent her money, even after she had married a young economist from Serbia and moved to Novi Sad. A letter in which her father reported to Schumpeter the killing of Mia and her husband by the Hungarian allies of Nazi Germany is a deeply stirring document of the cruelty of the regime and the war (HUG(FP)—4.5, Box 1, Folder "Letter on Mia's death").

[49] See, for instance, McCraw (2007, p. 229ff). In contrast, Schumpeter and his wife, who was an expert on the Japanese economy, were subject to investigations of the FBI and cleared of potential sympathies with the war enemy. Rothschild (2015, p. 234) reports on the relationship between Schumpeter and *Eduard März* (1908–87), a Jewish emigrant student at Harvard, who—after the end of the Second World War—found a "strangely peaceful and almost serene Schumpeter who had become reconciled with the world. März thinks that this may have been due to the fact that he had become more grateful to be in the US after having learned about the cruelties of the Nazi regime ("Thank God for America" became a frequent utterance)."

War, Schumpeter's lengthy elaboration of the wave-like evolution of capitalism was simply not of great appeal to the profession.

A few years later, however, Schumpeter wrote what would become his most famous book: *Capitalism, Socialism and Democracy* (henceforth, *CSD*).[50] While *TED* had laid out the basic theoretical framework, *BC* reached far back in history for its empirical validation. In contrast, *CSD* (1942/50) concluded Schumpeter's trilogy on the evolution of capitalism with a bold vision of where it might be headed. Arguably, it is his only book that happened to be in tune with one of the dominant public concerns of the time. Following the devastations of the Second World War and appearing on the verge of the Cold War (which was highly charged with ideological combat) Schumpeter posited an unsettling answer to a simple question: "Can capitalism survive? No. I do not think it can."[51]

From the eminent scholar of the evolution of capitalism, one would have expected to hear otherwise. And indeed, there are good reasons not to be canonical about this. On the one hand, Schumpeter's pessimistic outlook partly reflected his depressed mental situation during his later years. On the other hand, he never considered the statement a definite prediction, but rather an extrapolation of developments that he was concerned about. By bringing them to their logical conclusion, he hoped to call forth and strengthen the system's resilience against it.[52] Apparently his personal bet was on the growing socialization of society, albeit conceding that capitalism could still "have another successful run."[53] In any case, *CSD* is a masterful example of his reasoning by apparent paradoxes. Turning upside down the Marxist prediction of the collapse of capitalism due to its inherent flaws, Schumpeter argued that capitalism will indeed disband eventually, but as a consequence of its own success. In short, Schumpeter reasoned that, due to the growing routinization of innovation, "economic progress tends to become depersonalized and automatized," whereby capitalist enterprises render themselves superfluous through their own achievements:

> The perfectly bureaucratized giant industrial unit not only ousts the small or medium-sized firm and "expropriates" its owners, but in the end it also ousts the entrepreneur and expropriates the bourgeoisie as a class which in the process stands to lose not only its income but also what is infinitely more important, its function. (*CSD*, 1942/50, p. 134)

[50] After the disappointing reception of *BC*, he was surprised by its success, pointing out that he had pursued it with far less ambition and effort than his previous book. Despite this, it gained much popularity, especially after the publication of its second edition in 1947 (McCraw, 2007, p. 347ff; p. 371).

[51] *CSD* (1942/50, p. 61).

[52] As Schumpeter explained, scientific analysis "never yields more than a statement about the tendencies present in an observable pattern. And these never tell us what *will* happen to the pattern but only what *would* happen if they continued to act as they have been acting in the time interval covered by our observation and if no other factors intruded" (*CSD*, 1942/50, p. 61). In a later speech reprinted in the third edition of *CSD* (1942/50, p. 416), he also put it clearly: "I do not advocate socialism. Nor have I any intention of discussing its desirability or undesirability. [...] to make it quite clear that I do not 'prophesy' or predict it."

[53] *CSD* (1942/50, p. 163).

The reason for this is that the growing trustification of capitalism "takes the life out of the idea of property" and leads to an "evaporation" of its very substance. At the same time, capitalism's "rationalist attitude does not stop at the credentials of kings and popes but goes on to attack private property and the whole scheme of bourgeois values."[54] Monopoly capitalism thus induces a progressive socialization of the economy, which Schumpeter considered "culturally indeterminate."[55] He meant that, in principle, socialization is also consistent with the democratic method of arriving at political decisions through "a competitive struggle for the people's vote."[56]

Returning to the issue of money, the evolutionary trilogy of *TED*, *BC*, and *CSD* treated monetary questions almost exclusively from the perspective of the financing of entrepreneurial ventures, along with the mechanisms of propagation and adaptation they induce throughout the economic system. But Schumpeter never gave up on his plan for a general treatise on money, and monetary matters remained on his agenda in his teaching and public speeches (e.g., "The Future of Gold, Address to the Economic Club of Detroit", henceforth GOL; 1941). Furthermore, monetary theory continued to fare prominently in his final years, when he set out to write the *HEA*. Though also unfinished and incomplete, this huge monograph absorbed much of Schumpeter's time and effort, but again revealed the familiar productive mind at work.

As a final milestone of his career, Schumpeter was elected president of the *American Economic Association* in 1948. But even this important professional recognition could not lay his mind to rest. Keeping a busy schedule, he still had plans to return to the money book after first finishing *HEA*. Finally, the industriousness which had upheld his spirits for many years took its toll. Continuously over worked,[57] on January 8th, 1950, he died unexpectedly from a cerebral hemorrhage at the age of 66. Among the many obituaries that appeared, his friend Gottfried Haberler probably offered the most personal characterization: "He was a good laugher and could enjoy exuberantly a stimulating conversation, a good story, a brilliant joke, but he was fundamentally not a happy man."[58]

1.4 Aims, scope, and plan of the book

Schumpeter's major works were mostly informed by and aimed at a long-term perspective. Distinctively tying history with theory, he reached far back in time to understand what drives a system and determines its course. Historical and empirical research provided a laboratory for learning about the processes and

[54] *CSD* (1942/1950, p. 142f).

[55] "[A] society may be fully and truly socialist and yet be led by an absolute ruler or be organized in the most democratic of all possible ways; it may be aristocratic or proletarian; it may be a theocracy and hierarchic or atheist or indifferent as to religion" (*CSD*, 1942/50, p. 170).

[56] *CSD* (1942/50, p. 269). [57] McCraw (2007, p. 495). [58] Haberler (1950, p. 372).

dealing with the perpetual twists and turns of actual events. At the same time, he reached for a long-term vision through theoretical inspection and utmost abstraction, thereby seeking to distil a phenomenon's essential "nature" and function. Even though development unfolds as a "historical-genetic," that is, path dependent process, he believed that evolution ultimately tends to bring its "pure" elements to the fore. Consequently, he was convinced that good theory can supply the signposts indicating where a system is most likely headed in the distant future.

Schumpeter's characteristic emphasis on both history and theory also informed the plan for this monograph in which we simultaneously aim at three groups of readers: (i) non specialists with a curious mind, (ii) the "Schumpeterian economists," and (iii) those who pay attention to the history of economic thought.

The common point of reference is what we term *Schumpeter's venture money*. More specifically, we aim to lay out and proceed with our analysis along three "threads." The first thread is monetary history, more specifically the ongoing stream of innovations that has enhanced and broadened the scope of financing new ventures. The second thread is the complementary (but often unaligned) stream of ideas in the history of monetary thought. Finally, Josef Schumpeter himself, who envisioned his monetary theory of economic development from a thorough knowledge of economic history and the history of economic thought, is the third thread that binds everything together and establishes the boundaries of our endeavor.

To begin with, Part I provides a brief synopsis of the ongoing stream of "creative response" in monetary and financial history, as well as the scholarly struggle to understand and assimilate this in the history of monetary thought up to Schumpeter's time. It serves as an introduction to the nonspecialist, providing the general background.[59] Chapter 2 starts with a short account of the early origins of money as a social institution. Chapter 3 addresses the era of ascending capitalism that Schumpeter characterized by the merits of credit as an instrument with which to finance new commercial ventures. Such credit, broadly defined, was expanded in scope and volume for the financing of industrial development. Chapter 4 will turn our attention to this era.

Following the previous account of Schumpeter's varied and heterodox intellectual roots, the focus in Part II is on his monetary theory of economic development. Chapter 5 starts with the marginalist revolution and its consolidation of the classical monetary orthodoxy, leading directly to Josef Schumpeter's intellectual upbringing. In addition, some distinctions are drawn between Schumpeter and his intellectual kinship with the Austrian School.

[59] Unlike the remainder of this monograph, Part I draws exclusively from the existing literature and our original input is limited to an attempted compact presentation of the material at hand as well as its integration with the other focal themes. Consistently with the historical progression of explicit theoretical reflection and scholarly writing, references to the history of money and finance dominate the earlier chapters, whereas the evolution of monetary theory features more prominently in the later ones.

Since Schumpeter never completed the attempted treatise on money, much material of interest remained scattered across different sources. In part, it is only hinted at or implicit in his early works, and in part it received systematic treatment in lesser known articles or remained unpublished, whereas major portions were only published posthumously. The deliberate reconstruction of his monetary theory in Chapter 6 reveals, however, a strikingly original and coherent conception. In short, Schumpeter integrated a claim-theory of money with the expenditure-income approach. This culminated in his rationale of the non-neutrality of money, which matters for real production by affecting not only the general price level (as postulated by the monetary orthodoxy) but also relative prices, and hence the incentives to invest, through explicit structural relations.

Chapter 7 explores the basic premises of Schumpeter's monetary theory of economic development, in particular highlighting the role of "venture" money in financing innovation. It thereby identifies two characteristic forms of 'venture money': (i) the credit channel of "creative destruction," to which he attached particular theoretical importance, and (ii) the business case for modern venture capital, where entrepreneurs and early-stage investors realize the "promoter's profit" in the form of capital gains from the issue of new shares.

In practice, Schumpeter afforded much importance to both channels of venture money. While the literature provides some scarce information on his banking activities, his role as a kind of proto-venture capitalist went largely unnoticed. Drawing from the detailed study of documents at various archives in Austria, Part III concentrates on the detailed business history of both endeavors. Chapter 8 is dedicated to the history of the Biedermann joint-stock bank, whose president Schumpeter was from its foundation until 1924. While his banking activity has so far mainly been perceived as a speculative episode, here it is examined as a serious attempt to put his theoretical considerations of credit-based entrepreneurial development into practice. Despite his efforts, the project encountered severe economic turbulence in the spring of 1924. Its failure was due to unfavorable economic conditions, contradictory strategic orientations among the shareholder groups, and mistakes made by those in charge.

In addition to his banking activities, Schumpeter actively pursued the "promoter's profit" during his brief and unfortunate history as a proto-venture capitalist, a subject to which we turn in Chapter 9. He invested on a grand scale in the foundation of new industrial firms. Given the poor condition of the industrial sites after years of a war economy, the economic rationale appeared sound, but the financial scheme, timing, and practical execution were not. In addition to spending his own wealth, he borrowed heavily from his privileged bank account and raised considerable funds from third parties. Having established large leverage, he was unable to refinance short-term loans when Austria was hit with its major banking crisis in 1924. As the factories failed before they could produce any significant cash flow, Schumpeter learned the perils of high leverage the hard way. His personal role in the bank and industrial group are explained in Chapter 10, along with the financial consequences of the failures that overshadowed his life until the early 1930s.

Finally, Part IV casts light on the further legacy of Schumpeter's monetary ideas up to recent history. Chapter 11 first turns to the challenge posed by the extraordinary success of the Keynesian revolution. In contrast, Schumpeter's monetary ideas largely got lost in the following decades, which were dominated by the rivalry between Keynesian and neoclassical ideas, including their various attempts at synthesis. In short, the "caravan" had moved on without him. Chapter 12 then highlights selected traces of the "caravan's return." The tides had turned with the growing attention to financial frictions that began in the early 1970s. The new literature substantiated Schumpeter's concern for the financing of new ventures to be a non-trivial instance of the non-neutrality of money. In the 1990s, connections to Schumpeter also became more explicit in the literature. Triggered by a large body of empirical research, the nexus between finance and growth now features prominently, for instance, in Schumpeterian growth theory, as well as evolutionary agent-based models. Chapter 13 rounds off the narrative by examining three cases from recent history in which Schumpeter's vision appears to be particularly valid. One is the rise of venture capital in Schumpeter's close environment during his years at Harvard. Another example is the Great Recession of 2008–9, and the third example is the impact of digitalization on the further development of money. In the final epilogue, we characterize Schumpeter's monetary theory of economic development to be an old and often unattended variety that is still rich in substance.

PART I
HISTORY AND HETERODOX SOURCES

2
Early origins of money

> Money is one of the most perfect instruments which the human mind has devised [. . .]. In the simplicity of conception, in the variety of its applications and effects, it may be most aptly compared to the letters of the alphabet.
>
> (F. Wieser, 1914/27, p. 170)

Money is one of the oldest social institutions. Its practical import is so deeply engrained in the fabric of economic relations that monetary history necessarily predates any recorded history of deliberate theoretical thought. This chapter provides a short account of its early origins. It is of significance to our later discussion of Schumpeter's monetary theory of development for two reasons: first, the historical account illustrates the perpetual stream of new monetary arrangements and their importance to the real economy; second, the historical record puts into perspective the traditional preoccupation with metallism and the coinage of money as a means of exchange, which dominated the monetary orthodoxy at Schumpeter's time. While his opposition to the received canon was motivated by theoretical considerations, he certainly would have drawn much comfort and support from the modern historical record, had it been available to him. The upshot is that it warrants paying more attention to the phenomena of credit and account, which are also at the center of his conception. With a touch of irony we can say that the early history of money will also reveal the modernity of Schumpeter's vision.

2.1 Credit and interest

Comprehensive accounts of monetary history date back to about 10,000 years ago, when the neolithic revolution brought about agriculture in association with higher population growth. Increased commercial interaction contributed to the rise of complex social structures, and the record-keeping of the value of economic transactions was among the first needs to arise. Archaeological evidence from the Near East dating back to about 7000 BCE suggests that *clay tokens* were the first proto-financial tools, predating even the invention of writing (Table 2.1).[1] They

[1] Schmandt-Besserat (1992); Goetzmann (2016, p. 22ff). Berg et al. (2019, p. 65) refer to it as the early forms of a ledger technology.

Schumpeter's Venture Money. Michael Peneder and Andreas Resch,
Oxford University Press (2021). © Michael Peneder and Andreas Resch.
DOI: 10.1093/oso/9780198804383.003.0002

Table 2.1 Selected milestones in the early evolution of money

Time (ca.)	Location	Earliest known evidence of ...
		Before Common Era (BCE)
7000	Near East	Commodity **symbols** (clay tokens)
3200	Mesopotamia	**Credit** and interest (for agriculture, temple contributions, bridal gifts, etc.)
3100	Mesopotamia	**Writing** (clay tablets)
3000	Mesopotamia	**Contract** (*bullae*)
2500	Mesopotamia	**Compound interest** (for war reparations)
1800	Mesopotamia	**Equity partnerships** (for maritime trade)
1045	China	Use of **cowry** shells as money (probably much older)
6th century	Greek cities	**Metal coinage** (first in Ephesos, Lydia)
5th century	Greek cities	**Banking** (the *trapezitai* of Piraeus)
3rd century	India	Ancient **bills of exchange** (*adesha*)
221	China	Standardized Chinese bronze coin (*ban liang*)
216	Rome	**Corporation** (*societas publicanorum*)
		Common Era (CE)
211	Rome	**Life annuity** tables (e.g., for paying soldiers)
990s	China	**Private paper** exchange bills (*jiaozi*; Sichuan)
1024	China	**Paper currency** (by exclusive government authority)

symbolized specific economic commodities and were generally of a simple and abstract shape.

At the beginning of the Bronze Age, the innovation of irrigation agriculture in Mesopotamia allowed communities to settle year-round and develop first urban societies with growing populations, increased division of labor, and expanding trade relations that secured the supply of tin and other resources. Writing and credit soon became two indispensable elements of exchange.[2] As early as 3000 BCE there is evidence that in Mesopotamia clay tokens were stored in sealed lay balls, called *bullae*, a kind of contract which specified the commitment of future payments (e.g., tributes to the temple, taxes, or loans). Abstract symbols on the surface of these hollow and fist-sized envelopes of clay depicted the number and type of tokens inside. Later, the Sumerians began inscribing pictographs into clay *tablets* and the accounting symbols evolved into "cuneiform," the world's first writing. Goetzmann vividly portrays the practice:

> The oldest Uruk tablets were made circa 3100 BCE by scribes who took wet lumps of clay, shaped them into lozenges, and wrote on them with a wooden stylus. The stylus had a sharp end and round end—one end for lines and the other for dots.

[2] van de Mieroop (2005, p.17).

> Laid sideways, the stylus could also make triangular and cylindrical impressions. The combination of these formed a lexicon that scholars have now concluded was the first writing. (Goetzmann, 2016, p. 24)

Temples were the political and administrative center and the clay tablets were used to record the contribution and distribution of goods such as barley, cattle, or other means of subsistence. Agricultural shortfalls, the failure to meet obligatory contributions to the temple or social commitments, such as bridal gifts, and the capital needs of long-distance trade triggered *credit*, with its earliest appearance documented for the period of about 3200 to 1600 BCE.[3] Credit was generally short-term, typically in the form of an advance from the central storehouse, and had to be paid back during the next harvest. The loan contracts could be passed on to another person, although there is no indication that they were commonly traded.

Most credit called for *interest* in terms of additional payback at the end of the specified period. The Sumerian word for interest, *mash*, also means "calves,"[4] pointing at its agricultural roots as a fee on grazing and the natural increase of livestock. Apart from barley or silver, interest was often paid in the form of own labor or that of family members or a servant. Debt servitude caused social unrest and occasionally resulted in the annulment of debts or the release of debt slaves by royal decree.[5] Since loans were typically issued for a period shorter than an agricultural year, the notion of *compound interest* did not arise. The earliest evidence of it, however, was found in the context of war reparations in an inscription from about 2500 BCE, in which a rival city was commanded to pay rent plus cumulative interest for a reconquered territory.[6]

In the early second millennium BCE commercial credit was also common and insurance was even offered, if for an additional fee the loan was cancelled in the case of the loss of a shipment.[7] Documents from the city of Ur show that a kind of limited equity partnership existed, whereby liability was limited to the actual contribution and the profits were shared, conditional on the success of a maritime expedition.[8]

As time passed, more private contracts emerged and tax-farmers, for instance, acted as middlemen, balancing and converting the payments into silver. Shekels of silver became the common unit of currency with which the government set

[3] In later centuries, the Sumerian word *ur* also became the generic term for loan. "There is enormous variety in the formulation of loan records but the indispensable elements include what was borrowed, by whom, and from whom. How regularly, in which form, and when it had to be repaid was also indicated. Babylonian contracts were almost always dated, often to the day, [...]. Since many loans were an arrangement between two individuals, there were witnesses whose names were listed as well" (van de Mieroop, 2005, p. 21).

[4] As does the greek term *tokos*. The Latin term *pecus* means "flock." Goetzmann (2016, p. 44).

[5] van de Mieroop (2005, p. 28). [6] Goetzmann (2016, p. 35ff).

[7] Ferguson (2008, p. 185). [8] Goetzmann (2016, p. 46ff).

the price of commodities, labor, or penalties. Rather than being widely circulated, silver presumably mainly served as a *unit of account*:[9]

> Although they used a silver based pricing system, more than likely they recorded their small payments or obligations in accounts—like running a tab at a local store. They used silver as a "language" of accounts, but a grocer could not constantly and reliably weigh out shekels of silver while bargaining over barley, cress, and dates. (Goetzmann, 2016, p. 100)

2.2 Coinage

According to modern historical records, money and credit thus existed long before the invention of *coinage*, which evolved in the Mediterranean[10] from the early sixth century BCE onward. As is often emphasized in the economics literature, coinage offered greater flexibility in commercial transactions, especially in trade over long distances, where trust in an accurate and enforceable system of accounts was diminished. It avoided counter-party risk in the growing maritime trade of the Greek city states, when partners were often incapable of enforcing a loan contract of the kind that had appeared earlier in Mesopotamia.[11] In addition, small change reduced transaction costs in ordinary local commerce.

The first metal coinage may also have originated in China—presumably in order to mitigate the shortage of money as the economy outgrew the limited availability of cowry shells.[12] *Cowries* are among the oldest examples of money by means of a symbolic system of exchange and the pictograph of a shell still appears in many Chinese characters representing matters of commerce. While their use is confirmed by ancient documents dating from 1045 BCE, they were likely used before then. They evolved from an article of adornment into a means of payment between 3000 and 1122 BCE.[13] After the era of the "warring states"—each using a different currency, typically bronze cast into shapes of ordinary tools, such as spades and knives, it was only in 221 BCE that the Quin dynasty introduced a standardized bronze coin to China's first unified empire (the *ban liang*).

[9] See also Orrell and Chlupaty (2016, p. 17).

[10] The oldest troves were found in Ephesos in Lydia (which is near Izmir, now Turkey), Athens and other Greek city states. The earliest Lydian coins were made from a gold-silver alloy ("electrum").

[11] Some authors assert that long-distance trade existed before the introduction of coinage and that many coins had not circulated far. Alternate explanations therefore emphasize the context of warring city states. Related to and possibly mitigating the ancient practice of plunder, coinage may originate in the rulers' need to pay soldiers and more generally as a means of enhancing commerce and loyalty to the state. See Orrell and Chlupaty (2016, p. 21).

[12] Goetzmann (2016, p. 147ff).

[13] Peng (1994). The latter date signals the presence of *bronze cowries* in royal tombs (Goetzmann, 2016, p. 149).

2.3 Legal advances

In the fifth century BCE, the advancement of legal systems and public institutions to enforce common rules and contractual commitments was a major driver of financial development among Greek city states. An ancient banking business arose in the port of Piraeus, where the "trapezitai"[14] took deposits and provided loans for maritime trade and domestic business or backed expensive social obligations. The thicker the market, the more easily lenders could diversify their funding among distinct enterprises and thus accept the risk of shipwreck as well as facilitate other entrepreneurial ventures.

Written contracts allowed to document loans and commit debtors to certain payments. These were the basis of the ancient forms of *bills of exchange*,[15] which probably first emerged in India and Rome, and which later became an important instrument used to settle accounts among Arab merchants. One of the earliest recorded examples was the Indian *adesh*, which constituted orders of payment from a banker to a third person. In large towns it was used as a letter of credit among merchants.[16] It originated in the third century BCE during the Mauryan period, which had successfully rebelled against the Greek governors.

The Greek advances of the legal system became particularly influential in the Roman Empire, where money changers (*argentarii*) provided all kinds of banking services, ranging from taking deposits to carrying out money transfers or lending. Schumpeter, for instance, described the risk-bearing contracts drafted for maritime ventures:

> The outstanding case [...] is afforded by a contract that the Romans took from the Greeks, the *foenus nauticum*. This provided a method for the financing of maritime trade mainly by removing or relaxing the restrictions on the rate of interest in consideration of the clause that the "entrepreneur's" obligation as to both interest and capital lapsed in case his venture failed to succeed, i.e., that he owed only if ship and cargo landed safely.
>
> (BC, 1939, p. 615; see also Section 7.9)

Finally, one of Rome's distinctive own innovations was the *societas publicanorum*, a legal association of shareholders exclusively restricted to public contracts, but with special provisions that anticipated the modern corporation.[17] At a time when the empire was growing faster than its administrative capacity, the earliest documents mention this innovation in the context of procuring military supplies in 216 BCE.

[14] "Trapeza" denotes the table on which the financial businesses were conducted.
[15] Denzel (2008). [16] Reserve Bank of India (1998, chapter II, p. 1).
[17] Malmendier (2005, 2009).

Other public services included construction work, property rights, for example, for grazing, fishing or mining, and tax-farming. Unlike the regular "societas," the publican societies established a separate legal persona that was independent of its shareholders (the "publicani") and regularly bid for government contracts at public auctions. Shares were tradable, and during its heyday this system seems to have been widespread. Later, this form disappeared when such public contracts were no longer auctioned—*de facto* crowded out by public services. Since the special provisions had never been systematically integrated into the Roman legal system, they were practically forgotten during the following centuries.[18]

2.4 "Light and heavy"

In the ancient societies, the transition from a bartering to a monetary economy stimulated both the Chinese and Greek political philosophers.[19] In China, the outstanding example is the *guanzi*, a collection of essays attributed to the Jixia Academy in the city of Linzi.[20] It is composed of imaginary dialogues occurring in the seventh century BCE, but probably already composed by various authors during the fourth century BCE and continually revised up to about 26 BCE. In several passages it addresses money and points at its origins in government fiat: "The rulers cast coins to establish money."[21] Among economic explanations, the emphasis was placed on its functions as both a medium of exchange and a measure of value.

The *guanzi* has, in particular, come to prominence for its earliest known articulation of the law of supply and demand. Originally, the terms "light and heavy" simply referred to the weight of the coins, but they were eventually metaphorically extended to denote its purchasing power. A convenient way of expressing the value of money relative to that of goods was found: "If coins are heavy, then the myriad of goods will be light. If coins are light, then the myriad of goods will be heavy". In an often-quoted example, the *guanzi* relates the idea of relative scarcity and resulting differences in supply and demand to international trade:

> Now grain is heavy in our state, and light in the world at large. Then the other lords' goods will spontaneously leak out like water from a spring flowing downhill. Hence if goods are heavy, they will come; if light, they will go.
>
> (quotation from Peng, 1994, p. 96)

[18] Malmendier (2005, 2009).
[19] Peng (1994, p. 90).
[20] Goetzmann (2016).
[21] Quotation from Peng (1994, p. 94).

This advanced comprehension of economic relationships was also displayed in a comparatively abstract idea of money, in which the *guanzi* emphasized its (political) function as a general *measure of accounts*:

> If you grasp three coins, there is nothing there to warm you. If you eat them, there is nothing there to nourish you. The former kings used it to store up goods, to manage men, and to pacify the world. That which is used to order things is called a measure. A measure fixes height and subordination, so that things are not shifting. (quotation from Peng, 1994, p. 95)

2.5 Paper money

While the earliest appearance of metal coinage remains disputed, the Chinese were certainly the first to introduce *paper money*. As a primary example of historic specificity, this radical innovation resulted from particular challenges, as well as enabling and inducing factors, the confluence of which is owed to the specific technological, political, and economic circumstances of the time. Furthermore, the advanced theoretical understanding of monetary matters must also have been instrumental to this development.

To begin with, the Chinese were already familiar with and practically dependent on a fiat currency. Eschewing the scarcity of precious metals, such as gold and silver, coinage in China was mainly minted from the more readily available bronze or brass alloys. While requiring a strong government and sophisticated administration as the ultimate guarantee of the value that was enacted and stamped to the coin, this system had the benefit of ensuring a more flexible money supply, which the rulers could better adjust to growing populations and trade. The particular way in which the bronze coins were used was also rather uncommon by western standards:

> Coins were counted by tale rather than issued in different denominates, and the basic monetary unit was the single coin (*wen* or "cash"). Larger units were created by stringing coins together in units of 100 (*mo*) and 1,000 (*guan*) coins. The *guan* (or "string of cash") became the standard unit of account in state finance.
> (Von Glahn, 2005, p. 68)

A low intrinsic value together with a lack of higher denominations made this form of currency very cumbersome in commercial exchange. From the early ninth century onward, the Chinese government therefore operated depositories in its capital, where it offered promissory notes called *feiqian* or "flying cash" in exchange for bronze coins, which the merchants could later redeem in their provincial capitals.[22]

These deficiencies in commercial exchange were further exacerbated in the province of Sichuan, where coins were minted from iron instead of bronze. In addition, continued military harassment and conflict was driving monetary expansion to a point where inflation literally put a "heavy" burden on all kinds of transactions. In the 990s private merchants therefore began issuing their own "exchange bills" called *jiaozi*, which soon enjoyed growing circulation, but were also prone to abuse and led to a surge of legal disputes. By the year 1005 this development prompted the provincial government to enforce certain regulations,[23] while not restricting the total amount supplied. Private issue, however, remained precarious, as investments in illiquid assets such as real estate and other commodities curtailed the issuers' ability to redeem. Counterfeiting occurred as well. As a consequence, in 1024 the government assumed control as the exclusive authority for issuing paper currency.[24]

Finally, the innovation of fiat money by paper issues was only conceivable because of China's advanced knowledge in paper production and printing. More specifically, the substitution of hemp fiber with tree bark and carved woodblocks with metal plates enabled the issue of standardized, bright, and durable high-quality notes in great numbers.

Initially, the government issues of paper currency were successful and especially popular among the merchants in the growing tea trade, who frequently exchanged them at a premium above their nominal value.[25] In the course of time, however, radical economic reforms (including the nationalization of private enterprise), continual problems of counterfeiting, and growing military expenditures led to a depreciation of the paper currency to less than 10 percent of its face value by the year 1107.[26] Commodity vouchers, such as those based on the state's salt monopoly, gained in importance. But then, as in later periods, the Achilles heel of fiat money was the temptation of government authorities to excessively increase its issue in response to fiscal crises, thereby fuelling inflation.

From a western perspective, it is easy to blame the system of fiat money altogether, on the assumption that over time policy will inevitably give in to the temptation of inflationary practices. However, taking into consideration the broader historical context, and especially the role of military expenditures, one

[22] von Glahn (2005, p. 67).

[23] Only merchant houses with sufficient financial resources were allowed to issue notes that had to apply a standardized format, but bear the seals of the issuer. Instead of a standard denomination being applied, the value was inscribed on the bill.

[24] The issues were in two fixed denominations and had to be redeemed every two years with a commission fee of 3 percent. See von Glahn (2005).

[25] von Glahn (2005, p. 69).

[26] von Glahn (2005, p. 87).

may also conclude that the paper money's deteriorating valuation mainly mirrored the growing pressure on and declining prospects of the issuing Song rulers, which were eventually displaced by the Mongol Yuan dynasty:

> Yet the final demise of these early experiments in paper money should not obscure the notable success that Chinese governments attained in creating viable fiat currencies, particularly in Sichuan, the birthplace of the first paper currency. While its reach may have exceeded its grasp, the Song state developed a complex array of fiscal and monetary institutions, including paper currencies, that enabled the government to mobilize economic resources on an unprecedented scale. The durability of Song paper money not only as a means of paying taxes to the state, but also as the common currency of private trade, was indeed a remarkable achievement. (Von Glahn, 2005, p. 89)

The Mongol leader Kublai Khan (1215–94) would have agreed. He adopted the Song practice and issued his own fiat paper money. Based simply on the political power of enforcement, its existence must have come as a venerable shock to those who in ca. 1300 learned of it from the Venetian merchant *Marco Polo* (1254–1324). With the detailed title "How the Great Khan Causes the Bark of Trees, Made into Something Like Paper, to Pass for Money All over His Country," Polo's report presented fiat money as the "secret of alchemy in perfection":

> All these pieces of paper are issued with as much solemnity and authority as if they were of pure gold or silver; and on every piece a variety of officials, whose duty it is, have to write their names, and to put their seals. And when all is prepared duly, the chief officer deputed by the Khan smears the seal entrusted to him with vermilion, and impresses it on the paper, so that the form of the seal remains imprinted upon it in red; the money is then authentic. Anyone forging it would be punished with death.
>
> (Polo and Rustichello, edition of 1920, chapter 24)

The emperor's fiat also makes the money "pass current universally over all his kingdoms and provinces and territories," since "nobody, however important he may think himself, dares to refuse them on pain of death." Moreover,

> everybody takes them readily, for wheresoever a person may go throughout the great Khan's dominions he shall find these pieces of paper current, and shall be able to transact all sales and purchases of goods by means of them just as well as if they were coins of pure gold.
>
> (Polo and Rustichello, edition of 1920, chapter 24)

Foreign merchants must only sell their gold, silver, or gems to the emperor in exchange for paper, by means of which they can then pursue their purchases throughout his territory. Finally,

> several times in the year proclamation is made through the city that anyone who may have gold or silver or gems or pearls, by taking them to the mint shall get a handsome price for them. And the owners are glad to do this, because they would find no other purchaser gives so large a price. Thus, the quantity they bring in is marvellous, though those who do not choose to do so may let it alone. Still, in this way, nearly all the valuables in the country come into the Khan's possession.
> (Polo and Rustichello, edition of 1920, chapter 24)

The detail and historical accurateness of Polo's report suggest that his travelogue is original and based on his own experience. But there exists no firm evidence that he ever traveled further than the Black Sea, and some historians have suspected that he collected the narrations from other merchants coming from the East. Furthermore, he dictated his manuscript during his imprisonment in Genoa to fellow inmate Rustichello da Pisa, who was a professional writer of romances and likely embellished the tales, exaggerating Polo's role at the Chinese court. Perhaps this explains the otherwise astonishing fact that Polo's account of Chinese paper money apparently had no major impact on the development of European monetary thought, to which we will turn in the next section.

2.6 The "substance matter"

Economic analysis in the western hemisphere remained largely ignorant of and unaffected by the Chinese example of paper money. Similarly, scholars were not aware of the ancient scripts of the *guanzi*, which had hinted at the fundamental economic law of supply and demand much earlier than had European writings. Even Schumpeter's *HEA*, which is certainly one of the most encyclopedic accounts of the evolution of economic thought, does not mention them.

Schumpeter situated the beginnings of systematic analytical monetary thought with the Greek philosophers. Not unlike the early Chinese scholars, their economic analysis was rudimentary and mainly concerned with business in the context of a general theory of society and the state. However, the Greeks were already addressing two of the most enduring questions in monetary analysis: What is the "substance matter" and, relatedly, what are the constitutive functions of money? Thereby Schumpeter credited *Plato* (ca. 427–347 BCE) and *Aristotle* (384–322 BCE) with originating the two archetypes of monetary thought. According to Schumpeter, Plato had considered money as a "symbol devised for the purpose of facilitating exchange". More specifically, he referred to Plato's "canons of monetary policy—his hostility to the use of gold and silver," or "his idea of a domestic currency that would be useless abroad." Taken together, these examples indicate a concept in which "the value of money is on principle independent of the stuff it is made of."[27] Apparently, Plato was aware of the older and purely symbolic forms of money. In contrast, the growing diffusion of coinage had more time to impress the younger scholar Aristotle. According to Schumpeter, he had argued,

> that in order to serve as a medium of exchange in the markets of commodities, money itself must be one of these commodities. That is to say, it must be a thing that is useful and has exchange value independently of its monetary function—this is all that intrinsic value means in this connection—a value that can be compared with other values. (*HEA*, 1954, p. 62)

Furthermore, for Aristotle metal coins were the outcome of an evolution toward a superior form of commodity tokens with an intrinsic exchange value and highest "saleability." Explaining this superiority also led him to introduce the influential trinity of functions that money serves as (i) a medium of exchange, (ii) a measure of value, and implicitly also (iii) a store of value. He gave priority to the first function of facilitating exchange.

In short, Schumpeter portrayed Plato as the ancestor of anti-metallism and Aristotle as the earliest proponent of a commodity theory of money, which in the western hemisphere came to dominate monetary thinking up to the nineteenth century. To better organize this fundamental dichotomy, Schumpeter adopted the terms *metallism* and *cartalism* from *Georg Friedrich Knapp* (1842–1926).[28] Cartalism originates in the Latin word *charta*, which means the leaf of the Egyptian papyrus, or simply paper. For each view Schumpeter further adopts Knapp's distinction between their theoretical and practical forms:

> By Theoretical Metallism we denote the theory that it is logically essential for money to consist of, or to be "covered" by, some commodity so that the logical source of the exchange value or purchasing power of money is the exchange value or purchasing power of that commodity, considered independently of its monetary role. [...] By Practical Metallism we shall denote [...] the principle that the monetary unit "should" be kept firmly linked to, and freely interchangeable with, a given quantity of some commodity. Theoretical and Practical Cartalism may best be defined by the corresponding negatives. (*HEA*, 1954, p. 288)

[27] *HEA* (1954, p. 56).

[28] Knapp's *Die Staatliche Theorie des Geldes* was published in 1905. Recently, his ideas have experienced a revival as "neo-chartalism" or a self-proclaimed "modern money theory" (MMT). See, for instance, Wray (2000), the debates documented in Fiebiger (2012), or the criticism of Weber (2018) and Mankiw (2020).

Schumpeter admits to the ambiguities arising from such simple categorizations, and in particular refers to Aristotle as an example.[29] The general point, though, is that throughout the history of economic thought one always deals with a continuum of nuanced ideas that relate or overlap to varying degrees.

Aristotle's metallist concept of money prevailed throughout many centuries. One reason for this was that it perfectly aligned with the pre-eminent practical concern of the times, that is, the frequent debasement of coinage by the authorities. To western societies, which were not aware of either the Chinese example or of modern ideas about managing the money supply, that debasement was simply associated with the moral conviction of fraud. Given the historical context, it is no surprise that the scholastic philosophers of medieval times[30] endorsed the metallist interpretation of money and carried it onward up to the classical period of Adam Smith and others.[31] Given the available technology, markets, and political institutions of the time, they could point at many practical advantages of specie. Since "men are unable to make them easily by alchemy, as some endeavor to do,"[32] they posed bigger obstacles to counterfeiting and misuse by the authorities. Relatedly, precious metals were the only generally accepted currency in international trade. Overall, and again following Aristotle, the primary objective lay in the proper functioning of money as a means of exchange.

Practical cartalism arguably gained importance because the European rulers were often at war among themselves and this resulted in financial distress. However, unlike in China, the fragmented leaders would have lacked the fiat to back paper currency had the possibility crossed their mind. Hence, the different historical situation also led to different solutions and institutional arrangements—in particular, the emergence and diffusion of novel banking practices. These increased the supply of money or substitutes thereof, thereby ensuring the European rulers' liquidity in financing continued warfare and territorial expansion.[33] Their more enduring impact, however, was to establish increasingly refined tools of credit, which fuelled the fast growth of commerce and the ascent of capitalism.

[29] In the same footnote, Schumpeter conceded: "I am by no ways sure that I was right to class him with the theoretical metallists. [...] I prefer putting my doubts frankly before the reader to dogmatizing with a confidence I do not feel" (*HEA*, 1954, p. 290). The reason is that different writings of Aristotle include, on the one hand, references to the intrinsic value of money, but on the other hand also to its form as legal tender with the value set by law. See also Carruthers and Ariovich (2010, p. 25) or Cesarano (2014, p. 181).

[30] In addition to *Thomas of Aquinas* (1225–74)), Schumpeter (*WdG*, 1970, p. 44) refers in particular to *Jean Buridan* (1300–58) and *Nicole Oresme* (1320–82).

[31] *HEA*, 1954, p. 290.

[32] Quotation from Cesarano (2014, p. 187) referring to a text by Oresme from 1360.

[33] Goetzmann (2016).

3
Ascending capitalism

> [*Capitalism*] may be said to imply, first, private ownership of nonpersonal means of production, such as land, mines, industrial plants and equipment; and, second, production for private account, i.e., production by private initiative for private profit. But, third, the institution of bank credit is so essential to the functioning of the capitalist system that, though not strictly implied in the definition, it should be added to the other two criteria.
>
> (J.A. Schumpeter, 1946, p. 189)

The introduction of paper money in China had depended on a strong government within a large and unified empire. In contrast, similar developments were inconceivable in the fragmented European territories. As precious metals tended to drain off to markets with higher purchasing power, fiat money would have rapidly led to a shortage of internationally convertible currency. Instead, other instruments evolved. In the medieval feudal societies, finance had traditionally depended on the ownership of land as the foremost source of wealth and income. Over time, however, the excessive demand for resources by rivalrous European rulers, together with the continuous expansion of trade routes and international commercial relationships, offered opportunities for financial innovation, while the growing volume of transactions also led to increased specialization. Finance, thus, gradually evolved from auxiliary services into a sophisticated business. This chapter tracks some major developments of the era, ranging from novel instruments to the management of sovereign debt, commercial credit, and the origins of modern corporations, and addresses the early theoretical contentions that were induced by the expansion of financial innovation.

3.1 Sovereign debt

Without the benefit of fiat money, European rulers were continually struggling to balance their financial resources and expenditures. Among the earliest large organizations to thrive on novel financial services, the *Knights Templar* was a military monastic order that maintained a vast network of fortresses to protect pilgrims on their voyages to the Holy Land. It was founded in 1119 CE and active from about 1129 to 1312 CE. Its particular combination of military expertise,

Schumpeter's Venture Money. Michael Peneder and Andreas Resch,
Oxford University Press (2021). © Michael Peneder and Andreas Resch.
DOI: 10.1093/oso/9780198804383.003.0003

Table 3.1 Selected milestones of financial innovation up to the early eighteenth century

Time (ca.)	Location	Earliest evidence of ...
1129–1312	Pilgrim routes	**Multinational** banking (the *Templars*)
1172	Venice	**Government bonds** (forced loan on wealthy citizens)
1202	Pisa	Hindu-Arab **numerals** in Europe
13th to 16th century	Northern Italy and Europe	**Deposit banking**, fractional reserves; (negotiable) bills of exchange, money market
13th century	Various	Life annuities (monasteries, government)
1288	Falun	**Corporation** (oldest preserved shares)
1327	Germany	Corporate mining shares (*Kuxe*)
1347	Genoa	Marine **insurance**
1407	Genoa	Early **chartered bank** (*Casa di San Giorgio*)
1450	Venice	Systematic patent rights (glass makers)
1494	Venice	Description of double-entry bookkeeping
1555/1600	London	Trading companies (*Muscovy*; *East India Company*)
1602	Amsterdam	**Stock exchange** (fully tradable shares of *VOC*)
1609	Amsterdam	Pay by account in standardized currency (*Wisselbank*)
1633	London	Bank issue of **paper money**
1637	Amsterdam	Tulip mania
1694	London	**Bank of England** (joint-stock)
1671–1724	Various	**Probability** (de Witt, Bernoulli, Halley, de Moivre)
1720	Paris, London	Mississippi and South Sea **Bubble**

piety, and non-profit business made it a trusted financial institution, not just for depositing money and enacting long-distance remittances. Arguably, the Templars order was the first multinational banking organization (Table 3.1). As the recipient of generous donations, typically land property, it increasingly loaned money to the aristocracy, especially in Britain and France, where it became a "de facto royal treasury and accounting office."[1]

The particular dependence on sovereign lending, and hence politics, is also evident in the earliest history of the private banking business, which had its roots in a variety of merchant activities (see Section 3.2). For instance, large and diversified Florentine houses failed in 1345 after the British king defaulted on part of his debt. Later, the Medici family thrived on their close ties and expanding business with the Vatican, while the bank's downfall came with the family's expulsion from Florence in 1494.[2]

[1] Goetzmann (2016, p. 211). The Templars' later downfall was no less spectacular. After their military function had become obsolete, with their political neutrality and independence antiquated and their financial claims presenting an increasing burden to indebted rulers, the French king simply had their grand master and highest-ranking officials arrested and prosecuted.

[2] Cassis and Cottrell (2015, p. 14f).

Further financial innovations were propelled by continued warfare among the competing city states of Venice, Genoa, Pisa, and Florence. These all sought somewhat different solutions to funding their rising military expenditures.[3] Venice took a bold step when in 1172 it issued the first *government bond* through a forced loan (*prestiti*) on its wealthiest citizens, who earned interest on the debt instead of paying higher taxes.[4] In 1262 all Venetian debt was consolidated into a single fund of perpetual bonds (the "Monte Vecchi"), which the government could not retire, but the holders were allowed to trade on the secondary Rialto market. New loans were issued in times of need and the Venetian practice thus created a venerable market for government bonds.

At the time, however, bonds raised the moral dilemma of charging interest. Condemnation of usury was known in ancient India. Its explicit prohibition appears in Jewish writings from the eighth and seventh centuries BCE, in which the *Book of Deuteronomy* forbade charging interest for loans among the Israelites. Christianity and Islam later universally applied that principle to all loans.[5] As Aristotle had, they opposed the principle that "money begets money." Böhm-Bawerk later summarized the canonical repudiation of interest as follows:

> In the eyes of the canonists loan interest is simply an income which the lender draws by fraud or force from the resources of the borrower. The lender is paid in interest for fruits which barren money cannot bear. [In short,] interest always appears as a parasitic profit, extorted or filched from the defrauded borrower.
>
> (Böhm-Bawerk, 1884/90, p. 32)

Yet practical needs propelled the search for other solutions. One popular system involved was *life annuities*, as for example practiced in the monasteries or as part of marriage contracts. But annuities also offered an attractive alternative to public finance, since the implied insurance against the "risk of outliving one's resources"[6] allowed the issuer of an annuity to demand a compensation and hence eschew the ceilings on interest rates from the usury laws. With growing government demand, they became a popular instrument in many cities of northern Europe from the second half of the thirteenth century onward. Similarly to the Venetian bonds, in this system citizens had the opportunity to buy social security by investing current income and wealth, though the duration was limited to the purchaser's remaining life span.[7]

[3] Pezzolo (2016).

[4] Goetzmann (2016, p. 230). When the military expedition failed, the debt became permanent, though the doge was killed by an angry mob.

[5] Knoll (2008, p. 101ff). [6] Poterba (2005, p. 208).

[7] Goetzmann (2016, p. 258f) credits Girolamo Cardano (1501–76) with being the first to count and analytically compare frequencies. In 1671, Johan de Witt introduced the idea of using expected life duration to determine the value of an annuity. In addition to gambling, the valuation problem triggered many advances in the mathematical calculus of probability. In 1686, Jakob Bernoulli introduced the *law*

Finally, in 1407 the major creditors of Genoa formed the *Casa di San Giorgio*, which assumed the city's outstanding debt in return for the control of major revenue sources (e.g., customs duties). By issuing tradable shares, the company effectively transformed public debt into private equity and thus earned dividends in place of interest.

3.2 Merchant banking

Sovereign lending was not the only trigger of financial innovation. In the twelfth century, Northern Italy was a thriving commercial region with a variety of financial services that included money exchange, credit, the managing of accounts, or brokerage commonly conducted "over the counter" on wooden tables known as *banci*. For a long time, these banking activities remained informal and secondary to a merchant's other trades. Transfers between bank accounts from the late twelfth century in Genoa are among the earliest evidence of this type of activity. As an early example of financial regulation, Venice imposed a minimum capitalization requirement for exchange bankers in 1270.[8]

Among other factors, usury laws exerted growing pressure on the ancient practice of sea loans, where additional interest could buy the right to cancel a loan in case of shipwreck or similar losses. This incited the emergence of separate contracts for marine insurance in the form of legally valid payment for *securitas*. The earliest known such contract originates from Genoa in 1347.[9]

These and other financial innovations were fostered by progress on the intellectual front, in particular the application of commercial calculus and accounting. In 1202 Leonardo of Pisa (Fibonacci) introduced Hindu-Arab numerals in Italy and was the first to compare the present value of alternative cash flows. Another example is the Franciscan friar Lucca Pacioli. In 1494 he provided the earliest description of *double-entry bookkeeping* as an effective "technology of verification," whether debits and credits match.

Banks managed *deposits*, for instance, for fellow merchants and wealthy individuals. Traditionally, these meant the safe custody of fungible assets, which the depositor could claim at any time and for which the bank earned a fee as compensation. Interest was not an issue, since the terms of a deposit generally implied full reserves. This was, for instance, the kind of deposit the Templars had

of large numbers, Edmund Halley presented the first mortality table in 1693, and in 1724 Abraham de Moivre published a comprehensive mathematical treatise on the valuation problem. Poterba (2005, p. 214) concludes that the "basic framework for annuity valuation developed during this period" and "is very similar to that used today."

[8] Cassis and Cottrell (2015, p. 8f).

[9] The Prudential Insurance Company of America (1915, p. 4); Ferguson (2008, p. 185).

offered, while credit to sovereigns or others relied on their own vast riches. The alternative fixed term contracts had already been codified in Roman commercial law. Such time-limited deposits had to be returned by a specified date, until which the bank was free to use the funds for its own business. If the bank chose to further lend the money to other merchants, it effectively became an intermediary between savings and investment.

Still, many lenders faced opportunity costs that called for an economic equivalent to interest. The Florentine banks were particularly inventive in circumventing the restrictions imposed by the usury laws. They introduced the *deposito a discrezione*, which allowed borrowers to use the funds "at their own discretion", in return for which they were expected to pay a gift instead of interest:

> The bankers professed that discrezione was a free gift and not a contractual obligation. In fact, it was not recoverable by law and did not give rise to a legal claim until it had been written to the credit of the depositor in the banker's books. [... T]he Church forbade the taking of interest as usury, but it did not forbid the bankers to make gifts and to be kind and generous toward depositors. Of course, a banker could not help offering the same discrezione, or yield, as his competitors, lest he lose his customers. (de Roover, 1963, p. 102)

While business was often creative in establishing exceptions to the usury laws, doubts about their principal validity on theoretical grounds were rare. Böhm-Bawerk therefore commented dryly:

> Italy stood immediately under the eye of the Roman church. But Italy was the country in Europe that earliest attained a great position in trade and commerce; and on that account it was bound to be the first to find the pressure of the canon prohibition unbearable. The general attitude towards it may be explained by two considerations; that nowhere in Europe did the prohibition of interest remain in fact more inoperative, and that nowhere in Europe was it so late before the theorists ventured to oppose the Church's statute.
>
> (Böhm-Bawerk, 1884/90, p. 45f)

More deliberate steps toward overcoming the prohibition of interest occurred in the territories where the Roman church had a less direct influence. In England, Henry VIII substituted prohibition with regulation through a legal rate as early as 1545. "Thus the theoretical question whether loan interest was justifiable or not was practically answered before there was any theoretical economic doctrine."[10]

[10] Böhm-Bawerk (1884/90, p. 42). Later prohibition was briefly reimposed and finally abandoned in 1571.

In the same year, on the Continent the French Protestant *John Calvin* (1509–64) was among the first to take up the theoretical argument and reason that a loan enabled the borrower to employ money with a gain that justified the interest. In his letter *De Usuris* he argued that interest on commercial loans should be permitted (subject to qualifications, such as not being levied on people in urgent need). One year later, the French Protestant and legal scholar *Charles Dumoulin* (Molinaeus, 1500–66) published a more elaborate treatise on the topic.[11] Their ideas fell on fertile ground in the Netherlands, where in 1630 another French scholar *Claudius Salmasius* (1588–1653) triggered a wave of further debate. Among the most notable consequences, the Dutch Reformed Church finally admitted money lenders to the sacraments.

In the meantime, private banking further evolved through the growing practice of *fractional reserves* for demand deposits.[12] Larger banks increasingly realized that in the regular course of business they only needed to hold a fraction of the actual liabilities in assets available for current withdrawal. This freed up funds ("bank money") for either their own investments or loans, with the effect of increasing monetary circulation. According to Usher (1934), this development marked the origin of organized deposit banking.[13]

The discounting of *bills of exchange* became another means of circumventing the restrictive usury laws. The price difference between outgoing and returning bills could substitute the payment of interest—a method that was especially convenient for payments in different currencies. Typically held for the brief maturity of a few months (e.g., for the period between two trade fairs), they became a popular instrument of short-term commercial credit. Further facilitating the transfer of funds over long distances, bills of exchange gained importance with the expansion of far-reaching trade during the thirteenth and fourteenth centuries. The novel practices spread to north-western Europe, often via subsidiary establishments of the Italian merchant banks at the major trade fairs.

The large European *fairs* thus became important drivers of financial development. Given the many currencies of the fragmented political territories, money changers were in high demand. Furthermore, merchants regularly had to clear their accounts and settle outstanding debits and credits. When this was not instantly possible, so-called *lettres de foire* guaranteed the deferred payments.[14]

[11] Böhm-Bawerk (1884/90, p. 35).

[12] Usher (1934, p. 406; 1943); de Roover (1963); Binswanger (2015); or Cassis and Cottrell (2015, p. 8f). In contrast, De Soto (2002) suspects that fractional reserves explain incidences of default already seen in ancient Greek and Roman banks.

[13] "Deposit banking developed rapidly in all the more important commercial centres of Europe in the course of the thirteenth century. The wide extent of this development was undoubtedly fostered by the influence of the Templars and the Italian merchants following the fairs. The relative uniformity of the practice was also fostered at this time, and later by the influence of Roman law upon the commercial law" (Usher, 1934, p. 409).

[14] Situated in a favorable location between northern Europe and the Mediterranean, the Champagne fair enjoyed much success during the late twelfth and thirteenth centuries. At the time, it became

In contrast to such promises to pay, bills of exchange were used to order a payment. In late medieval times, these were not transferable but tied to the particular person referred to in the document. This required precisely the type of repeated personal encounter that the international fairs offered.

However, financial innovation, in particular the growing *negotiability* of bills, also contributed to the fairs' later decline. An important step was the possibility to endorse another person as the claimant of the payment, who was not mentioned in the initial document but only later noted, for example, on its back side. This practice is documented for Italian merchants at least as early as the beginning of the fifteenth century. Not only did it increase the negotiability of bills, but it also reduced the need to issue new ones. The growing negotiability of bills thus eroded the function of the exchange bankers in settling accounts among merchants at the fairs, while permanent market places benefited from the enhanced opportunities of circulation.[15]

In short, with "the help of endorsement and discount the bill of exchange had become a popular negotiable paper developing into 'international money.'"[16] The earliest financial markets then emerged from a dense network of merchant bankers in the international centers of trade that operated on a permanent basis.[17] For example, in Bruges the *Place de la Bourse* hosted north-western Europe's main money market until Antwerp's city fair became more popular in the sixteenth century. At the *Nieuwe Beurs* the exchange brokers of Antwerp established daily exchange rates and made the bills of exchange fully negotiable.[18] While bills of exchange established an order to pay, typically to a specific bearer by name, the alternative *letter obligatory* acknowledged a transferable debt payable to the bearer with longer maturities of up to one year. Only after the resolution of legal uncertainties with regard to transferability did they become a preferred instrument of commercial credit.

Similarly, the traditional bills of exchange became increasingly negotiable. For example, the Amsterdam Exchange Bank (*Wisselbank*) was founded in 1609 to increase the efficiency and reliability of commercial transactions, among other methods by denominating accounts in a standardized currency (the *florin banco*). Handling all the payments by account rather than the physical exchange of

Europe's principal bullion and money market (Cassis and Cottrell, 2015, p. 11). Further examples of large fairs that gained particular prominence were those in Lyon, Bruges, Antwerp, Frankfurt, and Leipzig. Later, their importance declined relative to the permanent centers of exchange in cities such as Venice in the fifteenth or Amsterdam in sixteenth century.

[15] "Thus, the fair places and fair bankers protested the longest and hardest against allowing endorsements, or at least repeated endorsement, as the practice of endorsing would have broken their monopoly in trading with bills of exchange at fairs for all times" (Denzel (2008, p. 12ff).

[16] Denzel (2008, p. 22). [17] Hicks (1989, p. 48); Battilossi (2016, p. 218).

[18] Cassis and Cottrell (2015, p. 12ff).

coins, it "pioneered the system of cheques and direct debits or transfers."[19] Not allowed to provide loans, the Wisselbank abstained from fractional reserves, and private cashiers began to offer commercial credit and other banking services.[20] Around that time, Amsterdam became the focal point of financial innovation, often considered the "birthplace" of modern corporations and the stock market.

In contrast, London still lacked a public exchange bank similar to that of Amsterdam, and by the middle of the seventeenth century commercial transfers had to rely on credit and trust within the merchant networks.[21] Providing professional mediation, scriveners had acted as loan brokers from the mid-sixteenth century onward, but they were increasingly replaced by lawyers. These subsequently turned to issuing notes that were drawn on deposits. Typically, they earned a brokerage fee instead of interest, but fractional reserves became common practice.[22] While the scriveners generally lent rather small amounts within a close personal network of clients, some of the goldsmiths started to exploit their connections to the Royal Mint on a bigger scale, adding deposit banking and by the 1670s also the issue of paper money to their regular trade in bullion.[23]

3.3 The corporation

The term corporation originates from the Latin word *corpus*, which designated a "body" of people authorized to act as a legal entity. In medieval societies, the townships, ecclesiastical communities, universities, and guilds shaped the early idea of "corporateness" in the sense of communities that qualified for particular privileges awarded by the crown, paid contributions in return and had to comply with certain regulations.[24] Its evolution was accordingly driven by the continuous tension between the striving for autonomy of particular groups of people on the one hand, and their coupling to the control and will of public authorities on the other.

The *Encyclopaedia Britannica* defines the corporation as a business organization of persons and material resources chartered by the state. Four key features make it particularly effective in raising large capital funds.[25] First of all, *juridicial*

[19] Ferguson (2008, p. 48).

[20] This was after lifting a ban on their activities in 1621 (Cassis and Cottrell, 2015, p. 20).

[21] "All English merchants and traders conducted their business within a web of credit so that prices for goods contained an interest element to the extent that price discounts were given when, unusually, a cash transaction was involved" (Cassis and Cottrell, 2015, p. 30).

[22] "However, it is clear that many took advantage of their clients' deposits, lending out a proportion via their own accounts over the periods when they were idle. Indeed, the intimate personal links that developed between scriveners and their depositors provided knowledge of the seasonal timing of both the receipt of clients' incomes and their expenditure habits" (Cassis and Cottrell, 2015, p. 32).

[23] The first issue by Henry Futter is dated 1633 (Cassis and Cottrell, 2015, p. 34). See also Binswanger (2015).

[24] Laski (2017); Micklethwait and Wooldridge (2003, p. 3–14).

[25] https://www.britannica.com/topic/corporation.

personality establishes a legal entity that can make contracts, hold property rights, sue, and be sued. Second, *indefinite duration* allows the corporation to outlive its founders and current owners. Third, the *transferability* of shares asserts flexibility through the ownership of securities instead of direct investments. And, finally, *limited liability* caps the potential loss of investors. Initially granted only as a rare privilege, it did not diffuse widely until the mid-nineteenth century.[26]

Some of Europe's oldest known corporate forms emerged in the traditional sectors of mining and grain mills. For example, *Stora-Enso* claims to have issued the oldest preserved corporate shares for its Swedish parent mining company *Stora Kopparberg* in 1288. Its royal charter goes back to 1347. Similarly, in Germany special mining shares (so-called *Kuxe*) are documented as early as 1327. In contrast to the practice of modern corporate stock, the holders had to partake and increase their investment in the case of capital calls, or other wise either sell their certificates or return them to the cooperative.[27] The same was true for the French *Honor del Bazacle* in Toulouse. Established through the merger of twelve watermill companies, it was formally incorporated in 1372.[28] Goetzmann relates its unique history to the particular persistence of Roman law that was maintained by local rulers and allowed for a flexible system of property rights and contracts.

In England, privileges encouraging foreign commerce and overseas ventures generated a major impulse for the evolution of the modern corporation. While the known trade routes were awarded to and controlled by the association of *Merchant Adventurers*, the prospect of new passages to unknown territories offered an opportunity to bypass the established guild and thereby generate new revenues for the debt-ridden crown.[29] Chartered in 1555, the *Muscovy Company* gave birth to a new method of venture finance, which became the template for other overseas trading companies to follow: forming a joint-stock company, the crown's privilege was monetized through the sale of tradable shares, which subsequently funded the expeditions.[30] But the new formula was no guarantee for success, as various failed endeavors proved the adventurous nature of the overseas charters. In contrast, the British *East India Company* was among the most profitable.[31]

As regards financial innovation, the *Vereenigde Oost-Indische Compagnie* (VOC) is of particular interest. Founded in 1602 through the merger of the trading

[26] Michie (2016, p. 242). [27] Goetzmann (2016, p. 303).

[28] See Sicard (1953); Goetzmann (2016); or Le Bris et al. (2019). As early as 1138 some founders had operated a partnership. In 1888 the company switched to the generation of hydroelectricity and in 1946 was absorbed into France's national public electricity utility (EDF).

[29] Goetzmann (2016, p. 308f); Laski (1917, p. 587). For instance, in 1496 the British king awarded the Venetian citizen John Cabot a monopoly for all trade with newly discovered territories in return for a 20 percent tax on profits.

[30] While exploring a north-east passage to China, the Muscovy actually prospered due to its exclusive trade rights with the Russian ports. As in the previous examples in Continental Europe, shareholders had to either partake in capital calls or sell their stock.

[31] Initially founded in 1600 by a temporary charter for fifteen years, it developed into one of the most powerful forces of British colonialism (Micklethwait and Wooldridge, 2003).

companies in various Dutch cities, it was initially chartered for ten years during which the investors' capital was locked into the venture. To compensate for the long-term commitment, shares were however made fully tradable. This move generated much liquidity and led to Amsterdam hosting the world's first formal stock exchange.[32] While the convenient transferability of shares at an early stage induced speculative trading, its development was also furthered by the VOC's later transition to permanent capital, allowance of limited liability, and annual dividend payments.[33]

When William of Orange conquered Britain during the *Glorious Revolution* of 1688, the advanced Dutch know-how in the financing of corporate ventures rapidly spread to London, where it not only met with a larger and deeper market, but also with a surging enthusiasm for business opportunities:

> This culture rested on the company as the central unit of enterprise, it involved an ever-widening public eager to invest and the development of intermediaries who promoted companies, bought and sold shares, wrote options, and made a market. It would take years for the legal and regulatory system to catch up to this new culture. (Goetzmann, 2016, p. 326)

The establishment of the *Bank of England* in 1694 was another major step in the financial evolution that took place during that era. Although it was founded in 1694 in response to the needs of sovereign debt and continued warfare, the Bank of England thrived on the privileges that it received in return for large loans to the state. It exclusively possessed the government's balances and the right to issue notes as a joint-stock company with limited liability.[34] Starting out as an exclusive bank to the state and the social elite, it later evolved to become the primary "banker's bank" and the central pivot of the British system of commercial credit. This development, however, was the outcome of a long period characterized by financial growth and turbulence as well as an unprecedented degree of theoretical reflection and discourse, which we will take up in the next section.

[32] Ferguson (2008); Lodewijk (2014). Alternate claims are made for the *London Stock Exchange*. It was founded in 1698 by John Castaing, who posted regular lists of stock and commodity prices in a coffee-house at *Change Alley*. Stockbrokers increasingly attended the place, since they were not allowed to operate at the *Royal Exchange*—reportedly because of their rude manners.

[33] Additional impetus came with the foundation of the *West India Company* (WIC) in 1621: "The speculative boon generated by the VOC and WIC worked as a hothouse for the city's financial market," known for its advanced "techniques, including the pledging of shares as loan collateral, repo transactions, forwards, and futures" (Geldeblom and Jonker, 2005, p. 199f).

[34] Only in 1826 did new legislation allow the establishment of other joint-stock banks, provided they operated at least 65 miles outside of London. In 1833 the geographic restriction was lifted for banks that did not issue notes. The Bank of England remained privately owned until its nationalization in 1946.

3.4 Early monetary contentions

The quantity theory

Theoretical metallism was commensurate to the preoccupation with the accumulation of gold and silver, especially during the heyday of mercantilism from the sixteenth to the eighteenth centuries. In the later classical period, mercantilism was the favorite foe to oppose with pride and rigor. In contrast, Schumpeter pointed out that mercantilism had never produced a coherent doctrine and that its economic considerations had mainly originated in the practical concerns of the time. For instance, the accumulation of precious metals typically related to a ruler's striving for political power, when specie was needed to purchase military equipment abroad or to keep allies aligned.

Historical events increasingly challenged the received wisdom and triggered a slow but important theoretical reorientation (Table 3.2). After the American conquests had brought about large inflows of precious metals to Europe, Jean Bodin (1530–96) was the first to point this out as the cause of rising prices and give it priority over other explanations, such as the debasement of coinage, the prevalence of monopolies, violent depredations during wartime, or excessive public expenditures. Schumpeter acknowledged Bodin's contribution, but credited Bernardo Davanzati (1529–1606) with having first expressed the *quantity*

Table 3.2 Selected milestones of monetary thought up to the nineteenth century

Author	Ideas
Jixia Academy (4th century BCE)	Money for exchange and measure of value; law of supply and demand
Plato (ca. 390–370 BCE)	Symbolic money facilitating exchange
Aristotle (ca. 340 BCE)	Commodity money facilitating exchange, measurement, and store of value
Calvin (1545)	Acknowledging interest on commercial loans
Jean **Bodin** (1568)	Inflow of precious metals raises prices
B. **Davanzati** (1588)	Quantity theorem in rudimentary form
William **Potter** (ca. 1650)	Cash-in-advance problem; paper for safe assets
William **Petty** (1665)	Velocity of ...
John **Locke** (1691)	...money
John **Briscoe** (1694)	Equation of exchange (w/o velocity)
John **Law** (1705)	Supply and demand; managed currency; issuing paper for expected capital gains
Richard **Cantillon** (1730)	Term *vitesse de la circulation*
F. **Galiani** (1750)	Utility and scarcity (*utilità e rarità*)
David **Hume** (1752)	Price-specie-flow mechanism; continuous and modest increase in money supply
P.N. **Christiernin** (1761)	Sticky wages and asymmetric price changes
Adam **Smith** (1776)	Real bills doctrine

theorem in its rudimentary form.[35] Like the early Chinese writings, he argued that gold had no value in use. He identified its function not as a measure of value, but in the command of other commodities, that is, its purchasing power. Still a staunch metallist, Davanzati argued that the scarcity of precious metals relative to commodities determines their value in exchange.[36]

Just as metallism helped denounce the practice of currency debasement, the quantity theory was instrumental in repudiating the mercantilist preoccupation with trade surpluses for the purpose of accumulating precious metals. It argues that an increase in the supply of circulating media raises general prices, but not output. In 1694, John Briscoe presented a first *equation of exchange* by setting the stock of money equal to prices times real income. But he failed to account for the velocity of money, an idea which had already been introduced in 1665 by William Petty (1623–87) and had been further elaborated by John Locke (1632–1704)[37] and Richard Cantillon (1680s–1734), who introduced the term *vitesse de la circulation*.[38] Schumpeter therefore credits John William Lubbock (1803–65) with providing the first elaborate formulation of the "equation of exchange" in 1840. Surviving many decades of heated contentions, the quantity theory peaked in influence and came to dominate monetary thought during the period from 1870 to 1914.[39] At the end of this period, the Fisher and Cambridge equations produced its definite formal representation. We will return to these for a more detailed discussion in the context of Schumpeter's own take on the quantity theory in Section 6.2.

Money supply and idle resources

As one of the early proponents of theoretical cartalism Schumpeter named the physiocrat Boisguillebert (1646–1714), who had considered money to be a pledge for future delivery in credit relationships. Further impetus came from the British land bank proposals, which suggested issuing bills secured by land or other property instead of specie. Schumpeter was critical of the idea in general, but lauded *William Potter* (1650), who had maintained that a lack of specie obstructs commerce in a country where precious metals are scarce:

[35] The *Lezione delle monete* of 1588. See also *HEA* (1954, p. 312ff).

[36] In a treatise from 1751, Ferdinando Galiani (1728–87), one of the forefathers of subjective value theory, characterized it by the expressive notion of *utilità e rarità*. According to Cesarano (2014, p. 198) and "[n]otwithstanding his uncompromising metallist stance, however, Galiani puts forward a comprehensive cartalist hypothesis based on the informational efficiency of money."

[37] Letter to a member of parliament in the year 1691.

[38] The *Essai sur la Nature du Commerce en Général* was published in 1730.

[39] Laidler (1991).

> though the store-house of the world be never so full of commodity, yet seeing the tradesman cannot afford to take it in, faster than he can find sale for what he has already, it follows, that if the people through their extreme poverty, are not able to take it off from the hands of the tradesman, the door in that respect is shut against trade, and by consequence against wealth. (Potter 1650, p. 56)

Taking poverty as sufficient evidence for the underemployment of resources, Potter insisted that an increase in the money supply would employ idle resources and raise output:

> On the other side, let it be supposed that money (or that which goes for such) does increase amongst them; it follows, that (they not hoarding it up, but laying it out in commodity, as fast as they receive it) the more their hands are filled with such money, by the increase thereof, so much the more does the sale of commodity, that is trading, increase; and this increase of trading does increase riches, and that so much the faster; because such riches increase men's expenses; therefore their trading, therefore their riches, and so perpetually; by which means then, you see the door is opened to the increase of wealth [...]. Therefore increase of money, or that which goes for such, not hoarded up, is the key of wealth.
>
> (Potter 1650, p. 56)

Potter likely influenced other non-metallists of the era, among whom Schumpeter for example singles out Nicholas Barbon (1640–98) and James Steuart (1707–80). They shared the believe that an increase in the money supply would raise the amount of spending and production. Another example is *John Law* (1671–1729), who supported the idea of a large national bank in Scotland that should increase the money supply by lending notes to be secured by land property. Law pointed out that Scotland not only suffered from an extraordinary scarcity of silver, but that its value depended on the international changes of demand and supply, upon which it had practically no influence. In contrast, land would have had the particular advantage that it could not increase in quantity or lose any of its uses.[40] Schumpeter related both Potter and Law to what he called *Becher's Principle*,[41] according to which people's expenditures on consumption are the prime mover of the economy—a theme which also fares prominently in Schumpeter's monetary foundations of the theory of economic development (Section 6.1).

[40] Law (1705, p. 34ff).

[41] He named it after the mercantilist Johann Joachim Becher (1635–82), who—fitting this special cast of characters—had to leave Vienna to escape his creditors. See *HEA* (1954, p. 283f; 294).

Managed currency

Although Law's land bank proposal was never adopted, his treatise introduced several advanced ideas. For instance, starting with the paradox of value, he originated the famous example of the demand and supply of "water and diamonds":

> Water is of great use, yet of little value; because the quantity of water is much greater than the demand for it. Diamonds are of little use, yet of great value, because the demand for diamonds is much greater, than the quantity of them.
>
> (Law, 1705, p. 1)

Exhibiting a clear mind with respect to economic value, Law acknowledged that prices must rise when the demand for money falls short of its supply, not intending to increase its quantity beyond full employment.[42] What set Law apart from the monetary orthodoxy, however, was that he consistently argued the case against metallism. In his own words, "money is not the value *for* which goods are exchanged, but the value *by* which they are exchanged."[43] According to Schumpeter, this "cuts the cable that so far has tied money to a commodity having 'intrinsic' value." Consequently, "since silver that serves as money has no other use than to buy goods, it might just as well be replaced by a cheaper material, in the limiting case by one that has no commodity value at all, such as printed paper".[44]

Of further interest to Schumpeter, Law had presented paper money as a natural progression in the evolution of monetary economies. First, the use of specie had enabled the transformation from barter to monetary exchange.[45] But that transformation was incomplete in that its restricted availability still left many resources underemployed. Law perceived that the further advance toward a managed paper currency could lift underdeveloped regions from their monetary constraints "as this addition to the money, will employ the people are now idle, and these now employed to more advantage: so the product will be encreased, and manufacture advanced" (Law, 1705, p. 42). In short, what appealed to Schumpeter was the demonstration

[42] Murphy (2009, p. 48) even suggests that Milton Friedman (1956) adopted his perspective when redefining the Quantity Theory in terms of the demand for money instead of its supply.

[43] Law (1705, p. 40; emphasis added).

[44] *HEA* (1954, p. 321f). Relatedly, "Law's argument admits of the following reconstruction: he first observed—a clear gain to analysis—that the use of a commodity as a means of circulation affects its value; from this it follows that the exchange value of the monetary commodity as money can no more be explained by its exchange value as a commodity than the latter can be explained by the former—although, of course, so long as the monetary commodity can freely move between its monetary and its industrial uses, the two must tbe equal" (*HEA*, 1954, p. 321).

[45] "As money encreased, the disadvantages and inconveniences of barter were removed; the poor and idle were employed, more of the land was labored, the product encreased, manufactures and trade improved, the landed-men lived better, and the people with less dependence on them" (Law, 1705, p. 4).

> "that there is an advantage other than cheapness and absence of worry about how to get and keep an adequate supply of money—it is that the quantity of money is fully manageable. This, then, seems to have been the work that gave birth to the idea of Managed Currency, which was subsequently lost to the large majority of economists until it forced itself upon them after 1919." (*HEA*, 1954, p. 321f)

Finally, John Law exemplifies the tenuous relationship between monetary thought and economic history. As an exception that proves the rule, his theoretical advances were driving historical events. When Law found the opportunity to vigorously realize his vision in practice as a finance minister of France, his success was indeed extraordinary, but short-lived, and resulted in a spectacular failure. Infamous for personally having fabricated history's first international large-scale financial crisis,[46] he simultaneously proved the power and extraordinary risks of a managed currency.

3.5 Financial bubbles

One important lesson from economic history that Schumpeter absorbed early on is that radical innovation, whether in production or finance, tends to shock the system and may induce a bubble of confidence and corresponding overinvestment. An early example was the Dutch options market, which in 1637 generated a futures bubble known as *tulip mania*. Similarly, the vivid stock markets soon led to a boom in company promotions. Furthermore, the charter of novel trade monopolies was a tempting means of restructuring the public debt of warring sovereigns. And the more desperate a situation became, the more reckless were the schemes they turned to. But the notorious epitome of a disastrous financial speculation was fabricated by John Law. The so-called *Mississippi Bubble* is particularly noteworthy for its radical combination of financial, fiscal, and monetary instruments that went far beyond anyone's imagination at the time.

The son of a goldsmith in Edinburgh, John Law had early learned the practice of banking but lost his family's fortune at the gambling tables in London. After a fatal duel he was convicted of murder and sentenced to death by the age of 23, but escaped prison and subsequently traveled to Amsterdam, later also to Italy and France. He excelled in his advanced knowledge of mathematical calculus, in particular probability theory, and soon earned a fortune running his own lotteries.

Reportedly, John Law met the French regent Philippe, successor to King Louis XIV, at the gambling dens in Paris.[47] With the regent's permission, Law started his scheme by setting up the *Banque Générale* in 1716. After private shareholders

[46] Kindleberger and Aliber (2005, p. 128).

[47] Micklethwait and Wooldridge (2003, p. 37).

were bought out by the state, he later converted it into the *Banque Royale*. The bank served to finance the consolidation of various trading companies into a single giant conglomerate, which held the monopoly rights of all French overseas trade: the *Compagnie des Indes*.[48]

The main plot was to take over public debt in return for the monopolies guaranteed to the company, which in turn traded its shares for the debt to investors. With public debt taken off the market, the interest rate declined, which further relieved the state of its enormous financial burden. Simultaneously, the Banque Royale issued notes that were loaned against the company shares[49] to the effect that the additional liquidity drove up share prices and nourished expectations of further gains. To dry up private derivative markets, Law also offered options for future purchases of the company shares. Furthermore, the company used the return on additional shares to lend money to the king, who could then repay the outstanding government debt, while the company also took over the national tax farms. When in February of 1720 the bank and the company formally merged, Law's plot seemed complete and the radical cure of the state's finance a success.

However, injecting liquidity into the market proved easier than keeping it under control. With the French king issuing additional money, share prices continued to shore and by far outpaced any realistic expectations of future profits from the new colonies:

> To conduct this trade, a grand new city was established at the mouth of the Mississippi: New Orleans, named to flatter the always susceptible Regent. Such visions, as we know, were not wholly without foundation, but their realization lay far in the future. To be sure, a few thousand impoverished Germans from the Rhineland, Switzerland and Alsace were recruited to act as colonists. But what the unfortunate immigrants encountered when they reached Louisiana was a sweltering, insect-infested swamp. Within a year 80 per cent of them had died of starvation or tropical diseases like yellow fever. (Ferguson, 2008, p. 144f)

Meanwhile, the monetary expansion caused hyperinflation at home. In May of 1720, Law attempted to curtail liquidity by reducing the value of shares and notes by about half, which however sparked a bank run to change shares for coin and finally caused the bubble to burst. By the end of the year, Law was dismissed of all positions and his property confiscated, and he again fled a country and spent most of his remaining life in Venice.

Law became a target of public mockery and ridicule, typically described in verse as a "quack and charlatan." Montesquieu famously credited him with "the secret of

[48] Also known as the Mississippi Company.

[49] Goetzmann (2016, p. 356) compares this form of collateralized borrowing to modern equity repurchase agreements (repo facilities).

catching the wind in balloons."[50] Among economists, he was doubly marginalized, first for his opposition to metallism, and second for his unprecedented failure in policy. From Hume and Smith to Marshall and many others, mainstream economists were at best ambiguous in acknowledging a certain genius, while stressing his "recklessness" and unbalanced nature. Even Keynes avoided any association of his monetary views with those of Law. Murphy therefore expresses his genuine surprise that "for Schumpeter there is no equivocation about Law" and for being "almost unique in that he is unstinting in his praise."[51]

Of course, Schumpeter understood and pointed at the deficiencies in Law's scheme—in particular, the danger of insatiable demands by the government, which resulted in the excessive issue of money and hyperinflation. However, he was unapologetic in his appreciation of the theoretical possibilities that Law had opened up. In his unfinished manuscript on money, Schumpeter drew a clear distinction between the method of issuing paper money and the way it was used. While he considered the first to be sound in principle, he blamed its excessive use, especially for the consumptive purposes of the French court, for having caused its collapse.[52] Later, in *BC* he described Law as having the positive attributes of a "banker-entrepreneur" and argued that the problem "was not that he created means of payment *in vacuo*, but that he used them for purposes which failed to succeed."[53] By the time he wrote the *History of Economic Analysis*, his praise had become outright flamboyant: "John Law [...], I have always felt, is in a class by himself. [...] He worked out the economics of his projects with a brilliance and, yes, profundity, which places him in the front rank of monetary theorists of all times".[54] Schumpeter thus credited Law with having a larger vision that long eluded economists and society. Similarly, Murphy points out that it took three centuries after John Law's birth to break the final link to metallic money through the United States' abandonment of the gold standard in 1971.[55]

All this stands in stark contrast with Law's direct impact on monetary history. Apart from the immediate pecuniary losses suffered by investors, an arguably bigger and more enduringly damaging effect was the consequent disinclination of the French market to embrace financial innovation. Seé argued that "for a long time people had little confidence in 'paper' and securities." Ferguson also concludes that "Law's bubble and bust fatally set back France's financial development, putting Frenchmen off paper money and stock markets for generations."[56]

However, the consequences were also felt beyond the French territories. Before the bubble burst, Law's scheme had had enough appeal to induce the British to found the South Sea Company, which accordingly culminated in the *South Sea Bubble*. A main difference, however, was that the South Sea Company did

[50] Quotation from Murphy (1997, p. 2ff). [51] Murphy (2000, p. 315f).
[52] *WDG* (1970, p. 55). [53] *BC* (1939, pp. 114, 250ff). [54] *HEA* (1954, p. 294f).
[55] Murphy (2000, p. 316). [56] Seé (1928, p. 67); Ferguson (2008, p. 154).

not control the Bank of England, since both organizations were backed by rival political factions.[57] This difference may explain the far lesser damage done to the London marketplace. The resolution of the crisis involved the nationalization of the South Sea Company by the government, which incurred deep losses for investors but saved the market from bigger turmoil.[58] Shortly before the bubble peaked, the so-called *Bubble Act* of 1720 established that all new corporations must obtain a royal charter, effectively restricting the promotion of new corporations and thereby cementing the market power of those already existing until the law's repeal in 1825. Even then, limited liability was subject to royal charter. Only in 1837 was this regulation lifted for ordinary companies, while limited liability was also extended to banks (1855) and insurance companies (1858).

These crises were not mere transitory shocks, but for a prolonged period they set the evolution of financial markets on a different path. As a consequence, during the eighteenth century financial innovation turned away from equities and back toward credit.[59] For example, in 1774 the market in Amsterdam floated the first closed-end mutual fund, turning bonds from governments and banks as well as plantation loans into tradable securities. The opening up of opportunities of diversification to smaller investors made this a significant financial innovation.[60]

3.6 Neutrality of money

With the spectacular failure of Law's financial venture and the simultaneous bursting of the Mississippi and South Sea Bubbles the quantity theory easily became the dominant intellectual doctrine. Expressing his "great doubt concerning the benefit of banks and paper-credit,"[61] *David Hume* (1711–76) was its most important proponent and the pre-eminent figure in the intellectual assault on mercantilism. Schumpeter denied him novelty,[62] but credited him with being "the first to show clearly and explicitly that [...] any quantity of money, however small, will do in an isolated country" and that "with perfect gold currency all round, every country will always tend to have the amount appropriate to its relative position in international trade."[63] The first part of his appraisal referred to the conventional quantity theory in closed economies: "If we consider any one kingdom by itself, it is evident

[57] The Whigs largely controlled the Bank of England, whereas the Tories backed the South Sea Company (Micklethwait and Wooldridge, 2003, p. 39).

[58] Micklethwait and Wooldridge (2003, p. 41).

[59] Goetzmann (2016, p. 383).

[60] Rouwenhorst (2005).

[61] Hume (1752, p. 29).

[62] Referring to Hume's essay "On Money," Schumpeter wrote that its "position in the history of economics, while not undeserved, is due to the force and felicity with which it formulated the results of previous work rather than to any novelties." On the same page he acknowledged that "it is always a 'major event' when an important concept is made explicit and workable, although it was—this is the usual case—implicitly present in previous arguments" (*HEA*, 1954, p. 291).

[63] *HEA* (1954, p. 316).

that the greater or less plenty of money is of no consequences, since the prices of commodities are always proportioned to the plenty of money" (Hume, 1752, p. 27). The second part referred to Hume's famous application of the quantity theory to open economies with international trade, in which he carved out the so-called *price-specie-flow mechanism*:

> It is difficult for a loss of balance to reach the point where it will do considerable harm to a nation. If half the money in England were suddenly destroyed, labor and goods would suddenly become so cheap that there would suddenly follow a great quantity of exports which would attract to us the money of all our neighbours. If half the money which is in England were suddenly doubled, goods would suddenly become more expensive, imports would rise to the disadvantage of exports and our money would be spread among all our neighbours. It does not seem that money, any more than water, can be raised or lowered anywhere much beyond the level it has in places where communication is open, but that it must rise and fall in proportion to the goods and labour contained in each state.
>
> (Hume in a letter to Montesquieu of 1749)[64]

Hume's emphasis on the neutrality of money, according to which its quantity has no lasting impact on production and international exchange relationships, became his most enduring contribution to monetary theory. Three important qualifications, however, are less frequently mentioned. The first plainly emphasizes the political motive, which was arguably the main reason for the mercantilist preoccupation with accumulating specie: "It is only the public which draws any advantage from the greater plenty of money, and that only in its wars and negotiations with foreign states."[65] The second is Hume's emphasis on sticky prices to explain why an increase in the money supply stimulates the economy for a transitional period. Third is his recommendation of "a gradual and universal augmentation of the money," because this "keeps alive a spirit of industry in the nation."[66]

At the time of Hume's writing, Sweden was in the midst of two progressive social experiments. One was the installation of parliamentary democracy in 1739, the other the introduction of an inconvertible paper currency in 1745. The idea was to increase growth, while tight control of imports would ensure the balance of international payments.[67] Consistently with both Hume's hypothesis of sticky prices and an initial restraint in the issue of paper, inflation stayed moderate for some years, but then it accelerated, among other reasons due to the financial

[64] Quotation from Arnon (2011, p. 17f). [65] Hume (1752, p. 27).
[66] Hume (1752, p. 32f).
[67] For this section on the *Swedish Bullion Debate*, see, for example, Rothbard (1995); Humphrey (2004); or Herger (2017).

burden of war. Attempts to curb inflation were initiated in 1762, but three years later a shift of parliamentary power led to a policy of monetary deflation with the aim to re-establish the old parity with silver. Monetary deflation, economic depression, and political turmoil followed, first ending the political experiment of parliamentary democracy through a *coup d'etat* in 1772, and then also bringing back absolute monarchy and the silver parity.

The British classical economists were probably aware of the historical events, but less so of the intellectual discourse taking place in the Swedish language. Most notably, *Pehr Niclas Christiernin* (1725–99) was a lecturer of economics at Uppsala, who was familiar with the treatises of Cantillon, Hume, and others.[68] Writing at the time of inflation he blamed the overissue of money as its primary cause. According to Rothbard, he thereby anticipated the later British bullionists by presenting an equilibrium theory of flexible exchange rates with inconvertible currency.[69]

But Christiernin also argued against the growing demand for a deflationary policy, which was meant to restore prices to pre-inflation levels. Informed by Hume's exposition of the quantity theory, he argued that the general price level was indeed irrelevant, but not its fluctuations. The reason he cited, as did Hume, was sticky prices, since "no one reduces the price of his commodities or his labor until the lack of sales necessitates him to do so. Because of this condition workers must suffer want and the industriousness of wage earners must stop before the established market price can be reduced."[70] Going beyond Hume, however, Christiernin emphasized that wages are stickier than general prices, causing an increase in real wages and a decline in the profit rate to the effect of further overall contraction. Implicitly, he thus presented a mechanism based on which money cannot be neutral. Finally, he emphasized that price adjustments are not only different but generally asymmetric, that is, they go up faster than they go down.[71]

3.7 The *real bills* doctrine

Meanwhile, in England the financial sector had continued to expand, and the new economic reality provoked political controversy and lively theoretical discourse. A first hint at the controversies to follow can be found in the writings of *Adam Smith* (1723–90). Hume was a mentor and close friend, which is why Schumpeter considered it to be "all the more significant" that in his monetary analysis Smith did not "commit himself to more than simple metallism."[72] In the *Wealth of*

[68] He received modest international recognition only after his *Summary of Lectures on the High Price of Foreign Exchange in Sweden*, originally written in 1761, was translated into English in 1971.
[69] Rothbard (1995, p. 220).
[70] Quotation from Humphrey (2004, p. 17f).
[71] Humphrey (2004, p. 17f).
[72] *HEA* (1954, p. 315).

Nations (1776),[73] Smith discussed the advantages of metal coins in a similar manner to Hume's earlier presentation. But he also deviated from the latter in two important respects. First, like many classic writers to follow,[74] he did not endorse the neutrality of money and stayed with its description as the "great wheel of circulation,"[75] which Hume had explicitly rejected.[76] This reservation is consistent with Smith's emphasis on the division of labor that requires money as an efficient medium of exchange and thereby contributes to the growth of productivity.[77]

Second, Smith accepted the reality of banks increasingly issuing paper that was not fully backed by specie, but instead relied on fractional reserves. While the division of labor, the "invisible hand," and the *laissez faire* policies remained his characteristic pivot, he reasoned a mixed monetary system as if it imitated pure metal circulation.[78] On the one hand, the issue of paper increased the efficiency of exchange:

> The substitution of paper in the room of gold and silver money, replaces a very expensive instrument of commerce with one much less costly, and sometimes equally convenient. Circulation comes to be carried on by a new wheel, which it costs less both to erect and to maintain than the old one. (Smith, 1776, p. 317f)

On the other hand, to earn profits and stay solvent, sound practice requires banks to only issue paper in exchange for *real bills* of adequate value, that is, short-term debts that are well-secured:

> When a bank discounts to a merchant a real bill of exchange drawn by a real debtor, and which, as soon as it becomes due, is really paid by that debtor; it only advances to him a part of the value which he would otherwise be obliged to keep by him unemployed and in ready money for answering occasional demands.
> (Smith, 1776, p. 331)

According to the *real bills doctrine*, pure self-interest forces banks to issue paper "responsibly," that is, only if it is backed by assets from a productive activity.[79] This leaves the quantity of money (in a narrow sense) unchanged, while the circulation

[73] Book I, chapter 4, *On the Origins and Use of Money.*

[74] Humphrey (1991) denies the popular notion that the economists of the classical epoch (i.e., ca. 1750–1870) subscribed to the hypothesis of neutral money. Schumpeter (*HEA*, 1954, p. 703) made a similar point: "I maintain that Ricardo, before him Wheatley, after him James Mill and McCulloch, held the quantity theory in this strict sense and that no other major writers did."

[75] Smith (1776, p. 317).

[76] "It is none of the wheels of trade: It is the oil which renders the motion of the wheels more smooth and easy" (Hume, 1752, p. 27).

[77] Smith (1776, Book I, chapter 4, p. 26). See also Arnon (2011, p. 34f).

[78] Arnon (2011, p. 48).

[79] Similarly, banks only offer private credit for consumptive purposes against sufficient collateral.

adapts to the amount of liquidity needed to finance real transactions. Thus, based on the principle of self-organization, unrestricted competitive banking prevents the creation of excess credit without invoking government regulation. At the same time, gold continues to regulate the system implicitly via the convertibility of competing bank notes to the international gold market.[80]

3.8 American independence

By the time Adam Smith published his *Wealth of Nations*, England's North American colonies had already launched their War of Independence (1775–83). Finance and commercial interests were not absent among its drivers and were obviously affected by the outcome. During colonial times British regulations were often at odds with the needs of a young, ambitious, and fast-growing society. The Bubble Act, which continued to restrict incorporation, is a case in point. One consequence was that America's first commercial banks were chartered late—in fact, only when needed to finance the revolution.[81]

The primary asset was ownership of land and the basic proposition for entrepreneurial ventures "was to acquire large, fertile tracts of land, divide them into lots, develop basic infrastructure, and then sell them to American and foreign settlers."[82] But British regulation constrained the development of new land by reserving western territories for the indigenous populations. As Goetzmann (2016, p. 388ff) points out, "[l]and speculation was a common thread that connected many of the leaders of the American Revolution."[83]

After independence, the most pressing problem was the huge war-related sovereign debt, much of it held by banks in Holland and France. *Alexander Hamilton* (1757–1804), the first secretary of the US Treasury, engineered a number of critical reforms to re-establish public credit and initiate a viable financial system for the new federation. One significant element of reform was the resumption of all debt at face value, refinanced by means of new foreign loans and government bonds. Another enduring element was the introduction of import tariffs, which

[80] Arnon (2011, p. 42).

[81] At the beginning of the Revolutionary War, the Continental Congress issued its own paper money (the *Continentals*) which soon depreciated heavily because of overissue and a lack of coordination between Congress and the states. In 1781 the *Bank of North America*, established in Philadelphia, became the first national charter (Downing, 2005).

[82] Goetzmann (2016, p. 389f).

[83] "Restrictions on land banks were also effectively restrictions on mortgage credit in the colonies, and restrictions on western expansion undermined the hopes on which the early American land companies had been built. It is not difficult to understand how the Washingtons, Adamses, Jeffersons, and Franklins would be tempted to support independence. Independent American colonies would be free to pursue a policy of western land development, mortgage banking, and optimal monetary policy. Finance, closely tied to collateralized lending and land speculation through incorporated companies, was an important driver behind the push to independence" (Goetzmann, 2016, p. 389f).

remained the principal source of federal revenues until the introduction of income taxes in 1913. Finally, Hamilton championed the establishment of a central bank, the First *Bank of the United States*, which in 1791 received a temporary charter for twenty years. It was a national commercial bank owned jointly by private stockholders and the federal government.[84] Its shares were among the earliest securities traded on the New York Stock Exchange, founded in 1792.[85]

Delayed by the political opposition of rivalrous state banks, the Second *Bank of the United States* was chartered in 1816. After its term ended, political opposition prevailed and initiated an era of *free banking*. From 1837 to 1862 only the states could charter banks that issued notes against specie. Such commercial banks had existed since the final years of the revolution, but after 1837 their charter was eased and typically required no special legislature. Ineffective supervision and bank failures followed. As a consequence, starting in 1863 new banking acts re-established a national system, which was based on federal charters and encouraged the development of a national currency.[86] Thus, a dual system emerged, in which banks could be chartered either at the state or the national level.

In short, by demonstrating the power of asset-backed money and transforming loans into currency, American westward expansion in certain ways validated the vision of land banks developed by John Law. In contrast with the global turn toward credit during that period, the young USA eschewed the "regulatory backlash in Europe against equity markets and paper money." Consequently, the "early American land companies took up where the bubble companies of 1720 left off."[87]

[84] McCraw (2012).

[85] Sylla (2005). Following a crash on the securities market early that year and subsequent regulatory restrictions, a group of brokers agreed on certain self-regulations, which included charging clients a minimum rate for commissions and establishing preferential dealings among the group, in what became known as the so-called *Buttonwood Agreement*.

[86] The national currency was to be backed by US Treasury securities, whereas state bank notes were taxed.

[87] Goetzmann (2016, p. 399).

4
Financing industrial development

> It may be more useful [...] to look upon capitalist finance as a clearing system that cancels claims and debts and carries forward the differences – so that "money" payments come in only as a special case [...] In other words: practically and analytically, a credit theory of money is possibly preferable to a monetary theory of credit.
>
> (J.A. Schumpeter, 1954, p. 717)

Continuing our brief sketch of the historical background and heterodox sources of Schumpeter's monetary theory, the period we finally turn to is characterized by powerful waves of innovation and a growing importance of finance. In England, it induced the classic controversies surrounding money, which are of particular interest to us for two reasons. First, they paved the way toward the monetary orthodoxy, which strongly dominated the field at the time Schumpeter started his enquiries. Second, the intense intellectual discourse produced many heterodox ideas – some incomplete or faulty, many pushed to the background and then partly forgotten, but nevertheless pointing at the shortcomings of the orthodox canon. They introduced alternative perspectives that were taken up and later modified by another generation of economists, which included Wicksell, Schumpeter, and Keynes. In Continental Europe, it was the emergence of banks actively engaged in promoting industrial development that left the biggest mark on Schumpeter's theoretical concepts as well as his later personal ambitions in banking.

4.1 The Industrial Revolution

When England became the birthplace of the *Industrial Revolution*, the promotion of new corporations was severely restricted and public euphoria for equity finance had diminished due to the previous financial crises.[1] As a consequence, critical infrastructure, including turnpike roads and canals, was often financed by partnerships among wealthy investors without recourse to public markets.

Explanations for why the Industrial Revolution first occurred in England during the period from about 1760 to 1840 emphasize a plethora of complementary

[1] Goetzmann (2016); Voth (2018).

Schumpeter's Venture Money. Michael Peneder and Andreas Resch, Oxford University Press (2021).
DOI: 10.1093/oso/9780198804383.003.0004

causes. These range from a relative abundance of natural resources[2] to the stability of institutions (e.g., political unity and centralization, confidence in the rule of law, the introduction of *intellectual property rights*; IPRs), military dominance, agrarian reforms, population growth, a landed upper class with commercial interests, an integrated domestic market combined with imperial expansion and overseas trade, religious tolerance, the Protestant work ethic, and entrepreneurial spirit. One way or another, these elements combined to foster technological progress and facilitate the emergence of a novel factory system. While their precise interaction and relative importance is disputed, this variety of conducive factors certainly increased the opportunities for "novel combinations" in the sense of Schumpeter's definition of innovation (Section 7.3).[3]

Financial innovation is remarkably absent from the narrative, which contrasts sharply with the evident connection between Britain's fast financial development and its commercial expansion during the previous period. The general explanation for this is that capital needs tended to be small for the early industrial ventures.[4] Entrepreneurs mainly relied on self-financing and informal funds from family, friends, or other partners, which were typically generated through close personal networks. More often than not, in the early days a gradual transformation of business was based on the accumulated profits of traditional artisans or tenant farmers, occasionally aided by local investors.[5] Only exceptional cases with large capital needs also involved wealthy merchants.[6]

Apparently, the preceding "financial revolutions" must have provided England with a privileged position at the start of the Industrial Revolution – not only in terms of having an advanced financial system with a comparatively broad and experienced class of investors, but also with respect to numerous indirect benefits. For example, military success and growing prosperity contributed to the country's own political stability and integration. Furthermore, the associated "commercial revolution" raised the general level of prosperity and relative abundance of capital available to new entrepreneurial ventures. Even if the wealthy merchant class only diverted its funds directly to investments in manufacturing in rare cases, its expenditures were bound to trickle down within the British economy through myriad economic relationships in the regular circulation of money. Finally, leading sectors of the Industrial Revolution, such as the cotton industry, benefitted from England's dominant position in overseas trade through the cheap and secure supply of raw cotton, in addition to the growing export markets. The latter allowed to

[2] For instance, high quality coal and iron, a large coastline, many navigable rivers, and weather conditions that were favorable to the spinning of cotton.

[3] For example, steam power was introduced to pump water out of the mines at a time when its later importance for transportation and manufacturing production could hardly have been anticipated.

[4] At least when compared to the funds raised for sovereign debts or overseas trade.

[5] Such as the drapers who funded the patents of Arkwright's spinning frames.

[6] Kindleberger (1975, p. 21f) mentions the iron and copper industries of South Wales.

exploit economies of scale and learning effects through the manifold incremental innovations that drove the bulk of actual productivity growth.[7]

During the Industrial Revolution most financial developments related to the continual growth, expansion, and specialization of the English banking sector. In the process, the growing influence and power of the Bank of England helped anchor England's monetary system and facilitate its increased use of fractional reserves. British financier *Walter Boyd* (1754-1837) provided an early description:

> The circulating medium of this city consists chiefly of Bank of England Notes, for converting which into gold and silver, when called for, the Bank keeps a large quantity of coin in its coffers, though not the full amount of the notes in circulation. The difference between the amount of the notes in circulation and the specie kept for paying them, is a clear addition to the powers of the money of the country. This is the first great augmentation, which the circulating medium of the country receives from the combined powers of Confidence and Capital.
>
> (Boyd, 1796/1811, p. 91f)

To this comes the second fraction:

> The sum of money which [...] every man of whatever description, finds it necessary to keep altogether unemployed [...] is generally deposited, not in his own strong box, but in the hands of his Banker; and this Banker, from being the depositary of a great number of such sums, finds, from experience, that the whole of these sums cannot, according to the natural course of things, be all wanted at once; but, on the contrary, while he possesses good credit, that a part of these deposits will fully answer all the calls that can be made upon him. [...] The sum he thus employs is another clear addition to the powers of the money of the country.
>
> (Boyd, 1796/1811, p. 91f)

Fractional reserves thus enabled a major expansion of monetary circulation. Quantitatively, and due to the larger size of their financial operations, sovereign debt and commerce must have benefitted most from the monetary expansion. But such a comparison can be misleading, because qualitatively – in terms of the structural transformation of productive systems – the impact for the small, nascent, and hence most vulnerable manufacturing activities may have been even bigger. Recent evidence highlights that in "stark contrast to textbook histories" the presence of country banks outside London caused major structural transformations in terms of (i) increasing the degree of industrialization within the local vicinity and

[7] Freeman and Soete (1997); Mokyr (1998, p. 47).

(ii) shifting employment from mature sectors toward newer industries that produced more specialized intermediate goods.[8]

In short, when technology became more advanced and expensive, the role of formal intermediation by attorneys, brokers, banks, insurance companies, and the stock market increased with the need for larger amounts of fixed capital. During the second half of the eighteenth century, country banking grew into a specialized industry, with most banks issuing notes against deposits or discounting bills of exchange.[9] While credit was predominantly short-term, British merchants, wholesale retailers and country banks could increasingly supply manufacturers with working capital by means of bills and overdrafts.[10] Though not yet generally providing long-term finance to industrial ventures, the banks' growing supply of working capital nevertheless made it easier for entrepreneurs to invest their own funds in the formation of fixed capital.

Conversely, the expansion of industrial activities contributed to the growing scope and importance of banking, fractional reserves, and paper money, which challenged the traditional canon of monetary thought. It is not by accident that the most advanced theoretical disputes of the time arose in the same country that led the Industrial Revolution. Remarkably, despite their inherent tensions and contradictions, both metallism and the quantity theory were largely victorious, as they were increasingly considered the unremovable safeguards of monetary stability. The next section will address the classic controversies surrounding money.

4.2 The classic controversies

The Bullion Debate

The creation of bank money had lifted many restrictions on monetary circulation. In the aforementioned report from 1796, the British financier Walter Boyd was outright enthusiastic:

> By the happiest exertion of the good sense of the country, in combining the effects of confidence with those of capital, the powers of our specie have been carried much beyond the limits fixed by its amount. By the wise introduction of a paper currency, constantly convertible into Gold and Silver, that currency has justly acquired all the powers which Gold and Silver possess.
>
> (Boyd, 1796/1811, p. 92)

The mood changed as early as the following year, when these "powers" were tested by a bank run following rumours of a French invasion. After several country banks

[8] Heblich and Trew (2019).
[9] Cassis and Cottrell (2015, p. 52f).
[10] Mokyr (1998, p. 63f).

failed and the Bank of England had run short of reserves, the *Bank Restriction Act* suspended the convertibility of paper into specie.[11] Fractional reserves thus proved vulnerable to a national crisis and war forced England to repeat the Swedish experiment of inconvertible money.

Much as in the Swedish experience, inflation remained modest in the early years after suspension, and then only gradually increased. The longer suspension continued, the more it was resisted. The self-same Walter Boyd can provide a good example of the shifting mood. While he had earlier criticized the Bank of England for issuing insufficient notes to support the credit needed by business, he then became a leader of the *bullionists*' early campaign for resumption to full convertibility. More specifically, he accused the Bank of England of having caused high inflation by issuing too many notes "uncontrolled by the obligation of paying them, in specie, on demand." Boyd considered the quantity theory to be "invariable in its operation, as the law of gravitation."[12] Conversely, monetary experiments no longer received his approval. In a letter to William Pitt he wrote:

> *Innovation* has been the great danger against which your administration has laboured, and in many respects with success, to defend this country. But is there, in the annals of history, any innovation more remarkable or more dangerous than this was? Can any two things be more essentially different than the circulation of paper, constantly convertible into specie, and that of paper, so convertible, only at the pleasure of the Corporation which issues it? (Boyd, 1800/11, p. 74f)

Schumpeter expressed clear reservations about the bullionist cause. With regard to the war inflation during restriction, he remarked that "to the modern student who is inured to stronger stuff, the most striking feature of the subsequent inflation is its mildness" and that it "was in fact this very mildness of the inflationary process that made diagnosis so difficult" and hampered the efforts of the early bullionists to overturn restriction.[13]

When inflation gained momentum, the bullionists found a new leader of the debate in *David Ricardo* (1772–1823), who came to prominence by raising their cause in a series of public letters and subsequently joined a parliamentary committee chaired by Francis Horner. In 1810, the committee's famous Bullion Report largely followed his conclusions and recommended resumption to the gold standard within a period of two years.[14] Failing to win a majority in parliament,

[11] Initially, suspension was meant to last for 6 months after England concluded stable peace with France.

[12] From Boyd's *Letter to William Pitt* (1800/11, pp. 4, 7).

[13] *HEA* (1954, p. 690f). The most prominent proponents besides Boyd were Lord King (1803) and John Wheatley (1804).

[14] The report, which was probably drafted by Horner, William Huskisson, and Henry Thornton concluded that "the system of the circulating medium of this country ought to be brought back, with as much speed as is compatible with a wise and necessary caution, to the original principle of cash

Ricardo further pursued his agenda by penning the influential pamphlet on *The High Price of Bullion* (1811). In a sweeping synthesis of arguments ranging from those of Hume and Smith to those of fellow bullionists Lord King and John Wheatley, and combining them with much empirical detail, Ricardo aptly summarized the bullionist agenda:

> The only legitimate security which the public can possess against the indiscretion of the Bank is to oblige them to pay their notes on demand in specie; and this can only be effected by diminishing the amount of bank-notes in circulation till the nominal price of gold be lowered to the mint price. (Ricardo, 1811, p. 99)

Ricardo's obstinacy paid off when in 1819 parliament finally passed a law to reinstate resumption by 1821. His major original contribution to monetary thought, however, was the "ingot plan."[15] The idea was to ease the resumption of the gold standard by restricting the conversion of notes to bullion rather than gold coins, which would then practically remain out of circulation. It effectively combined the benefits of the higher efficiency of paper circulation with the stable value of a convertible gold standard – an idea that was of eminent importance to the further development of monetary policy. Schumpeter's verdict on Ricardo was nevertheless very hostile. He expressed respect for Ricardo's analytical skills, but severely disapproved of his approach of reducing economic problems to stylized long-run equilibrium outcomes:

> His interest was in the clear-cut result of direct, practical significance. In order to get this, he cut that general system to pieces, bundled up as large parts of it as possible, and put them in cold storage – so that as many things as possible should be frozen and "given." He then piled one simplifying assumption upon another until, having really settled everything by these assumptions, he was left with only a few aggregative variables between which, given these assumptions, he set up simple one-way relations so that, in the end, the desired results emerged almost as tautologies. (*HEA*, 1954, p. 472f)

Yet Schumpeter was no less critical of the anti-bullionists, whom he considered to be an unequal match: "The considerable success [...] was due not only to Ricardo's force and brilliance but also to the lack of these qualities in

payments at the option of the holder of Bank paper" (reprinted in Cannan, 1919, p. 68). When it failed to win a majority in the parliamentary vote, public attention shifted to other problems and even inflation seemed to give way to deflation.

[15] Ricardo (1816). He first mentioned it in the appendix of the fourth edition of Ricardo (1811) and made some adaptations to it in Ricardo (1824).

his opponents."[16] Among them, Schumpeter acknowledged Thomas and Mathias Attwood, leaders of the *Birmingham Currency School*, as the most original contenders. Its disciples were frequently described as crude inflationists,[17] and Schumpeter also held against them that they did not systematically work out their principles. In his view, Thomas Attwood, in particular, lost any professional respect due to his political agitation and "phraseological overstatement." As a consequence, "professionals did not take him quite seriously. They were wrong, however," Schumpeter continued, because his diagnosis

> had the merit of serving as a magnifying glass that enabled him to see what the leading economists of the period refused to see, namely, that an ideally managed paper money could avoid some consequences of the gold automatism, which are in fact functionless. *HEA* (1954, p. 714f)

Finally, he credited Attwood for anticipating the notion of resumption, even if at a reduced gold value of the pound, which would only return in 1919.

Characteristically, in Schumpeter's *History of Economic Analysis* the one real hero to emerge from the bullion controversy eschews any categorization within the partisan political camps: *Henry Thornton* (1760–1815), he announced with a flourish, "must be saluted at once." Furthermore, his *Enquiry into the Nature and Effects of the Paper Credit of Great Britain* (1802/1939) "is an amazing performance," which "anticipated in some points the analytic developments of a century to come. No other performance of the period will bear comparison with it."[18]

If Schumpeter's judgement sounds extravagant, Hayek (1939) was no less exuberant:[19]

> the appearance of the *Paper Credit* in 1802 marks the beginning of a new epoch in the development of monetary theory. Although Thornton's merits have long been overshadowed by the greater fame of Ricardo, it has now come to be recognized that in the field of money the main achievement of the classical period is due to Thornton. (Hayek, 1939, p. 36)

In the face of radical financial innovations surrounding the increased use of paper credit, Schumpeter argues that during this period "it was the practitioners who

[16] *HEA* (1954, p. 708). Robert Torrens (1780-1864) was an exception that Schumpeter referred to with explicit sympathy. Another prominent example was Sir Francis Baring (*HEA*, 1954, p. 696).

[17] Mises (1912/53, p. 264); Viner (1937, p. 281f).

[18] *HEA* (1954, 714f), p. 689.

[19] Thornton was widely known and respected at the time, but practically fell into oblivion after Ricardo's monetary doctrine came to dominance. Hayek brought him back to widespread notice when in 1939 he edited a reprint of Thornton's *Paper Credit* (1802/1939). This huge reversal that he initiated in the general appreciation of Henry Thornton is probably unprecedented in the history of economic thought.

were in the vanguard of analytic advance, and research workers of different types were in most cases content to take their clues from them".[20] Thornton was precisely that – a respected banker with practical experience, who understood better than his contemporaries the nature and extent of the paper credit revolution.[21]

However, Thornton also displayed a complex and independent mind. In the midst of the political controversy, he had for many years defended restriction and the operations of the Bank of England as necessary measures. In 1802, that is, during the first wave of the bullion debate, he aligned with the anti-bullionists by arguing that non-monetary factors such as bad harvests and high foreign expenditures related to the war had caused the increase in prices and the deterioration of the exchange rate. Consequently, one could not blame the Bank of England for an overissue of banknotes. However, later in the Bullion Report he recommended resumption, reflecting his growing concerns about the monetary causes of inflation,[22] the Bank of England's adherence to the real bills doctrine, and possibly also a change in viewpoint regarding the government's influence on the Bank's decisions.[23]

The impossibility of an easy association with either political camp likely contributed to the later neglect of Thornton's work. Even after its rediscovery in the twentieth century, authors could not agree on how to receive it and would call him a moderate bullionist, a moderate anti-bullionist, or even "an anti-bullionist in sheep's clothing."[24] Hayek, however, contended that Thornton had not altered his own theoretical position, but consistently applied it to a changing apprehension of the political and empirical circumstances.[25] Using Schumpeter's terminology, we may say that Thornton was a practical cartalist during the times of monetary crisis,[26] but that he became a practical metallist after adjusting his

[20] *HEA* (1954, p. 688).

[21] Thornton was also a member of parliament and mainly known for his evangelical mission and commitment to social causes – in particular the abolition of the slave trade. Though he was a prolific writer, economics was nevertheless a rare and exceptional topic. See Murphy (2009, p. 189ff).

[22] At the time, there existed no precise data or measures of inflation. The debate instead focused on the depreciation of the price for minted coins, which was tied to and negatively affected by the issue of paper, relative to the international market price of gold bullion. See also Thornton (1802/1939, pp. 149, 192).

[23] Later attempts to empirically test the bullionist hypothesis mostly failed at identifying a significant causal effect (e.g., Officer, 2000). Hendrickson (2018), however, presents econometric evidence in support of the bullionist's claim, showing that the increased note issue caused prices to rise and a depreciation of the exchange rate. His findings also suggest that the Bank of England served to monetize part of the expenditures by the government.

[24] Rothbard (1995, p. 186).

[25] Hayek (1939). So do Hicks (1982); Skaggs (1995); and Arnon (2009).

[26] "In a commercial country, subjected to that moderate degree of occasional alarm and danger which we have experienced, gold is by no means that kind of circulating medium which is the most desirable. [...] If, during the war, it had been our only medium of payment, we might sometimes have been almost totally deprived of the means of carrying on our pecuniary transactions; and much confusion in the affairs of our merchants, great interruption of manufacturing labour, and very serious evils to the state, might have been the consequences. Paper credit has, on this account, been highly important to us" (Thornton, 1802/1939, p. 276).

previous confidence in the Bank of England and apprehending the situation, such that convertibility was needed to keep the government in check. We may also say that he gave priority to principles over political alliances.

Yet Thornton's theoretical position is equally difficult to categorize. Indeed, he simultaneously enchanted and frustrated both sides by dismissing the bullionist's claim of neutral money as readily as the real bills doctrine, which the anti-bullionists held dear.[27] Schumpeter therefore refrained from classifying him into either of the contemporary factions, instead portraying him as a precursor of theoretical developments to follow.[28] In other words, if Thornton was far ahead of his time, one should not put him in a category with his contemporaries. We follow Schumpeter's strategy, setting aside the bullion debate and turning our attention to Thornton's own theoretical contribution.

Paper Credit

In the years following restriction, professional attention, public controversies, and parliamentary testimonies[29] induced Thornton to write his book on *Paper Credit*. Despite the highly political circumstances and the questions at stake, his main contribution was theoretical, namely to explain the emergence, nature, and impact of a growing paper circulation that may not be convertible to commodities of intrinsic value.

For more than two millennia, that is, from Aristotle in the fourth century BCE to Adam Smith and the classical epoch up to Carl Menger and the neoclassical revolution at the end of the nineteenth century, the widely accepted economic explanation of the origin of money was based on its convenience and efficiency as a medium of exchange. Consequently, credit was only a subsidiary phenomenon and sophisticated payment systems, such as bank deposits or convertible papers, explained as having developed from it. Schumpeter called these "monetary theories of credit" and contrasted them with "credit theories of money."[30] He attributed

[27] Consequently, the online *History of Economic Theory* (*HET*) describes him as "occupying a curious intermediary position" (see http://www.hetwebsite.net/het/schools/bullion.htm).

[28] "[…] in matters of monetary as of general theory, Ricardian teaching is a detour and that it slowed up the advance of analysis, which could have been much quicker and smoother had Thornton's lead been followed – had Ricardo's force not prevailed over Thornton's insight" (*HEA*, 1954, p. 704).

[29] See, for example, his expert testimony to a parliamentary committee in 1797; reprinted in Hayek's edition of Thornton (1802/1939).

[30] The term first appeared in Wicksell (1898/1936, p. 105). Among later proponents of a "credit theory of money," Macleod (1866) and Hahn (1924) provided the most radical statements. Both remained relatively obscure, but were appreciated, for example, by Skaggs (1998) and Hagemann (2010). Arnon (2011) further identifies it with the work of, for example, Bagehot (1873); Wicksell (1898/1936); and John Hicks. Messori (2003) links it with Schumpeter's theory of cycles.

the latter to Thornton, who had turned the received canon upside down by commencing his treatise with the bold assertion that credit logically exists prior to money:

> Commercial credit may be defined to be that confidence which subsists among commercial men in respect to their mercantile affairs. [...] Even in that early and rude state of society, in which neither bills nor money are as yet known, it may be assumed, that if there be commerce, a certain degree of commercial credit will also subsist. [...] it must happen, even in the infancy of society, that one man will deliver property to his neighbour without receiving, on the spot, the equivalent which is agreed to be given in return. It will occasionally be the interest of the one party thus to wait the other's convenience. [...] This commercial credit is the foundation of paper credit; paper serving to express that confidence [...] which might otherwise be merely verbal. (Thornton, 1802/1939, p. 75f)

By example of the clearing operations of the London banks, he further demonstrated that bank notes and deposits served the same purpose as means of payments.[31] Schumpeter embraced this comprehensive concept of "all we pay with,"[32] but also stressed that Thornton did not explicitly equate it with money, which he tended to define conventionally as a commodity. The important point, which was different from the approaches of Adam Smith and others, was that not the quantity of money as such was defined, but that the actual expenditures determined the impact on prices or output:

> The quantity of circulating paper, that is, of paper capable of circulation, may be great, and yet the quantity of actual circulation may be small, or *vice versa*. The same note may either effect ten payments in one day, or one payment in ten days; and one note, therefore, will effect the same payments in the one case, which it would require a hundred notes to effect in the other.
> (Thornton, 1802/1939, p. 96)

Thornton dismissed the classical assumption of a constant speed of circulation, which had simplified the quantity theory to exactly proportional effects. In contrast, Thornton pointed at various causes of variation in the velocity of money. One relates, for instance, to *liquidity preferences*, in the sense that circulation tends

[31] "Merely by the transfer of the debts of one merchant to another, in the books of the banker, a large portion of what are termed cash payments is effected at this time without the use of any bank paper, and a larger sum would be thus transferred" (Thornton, 1802, p. 75f, p. 101; see also p. 134).

[32] *HEA* (1954, p. 698f).

to rise with the general state of confidence as people tend to "provide less amply against contingencies," while another factor is the opportunity cost of holding cash, that is, "the loss of interest arising from a detention of notes."[33]

Thornton remained in the shadow of David Ricardo, whose doctrine became the canon of monetary theory, while his own ideas faded into oblivion. It took almost a century for them to reappear, unacknowledged and possibly rediscovered independently, but further developed in the work of Wicksell, Schumpeter, and Keynes.[34] By starting with credit as a radically different pivot of analysis, he had come across an astonishing number of new theoretical insights, the full import of which was beyond the grasp of his contemporary peers, and most likely also of his own. Compared to his own rather rudimentary presentation, they have become much clearer in retrospect, with later writers developing similar ideas into comprehensive theorems.

One example is Thornton's understanding of the role of interest. Apart from the establishment of legal restrictions aimed at curtailing usury, the classical interpretation in the tradition of Hume and Smith was that interest reflects the rate of profit on real capital. In contrast, Thornton related the bank rate of interest to the current rate of profit,[35] thus hinting at the equilibrium of both the money and goods market to determine the quantity of total circulation. At the time, economists focused on the quantity of money and largely ignored the rate of interest as a relevant variable. Indeed, the loan rate of the Bank of England was limited by an upper bound of 5 percent, which reflected traditional concerns over usury. While that may have drawn earlier criticism because of its interference with free market forces, Thornton explicitly reasoned that the fixed interest rate restricted the capability of the Bank of England to respond to changing market conditions.

Another example is the role of money in international trade, where Thornton generalized Hume's specie-flow mechanism to situations involving inconvertible currencies. Hayek (1939, p. 48) considered it to be the first exposition of the purchasing power parity theory: instead of reducing prices for exports and increasing prices for imports that are commonly valued in specie, domestic inflation now produces "a fall in the price at which the overabundant bills on England sell in the foreign market."[36] In other words, he conceived that arbitrage eliminates price differences between the foreign and domestic economy through corresponding

[33] *HEA* (1954, p. 96f).

[34] See Arnon (2011, p. 365). Unfortunately, neither Wicksel nor Keynes gave proper attribution to Thornton and it therefore remains an open question as to whether they received the initial ideas from him or rediscovered them on their own. The same situation also applies to Schumpeter's early work, which hardly mentions Thornton. However, one may say that he made good with his later accolades in the *HEA*.

[35] Thornton (1802, p. 254).

[36] Thornton (1802/1939, p. 199).

adjustments in the exchange rate, thus mitigating their impact on the balance of trade.

From its origins, paper credit had the advantage of sparing the expensive use of precious metals. In the course of economic development and the expansion of commercial transactions, Thornton concluded that paper must further gain in importance:

> If there may be a convenience in giving credit in the infancy of society, when the interchange of commodities is small, there may be, at least, the same convenience when goods begin to be multiplied, when wealth is more variously distributed, and society is advanced. (Thornton, 1802/1939, p. 76)

However, paper credit does not just grow with development; it also enhances development through various channels that ultimately tend to lower prices through an increase in productivity. Money in the form of paper credit is thus no longer neutral for several reasons. One of these is the familiar explanation of lowered transaction costs: "Paper credit, also, promotes general cheapness, by sparing much expence and trouble in weighing, counting, and transporting money; and by thus facilitating more particularly the larger transactions of the merchant."[37] Second, and relatedly, paper credit broadens the market by extending the option to buy or sell to more people. Both are consistent with Adam Smith's classic standpoint that larger markets increase competition and the division of labor, which had set him apart from Hume's quantity theory emphasizing neutral money.

The third mechanism, however, stands in explicit opposition to Smith and the classical view. They believed that investment must equal savings, and banks therefore cannot contribute to the addition of productive capital, only rendering a greater part of it active by means of intermediation. In contrast, Thornton understands credit to be an additional source of investment and therefore insists that "the use of paper furnishes even "additional" stock to the country." As an example, he refers to the purchase of new and technically superior machinery.[38]

The latter effect arises from the different speed of adjustment of wages and the prices of goods. In the case of deflation, he concludes, as Christiernen had done earlier, that the slower response of wages depresses profits and "would occasion much discouragement of the fabrication of manufacturers."[39] In the case

[37] Thornton (1802, p. 272f).

[38] "Thus, for example, the use of a new sort of machinery which costs less in the erection than that which was employed before, and which just as effectually does the work required, since it enables the owner to have always more goods in the course of manufacture, while he has exactly the same means of manufacturing them, might not improperly be described as adding to the stock of the country" (Thornton, 1802, pp. 176 and 272).

[39] Thornton (1802, p. 119). We are not aware of any evidence proving that Thornton knew of Christiernen's analysis. But in 1811 he referred to the Swedish example in a speech defending the Bullion Report (see Appendix in Thornton 1802/1939, p. 339). Laidler (2000, p. 4) further reports that

of inflation, he points at the unfair distributional consequences: "Much pressure may have been felt by the lower classes of people, whose wages are seldom raised until sometime after the occasion for a rise has begun to exist."[40] Yet, in the course of the argument he also produced the first printed statement of what later became known as Wicksell's doctrine of "forced savings":[41]

> It must be also admitted, that, provided we assume an excessive issue of paper to lift up as it may for a time, the cost of goods though not the price of labour, some augmentation of stock will be the consequence; for the labourer, according to this supposition, may be forced by his necessity to consume fewer articles, though he may exercise the same industry. But this saving [...] will be attended with a proportionate hardship and injustice. (Thornton, 1802/1939, p. 239)

Another point well taken by the bullionist campaigners, was Thornton's rebuttal of the real bills doctrine. Although principles of prudent lending are in the self-interest of bankers, much uncertainty prevails in practice. Consequently, to "determine what bills are fictitious, or bills of accommodation, and what are real, is often a point of difficulty."[42] In addition, one cannot rely upon sound banking practices to restrict paper credit to a non-inflationary amount, because once in circulation "real bills [...] may be multiplied to an extremely great extent; and, moreover, that it is only necessary sufficiently to extend the customary length of credit, in order to effect the greatest imaginable multiplication of them."[43] Again, this point brings Thornton's analysis close to Wicksell, who elaborated the idea of a "cumulative process" (see Section 5.3).

In conclusion, Henry Thornton was a most forceful opponent of the quantity theory, based on which money supply could only affect prices without any impact on the real economy. Unlike Smith, who was cautious in his objections, and unlike the anti-bullionists, who too easily adopted Smith's doctrine of real bills as an excuse to oppose the resumption of convertible paper, he provided a thorough

Thornton's family had traded lumber with the Baltic. Referring also to the Baltic connections of Tooke and Joplin, he concludes: "Though there is no direct evidence of a Swedish influence on British debates, the conjecture is plausible."

[40] Thornton (1802, p. 190).

[41] Hayek (1932) sketched the history of the idea of forced savings from Bentham and Thornton to Wicksell, Mises, and Schumpeter. Schumpeter "Gründungsgewinn in Recht und Wirtschaft" (GRW; 1911, p. 108f; *HEA*, 1954, pp. 724, 1115) awarded the expression to Mises and acknowledged Bentham, but emphasized the intellectual lineage of Thornton, Malthus, and Wicksell. There has been some discussion in doctrinal history about whether priority should be given to Bentham or Thornton. Though Bentham only had it published in 1843, Hayek (1932) argued that it had received its final form by 1804 but had probably been sketched earlier. However, he also argued that Thornton had worked on his *Paper Credit* for a period of about six years. Schumpeter politely concluded: "According to the rules I follow in matters of priority, I have, however, no choice but to date [Bentham's] theory 1843, although Professor von Hayek is presumably correct in thinking that Bentham made its contents known to his economist friends" (*HEA*, 1954, p. 724). See also the brief discussions in Viner (1937, p. 188).

[42] Thornton (1802/1939, p. 89).

[43] Thornton (1802, p. 253).

analysis and kept his theoretical arguments separate from his political advice. More specifically, he believed that an increase in the money supply could affect either prices or real production, depending on the initial conditions, and he explicitly distinguished between an economy that is in a situation of underemployment and one that is not:

> When the Bank of England enlarges its paper, it augments, in the same degree [...] its loans to individuals. These favoured persons immediately conceive, and not without reason, that they have obtained an additional though borrowed capital, by which they can push their own particular manufacture or branch of commerce [However] it is obvious, that the antecedently idle persons to whom we may suppose the new capital to give employ, are limited in number; and that, therefore, if the encreased issue is indefinite, it will set to work labourers, of whom a part will be drawn from other, and, perhaps, no less useful occupations; [consequently,] there are some bounds. [Hence, he feels] obliged to admit, that, although additional industry will be one effect of an extraordinary emission of paper, a rise in the cost of articles will be another.
>
> (Thornton, 1802/1939, p. 236f)

Thornton concluded that such a delicate balance required more than the classic principles of *laissez-faire* and wanted the Bank of England to deliberately take responsibility for managing the credit system in the public interest. To this end, he demanded that it should assume a comprehensive role as lender-of-last-resort. As the last source of both cash and credit, the Bank of England should act according to its double responsibility as guardian of the currency and of the credit structure.[44]

Finally, in what Schumpeter referred to as "the Magna Charta of credit management,"[45] Thornton prescribed the principles of prudent central banking:

> To limit the total amount of paper issued, and to resort for this purpose, whenever the temptation to borrow is strong, to some effectual principle of restriction; in no case, however, materially to diminish the sum in circulation, but to let it vibrate only within certain limits; to afford a slow and cautious extension of it, as the general trade of the kingdom enlarges itself; to allow of some special, though temporary, encrease in the event of any extraordinary alarm or difficulty, as the best means of preventing a great demand at home for guineas; and to lean to the side of diminution, in the case of gold going abroad, and of the general exchanges continuing long unfavourable; this seems to be the true policy of the directors of an institution circumstanced like that of the Bank of England. To suffer either the solicitations of merchants, or the wishes of government, to determine the measure of the bank issues, is unquestionably to adopt a very false principle of conduct. (Thornton, 1802/1939, p. 259)

[44] *HEA* (1954, p. 696). [45] *HEA* (1954, p. 729).

The currency debate

With England's resumption to the gold standard in 1821, the bullion debate effectively concluded. In the controversies that followed, contenders on either side accepted convertibility largely in the shape of the classical Ricardian doctrines.[46] But recurrent crises increasingly shattered confidence in convertibility as in itself sufficient to achieve the stability of the price system and foreign balances, while a prolonged deflationary trend took its toll on growth and employment. Public attention thus increasingly turned toward questions of governance and the organization of banking, with a focus on the short-run problems of how to manage the currency.[47]

The Bank of England enjoyed privileges which had increasingly led it to evolve into the "banker's bank," or what Francis Baring in 1797 referred to as the lender of *dernier resort*.[48] But it had never been formally charged with that responsibility to act in the public interest. Conversely, being a joint-stock company implied that its shareholders were legally entitled to expect high dividends. Thornton had already pointed at the governance problem. His consideration was to defend the Bank of England's *de facto* monopoly in the issue of bank notes within London as well as its country-wide monopoly in the supply of specie along three main arguments: the monoply would (i) ensure compensation for foregone opportunities to the bank's private shareholders;[49] (ii) impose an undivided responsibility of the bank's directors to the public interest; and (iii) act as a safeguard against competitive pressures that may lead to excessive lending:

> If a rival institution of the Bank of England were established, both the power and the responsibility would be divided; and, through the additional temptation to exercise that liberality in lending, which it is the object of competition to promote, the London notes, and also the country bills and notes, would be more liable to become excessive. Our paper credit would, therefore, stand in every respect on a less safe foundation. (Thornton, 1802/1939, p. 229)

John Wheatley (1803) further demanded that the Bank of England be awarded a national monopoly for issuing notes.[50] And Ricardo (1824) drafted his *Plan for the*

46 Schumpeter remarked, that the "first thing that strikes the modern observer when he looks back upon that controversy is the extent of fundamental agreement between the two 'schools'. Neither contained any radical monetary reformers. Both were equally averse to monetary management or any thoroughgoing control of banking and credit. [...] That is to say, both groups consisted of laissez-faire men. Moreover, both groups were staunch supporters of the gold standard and, in particular, of the regulation of foreign exchanges by free gold movements" (HEA, 1954, p. 696).

47 Viner (1937, p. 221).

48 In *Observations on the Establishment of the Bank of England*. See also Thornton (1802/1939, p. 127).

49 "The national bank, indeed, may fairly be called upon, in consideration of the benefits enjoyed through its monopoly, to submit to a considerable expence in supplying gold for the country" (Thornton, 1802/1939, p. 181).

50 "The most eligible mode appears to me to be that the bank of England should possess the exclusive privilege [...] of regulating the whole paper currency of the country; that the circulation of the notes

Establishment of a National Bank, which was published posthumously. Therein, he declared that the "Bank of England performs two operations, which are quite distinct, and have no necessary connection with each other: it issues a paper currency as a substitute for a metallic one; and it advances money in the way of loan, to merchants and others."[51] He then also called for a national monopoly in the issue of paper money,[52] but unlike Thornton or Wheatley he aimed to deprive the Bank of England of this privilege. Instead, his plan was to "transfer the profit which accrues from the interest of the money so issued from the Bank, to Government."[53] The new organization should be guided by independent commissioners, who must regulate the issue of notes such that they "never, on any pretence, lend money to Government, nor be in the slightest degree under its control or influence."[54]

In the ensuing great classical controversy, which lasted from about 1825 to 1865, Ricardo's insistence on the functional separation of paper issue and the credit system was a main contention of the so-called *Currency School*.[55] To this one must add the school's emphasis on a strict rule to guide the quantity of paper issued with a 100 percent convertibility to gold.[56] While the Currency School thus shared the bullionist concern for convertibility,[57] the demand for a strict rule-based regulation of the currency without any discretionary interventions went beyond their cause. Viner summarized the *currency principle* as follows:[58]

> A mixed currency would operate properly only if it operated precisely, as would a metallic currency, i.e., only if any efflux or influx of gold resulted in a corresponding (absolute, not proportional) decrease or increase in the quantity of the currency. (Viner, 1937, p. 221)

Schumpeter summarized the "currency principle" in a similar but more comprehensive manner with the following two assertions: first, that one needs special

of country banks should be declared beyond a given period illegal; and that the bank should substitute the same or nearly the same in their stead" (Wheatley, 1803, p. 128).

[51] Ricardo (1824, p. 276).

[52] The alternative "free banking principle" would deny such a monopoly. For elaborate discussions, see White (1984) or Arnon (2011).

[53] See Ricardo (1824, p. 281). Sraffa (1951, p. 272) remarks that in 1814 Say had made a similar proposal for a national bank in an unpublished paper submitted to Ricardo, who first mentioned the idea in his *Principles* in 1817. Furthermore, the difference in opinion with Wheatley is worth noting, since Ricardo's monetary views are often portrayed as merely reflecting his. Schumpeter, for example, repeatedly refers to the "Wheatley-Ricardo" line of arguments.

[54] Ricardo (1824, p. 282); and the Commissioners should not be removable from their office, but by the Houses of Parliament.

[55] Goodhart and Jensen (2015).

[56] Thomas Joplin (1790–1847) was the first to propose a 100 percent reserve system of banking (*HEA*, 1954, p. 723). Goodhart and Jensen (2015) also mention alternative rules to come later but maintain the currency principle, such as Friedman's k-percent rule, Fisher's price-level, and an inflation target.

[57] Though this did not hinder former anti-bullionists, like Torrens, from joining their camp.

[58] Viner (1937) considered Robert Torrens (1780–1864), S.J. Loyd (Lord Overstone; 1796–1883), as well as G.W. Norman (1793–1882) to be the most important representatives of the Currency School, and Thomas Tooke (1774–1858), John Fullarton (1780–1849), James Wilson (1805–60), and James W. Gilbart (1794–1863) to be the most important spokespersons of the Banking School.

restrictions on the issue of notes to assure convertibility. And, second, that the notes issued by the Bank of England are mere gold certificates rather than instruments of credit.[59]

The Bank Act of 1844 ("Peel's Act") largely followed the proposals of the Currency School. It awarded the Bank of England the exclusive privilege of issuing new notes in England and Wales, which, apart from being backed by a restricted amount of government debt, had to be 100 percent backed by gold. Furthermore, following the Currency School, bank deposits were not affected by this regulation. Finally, it strictly separated banking and the issue of notes into distinct departments. Subsequently, the Bank Act had to be suspended several times in the course of a crisis.

The Currency School narrowly defined money along the lines of Ricardo, that is, without including deposits or other means of payment. This helped keep its strict monetary rule manageable, but was also arguably an "Achilles heel" that the proponents tended to ignore.[60] In contrast, the rival "Banking School" enjoyed exploiting this weakness. Viner summarized their opposite view in the following *banking principle*:

> The amount of paper notes in circulation was adequately controlled by the ordinary process of competitive banking, and if the requirement of convertibility was maintained, could not exceed the needs of business for any appreciable length of time. (Viner, 1937, p. 223)

Schumpeter summarized the "banking principle" again with two main assertions: first, that, given proper governance by the Bank of England, the convertibility of notes was sufficient to achieve monetary stability. But, second, if nevertheless needed, the regulation of notes alone could not deal with the problem because it ignored the similar impact of bank deposits.

The first assertion relied on Fullarton's *principle of reflux*. This asserts that, in contrast with the real bills doctrine, the mechanism of self-regulation does not require the bank's prudent supply of credit, but originates in the demand for loans. Simply stated, even if banks were to overissue notes, people would only demand them for real transactions. Otherwise, non-interest-bearing notes flow back into the interest-bearing bank deposits. Hence, Fullarton concluded: "It may rest with the banker to issue, but it is the public which circulates; and without the concurrent action of the public, neither the power nor the will to issue can be of any avail."[61]

The principle of reflux may have been an argument with which to counter Thornton's earlier criticism of the real bills doctrine. But those who opposed

[59] *HEA* (1954, p. 727). [60] Goodhart and Jensen (2015, p. 7).

[61] Fullarton (1844, p. 86). See Le Maux (2012) for a comprehensive characterization of the various channels of bank demand debt and liquidity flows in a "matrix of reflux."

the Banking School maintained that the case of self-regulation of paper credit remained on weak footing – the reason for this being that the situation can be quite different when banks act together. For example, if they happen to jointly lower interest rates or credit standards, they will also increase the overall demand for credit.[62]

The second assertion emphasized, just as Thornton had done, that all means of payment matter in the formation of prices. Similarly to Thornton, Tooke shifted the focus from the quantity of money to actual expenditures and income: "That the amount of bank notes in the hands of the public is determined by the purposes for which they are required."[63] He is therefore generally credited with originating the "income theory of money," which stresses that not the money supply, but the total income and related expenditures determine prices. The simple logic is that, if income increases, spending will also increase and prices must rise. A more intricate theoretical implication is that income flows replace the money stock in determining prices. And assuming that the money supply always adjusts endogenously to the demand of circulation, Tooke's radical conclusion is that the issue of banknotes can neither increase nor decrease the quantity of circulation. Consequently, the quantity of money has no impact on prices, but "on the contrary, the amount of the circulating medium is the consequence of prices."[64]

While Schumpeter acknowledged Tooke's contribution to an *income theory of money*, he did not hide his disappointment in its realization:

> But as left by Tooke, it is open to a criticism that greatly reduces its importance: those revenues are obviously not ultimate data; prices determine them as much as they determine prices; and in the complex of factors that generate them, quantity of money has its place.[65] *HEA* (1954, p. 710)

To summarize, the Banking School criticized the strict currency principle on the grounds that (i) it was neither necessary, because of the market's sufficient capacity for self-regulation, (ii) nor was it effective, because of deposits and other unregulated means of payment; but it nevertheless did harm by (iii) unduly interfering with the liquidity demands of trade.

However, the Banking School never presented a concise alternative plan for dealing with crises. A different reading to Viner's or Schumpeter's presentation of the "banking principle" therefore emphasizes its sympathy with policy discretion.[66] This inference, however, is rather implicit and stands at odds with the

[62] See Viner (1937, p. 238ff), who refers, for example, to statements by Joplin or McCulloch.
[63] Tooke (1844, p. 122). [64] Tooke (1844, p. 123f). [65] *HEA* (1954, p. 710).
[66] Arnon (2011); Goodhart and Jensen (2015).

school's general *laissez-faire* attitude.[67] From this perspective, one may agree with Viner that both schools generally remained hostile to discretionary management.[68]

Bimetallism and the gold standard

Economists embraced the commodity theory on the supposition that the intrinsic value of precious metals warranted stability in the value of the monetary unit. It was, however, history that mattered in the choice of a particular standard. Drawing from Roman heritage, silver coins dominated the European monetary system at the beginning of the second millennium. After Florence and other Italian cities introduced gold coins in the early thirteenth century, both metals remained in circulation, but (except in Britain) silver remained more widely used well into the nineteenth century.[69] Difficulties in defining the common unit of account as legal tender gave birth to *Gresham's Law*:[70]

> When two sorts of money are current in the same nation, of like value by denomination, but not intrinsically, that which has the least value will be current, and the other as much as possible hoarded, or exported. [In short,] [b]ad money always drives good money out from circulation. (Macleod, 1890, Vol. 2, p. 436)

From the early thirteenth to the nineteenth century, gold and silver coins had typically coexisted as legal tender at a fixed exchange rate.[71] In view of the above difficulty, the long endurance of *bimetallism* is, however, surprising and calls for an explanation. The most compelling of these refers to the enhanced resilience of the monetary system, due to the greater flexibility and stability of prices. In keeping with the *parachute effect*,[72] an independent increase in the supply of either gold or silver displaced the use of the other medium of exchange, since it was then accordingly overvalued at the mint. To the extent that this happened, such external variations were absorbed within the system and did not affect the total

[67] The best indication comes from the parliamentary hearings of Tooke as reported by Arnon (2011, p. 243). For example, when pressed to propose his own policy plan, Tooke typically suggested improving the governing body of the Bank of England. Or, when asked about specific limits and rules for the determination of interest rates, he denied the need for a regulation, but recommended to "leave it to the discretion of some man or some body of men, no doubt, they are fallible in their judgement." Thus, the reference to discretionary policy may follow from a lack of own prescriptions for how to avoid or cope with crises.

[68] Viner (1937, p. 389). [69] Laidler (1991, p. 29f).

[70] Henry Dunning Macleod (1821-1902) attributed the origin of the law to the Greek philosopher Aristophanes, but named it after the British merchant Thomas Gresham (1519–79), who was the founder of the Royal Exchange in London. See also Macleod (1866, p. 219).

[71] Redish (2016, p. 326f).

[72] According to *Michel Chevalier* (1806–79), bimetallism tended "to absorb the depreciating and to set free the appreciating monetary metal and so to stabilize the value of the monetary unit, at least as long as the latter was not entirely displaced" (*HEA*, 1954, p. 716f).

money supply and hence prices. This inbuilt resilience was one reason why the case of bimetallism was of particular theoretical interest to Schumpeter, who devoted considerable attention to it in one of the missing chapters of the money book.[73] Another reason he pointed out was that, by fixing exchange ratios between the two metals, authorities had to move beyond an orthodox understanding of money as defined by their strict commodity value. Bimetallism thus introduced significant elements of a "managed currency." Finally, he argued that monometallism had displaced it even when it was against the national interest, thereby highlighting path dependency and the interrelatedness of international monetary systems.

The monetary orthodoxy was less intrigued by these theoretical possibilities. It generally acknowledged that the parachute effect reduced undesired variations in the price level, but mostly agreed with Jevons that bimetallism had an inherent tendency to result in alternating monometallism. Similarly, in reference to Menger's criterion of maximum "saleability" (Chapter 5), Mises argued that the increasing global integration of markets eventually had to induce the various territories to converge to one of the two metals as the general medium of exchange.[74] Against this background, Schumpeter believed in the historical longevity of bimetallism and blamed policy for its demise. With typical poignancy, he concluded that bimetallism was not abandoned because it had failed, but rather failed because it had been abandoned.[75]

In any case, bimetallism had offered a larger monetary base to countries with scarce precious metals. Over time, this advantage may have lost significance due to the increased circulation of bills of exchange and bank money. Its own advanced financial system may therefore be one of the deeper reasons for Britain's leadership in the transformation to monometallism. With regard to the particular events that brought it about, however, Laidler concludes that "Britain's movement to a Gold Standard in the eighteenth century was the accidental outcome of an attempt to place her currency on a bimetallic basis at an inappropriate, fixed, relative mint price for the metals."[76] In short, confronted by growing gold supplies from Brazil, Sir Isaac Newton, then master of the mint, failed to sufficiently reduce the price of gold coins in 1717. Overvaluation meant that the gold price of silver was too low, and, consistently with Gresham's Law, gold became the dominant medium of exchange. Subsequently, Britain officially adopted the gold standard in 1821. Similarly, in 1834 the overvaluation of gold triggered a *de facto* gold standard in the US (which led to its official adoption in 1879).[77] When in 1873 Germany adopted the gold standard, it "tipped the balance" and "evoked a chain reaction."[78]

[73] Available at the Harvard Archives: HUG(FP) – 4.77 Box 9. [74] Mises (1912/53, p. 8ff).

[75] HUG(FP) – 4.77 Box 9 "Mss and typs and notes, Published?"; Folder "Schumpeter – Money Ch. XIV, (2 of 4)," unnumbered 4th sheet.

[76] Laidler (1991, p. 32). Similarly, Eichengreen (2019a, p. 5) refers to the gold standard as "one of the great monetary accidents."

[77] Frieden (2015). [78] Eichengreen (2019a, p. 14f).

As a consequence, France also restricted the minting of silver coins, and network effects and the decline in the global demand and value of silver made the process irreversible and forced other countries to follow.

In this process, the case of the Austro-Hungarian monarchy drew particular theoretical interest. The prolonged series of costly wars had much deprived it of specie and forced it (more than any of the other leading economies) to augment its circulation through treasury and bank notes. As early as the first half of the nineteenth century, paper money had surpassed metal coins in the current circulation of cash, and during urgent crises, cash was almost entirely composed of paper.[79] According to Schumpeter's teacher Friedrich Wieser, this managed currency proved surprisingly effective:

> The disturbances of the year 1848 made it necessary to exempt the bank from the obligation to redeem its notes. Since then, the Austrian public has become so accustomed to paper, the precious metals have so completely disappeared from circulation, during this long time, that a return to specie seemed to many a vexatious and costly undertaking. If the wish of the great mass of the people had prevailed, Austria would never again have given up the paper standard.
>
> (Wieser, 1893, p. 380)

Given the pronounced depreciation of silver, Wieser argued that the paper currency provided more stability than a pure silver standard or the free coinage of silver would have done: "Silver had become of less value than paper! Or, more exactly, a silver gulden was indeed worth as much as a paper gulden, but the fine metal contained in a silver gulden [...] was worth less than a 'gulden of the Austrian standard.'"[80] To Wieser, this observation raised an eminent theoretical question:

> If, now, our silver gulden so long maintained a purchasing power so far in excess of their bullion value, whence did they derive this value? [...] Is there not, then, in this case, a clear example of a money whose value, in defiance of all theory, is determined quite independently of any relation to a metallic basis?
>
> (Wieser, 1893, p. 386f)[81]

[79] Jobst and Kernbauer (2016, p. 53).

[80] Wieser (1893, p. 386).

[81] See also Schumpeter's very similar argument in *TED* (1911/34, p. 49): "The suspension of coinage on the one hand and the prohibition of melting on the other likewise offer us examples from experience of the independent character of the value of money."

For the monetary standard, Wieser therefore explicitly preferred paper to silver, and in principle also paper to gold. The latter he accepted only for pragmatic reasons:

> Money is like speech; it is a means of intercourse. He who would have dealings with others must speak their language, however irrational he may find it. [...] If Europe errs in adopting gold, we must still, for good or evil, join Europe in her error, and we shall thus receive less injury than if we insist on being "rational" all by ourselves. (Wieser, 1893, p. 388f)

British monetary orthodoxy

After the Banking Act of 1844, the theoretical controversies in England ebbed away. To a large extent this was due to John Stuart Mill's influential consolidation of the prevalent views into what Fetter called the "British monetary orthodoxy."[82] Schumpeter also emphasized that "it was primarily in Mill's formulation that the work of the first half of the nineteenth century reached the writers of the second half."[83] He referred to Mill's version of the quantity theory as an example of his special ability to synthesize the central components of a theorem with valid objections against it. Mill had admitted that purchases on credit also matter, that velocities of money can change, and that the amount of total circulation relative to that of goods determines prices. "Thus, there is hardly any difference left between Mill's version of the quantity theory and the views of its opponents, contemporaneous or later."[84] Nevertheless, Mill stayed firmly committed to a strict version of the quantity theory and at the same time subscribed to the conventional commodity view.[85]

A second major figure of enduring influence was *Walter Bagehot* (1826–77), the early editor of the British magazine *The Economist*. Like Mill, he supported convertibility. However, he was less concerned with the theoretical arguments and instead displayed much depth and acumen in his analysis of the practical workings and policy needs of the monetary system. In *Lombard Street*, Bagehot famously championed the cause of deliberate central banking. Curiously, he never referred to and was probably not even aware of the earlier work by Henry Thornton.[86]

[82] Fetter (1965). [83] *HEA* (1954, p. 689f). [84] *HEA* (1954, p. 705). See also Mensic (2014).

[85] "Money is a commodity, and its value is determined like that of other commodities, temporarily by demand and supply, permanently and on the average by cost of production" (Mill, 1848/71, p. 351).

[86] Arnon (2011, p. 283).

Bagehot started with the observation that English commerce had become "essentially a trade on borrowed capital," which lay at the root of its striving success. Yet credit was nothing but "a set of promises to pay," which literally invoked the needed confidence in the soundness of the system. "Money will not manage itself," but as in other trades, the natural system would be one of many competing note-issuing banks "of equal or not altogether unequal size."[87]

The Bank of England had not assumed its particular role as the "banker's bank" through abstract economic laws, but rather as a result of historical circumstances and political decisions. Thanks to this system, public confidence had grown and, reasoning from an institutional perspective, Bagehot rejected the idea of an alternative "free banking" regime.[88] In short, "[a]ll banks depend on the Bank of England, and all merchants depend on some banker." And, consequently, "all our credit system depends on the Bank of England for its security."[89] More than seventy years after Thornton, Bagehot had to repeat the demand for the Bank of England to accept its responsibility as the guardian of the national banking reserves, and further called for it to improve its governance and administration.[90]

Business sentiments fluctuate and the interest rate is the ordinary means of managing the money market. During good times, the bank must accumulate sufficient reserves, because the true test of its loyalty to the public interest arises in times of crisis. It is then that the bank's policy must act against the natural instinct of hoarding to protect its reserves:

> A panic, in a word, is a species of neuralgia, and according to the rules of science you must not starve it. The holders of the cash reserve must be ready not only to keep it for their own liabilities, but to advance it most freely for the liabilities of others. They must lend to merchants, to minor bankers, to "this man and that man," whenever the security is good. In wild periods of alarm one failure makes many, and the best way to prevent the derivative failures is to arrest the primary failure which causes them. (Bagehot, 1873, p. 51)

To summarize, during this period British monetary orthodoxy evolved from a general consensus to protect the gold standard of its currency into a growing acceptance of central banking that was ideally characterized by, among other aspects, the independence of government, the monopoly in the issue of notes, and the management of the nation's gold reserves. In return, the Bank of England

[87] Bagehot (1873, pp. 16, 22, 20, 67).

[88] "Credit in business is like loyalty in Government. You must take what you can find of it, and work with it if possible. A theorist may easily map out a scheme of Government in which Queen Victoria could be dispensed with. [...] but for practical purposes, it is not even worth while to examine" (Bagehot, 1873, p. 68).

[89] Bagehot (1873, p. 35).

[90] "We should diminish the 'amateur' element; we should augment the trained banking element; and we should ensure more constancy in the administration" (Bagehot, 1873, p. 73).

increasingly had to accept its responsibility as "lender of last resort" and act in the public interest. According to the *Bagehot principle*, in the case of crisis this implied generously expanding the money supply by applying a policy of large-scale and preventative lending in order to contain the spread of panic.

4.3 Varieties of capitalism

If we apply Schumpeter's definition of capitalism as "that form of private property economy in which innovations are carried out by means of borrowed money, which in general, though not by logical necessity, implies credit creation,"[91] it is interesting to note that, despite the hegemony of British monetary thought and the global dominance of its gold standard, capitalism, and in particular the organization of finance, evolved along a variety of different paths. This section briefly highlights some major developments.

Among the threads common to all western economies, sovereign debt continued to consume the major portions of financial intermediation, especially among the "state banks" (e.g., Bank of England) as well as the large *private banking* houses. After many governments lifted restrictions on limited liability, *joint-stock banks* rapidly diffused during the nineteenth century.

Growing markets allowed for increased differentiation and specialization. During the nineteenth century, industrialization and the general expansion of commercial relationships raised the need for current means of payment as well as long-term capital. In various places, financial markets further evolved to increase their supply and efficiency in use, but did so along remarkably different trajectories. This differentiation of financial systems during that period was a core part of the emerging 'varieties of capitalism.'[92] Having different stages of development and socio-political environments, the respective territories faced different challenges, which led to diverse institutional solutions and according differences in the relative importance of the various forms of financial intermediation.

English banking

In England, two functions of intermediation evolved into characteristic activities in addition to traditional merchant banking. One was conventional *commercial banking* by "institutions that accept deposits payable on demand and originate loans with personal and corporate customers."[93] The other was *investment banking*,

[91] Schumpeter (1939, p. 111). [92] Hall and Soskice (2001).

[93] Westerhuis (2016, p. 110). The following passages are mainly based on Cassis and Cottrell (2005); Fohlin (2007, 2016); Michie (2016); Westerhuis (2016); and Voth (2018).

"whose fundamental job is to help finance the long-term capital needs of business and governments," either through stocks or bonds, and either through own capital or the intermediation of securities.[94] Though investment banking has a long history based on this general description, the modern usage of the term refers more specifically to the underwriting and placement of securities, which can be government bonds, corporate bonds, or equity. It thus emerged as a form of banking due to the growing importance of incorporation and external finance during the era.

While in most places banks were free to combine different types of business (including the various forms of merchant banking) and certainly did so in innumerable ways, the term *universal banking* characterizes the combination of the above two ideal types, where savings deposits not only contribute funds for short-term loans, but also serve long-term capital needs. On the one hand, this fostered industrial development by broadening the banks' resource base. Yet on the other hand the qualitative transformation of assets from deposits and capital with a short maturity to long-term loans and securities presented additional challenges to liquidity management and increased the risks of banking crises.

The English system refrained from adopting universal banking and maintained a characteristically high degree of specialization. Bankers in London kept their international orientation and attention focused on merchant activities, while some private partnerships further developed into investment banking. Conversely, the country banks supplied working capital through short-term credit to local industries. A particular instance of specialization came in the form of so-called *company promoters*, who at the end of the nineteenth century became notorious for buying up private companies in order to sell their shares on the public market.[95] Apparently, in England a wealthy and financially sophisticated social class was conducive to this marked degree of specialization among financial services.[96]

Continental Europe

On the Continent, the ambition and need to catch-up with England's industrialization became an important driver of change. However, catching up seemed to have become more difficult as industrialization progressed, requiring increasing amounts of capital investments. England's advanced capital markets would in principle have suggested a strengthening of its comparative advantage and industrial leadership. On the Continent, meanwhile, financial innovation was once more changing the nature of the game, as banks increasingly learned to compensate

[94] Fohlin (2016, p. 133).
[95] Nye (2014); Fohlin (2016, p. 141).
[96] Bagehot's (1873, p. 139).

Table 4.1 Selected milestones of financial innovation up to the twentieth century

Time (ca.)	Location	Earliest known evidence of ...
1774	Amsterdam	Closed-end **mutual investment funds**
1780	US	Inflation-indexed bonds
1788	Vienna	Joint-stock **development bank** (*Schwarzenberg Bank*)
1790	US	US patent law (IPRs as tradable assets)
1822	Brussels	Joint-stock universal bank
1848, 1850s	Cologne, etc.	German universal banks
1852/1864	Paris	*Credit Mobilier, Société Générale*
from 1860s	US	US investment banking (Civil War; infrastructure)
1890s	US	Reforms of NYSE (e.g., clearing, annual reports)

for this gap by providing funds for industrial developments.[97] Offering more than mere mediation between savings and investments, they exploited the flexibility and power of fractional reserves in pursuit of the new technological opportunities.

Cassis and Cottrell (2005, p. 143) trace the origin of joint-stock industrial development banks back to the short-lived *k.k. oktroyierte Wiener Commerzial-, Leih- und Wechselbank* in Austria. Backed by Vienna's high aristocracy,[98] it was chartered in 1788, but failed by 1811 (Table 4.1). In addition to merchant and deposit banking, bills-of-exchange and collateralized loans, it also offered credit against securities for entrepreneurial finance and in 1801 founded a spinning mill, which was Austria's first successful large-scale factory.[99] It also set an example of development banking as a form of highly involved active investment. The bank had initially sent agents to absorb knowledge from England and eventually recruited a British mechanic, who successfully ran the spinning mill and launched a wave of similar company promotions in the region. Only a few years after the successful promotions, the bank withdrew from the company and left its further development to the shareholders.[100]

In 1822, a group of private bankers in Brussels founded the *Société Générale de Belgique*, which is the oldest example of a large-scale *universal bank*.[101] A broad network of branches supplied many savings deposits, while in the 1830s financial crisis forced the bank to turn bad industrial loans into equity. It thus entered "mixed banking," if so defined by the combination of credit and equity investments.[102]

[97] The following passages are mainly based on Gerschenkron (1962); Fohlin (2016); and Burhop et al. (2019).

[98] It was therefore nicknamed the "Schwarzenbergbank" (Matis, 2005).

[99] The "k.k. priv. Pottendorfer Garnmanufaktur Gesellschaft." See Butschek (2011, p. 92).

[100] Freudenberger (1996); Butschek (2011, p. 100ff).

[101] The bank was initially founded under Dutch ruler William I as the "Société Générale pour favoriser l'Industrie Nationale des Pay-Bas" and renamed after Belgium gained its independence in 1830.

[102] Cassis and Cottrell (2005, p. 163).

More generally, in the second half of the nineteenth century, the growing capital needs and opportunities of industrialization prompted traditional banks to diversify and thereby become, or newly establish, universal banks. For example, in 1852 the French Pereire brothers founded the *Crédit Mobilier* as a joint-stock bank with limited liability. It famously promoted industrial companies and infrastructure, in particular railways, but it also promoted one of the earliest German universal banks.[103]

Though it was itself short-lived, the Crédit Mobilier initiated an early boom in corporate *investment banking* and induced the foundation of other joint-stock banks that had greater longevity. One example was the French *Société Générale*, which was founded in 1864. Another example was the *Oesterreichische Credit-Anstalt*, which was founded in 1855 as the first universal bank of the Austro-Hungarian Empire. Other banks followed, but taken together their impact on entrepreneurial finance was limited:

> Like many of their counterparts in other countries, the large Austrian banks initially focussed on railway financing and remained primarily engaged in the conversion of large, relatively safe firms. On the commercial side of their business, they secured their credits with the best-quality securities. Thus, the banks' investment services tended to exclude smaller, potentially riskier ventures.
>
> (Fohlin, 2016, p. 147f)

Germany is known to have developed the foremost example of the system of universal banking. It began in 1848 with the restructuring and incorporation of the Cologne bank, followed by other banks that were incorporated during the 1850s, investing in the build-up of railways and industry.[104] As many of the banks failed, it was only in the 1870s, after Germany had overcome its territorial fragmentation, liberalized company law, and established its central bank,[105] that large joint-stock universal banks, such as the *Deutsche Bank*, *Dresdner Bank*, and *Darmstädter Bank* began fuelling the rapid industrialization and growth of the country.

The large universal banks entertained close and manifold ties with industry, simultaneously combining commercial, investment, and brokerage services, in addition to running their traditional lending operations. Particularly after the boom in incorporations during the 1890s, they underwrote corporate bonds and equity issues, held industrial shares, and exercised proxy voting rights for those

[103] The *Bank für Handel und Industrie* in Darmstadt. Fohlin (2016, p. 145).

[104] Fohlin (2016, p. 146). See also, Borchardt (1961), who doubts that during the first half of nineteenth century capital shortages were much of a barrier to German industrial development. Instead, he points at low demand for credit and a general reluctance to incur debts as some of the potential causes for social disrepute. While Japan developed another renowned example of bank-based corporate finance, Hoshi and Kashyap (2001) emphasize the dominance of equity finance in the *Meiji* period of modernization prior to the military build-up in the 1930s.

[105] The *Reichsbank* in 1876.

who deposited bearer shares with them. This gave them powerful representation on the company boards, reduced informational asymmetries, and thereby also eased the provision of long-term credit. Corporate finance was further strengthened in 1892 with the introduction of the *Gesellschaft mit beschränkter Haftung* (GmbH)—an important innovation, which established the principle form of *private limited liability companies* (PLLCs).[106]

These historical examples of banking certainly influenced Schumpeter's perception of the capitalist function in economic development as well as his short-lived and ill-fated personal ambitions in that industry (Chapter 8). Characteristically, he described them as follows:

> [B]anks of the *mobilier* type themselves acquire parcels of stock, either because this strengthens their hold on the current business of customers and their claim to manage the future issues of the same concerns, or because they wish to influence the latter's business policies – particularly to acquire positions of strategic value in negotiating amalgamations – or because a given issue is not yet ripe for introduction to the public, or because they intend to trade in it permanently, or simply in order to profit by appreciation. (*BC*, 1939, p. 647)

Generally acknowledging the spectacular success of the German model of industrial development, the contemporary historical narrative, however, tends to be cautious about the specific contribution of its financial system:

> Though the German universal banks have been credited with offering a venture-capital like set of financial and managerial services through all stages of development, more recent revisions of the historical accounts suggest that the universal banks' activities looked more like those of other commercial/universal banks of the time [...]. While the banks sometimes needed more time than planned to place shares, at least by the 1880s, these banks engaged rather conservatively in the holding of industrial equities for their own account. (Fohlin, 2016, p. 146)

The upshot is that, despite the distinctive importance of banking activities for industrial development in Continental Europe, start-up finance was also mainly covered by individuals, family, and personal networks, whereas retained earnings and credit usually paid for ongoing investments and growth.[107] Furthermore, recent research has highlighted the role of the many small community savings banks in the financing of local infrastructure, in addition to the provision of credit to small and medium-sized businesses.[108]

[106] Guinnane (2010). The British equivalent was established in 1906.
[107] Pierenkemper (1990).
[108] Lehman-Hasemeyer and Wahl (2017). The first German savings bank was founded in Hamburg in 1778. Its primary purpose was to offer savings opportunities to the wider population, and thereby also provide local communities with better access to finance. In 1854 Prussia demanded that all its counties establish at least one.

North America

The worn phrase of "pushing frontiers" still best characterizes the development of the young United States of America. Freed from British regulation, the new federation further expanded its economic frontiers with the promotion and incorporation of new businesses. Many aimed at building infrastructure, such as canals, turnpikes, and railroads, and the growing acceptance of limited liability made it easier to raise funds. There was sizeable public support, for instance, for land grants, exclusive monopolies, or bonds backed by the government and municipalities.[109] However, during the early nineteenth century, intermediation through investment banking services also arose in various commercial activities (e.g., money brokers, mercantile firms, and commercial and private banks). By the 1850s, these services had become increasingly specialized.[110] Yet, once again, it was the financing of public debt that mattered most when at the beginning of the Civil War (1861–65) the issue of war bonds initiated the establishment of the first modern American investment bank by Jay Cooke in Philadelphia.

In addition to public debt, the railway boom and the rise of "heavy" industries increased the need for external finance, thereby creating fertile ground for financial intermediation. After 1864, national commercial banks took deposits, issued notes, and more generally provided working capital and liquidity as well as payment services,[111] but were not allowed to participate in investment banking. This facilitated the entry and growth of specialized investment banks, which were not allowed to take deposits or issue notes. Most were organized as private partnerships in which European immigrants played a major role. In addition to their privileged access to European investors, a reputation for professional management and reliable returns were their principal assets in raising funds.[112] Though commercial banking and investment banking were technically separated, thanks to growing markets and financial strength, some houses developed characteristics of universal banking. For instance, investment bankers like J.P. Morgan owned shares and were represented on the boards of commercial banks, while bigger commercial banks integrated investment subsidiaries of their own.[113]

Among particular instruments, investment banks popularized the principle of *preferred stock*, which originated earlier in British infrastructure projects (in part to sidestep the regulation of the debt-equity ratio). Less secure than debt securities,

[109] Chandler (1977, p. 90). [110] Fohlin (2016, p. 150f).

[111] Fulford (2015) identifies a significant and positive causal impact of national banks on the regional output per capita. Furthermore, he shows that national banks fostered structural change in terms of a growing specialization of production according to locational advantage. In the rural areas this meant a faster expansion of agriculture relative to manufacturing.

[112] Baskin and Miranti (1997, p. 138). To name a few examples, J.P. Morgan was the son of a London banking family, while Kuhn Loeb, Goldman Sachs, and the Lehman Brothers were part of the German-Jewish community.

[113] Carosso (1970); Fohlin (2016, p. 151f).

but preferable to common stock when it came to dividend payments and claims in cases of liquidation, this hybrid form of holding shares represented a crucial step in acquainting the American public with common stock. Akin to traditional partnership interests, early stockholders expected relatively fixed annuities. One likely reason for this was that dividend payments were a comparatively robust signal, given the poor state of investors' information on the value of assets. In the late nineteenth century, opportunities for fast growth, high capital needs, and high leverage caused some American companies to drop the practice of first paying out profits and then issuing securities for new investments. Instead, they increasingly used *retained earnings*, thereby substituting future capital gains for current dividends as the financial reward for their shareholders.[114]

At the time, the anticipation of capital gains also incited growing speculation with company shares on the stock market. In the 1890s, bursting bubbles and the re-organization of the railroad companies prompted a number of critical reforms at the New York Stock Exchange (NYSE). By establishing a clearing mechanism for its members and asserting requirements for annual reports with audited balance sheets and profit-loss statements, it simultaneously boosted the confidence of investors and offered a quality signal to the benefit of its listed companies.[115]

Finally, the image of the US "pushing frontiers" also accords well with regard to the boundaries of technological *innovation*. A distinctive strength of the US system was its early recognition of IPRs as tradable assets. This created early markets for technology, which enabled highly specialized inventors to establish an independent business during the late nineteenth century.[116] Later, the rising cost and complexity of invention, together with the strategic advantages of keeping these in-house, favored the formation of research and development (R&D) laboratories within larger companies, some of which originated in the earlier inventor-led business model.[117]

At the time, however, banks or securities markets were only of limited importance to the financing of new enterprises. For example, when studying the financing of inventions in Cleveland between 1870 and 1920, Lamoureaux et al. (2007, p. 40) concluded that

> formal financial institutions did not play a leading role in the creation of new enterprises. Instead, entrepreneurs seeking to exploit new technologies typically

[114] Baskin and Miranti (1997, pp. 152, 193).

[115] Neal and Davis (2007, p. 140) referring to Sobel (1965).

[116] Lamoreaux and Sokoloff (2007, p. 4ff). Royal privileges for inventors have a very long history. The first systematic application of patent rights originated with the protection of Venetian glass makers in 1450. The first US patent law dates from 1790 and distinctly provided for the tradability of patents. Unlike the European system, the US system awarded these to the first inventor (instead of to the first to file), required its immediate publication, and charged much lower fees.

[117] Lamoreaux and Sokoloff (2007, p. 14) point, among others, to the example of General Electric.

> raised capital directly from wealthy individuals. These investors bought substantial shares in the equity of new firms, held on to their investments for long periods of time, and often played an important and ongoing role in management.
> (Lamoreaux et al. (2007, p. 40)

Still, financial institutions and industry clearly co-evolved. Leading manufacturers, for instance, founded banks to supply themselves with working capital in the form of short-term commercial credit. However, the "bottom line is that these institutions were not directly involved in the founding of new companies."[118] Even when the automobile industry emerged at the beginning of the twentieth century, local networks and internal finance dominated its early development. Only at later stages was the stock market used to raise funds for investments in the large companies or for the purpose of mergers and acquisitions, which enabled industrial consolidation.[119]

4.4 Concluding remarks

Aiming to provide a thorough introduction to Schumpeter's own vision and conception, this brief history of money and monetary thought—as sketched in this first part of the book—has brought us to Schumpeter's own lifetime. Though the deeper connections will become apparent later, a few preliminary examples may illustrate the varied soil from which he drew inspiration. One early source was *William Potter* (1650), whom Murphy credits with being the first to emphasize the cash-in-advance problem, and whose analytical work Schumpeter explicitly lauded.[120] Another peculiar source was *John Law* (1705). Arguing from the context of an underdeveloped Scottish economy, Law had reasoned that out of equilibrium a change in the money supply could mobilize idle resources and therefore have a real impact on production, not just prices. This perspective naturally resonated with Schumpeter, whose concept of the creative entrepreneur provided for the perpetual emergence of new opportunities and made disequilibrium a general characteristic of the economic process (see Chapter 7). A further striking example is Schumpeter's close connection to Henry Thornton. We find their intellectual kinship in the credit theory of money, the implied endogeneity of the monetary system and real production, as well as in their shared attitude toward the quantity theory. Both are critical of the latter, considering it simplistic and misleading, but also accepting its validity in the long-term, *if* resources are fully employed. They share a profound concern about the perils of inflation, but are equally difficult

[118] Lamoureaux et al. (2007, p. 45). [119] Tedlow (2001); O'Sullivan (2007).
[120] Murphy (1997, p. 45ff); *HEA* (1954, p. 294).

to categorize with regard to the ideological debates on the monetary policy of their times.

Yet, above all, Schumpeter took seriously the historical fact of financial innovation in enabling the evolution of complex social interaction. As Goetzmann summarized, "finance has vastly improved our species' ability to reduce existential risks and to allocate resources through time to foster growth."[121] Against the orthodoxy of his time and its growing preoccupation with static equilibrium, Schumpeter was determined to assimilate this lesson from financial history into a *monetary* theory of development.

[121] Goetzmann (2016, p. 3).

PART II

SCHUMPETER'S MONETARY THEORY OF DEVELOPMENT

5
Marginalism and the Austrian School

> [T]he whole study of relative prices is based on the conception of marginal utility; and in the determination of the *average* price level, and consequently of the actual level of money prices, this principle plays practically no part, or only a very indirect part.
>
> (K. Wicksell, 1898/1936, p. 18)

In this second part of the monograph, the focus lies on Schumpeter's monetary theory of development. We will investigate it in three steps. To begin with, the current chapter addresses his intellectual upbringing in the midst of the marginalist revolution and how he drew the lines to his intellectual kinship of the Austrian School. Chapter 6 then explores the essential general building blocks of his monetary theory, which are little known and spread throughout several different publications. Finally, Chapter 7 applies these to devise a concise reconstruction of his theory of economic development, paying due attention to its often neglected monetary side.

Schumpeter was a progeny of the *marginalist revolution*. Studying in Vienna with two of its main proponents, his own method and concepts were thoroughly rooted in its fundamental premises. Here, we focus only on the monetary side of the early marginalist tradition. First, we turn to its founders (Jevons, Walras and Menger), then to Schumpeter's teachers in the Austrian School (Böhm-Bawerk and Wieser). We further discuss selected aspects of the monetary theory of Knut Wicksell, who systematically applied the marginalist principles to monetary matters. Finally, we ask how Schumpeter related to the monetary theories of Ludwig Mises and Friedrich Hayek.

5.1 The marginalist revolution

The "marginalist revolution" was initiated in the 1870s with the landmark contributions of *William Stanley Jevons* (1835–82), *Carl Menger* (1840–1921), and *Leon Walras* (1834–1910).[1] Independently of the former, Walras (1874) integrated

[1] Important forerunners were Heinrich von Thünen (1780–1850), Karl Heinrich Rau (1792–1870), Antoine-Augustin Cournot (1801–77), and Hermann Heinrich Gossen (1810–58). See, for instance, Kurz (2016, p. 57ff) for a critical discussion and comparison with the classical system of Smith and Ricardo.

Schumpeter's Venture Money. Michael Peneder and Andreas Resch,
Oxford University Press (2021). © Michael Peneder and Andreas Resch.
DOI: 10.1093/oso/9780198804383.003.0005

the marginalist principles into a general equilibrium theory of the economy. During the following decades, marginalism thoroughly upset the received classical doctrine on economic value. In short, "[t]he value of commodities is derived wholly from their utility, but the utility they afford is not wholly convertible into value." The reason is that "value should express, not total utility, but only a part of it, [...] the 'marginal utility' as we say."[2]

The immediate concern of the Marginalist School was the theory of value and the according problem of distribution. Conversely, money remained a side issue up to the seminal work of Wicksell (1898/1936). Among the notable exceptions to this, in his earlier work Jevons contributed to the statistical approach of measuring price indices,[3] and later applied it to the idea of indexing debt contracts (Table 5.1). Furthermore, he pointed at a fourth function of money: the *standard of deferred payments* in the sense of an accepted unit with which to settle debts.[4]

Another example is Walras' concept of *encaisse désirée*. Its demand corresponds with the cash people desire to hold for the service of future transactions and to which the principles of marginal utility therefore apply. Similarly to physical capital, this money is a means of intertemporal reallocation and the markets are assumed to clear when interest rates bring the aggregate of desired cash into equilibrium with the total amount of money.[5] According to Schumpeter, this "great master of universal interdependence" thereby originated a consistent system for determining absolute money prices, but subsequently did not go through with it.[6] Remaining strictly within the realm of the quantity theory, he assumed for the most part that variations of the interest rate did not affect the total amount of transactions and hence the demand for cash. By distinguishing between the *numeraire*, which can be an arbitrary commodity for expressing prices relative to a common denomination, and the *monnaie*, which represents the actual means of exchange, he effectively isolated relative price relationships from their absolute level in money prices. Consistently with the quantity theory, money thus remained neutral and the analysis firmly within the boundaries of long-run equilibrium tendencies.[7]

In contrast, the Austrian Marginalist School cared less about static, long-run equilibria, instead showing a strong interest in the phenomena of social coordination. Menger (1871) emphasized, among other aspects, the principle of subjective value (as opposed to intrinsic, e.g., cost-based value), uncertainty, and incomplete or unevenly distributed information. Accepting a fundamental indeterminateness

[2] Wieser (1891, p. 2).

[3] Assuming multiplicative instead of additive errors, Jevons (1865) proposed taking the geometric mean of price ratios. See Diewert (1993, p. 37).

[4] Jevons (1875).

[5] Laidler (1991, p. 551f) points out that Alfred Marshall originated a cash-balance approach as early as 1871, but first published it only one year after Walras in 1887. The Cambridge equation distinctly emphasized the demand for money and its precautionary function as a store of value, in contrast with the classical focus on transactions. See Section 6.2.

[6] *HEA* (1954, p. 1024f).

[7] Becker and Baumol (1952).

of final economic outcomes, the analytical interest turned toward processes, in particular the forces that affect the selection of alternative potential realizations.

The individualist and subjectivist approach relates directly to the enduring emphasis of the Austrian School on structure and spontaneous order, of which Menger's theory of money is a good example. Focusing on the genesis of money as a medium of exchange, he stressed the different "saleableness" of goods, defined as the "greater or less facility with which they can be disposed of at a market at any convenient time at current purchasing prices."[8] Since individuals aim to exchange less saleable for more saleable goods, it is through mere economic self-interest that money emerges as a social institution: "the spontaneous outcome, the unpremeditated resultant of particular, individual efforts of the members of a society."[9]

Menger's perspective on the nature of money remained within the conventional Aristotelian emphasis on its function as a medium of exchange in which the precious metals exhibit intrinsic advantages, such as their durability, homogeneity, and divisibility, along with a lower fluctuation of prices. Consequently, "their saleableness is far and away superior to that of all other commodities."[10] Once adopted as a medium of exchange, increasing returns render such advantages self-reinforcing and cumulative. In other words, money did not need to be generated by law: "In its origin it is a social, and not a state-institution." This does not imply, however, that Menger discounted the role of government, since "by state recognition and state regulation, this social institution of money has been perfected and adjusted to the manifold and varying needs of an evolving commerce."[11]

In short, Menger's emphasis on spontaneous order and unrestricted interaction among self-interested individuals remained a distinctive characteristic of the Austrian School, and his careful theoretical analysis is still a hallmark of evolutionary institutional reasoning. The monetary core of his analysis, however, was not novel. It essentially fit the orthodoxy of the time and complemented the static equilibrium perspective with a plausible and well-reasoned process theory. Schumpeter therefore concluded that Menger's theory of the origin of money, "though a masterly performance so far as it went, was simply a descendant from Davanzati's."[12]

5.2 Early Austrian School

At the University of Vienna, Schumpeter had studied with Eugen von *Böhm-Bawerk* (1851–1914) and Friedrich von *Wieser* (1851–1926), who were not only good friends and brothers-in-law, but also stood out as Menger's most important

[8] Menger (1892, p. 244). [9] Menger (1892, p. 250); Peneder (2001, p. 5f).
[10] Menger (1892, p. 252). [11] Menger's (1892, p. 255). [12] *HEA* (1954 p. 1085f).

disciples. Schumpeter repeatedly emphasized that, through their teaching and further theoretical developments, both should be considered co-founders of the Austrian School along with Menger.[13] Common usage, however, refers to Menger as the founder, and to Wieser and Böhm-Bawerk as the *first generation* of the school.

Böhm-Bawerk (1889/91) is most famous for originating the Austrian capital theory. He insisted that physical capital was an intermediate product of nature and labor and rejected treating it as an independent factor of production.[14] Furthermore, he explained capital as the product of investment, which is a time-consuming process that enhances the productivity of the primary inputs:

> [A] a greater result is obtained by producing goods in *roundabout* ways than by producing them directly. Where a good can be produced in either way, we have the fact that, by the indirect way, a greater product can be got with equal labour, or the same product with less labour.
>
> (Böhm-Bawerk, 1889/91, p. 34; emphasis added)

Investments come at the cost of delayed consumption and, according to Böhm-Bawerk, "present goods are, as a rule, worth more than future goods of like kind and number."[15] These positive *time preferences* result from the higher uncertainty we must account for in the valuation of future goods, but are also forced upon us by the immediate perception of the present "through our senses," whereas "the future we must anticipate and picture."[16] In short, the investment decision must balance out the aspired gains in productivity with the "pain" of delayed consumption of those inputs which enter the roundabout method of production. To achieve productivity gains, entrepreneurs purchase means of production from labor and nature, and generate a surplus that increases with the extension of the average period of production.

One aspect of Böhm-Bawerk's conception, that later proved particularly influential for Schumpeter's monetary theory of development, was that,

> a value increment arises as soon as the present means of production have begun in the hands of the entrepreneur to grow toward their consumptive maturity—and this value increment forms the basis of the net return to the entrepreneur's capital. (TGE, 1952, p. 180)[17]

Böhm-Bawerk thus arrived at an alternative explanation of interest that "arises from an exchange of present against future consumers' goods and is essentially a

[13] *Ten Great Economists TGE* (1952, p. 89); *HEA* (1954, p. 844).
[14] Böhm-Bawerk (1889/91, p. 78).
[15] Böhm-Bawerk (1889, p. 160).
[16] Böhm-Bawerk (1889, p. 163).
[17] *TGE* (1952, p. 180).

premium (*Agio*), attaching to the former."[18] According to the neoclassical principles of price formation, the interest rate adjusts to the level at which the marginal productivity gains of further capital deepening are equal to the marginal loss of utility from postponing consumption, thereby achieving an optimal level of investment for given individual preferences and technological constraints.

In the same year in which Böhm-Bawerk published his theory of capital and interest, Wieser (1889/93) presented the subjectivist foundation of value theory on the principle of "alternative cost," or "opportunity cost," as it became better known.[19] Wieser originated the term "marginal utility" (*Grenznutzen*) and established the method of "imputation," by which the output prices of finished products are divided into the values of the factors of production.[20] With respect to money, Wieser acknowledged the difficulty of explaining its value exclusively in terms of subjective preferences and distinguished between the subjective use value of goods on the one hand and prices as objective exchange values of money on the other. Accordingly, prices reflect "the anticipated use value of the things which can be obtained for it,"[21] but also emerge as an objective datum from the market process. While it is derived from subjective marginal utilities, the objective exchange value acquires a different quality as a definite magnitude of payments needed to purchase particular goods. Schumpeter would later describe these as the "sediment" of a "social system of individual values."[22]

The strong intellectual kinship among the three founders of the Austrian School should not lead one to assume that they were a particularly homogenous force. Rather, one may infer that the early proponents drew much inspiration from a fertile culture of intellectual dispute. For example, Friedrich Wieser dissented strongly from Böhm-Bawerk's theory of capital and interest. Not only did he prefer to treat capital as an independent factor of production,[23] but he also remained "fundamentally opposed"[24] to the general validity of positive time preferences. While Böhm-Bawerk had acknowledged that the anticipation of future wants induced people to make provisions for prospective needs, Wieser emphasized that a willingness to postpone consumption was imperative to the development of

[18] *HEA* (1954, p. 928).

[19] The latter term was coined by Green (1894, p. 222f): "[C]ost consists for the most part of the sacrifice of opportunity."

[20] Kurz (2016, p. 72).

[21] Wieser (1889/93, p. 61); see also *TED* (1911/34, p. 50). In German, Wieser used the terms "Tauschwerth" for the former and "Verkehrswerth" for the latter. An alternative more literal yet potentially confusing translation would thus be "exchange value," referring to subjective utility, and "market" or "sales value," referring to transaction prices.

[22] *TED* (1911/34, p. 56).

[23] See Wieser (1914/27, p. 73): "Capital, though due to human effort, though historically it may be the product of labor, has become an independent factor of production in the practical economic organization. Labor and free nature alone are no longer sufficient to create it. It is a productive factor *sui generis*; practice and therefore also economic theory have to take into consideration its unique nature."

[24] Wieser (1914/27, p. 142).

modern civilization: "Efficient economy requires that the future satisfaction and need shall not be deemed less important than the vividly experienced desire of the moment."[25] Menger and Schumpeter also disagreed with Böhm-Bawerk's theory of capital, prompting its most important later proponent F.A. Hayek to question its designation as the Austrian theory of capital.[26]

Another case in point is Wieser's reservations regarding the paradigmatic individualism of Menger's theory of money. Menger had portrayed money as the outcome of what we may today call cognitive leadership[27] and the mere self-interest of those who follow a successful example. In contrast, Wieser placed emphasis on the distinctive quality that adoption by the masses adds to the process: while "success is the driving force that moves the masses to copy the example of the leaders," the masses establish "the universal practice which gives to a rule its binding force and social power."[28] However, the mass habit of accepting money also creates an obligation:

> [M]oney represents something more and stronger than the will of participating individuals. [It] is no longer the mere result of the individual aims of leaders whom the masses follow. [Instead, money can] release a power which produces results far beyond those set by the masses or desired by the leaders.
>
> (Wieser, 1914/27, p. 165)

In contrast with Menger's emphasis on spontaneous order and the intrinsic advantages of specie, Wieser considered the evolution of money to be in flux, pointing at a historical tendency toward dematerialization of money by means of a growing separation of its services from the substance matter:[29]

> I confess to the often fought and, I believe, not refuted heretical opinion that [...] money is conceivable which, without receiving any value from its materials, i.e., without receiving any value from its "use," would quite exclusively serve circulation and would thus be good money held in full value.
>
> (Wieser, 1904, p. 167)

Consistently with his historical account of the Austrian experience with paper money (see Section 5.4), he thereby embraced the theoretical possibility of a managed currency without intrinsic material value. This was only limited by the need for a stable international currency for the purpose of international exchange. For this task, gold was still the best option available, as it is in principle

[25] Wieser (1914/27, p. 36). [26] Hayek (1941, p. 46). [27] Witt (1998).
[28] Wieser (1914/27, p. 162ff). [29] Wieser (1927, p. 693).

self-organized and operates independently of political intervention. While later expressing sympathy with Keynes' suggestion of a managed world currency off gold, he also considered this utopian—due to doubts about the prospect of necessary "world peace" and, more generally, doubts about whether the nations would be capable of sufficient policy coordination in the near future.[30]

Finally, Wieser sympathized with Tooke's income approach, based on which money incomes drive expenditures and therefore prices.[31] In association with his own theory of imputation, Wieser was able to put this on a stronger theoretical footing:

> The value of money is formed through exchange relationships—in the theory of monetary value, therefore, only those quantity relations are to be examined which emerge by way of exchange. Ultimately, the value of money is only formed in those transactions which relate to consumer goods. If productive goods or means of acquisition of any kind are otherwise exchanged, then independent prices are not formed there, but their prices are adjusted to those which exist for consumer goods and these decide the value of money—a functional theory of money must therefore above all adhere to those quantitative relationships which have an effect on the exchange of consumer goods. (Wieser, 1909, p. 214)

For Wieser, the crucial question was which quantity determined prices: "In the older theory this quantity was the material stock of money. Actually it should be represented by the entire sum of the income of the economy which is available under the expanded form of money."[32] His reference to "older" theory also included Menger, who stressed that expenditures misrepresent the demand for money, since they fail to include the cash balances held idle as reserves for potential prospective needs.[33] However, sticking to his aim of understanding the structure of price determination, Wieser concluded that "in a static economy, the general level of prices is determined by the newly produced natural consumption values on the one hand and monetary income on the other."[34] Thus, he agreed that monetary circulation adjusts endogenously to the needs of trade and, with rising demand, will even find new ways to better organize means of credit payment. Unlike Tooke, however, he asserted that the "misapplication" of credit that failed to facilitate actual trade must inevitably lead to an increase in prices.[35]

[30] Wieser (1927, p. 715f). [31] Mensik (2014). [32] Wieser (1914/27, p. 262).

[33] Menger (1909, p. 110ff); Streissler (1973) and Chaloupek (2010) argue that Menger had anticipated elements of Keynes' later emphasis on "liquidity preferences" (see Chapter IV).

[34] Wieser (1914/1927, p. 264). [35] Mensik (2014, p. 387).

5.3 Knut Wicksell

Notwithstanding his thorough respect for his teachers in Vienna, Schumpeter maintained that *Knut Wicksell* (1851–1926) had presented the best formulation of the Austrian doctrine. Wicksell was a trained mathematician, whose interest increasingly turned toward economics after he had traveled the Continent in 1887 and also attended lectures by Carl Menger. Writing in German and Swedish, however, his ideas were little known outside the two language realms. For example, his most important work, *Geldzins und Güterpreise*, was written in 1898, but not translated into English until 1936 (*Interest and Prices*).[36] Acknowledging the influence of the early Austrians, in particular Böhm-Bawerk's capital theory, his analysis certainly had a significant impact on the younger generation of Schumpeter, Mises, and Hayek, as well as the Swedish School and Keynes.

Wicksell initially set out to rectify the quantity theory of money:

> The Quantity Theory is *theoretically* valid so long as the assumption of *ceteris paribus* is firmly adhered to. But among the "things" that have to be supposed to remain "equal" are some of the flimsiest and most intangible factors in the whole of economics—in particular the velocity of circulation of money.
>
> (Wicksell, 1898/1936, p. 42)

Consistently with this ambivalent statement about the quantity theory, Wicksell had some sympathy for the alternative income approach. After discussing the work of Tooke and others, however, he disagreed that they had produced any systematic theory and concluded: "Relatively at any rate; the Quantity Theory is the most competent of all the methods of interpretation that have so far been advanced of the oscillations of the general price level."[37] Furthermore: "If the Quantity Theory is false—or to the extent that it is false—there is so far available only one false theory of money, and no true theory."[38]

Like Schumpeter, Wicksell was disappointed that the marginal revolution had not yet made a decisive difference in the field of monetary analysis: "Jevons, Walras, and Menger, have entered fairly deeply into questions concerning money. But their treatment of such questions runs, for the most part, in the old ruts."[39] While Wicksell initially set out to examine the quantity theory, he ended up developing an original explanation of the formation of aggregate price levels. It may be a matter of taste whether one considers his analysis a modification or "augmentation" of the quantity theorem as a macroeconomic identity, or whether one considers it an alternative theory to its interpretation as an equilibrium

[36] Though a brief English summary was published in 1906.

[37] Wicksell (1898/1936, p. 50).

[38] Wicksell (1898, p. xxiii).

[39] Wicksell (1898, p. 18).

condition.[40] In any case, the latter highlights the difference between money supply and the interest rate as two prime movers of the price level, with all its implications for the choice and design of adequate policy instruments.[41]

It is also consistent with the fact that Wicksell was not shy about breaking with the monetary orthodoxy in fundamental ways. To begin with, he consequently pointed out that absolute prices are purely a matter of convention, which depend on the chosen monetary standard.[42] Accordingly, he explicitly carried the marginalist revolution to its obvious conclusion on the question of theoretical metallism:

> No theorist can today lend his support to the traditional conception that money possesses in itself an independent and more or less invariable, intrinsic value, against which the exchange values of real commodities are, as it were, compared or measured; [...] the modern theory of value must have put a definite end to this manner of approach. The value of an object is merely the importance that we ascribe to its possession for the purpose of gratifying our wants.
>
> (Wicksell, 1898/1936, p. 29)

Nevertheless, money is not an ordinary good: "It is its purchasing power over commodities that determines its utility and marginal utility, and it is not determined by them."[43] As an intermediary of purchasing power, money can take various forms, and Wicksell discusses these in terms of the situation of (i) a pure cash economy, (ii) a mixed system with cash and simple credit, and, finally, (iii) the case of a pure credit economy. Contrasting such ideal types allowed him to highlight the way in which

> the *ex novo* and endogenous nature of credit money modifies the [...] coordination between savings and investment. More precisely, while in a barter economy these two magnitudes are defined in real terms, in a monetary economy credit money may to a certain extent become a substitute for real savings.
>
> (Festré, 2006, p. 334).

Therefore, the pure credit economy meant more than a mere hypothetical situation: "There can scarcely be any doubt that the use of bills might, under favourable conditions, have developed so far as to have dispensed almost completely with the use of money" (Wicksell, 1898/1936, p. 65). Or, supposing that the system

[40] Arnon (2011, p. 345).

[41] According to Laidler (1991, p. 188), "Marshall, Fisher, Hawtrey, and other leading quantity theorists also understood how a managed currency could be made to work, but unlike Wicksell they stopped short of advocating it," because "they feared the discretionary power that its introduction might give to policy-makers" (Laidler, 1991, p. 188).

[42] Wicksell (1898/1936, p. 4). [43] Wicksell (1898, p. 29).

> is developed up to the point where everybody possesses a banking account. Then all payments could be effected by such bookkeeping transfers, except possibly those for which small change suffices. It is true that a substantial amount of capital would be required to instil confidence and to meet unavoidable risks.
>
> (Wicksell, 1898, p. 68)

At the end of the nineteenth century, at a time when the gold standard was still firmly in place in many countries, Wicksell thus envisioned the hypothetical case of a pure credit economy that could in principle operate without any cash. His purpose, however, was above all theoretical: to deprive the quantity theory of its foundations,[44] in order to eliminate any changes in the monetary base as an interfering factor of his analysis of interest and prices. As Laidler emphasized in his critique of the Neo-Wicksellian approach,[45] this conscious restriction must be kept in mind when applying Wicksell's tools in the analysis of actual monetary policy. The crucial step in Wicksell's analysis is the distinction of what he called the "natural rate" of interest and the money rate of interest. While the former descends directly from Böhm-Bawerk's marginal productivity of capital, the classical explanation of interest treated the money rate and the real rate of return as fundamentally equivalent. Yet Wicksell went one step further. Acknowledging that the money rate is formed on the credit market by the demand and supply for loans, he asserted that it does not necessarily equal the rate of return on capital, and that their exact coincidence is even unlikely.[46] Though the real rate of return must have an influence on the demand for loans, other factors may interfere as well. When compared with the system of Walras, the money rate is no longer set equal to the rate of return, but becomes an additional variable and its correspondence with the real rate becomes an additional equilibrium condition.[47]

As an equilibrium condition, general price stability requires that the money rate correspond to the natural rate of interest, which anchors the system and is determined in the real economy. Conversely, differences between the two rates upset the price level and set in motion a *cumulative process*: If the loan rate is below the real rate, the expansionary impulse causes inflation, whereas a loan rate above the real rate of return will cause a contractionary deflation of prices. These price changes are cumulative in the sense that a return to equilibrium will not reverse them but only establish a new price level. If, however, and for whatever reason, a difference between the two rates is maintained, the price changes will continue without limit. In conjunction with according anticipations in the market, they may also accelerate.[48]

[44] Wicksell (1898, p. 76). [45] See Laidler (2006) on Woodford (2003).
[46] Wicksell (1898/1936, p. 106). [47] *HEA* (1954, p. 1118). [48] Wicksell (1898, p. 96).

Table 5.1 Selected milestones of monetary thought in the nineteenth century

Author	Ideas
Francis **Baring** (1797)	Lender of last resort
Henry **Thornton** (1802/1939)	Credit theory of money; forced saving; cumulative process; purchasing power parity theory
David **Ricardo** (1811)	Ingot plan
John **Fullarton** (1844)	Principle of reflux
Thomas **Tooke** (1844)	Income theory of money
J.W. **Lubbock** (1840)	Elaborate equation of exchange
J.S. **Mill** (1848/71)	Synthesis of monetary orthodoxy
A. **Marshall** (1871)	Cambridge cash-balance approach
Walter **Bagehot** (1873)	Monetary expansion to contain panic
W.S. **Jevons** (1875)	Standard of deferred payments; statistical approach to index numbers (1865)
L. **Walras** (1886)	*Encaisse désirée*; *numéraire vs monnaie*
F.Y. **Edgeworth** (1888)	Economies of scale in reserve holdings
Carl **Menger** (1892)	Evolution of money as a social institution
E. **Böhm-Bawerk** (1889)	Positive time preferences; *agio* theory of interest
Friedrich **Wieser** (1889/93)	Imputation; income theory of money
Knut **Wicksell** (1898/1936)	Real *vs* money rate of interest; interest rate policy (anticyclical)

In short, a permanent deviation of the two rates "exerts a progressive and cumulative influence on prices."[49] In a credit economy, the central bank can no longer exert much control over the actual money in circulation. Furthermore, the natural rate of return is neither directly observable, nor very amenable to public intervention. But the development of prices "provides a reliable test of the agreement or diversion of the two rates." This leaves the loan rate as the obvious policy tool for which Wicksell offered a simple rule of prudent interest rate policy:

> For the current level of commodity prices provides a reliable test of the agreement or diversion of the two rates. The procedure should rather be simply as follows: So long as prices remain unaltered the banks' rate of interest is to remain unaltered. If prices rise, the rate of interest is to be raised; and if prices fall, the rate of interest is to be lowered; and the rate of interest is henceforth to be maintained at its new level until a further movement of prices calls for a further change in one direction or the other. (Wicksell, 1898/1936, p. 68; emphasis removed)

Finally, Wicksell acknowledged that, in an open economy, additional concerns about the exchange rates or the balance of payments factor in. The solution he conceived was the international coordination of monetary policy. The pursuit of international stability of world prices and balances of payment would be its joint

[49] Wicksell (1898, 120f).

objective, while going off gold and introducing an international "ideal standard of value"[50] was the necessary pre-condition.

To conclude, Wicksell influenced both the Austrian School and Keynes and had a significant impact on Schumpeter, foremost by putting monetary analysis and the determination of the price level back on the agenda. More specifically, Wicksell's independent determination of the money rate of interest, interacting with the real rate via equilibrium conditions, discharged the classical identity of the two. Furthermore, as Schumpeter would later do, he conceived the business cycle to be initiated by "real" causes, but simultaneously addressed the monetary mechanisms of propagation.[51] Finally, Wicksell's method of starting from a hypothetical "pure cash" economy and then developing the more complex cases may have inspired Schumpeter's strategy of first contrasting his theory of development with the hypothetical antipode of a "circular economy."

5.4 Drawing the lines

Apart from its impact on Wicksell, who was little known outside the German and Swedish language realms, the marginalist revolution had little influence on the monetary doctrines of the time. It mainly helped refine the orthodox views and align these with the new method. As Schumpeter concluded, the majority of writers accepted the definition of money as the most saleable commodity, by which, according to him, "practically all must be classed as theoretical metallists."[52] In accordance with Menger, metallism was often defended, due to its historical development and the presumed superiority of metal coinage. Alternate views emerged from a legal perspective. Neither explanation was to his satisfaction.

Historical and legal rationales

The leading economists of the time perceived that the historical record of the evolution of money favored the commodity view, and they stressed the advantages of precious metals in the exchange of goods. It seems that they were not aware of the economic significance of clay tokens and tablets in Mesopotamia, or of other symbolic forms of circulation, which now hold an important place in the historical record (Chapter 2). Schumpeter also remained more cautious about the origin of credit than the current historical record would warrant.[53]

[50] Wicksell (1898, p. 193).

[51] Ingrao and Sardoni (2019). [52] *HEA* (1954, p. 1087).

[53] "We do hold that credit creation goes back very far, quite as far as capitalism does according to any definition, but we neither need nor do hold, that it played a decisive role from the outset" (*BC*, 1939, p. 230).

In his opposition to the commodity view, Schumpeter attached importance to the priority of a theoretical rationale over that of the historical-genetic origin of money. In short, he argued that "the essence of the matter became crystallized only in the course of history, and it is precisely the most modern forms of manifestation that are here the purest logically and the simplest substantively."[54] One such important manifestation is in the degree of security a society can attach to its money as legal tender:

> It is, of course, clear that in primitive conditions only money made of an intrinsically valuable material can obtain its definite market valuation and continue to circulate. Money made of valueless material presupposes so high a standard of legal security, that in international trade even today only money based upon "valuable" material functions smoothly. (MSP, 1917–18/56, p. 157)

This emphasis on the enforcement of legal tender warrants a look at Georg Friedrich Knapp's *State Theory of Money*, which challenged the orthodox commodity view with a deliberate emphasis on the role of government fiat. In short, it postulated that "money is a creature of law" and that, accordingly, the "soul of currency is not in the material of the pieces, but in the legal ordinances which regulate their use."[55] Money is thus a social institution, which historically first acquired its special use through custom and later through law.

Knapp's state theory became popular among German-speaking scholars, but was also well received, for instance, by Keynes. Schumpeter certainly agreed with calling money a social institution. In his money book, he devoted the entire second chapter to a "sociology of money." A far cry from denying the importance of custom and law for the particular forms and realizations of a monetary system, he nevertheless called the state theory a mere "tempest in a teapot":[56]

> Money is as little and in no other sense a creature of the law than is any other social institution such as marriage or private property. [...] Marriage and property, too, are regulated by law and to that extent their concrete forms are of course creatures of the prevailing legal system. But no-one can explain marriage or property by this legal system. Rather, the relevant legal provisions themselves are comprehensible only on the basis of the social nature and the social functions of the relations and modes of behaviour which these legal provisions regulate.
>
> (MSP, 1917–18/56, p. 160)

The above statement is in full concord with his peers from the Austrian School of economics. In the tradition of Carl Menger they all insisted on the need for and

[54] Conversely, "it is a prejudice to believe that either what happens first historically or what is culturally more primitive is also necessarily the simpler logically and the less complicated" (*WDG*, 1970, p. 35).

[55] Knapp (1905/24, p. 1ff).

[56] *HEA* (1954, p. 1090).

prioritization of an economic explanation, which could explain the use and value of money in terms of the logical requirements of the market system. Despite their fundamental agreement, Schumpeter's relationship to the Austrian School was somewhat ambivalent and deserves further explanation in the following section.

"Only fish swim in schools"

Among his closer Austrian peers, Schumpeter had a genuine admiration for Menger, but this did not stop him from propagating a different vision of the nature of money. Similarly, Böhm-Bawerk's theory of capital and interest was a major influence, which he nevertheless challenged, much to the dismay of his teacher. His strongest intellectual kinship was with Friedrich Wieser. Both had a similar overall vision of economic development and emphasized the income approach and endogenous money.

Consistently with Schumpeter's distinctly individual personality, there is no simple answer to the recurrent question of whether or not he should be considered a member of the Austrian School. However, it is a fact that he studied with its co-founders, and there is no way to deny their influence on his academic upbringing. The Austrian School is therefore, so to speak, part of his intellectual "genetic" blueprint. This is most evident in the common attention to structures and processes, that is, the economic dynamics and emergent properties of a system that originated in individual choices and structural change. Relatedly, they distrusted the notion of perfect competition and shared a disequilibrium view of the economy. When compared to mainstream economic theory, this amounts to a substantial degree of concordance between Schumpeter and his Austrian "kin."

Another fact, however, is that Schumpeter never wanted to be part of any such group. He notoriously proclaimed that "only fish swim in schools."[57] *Ludwig Mises* (1881–1973) explicitly declared Schumpeter not to be part of the Austrian School, whereas Schumpeter regarded Mises as "the founder of a school of his own."[58] Arguably, the two represent an instance of speciation along differences that already existed within the so-called first generation. According to Streissler, Schumpeter "was an economist in the liberal tradition—admittedly more in the somewhat muted tradition of Wieser than that of the austere Böhm-Bawerk, which Mises and Professor Hayek followed."[59] If Mises, and to a limited extent Schumpeter, represent the second generation of the Austrian School, *Friedrich Hayek* (1899–1992) and *Gottfried Haberler* (1900–95) were the most notable proponents of its third generation. However, all this need not mean much, since even Schumpeter's intense dispute with Böhm-Bawerk was characteristic of the school's intellectual

[57] Stolper (1994, p. 88). [58] *HEA* (1954, p. 1086) and Vanberg (2015, p. 95).
[59] Streissler (1983, p. 357); see also Wasserman (2019).

heritage (Section 7.10). Schumpeter generally remained on good terms with the Austrian economists, his friendship with Gottfried Haberler at Harvard serving as a case in point.[60] Similarly, his high esteem for Friedrich Hayek was genuine. The same does not necessarily apply to Ludwig Mises, though a certain mutual and polite restraint suggests a shared sense of relationship.[61]

One obvious difference to the school of thought of his Austrian kin was Schumpeter's admiration for the competing marginalist tradition of Walras.[62] This also relates to an important fault line with respect to the philosophy of science. In his introduction to *HEA* (1954), Schumpeter stressed the need for a variety of methods in economics, including history, sociology, statistics, and pure theory. He was thereby addressing Hayek's critique of "scientism," a term used "to denote the uncritical copying of the methods of mathematical physics in the equally uncritical belief that these methods are of universal application."[63] Schumpeter agreed "in principle," but argued that Hayek had raised the wrong question. Even if certain tools were developed first, for example, in physics, this does not imply "that there is anything specifically 'physicist' about this particular kind of language." The same can be said about "concepts of physics, such as equilibrium potential or oscillator, or statics and dynamics, which turn up of themselves in economic analysis just as do systems of equations." And, referring to the Austrian theory of marginal utility, he added that it "cannot be a crime to formulate their reasoning correctly."[64]

The index method

With regard to money, one major disagreement concerned the measurement of the price level and its changes. As they are familiar with index numbers from undergraduate courses in statistics, current students of economics tend to take these for granted. They would probably not understand why Schumpeter dedicated many pages to explaining them in a separate chapter of his "money book" (*WDG*, 1970). However, as the heading "theory of the price level" indicates, the very legitimacy of price indices was hotly contested, especially among Schumpeter's Austrian

[60] Boehm (2015).

[61] Though Mises and Schumpeter knew each other well from their common years of study in Vienna, McCaffrey surmises that they only met once while both were living in the US. The occasion was a lecture Mises gave at Harvard University. Finding no indication of open hostility, but "only a silent acknowledgement of differences," McCaffrey quotes from the memoirs of Ludwig's wife, Margit Mises: "During our stay in Cambridge I met, for the first and only time, Professor Joseph A. Schumpeter, who had just been married for the third time. His new wife was an elegant and intelligent American. They kept a lovely, well-run home. The discussion at lunch was lively but careful, both men aware of their parts as host and guest. Schumpeter knew of course that Lu did not agree with many of his views" (Margit Mises, 1976, p. 64; as quoted in McCaffrey, 2014).

[62] Similarly, though in a less apparent way, Schumpeter disagreed on the issue of socialist calculation (Vanberg, 2015, p. 96f).

[63] *HEA* (1954, p. 17). [64] *HEA* (1954, p. 18).

peers. Though Schumpeter had championed the demand for micro-foundations of economic analysis and coined the term "methodological individualism" in WHN (1908), he never adhered to the radical subjectivism of Mises and Hayek.[65] As a consequence, he was also less dogmatic about methods of aggregation and analyses of macroeconomic phenomena. Unlike the "small but distinguished group who believe neither in price index numbers nor in the price-level concept itself,"[66] Schumpeter, like Wieser and Wicksell before him, accepted prices as objective data that result from the market process. He thus eschewed the Austrian fixation on subjective values, which would only allow a direct appraisal of one's preferences for specific choices. According to Mises, however,

> Schumpeter also starts from the erroneous idea that we need a measure of value in order to be able to compare values with each other. The value judgement, however, by no means involves the comparison of two "value quantities"; it is nothing other than the comparison of two feelings, [whereby this] subjective use value is inaccessible to any measurement. (Mises, 1912/53, pp. 24, 19)

To the contemporary reader, who is accustomed to macroeconomic concepts from introductory courses in economics, this emphasis on subjectivist principles applied to money values must sound peculiar and disconcerting. However, one easily overlooks the fact that the problem in aggregation is not that agents are heterogenous—or "feelings" would be intangible—but that preferences are strictly ordinal. Hence, subjective utility lacks a proper metric or cardinal scale for measurement. As Mises put it,

> subjective valuation, which is the pivot of all economic activity, only arranges commodities in order of their significance; it does not measure this significance. And economic activity has no other basis than the value-scales thus constructed by individuals. (Mises, 1912/53, p. 39)

Having been raised in the Austrian tradition, Schumpeter understood these objections all too well. In a courteous review of the second edition of *Theorie des Geldes und der Umlaufmittel*, in which Mises had repeatedly criticized Schumpeter for his advocacy of index numbers, Schumpeter in turn pointed out that Mises was "decisively overshooting the target" with his assertion of the fundamental inadequacy of the method. Relatedly, he dryly remarked that the reader "cannot follow wherever the temperament [of Mises] leads."[67]

Behind this methodological controversy, the theoretical issue at stake was none other than the constitutive function of money. In the same review, Schumpeter

[65] Arena (2015, p. 79).

[66] *HEA* (1954, p. 701). Schumpeter explicitly refers to Mises, Hayek, and, "with some qualifications," Haberler. Among them, Schumpeter considered Mises "the foremost critic of the price-level concept" (*HEA*, 1954, p. 1099).

[67] "Geldwerttheorie und Währungspraxis" (RGU; 1924, p. 2).

summarized that, according to Mises, "money is essentially based on the role of the medium of exchange," and that he "rigorously recognizes as real money only the goods that actually serve as such medium of exchange due to their special saleability. Even banknotes appear as money surrogates."[68] And Mises indeed opined that, "[a]lthough it is usual to speak of money as a measure of value and prices, the notion is entirely fallacious. So long as the subjective theory of value is accepted, this question of measurement cannot arise." The reason for this being that subjective values are a psychological judgement which, according to him, "in no way involves the idea of measurement."[69] Mises thus stood in direct opposition to Schumpeter, who in *WHN* had postulated the standard of value to be the second constitutive function of money after that of facilitating exchange. Schumpeter had thereby strictly distinguished between prices and the subjective utility of having certain goods and services at one's disposal, and had established that the former can be expressed in multiples of any arbitrary unit chosen as the common unit of account.[70] Later, in MSP (1917–18/56) he elevated that unit of account to be the truly indispensable function of money (see Chapter 6).

Even when Mises acknowledged some practical use of index numbers, his strict epistemological stance bound him to conflate them with the aggregation of subjective utilities.[71] In contrast, Schumpeter only applied them to prices and even avoided Wieser's expression of "objective value" to avert a confusion of terms. In later editions, however, Mises had to concede to reality. He added two paragraphs, concluding that "[t]he practical utility of all these calculations for certain purposes is beyond doubt; they have proved their worth in quite recent events. But we should beware of demanding more from them than they are able to perform."[72] Arguably, this settled the disparity between Schumpeter and the Austrians regarding the issue of index numbers.

Any such differences, however, should not veil the fundamental concord regarding a general monetary vision, which Schumpeter, Mises, and Hayek owed to the distinctive influence of Knut Wicksell (and relatedly to that of Henry Thornton).[73] Agnes Festré summarized their common point of departure:

> In contrast to the orthodox monetary view, these authors consider that the introduction of the organization of bank credit in the field of economic theory implies

[68] RGU (1924, p. 2). [69] Mises (1912/53, p. 38f; see also p. 45).

[70] To illustrate the distinction, Schumpeter explained the following statement as indeed problematic: "That amount of goods is worth a thousand apples to me." Whereas, conversely, the following expression would be logically sound: "For this quantity of goods I would give at the most a thousand times this apple" (*WHN*, 1908, p. 290).

[71] "All index number systems, in so far as they are intended to have a greater significance for monetary theory than that of merely playing with figures, are based upon the idea of measuring the *utility* of a certain quantity of money" (Mises, 1912/53, p. 193; emphasis added).

[72] Mises (1912/53, p. 194).

[73] Unfortunately, we cannot ascertain whether Schumpeter first encountered these ideas by reading Thornton or in the later work of Knut Wicksell. A first reference to Henry Thornton appears in Schumpeter (1917–18/56, p. 704), many years before Hayek (1939) contributed significantly to his contemporary prominence.

> radical changes within the economic system. Indeed, as soon as one accounts for the existence of a banking system, money ceases to be exogenous and the mere counterpart of real exchanges. The *ex novo* and endogenous nature of credit-money modifies the conditions under which the mechanisms of co-ordination between savings and investment operate [and] may allow the emergence of global disequilibria. (Festré, 2002, p. 443)

Unlike Wicksell, who aimed to integrate the credit economy into a general equilibrium framework, Schumpeter, along with Mises and Hayek, applied the endogenous supply of bank money to develop distinct disequilibrium views of the economy. The cumulative process of Thornton and Wicksell was an essential element in this. For Schumpeter, the initial impulse originated with the real economy, just as Wicksell had assumed. As the subsequent chapters will investigate in detail, innovation is the initial driver, but endogenous money a foremost mechanism of propagation in his monetary theory of development. Furthermore, he portrayed finance itself as a social technology that evolves and thereby fosters development, and recurrent crises as the two faces of dynamic disequilibrium.

Mises and Hayek pursued a different path. Mises, in particular, took a gloomy view of banking. He elaborated a detailed explanation of the cumulative process, starting with the primary impulse of monetary expansion by profit-seeking banking operations. Despite his sympathy for the "currency principle" (Section 4.2), he argued that it was not implemented consistently enough:

> [S]omething was overlooked in the calculations of the Currency Theorists. They did not realize that unbacked deposits were substantially the same as unbacked notes, and so they omitted to legislate for them in the same way as for the notes. (Mises, 1912/53, p. 370)

In other words, the Currency School's disregard for endogenous bank money had subverted its own reforms, because "fiduciary media, suppressed as bank-notes, developed in the form of deposits."[74] Mises further argued that competition forces the banks to extend credit, which lowers the interest rate below its equilibrium value, causes overinvestment, and distorts the relative prices between producer goods and consumer goods. At first, the former will rise against the latter, which in the tradition of Böhm-Bawerk causes a "lengthening" of the production period. Later, the inevitable counter-movement has the opposite effect of "shortening" it. "In either case there is a loss of value," since "goods which could have satisfied more important wants have been employed for the satisfaction of less important."[75] According to Hayek, Mises had transformed Wicksell's theory into a satisfactory

[74] Mises (1912/53, p. 370). [75] Mises (1912/53, pp. 364, 370).

explanation of the credit cycle. Himself introducing, for instance, the notion of *intertemporal equilibrium*, Hayek further developed it into a comprehensive monetary explanation of the business cycle. Unlike Schumpeter, he was agnostic about the manifold different factors, which may initiate the cumulative process. Though "it is to monetary causes that we must ascribe the divergences of the pricing process" and the consequent "periodically recurring disproportionalities in the structure of production."[76]

The gold standard

Schumpeter, Mises, and Hayek were all born into the era of the *classical gold standard*, a period from about 1879 to 1914.[77] From a historical perspective, the "exchange rate stability and mechanical monetary policies that were its hallmarks were exceptions rather than the norms."[78] However, during that time monetary orthodoxy firmly embraced metallism as the undisputed embodiment of "sound money":

> the norm was a commodity-based monetary system, with the liabilities of banks being convertible at a legally stipulated rate into gold or silver (or both). Under such an arrangement, the value of money was ultimately the value of the precious metals. (Laidler, 1991, p. 10)

To the economic theorist, the situation at the time was peculiar, in so far as the classical economists had long opposed the mercantilist preoccupation with the accumulation of precious metals. Furthermore, they understood that variations in the discovery of metal ore and the efficiency of mining were the cause of unwanted price fluctuations. In the hands of Wicksell, the quantity theory had "finally undermined the idea that there was something "natural" about the market value of gold rendering it specially suitable as a basis for the monetary system."[79] However, at the time Knut Wicksell was still largely unknown, Henry Thornton had been thoroughly forgotten, and John Law considered the embodiment of reckless government to be forestalled by sound economic principles. Ricardo's doctrine prevailed, as general economic theory had failed to assimilate the growing importance of banking and credit. And even when the role of credit as a circulating medium was explicitly acknowledged, such "fiduciary" money remained in a separate category. The leading authorities, including Jevons, Menger, and Walras, considered money proper to be foremost a commodity for facilitating exchange.

[76] Hayek (1929/33, pp. 182f, 139). [77] Redish (2016, p. 329).
[78] Eichengreen (2019a, p. 38). [79] Laidler (1991, p. 194).

The socialist *Karl Polanyi* (1886–1964) poignantly described the universal rule of monetary orthodoxy:

> Belief in the gold standard was the faith of the age [...]. Whether the gold itself has value for the reason that it embodies labor, as the socialists held, or for the reason that it is useful and scarce, as the orthodox doctrine ran, made for once no difference. The war between heaven and hell ignored the money issue, leaving capitalists and socialists miraculously united. Where Ricardo and Marx were at one, the nineteenth century knew not doubt. (Polanyi, 1944, p. 26)

Representing the opposite political spectrum, Ludwig Mises also confirmed that "[s]ound money meant a metallic standard" and that "[t]hose who disputed the eminence of the gold standard were dismissed as cranks by the representatives of the official doctrine—professors, bankers, statesmen, editors of the great newspapers and magazines." Mises distanced himself from this "blunder of tactics," but believed that the "essential principles of the sound-money doctrine were and are impregnable":[80]

> Gold must be in the cash holdings of everybody. Everybody must see gold coins changing hands, must be used to having gold coins in his pockets, to receiving gold coins when he cashes his pay check, and to spending gold coins when he buys in a store. (Mises, 1953, p. 451)

While Mises was a fervent proponent of the classical gold standard, Schumpeter was not. But neither was Wieser nor Hayek. They all acknowledged that gold was not an ideal money. In the early years, Hayek still pointed at the lack of a theory guiding the transition toward a managed currency.[81] Later, he advocated the "denationalisation" of money by means of free competition between privately managed currencies:

> The *political* impossibility that governments will achieve it does not mean there is reason to doubt that it is *technically* possible to control the quantity of any kind of token money so that its value will behave in a desired manner, and that it will

[80] Mises (1953, p. 415).

[81] "So long as we do not see more clearly about the most fundamental problems of monetary theory and so long as no agreement is reached on the essential theoretical questions, we are also not yet in a position drastically to reconstruct our monetary system, in particular to replace the semi-automatic gold standard by a more or less arbitrarily managed currency. Indeed, I am afraid that, in the present state of knowledge, the risks connected with such an attempt are much greater than the harm which is possibly done by the gold standard" (Hayek, 1931/5, p. 127).

> for this reason retain its acceptability and its value. It would therefore now be possible, if it were permitted, to have a variety of essentially different monies.
> (Hayek, 1976/90, p. 32)

Early on, Schumpeter (*TED*, 1991/34, *MSP*, 1917–18/56) embraced the theoretical possibilities that Law, Thornton, and Wicksell had opened. His clear repudiation of "theoretical metallism" marked a conscious and consequential break:

> Money is not a commodity—not even when it happens to consist of a valuable material. For as soon as the latter is used as money, it must necessarily cease to fulfil its role as an economic good. [Therefore,] it is not essential for money to consist in something, or to be covered by something, that has an economic value of its own. (MSP, 1917–18/56, p. 161)[82]

John Maynard Keynes (1923) more drastically proclaimed the gold standard to be "a barbarous relic." Like Schumpeter, he understood that the theoretical case for a commodity value of money could not be maintained. Still, the widespread dominance of the gold standard called for an explanation. Keynes argued that gold had provided a reasonably stable standard of value in the past, which he doubted would last. Furthermore, he criticized the widespread skepticism of governments' ability to properly manage a currency, and ultimately denied the gold standard any economic rationale: "Conservatism and scepticism join arms—as they often do. Perhaps superstition comes in too; for gold still enjoys the prestige of its smell and colour".[83]

In a similar vein, Schumpeter pointed at the non-economic factors behind the prevalence of the gold standard, which "was looked upon as the hallmark of honesty and respect for it was a matter of national honor and prestige."[84] However, unlike Keynes and in accord with his Austrian kinship, he remained sceptical of the governments' ability to manage the currency. While he definitely dismissed theoretical metallism, he also acknowledged that practical metallism provided a valid point in its fear of abuse through the overissue of inconvertible paper and the resulting perils of inflation. Owing to the intrinsic value of precious metals, the rationale of a commodity standard was derived precisely from the fact that it could not be easily managed: "Centuries of sad experience have taught us that money which does not consist of something that has a value of its own will be tampered with." Consequently, people require "that neither governments nor anyone else shall be able to manufacture it at will. Gold cannot be manufactured at will."[85] He thus recognized a virtue in the discipline which practical metallism had imposed on governments.

[82] See also GOL (1941, p. 2).
[83] Keynes (1923, p. 172)
[84] GOL (1941, p. 4).
[85] GOL (1941, p. 3).

This seemingly ambivalent position mirrors that of his teacher Friedrich Wieser (Section 5.2), even though Schumpeter was more articulate and analytical in expressing it. The distinction between theoretical and practical metallism allowed for an institutional explanation of the historical prevalence of gold, despite its untenable theoretical foundation. At the same time, it enabled Schumpeter to reason and disambiguate his own position on the gold question. His priority was with the theoretical argument which, however, included the historical specificity of institutional arrangements and their potential to evolve. He believed that, in the due course of time, novel and more effective arrangements would likely act as a substitute for secondary characteristics, whereas the ongoing evolution of technological and social systems would bring money closer to its indispensable, and hence most essential, economic functions.

The gold question also illustrates the different attitudes of Schumpeter and Keynes toward policy. Both denied the commodity standard any valid theoretical rationale. But, beyond this, Keynes was actively involved in the search for new ideas to reform the international monetary system. For example, in 1922 he and Ralph Hawtrey contributed to the *Genoa resolution*, which called for the possibility to augment central bank reserves with interest-bearing foreign assets and thus move toward an international *gold-exchange standard*.[86] In contrast to Keynes' clear political orientation, Schumpeter would, for instance, open a speech on the gold question with the following quip: "I am not running a drug store. I have no pills to hand out; no simple solutions for any practical problems that may arise. For these problems are largely political and it is up to you to say what you want, and to fight for it".[87]

His speech then took many dialectic turns, delighting in attracting attention by crushing the expectations and popular preconceptions of the audience, while ultimately aiming to please and recapture the audience's sympathy—in this case, by playing the popular card of skepticism regarding government discretion. In all this, he did not try to disguise any inherent ambiguities but rather laid them bare and thrived on them, so as to puzzle and entertain the audience. Finally, he summarized the role of gold as an international anchor and standard of value as follows:

> A common unit of legal tender defined in gold would be a useful element in such an arrangement. But it would not be necessary. It is precisely the virtue of an unfettered gold standard that a system of different national units would do almost as well, provided only that all were defined in terms of gold and that gold could move freely from one constituent part of the bloc to any other.
>
> (GOL, 1941, p. 6)

[86] Eichengreen (2019a, p. 55ff). This resolution failed due to US resistance, as did Keynes' later attempt to dissuade Churchill from returning to the gold standard.

[87] GOL (1941, p. 1).

To summarize, Schumpeter, along with Mises and Hayek, rejected any notion of theoretical metallism or the corresponding attributes awarded the precious metals. At the same time, they similarly acknowledged—from shared historical experience[88] and depending on specific institutions—the practical benefits of a commodity standard in terms of restricting government discretion, as well as the role of gold as a useful anchor for international exchange. Despite such concessions to monetary orthodoxy, and exactly like Law, Thornton, and Wicksell before him, Schumpeter in particular insisted on the possibility of a national system of managed currencies. Nevertheless, according to his own typology, only Keynes qualified as a resolute theoretical and practical anti-metallist. In contrast, one must more ambiguously classify Schumpeter together with his Austrian kin as theoretical non-metallists,[89] but also as practical metallists subject to the following qualifiers:

(i) Mises was an unconditional supporter of the classical gold standard, taking for granted that policy would not manage a currency to the benefit of the public.
(ii) Hayek preferred a managed currency, *if* it were less prone to variation than the supply of gold. Later, he considered free competition between privately managed currencies to be the ideal safeguard for their stability (see next Section).
(iii) Schumpeter most clearly sympathized with the principle of managed currencies, but conceded to the advantages of gold *as long as* policy institutions were not capable of managing currencies effectively. Characteristically, he emphasized the role of a gold-exchange standard as an anchor for the settling of international *accounts*.

Currency competition

In the 1970s, after the dollar's convertibility to gold had ended and the Bretton Woods system of fixed exchange rates collapsed, Hayek again turned his attention to the question of the proper design of a monetary system. Championing the case of free competition between privately managed currencies,[90] he was careful

[88] See Chapter 8 on how the period of hyperinflation in Austria affected Schumpeter's personal fortune during the early 1920s.

[89] Although Schumpeter suggested otherwise in the case of Mises: "Since, according to the metallist view, the theory of money derives directly from the logically prior theory of barter, metallist theories are (roughly or exactly, I am not quite sure) what L. von Mises has called catallactic theories of money" (*HEA*, 1954, p. 288f).

[90] Hayek (1976/90). At the time he was not aware of the earlier contribution by Benjamin Klein (1974), which he acknowledged in later editions.

to distinguish his proposal from the historical instances of free banking.[91] He considered that free banking was a valid principle as long as the commercial banks, which were allowed to issue notes in terms of a single national currency, had to redeem them in specie. It became, however, inconsistent and "wholly indefensible" once the issue of legal tender money by privileged central banks had replaced it.[92] Instead, Hayek suggested abolishing the national monopoly of legal tender and open currencies to free competition. Thereby he acknowledged that, similar to free banking, historic attempts toward "free money"[93] had been largely inflationist. Furthermore, Gresham's law stating that bad money drives out good currency (Section 4.2), was generally referred to in support of the monopoly of central banks. Against this, Hayek argued that Gresham's law only applies if exchange rates are fixed. For a monetary regime with variable exchange rates he expected an opposite impact:

> [T]he inferior quality money would be valued at a lower rate and, particularly if it threatened to fall further in value, people would try to get rid of it as quickly as possible. The selection process would go on towards whatever they regarded as the best sort of money among those issued by the various agencies, and it would rapidly drive out money found inconvenient or worthless.
>
> (Hayek, 1976/90, p. 41ff)

In practical terms, this requires the full liberalization of international capital flows among participating countries including, for instance, the abolition of exchange controls, the freedom of foreign banks to open branches on the same terms as domestic ones, or the "full freedom to use any of the currencies for contracts and accounting."[94] Displaying his trademark confidence in the virtues of long-run competitive equilibrium, Hayek reasoned that (in the absence of government intervention) only the most stable currencies will survive:

> I have now no doubt whatever that private enterprise, if it had not been prevented by government, could and would long ago have provided the public with a choice of currencies, and those that prevailed in the competition would have been essentially stable in value and would have prevented both excessive stimulation of investment and the consequent periods of contraction.
>
> (Hayek, 1976/90, p. 14)

It was no coincidence that he introduced these ideas during a period of high inflation and turmoil in the international monetary system. Accordingly, in "Hayek's

[91] See, for example, White (1984) or Capie and Wood (1990).
[92] Hayek (1976/90, p. 90).
[93] For instance, the *Freigeld* of Silvio Gesell (1919/49).
[94] Hayek (1976/90, p. 23).

vision, currencies would compete primarily as stores of value. Those with credible issuers that could maintain the currency's value would succeed, whereas others would be driven out of the market."[95] Nevertheless, the proposal does not seem to have had much impact at the time. It was only much later that his ideas were adopted by a vigorous new movement, which combined his libertarian ideals with the ingenuity of the internet generation. After the Great Recession of 2008–9, and exploiting the opportunities offered by new digital technologies, they began to challenge the conventional institutional boundaries of money in a variety of initiatives to launch private cryptocurrencies such as *Bitcoin* or *Libra*. We will come back to these cases in Chapter 13.

The heresy

Unlike the monetary orthodoxy and related to the aforementioned interest in the impact of credit and bank money, neither Schumpeter, Mises, nor Hayek considered money to be neutral with respect to real production and relative prices. However, Mises and Hayek placed the emphasis on the potential disruption that variations in the supply of money can impose on the efficient coordination of markets. They aimed to amend the orthodox canon by assimilating the impact of bank credit as an endogenous source of the money supply. In the case of credit, Mises and Hayek rejected the banking school's belief in self-correcting market forces. Instead they aimed to fix the currency principle, while staying close to its spirit of austere monetary policy. Yet the overall appraisal of the monetary system remained gloomy, and the non-neutrality of money was mainly considered a source of trouble, upsetting the smooth and idealized adjustment of individual plans toward equilibrium. As Klausinger concludes:

> Hayek conceived the money economy in such a way that money explicitly occurs only as a potential disruptive factor by enabling the central price for intertemporal coordination, the money interest rate, to deviate from the equilibrium (of an equivalent barter economy). The question of what function money performs in this economy remains unregarded. (Klausinger, 1991, p. 104)

Even for Schumpeter's Austrian "kin," the greatest achievement was to keep to a minimum the distortions the monetary system caused relative to the ideal of an intertemporal equilibrium analogously to a pure barter economy. Hayek, however, at least indirectly acknowledged the beneficial role of money in the process of development when he objected to the idea of keeping the amount of deposits stable

[95] Brunnermeier et al. (2019, p. 8).

in order to eliminate cyclical fluctuations. He considered it utopian to abolish bank money and thereby reduce the role of banking to that "of brokers, trading in savings."[96] Furthermore, a 100% reserve requirement as called for by Irving Fisher in the 1930s (and later known as the Chicago Plan) would not be desirable, since

> [t]he stability of the economic system would be obtained at the price of curbing economic progress. The rate of interest would be constantly above the level maintained under the existing system, [implying that the] utilization of new inventions and the "realization of new combinations" would be made more difficult. (Hayek 1929/33, p. 190)

Hayek thus explicitly accepted the gist of Schumpeter's monetary theory of development, even though he never attempted to assimilate it into his own approach. Schumpeter, in turn, had always acknowledged and taken seriously the downsides of endogenous money. In contrast with the Austrian theory, however, his approach offered a characteristically brighter outlook on the nexus between finance and growth, highlighting the mutability and positive function of money in the process of economic development. Thus, having drawn a sharp dividing line against the orthodox doctrine, Schumpeter was aware that

> this again leads us to two heresies: first to the heresy that money, and then to the second heresy that also other means of payment, perform an essential function, hence that processes in terms of means of payment are not merely reflexes of processes in terms of goods. In every possible strain, with rare unanimity, even with impatience and moral and intellectual indignation, a very long line of theorists have assured us of the opposite. (*TED*, 1911/34, p. 95)

The next chapter will collect and arrange the essential building blocks with which Schumpeter crafted his concept of the *non-neutrality* of money in the process of economic development.

[96] Hayek (1929/33, p. 190) referred to the monetary theory of business cycles by *Ralph G. Hawtrey* (1879–1971).

6
Non-neutrality of money

> The condition of a people's monetary system is a symptom of all its conditions.
>
> (J.A. Schumpeter)[1]

Schumpeter's monetary theory is best known for shunning the orthodox postulate of "neutral money," which by determining only the nominal value of transactions does nothing more than cover the real magnitudes of an economy, like a *veil*. Classical theory was thus entitled to ignore money and focus exclusively on the relationship between relative prices and production.[2] Opposing the orthodox view, Schumpeter deliberately expressed "denial of the proposition that, with the exception of what may be called monetary disorders, the element of money is of secondary importance in the explanation of the economic process of reality." Instead, he aimed for a monetary analysis where "[m]oney prices, money incomes, and saving and investment decisions bearing upon these money incomes [...] acquire a life and an importance of their own."[3] Positing an alternative metaphor, he compared money to a *skin*, meaning that it is in no way detached from but forms an integral part of the living organism (see Section 6.4). It is in this sense that he declared the monetary system to be an aggregative symptom of the economy's overall conditions.

6.1 The claim theory

Schumpeter identified the financing of entrepreneurial ventures as the vehicle through which investors simultaneously enable economic development and generate fluctuations and instability, these being two sides of the same coin. Rejecting both the commodity view and the alternative state theory, he insisted on a genuine economic explanation of money. To understand its essential nature, an

[1] Undated; from the "Original manuscript of Money, in German and English, Chapt. 1–2," HUA – HUGFP66.55 Manuscript on Money, Box 1, p.1.

[2] Patinkin (1956/89) attributed the first use of the term "veil of money" to Robert Liefmann in 1917. It was, however, Böhm-Bawerk (1889/91, p. 214) who apparently originated the metaphor, when he argued that money throws "a veil difficult to penetrate." According to Boianovsky (1993, p. 725), he influenced the later use of the term by Fisher, Schumpeter, Pigou, and Robertson. See also Klausinger (1990) and Chaloupek (2010).

[3] *HEA* (1954, p. 277).

Schumpeter's Venture Money. Michael Peneder and Andreas Resch, Oxford University Press (2021). © Michael Peneder and Andreas Resch.
DOI: 10.1093/oso/9780198804383.003.0006

enumeration of the various functions in which money is of avail to practical purposes would not suffice. Instead, he aimed to identify which functions render the social institution of money indispensable. In this sense, he considered only two to be constitutive. One is the function of money as a "medium of exchange" and the other as a "standard of value." Conversely, he considered money a convenient medium for the "store of value," but not the only (and therefore necessary) one. In turn, Jevons' "standard of deferred payments" derives from a general standard of value.[4]

Since Aristotle, economists have given priority to the function of money as a medium of exchange. This was particularly true for the Austrian approach in the tradition of Menger, who had explained the evolution of money as the market-driven spontaneous order, which must eventually converge toward a good of utmost saleability. By assimilating the individual choice of preferred cash balances into their theory, Marshall, Walras, and Menger had also drawn attention to its function as the most liquid store of value. Unlike them, Schumpeter placed his distinctive emphasis on the role of money as a common *unit of account*. While money was evidently important in facilitating exchange, he sought its deeper meaning in the abstract function of a standard of value.

In *WHN* (1908) Schumpeter flamboyantly elaborated the importance of money to the formation of equilibrium prices through *indirect trade*, that is, by means of the trade-offs already accounted for after comparing the relative prices before an actual exchange.[5] In other words, a pure barter economy cannot manage to eliminate all arbitrage opportunities and therefore cannot approach the eficiency of general equilibrium.[6]

Clearly, this function goes beyond the mere facilitation of individual transactions. Schumpeter made this point with reference to Walras' equilibrium system, which critically depended on the *numéraire* as a common denominator. Implicitly, Walras had demonstrated the unit of account to be an indispensable part of the theoretical fabric of general equilibrium. Schumpeter had only to twist Walras'

[4] *WHN* (1908, pp. 282, 290f).

[5] *WHN* (1908, p. 274ff). Note that Mises (1912/53, p. 5) rejected Schumpeter's claim that indirect trade necessitates the institution of money. In contrast, Schlesinger (1914, p. 81) praised him as well as Walras for having built the bridge between money and general economic theory by demonstrating the need of indirect exchange to achieve equilibrium. Elaborating the determinants of cash balances, Schlesinger (1914, pp. 87–103) anticipated Keynesian explanations of the demand for money (ÖBL 1815–1950, 1992, p. 193), which he attributed to the overall need for transactions, business fluctuations, and the foregone interest as the price for insurance against the lack of cash. In a review of Schlesinger's dissertation, Schumpeter (1915, p. 241) had special praise for this part. *Karl Schlesinger* (1889–1938) wrote his dissertation under Böhm-Bawerk and later became director of the Anglo-Austrian Bank. He will come back into the picture when we discuss Schumpeter's financial ventures as director of the Biedermann Bank (Chapter 8).

[6] Brunnermeier et al. (2019, p. 7) illustrate this point with a simple example: "In an economy with n goods, there are n(n − 1)/2 relative prices that would have to be tracked in the absence of a unit of account. With money that serves as a unit of account, only n prices need to be tracked: the price of each good in units of money.

angle of perspective, and he did so in a peculiar way. To him, the arbitrary element of the *numéraire*, a mere technical coefficient, was the essential function of money. And, in contrast, its concrete realization in the form of *monnaie*, which Walras, like others, demanded to be considered a definite and valuable commodity, was nothing but an arbitrary element—at least as far as pure theory goes.

Later, Schumpeter illustrated the necessity for money as a unit of account by means of the opposite hypothetical case of a pure socialist economy. In his money book (*WDG*, 1970) he devoted the entire fourth chapter to this subject, arguing that a socialized clearing mechanism may eventually dispel the need for direct monetary transactions, just as coin and other currency had eliminated the need for physical barter. He insisted that even an idealized socialist system must be monetized by some common unit of account. Stripped down to its essential logic, to him this was where the indispensable nature of money resided. To emphasize his point Schumpeter used the old term *Rechenpfennige* in the title of the original German edition of MSP (1917–18/56). In early times (i.e., before mathematical calculus was generally performed in writing), these *Rechenpfennige* were small metal tokens ("counters") that looked like coins, but were used as an auxiliary means of calculation.

In *WDG* Schumpeter then set out to identify the particular carriers of the social accounts and trace their manifold interactions, aiming for a general "theory of the economic process in terms of expenditure flows."[7] As Marget explained, he wanted to go beyond the comparison of successive equilibria in comparative statics and instead

> start from the proposition that what happens in so-called "transitional" processes may very profoundly alter the actual course of subsequent events. We therefore require an analytical apparatus that will do full justice to the mechanics of *change*, in the sense of providing a description of every step in the processes of change at which decisions are taken that could change the level or direction of those flows of money and of objects sold for money which, in an economy such as ours, are the realized events of economic life. (Marget, 1951, p. 117)

At a time when money was generally conceived in its material form, either as a medium of exchange or a store of value, Schumpeter approached his task by identifying the principal function of money as the social clearing of current accounts:

> But let us not forget that contractual figure which, better than anything else, demonstrates the meaning of money and is much more suited than the act

[7] Marget (1951, p. 113).

> of handing over coins to make it clear to us what the monetary institution is about, namely the current account agreement. [...] After all, the demands and obligations arising from economic life, as well as the cash payments made, are thus stamped to what they are, namely to mere invoice items.
>
> (*WDG*, 1970, p. 127)

Following Wicksell's earlier example of a pure credit economy – but long before the age of electronic payments and digital currencies (Chapter 13) – Schumpeter clearly envisioned a system of universal current accounts consistent with the modern idea of a general ledger[8] to be the purest form and logical conclusion of a monetary system:

> The generalized notion of this current account relationship, i.e. the idea that *everyone's* economic acts are recorded on a real or imaginary current account, is extremely revealing and so useful for grasping the social connections and processes that make up the monetary and credit system that one could call it the *basic concept of monetary theory*. (*WDG*, 1970; emphasis added)

The key point here is that Schumpeter regarded money neither as a commodity nor a good, but as a *claim ticket to goods*. It originates in the liability of an issuer, who is trusted to hold the according assets. Consequently, the monetary system is foremost an institution of social accounts and the attention accordingly shifts from money as a definite object to its representation of "shares in the mass of goods."[9] Or, as he liked to point out, using money as a unit of account "changes as little as the use of chips changes the essential nature of a game."[10]

Schumpeter ascribed the claim *analogy* to the German banker *Friedrich Bendixen* (1864–1920), and even earlier to J.S. Mill.[11] But Mises explicitly attributed the claim *theory* to Schumpeter. Without agreeing to it, he acknowledged its broader theoretical significance as "an ingenious attempt [...] by Schumpeter to arrive at a real theory of the value of money."[12] In hindsight, we may easily agree. By increasing abstraction—which in Schumpeter's case was also meant to anticipate the essential functions likely to emerge and prevail in the further evolution of money, its function as a standard of value has progressively absorbed its function as a medium of exchange. It ultimately transformed the

[8] "The concept of a general ledger is the abstract notion that all economic actions in the real world (all transactions, all exchange, contract, and production) can be hypothetically mapped to a general ledger that records that change in a state of the data of an economy" (Berg et al., 2019, p. 59).

[9] MSP (1917–18/56, p. 162).

[10] Similarly, one "cannot ride on a claim to a horse and everybody realizes that the creation of such a claim does not increase the available quantity of horses" (*MSP* (1917–18/56, pp. 153, 167).

[11] MSP (1917–18/56, p. 153).

[12] "Even in the writings of Bendixen, who would have been glad to see his obscure arguments called a claim theory, the claim concept has no greater significance ascribed to it" (Mises, 1953, p. 470).

traditionally object-based system of payments into an integrated symbolic ledger of social accounts.[13]

Expanding on the idea of social "claims," Schumpeter attached particular importance to the fact that in the market economy, and apart from purely redistributive activities, everybody must submit to the condition that a money income is obtainable only against an equivalent contribution to production. "In this way, every productive contribution in the market automatically implies a definite quantity of consumer goods. This is *real income*."[14] Consequently, everybody looks upon money income (which may originate in either productive or redistributive activities) from the point of view of the commodities which can be acquired with it—exactly as in the case of a claim ticket. Like Wieser, Schumpeter thus regarded money income as "merely the monetary expression of the goods consumed."[15]

Unlike Wieser, but in accordance with Böhm-Bawerk, Schumpeter did not treat physical capital as an independent factor and corresponding source of income *sui generis*. Instead, he consistently referred to it as the "produced means of production." Hence, "money income is acquired on the market for the means of production only to be spent on the other market for consumer goods," whereas households "can spend in the market for consumer goods only the same money that they have received in the market for the means of production." Explicitly referring to Wieser, he emphasized the fundamental equality of total incomes and social product: "Income units, and not the money units as such, are the true 'entrance tickets' to the fund of goods" and money income is "merely the monetary expression of the goods consumed."[16]

Independently of the particular clearing processes in a market economy, a hypothetical socialist system would also require some form of claim ticket to the fund of goods, and hence monetization:

> If, in place of money, some central authority were really to issue receipt vouchers for productive contributions, and these receipt vouchers were at the same time claim tickets on the consumption fund of the economy, then we should have before us one of the possible forms of a social clearing system.
>
> (MSP, 1917–18/56, p. 154)

[13] Though Schumpeter's attention to a proper ontology of money had largely disappeared from the radar of economics during the following decades, it recently resurged in a lively debate between Geoffrey Ingham and Tony Lawson. Ingham, in particular, is much in accord with Schumpeter's conception, concluding that the value of money "is *ontologically* grounded in its debt settling and purchasing power not from any pre-existing tradable- but unspecified-value." Consequently, "all money is a token credit denominated in money of account" (Ingham, 2018, p. 841). See also Lawson (2016, 2018).

[14] *MSP* (1917–18/56, p. 152; emphasis added).

[15] *MSP* (1917–18/56, p. 153).

[16] *MSP* (1917–18/56, pp. 153, 162).

To conclude, the value of money is "nothing but the purchasing power of the income unit," and the "problem of the value of money is simply the problem of its purchasing power, or, in turn, the problem of the money price of individual commodities."[17] While the subjective utilities of goods consumed remain instrumental in grading people's real income, the term "value of money" now exclusively refers to prices as objective data of the market. By accepting the latter as an aggregate datum, Friedrich Wieser had already put one foot outside the strict Austrian preoccupation with subjectivism, but the other foot remained inside, because he stressed the subjective origin of the individual valuation of money. In contrast, Schumpeter dropped Wieser's notion of a "subjective value of money" and consistently referred to the subjective valuation of income. Treating money and prices solely as "objective" aggregate data, he arguably stepped outside with both feet. But as discussed in Chapter 5, this emancipation from the Austrian doctrine was necessary in order for him to focus on the function of money as a measure of value and social accounts.

Again, consistently with Wieser, but in a departure from the monetary orthodoxy and the Cambridge tradition, which both typically referred to money in terms of notes and coins,[18] the above considerations led Schumpeter to argue for a comprehensive functional definition of money. However, this was restricted to concrete payments as an enactment of the purchasing power granted by a claim: "To the extent that they are in actual, though not necessarily general, circulation," his pure flow concept of money included: (i) all "commodities which in fact circulate as money"; (ii) "money made of a material the market price of which is less than the purchasing power of the monetary unit made of it"; (iii) bank notes; (iv) bank deposits (current accounts and clearing accounts); (v) "all payments which are disbursements out of income and are handled exclusively by compensation"; and, finally, (vi) "money credit instruments and claim titles of all kinds."[19]

Once more, Schumpeter found one of his sharpest critics in Ludwig Mises, who accurately pointed out that his definition of money neglected all stocks (including hoards, reserves, and other claims "waiting to be employed"), though these fulfilled an economic function as stores of value.[20]

6.2 The quantity theory

In addition to the era of the prevalence of the classical gold standard, Schumpeter was born into what Laidler coined as the *Golden Age of the Quantity Theory*, which similarly peaked in the period from about 1870 to 1914. The quantity theory

[17] *MSP* (1917–18/56, pp. 155, 165ff). [18] Laidler (1991, p. 124).
[19] MSP (1917–18/56, p. 168ff). [20] Mises (1953, p. 472).

explained long-run variations in price levels solely with changes in the stock of a currency that had to be accordingly managed. In the classical monetary debates, the growing importance of credit and banking had fuelled opposition to the quantity theory. Yet it still remained largely uncontested after Mill had assimilated the impact of circulating credit on prices. Consequently, Wicksell (1898/1936) considered it the only existing monetary theory (Section 5.3).

From a theoretical perspective, the gold standard and the quantity theory made for an uncomfortable match and their simultaneous dominance during that time constitutes a kind of conundrum in the history of monetary thought. Laidler repeatedly discusses their inherent tensions and argues that "the quantity theory was usually associated with the case for bimetallism and was treated with much hostility by the advocates of 'sound money.'"[21] Relatedly, Milton Friedman referred to the alleged "crime of 1873," when the US abandoned bimetallism in favor of the gold standard as "a mistake that had highly adverse consequences."[22] Schumpeter also addressed this inconsistency: "Occasionally, one finds also a metallist quantity theory, according to which the price level would move in proportion to changes in the quantity of gold money."[23] But for this to hold, one must assume that other means of circulation change in exact proportion and, in particular, that the ratio of credit to gold is either constant or at least changing very slowly. To Schumpeter this assumption was "completely unacceptable."[24]

Conversely, "the basic idea of the quantity theory," Schumpeter argued, "follows immediately and necessarily from the claim theory."[25] This is because,

> the real importance of "claim tickets" giving title not to definite objects but to shares in the mass of goods, must decisively depend upon the number of these claim tickets. The case may be likened to a game in which chips represent the players' share in the common pool; the total number of chips clearly decides the size of the share represented by each chip. (MSP, 1917–18/56, p. 162)

The "golden age" of the quantity theory culminated in two formal representations, which came to dominate monetary thought throughout Schumpeter's early career. The first was *Fisher's equation of exchange*, in which *Irving Fisher* (1867–1947) related the stock of money M and the velocity of circulation V (the "money side") to the total value of purchases, expressed as the sum of prices p times quantities q for n goods (including intermediate goods l and final goods c). The latter equal the product of average prices P and total transactions T (both measured

[21] Laidler (1991, p. 50). [22] Friedman (1992, p. 78). [23] MSP (1917–18/56, p. 174).

[24] "Once it is perceived that the relation between credit-money and gold money is non-essential and is in only a few cases roughly enforced by legislation and payments habits, much of the old doctrine must be thrown overboard" *MSP* (1917–18/56, p. 174).

[25] MSP (1917–18/56, p. 163).

as indices). Distinguishing between "actual" money M and deposits M', as well as their respective velocities, his equation of exchange appears as:[26]

$$MV + M'V' = \sum_{n=1}^{l+c} p_n q_n = PT \tag{6.1}$$

Fisher (1911/20) remained within the classical tradition, which had focused on transactions and defined money in a narrow sense. But he also augmented it by separating out the additional impact of circulating credit on prices. The latter absorbed the advances in Mill's synthesis and enhanced its credibility as a consistent and general quantitative relationship. In *WHN* Schumpeter considered this the endurable core of the theory (though of limited import).

One significant advance of Fisher's equation was the clear statement of the assumptions that were necessary for a strict interpretation of the quantity theory. Unlike Schumpeter, he reasoned that bank reserve policies together with individual convenience and habits cause M and M' to stay within fixed proportions:

> It has even been argued that this interposition of circulating credit breaks whatever connection there may be between prices and the quantity of money. This would be true if circulating credit were independent of money. But the fact is that the quantity of circulating credit, M', tends to hold a definite multiple of money. (Fisher, 1911/20, p. 50)

From this it follows that "the level of prices varies directly with the quantity of money in circulation, provided the velocity of circulation of that money and the volume of trade which it is obliged to perform are not changed."[27] Thus, Fisher considered money to be the "active" exogenous variable to which prices are adjusted.

The *Cambridge equation* offered an alternative representation of the quantity theory. We owe its first comprehensive exposition to Pigou, but essential parts originate in the oral lectures of Alfred Marshall from the 1870s.[28] While arriving at the same relationship and results as the equation of exchange, attention shifted from the money supply to the demand for money in circulation M^d, which depends on the propensity to hold the cash balances k, price level P, and real income Y in equilibrium $M^d = M$, and hence

$$M\frac{1}{k} = PY \tag{6.2}$$

[26] Fisher (1911/20, p. 48). Fisher (1911/20, p. 25) explicitly acknowledged, among others, Newcomb, Edgworth, and Kemmerer for earlier representations.

[27] Fisher (1911/20, p. 50).

[28] Pigou (1917); Laidler (1991, p. 53ff).

When compared to Fisher's equation of exchange, the inverse of the propensity to hold cash $1/k$ replaces the velocity of money V and total income Y substitutes for the sum of transactions T. Despite their formal equivalence, which Pigou explicitly stressed,[29] the two approaches differ in their perspective. When the demand for the stock of cash balances was substituted for the concept of transaction velocity, the focus inevitably shifted from the money function as a medium of exchange to the money function as a liquid store of value, and from the money supply to its demand. Despite these differences, Laidler above all emphasizes the continuities between Fisher, the Cambridge School, and the classical approach.[30]

To summarize, the quantity theory entails three major tenets for long-run equilibrium outcomes. First, there has to be a strict *proportionality* of variations in prices and the stock of money. Second, *causation* goes from exogenous changes in the quantity of money to prices ($P=f(M)$). And, third, *neutrality* makes money a mere "veil," which does not affect real economic variables in the long run. This is because the variables are already determined by the general equilibrium conditions of exchange, which depend on exogenous variations in technology, tastes, resources, and so forth.

Starting with his earliest writings in *WHN*, Schumpeter would not agree to either. In MSP he explicitly opposed Fisher's assumption of fixed proportionality between bank reserves and bank money, and even more so the implicit assumption of a constant ratio of credit to gold. In the course of their careers he and Fisher became close friends and, in a peculiar attempt to reconcile their views, Schumpeter later reasoned that Fisher "cannot be classed with quantity theorists except in a special sense":

> First, he stopped short of the quantity theorem in its fullest possible sense by admitting the influence of T on both V and M [and] this weakens the theorem considerably, at least as a long-run proposition, because it introduces a relation between the "independent variables" that interferes with the direct effects of variations in T on P. (*HEA*, 1954, p. 1102)

Second, Schumpeter reasoned that the quantity theorem

> does not hold in what Fisher calls "transition periods." But actually, since the economic system is practically always in a state of transition or disequilibrium, phenomena that *seem* incompatible with the quantity theorem and have in fact furnished many of their arguments to its opponents are almost always in evidence. By paying careful attention to them [he] merely supplemented the information that the quantity theorem conveys. [But] we might say with almost equal justice that, in a large and particularly valuable part of his work, he shelved it.
> (*HEA*, 1954, p. 1102)

29 Pigou (1917, p. 53). 30 Laidler (1991, p. 82f).

Finally, he pointed out that *M*, *V*, and *T* were only proximate causes of *P*, reflecting manifold indirect causes, which to Fisher were also the more interesting causes for the purpose of dynamic analysis.

6.3 The income-expenditure approach

Schumpeter also took issue with some of the core terminology of the quantity theory. In particular, he objected to the popular concept of the *velocity* of money. Originating in the early eighteenth century (Chapter 3), it implicitly suggested a sequential use of the monetary unit in circulation. This is explained by the historical context, since at the time economists had yet to appreciate the theoretical import of fractional reserves, through which the same bank deposits enable multiple simultaneous payments. In contrast, Schumpeter emphasized that "most bank money is created only at the moment when it is needed in circulation, or shortly before," and hence "the distinction between existing and circulating quantity of money loses in significance."[31] In short, the notion of "velocity" does not convey an accurate image of what happens in a modern credit economy.

Furthermore, Schumpeter opposed the idea that each time a monetary unit changes hands it also affects general prices. On the contrary, he argued that "it is a matter of complete indifference through how many hands a sum of money must go in order to be transferred from one income into another. If a change of hands means such a transfer, it has the effect of an increase in the quantity of money by an equal amount." But "if a sum enters a firm or household only to be passed on without any counterpart in the satisfaction of wants, then it has no such effect."[32]

He illustrated the point with the case of two countries differing only in their degree of vertical specialization in production. If in one economy the value chain is more fragmented into independent user-supply relationships, its velocity of circulation and hence the quantity of money must be higher than in the other economy, where production is more integrated. Because of the proportional increase in the turnover of commodities, differences in the volume of circulation would, however, not affect the general price level. Velocity in the above sense therefore also does not appear to be the accurate concept.

This led Schumpeter to reinterpret the equation of exchange from the perspective of the income approach in the tradition of Tooke, Mill, and Wieser. The income theory is a *flow concept* and explains the formation of prices with the interaction of nominal expenditures on the one hand, and the stream of production in real terms on the other. Thereby, "only that part of the quantity of money which actually circulates confronts commodities and has an immediate relation to the sum of

[31] MSP (1917–18/56, p. 200; see also pp. 177ff and 203).

[32] *MSP* (1917–18/56, p. 180).

incomes. It alone fulfils the basic function of money."[33] A potential downside, however, is that Schumpeter "must exclude the sums that circulate on the market for income-yielding assets – on the real estate market, the mortgage market, the stock market, and so on," assuming that "these sums exert no direct influence on purchasing power."[34] These yields only count when spent in consumption or on further means of production.

What made this approach attractive to Schumpeter and Wieser before him, is that,

> like the cash balance approach, it points to individual behaviour; more than the cash balance approach, it removes mere quantity of money from the position of a proximate "cause of the price level" and substitutes for it one that is still nearer to prices – income, or even consumer expenditure; finally it relieves the theory of money prices from such questions as what is to be considered as money. The effect of an increase of money upon prices is indeterminate so long as we do not know who gets the additional money, what he does with it, and what the state of the economic organism is on which the new money impinges.
>
> *HEA* (1954, p. 1110)

Schumpeter then defined the theoretically precise measure as the number of times a monetary unit "traverses the circular flow from the consumption sphere back to the consumption sphere," which means each time it becomes "an element of money income and is spent as such."[35] Distinctly referring to final consumption instead of total transactions, Schumpeter called this measure *efficiency*:

> Then we end up with the turnover of the national product between companies and households on the one hand and the turnover of the productive services between households and companies on the other hand and win the term which we want to call *efficiency* of coins or units of credit. This efficiency is measured by the number of times a coin or credit unit is spent by households on consumer goods – *serving the national product* – during the observation period.
>
> (*WDG*, 1970, p. 242)

In *HEA* Schumpeter highlighted the advantages of this approach with reference to J.S. Mill. First, he pointed out that starting from total expenditures corresponds to using the sum of monetary units (however defined) times their velocity. But this allows

> to separate the two constituents of what is usually labelled as velocity: the rate of spending, which is certainly variable, and velocity in a narrower sense, which,

[33] MSP (1917–18/56, p. 175); see also Wieser (1927) or Kunwald (1934, p. 2); Mensik (2014).
[34] MSP (1917–18/56, p. 176). [35] MSP (1917–18/56, p. 179).

> being determined by habits of payment, the degree of concentration of industry, and the like, may in fact, normally at least, be treated as an institutional constant. (*HEA* 1954, p. 705)

While the reference is to J.S. Mill, it describes precisely the plot Schumpeter himself applied by separating the notion of "efficiency" into a subjective and objective component. The first was personal *disposition* and accounted for differences in the demand for money, such as the individual propensity to hold cash. Schumpeter emphasized that efficiency must therefore vary for different social groups, with poorer people generally spending their income more rapidly. The second component, which he called *frequency*, depends, for example, on the technical nature of a payment system. Consequently, efficiency must also vary for different types of money.[36] Taken together, the above amendments to Fisher's equation of exchange amount to a different definition of V, which now represents "efficiency" as the product of "disposition" and "frequency."

Connecting production with expenditures on final demand ultimately requires a consistent definition of what constitutes a sector. The modern literature on global value chains has brought some clarifications concerning concepts and terminology. Herrendorf et al. distinguish two alternative approaches and emphasize that each of them is internally consistent.[37] The *consumption value added* approach is the familiar one, where separate production functions represent the distinct value-added components of final consumption. We know it from common representations in the microeconomic textbooks or, for instance, from the organization of economic activities in the national accounts. The utility of producing a final good, let's say a new dress or suit, is thus unbundled from the intermediate services provided, for instance, by the transportation or retail sectors. In contrast, but consistent with the Austrian theory of distribution and method of imputation, Schumpeter applied what Herrendorf et al. call the *final consumption expenditure* approach. It defines the production functions for different goods of final consumption, and hence must include all value increments from other "produced means of production." In modern terminology, Schumpeter's idea of the production function thus corresponds to that of a vertically integrated value chain, where labor and natural resources are the only primary inputs.

Consequently, what counts for the formation of consumer prices p^c for n final consumption goods q^c is the volume of expenditures on final consumption E^c from nominal income I. In his equation of exchange, savings matter only indirectly by reducing the efficiency of monetary circulation. Schumpeter therefore equates I with the total expenditures on final consumption – that is, only with the income which is effective in terms of consumption. Its sum defines total demand, which

[36] *WDG* (1970, p. 181).

[37] Herrendorf et al. (2013). See also Peneder and Streicher (2018, p. 93).

depends on the quantity of circulating money M (broadly defined) times its *efficiency* V.[38] By eliminating all transactions for intermediate goods Q^I from Fisher's equation, Schumpeter related total expenditures on final consumption goods E^c to the product of the *consumer price index* P^c times *real income* I^c, which he expressed in terms of the goods actually consumed.

While formally equivalent to Fisher's fundamental equation of exchange, the following restatement highlights the distinctive interpretation in terms of consumer prices P^c and real income I^c:

$$E^c = MV = \sum_{n=1}^{c} p_n q_n = P^c I^c \tag{6.3}$$

Despite the considerable attention Schumpeter had devoted to his refinement of the equation of exchange, he regarded it as "only a truism," an identity which is neither "a tautology in the proper sense," nor meant to "express a definite causal connection." All it says is that, "if two of the three magnitudes that it contains – the quantity of money in circulation, efficiency, and the product sum – are given, the third is thereby determined."[39] Overall, we may compare his effort to that of house-cleaning, meant to remove obstacles and inconsistencies that might get in the way of furnishing his main aim: establishing the non-neutrality of money.

6.4 Money and real production

Schumpeter's opposition to the monetary orthodoxy centered on its postulate of neutrality. According to this, money determines general prices, but in equilibrium with full employment it has no effect on production and hence real income in terms of goods consumed. As previously mentioned, in contrast to the monetary orthodoxy, which had portrayed money as a mere veil on top of real economic relationships, Schumpeter envisioned money as a *skin* and therefore an inextricable part of the economy as a living organism:

> No one objects when we say that the skin condition of an animal's body depends on the condition of all its organs, but, at the same time, that the condition of the skin is an essential element in the condition of all the other organs. Just as little objection should be raised to our present inverse proposition: namely, that

[38] MSP (1917–18/56, p. 182).

[39] *MSP* (1917–18/56, , p. 183). As regards the current empirical record, Teles et al. (2015) find that the often reported strong (almost one-to-one) correlation between the quantity of money (*M*1) and inflation does not hold for countries with moderate inflation rates (below 12%), except if money growth is adjusted by subtracting GDP growth and adding, for instance, nominal interest rates. If monetary policy targets inflation, the correlation generally breaks down for lack of variation.

> currency policy and the existing state of the currency in principle always exert an important influence on what a people wills or does and on all elements of its social and economic condition. (Schumpeter, undated, p. 4f)[40]

In order to advance his own proposition of non-neutrality, Schumpeter first had to come to terms with the quantity theory. In doing so, he explicitly denied the most popular argument for its refutation:

> [I]t is no answer to argue that all productive capacity is hardly ever exploited to the full, so that, in the case under discussion, these reserves could be called upon. If it was advantageous before the rise in the price level not to utilize the productive apparatus fully, it remains advantageous after the rise too, for none of the possible causes of under-utilization is thereby removed. (MSP, 1917–18/56, p. 190)

Instead, to prepare his own case against the neutrality of money, he carved out three general propositions that follow from the fundamental equation of exchange: The *first proposition* states that "[n]o change in the magnitudes of which the product sum $p_1q_1 + p_2q_2 \ldots + p_cq_c$ consists can directly influence the product sum itself."[41] Attention thus turns to the economy's price structure, since for a constant monetary circulation MV the demand for one good always implies "to surrender for this good a definite quantity of another"[42] or, relatedly, that the change in relative prices must absorb variations in the money demand for individual goods p_nq_n. Consequently, the latter cannot cause any changes in aggregate circulation MV directly via an impact on the total expenditures in final consumption p^cI^c.

The *second proposition* claims that variations of the general price level must originate from monetary impulses – that is, changes in the quantity M or efficiency V, whereas every change in MV causes a corresponding adjustment in the product sum P^cI^c.[43] Taken together, the two propositions establish a one-way causal relationship, where changes in the monetary aggregate affect general prices and therefore also the money price for each individual good. In contrast, changes on the "goods side" are absorbed by the system of relative prices, and hence have no impact on the money aggregate. What the quantity theory then further adds to the above propositions of the equation of exchange are the assumptions that V and Q are constant, thus neutralizing the elements of efficiency and production. By necessity, the quantity of money then becomes the driving force to which only prices adjust. In turn, if all monetary impulses are absorbed by general price changes, money must be neutral with respect to what happens in the real economy. Schumpeter acknowledged that this

[40] From the "Original manuscript of Money, in German and English, Chapt. 1–2," HUA – HUGFP66.55 Manuscript on Money, Box 1, p. 1.

[41] MSP (1917–18/56, p. 184). [42] *MSP* (1917–18/56, p. 185).

[43] *MSP* (1917–18/56, p. 187ff).

> contains a simple truth: an increase in the sum of incomes is not an addition to the reservoir of goods, but only an increase in the "claim tickets" thereto. The real content of these claim tickets must fall, the price level rise, the quantities of commodities remain unaffected. If all prices rose uniformly and simultaneously, their rise would be nominal only and the matter would end there.
>
> (MSP, 1917–18/56, p. 189f)

Yet, of course, this is not where Schumpeter would put the matter to rest. In accordance with his Austrian peers and upbringing, Schumpeter soon pointed at the heterogeneity of price effects from monetary expansion:

> If, for example, the increase occurs unevenly, e.g. only in a part of our economic subjects, which must be by far the most frequent case, then at least a shift in the purchasing power of the same will take place first. All those who have a fixed income will be disadvantaged at first, and production and consumption will try to take other paths. However, we will react against this process, but by the time this happens, fundamental changes in the former state of the economy may have taken place in such a way that a return to it is impossible. (*WHN*, 1908, p. 295)

Money illusion, a concept known at least since Hume and Christiernen (Chapter 3), reinforces the real effects of differential price changes:

> [I]ncreases in the quantity of money never occur uniformly for all people. Further, people are never completely aware of the nature of the process, so that, at least for some time, they act as if they received higher incomes while the sum of incomes remains constant. For both reasons, prices never rise uniformly – neither the prices of consumer goods relative to each other nor the prices of consumer goods relative to those of the means of production. Thereby the price rise ceases to be merely nominal. It means a real shift of wealth on the market for consumer goods and a real shift of power on the market for the means of production, and it affects the quantities of commodities and the whole productive process.
>
> (MSP, 1917–18/56, p. 191)

Schumpeter conceded that monetary expansions produce many transitory effects, including a drop in real wages or a redistribution of rents, which will not affect the aggregate economy in the long run. Some impacts, however, are irreversible and set the economy on a different path:

> But very frequently such re-establishment of the *status quo* is impossible. Newly-won positions may be permanently held and old ones permanently lost, and much in the life of the economy may thereby change – forms of business organization, direction and methods of production, etc. Much that is new may have received just the impulse, much that is old just the *coup de grace* which had been lacking.
>
> (MSP, 1917–18/56, p. 191)

In short, monetary expansion can lead to persistent changes in industrial structure. But whether, in what form, and to which extent these changes happen depends on the institutional particulars of the monetary and productive system: "It is decisive for these effects where, in the body economic, the increase of money appears."[44]

The argument is then illustrated with several examples of monetary expansion. In one of these cases, Schumpeter refers to lucky gold panners and their suppliers, all of whom spend the minted pieces of gold entirely on consumer goods. As the total production of goods does not change, the additional circulation results in higher prices. Still, there are distributional effects, since the larger real income of the gold panners and their suppliers is offset by the reduced real income of all others, who must pay higher prices without enjoying an equivalent rise in their money income.

In another example, Schumpeter assumes that the gold panners invest all their gains. They can do so either by acquiring the means of production to run a business of their own, lending money directly for industrial purposes, or by using bank deposits for intermediation. Now, the immediate impact would be an increase in the price of the means of production, including labor, before the increase of prices spreads to the market for consumer goods. With regard to distribution, those who supply the means of production temporarily earn a higher real income at the cost of those who do not. This corresponds to a specific instance of *forced savings*, introduced by Thornton and Wicksell (Section 4.2), which distinctly enables the reallocation of purchasing power toward the further accumulation of means of production, that is, capital formation in its conventional sense.

With his *third proposition* Schumpeter invoked the idea of endogenous money, the supply of which adapts to changes in demand through the creation of credit. The first proposition had barred any direct impact of changes in the particular instance of $p^n q^n$ on the product sum PI. However, by assuming that credit renders the money supply endogenous to its demand, the former can nevertheless affect the monetary aggregate MV. And because of the second proposition the change in individual prices can then also exert an indirect influence on the product sum on the goods side of the equation. This would not only affect aggregate prices but also have an impact on production and real incomes.

In the case of commodity money, the classical economists already understood that an increase in the value of gold increased searching and mining efforts, and thereby increased the total quantity of specie. From this it follows, "even from the standpoint of the most rigorous quantity theory, not only that the quantity of gold money determines prices, but also that in principle prices likewise determine the quantity of gold money." Thus, "the quantity of gold 'depends' upon the purchasing power of money," which affirms "a two-way mutual causality."[45]

[44] *MSP* (1917–18/56, p. 192).

[45] *MSP* (1917–18/56, p. 199).

In the case of bank money, the situation is more complex and takes on greater economic significance. Since the costs of production are negligible, the connection between the value of money and its material substance no longer matters. Neither does the distinction between money and circulation, because the creation of bank money occurs almost synchronously with its spending. Yet in this case the demand for credit provides the impulse for an increase in the money supply, whereby the particular impact of money on production and real income depends on the specific interaction between consumers, entrepreneurs, and finance.

Although he embraced the concept of endogenous money, Schumpeter was critical of the received doctrines from the banking school (Section 4.2). He agreed that "[n]o more bank money can be created than is demanded by the business world,"[46] but he considered Fullarton's principle of reflux a gross exaggeration. He denied that bank credit was sufficiently elastic to adapt the money supply perfectly to changes in production thereby leaving commodity prices largely unaffected. Quite to the contrary, Schumpeter insisted on the importance of such price effects and aimed to integrate them in his explanation of economic development and business fluctuations:

> The case is quite clear: we have an increase in the quantity of bank money that normally prepares the way for an expansion of production and one that precedes the increase in commodities. The upswing consists in the creation of many new firms, the modernization and extension of old ones, and the full utilisation of all productive capacity. This requires means of production and, to acquire them, increased or new bank credits. [...] The prices of means of production rise, so does the income of their owners, who eventually spend more and thereby raise the prices of consumer goods. [...] If the credit is used as working capital, it will normally not be long before the corresponding commodities appear on the market and the much-praised parallelism between the flow of bank money and the flow of commodities is restored. (MSP, 1917–18/56, p. 203)

The upshot is that, even if changes in the price or quantity of individual goods can have no direct effect on the product sum *PI*, the endogenous response from credit money can account for indirect effects on it via the money aggregate *MV*. Yet he also cautioned that this "happens necessarily and automatically only in some cases."[47]

Before turning to those cases, we may briefly recapitulate the three mechanisms already known from the earlier literature, through which an increase in the money supply may enhance production. In Section 3.6 we first encountered Hume's notion of "money illusion" caused by the delayed reaction of prices to a change

[46] *MSP* (1917–18/56, p. 201). [47] MSP (1917–18/56, p. 198).

in expenditures and, second, Christiernen's related argument of a further delay in the response of wages to other price changes and the consequent variations in the profit rate. To these we must add as a third element the mechanism of "forced saving," as first spelled out by Thornton[48] (Section 2.5). However, these were generally considered auxiliary impacts of a temporary nature, and if anything received attention, it was their undesirable impact on income distribution.

Schumpeter also emphasized the unfair distributional consequences of inflation, particularly when they were caused, for instance, by an increase in war-induced treasury bills.[49] In the case of an endogenous expansion of credit, however, he distinctly stressed its potential to stimulate productive investments. This, finally, brings us to Schumpeter's core hypothesis on the *nexus of finance and growth*:

> The price-raising effect of bank money gives rise to the phenomenon of "forced saving." Without wishing to save, people are forced to do so by the reduction of their real income through the rise in prices. This releases means of production and the stock of goods at the disposal of the economy for productive purposes is increased, its fund for immediate consumption is diminished. [As a consequence, banking operations enrich] the productive apparatus of the economy. They cause a shift in purchasing power among individuals and, if this shift favours the expansion of production, a transfer of means of production to those individuals to whom credits are granted by means of newly created money.
>
> (MSP, 1917–18/56, p. 205)

The advantage is that monetary expansion can stimulate further production. Yet, due to increased production, the initial increase in prices is only temporary. It is even likely to be more than compensated, because of improvements in the method of production. Such productivity growth implies a higher real income, and "if this difference itself is again invested, the process would have to repeat itself."[50] Thus, the initial increase in the quantity of money can stimulate growth and development.

6.5 To recap, briefly

Schumpeter excelled in his genuine interest in, detailed knowledge of, and command of economic history and thought. Not only did this supply him with a broad repository of economic ideas, but it also prompted him to cultivate a critical attitude toward the received doctrines, understanding that any established canon

[48] Humphrey (1986, p. 21).
[49] See "There is Still Time to Stop Inflation" (INF) (1948).
[50] *MSP* (1917–18/56, p. 194).

may eventually be overtaken by a stream of novel ideas. Consistently with his own definition of innovation, he mainly conceived his theory through the original and creative combination of ideas that already existed, but were often obscure and had either been condemned or ignored by his peers.

This chapter has presented a brief synopsis of the key ingredients of Schumpeter's monetary theory, outlining how he collected various threads from the diverse and heterogenous sources of economic thought, then recombining and sculpting them into a forceful and distinctive concept of his own. While his writing on monetary matters is spread across multiple sources, one may summarize his endeavor in the following three integrative logical steps:

- First, he picked up and elaborated the *claim theory* into a general vision of money as a purely symbolic system of social accounts.
- Second, he put the quantity theory into a straightjacket of diminished relevance and refocused it in the *income-expenditure* approach, which better served his interest in the long-term development of real incomes.
- Finally, he applied further threads from the heterodox literature, most notably the notions of "endogenous credit" and "forced savings," in order to link money with the *real economy*.

Thus, lifting the veil of money and rebutting the postulate of its neutrality, his main assertion was that the endogenous supply of credit renders changes in the price structure an important driver of economic development. All of this amounts to a significant achievement and contribution to monetary theory. Yet, how well does this go together with his general economic vision?

As the saying goes, the proof is in the pudding. And Schumpeter served it early on—before ever explicating the full recipe and its ingredients—in his acclaimed *TED* of 1911. In the next chapter, we will attempt a detailed exposition of this work, in particular paying attention to its often neglected monetary side.

7
Finance and economic evolution

> [W]hat we are about to consider is that kind of change arising from within the system which so displaces its equilibrium point that the new one cannot be reached from the old one by infinitesimal steps. Add successively as many mail coaches as you please, you will never get a railway thereby.
>
> (J.A. Schumpeter, 1911/34, p. 64)

Schumpeter's ideas were spread throughout a voluminous output, some of which was, however, never translated into English or, if so, only with a considerable delay. Frequently, the secondary literature has embraced only particular ideas that apply to separate disciplines, such as those specializing in entrepreneurship, innovation, and technological change, industrial organization and dynamics, growth theory, business cycles, or public choice. Typically, it has also focused on selected arguments, even popular phrases or quips. As a consequence, it is easy to miss the inner coherence and multiple ties connecting the various parts of his *oeuvre*.

Arguably, *Theory of Economic Development* (*TED*; 1911/34) was his most accomplished and pivotal work. Practically all of his major original publications, whether explicitly or implicitly, expanded on selected themes contained within it. In *WHN* (1908) he had already foreshadowed his further plans, after clearing the terrain by surveying the canon of established theory. This established a solid foundation for the development of his own vision, whereby his distinctive interest in the heterodox sources provided him with a large repository of additional threads to process. *TED* then began with an eclectic synopsis of the received canon, imaginatively collapsing into what Schumpeter called the "circular flow" of a stationary economy. Conversely, *TED* laid out the theoretical basis for what he would later elaborate in his two-volume *BC* (1939). Furthermore, it hinted at a tendency toward progressive trustification of capitalism, which became the popular theme of *CSD* (1942/50). Finally, Schumpeter set out to elaborate a general and dynamic monetary theory, yet failed to see it through. The treatise remained fragmentary, published posthumously in *WDG* (1970).

This chapter highlights Schumpeter's *monetary* theory of economic development and its genuine account of the *nexus* between finance and the real economy.

Schumpeter's Venture Money. Michael Peneder and Andreas Resch, Oxford University Press (2021).
DOI: 10.1093/oso/9780198804383.003.0007

In his theory, innovation and "creative destruction"[1] critically depend on the creation and reallocation of purchasing power through finance. After having discussed the general aspects of his monetary theory in the previous Chapter 6, the following brief reconstruction builds on the structure and stream of arguments in *TED*, while assimilating, where appropriate, Schumpeter's further elaborations on selected themes in his later publications along six basic premises:

1. Entrepreneurial ventures navigate an uncertain but open "sea" of opportunities.
2. Innovation requires the prior investment of effort and money in pursuit of temporary monopoly gains.
3. Entrepreneurs exploit such opportunities by initiating and implementing discontinuous change.
4. Venture investors trust the entrepreneurs' vision and provide them with the purchasing power needed to control the means of production in advance.
5. Successful innovations induce imitation. Their progressive diffusion annihilates the temporary monopoly surplus, thereby decreasing prices, raising demand, and fostering the overall growth of real income.
6. Innovations do not occur independently, but are instead clustered, generating various overlapping waves of fluctuations in the overall business activity.

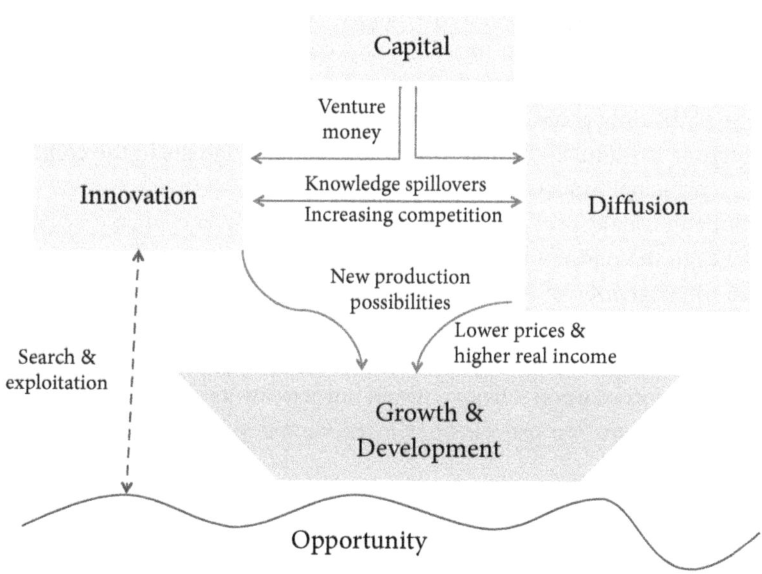

Figure 7.1 Depicting Schumpeter's "ad-*venture*" model of development

[1] Schumpeter introduced the notion of "creative destruction" relatively late, considering it "the essential fact about capitalism" in *CSD* (1942/50, p. 83). Despite its enormous popularity, Schumpeter later preferred the less martial expression of "creative response" (CRH, 1947).

Taken together, the specific realization and dynamic interplay of these elements enables and shapes the characteristic process of development in capitalist economies. Having once been asked to explain Schumpeter's theory of economic development within five minutes, we do not want to hide how we responded to the task with the graphic illustration in Figure 7.1.

7.1 Definition and scope

True to his Austrian upbringing and attention to epistemic foundations, Schumpeter first of all acknowledged the fundamental unity of all social facts and avowed himself to a need for theoretical abstraction:

> The social process is really one indivisible whole. Out of its great stream the classifying hand of the investigator artificially extracts economic facts. The designation of a fact as economic already involves an abstraction, the first of the many forced upon us by the technical conditions of mentally copying reality.
>
> (*TED*, 1911/34, p. 3)

Emphasizing its abstract nature, the theory of economic development "is not at all concerned with the concrete factors of change, but with the method by which these work, with the *mechanism of change*."[2] More precisely, *economic* activity always means the satisfaction of wants, and consumption is therefore "the only end of all production." The latter refers to the combination of labor and natural resources as the only generic factors of production, whereas all "produced means of production" are derived factors, which themselves originate in the combination of the two principal inputs.[3]

Schumpeter usually preferred the term *development* over *change*, since the latter also applies to the manifold continuous adjustments of an equilibrium system in response to exogenous events. Similarly, the mere growth of production would call forth "only processes of adaptation of the same kind as the changes in the natural data." In contrast, development specifically refers to the changes of a system which "are not forced upon it from without but arise by its own initiative."[4] He thus defined development as a process of *endogenous* and *qualitative transformation*.

7.2 Limits to growth

The *first basic premise* of Schumpeter's evolutionary theory of development is that the system must be open to new opportunities. To him, "[t]echnological

[2] *TED* (1911/34, p. 61). [3] *TED* (1911/34, p. 10ff). [4] TED (1911/34, p. 63).

possibilities are an uncharted sea"[5] with no definite boundaries to innovation, at least known, neither from running out of feasible technological changes nor an ultimate saturation of demand. On pure logical grounds one cannot preclude either, and the recurrent fear of secular stagnation is a reasoned possibility that Schumpeter acknowledged.[6] But he also argued that the historical record of technological change suggests otherwise. Like Wieser, but unlike, for instance, Keynes,[7] he believed in the common psychological trait of people continuously "discovering new directions of desire."[8] Because, "as higher standards of life are attained, these wants automatically expand and new wants emerge or are created, satiety becomes a flying goal, particularly if we include leisure among consumers' goods."[9]

In Schumpeter's time, the ecological limits of growth were not yet a general concern. Their ever-growing current importance, however, warrants a short side reference to the Austrian theory of value. In his contribution to modern welfare economics, Friedrich Wieser distinguished between exchange value ("Tauschwerth") in terms of the subjective *utility* of goods on the one hand and transaction value ("Verkehrswerth") in terms of objectively given prices on the other (Section 5.2). He consequently stressed that "price is a social fact, but it does not denote the estimate put upon goods by society."[10]

Wieser's immediate concern was the difference between average utility as a measure of subjective well-being and marginal utility as a determinant of prices—for example, in the case of a monopoly raising prices to the disadvantage of consumers. Today, we may also think, for instance, of negative externalities from environmental degradation, or the accurate measurement of welfare beyond the common national product, which is generally based on transaction prices.[11] In what he considered a rare case of conflict between subjective utilities and objective transaction values, Wieser left no doubt as to the proper prioritization: "The highest principle of all economy is utility. Where value and utility come into conflict, utility must conquer; there is nothing in the nature of value which could give it the ascendency."[12]

Similarly to Wieser, Schumpeter stressed the importance of income distribution in the determination of social value, which follows from the principle of diminishing marginal utility in consumption:

> It is important to note that, for the purposes of a theory of utility and value, it is not sufficient to know merely the quantities of goods existing [...]. Not only must the sum of individual wealth be given, but also its distribution among

[5] *CSD* (1942/50, p. 118). [6] *BC* (1939, p. 1035); *CSD* (1942/50, p. 111ff).
[7] Keynes (1930b). See also Rayo and Becker (2007a,b) or Pecchi and Piga (2008).
[8] Wieser (1914/27, p. 26). [9] *CSD* (1942/50, p. 131). [10] Wieser (1889/93, p. 64f).
[11] Jones and Klenow (2016); Stiglitz et al. (2018). [12] Wieser (1889/93, p. 54).

> individuals. Marginal utilities do not depend on what society as such has, but on what individual members have. [...] The distribution of wealth is important for determining values and shaping production, and it can even be maintained that a country with one and the same amount of general wealth may be rich or poor according to the manner in which that wealth is distributed. ("On the Concept of Social Value" (CSV), 1909, p. 214f)

If we apply the Austrian value theory to the contemporary problems of growing inequality and degradation of the natural environment, the often-conceived transformation to more sustainable and ecological means of production would *ceteris paribus* add to a society's utility and well-being, and hence also to real income in terms of the quality of life people can afford. An insight revealed in this side note is that such a transformation goes together with qualitative change and a rising standard of living, which points exactly at the deeper and very contemporary meaning of Schumpeter's definition of economic development.[13] Clearly, his vision reached *beyond GDP*.

7.3 Innovation and competition

Defined as the novel combination of factors of production,[14] innovation is the central pivot of Schumpeter's theory of development, the linchpin of a system's endogenous qualitative transformation. These innovations are not confined to technological change, but must be understood very broadly, ranging from the introduction of (i) new products and (ii) processes to the use of (iii) new resources, (iv) the discovery of new markets, or (v) changes in the industrial organization of a market (such as the creation or breaking up of a monopoly).[15]

However, innovation calls for the prior investment of effort and money to search for and exploit opportunities. This invokes the question of appropriate incentives for innovation, and thus leads to the *second basic premise* of Schumpeter's theory of development. To begin with, he emphasized three generic reasons for the difficulties that "every step outside the boundary of routine" causes.[16] The first lies in the objective task of carrying out new combinations: instead of being able to follow an established routine, one must work out the details of a plan, assess its viability, and make it operational. The second barrier is psychological, involving the effort needed to overcome one's own reluctance to embark on a new venture:

[13] Peneder (2017).

[14] More precisely, "[i]f, instead of quantities of factors, we vary the form of the function, we have an innovation" (BC, 1939, p. 87).

[15] *TED* (1911/34, p. 66).

[16] *TED* (1911/34, p. 84ff).

> The very nature of fixed habits of thinking, their energy-saving function, is founded upon the fact that they have become subconscious, that they yield their results automatically and are proof against criticism and even against contradiction by individual facts. (*TED*, 1911/34, p. 86)

Finally, unlike established modes already taken for granted, innovations must first gain acceptance from the social environment: "In matters economic this resistance manifests itself first of all in the groups threatened by the innovation, then in the difficulty in finding the necessary cooperation, finally in the difficulty in winning over consumers" (*TED*, 1911/34, p. 86). Proper economic incentives to accept the incurred cost of search and exploitation require the anticipation of a pecuniary profit in reward. Yet, based on the assumption of perfect competition, the marginalist reconstruction of the classical economy and its principles of distribution (as demonstrated in Wieser's method of imputation) allow no such surplus. Schumpeter hence pointed out that, in perfect equilibrium, "net profit cannot exist," because "the prices of the means of production must under free competition be such that they exhaust the price of the product."[17]

To solve the problem, Schumpeter identified the particular reward arising from innovation as the creation of temporary monopoly profits: "Since the entrepreneur has no competitors when the new products first appear, the determination of their price proceeds wholly, or within certain limits, according to the principles of monopoly price."[18] Only as competitors catch up and adapt to the new situation will the innovation diffuse and the surplus vanish. Even then, the remaining entrepreneurial profit is a net gain, meaning "that it is not absorbed by the value of any cost factor through a process of imputation."[19]

Despite this seemingly straightforward reasoning, rents from innovation and according price-setting power have far-reaching theoretical consequences. They alone account for the endogenous explanation of innovation, growth, and development from proper incentives that arise within the economic system. Growth theory took several decades until it managed to account for this within concise formal models.[20]

7.4 The entrepreneurial function

Combining influences from both the Austrian School and the German historical tradition, the *third basic premise* of the theory of development can be found in the

[17] *TED* (1911/34, pp. 31, 150). At best, such a surplus can occur during the transition from one equilibrium to another.

[18] *TED* (1911/34, p. 152). In *HEA* (1954, p. 894) Schumpeter praised John Bates Clark (1847–1938) for being "the first to strike a novel note by connecting entrepreneurial profits [...] with the successful introduction into the economic process of technological, commercial, or organizational improvements."

[19] *BC* (1939, p. 105).

[20] See, for instance, Aghion and Howitt (1992, 1998).

particular emphasis that Schumpeter placed on the function of entrepreneurial leadership.[21] Characteristically, he did not simply assume that pecuniary incentives would automatically and by themselves surmount the aforementioned barriers to innovation. And, while acknowledging that one generally "must start from the satisfaction of wants, since they are the end of all production,"[22] many of them would remain latent. For the most part, it is therefore up to the entrepreneurs to initiate discontinuous change:

> Yet innovations in the economic system do not as a rule take place in such a way that first new wants arise spontaneously in consumers and then the productive apparatus swings round through their pressure. We do not deny the presence of this nexus. It is, however, the producer who as a rule initiates economic change, and consumers are educated by him if necessary; they are, as it were, taught to want new things, or things which differ. (*TED*, 1911/34, p. 65)

Consumers' resistance to change is one of the barriers to innovation, which entrepreneurs must learn to overcome.[23] There are exceptions: for instance, "[i]n every social circle, particularly if it be not too large and if its members enjoy a certain minimum of means and leisure [...] we observe leaders of fashion, specialists in creating new forms and habits of private life."[24] Schumpeter thus acknowledged "user innovations,"[25] but considered these an exception to the rule. More generally, however, discontinuous change requires individual leadership, and this explains why innovations are not carried out simultaneously by all firms, but rather occur unevenly.[26]

Admitting it to be irrelevant for the main economic mechanism, Schumpeter allowed himself a much-quoted side note, in which he attempted a brief psychological characterization of the entrepreneurial type. In it, he considered this person typically "more self-centred than other types"[27] and distinctly driven by three kinds of personal motives: "First of all, there is the dream and will to found a private kingdom," which "is specially strong for people who have no other chance of achieving social distinction." He added that the "sensation of power and independence loses nothing by the fact that both are largely illusions." Second,

[21] Streissler (1994) mentions, among others: Gottlieb Hufeland (1760–1817), who stressed the importance of entrepreneurs; Karl Heinrich Rau (1792–1870), who emphasized the distinctive need for combining factors of production; and A.F. Riedel, who elaborated on the task of innovation (in 1838). Balabkins (2003) singles out Albert E.F. Schäffle (1831–1903), who taught temporarily in Vienna, served as Austrian minister of commerce, and discussed innovation in the context of intellectual property. Finally, Karayiannis (2005) mentions the influence of J.B. Clark, who emphasized profits from cost-reducing innovations.

[22] *TED* (1911/34, p. 65).

[23] "[T]o produce satisfactory soap, it was also necessary to induce people to wash—a social function of advertisement that is often inadequately appreciated" (*BC*, 1939, p. 243).

[24] *BC* (1939, p. 74). [25] Hippel (1986). [26] *TED* (1911/34, p. 87); *BC* (1939, p. 97).

[27] *TED* (1911/34, p. 91).

"there is the will to conquer: the impulse to fight, to prove oneself superior to others, to succeed for the sake, not of the fruits of success, but of success itself. From this aspect, economic action becomes akin to sport." And, finally, "there is the joy of creating, of getting things done, or simply of exercising one's energy and ingenuity." The latter trait means that the entrepreneur typically "seeks out difficulties, changes in order to change, delights in ventures."[28]

We may summarize the three motives under the headings of (i) power and independence, (ii) ambition, and (iii) joy in creative ventures. Arguably, the first depends most directly on pecuniary gains and the third the least, while the second takes an intermediate position.[29] Only for the third motive did Schumpeter convey an idealized image of the creative venturer, whereas the two others are portrayed as rather pathological cases. Consequently, he does hold "that entrepreneurs have an economic function as distinguished from, say, robbers. But we neither style every entrepreneur a genius or a benefactor to humanity."[30] In short, what matters for Schumpeter's theoretical apparatus is the function of entrepreneurship, where the principal performer is "merely the bearer of the mechanism of change":[31]

> The carrying out of new combinations we call "enterprise"; the individuals whose function is to carry them out we call "entrepreneurs." These concepts are at once broader and narrower than the usual. Broader, because in the first place we call entrepreneurs not only those "independent" businessmen in an exchange economy who are usually so designated, but all who actually fulfil the function by which we define the concept, even if they are, as is becoming the rule, "dependent" employees of a company. [At the same time, the] concept is narrower than the traditional one in that it does not include all heads of firms or managers or industrialists who merely may operate an established business, but only those who actually perform the function. (*TED*, 1911/34, p. 74)

In a radical break from previous practice, Schumpeter replaced the traditional occupational notions of entrepreneurship with a specific economic function. Others had pictured entrepreneurs as mere undertakers, owners of capital, or managers, if they were considered at all, and generally focused on capital and labor as the two principal factors of production. Relatedly, Schumpeter dispensed with the popular emphasis on risk-bearing and referred it to the separate capitalist function.[32] Compared to alternative notions of entrepreneurship, Schumpeter's concept exhibits a clearer definition and purpose, but is nevertheless narrow in scope. In a practical sense, it is interchangeable with innovation.[33]

[28] *TED* (1911, p. 93f). [29] *TED* (1911, p. 94). [30] *TED* (1911, p. 90).

[31] *TED* (1911, p. 61).

[32] He thus anticipated later notions of "corporate entrepreneurship." See, for instance, Burgelman (1983a,b).

[33] Block et al. (2017) surveyed the empirical literature on the "Schumpeterian entrepreneur." See also Grebel (2007) for a contemporary perspective.

The most important theory among competing functional theories of entrepreneurship is that proposed by the later Austrian School.[34] Instead of innovation, they mainly identified entrepreneurship with arbitrage—that is, the function of alerting entrepreneurs to coordinate demand and supply through the discovery and exploitation of exogenously given imbalances in prices. Another influential concept is the human capital theory,[35] which emphasizes, among other aspects, the adoption and implementation of new technologies by entrepreneurs. All three theories generally share a disequilibrium view of the economy. However, there are some important differences. While Schumpeter considered the entrepreneur to be the source of disequilibrium, the others treat the entrepreneur as an equilibrating force.

Essentially, the three distinct theories of entrepreneurship are complementary, as each points at different functions that are invariably important for the effective and efficient operation of the economic system:[36] As a disequilibrating force, entrepreneurship (i) creates new opportunities by means of innovation; as an equilibrating force, the alert discovery and exploitation of given opportunities (ii) improves market co-ordination through the detection and elimination of imbalances in the price-quantity relationships and (iii) incites technology diffusion through the adoption of novel practices and techniques. Some firms may simultaneously conduct all three functions at a time, whereas others specialize in exploiting opportunities of a particular kind, and yet others may experience the three modes at different times. But their common characteristic is always the *pursuit and exploitation of opportunities* for profit, which in general behavioral terms sums up that which is unique about what the entrepreneur does.

With these three basic premises in mind, we may finally inquire about the specific role of money in the process of development. In doing so, Schumpeter's strategy of contrasting development with the hypothetical benchmark of a circular flow is particularly instructive.

7.5 Breaking the circular flow

Schumpeter always defended the use of equilibrium models as the "description of an apparatus of response," which provides the "bare bones of economic logic which, however abstract or remote from real life it may be, yet renders indispensable service in clearing the ground for rigorous analysis."[37] In his early work,

[34] In particular Hayek (1945) and Kirzner (1997).
[35] For instance, Schultz (1975); Lazear (2004).
[36] See Peneder (2009).
[37] *BC* (1939, p. 68). To this he adds "that these assumptions are very far from reality; but we hold that the logical schema of that theory is yet right 'in principle' and that deviations from it can be adequately taken care of by introducing friction, lags, and so on, and that they are, in fact, being taken care of,

Schumpeter followed *J.B. Clark* (1884–1963) in distinguishing between "static" and "dynamic" analysis, but already expressed his dissatisfaction with the received terminology.[38] When *Ragnar Frisch* (1895–1973) later defined dynamics more concisely as a system of economic variables that relate to different points of time,[39] Schumpeter learned to distinguish more precisely between a stationary system (including steady state growth) on the one hand, and development as an evolutionary process of qualitative transformation and structural change on the other.[40]

His theory of economic development consequently starts with the abstract benchmark of a stationary economy in equilibrium with rational and fully informed agents, perfect competition, and zero entrepreneurial profits. Characteristically, this model of the "circular flow" cannot explain the emergence of new enterprises or innovations, nor does it aim to do this (Figure 7.2). Based on this model, firms are already in operation, and technology and preferences are exogenous. Their task is adaptive, seeking the efficient management of operations

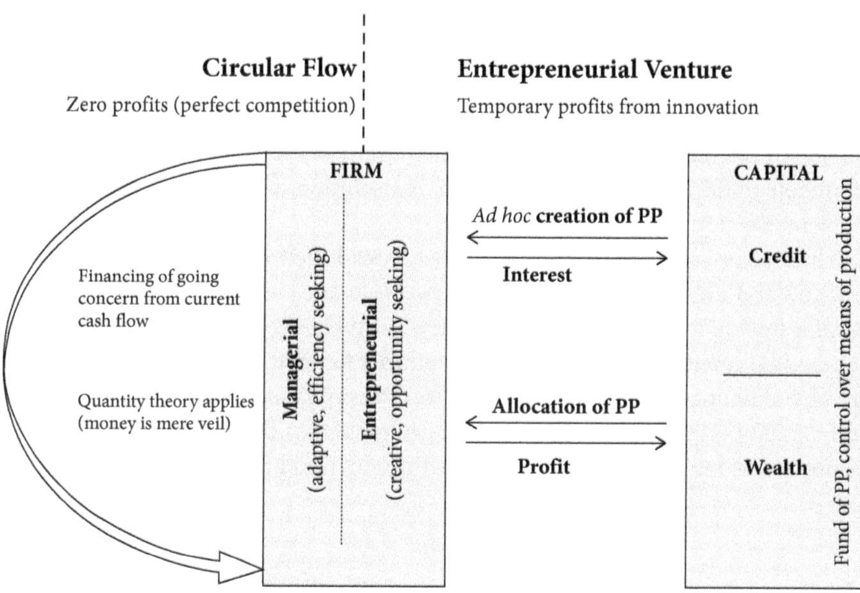

Figure 7.2 Breaking the "circular flow"

with increasing success, by recent work developing from the traditional bases. We also hold, however, that this model covers less ground than is commonly supposed and that the whole economic process cannot be adequately described by it or in terms of (secondary) deviations from it" (*BC*, 1939, p. 98).

[38] *WHN* (1908, p. 182).

[39] See Louca (2015) on the relationship between Schumpeter and Frisch.

[40] See Hagemann (2003, p. 56) and Andersen (2011, p. 40); or *HEA* (1954, p. 868) for Schumpeter's appraisal of the original dichotomy by J.B. Clark.

within a given business environment. Running on ordinary routines, the firms also have no need for leadership in the above sense.[41]

In the circular flow, money is therefore a practical device with which to ease transactions, and its stream is opposite to that of goods. Yet, stripped down to its bare logic, the economy can in principle do without it through the synchronisation of expenditures and cash flows. Consequently, the quantity theory applies and money is a mere veil, which affects price levels, but no real economic relationships. And just as in the equilibrium of Walras, the comprehensive system of mutual interdependencies can be explained by a common standard of value to denote relative prices (the "numéraire"), as well as an anchor of the absolute price level (the "monnaie").[42]

Schumpeter then contrasted the stationary system with his vision of economic development through entrepreneurial ventures.[43] Individual leadership now matters. It is necessary to break out of the received routines and pursue new profit opportunities. While the entrepreneur "swims with the stream in the circular flow which is familiar to him, he swims against the stream if he wishes to change its channel."[44] And only here does a distinct import of the monetary system to the real economy arise from the particular need to pre-finance innovation. Whereas an ongoing stationary system can use its current returns to self-finance its expenditures and maintain production, the entrepreneurs cannot by themselves provide the means with which to get a new venture started. They need investors to fund their initial search and exploitation as a solution to the old *cash-in-advance* problem (Section 3.4).

Schumpeter consciously picked up that thread, tied it to the entrepreneurial function and identified a clear *nexus* between finance and growth. To break the circular flow of a stationary economy, new ventures need investors who trust in (lat. *credit*) the entrepreneur's vision and capacity for redemption, and who provide the capital defined as the purchasing power to control needed means of production. Schumpeter thereby postulated a pure monetary concept of capital, which "is not goods but balances, not a factor of production but a distinct agent which

[41] Although the "assumption that conduct is prompt and rational is in all cases a fiction," it is "sufficiently near to reality, if things have time to hammer logic into men" (*TED*, 1911/34, p. 80; see also p. 84); see also Bachinger and Matis (2009, p. 557ff).

[42] In reference to this chapter Samuelson declared that he was "struck by the degree to which the exposition is poetic in form. It is like a parable, and its wisdom lies between, as much as within, the lines" (1943, p. 61).

[43] According to Goodwin (1990, p. 39), he "elaborated the fundamental notion of the profit motive as the driving force, but did so in the spirit of Marx, not Walras, that is, that it not only drove price toward cost but also that, to restore and maintain profit, the structure of production was repeatedly altered, thus engendering a kind of perpetual morphogenesis of the economy and of the society created by it." In a similar vein, Josef Steindl emphasized that "[i]t is not the scarcity of real capital that enables the existence of profit, but the scarcity of risk capital." Steindl (1987, p. 17). See also Hanappi (2015) on the relationship between the two "theoretical mavericks" Schumpeter and Goodwin.

[44] Steindl (1987, p. 79f).

stands between the entrepreneur and the factors."[45] By substituting entrepreneurial rents from innovation for the zero-profit condition, investors who can anticipate the pecuniary gains have an incentive to fuel development by financing the new ventures. Their provision of financial capital enables entrepreneurs "to buy before they sell," and hence to overcome the cash-in-advance barrier to innovation.[46]

Entrepreneurs with sufficient accumulated wealth of their own can self-finance the needed investments. Others must seek external sources. But where do these funds of purchasing power come from? According to Schumpeter, the most common explanation is again misleading:

> But we may not even start from total "savings." For its magnitude is explicable only by the results of previous development. By far the greater part of it does not come from thrift in the strict sense, that is from abstaining from the consumption of part of one's regular income, but it consists of funds which are themselves the result of successful innovation. (*TED*, 1911/34, p. 72)

In short, capital accumulates from surplus income, which according to Schumpeter's strict assumptions must originate from entrepreneurial profits, that is, from innovation broadly defined. Investors must first enable this innovation by financing the necessary search and exploitation of perceived opportunities in advance. If own wealth from past savings and hence surplus income is missing, the core function of "Schumpeterian" banking is to create the needed purchasing power *de novo* through credit. Driven by the anticipation of entrepreneurial profit from innovation, this initial credit then kick-starts the further capital formation from retained earnings, dividends, or interest paid. In the stream of development, the real and the monetary side of the economy thus become inextricably interwoven.

Consequently, the capitalist function of directing the stream of purchasing power among alternative uses, applied specifically to the purposes of the entrepreneurial venture, brings us to the *fourth basic premise* of Schumpeter's monetary theory of development:

> The function of capital consists in procuring for the entrepreneur the means with which to produce. It stands as a third agent necessary to production in an exchange economy between the entrepreneur and the world of goods. It constitutes the bridge between them. (*TED*, 1911/34, p. 117)

The capitalist, hence, is the "*ephor* of the exchange economy," who "makes possible the carrying out of new combinations, authorizes people, in the name of society as it were, to form them."[47] And finally— concealed by the bulk of speculative

[45] *BC* (1939, p. 129). [46] Messori (2003).

[47] *TED* (1911/34, p. 74; emphasis added). Note that here Schumpeter referred to the "banker," whom he considered the "capitalist *par excellence*." See also footnote 82.

operations in pursuit of arbitrage—the financial markets are "always, as it were, the *headquarters* of the capitalist system, from which orders go out to its individual divisions, and that which is debated and decided there is always in essence the settlement of plans for further development".[48]

The upshot is that innovations depend on the system's capacity to pre-finance the necessary efforts. Both entrepreneurs and capitalists must invest their respective resources and through their creative vision, pursuit, and exploitation of opportunities become the prime movers of growth and development.

7.6 Diffusion and aggregate growth

Innovations are not isolated events, as they become the source of further investment opportunities. This brings us to the *fifth basic premise* of the theory of economic development. Major innovations kick-start a process of *diffusion*, by which other entrepreneurs gradually populate the new economic spaces thus opened. It is only a matter of time until innovations leak and generate positive spillovers to other firms which learn to adopt new techniques, imitate, or even challenge the incumbent with their own variation on the innovation. As other firms follow, the path of innovation "becomes progressively smoothed for successors by accumulating experience and vanishing obstacles."[49] However, with the declining costs of imitation, the competitive advantage from the initial innovation also shrinks, competition increases, and the surplus profits must ultimately vanish. In other words, the particular speed and duration of diffusion depend on the precise form of diminishing costs and returns of imitation.

While innovations are pursued to reduce competition, the temporary nature of success implies that expectations regarding the intensity and nature of competition also affect the incentive to undertake the entrepreneurial venture in the first place. This involves a fundamental endogeneity of competition and innovation, which is another reason why the outcomes depend on the particular conditions of the respective markets and technologies. In the end, it is the widespread diffusion of new productive knowledge that fuels the aggregate growth of per capita income via the associated expansion of goods or services and decline of prices. The latter is responsible for the rise in real purchasing power that brings the benefits of innovation not only to a few pioneering users, but also to the mass of consumers.

[48] *TED* (1911/34, p. 126; emphasis added). Schumpeter used the term "money market" very broadly in the sense of "financial markets." Though he acknowledged the distinction between money markets for short-term loans and capital markets for trade in long-term assets in a reference to Spiethoff (*TED*, 1911/34, p. 124), he did not adopt it for his own theoretical purposes. Braunberger (2016, p. 15) explains this by Schumpeter's emphasis on the short-term nature of interest. See also Kurz (2015).

[49] *BC* (1939, p. 131).

Thereby, "credit creation spreads from its "logical" source, financing of innovation, throughout the system. It intrudes by way of credits being created for any kind of expansion that cannot be financed by existing funds."[50]

7.7 Business cycles and crises

Aggregate growth is not where the model ends. Turning to the problem of recurring fluctuations of economic activity, Schumpeter again argued that the primary impulse emerges from innovation. In short, his *sixth major premise* is that innovations do not occur independently of each other, but are instead *clustered*.[51] Economic fluctuations occur "because the new combinations are not, as one would expect according to general principles of probability, evenly distributed through time." Instead, they typically "appear, if at all, discontinuously in groups or swarms."[52] This is "because the apperance of one or a few entrepreneurs facilitates the appearance of others, and these the appearance of more, in ever-increasing numbers,"[53] which means that in the course of diffusion the initial barriers to innovation progressively level off. In the words of Oskar Lange, the clustering of innovation reflects the declining risk of failure during periods in which the system finds itself in the close neighborhood of equilibrium.[54]

While considering business cycles a fundamentally institutional and historical phenomenon,[55] Schumpeter proceeded with his theoretical argument by means of three abstract "approximations."[56] The first relies on the anticipation of gaining a share in the surpluses of innovation, which induces the initial wave of diffusion and at the same time annihilates the very same profits. The impulse for rising prosperity might thus simply end when the newly opened opportunities become gradually exhausted. But this is not the point Schumpeter pressed. Instead, he emphasized endogenous economic factors. One was the growing shortage of human capital—in his terms, the progressively diminishing qualifications of the new entrepreneurs who enter a market. Another factor was credit deflation, which occurs when the successful entrepreneurs pay off their debts, thereby reducing the monetary circulation. But foremost it is the spread of innovation, which lowers general prices and thereby terminates the phase of growing prosperity. The

[50] *BC* (1939, p. 159).

[51] "If the new enterprises in our sense were to appear independently of one another, there would be no boom and no depression as special, distinguishable, striking, regularly recurring phenomena" (*TED*, 1911/34, p. 224).

[52] *TED* (1911/34, p. 223). [53] *TED* (1911/34, p. 228). [54] Lange (1941, p. 192).

[55] "In a society with private property and competition, this process is the necessary complement of the continual emergence of new economic and social forms and of continually rising real incomes of all social strata" (*TED*, 1911/34, p. 255). See also *BC* (1939, pp. 144 and 156).

[56] For elaborate discussions, see, for example, Clemence and Doody (1950, p. 9ff) or Andersen (2011, 174ff).

consequent recessions thus also originate in the clustered occurrence and spread of innovations: "While the disturbance caused by a continuous appearance of entrepreneurs could be continuously absorbed, the swarm-like appearance necessitates a special and distinguishable process of absorption."[57] In the first approximation, the recurring downturn is thus an inevitable part of economic development, during which the system adapts to new conditions: "It fulfils what the boom promised. [...] The stream of goods is enriched, production is partly reorganised, costs of production are diminished, and what at first appears as entrepreneurial profit finally increases the *permanent real incomes of other classes*".[58]

It is with the "second approximation" that Schumpeter introduces the elements of error, excess, and financial speculation. While the boom further feeds on the above rise of real incomes, the households, businesses, and investors alike fail to accurately anticipate its temporary nature and become overly optimistic in their economic plans. Furthermore, the financial sector increasingly provides unproductive loans for private consumption or to businesses which merely expand "on old lines."[59] As the monetary circulation runs ahead of production, prices rise and further increase the scope of financial speculation and the general fragility of the system. Consequently, according to Marshak the second approximation is characterized by the impact of price changes on net borrowing (or repayment of debt).[60]

Historically, the spread of limited liability had increased the potential scope of moral hazard and Schumpeter understood, just as Thornton and Wicksell had before him, that by expanding the mutual lines of credit banks may continue to lend to insolvent clients in order to hide bad loans and "gamble for resurrection."[61] Yet, ultimately, the secondary wave must break in an often-painful liquidation of unmet promises and obsolete assets. Unlike the mere adaptation to changing conditions in the first approximation, the excess of the second wave tends to turn into exaggerated pessimism, where people fail to accurately anticipate the forthcoming recovery. The subsequent "abnormal" depression leads to excessive liquidation of assets and firms that would under normal conditions be productive, causing high unemployment and economic hardship.

While both approximations originate in the process of economic development, only the first is a necessary part of it. Schumpeter thus affords logical priority to what he considers the primary mover, which triggers a great mass of further events

[57] *TED* (1911/34, p. 231). [58] *TED* (1911/34, p. 245).

[59] *BC* (1939, p. 147). Hayek probably adopted a similar distinction between the "primary" and "secondary" causes of business cycles from Schumpeter (Klausinger, 2008, p. 15); see also Bachinger and Matis (2009, p. 583ff).

[60] Marshak (1940, p. 891).

[61] Keuschnigg and Kogler (2020, p. 3). See also Schlesinger (1914, p. 122) and "Book Review of Schlesinger Karl, Theorie der Geld- und Kreditwirtschaft" (BRS; 1915).

that occur in the process of the secondary wave. However, the different levels of abstraction easily distort their general perception:

> Indeed, the phenomena of this secondary wave may be and generally are quantitatively more important than those of the primary wave. Covering as they do a much wider surface, they are also much easier to observe; in fact, they are what strikes the eye first, while it may be difficult, especially if the innovations are individually small, to find the torch responsible for the conflagration. This is one reason why the element of innovation has been so much neglected by the traditional analysis of the business cycle: it hides behind, and is sometimes entirely overlaid by, the phenomena of what appears at first glance to be simply a general prosperity. (*BC*, 1939, p. 146)

To conclude, Schumpeter argued that economic development "systematically produces alternating phases of prosperity and depression," but explicitly denied any constant periodicity of such fluctuations. Instead, their duration must "depend on the nature of the particular innovations that carry a given cycle, the actual structure of the industrial organism that responds to them, and the financial conditions and habits prevailing in the business community in each case."[62] Furthermore, their empirical observation is hampered by the interference of what in a "third approximation" he considered "an indefinite number of wavelike fluctuations which will roll on simultaneously" and with distinct periodicity.[63]

Arguably, the term business "cycle" therefore misled many critics, if they adhered to its literal meaning.[64] However, in contrast with the common macroeconomic approach, Schumpeter had presented a model of economic evolution and placed according emphasis on irregularity and historical specificity in order to explain recurrent fluctuations. For instance, Marshak acknowledged Schumpeter as "a student of economic history *and* theory—suspicious of 'closed systems' "[65] and knew to receive *BC* as a general history of capitalism. According to McCraw, it also previewed modern business history.

The welfare connotations of Schumpeter's theory, however, ran completely counter to the common focus on stability.[66] By the time he wrote *BC*, Schumpeter

[62] *BC* (1939, p. 143).

[63] *BC* (1939, p. 161ff). Schumpeter illustrated the apparent irregularity of their joint outcome by drawing three simultaneous sine waves, representing short Kitchin cycles of about three years, intermediate nine-year Juglar cycles, and Kondratieff-type long waves of more than fifty years (p. 212ff). Later theories of the business cycle would emphasize the different durability of various kinds of investment goods, such as inventories, fixed capital, or R&D. See Hagemann (2003, p. 63f) and Andersen (2011, p. 187ff) for further discussion, as well as Louca (2007) and Silverberg (2007) on "long-waves."

[64] Andersen (2011) makes this point. One may also compare the influential and very critical review of Kuznets (1940) with the sympathetic one of Marshak (1940), as well as the elaborate defence by Clemence and Doody (1950).

[65] Marshak (1940, p. 894). [66] Andersen (2011, p. 157ff).

had become aware that "scientific analysis of an organic process easily creates the impression that the analyst 'advocates' letting that process alone." In particular, the excesses of the second wave are no longer constitutive to economic development and may instead impede it. He therefore attached importance to declaring that his "analysis lends no support to any general principle of *laisser faire*" and "does not in itself constitute an argument for letting things take their course or trusting to 'the restorative forces of nature.' "[67] Instead, he pointed at the need for government action—particularly in cases of "abnormal" depression, though not as much during the ordinary course of business fluctuations.

His policy recommendations were typically pragmatic, but not very detailed. First, he put the emphasis on the least controversial recommendation: improving business cycle forecasts. Second, he sided with the counter-cyclical use of fiscal stimuli, arguing that the

> postponement of new construction by government enterprises or by great combines to periods of depression appears from our standpoint as a moderation of the consequences of the swarm-like appearance of new combinations and as an attenuation of the inflation of the boom and the deflation of the depression, hence as an effective means of alleviating the cyclical movement and the danger of crises.
> (*TED*, 1911/34, p. 253)

He was, however, critical of general monetary stimuli, since he believed that the indiscriminate expansion of credit would merely raise inflation. Conversely, he acknowledged the theoretical possibility of using credit facilities to discriminate in favor of only viable businesses that were temporarily under stress from an abnormally deep crisis.[68]

But with regard to central bank policy Gottfried Kunwald (1869-1938) also warrants some attention. He had studied with Carl Menger at the University of Vienna and later became Schumpeter's most important partner at the Biedermann Bank (Chapter 8). He asserted that a timely and proper management of expectations was the essential remedy for depression. As Schumpeter had argued, depressions originate in the excesses of the boom. Kunwald therefore advised swift intervention by the central bank to break potential waves of speculation as soon as securities become overprized.[69]

[67] *BC* (1939, pp. vi, 155).

[68] To this Schumpeter added two qualifications. First, he pointed out that the technical requirements for such a policy were not yet available. Second, he emphasized that "such a policy would lead far into a special variety of economic planning, which would infinitely increase the influence of political factors upon the fate of individuals and groups." While declaring that "this involves a political judgement which does not concern us here" (*BC*, 1939, p. 254), his personal and even moral indignation toward it becomes apparent in a miscarried comparison to policies of "racial hygiene" which followed.

[69] Kunwald (1934, p. 151f).

7.8 Credit and creative destruction

In the process of capital formation, Schumpeter's recursive reasoning necessarily leads back to the situation in which entrepreneurs first aim to break out of the circular flow, but do not yet have (sufficient) accumulated surplus income at their own disposal. Ultimately, the necessary advance payment must then originate in the *ad hoc* creation of purchasing power, that is, money, through bank credit. And, according to Schumpeter, "this is the source from which new combinations *are* often financed, and from which they would have to be financed *always*, if results of previous development did not actually exist at any moment" *TED*(1911/34, p. 73). Therefore, the "creation of purchasing power characterises, in principle, the method by which development is carried out in a system with private property and division of labour."[70] With respect to economic development, the banker's characteristic role then becomes that of a producer of purchasing power, rather than the conventional one of financial intermediation. To him, credit creation in the above sense was the "monetary complement of innovation."[71]

To many economists at the time, this must have conjured the image "of catching the wind in balloons," as encountered in the context of John Law's miscarried financial ventures (Section 3.5). In their notorious dispute on the dynamic theory of interest (Section 7.10), Böhm-Bawerk did indeed bring up the charge that "Schumpeter is much closer than he suspects and perhaps also wants, at the side of Law and McLeod, and unfortunately quite far away from Hume."[72] But more to the point, he summarized the particular offense which monetary orthodoxy took at Schumpeter's radical exposition:

> According to Schumpeter, capital is not a stock of goods, but "purchasing power," and in the developed capitalist national economy this is offered preferably by the issuing banks in the means of credit payment issued by them beyond the metallic cover; so preferably that Schumpeter, with his own tendency to dialectically push the thoughts to extremes, declares the uncovered means of credit payment "in principle" even for the sole source of credit granted to entrepreneurs. For technical banking reasons, however, the amount of loan money can never be spent in a completely unlimited amount, but only in such a limited multiple of the cash stock held by the issuer that the latter "with regard to the possible presentation of loan money" will probably suffice to redeem the presented amounts. (Böhm-Bawerk 1913a, p. 30)

There can be no doubt that Schumpeter was aware of the connection to his heterodox ancestors in monetary thought, as well as of the potential disrepute it

[70] *TED* (1911/34, p. 73). [71] *BC* (1939, p. 111). [72] Böhm-Bawerk (1913a, p. 31).

could cause among his peers. But what many critics failed to notice or mention was his careful elaboration of how the *ad hoc* creation of purchasing power through credit connects the individual venture with the overall money supply. The creation of credit offers no free lunch but leads to far-reaching macroeconomic consequences as well as particular trade-offs felt at the level of markets and individual firms. Consistently with his later representation of the fundamental equation of exchange, the additional money in circulation must not only raise prices in the aggregate but also alter the distribution of purchasing power in terms of the claims on a yet unimproved social product. And this is the specific method with which credit propels *creative destruction* as a fundamentally monetary process:[73]

> [I]n our case a different employment of the system's productive powers cannot be achieved otherwise than by a disturbance in the relative purchasing power of individuals. [...] For in the circular flow there would be no idle stocks for the needs of the entrepreneur. (*TED*, 1911/34, p. 96)

For example, credit for the purpose of a particular investment not only raises the purchasing power of the entrepreneur who received it, but also more generally the price of productive services. This inevitably weakens the purchasing power of others (if not the suppliers of productive services, then their suppliers, etc.) and thereby withdraws goods from their previous use. By tying together the cash-in-advance problem, his theory of entrepreneurial profit, and certain elements from the idea of forced savings,[74] Schumpeter identified the specific function of credit in the process of economic development, which is "in enabling the entrepreneur to withdraw the producers' goods which he needs from their previous employments, by exercising a demand for them, and thereby to force the economic system into new channels."[75] Applying the *claim* theory of money (Section 6.1) adds another flavor:

> By credit, entrepreneurs are given access to the social stream of goods before they have acquired the normal claim to it. [...] Granting credit in this sense operates as an order on the economic system to accommodate itself to the purposes of the entrepreneur, as an order on the goods which he needs: it means entrusting him with productive forces. It is only thus that economic development could arise from the mere circular flow in perfect equilibrium. (*TED*, 1911/34, p. 107)

[73] See also *CSD* (1942/50, p. 83).

[74] Schumpeter, however, also pointed at differences to the concept of "forced savings" in his exposition. For example, "it is primarily the purchasing power of other firms that is reduced," whereas the "reduction of the 'real' purchasing power of some households [...] is compensated in part by the increase in the real purchasing power of others." Furthermore, their "voluntary saving may so superimpose itself on credit creation as to neutralize some of the effects of the latter" (*BC*, 1939, p. 112).

[75] *TED* (1911/34, p. 106).

Therein, Schumpeter gave logical priority to the credit channel of creative destruction, which pre-conditions the familiar substitution and income effects on the product market. In short, he identified three distinct but related channels through which new combinations displace old ones. To begin with, there are the increased costs for old businesses due to the credit-induced inflation in the market for intermediate goods; then "later their receipts are reduced, first in those businesses with which the innovation competes, but then in all old businesses, insofar as consumer demand changes in favor of the innovation."[76]

Finally, the credit inflation is only temporary, since the entrepreneurs must redeem their advances, and—if the ventures are successful—will also increase the supply of goods or services in the real economy. Unlike credit for consumptive purposes, in the long run "there is no credit inflation at all in this case—rather deflation—but only a non-synchronous appearance of purchasing power and of the commodities corresponding to it."[77] After redemption, the interest and entrepreneurial profit remain in circulation.

What then are the limits of such a credit expansion? In the first instance, one should assume, as Adam Smith had done in the real bills doctrine (Section 3.7), that banks only lend money if they expect the funded projects to be profitable. Only then will their creation of additional purchasing power not raise inflation but be (more than) balanced by the increasing stock of goods and services. Conversely, if ventures fail, they raise the demand for productive services without an according increase in production, affecting prices in the same way as consumptive credit. Consequently, the natural limit of a non-inflationary credit expansion would be defined by the availability of profitable entrepreneurial ventures.

But, similarly to Thornton, Schumpeter pointed out that this limit was "extremely elastic. A bank does not expand its credit single-handedly. It does so when others are doing the same."[78] While the associated loss should in principle discipline the lending practices of individual banks, the banking system together can temporarily lift this restriction, if banks refinance their losses among themselves through the further creation of credit. This can be induced, for instance, by the joint anticipation of further price increases resulting from the very same inflationary forces. In addition, financial practice aims to exploit the situation through further speculation, whereby the "vast scope for irresponsibility and misconduct" is "immeasurably increased by the fact that the evolution of an environment's system of moral ideas and legal safeguards tends to lag behind its economic evolution."[79] A process of *cumulative causation* thus aggravates the situation and, if uninterrupted by legal restrictions and public authorities, such as the central banks, can generate financial cycles, hyperinflation, and correcting crises, including notorious waves of bank failures—patterns which find sufficient

[76] *TED* (1911/34 p. 232). [77] *TED* (1911/34, p. 110). [78] *BC* (1939, p. 121).
[79] *BC* (1939, p. 410).

support in the historical record.[80] In a nutshell, the effect of credit on prices depends on whether the additional money in circulation is used for productive purposes, and whether the ventures succeed in increasing the supply of saleable goods and services.

Among the various ways in which capitalists allocate purchasing power, the power of banks to "produce" it via credit and additionally affect its allocation through indirect price effects was Schumpeter's main theoretical thread for advancing a monetary explanation of economic development. Additionally, from a historical perspective, his emphasis on the role of banking in fostering industrial development was empirically well founded. Especially in Austria, Germany, and other Continental European countries, banks played an important role in providing long-term corporate financing. The large universal banks, in particular, entertained close and manifold ties with industry, simultaneously combining commercial, investment, and brokerage services, in addition to their traditional lending operations (Section 4.3). However, capital needs generally tended to be low during the early phases of industrialization.[81] When the railway boom and rise of heavy industries later increased the demand for external finance, Baskin and Miranti maintain that

> [t]raditionally, it has been easier to establish viable markets for debt, rather than equity, securities. In the past, corporations have mainly relied on borrowing to raise the bulk of funds from outsiders. The perfection of large-scale impersonal markets in common stock has been only a comparatively recent development.
>
> (Baskin and Miranti, 1997, p. 15)

One consequence was that the early Schumpeter did not consider the difference between foreign and own capital in affecting its principal economic function of allocating purchasing power to the entrepreneur. Only in his later work, particularly *CSD* (1942/50), did he discuss the advantage of large firms in terms of their greater resources for self-financed research activities thus indirectly acknowledging the benefits of own equity in the presence of capital market frictions. Yet, arguably, Schumpeter's conception amounted *in the main* to a credit theory of entrepreneurial innovation and economic development. From a contemporary perspective, however, and especially in the context of financing innovation, his emphasis on credit and banking, while turning a seemingly blind eye to the specific role and importance of equity, merits some additional reflection. While this section has explained his focus on credit, in the next section we are going to explain what warrants the above emphasis on "in the main."

[80] Kindleberger and Aliber (2005).

[81] Frost (1954, p. 184); Kindleberger (1984, p. 191ff).

7.9 Promoter's profit

For Schumpeter, the choice of individual financing instruments was foremost a technical question, in which he showed comparatively little theoretical interest. Credit held a special place in his conception, because of the particular combination of entrepreneurial ventures, investors' choices, and macroeconomic consequences via the endogenous growth of the money supply and according effects on the structure of prices. Furthermore, in accord with a frequent practice among German-speaking economists, Schumpeter often used the term "credit" synonymously with capital and referred to the "banker" as the capitalist or, more generally, the financier.[82] It would be wrong, therefore, to infer that he considered credit a superior instrument from the perspective of the individual venture. In one of his rare discussions of the financing instruments he clearly expressed the opposite view:

> [I]f it is true that long-term enterprises are financed by short-term credit every entrepreneur and every bank will try for obvious reasons to exchange this basis as soon as possible for a more permanent one, indeed will regard it as an achievement if the first stage can be completely jumped in an individual case. In practice this approximately coincides with replacing purchasing power created *ad hoc* by that existing already. [...] In the first place, *shares* or *bonds* are created and their amounts are *credited* to the enterprise, which means that banking resources still finance the enterprise. Then these shares and bonds are disposed of and gradually are paid for [...] by the subscribers out of existing supplies of purchasing power or reserves or savings. Thus, as it may be expressed, they are resorbed by the community's savings. (*TED*, 1911/34, p. 111; emphasis added)

In short, Schumpeter understood the advantages of equity for individual ventures. Yet, while long-term finance is what entrepreneurs need and strive for, short-term loans may often be all they can get. More generally, to Schumpeter the capitalist function is synonymous with *risk bearing* and in this regard invokes the prioritization of equity over debt finance. Among the historical examples he cites for this in *BC*, he often places emphasis on the cases where external investors shared the risks more broadly. For instance, when referring to the Roman *foenus nauticum* he pointed out "how perfectly this contract expresses the aspect that to us is the essential one,"[83] which means that investors carried the risks of maritime ventures in addition to financing them (Section 2.3). Another case in

[82] Streissler (1982, 1994) points in particular at the influence of *Karl Knies* (1821–98) and *Rudolf Hilferding* (1877–1941). For example, in *BC* (1939, p. 647) Schumpeter refers to funding "debts by the issue of bonds or stock"; see also footnote 47.

[83] *BC* (1939, p. 615).

point are the "banks which on principle participate in the ventures they finance" and which Schumpeter—for lack of a more accurate expression—described as the "crédit mobilier type." They acquired "parcels of stock," among others, "in order to profit by appreciation." It was in particular after the boom of incorporations in the late 1890s that these and other large banks underwrote corporate bonds and equity issues, held industrial shares and exercised proxy voting rights for those who deposited bearer shares with them. This provided them with powerful representation on the company boards, reduced informational asymmetries, and thereby also affected their readiness to provide long-term credit (Section 4.3).

While many banks acted as mere agents, who earned a fee on their service of underwriting and intermediation, the profitable business of promoting and listing new joint-stock companies also raised a profound theoretical issue. The particular attention which the Austrian School paid to the theory and distribution of value, the Marxist criticism of financial capitalism, and Schumpeter's take on entrepreneurial profit from innovation all nourished a specific interest in the origin of the large surplus that became apparent in many company valuations.

At the time, venture capital in its modern form and professional organization was not yet known. However, arguably, *Rudolf Hilferding* (1877–1941) and Joseph Schumpeter anticipated key features of what would later become its characteristic business model. Together with Ludwig Mises, both had attended Böhm-Bawerk's famous seminar in 1905. They were well acquainted and developed their ideas within a similar intellectual environment. Despite their different ideological backgrounds— Hilferding became the spearhead of Austro-Marxism and later also finance minister in Germany—both reportedly developed "a cordial friendship" and by 1905 had conceived many of their fundamental ideas.[84]

Hilferding championed the concept of the *promoter's profit* ("Gründergewinn"). In modern terminology, these are the capital gains from the founding, expanding, or restructuring of a business that are realized by selling new shares. His concept thus corresponds in many respects to the contemporary business model of private equity and, more specifically with regard to start-ups, venture capital. Hilferding stands out in considering such a disbursement of new shares, privately held by the promoters of a new (or restructured) firm, to be a source of income *sui generis*.[85] It is not only fundamentally distinct from loans that earn interest, but also from the public trade of equity on the stock exchange, since the latter implies the principle of arbitrage according to which the share yields tend to equal the risk-adjusted money rate of interest. Moreover, the gains from the public trade have no direct impact on the further accumulation of productive capital, instead tending to stay within the realm of speculation. In contrast, shares that are privately held may temporarily

[84] Michaelides and Milios (2005, p. 101; 2015); see also Kurz (2011) and Greitens (2012).
[85] Hilferding (1910/81, pp. 109, 112).

eschew arbitrage and earn a promoter's profit in addition to regular interest.[86] In accordance with his Neo-Marxist perspective, he considered the promoter's profit to be a powerful source of accumulation, fostering the concentration of industrial capital in the hands of ever more powerful financial organizations through the simultaneous use of loan and equity instruments.

Among the arguments raised against his concept, Hilferding was criticized for not explaining how the promoter's profit arose in the first place.[87] In contrast, Schumpeter readily absorbed the promoter's profit as a special kind of entrepreneurial profit, which constituted a more general source of income. In doing so, he distinguished between monopoly revenues from innovation and the according capitalized gains in company value:

> And yet two quite different economic phenomena exist. The carrying out of the monopolistic organisation is an entrepreneurial act and its "product" is expressed in profit. Once it is running smoothly [...] it has become a monopoly revenue. Profit from founding a business and permanent return are distinguished in practice; the former is the *value of the monopoly*, the latter is just the return from the monopoly condition. (*TED*, 1911/34, p. 152; emphasis added)

Schumpeter thus depicted the capital gains as the value increment that is due to the anticipated future returns from a successful innovation. The promoter's profit originates in the temporary entrepreneurial rents from innovation, which are capitalized by the issue of new shares. He considered it to be the purest form of entrepreneurial profit:

> It may now be briefly observed that profit as here conceived is the main element of the phenomenon which is described as promoter's profit. Whatever promoter's profit may be in addition, its basis is the temporary surplus of receipts over cost of production in a new enterprise. The promoter may indeed be, as we saw, the purest type of the entrepreneur genus. He is then the entrepreneur who confines himself most strictly to the characteristic entrepreneurial function, the carrying out of new combinations. (*TED*, 1911/34, p. 137)[88]

Wieser agreed with his explanation[89] and explicitly considered it a serial business: "In the case of the stock-company, as a general rule, the promoters promptly

[86] That is, until "they are then evened out by the flow of newly accumulated quantities of surplus value into those spheres which have the highest promoter's profit" (Hilferding, 1910/81, p. 188).

[87] Greitens (2012, p. 69).

[88] Schumpeter, however, used the term "promoter" sparingly, because in the common language of his time it meant "frequently only an agent intervening on commission, who does the work of financial technique in floating the new enterprise" (*TED*, 1911/34 p. 78). See also Section 4.3.

[89] "Promoter's profits are a particular kind of entrepreneur's profit. They are the reward for 'undertaking the enterprise'. These profits collect in advance on a capitalization of the profits of the enterprise" (Wieser, 1914/27, p. 360).

retire from the enterprise and make room for the stockholders who come in subsequently."[90] In contrast, Hilferding and Schumpeter conceived the promoter's profit as a more general concept. Schumpeter explicitly distinguished it from the mere underwriting of new stock companies, emphasizing that it "applies only to the real promoter and not to the agent who sometimes performs the technical work of forming a company and frequently goes by the same name." The point was, of course, that the typical activity of "promoters" at the time was to underwrite a new public offering, which earns a regular fee for the service of intermediation but neither creates nor merits the capital gains which underlie their concept. Furthermore, he stressed that the promoter's profit is not confined to the founding of a start-up business, but extends to new ventures in existing firms, since "everything new that is created in a company is not in most cases perfected with the promotion of it," and people therefore "often continually embark upon new enterprises."[91]

Schumpeter explicitly pointed at the existence of capital market frictions and corresponding conflicts between entrepreneurs and investors: "If, during the founding of a business, everything was to proceed correctly and with ideal perfection and foresight on all sides, the profit would be what remained in the founder's hands. Of course, in practice it is quite different."[92] In other words, in perfect capital markets, the entrepreneurs can raise loans and pay interest, but keep the full entrepreneurial rent. However, when information is not perfect and credit is thus constrained, entrepreneurs must find ways to bridge the financing gap by raising long-term capital, typically giving equity to external investors, who then claim their share in the surplus.

Financial frictions explain the inherent conflict between entrepreneurs and investors over corporate control and the according distribution of the surplus. Hilferding argued that the financial organizations gradually gain control over industrial capital via the accumulation of the promoters' profits. Schumpeter, however, remained guarded about the ultimate distributional consequences. He stressed that external finance enables new ventures and that the surplus also contributes to the accumulation of capital within the firm, thereby strengthening its self-financing capacity. In his analysis, the distribution of the gains from the accumulation of capital between entrepreneurs and outside investors therefore remains indeterminate. The upshot is, that both "real" production and venture finance critically depend on each other and must cooperate in the pursuit and exploitation of entrepreneurial profit. But, given imperfect capital markets, they are also systematically in conflict about its later distribution. In a sense, these contrary ideological views of Schumpeter and Hilferding still represent the opposing political attitudes toward modern venture capital held today.

[90] Wieser (1914, p. 359). [91] *TED* (1911/34, p. 137f).

[92] TED (1911/34, p. 137f). See also "Gründungsgewinn in Recht und Wirtschaft" (GRW, 1911).

7.10 Interest on capital

Our discussion has so far left out Schumpeter's theory of interest, with its notorious denial of a positive rate in a stationary economy. One reason for this is that the famous dispute surrounding it has often overshadowed and distracted from the more essential elements of his monetary theory. The other is that we did not require it in the line of arguments connecting his monetary theory to that of economic development. In short, we consider it an intellectually interesting but non-essential outgrowth of Schumpeter's delight in carrying a logical argument to its radical conclusion. Taking proper account of the underlying assumptions generally leads to a confirmation of the logical consistency of his argument, but also simultaneously to the acknowledgement of its diminished economic relevance. In a certain way, his reasoning resembles the reductionism of those formal theoretical models, which he greatly admired. However, by not applying the mathematical apparatus himself, his assumptions were often not sufficiently explicit and the complex line of arguments difficult to defend without first invoking all the priors, as developed throughout *TED*.

Contemporary peers were upset by his seemingly frivolous denial of the relevance of phenomena of apparent empirical importance, such as time preferences, capital accumulation in non-innovating firms, or consumer credit and savings. While Schumpeter never denied the role of savings in abstaining from consumption out of regular income, it was of secondary importance to his theory of development. Similarly, he acknowledged that interest reflects different time preferences in the case of consumer credit—but, again, these do not explain the essential characteristics of capitalist development. The fiercest rejection came from Böhm-Bawerk, who was not only Schumpeter's teacher but also the leading authority on capital and interest.[93] This strong repudiation certainly contributed to the widespread opposition to, or even worse, indifference toward his monetary theory, and therefore meant a major setback. Arguably, this dispute sealed Schumpeter's transition from an independently minded infant prodigy to the notorious "prodigal son" of the Austrian School.

To briefly summarize, Schumpeter was exclusively concerned with productive interest on capital. Though he acknowledged the independent existence of interest on consumptive loans or government credit, these never entered his theory as essential in the sense of indispensable elements of economic development. Furthermore, he distinctively defined capital in monetary terms as purchasing power rather than a stock of goods, as was the case in Böhm-Bawerk's theory. Nevertheless, Schumpeter liked to stress that he followed his teacher in considering entrepreneurial profit to be the origin of a price *agio*, part of which can be paid as

[93] Böhm-Bawerk (1913a,b); Schumpeter (1913).

interest to creditors. Consequently, he defined interest as "a premium on present over future purchasing power."[94]

At first, Schumpeter literally trailed Böhm-Bawerk in refuting the older theories that had aimed to explain interest, for instance, as a cost of production or a premium on abstinence. However, he framed their theoretical problem more deliberately within the perspective of the hypothetical stationary economy of the circular flow (Section 7.5). In its ordinary course, the entirety of the values produced must thus accrue to the services of labor and land, whereas the produced means of production merely constitute an intermediate step in the method of imputation rather than an independent third factor of production. This is because perfect competition drives down their prices to the total value of the products imputed to them.[95]

Wieser's method of imputation using the marginalist method had thus raised the pending question about the origin of interest as a separate category of permanent income. Böhm-Bawerk had found a solution in his postulate of positive time preferences (Section 5.2). But Schumpeter, like Wieser, bluntly denied their validity as a generic cause of interest and thus pulled the rug out from under Böhm-Bawerk's explanation. Instead, Schumpeter substituted it with his concept of entrepreneurial profit: "In the absence of consumers' time preference, innovation, or the expectation of profits in our sense of the term, is now the only factor to produce, in an otherwise stationary and undisturbed world, a positive premium on present balances" (*BC*, 1939, p. 602). That surplus from innovation, however, does not exist in the stationary system of the circular flow. This is because "*ex hypothesi* all arbitrage gains have already been made and are therefore excluded."[96] The advantage was that, given the previous assumptions and by accepting only endogenous innovation as the sole source of entrepreneurial profit, Schumpeter inevitably arrived at his postulate of the non-existence of interest for productive purposes in the stationary economy: "The true equilibrium rate, i.e., the rate that would obtain in a stationary process perfectly equilibrated in all its elements and displaying no tension at all, would as we know be zero" (*BC*, 1939, p. 603).

To Böhm-Bawerk and many of his followers, this was untenable. When launching his mighty critique[97] he pulled no punches and mocked Schumpeter for being "intoxicated by a brilliant idea."[98] Or, more to the point:

[94] *TED* (1911/34, p. 157).

[95] *TED* (1911/34, p. 162ff). In defence of Schumpeter's theory of interest, Samuelson (1943) denied the relevance of the Austrian method of imputation and took issue with the fact that his teacher and mentor had applied the argument equally to industrial equipment, machinery, seed-corn, and the breeding of livestock.

[96] *TED* (1911/34, p. 189f).

[97] Initially about sixty pages, then another unconciliatory final remark of fifteen pages in reply to Schumpeter's written defence, itself about forty pages.

[98] Böhm-Bawerk (1913a, p. 2). And furthermore: "It is a pity that spirit and power of speech, an eminent skill in the dialectical joining of words, in this case did not mate with a higher degree of

> I will not hold back for a moment the judgement that, despite all the recognition of the high personal qualities of the author, I consider his "dynamic" interest theory to have been completely unsuccessful and misleading. The interest on capital is and remains that for which all the world has always held it with good reason: a static branch of income. (Böhm-Bawerk, 1913a, p. 2)

In the engaging intellectual debate that followed,[99] both failed to find a common interpretation of their differences. At the heart of the matter was their distinct attitude toward time preferences, which made the two approaches irreconcilable. But this was a purely behavioral assumption and neither Böhm-Bawerk nor Schumpeter had much to say about its empirical relevance in the creation of credit.

This may be one reason why Böhm-Bawerk mainly attacked Schumpeter for his narrow definition of entrepreneurship, which he considered to exclude the vast majority of actual business leaders. However, he thereby chose a battleground that was not to his own advantage. As discussed in Section 7.4, Schumpeter's theory of entrepreneurial profit from successful own innovation was indeed narrow but well-elaborated. In contrast, Böhm-Bawerk's concept was rather rudimentary, considering entrepreneurs in a conventional manner as the owners of the means of production. However, he raised an important objection when arguing that Schumpeter's "heroic" entrepreneur, who earns a profit from own innovation, represents a small minority of firms. He doubted that these can more generally explain the actual scope and importance of interest in the economy.

This critique forced Schumpeter to further explicate his theory of entrepreneurial profit in his reply to Böhm-Bawerk.[100] In short, he explained that the imitation of an innovation does not instantaneously transform the markets into a situation of perfect competition with zero profits. Instead, innovations take time to diffuse. For instance, high fixed costs in production together with the different age of existing capital stocks make it unlikely for innovations to spread uniformly. In addition, many innovations are not one-shot affairs but go through stages of continuous refinement, strengthening the vintage effects, whereby a variety of "new combinations" at different stages of their maturity permeate the market. Schumpeter hence became more explicit in acknowledging that these firms still earn a profit—less than in a monopoly, but more than in a situation of perfect competition—and that this profit must decrease in the further course of the diffusion of an innovation. Only if the system reaches the hypothetical limit of a uniform distribution and according perfect competition among homogenous

patience and self-criticism. The highly gifted author seems to create extremely easily and quickly; an enviable, but as you can see, possibly also a dangerous gift from God" (Böhm-Bawerk 1913a, p. 61).

[99] Böhm-Bawerk (1913a,b) and Schumpeter (1913); see also, for example, Hahn (1924, p. 127, fn 115), Hagemann (2010), or Kurz (2012).

[100] "Eine 'dynamische' Theorie des Kapitalzinses" (INT; 1913, p. 636).

firms will profits actually vanish. Before that happens, however, other innovations are likely to fuel the entrepreneurial process anew.

To conclude, even though the mass of firms is not entrepreneurial in the Schumpeterian sense, these non-innovating firms can still make a profit and hence pay interest to secure the funding of their investments. To Schumpeter, the important theoretical point was that in all those instances the creative act of innovation was still the primary source of a positive net return. It triggers all the profits earned throughout the following cascade of adaptive imitations. The latter are only a secondary and diminishing source of net returns, because they depend on something that is there to be imitated and has not yet been completely diffused.

Arguably, Schumpeter thus successfully defended the logical consistency of his theory. Yet from here it is not far-fetched to reason analogously that any lengthening of the production period can be considered either an innovation itself or an act of imitation in the above sense. Böhm-Bawerk's "roundabout" method of production is then only a special case of Schumpeter's principle of "novel combinations" and the latter the generic explanation of the deeper source of capital formation, credit, and interest. Furthermore, following Schumpeter's rationale, the profits from the lengthening of the production method themselves can only be temporary.[101] Schumpeter did not make this implication explicit, but Böhm-Bawerk's strong reaction to his theory suggests that he was well aware of its fatal implications for the relative relevance of his capital theory.

As an afterthought, we should recall that the younger members of the Austrian School, in particular Mises, Hayek, and Kirzner, later developed a broader concept of entrepreneurship (Section 7.4). Like Schumpeter, they emphasized its opportunity-seeking nature, but in contrast they did not place the focus on endogenous innovation, instead highlighting the entrepreneurs' alertness to given frictions in the markets. These continuously interfere with the equilibrium tendencies and thus regularly offer new opportunities to make a profit, for example, from arbitrage or from moving faster than competitors in response to (exogenously) changing tastes and technology. If such profits are not mere exceptions but occur frequently, the exploitation of novel opportunities other than those arising from own innovation can equally establish the demand for advance means of payment and hence become an independent source of the price agio from which interest is to be paid. Though one still cannot consider this a stationary economy in the sense of a frictionless circular flow, Schumpeter's claim of endogenous innovation as the only constitutive source of interest also does not hold.

Schumpeter never revised his position, but in his unfinished "money book" he significantly downplayed the claim for zero interest in the stationary economy. Mentioning it only briefly, he took care to emphasize that, even in the circular

[101] *INT* (1913, p. 610).

flow, savings together with interest for consumptive purposes can contribute to growth through the steady expansion of the means of production.[102] Apparently he was in agreement with *Paul Samuelson* (1915-2009), who defended the logical consistency of Schumpeter's argument, but also considered it insignificant to his theory of development:

> As stated the argument can hardly be controverted. Technological development may produce a positive rate of interest, but after it ceases, only time preference can keep the rate up. [But also] Schumpeter's theories of development and of the cycle would be unaltered in essentials if there were a non-zero rate toward which interest were tending. Similarly, these theories would require no modifications if interest simply approached a zero rate without ever reaching this limit. (Samuelson, 1943, p. 67)[103]

Despite Samuelson's vindication of his teacher's theory of interest on capital, Böhm-Bawerk's critique was long echoed by renowned economists, including Lionel Robbins, Frank Knight, and George Stigler. In his reply to Böhm-Bawerk, Schumpeter anticipated the unavoidable bearing the dispute was going to have on his standing among monetary economists:

> Whatever the outcome of the discussion, the fact remains that my theory has made a thoroughly unfavourable impression on the highest authority in this matter and that, however else the fate of my theory may be, the weight of one of the few great names of our science will always weigh against it.
>
> (INT, 1913, p. 600)

For the young rising star economist, this was likely the first major setback of his professional career. Yet other and far more tangible defeats would soon follow. Schumpeter's boundless ambition would once again play a significant role when he attempted to simultaneously incorporate two principal roles in his venture theory of economic development. Temporarily leaving the academic sphere, he tried his luck in the real world of finance, becoming both the director of one of Vienna's most renowned banks and a "proto-venture capitalist" pursuing promoters' profits from the founding of new enterprises. Both of these financial ventures failed spectacularly. The following chapters in Part III of this monograph will elucidate their history.

[102] *WDG* (1970, pp. 114, 118).

[103] See also Samuelson (1943, p. 61): "Schumpeter's theory of a zero rate of interest could be dispensed with, and no great harm would be done to his theory of the cycle or of development. Instead of tending to rebound to a zero rate, the interest rate would tend, after a period of innovation, to return to some other rate, alleged to represent an intrinisic rate of time preference or impatience, or any other broad margin."

PART III
SCHUMPETER'S FAILED FINANCIAL VENTURES

8
The Biedermann Bank

> The founding of a new bank is [...] in the opinion of the applicants one of the best ways to truly interest foreign capital in the tasks of our national economy, and to make it do truly fruitful work for Austria with all its risks.
>
> (Schumpeter et al., 1921)[1]

The previous parts have dealt with the emergence of monetary orthodoxy, as well as how Schumpeter overcame these positions through his own monetary theory of development. The three chapters of Part III are dedicated to Schumpeter's efforts to put his theoretical expertise into practice. After his political activities during the First World War and his interlude as state secretary for finance—mentioned in the biographical remarks of the introductory Chapter 1, he did not wish to return to his former job as an economics professor in the Austrian provincial capital of Graz. Rather, from 1921 onward, he intended to make a fortune as a banker and venture investor.[2] On the basis of economic considerations, Schumpeter was convinced that he would invest in an upswing[3] and thus achieve rapid success. However, he was confronted with adverse economic circumstances and certainly made mistakes himself as a beginner in the field of practical entrepreneurship.

In this chapter, an overview of the economic background of his entrepreneurial attempts is followed by a detailed study of Schumpeter's efforts as president of the Biedermann Bank and as the co-founder of an industrial group. Finally, in Chapter 10, the role he played in these ventures and the personal consequences of his entrepreneurial efforts are elucidated. This period of Schumpeter's life has already been described, and clever and accurate interpretations have been provided. However, in these studies details are at times incomplete or even incorrect.[4]

[1] "Die Gründung einer neuen Bank ist [...] nach der Überzeugung der Einschreiter eines der besten Mittel, ausländisches Kapital für die Aufgaben unserer Volkswirtschaft wirklich zu interessieren und für österreich wirklich fruchtbare Arbeit mit all ihren Risiken leisten zu lassen." ÖStA, AdR, BmF, Zl 16,038/21, Letter of Schumpeter and seven other applicants to the Federal Ministry of the Interior and Education, Notice of receipt February 19, 1921.

[2] Preliminary results for the following chapters have already been published in Resch (1997); Resch (2013); and Peneder and Resch (2015).

[3] See *Wiener Völker Echo*, No. 1, 1921, p. 26; and several articles in *Die Börse*, 1920 and 1921, published in Stolper (1993, pp. 17–39).

[4] The most important analyses can be found in Allen (1991) and Stolper (1994). Allen called upon several contemporary witnesses, enabling him to give a very vivid picture of the time, which, however,

Schumpeter's Venture Money. Michael Peneder and Andreas Resch,
Oxford University Press (2021). © Michael Peneder and Andreas Resch.
DOI: 10.1093/oso/9780198804383.003.0008

For this reason, the following section attempts to evaluate the available source material in great detail to provide a comprehensive picture.

8.1 General economic background

During and after the First World War, the economic and social environment in Austria suffered radical upheaval.[5] The Habsburg Empire had fought to the point of total economic exhaustion. In the area of the newly founded Republic of Austria in 1920, GDP was around 35 percent lower than it had been in 1913. Because of the division of the monarchy into seven national states, the Viennese banks, traders, and industrial firms lost important segments of their former domestic markets. Many industrial firms with plants situated in different regions of the former monarchy involuntarily became international companies and had to adapt their activities to the nationalist economic policies in the new states, which increased their overall costs.[6]

Further economic problems resulted from the devaluation of war bonds and depreciation of the Austrian currency, which accelerated to hyperinflation by 1921. Finally, by September 1922 the Austrian *Krone* (henceforth krone, pl. kronen) had fallen to a fourteen-thousandth of its pre-war value. In autumn 1922, stabilization was achieved through an international loan organized by the League of Nations and guaranteed by several states, among them the United Kingdom. The corresponding agreements were laid down in the three so-called "Geneva Protocols." The price of this was a pronounced austerity policy and tight monetary regime after 1922. Under these conditions, the newly established Austrian Central Bank (Oesterreichische Nationalbank) came under foreign—in particular British—control.[7] As a result of this, real interest rates remained at around 10 percent, even for first-class clients, during the entire First Austrian Republic. At the same time, the real economy suffered a stabilization crisis in 1923, while the Viennese stock market experienced a bull market, because many speculators believed that the appreciations of the stock prices had not kept pace with inflation, which meant that some room for further increases was expected. When the bull market ended toward the end of the year 1923, a speculative wave against the French franc set in, which completely failed in March 1924. To cover the accrued debts, massive stock sales followed in Vienna, which led to a stock market crash and ultimately to a severe banking crisis. The share index on the Vienna Stock Exchange first rose from 502 points (September 1922) to 2,686 points (December

contains several errors in detail. Stolper has evaluated the written sources more comprehensively, but since then new sources, such as the estate of Gottfried Kunwald, have become accessible.

[5] Rothschild (1947); Sandgruber (1995, pp. 335–402); Butschek (2011, pp. 171–250).

[6] Resch (2010). [7] Kernbauer (1991, pp. 61–85); Jobst and Kernbauer (2016, pp. 161–6).

1923), then fell to 1,141 points by July 1924. In this situation, the newly founded Austrian Central Bank provided some relief through the generous discounting of bills of exchange, and the big Viennese banks set up a support fund in order to rescue several distressed financial firms. Around the turn of 1924/5, the schilling was introduced as the new currency, with an exchange ratio of 10,000 kronen to 1 schilling.

During the inflation period, numerous banks tried to profit from speculative opportunities with currencies and stocks, while the overall conditions for sound business deteriorated. The number of joint-stock banks in Austria (most of them located in Vienna) increased from twenty-seven (1913) to seventy-six in 1923 and dropped to forty during the ensuing crisis up to 1927. There are no reliable statistics for private banks, but according to the "Bankierbuch," which was published in the financial yearbook *Compass*, their numbers increased from 216 in 1918/19 to 378 in 1923/4 and plummeted to 169 by 1928/9.[8] During the growth phase that emerged, albeit on an unsound basis, up to 1923, the banks had to compete for employees, which meant that their union was able to negotiate high wage agreements, high severance pay entitlements, and complete permanence after relatively short periods of employment. The large number of new hires under these conditions meant that during and after the bank crisis of 1924 the Austrian financial institutions suffered from heavy cost burdens due to a surplus of employees who had high wage claims and could only be made redundant at high costs, if at all. The total number of persons employed in Vienna in the financial sector first increased from 19,331 in 1910 to 41,128 in 1923, and then as a result of the ensuing bank crises dropped back to 21,597 by 1934.

Austrian industry also suffered from a notoriously depressed business environment. The Austrian GDP index (1913=100) recovered from 66.4 in 1920 to 80.1 in 1922, decreased to 79.3 in 1923, and recovered to 88.5 (1924) and 94.5 in 1925. While pre-war GDP was surpassed in 1928, industrial production was never restored to its pre-war level.[9]

In Austrian entrepreneurial history, two narratives are used to characterize the development of the business elites after the war. The first narrative emphasizes the decline of old bourgeois elites and "old money" due to the lost war and inflation, while the other hints at the chances for alert entrepreneurs to use opportunities arising from the upheavals and discontinuities. It is obvious that Schumpeter himself attempted to be one such alert winner. He recognized that the unstable financial developments and restructuring of the former common Habsburg markets allowed for speculative dealings, and that industrial niches in the new protectionist national states offered opportunities for start-ups betting on import substitution or innovative products. Schumpeter attempted to base a third career on this insight, after concluding his activities as a professor of economics and secretary of state for finances.

[8] Resch (2018, pp. 81–93).

[9] Resch (2018, p. 84).

8.2 The roots of the banking project

In his attempts to become bank president, Schumpeter had to overcome major bureaucratic obstacles. Ultimately, the merger of two different projects that complemented each other led to (provisional) success. On the one hand, he himself undertook to found a new bank together with members of Austrian and international business elites. On the other hand, one of the leading Austrian universal banks, the Anglo-Oesterreichische Bank (Anglo-Austrian Bank), intended to convert a Viennese private bank named Biedermann Bank into a subsidiary joint-stock bank, while at the same time itself being transformed from an Austrian into a British firm during the economically turbulent years of 1921 and 1922. Both of these plans met with distinct difficulties, which were overcome by merging them into one common banking project.

Before the First World War Austria had developed a bank-centered capital market (see Chapter 4), while the market for equity capital via joint-stock exchanges remained somewhat underdeveloped.[10] Under these circumstances, it is easy to comprehend why Schumpeter considered banks crucial organizations for entrepreneurial finance in his early theories of entrepreneurship, innovation, and development, and understandable that he himself was keen to become a banker. Yet, due to strict regulations, the foundation of a joint-stock bank was a tedious process. To obtain a license, the consent of two ministries was necessary: that of the ministry of finance and that of the ministry of the interior. If Schumpeter had been content with the establishment of a private bank, he would have avoided many bureaucratic difficulties, as private banking was a completely free trade in Austria until the middle of the 1920s. However, he anticipated favorable treatment of his banking project by the relevant authorities, because it had been customary in imperial Austria to grant former ministers of finance a bank license once they left office. Despite these positive initial prospects, the project did not evolve as smoothly as he expected and he had to make considerable adjustments during its course.

Schumpeter's most important companion during his banking endeavors, which took place between 1921 and 1925, was business lawyer Gottfried Kunwald (1869–1938).[11] Kunwald, who came from an assimilated Jewish bourgeois family in Vienna, had studied law and economics at Vienna University after graduating from the prestigious Catholic "Schottengymnasium" secondary school. Kunwald had

[10] Compared to other European Countries, Austria-Hungary had an underdeveloped market for equity capital and lagged behind with respect to the number of joint-stock companies. While the number of this kind of firms increased from 653 to 3,566 in the Netherlands between 1886 and 1912 and in Italy from 583 to 1,215, Austria-Hungary only experienced weak growth from 380 to 557 (Resch and Stiefel, 2011, p. 120). In Germany, there was also a system of strong universal banks but here this sector was complemented by a well-developed stock market (Burhop et al., 2019).

[11] For Kunwald, see Herrnstadt-Steinmetz (1993); Weissensteiner (2004); Enderle-Burcel (2018, pp. 40–78).

an excellent network of contacts to the leading Christian Social Party politicians, among them Ignaz Seipel and Heinrich Mataja. Seipel, who was a Catholic prelate and professor of moral theology, was Austrian Chancellor from 1922 to 1924 and again from 1926 to 1929. Mataja, an avowed anti-Semite, was secretary of the interior from 1918 to 1919 and foreign minister from 1924 to 1926. Kunwald functioned as the most important economic advisor to Seipel, who successfully stabilized the Austrian currency in 1922. Kunwald was also a partner of art trader Würthle & Sohn, published a culture journal (*Der Merker*), and invested in a printing and publishing group formed by the Austrian banker and speculator Richard Kola before and after the First World War. Furthermore, he was a corporate attorney of the Anglo-Oesterreichische Bank, which was probably his most important single client. Kunwald shared Schumpeter's interest in monetary theory and economic development.[12]

Today, Kunwald's estate is preserved at the Austrian State Archives. The extensive files allow for detailed insight into how Kunwald and Schumpeter cooperated during the course of the Biedermann Bank project. For example, some pieces of paper scribbled in Schumpeter's handwriting show how they attempted a kind of a mind-mapping procedure to assess possible partners and persons useful to the project. These papers[13] show that they were very aware of the importance of social capital and make clear that Schumpeter's bank project was from the outset intended as an international venture. The sheets bear headings such as "Entente Leute" (people of the entente), "Journalisten" (journalists), "Bankleute" (bank people), "Politiker" (politicians), "Industrielle" (industrialists), and "Beamte" (public officials). Among the "people of the entente" one finds names like Allizé,[14] Segré,[15] and several British personalities like Lindley, Cunningham, Halstead(-Porter), Bartlett, and Phillpotts. The other categories include leading Austrian personalities. Among the bank people, Schumpeter and Kunwald listed eminent bankers such as Rothschild, Thorsch, Bisteghi, Kola, Rosenberg, Schwarz, Treichl, Sieghart, and Castiglioni.

8.3 "Österreichische Bank" (Austrian Bank Ltd)

After preliminary considerations with regard to basic structures and possible personal participation, the bank project began to take shape in early 1921. Schumpeter found several eminent industrialists and (former) aristocrats[16] as partners.

[12] Kunwald (1934).
[13] ÖStA, Bestand GK, 616-1, Box 850, File 1269 Schumpeter, sheet numbers 332 to 338.
[14] Henri Allizé (1860–1930), French diplomat.
[15] Salvatore Segré Sartorio (1859–1949), Italien entrepreneur and politician.
[16] Nobility was abolished in Austria in April 1919 by the "Adelsaufhebungsgesetz" (Law on the abolition of nobility).

Together, they applied to the Austrian Ministry of Finance and the Ministry of the Interior and Education for a license to found a new joint-stock bank named Österreichische Bank (Austrian Bank). Schumpeter's peers as applicants were the banker Rudolf Bisteghi, Baron Demetrio Economo (board member at Banca Commerciale Triestina, Assicuratione Generali and several industrial firms), Ferdinand Prince Montenuove (an aristocratic owner of a large estate), (former) count Rudolf Hoyos-Sprinzenstein (owner of a large estate), Friedrich Krassl-Traisenegg (board member at several financial and industrial firms), and Eugen Miller-Aichholz (an Austrian industrialist). The application was filed by the business lawyer of the group, Rudolf Maria Braun-Stammfest, who also played an important role in Schumpeter's industrial activities, which are analyzed in Chapter 9.

The founders stated that a quarter of the capital stock of 240 million kronen was to be raised by the concessionaires, another quarter by a Hungarian financial group, and about half by foreign, mainly English, financial circles.[17]

The two competent ministries were very reluctant to provide new bank licenses due to the mushrooming of dubious banks after the war. Since the applicants had anticipated this attitude, they attempted to provide arguments for why their firm would be different to the other new banks and would serve as a useful enrichment to the Austrian economy. It was most likely Schumpeter who penned these economic explanations.

The applicants put forward three arguments in favor of their project. First, they announced that it would attract foreign capital for the Austrian economy, above all for small and medium-sized industrial enterprises, which suffered from scarce domestic capital supply and high interest rates. The reference to the importance of credit for good industrial development bore clear "Schumpeterian" handwriting. Second, the applicants themselves conceded that too many new banks had already been founded, which might result in a banking crisis after the stabilization of the currency. Yet they emphasized that, in contrast to the majority of other banks, they did not aim to capitalize on the opportunities for speculative deals on short notice, but that they intended to enter into stable business relations with foreign capital groups. Third, they stated that their bank would provide stability and valuable financial services during the banking crisis that was to be expected due to the unsustainable business model of most of the other new banks. Thanks to their stable relations with foreign capital groups and sound business practices, they would be able to continue their function as a capital supplier to Austrian medium-sized industries while many other banks would be unable to do so.[18]

[17] ÖStA, AdR, BmF, Zl. 16,038/21, Letter of the applicants to the Federal Ministry of Finance, notice of receipt from February 19, 1921. At the same time, the application was also sent to the Federal Ministry of the Interior.

[18] ÖStA, AdR, BmF, Zl. 16,038/21, Letter of the applicants to the Federal Ministry of Finance, notice of receipt from 19 February 1921.

In an immediate reaction, the Ministry of Finance stated that the name Österreichische Bank could not be sanctioned because a firm named like that might be confused with the Austrian Central Bank. Furthermore, the responsible official in the Ministry of Finance, Dr Reissenberger, responded that he shared the view that too many new banks had already been founded and that a banking crisis was to be expected. He concluded that no further new bank concessions ought to be granted, noting in the file: "These considerations speak against the creation of new banks at all."[19]

8.4 Founding of the Biedermann joint-stock bank

Reissenberger came up with a solution for the applicants. The Ministry of Finance communicated three pre-conditions to Schumpeter for the granting of a bank license, despite the general caveats. The first was that he had to provide subscription agreements for the total nominal capital to be paid in in cash. Second, he had to provide evidence of the participation of foreign groups that would offer an "eye-popping advantage for the Austrian economy." Third, the new bank had to absorb one other weaker financial institution, whether it be a private bank or a limited liability company, in order to not increase the total number of banks. In a letter, the Ministry of Finance assured Schumpeter that he would obtain a license for this project as soon as the subscriptions for the capital were procured.[20]

Just as Schumpeter obtained his conditional approval for a license, the previously mentioned banking project Anglo-Oesterreichische Bank had progressed to the point that it could offer itself as a cooperation partner to fulfill these pre-conditions. After the war, the well-established Anglo-Oesterreichische Bank was converted from an Austrian to an English firm and renamed Anglo-Austrian Bank Ltd, due to the debt situation in London. In short, both the Anglo-Oesterreichische Bank and the Anglo-Austrian Bank Ltd were referred to as "Anglobank" in contemporary reports, as is henceforth done in this text. Meanwhile, as Anglobank was going to become an English firm, this company intended to re-establish the oldest Viennese private bank named M.L. Biedermann & Co. as a joint-stock bank, which would act as a local subsidiary.

The Anglo-Oesterreichische Bank[21] had been founded in 1863, despite resistance from local incumbents like the house of Rothschild and the largest universal bank, Oesterreichische Credit-Anstalt für Handel und Gewerbe which was also within the sphere of the Rothschilds. The Anglo-Oesterreichische Bank was a

[19] "[...] diese Erwägungen sprechen gegen die Gründung neuer Banken überhaupt." ÖStA, AdR, BmF, Zl. 16,083/21, Sektion I, Department II, Notes of Dr Reissenberger.

[20] ÖStA, AdR, BmF, Zl.16,038/21, Draft of the letter in the file.

[21] The history of the Anglo Oesterreichische Bank and the Anglo Austrian Bank Ltd is documented in Natmeßnig (1998).

British foreign bank established under the leading participation of the London-based private bank Glyn, Mills & Co. After the bank recovered from the 1873 economic crisis, it developed as an equal competitor and business partner to the other Austrian universal banks. In terms of total assets, the company was the fifth largest Viennese bank before the First World War. Business developed very well in Central and Eastern Europe. Above all, the bank was able to acquire extensive industrial holdings in Bohemia and investments into petroleum mines and refineries in Galicia[22] thanks to the successful initiatives of its leading industrial expert Hugo Schwarz, who in 1919 held some thirty-five board positions in industrial firms belonging to the group of the Anglo-Oesterreichische Bank.[23]

However, before the war the Anglobank accumulated high debts in London due to failed dealings with bills of exchange that were finally rediscounted by the Bank of England. During the years between 1914 and 1918, the branch in London was sequestered according to the Enemy Trading Act and further business activities were not allowed. After 1918, a trustee realized the assets in the United Kingdom, but after that the Bank of England still had outstanding receivables of 3 million pounds and thus became the main creditor. Austrian business was weakened due to the war and post-war inflation. In May 1920, the governor of the Bank of England, Montague Norman, suggested converting the Anglo-Oesterreichische Bank into a British firm and the receivables into shares.[24] After complicated negotiations, an agreement was reached based on which the Bank of England was allotted 53.57 percent, a syndicate of other British Banks 16.67 percent, and the former Austrian shareholders 29.79 percent of the share capital of the newly established Anglo Austrian Bank Ltd.[25] The headquarters were transferred from Vienna to London, and the Vienna location continued as a branch. Due to the majority stake of the Bank of England, Montague Norman was able to exercise direct control over the bank. The new bank was formally established in London on March 27, 1922.

The chief negotiator of the Austrian group of former shareholders was Dr Wilhelm Rosenberg, a board member of the old Anglo-Oesterreichische Bank. During the complicated procedures, he gained Norman's full trust. Sir Herbert Lawrence, a representative of the British Bank syndicate, became president of the board of the new company, and Norman appointed his confidant, Michael Spencer-Smith, vice president. Other British board members were Peter Bark (former minister of finance in Russia), Ernest W. H. Barry, Sir Ernest Maes Harvey, Sir John Gordon Nairne, Sir Henry Strakosch, and George Malcolm Young. In addition to these, five managers of the former Anglo-Oesterreichische Bank became members of

[22] After some military conflicts, which followed the First World War, Galicia became a part of Poland in the early 1920s.

[23] *Compass*, Vols 2 and 3, 1919, p. 449.

[24] Natmeßnig (1998, pp. 158–235); *Compass*, Vol. 1, 1924, p. 288.

[25] These figures are given in Natmeßnig (1998, p. 183).

the new board: Wilhelm Rosenberg, Hugo Schwarz, Max Chevalier de Anhauch, Paul Engel, Gustav Korner, and Hans Simon. The management committee of the Viennese branch was composed of Rosenberg, Engel, Korner, Schwarz, Simon, and George Malcolm Young, whom the Austrians regarded as a local overseer of Norman.

At the same time, the Czechoslovak assets of the former Anglo-Oesterreichische Bank, which mainly consisted of valuable industrial holdings, had to be transferred to a separate bank in Prague due to specific national economic laws in that country. Yet the Anglo Austrian Bank Ltd kept 100 percent of the shares of the newly founded Anglo-Československá Banka.[26]

While the conversion of the Austrian Anglo-Oesterreichische Bank into the British Anglo-Austrian Bank Ltd was under way in 1921, the Viennese management of the bank attempted to acquire a future allied company in Austria, which was to be run in the local currency and remain somewhat more distant from the control of London. In this context, Rosenberg thought of the Biedermann Bank, because close contacts already existed with this company.

M.L. Biedermann & Co., founded in 1792 by Michael Lazar Biedermann, was the oldest active private bank in Vienna. The institution had played an important role in the financial history of Vienna since the Napoleonic wars. Many customer families, among them members of the Austrian and Bavarian high nobility, had relations to the bank that dated back several generations. During the first half of the nineteenth century, the bank was successful in trade with raw wool and cooperated with other banks such as the Viennese Rothschilds in dealings that served the financial needs of the Austrian state. These activities allowed for establishing firm relations with the London capital market. In 1852, Johann Klein joined the company. He worked his way up to become an authorized signatory and partner and contributed to the bank's further successful development. Yet from the 1850s onward, the private banks gradually lost importance amidst the establishment of new universal banks. During and after the war, the bank was further weakened economically.[27]

In 1918, the open partners Robert Biedermann Baron of Turony and Johann Klein withdrew into private life and Arthur Klein became the only fully liable partner. Klein hired a new authorized officer, Isidor Modern, and the bank set up a branch in Budapest to maintain its extensive business relations with Hungary.[28]

[26] In general, the Czechoslovak government insisted, due to nationalist economic laws, that all banks had to have a majority of domestic shareholders. Yet, the Anglo Austrian bank obtained an exception, as it assisted in the placement of a Czechoslovakian bond in London together with the Bank of England (Natmeßnig, 1998, pp. 205–30).

[27] ÖStA, AdR, Bankkommission, Box 21, File 7, Biedermann Bank, Templates to the I. Ordinary General Assembly of M.L. Biedermann & Co. Bankaktiengesellschaft, October 17, 1922, p. 9; Allen (1991, p. 185).

[28] *Neue Freie Presse*, January 5, 1919, p. 13; February 10, 1921, p. 12; *Zentralblatt*, 1919, p. 71.

At the same time, several Members of the Biedermann and Klein families were registered as limited partners.

As a further limited partner, the firm Ofenheim & Co. got involved.[29] This company in turn was linked with Anglo-Oesterreichische Bank, which seems to have partially financed the silent partners' contributions.[30] Ofenheim & Co. was a renowned enterprise in the petroleum and private banking businesses in the Austrian-Hungarian Monarchy and the United Kingdom, with offices in Vienna and London.[31] Viktor Ofenheim von Ponteuxin had been a pioneer of Austrian railway construction from the 1850s to the early 1870s and had managed to establish close contacts with British investors for the financing of these projects. He withdrew from the railway business after conflicts with the government and several court cases. His son Wilhelm Ofenheim von Ponteuxin invested in the oil industry and acquired several patents for petroleum technology during the last quarter of the nineteenth century.[32] The Ofenheim group participated in several petroleum firms, among others the Internationale Petroleum AG, Budapest, and Anglo-Galician Oil Company Ltd, London, which ran oil mines and refineries in Galicia, the easternmost province of the Austrian half of the Habsburg Empire. Ofenheim and the Biedermann Family also had stakes in the Aktiengesellschaft für österreichische Mineralölprodukte in Vienna. From 1904 to 1906, the Anglo-Galician Oil Company was liquidated and replaced by the Galizische Naphta-Aktiengesellschaft "Galicia," again with Ofenheim and other Austrian and British investors as shareholders.

Biedermann's new limited partners made it possible to overcome current financial shortages, but the bank needed further restructuring to secure its future prospects. The main interested groups—the families Klein and Biedermann, Ofenheim & Co. and the Anglo-Oesterreichische Bank—decided to convert the firm into a joint-stock bank, but they did not have the necessary official authorization to do so. In this situation the Schumpeter group, in possession of the precious license, joined forces with the Biedermann group, which could provide for underwriters required to make sure the payment of the nominal capital in cash.

[29] Robert Freiherr von Biedermann, Johann Klein, Rudolf Freiherr von Biedermann, Gräfin Lucie von Seher-Thoss née Biedermann, and Reichsgräfin Stefanie von Attems-Petzenstein, née Freiin Biedermann von Turony held silent partnerships to the amount of 100,000 kronen, and Ofenheim & Co. to the amount of 200,000 kronen. ÖStA, Bestand GK, 616–1, Box 756, File 236, Excerpt from the Commercial Register of Companies of the Commercial Court in Vienna, M.L. Biedermann & Co.; Bankierbuch (list of banks and bankers) in *Compass*, Vol. 1, 1920, p. 407; *Neue Freie Presse*, June 23, 1921; Stolper (1994, p. 306).

[30] ÖStA, Bestand GK, 616–1, Box 756, File 236, Excerpt from the Commercial Register for Companies of the Commercial Court in Vienna, Volume II, p. 572, M.L. Biedermann & Co.; and Box 756, File 241, Letter concept Kunwald to the Federal Chancellery, June 19, 1924, p. 9.

[31] Vienna IV, Gußhausstraße 3 and London, 28 Bishopsgate Street. Österreichischer Zentralkataster 1908, Vol. 1, Wien, Vienna 1908, p. 185.

[32] Schlegel (1987); ÖBL, Vol. 7, 1977, p. 215.

Kunwald, who was in touch with both groups, probably set up the collaboration. In February 1921, General Council (Generalrat) Hugo Schwarz proposed having the Biedermann group as underwriters for Schumpeter's banking project.[33]

On March 25, 1921, Schumpeter appeared in person at the Federal Ministry of Finance to inform director general (*Sektionschef*) Dr Pollák that his banking project had been amended in accordance with the guidelines issued by the ministry, and that the applicants now intended to convert M.L. Biedermann & Co. into a joint-stock bank. In a letter issued the same day, the minister of finance officially notified Schumpeter that he would grant a definitive bank licence as soon as the subscription declarations for the entire share capital had been submitted.[34]

On April 6, Schumpeter, Rosenberg, Klein, and Kunwald held a meeting at Kunwald's office, during which they drew up a memorandum outlining the main provisions for their cooperation.[35] Schumpeter's aim was not to submit a list of underwriters other than that agreed with the Biedermann group (Biedermann Bank and Anglo-Oesterreichische Bank). The Biedermann group and Schumpeter agreed on a list of underwriters, which consisted of long-term-committed founders and some interim financiers. After the formal incorporation, the new joint-stock bank attempted to take over the business of the old Biedermann private bank, while the owners of these assets would use the means they were getting to acquire the shares, which were temporarily paid in by the interim financiers. As mentioned above, it was intended that a syndicate dominated by the Anglo-Oesterreichische Bank would ultimately emerge as a majority shareholder.

In the memorandum, Schumpeter and Kunwald were entitled to 120,000 shares in the new bank and the old, private Biedermann Bank agreed to grant them a low-interest loan for this investment. In order to secure a strong position for the Anglo-Oesterreichische Bank, shares with a nominal value of at least 100 million kronen, underwritten by Biedermann Bank and Ofenheim & Co., were to be transferred to a syndicate led by Anglobank.

Furthermore, the old Biedermann private bank agreed to act in accordance with Schumpeter in setting up the new bank and appointing the managers and staff. They had already agreed on a provisional list of board members and the executive committee of the new Biedermann joint-stock bank. At this stage, they envisaged appointing Schumpeter, Klein, Kunwald, Modern, Rosenberg, and Schwarz as executives. Further appointments to leading positions were regulated, in particular stating that Schumpeter was to become president and Kunwald vice president of the board for at least five years. Both would receive an annual salary of 600,000 kronen. Schumpeter was to also obtain an "adequate presidential room" and a

[33] ÖStA, Bestand GK, 616–1, Box 756, File 236, Memorandum from April 6, 1921.

[34] ÖStA, AdR, BMF, Zl. 16,038/21, Note in the file.

[35] Two drafts of this memorandum are handed down in ÖStA, Bestand GK, 616–1, Box 756, File 236 and Box 757, File 247.

Table 8.1 Underwriters of M.L. Biedermann & Co., Bankaktiengesellschaft

Underwriters	Amount (000,000 kronen)	% of all shares
M.L. Biedermann & Co. in its own name	109	45.4
M.L. Biedermann & Co. signs on power of attorney for S. Japhet & Co. Ltd, London	9	3.8
Ofenheim & Co. in its own name	20	8.3
Ofenheim & Co. signs on power of attorney for Albert McNamara, an industrialist in Shrivenham	18	7.5
Ofenheim & Co. signs on power of attorney for Cyril Butler-Kendall, an industrialist in London	18	7.5
Ofenheim & Co. signs on power of attorney for George Wilson, an industrialist in Shrivenham	18	7.5
Dr Joseph Schumpeter	48	20.0
Total	240	100.0

Source: ÖStA, AdR, BMF, Zl. 34,021/21, duplicate in the file.

two-horse carriage with a spare horse, while Kunwald would receive a two-horse carriage without a spare horse.

In mid-April 1921, together with Schumpeter, the companies M.L. Biedermann & Co. and Ofenheim & Co. formally submitted an application to the Ministry of Finance and the Ministry of the Interior to obtain a licence for the establishment of "Bankhaus M. L. Biedermann & Co., Aktiengesellschaft."[36] As previously agreed, the share capital should amount to 240 million kronen. M.L. Biedermann & Co., Schumpeter and friends, Ofenheim, the British financier R.S. Colby, the petroleum entrepreneurs Sir Kandle and Ellen, and the London broker firm Japhet were named as underwriters.

Less inflow of foreign capital was planned than in the original project, as firms like Biedermann and Ofenheim would ensure the adequate soundness and financial strength of the applicants. The contributions by the various formal founders are detailed in Table 8.1.[37]

8.5 Distribution of capital shares

The founding of M.L. Biedermann & Co., Bankaktiengesellschaft took place on July 16, 1921.[38] Immediately thereafter, the business of the old Biedermann Bank was taken over and this company entered liquidation. While with respect

[36] ÖStA, AdR, BMF, Zl. 16,038/21, Letter from Braun-Stammfest, which arrived at the ministries on April 15, 1921.

[37] ÖStA, AdR, BMF, Zl. 34,021/21, copy of the original letter.

[38] Stolper (1994, p. 306).

to the authorities the abovementioned underwriters had to formally pay for the shares, their actual placement was taken over by a syndicate organized by the Anglo-Oesterreichische Bank. The activities of this syndicate are of particular interest, as they show how the promoters tried to realize their promoters' profits.

In addition, the placement of the shares determined the balance of power in the supervisory bodies of the new bank. In the course of these transactions, the old M.L. Biedermann & Co. private bank received 125,000 shares with a total nominal value of 50 million kronen (20.8%) for the transfer of its business, which became the property of Arthur Klein and the other owners during the liquidation of the firm. The Anglo-Oesterreichische Bank directly acquired 17,500 shares with a nominal value of 7 million kronen (0.9%). The remaining 457,500 shares with a nominal value of 183 million kronen (76.3%) were taken over by a syndicate led by Anglobank. This consortium intended to sell 275,000 shares with a nominal value of 110 million kronen on the market and block the rest (182,500 shares, 73 million kronen, 30.4%) for eight years on behalf of the syndicate management in order to ensure their control over the bank. The largest participants in the syndicate are shown in Table 8.2.

The syndicate collected 192.15 million kronen from its members to acquire a total of 457,500 shares. By the time it settled its accounts in April 1922, it had increased the value of its assets to 304.47 million kronen by marketing 275,000 shares, with all expenses and fees for the syndicate and the formal underwriters mentioned above deducted. The gross assets before payment of various fees had mounted to almost 350 million kronen and the syndicate had kept 182,500 shares, as mentioned above, which were probably still booked at their purchase price. The reported increase in assets must therefore have been achieved by marketing the 275,000 shares that had been sold at a total price of some 273 million kronen or around 990 kronen per share. Given this market price, the value of the 182,500

Table 8.2 The ten largest participants of the first Biedermann syndicate

Name	No. of shares	% of all shares
Klein, Arthur	150,000	25.0
Anglobank Vienna	81,000	13.5
Modern, Isidor	46,000	7.7
Seherr-Thoss, Lucy, née Biedermann	30,000	5.0
Arons & Walter, Germany	15,000	2.5
Storfer, Bernhard	13,725	2.3
Halporn, Wilhelm	12,150	2.0
Ofenheim & Co.	10,000	1.7
Anglobank Czernowitz	9,150	1.5
Klein, Johann	8,775	1.5

Source: Calculated after ÖStA, Bestand GK 616–1, Box 757, File 247, sheet 3, List I "Syndicat."

shares blocked by the syndicate had risen by some 104 million kronen or 134 percent. All in all, the total value of the syndicate had risen from paid-in 192.15 million kronen to around 407.5 million kronen, which meant a gain of around 210 percent. However, in 1921 inflation had accelerated to a rate of around 230 percent, causing a slight loss in real terms. At least the investors had managed to preserve most of their real monetary values during this period of depreciation and the remaining stock of 182,500 shares allowed hope for further value increases.[39]

The takeover of the old Biedermann Bank and the activities of the syndicate determined the initial owner structure of the new Biedermann joint-stock bank. Very clearly, the former principal owner Arthur Klein held the largest share package by far, and the Anglo-Oesterreichische Bank had a strong voice through its own share-holding and control over the blocked syndicate shares.

According to the agreement from April 6, 1921, Schumpeter and Kunwald would have been entitled to buy 120,000 shares, financed by a cheap loan from the old Biedermann Bank. However, while the syndicate was operating, the plans were amended to the effect that they would receive around 15 million kronen out of the syndicate's profits, but would not participate as shareholders. According to the Austrian Central Bank's online calculator for historical Austrian currencies,[40] in late 1921, this payment, which was booked under fees, corresponded to a current value (2018) of around 500,000 euros. Thus, the Biedermann project had started off very well for Schumpeter: He received a substantial promoter's profit and assumed the well-paid position of the bank's president, which was associated with prestige and promised to provide a basis for further profitable business.

The business development of both the Anglobank and the Biedermann Bank started very hesitantly after their reconstruction in 1921/2. The industrial assets of the Anglobank were adversely affected by the consequences of the war and the disintegration of the former monarchy and, beyond this, business development was hampered by an internal cultural conflict resulting from the shift of control from Vienna to London. The organization had a strong business tradition as a leading Viennese universal bank with solid industry relations. Board member Hugo Schwarz had been the leading industry expert in the "old" Anglo-Oesterreichische Bank, with strong ties to manufacturing firms in Bohemia and the petroleum business in Galicia. At the same time, the new English rulers, above all Montagu Norman, intended to take a different course of business. In general, as already mentioned in Chapter 4, "English banking" was more orientated toward short-term business, finance of trade, and a strong focus on liquidity.[41] In contrast, traditional "Continental banking" meant investing in industrial relations and

[39] ÖStA, Bestand GK 616–1, Box 757, File 247, Biedermann-Syndikat I.

[40] https://www.oenb.at/docroot/inflationscockpit/waehrungsrechner.html (December 5, 2019).

[41] For the traditions of "English banking," but also for more differentiated views, see for example, Cottrell (1994, pp. 1137–61); Collins (2012, pp. 92–122); Michie (2016, pp. 16–124); or Voth (2018, pp. 173–93).

even relevant share holdings of related industrial firms to maintain a large bank-industry group. This strategy tied up considerable resources and therefore stood in contrast to the liquidity orientation. Furthermore, all steps taken by Viennese managers had to be approved by London headquarters, which rendered business operations very cumbersome and hampered quick decisions.

Another source of conflict came from different cultures of corporate governance and employer-employee relations. In Austrian banks, the functionaries usually had great freedom to own trades and businesses, which often allowed for advantageous dealings, in some cases through insider knowledge. The British owners stopped this type of activity. Moreover, in view of the weakened business situation, they granted lower compensation than the other Viennese banks. Consequently, some key employees started to look for other jobs. Very soon there were rumours in the local press that even certain board members, such as Schwarz, were prepared to move to other banks.[42]

Due to various start-up difficulties, the bank was not able to present its 1922 balance before the end of September 1923 and had to announce disappointing results. The always well-informed business magazine *Der österreichische Volkswirt* (*The Austrian Economist*) commented that the Anglobank had failed to participate in the "extraordinary economic activity of Austrian banks in recent years." They emphasized that "the confidence of the London administration did not turn to all Austrian board members and a number of personal crises arose from this." Aside from the weak development in Austria, heavy losses of the Anglo-Československá Banka contributed to the weak result. A further capital injection of 400,000 pounds, planned from the outset, had only been carried out toward the end of 1922 against priority shares and predominantly invested in British Treasury bills. This had therefore also not benefited Continental European business. Overall, the bank paid a 6 percent dividend on preference shares, which mainly belonged to British investors, and a zero dividend on the other shares.[43]

As a consequence of the cultural conflict, in some cases the "Austrians" were inclined to carry out business without informing London headquarters. For example, insiders realized that investments in other local banks, above all in the Internationale Handelsbank and Austro-Holländische Bank, were made at the initiative of Schwarz while Rosenberg was in London for consultations.[44] Both of

[42] See, for example, *Die Börse*, May 25, 1922, p. 5; *Der Montag*, January 22, 1923, p. 5; *Neues Wiener Journal*, March 14, 1923, p. 11; *Die Bilanzen*, August 8, 1925, p. 345f.

[43] *Die Bilanzen* (Supplement to *Der österreichische Volkswirt*), August 8, 1925, p. 345f. Wolfgang F. Stolper informed us in a letter from July 21, 1999 that his father Gustav Stolper wrote these balance sheet reviews of Biedermannbank since at the time he was an editor of *Der österreichische Volkswirt*. Due to his close personal friendship with Schumpeter they were always written in a friendly and polite manner, even in times when the bank suffered of severe economic problems.

[44] ÖStA, Bestand GK, 616–1, Box 756, File 241, Kunwald to Federal Chancellors Office, letter concept, June 17, 1924.

these investments will be analyzed in further detail later, because they were carried out together with the Biedermann Bank.

Since the Anglo-Austrian Bank Ltd was an influential shareholder of the Biedermann Bank, the structural problems also affected this bank. In a similar manner to the Anglobank, the Biedermann Bank also got off to a slow start.

The following analysis reveals the structure of the groupings that influenced the Biedermann Bank by elucidating the composition of the boards and other indications of the weighting ratios among the shareholder groups.

After the first syndicate had placed the shares and established an owner structure under predominance of the Anglobank and Arthur Klein, two further share issues took place around the turn of 1921/2 and September/October 1922, which slightly extended the group of firms and persons with a voice in the Biedermann Bank. Initially, nominal capital was raised from 240 to 500 million kronen, and in a second step to 1 billion kronen. During this phase, in addition to Arons & Walter, other eminent investors from Germany were won for the project, including the private bank Gebrüder Arnhold in Dresden and Julius Hepner, a formerly Russian financier who now acted from Berlin and Frankfurt am Main, in several cases together with Gebrüder Arnhold. Gebrüder Arnhold was among the five biggest German private banks during the early 1920s and maintained widely ramified industrial relations. They owned holding companies for brewing industries, porcelain industries, and electrical industries, among others.[45] Like the old Biedermann Bank, they had established strong industrial relations and could be seen as partners for similar future business relationships.

Biedermann shares were not yet listed at the Vienna Stock Exchange but traded as "Exoten" (exotic values) on informal private markets. Some Viennese private banks periodically published price lists of shares that were not traded on the stock exchange. According to one such list, named "Kursblatt exotischer Wertpapiere" (price sheet of exotic securities), prices for shares with a nominal value of 400 kronen rose to 700 kronen in September 1921 and to 1,200 kronen in September 1922.[46] This allowed the major shareholders to carry out the two capital increases in which they allocated large blocks of shares to themselves at prices somewhat below market value, sold chunks of these securities in syndicates, and retained control of the bank with the blocks of shares they themselves held.

The first capital increase from 240 to 500 million kronen was decided at an extraordinary general meeting on December 20, 1921. Existing shareholders were entitled to purchase 400,000 shares at 700 kronen each, and the remaining 250,000 shares went to a consortium led by Anglobank and managed by Kunwald. The consortium sold shares until the profits were sufficient to give the remaining shares to members free of charge. When the consortium was liquidated in March 1922,

[45] Köhler (2008, p. 207f).
[46] Quoted after *Compass*, Vol. 1, 1923, p. 387.

the members obtained 143,750 shares. The free shares were blocked to secure common control over the bank. Beyond consortium participation, many investors used their subscription rights based on their previous shareholding from the first issue and bought further shares at prices below the present market value.

The third share issue took place in the same manner after September 22, 1922. This time 1.25 million new shares of 400 kronen each were issued. The existing shareholders were entitled to purchase 625,000 shares at 1,200 kronen each, and a syndicate took the same amount. When this consortium settled its accounts in March 1923, the participants received a total of 488,802 shares, financed from the sale of 136,198 shares. The marketing of this issue was eased by the fact that the stocks were formally listed at the Vienna Stock Exchange on November 11, 1922. The initial quotation was made at a price of 4,000 kronen. Again, some of the syndicate members also exercised subscription rights as shareholders. According to a list drawn up in 1923, specific large shareholders acquired major chunks of the second and third issue.

Table 8.3 shows that the fourteen selected investors together acquired more than 40 percent of the new shares of the second and nearly 49 percent of the third issue. Most of them had already participated significantly in the first share issue and together they controlled the company, especially since small shareholders hardly participated in the general meetings. The composition of shareholders again shows the strong position of the Anglobank with its own shareholdings and investments by Rosenberg. At the same time, the former major owners of the Biedermann private bank, the Klein and Biedermann families, still held strong positions. In addition to these shareholders, the German investors (Gebrüder Arnhold, Arons & Walter) and leading Biedermann functionaries (Schumpeter, Kunwald, Modern, the Halporn brothers, and Treichl) must have had a relevant say in the bank. While Anglobank stood for prudent "English banking," which focused on liquidity and short-term business, all other major investors were more likely oriented toward "Schumpeterian banking," which favored investment in industries, start-ups, and innovations and aimed to seize opportunities agilely. Without a doubt the same contradictions of English *vs* Continental banking existed among the Biedermann shareholders as existed within the Anglobank itself.

The balance of powers resulting from the acquisition of shares was also reflected in the composition of the Biedermann Bank board. Josef Schumpeter was president, with former majority owner Arthur Klein and Gottfried Kunwald acting as vice presidents. The Biedermann and Klein families were further represented by Baron Elek Biedermann von Turony and Gräfin Lucy Seherr-Thoss née Biedermann, and the German banks by Eugen Schiff (Arons & Walter), Dr Heinrich Arnhold (Gebr. Arnhold), and Julius Hepner.

Further members of the board from the start were Count Felix Gustave Bruselle, Dr Josef (Count) Ezdorf, Bernhard Janowitzer, Josef Kraus, Baron Otto Lindenfels-Thumsenreuth, Isidor Modern, and Dr Hans Scanavi. Until the end of

Table 8.3 Biedermann syndicate: important shareholdings of the second and third issue in 1923

Name	2nd issue (%)	3rd issue (%)	Remarks
Anglo Austrian Bank Ltd, Vienna Branch	10.7	7.7	Transformed from Anglo-Oesterreichische Bank ("Anglobank") in March 1922
Hepner Julius, Berlin, Frankfurt am Main	7.2	6.6	Russian businessman, speculative dealings with Bankhaus Gebrüder Arnhold
Gebrüder Arnhold, Dresden and Berlin	7.0	3.6	Eminent German private bank with holding companies for brewing, porcelain, and electrical industries, etc.
Klein, Arthur, vice president	4.6	9.7	Former major owner of M.L. Biedermann & Co.
Seher-Thoss, Lucy Gräfin, Budapest	2.2	1.7	Member of the Biedermann family
Schumpeter, Josef	1.4	2.8	President of Biedermann Bank
Kunwald, Gottfried	1.1	2.7	Vice president of Biedermann Bank
Modern, Isidor	1.0	6.7	Director of Biedermann Bank
Schwarz, Hugo	1.0	2.6	Leading industrial expert of Anglobank
Rosenberg, Wilhelm (estate)	1.0	0.9	Leading manager of the Viennese branch of Anglobank
Arons & Walter, Berlin	1.0	0.2	Eminent private Bank in Berlin, lead by Barthold Arons, Hermann Walter and Walter Schiff
Halporn, Paul	1.0	1.2	Director of Biedermann Bank
Halporn, Wilhelm	1.0	1.2	Director of Biedermann Bank
Treichl, Alfred	–	1.2	Moved from Anglobank to Biedermann Bank in late 1922
Total	40.2	48.8	

Note: Names revised and completed.

Source: ÖStA, Bestand GK, 616–1, Box 756, File 240, General Assembly of Biedermann Bank 1923, List of blocked Biedermann shares, 2nd and 3rd issues.

1921, four leading personalities of the Anglobank, Dr Wilhelm Rosenberg, Max Cavaler de Anhauch, Paul Engel, and Hugo Schwarz joined the board. In addition, the following investors became board members before the end of 1921: Dr Rudolf Maria Braun-Stammfest, Max Edlauer, Josef Fischl, and Berthold Storfer. Edlauer's firm Schuch Edlauer was the owner of the house at Plankengasse 3 in Vienna, which was acquired by the Biedermann Bank in 1921 as the new company headquarters. A seat on the board seems to have been part of the deal.[47] Storfer was a very active businessman who invested in a broad range of banking and trade ventures in Vienna and Central and south-eastern Europe.[48]

It is obvious that Schumpeter, the German bankers, Kunwald, Storfer, and several others stood for Continental banking. As head of the Viennese branch of the Anglobank and a confidant of Norman, Rosenberg seems to have acted as a kind of warden for London, while Schwarz and to a lesser degree Anhauch represented the dissidents against English banking in the Anglobank.

The Biedermann board of directors, which was responsible for operative business, originally consisted of Modern and the Halporn brothers. Around the turn of 1922/3, Schumpeter, Klein, and Kunwald also became directors. During 1922, the Anglobank transferred some of its personnel to the Biedermann Bank. In the course of this transaction, Alfred Treichl was appointed as a further director. These actions temporarily aggravated the relations between the "Anglobank people" and the incumbent Biedermann bankers. In July 1922, although physically handicapped and therefore barely able to travel, vice president Kunwald had to go to the spa town of Bad Gastein, where director Modern was on holiday, to convince him to accept Treichl's appointment and cooperate with him. They agreed that Modern would not be subordinate to Treichl, that he would remain responsible for stock market dealings and placements of shares, that relevant matters would be decided among the colleagues, and that no one would be allowed to enact "faits accomplits". Kunwald wrote to Anglobank board member Simon: "The fact that I drove two nights to talk to him, of course, made a big impression on him. I don't think it would have gone as smoothly without that outfit."[49]

This antagonistic power constellation between "English" and "Continental" bankers left its traces in the strategic orientation of the bank, as documented in several of the enterprise's publications. The company statutes were mainly written to the liking of Schumpeter's vision. They were probably an adapted version of first drafts penned by himself and friends for the original "Österreichische Bank" project. The objectives of the company were defined as the acquisition of the former firm M.L. Biedermann & Co. and the continuation of this business, with the aim of focusing on commerce, finance, and real estate. Above all, the aim of the bank should be

[47] *Die Börse*, June 1, 1922, p. 12. [48] Anderl (2012).

[49] ÖStA, Bestand GK, 616–1, Box 851, File 1270, Dr. Simon, Letter from Kunwald to Simon, July 28, 1922.

> to open the international monetary market for the Austrian medium-sized industry, to cultivate and renew the economic relations of those industries with the successor states of the Habsburg Empire and the Balkans and to develop any production possibilities of the Austrian small and medium-sized industries.[50]

In contrast, the company report for 1922 defined the fundamental business principles in a way that was more in tune with "English banking". It was said that the intention of the founders was

> not the incorporation of a new bank but of a banking house based on stocks, a joint stock company which would take ownership of 130 years of trust in the private Biedermann Bank as the most precious possession, and would look after this possession in a new way to develop it further as custodian of entrusted fortunes as caretaker of the customers and as a reliable indispensable intermediary on the capital market.

Furthermore, "unconditional liquidity in an amount which exceeds the extent of practices of continental banking" was emphasized as the most important prerequisite for fulfilling the role of a "real and true banker who deserves this honourable title."[51]

8.6 Business development in 1921 and 1922

In practice, the Biedermann Bank's business only managed to develop very hesitantly on the basis of these contradictory strategies. As mentioned above, in August 1921 the newly founded firm bought a new business location in the city of Vienna. The bank's management seems to have underestimated the difficulties of the adaption of the bank's operations. Delays in the renovation and repair of the house hampered business activities for several months.[52] In 1922, the first full year of business activities, the bank was affected by hyperinflation up to September, as well as the subsequent stabilization of the Austrian currency. An inflation rate of more than 3,000 percent meant that all monetary values shrank to less than a thirtieth.

[50] ÖStA, AdR, BmF, Bankkommission, Box 21, File 7, Statutes of M.L. Biedermann & Co., Bankaktiengesellschaft in Wien, Vienna 1921, p. 4.

[51] ÖStA, AdR, BmF, Bankkommission, Box 21, File 7, Templates to the Second ordinary General Assembly of M.L. Biedermann & Co., Bankaktiengesellschaft, p. 9.

[52] ÖStA, AdR, BmF, Bankkommission, Box 21, File 7, Templates to the first ordinary General Assembly of M.L. Biedermann & Co., Bankaktiengesellschaft, p. 10f.

A look at the balance sheets of Biedermann Bank shows that the institution was not able to keep pace with this development. While the monetary devaluation factor was around thirty, the total balance sheet sum grew by only a factor of ten from 4 billion kronen at the end of the business year 1921 to 42.6 billion kronen in 1922. Due to the two capital increases mentioned above, the nominal value of shares increased from 0.24 to 1 billion kronen, and a capital reserve of 0.9 billion kronen was formed. Furthermore, according to the business reports, retained earnings amounted to 0.01 and 2.28 billion kronen in the two consecutive years. Adding up these figures reveals that the equity component rose from 6.3 to 9.8 percent. In real terms, the balance sheet total shrank to one-third and equity diminished by 42 percent, despite the two capital increases.

Although the accounting system used during the first half of the twentieth century did not meet present standards, the asset structure given in the balance sheets allows for some insight into the structure of business development. In 1922, around 58 percent of the means were invested in debtors and 29 percent in bank deposits. The astonishingly high share probably reflects the orientation toward high liquidity in accordance with "English banking". Even if the holdings of foreign currency counteracted the inflation in Austria, it is doubtful that bank deposits were a profitable asset category during hyperinflation. Less than three-fifths of assets were held as outstanding debts. This category included the debts of companies with solid business relations with the bank, and the bank to a certain degree likely financed speculative customer dealings with securities as collateral. Fewer than 13 percent of the assets were either securities held by the bank or participations in syndications and capital contributions. These business areas comprised investment banking activities, such as participation in capital increases and bond issues, as well as own investments in other firms. Biedermann Bank carried out some transactions on its own and some together with the Anglobank. Dealings in Germany mostly came through cooperation with Bankhaus Arnhold (Dresden, Berlin).

Biedermann Bank also invested in several subsidiary financial firms. The most important of these was the Internationale Handelsbank in Vienna (International Trading Bank). Together with Biedermann Bank, Anglobank became the biggest shareholders in the course of a capital increase of this bank during the second half of 1921. Thereafter, Internationale Handelsbank and Biedermann Bank, together with the Landwirtschaftsgesellschaft (an organization of formerly noble agrarians) and a group of Dutch investors, converted a small bank in need of restructuring into Austro-Holländische Bank (Austrian-Dutch Bank). Furthermore, Biedermann Bank participated in the private bank Fischer, Krása & Cie (Prague) with a limited partnership contribution, and the branch of the Biedermann Bank in Budapest was converted into an autonomous limited partnership named Biedermann & Co. Bankkommanditgesellschaft in cooperation with the Anglobank.

Finally, in October 1922, as the last firm of the group, the Austrian Branch of the Hungarian Credit and Intermediary Bank (Hitel- és Közvetitö bank r. t.) was converted into Wiener Handelskreditbank A. G. by the Anglobank together with Biedermann Bank.[53] Although this bank was not explicitly mentioned as a related firm in the company reports, it is clear that the company belonged to the surrounding sphere, since several functionaries—among them Ezdorf, Klein, Kunwald, and Schumpeter—were on both of the company boards.[54]

During the years 1921 and 1922, Biedermann Bank participated in a moderate number of equity transactions, among others the capital increases of three Austrian banks, two German banks, and several industrial firms. Among the banks were Wiener Bankverein and Deutsche Bank. Until the end of 1922, the industrial group, which was related to Biedermann Bank comprised around ten Austrian, three Hungarian, and four German firms. The range of companies extended from modern businesses as electricity suppliers in Austria and Germany and producers of new materials (a factory for synthetic leather in Saxony) to firms which bet on import substitution in the successor states of the former Habsburg Empire (a soap factory in Austria and factories for cigarette paper in Hungary and Austria) and firms without any distinctive innovative perspectives.[55]

Some industrial relations dated back to the era of the former private Biedermann Bank (e.g., the Eos works for shipbuilding, Schubert special machines, and the Rhombus publishing house in Vienna), some firms were converted into joint-stock companies in cooperation with the Anglobank (e.g., Universale Bau AG, the Hofmann & Czerny piano factory and the Oscar Schubert factory for special machines), and some investment relations were established thanks to the German shareholder Gebrüder Arnhold (e.g., Sachsenwerk Licht und Kraft-AG, Deutsche Kunstleder AG, Kötitz, Sachsonia, Bank für Brauindustrie AG Berlin, Deutsche Wasserkraft, and Elektro AG). Finally, a participation in the capital increase of "Iriag" Internationale Rohölindustrie AG was carried out together with Internationale Handelsbank.

All in all, the industrial group related to Biedermann Bank consisted of around fifteen to twenty small and medium-sized industrial companies.[56] The share of capital contributions and syndicate participations shows that the volume of equity

[53] *Compass*, Vol. 1, 1923, pp. 390 and 1373.

[54] *Compass*, Vol. 1, 1923, pp. 387 and 1373.

[55] Among the companies that relied on import substitution were "Riva" Parfumerie & Seifenindustrie AG (Perfumery and soap industry), Altesse Gaza AG, Austria, and Samum Altesse Zigarettenhülsen und Papierfabrik, Austria and Hungary (Factories for cigarette paper). Examples of firms with no perceivable innovative approach were "Mefra" AG für Garnerzeugung, Vienna, a traditional cotton mill, "Hungaria" Hutstumpen- und Hutfabrik AG (factory for hats and hat bodies), Hungary, or Ungarische Salamifabrik AG (factory for Hungarian salami), Budapest. ÖStA, AdR, BmF, Bankkommission, Box 21, File 7, Templates to the second ordinary General Assembly of M.L. Biedermann & Co., Bankaktiengesellschaft, p. 13f.

[56] ÖStA, AdR, BmF, Bankkommission, Box 21, Templates to the third ordinary General Assembly of M.L. Biedermann & Co., Bankaktiengesellschaft, September 27, 1924; *Compass*, Vol. 1, 1924, p. 318.

Table 8.4 Annual accounts of Biedermann Bank from 1921 to 1925

Accounts	1921 Billion kronen	in %	1922 Billion kronen	in %	1923 Billion kronen	in %	1924 Billion kronen	in %	1925 Billion kronen	in %
Balance sheet total	4.027	100.0	42.621	100.0	264.247	100.0	135.896	100.0	118.231	100.0
Liabilities										
Shares (nominal)	0.240	6.0	1.000	2.3	2.500	0.9	2.500	1.8	6.250	5.3
Agio fund and reserves	0.000	–	0.947	2.2	33.836	12.8	4.836	3.6	6.250	5.3
Creditors and deposits	3.710	92.1	37.148	87.2	218.302	82.6	127.896	94.1	105.548	89.3
Profit	0.077	1.9	3.525	8.3	9.609	3.6	0.664	0.5	0.182	0.2
Assets										
Cash	0.025	0.6	0.506	1.2	3.367	1.3	3.455	2.5	2.130	1.8
Real estate	0.024	0.6	–	0.0	0.000	0.0	3.500	2.6	7.885	6.7
Securities	0.237	5.9	3.000	7.0	16.230	6.1	9.017	6.6	4.166	3.5
Syndicates and capital contributions	0.201	5.0	2.380	5.6	16.629	6.3	14.212	10.5	0.000	0.0
Debtors (advances on securities included)	3.540	87.9	24.524	57.5	203.765	77.1	84.756	62.4	89.570	75.8
Bank balance	–	–	12.210	28.6	13.871	5.2	11.497	8.5	4.282	3.6
Bills of exchange	–	–	–	–	10.386	3.9	9.458	7.0	10.199	8.6

Continued

Table 8.4 *Continued*

Accounts	1921 Billion kronen	in %	1922 Billion kronen	in %	1923 Billion kronen	in %	1924 Billion kronen	in %	1925 Billion kronen	in %
Earnings statements										
Earnings										
Interests	0.049	22.3	1.609	18.3	5.666	21.1	–	–	–	–
Interests and commissions	–	–	–	–	–	–	10.636	61.6	4.606	54.4
Commissions	0.019	8.6	1.948	22.2	12.071	44.9	–	–	–	–
Earnings from foreign exchange, securities, and syndicated business	0.151	68.7	5.227	59.5	8.495	31.6	–	–	–	–
Diverse earnings	–	–	–	–	–	–	6.169	35.7	3.858	45.6
Retained earnings	–	–	0.006	0.1	0.675	2.5	0.459	2.7	–	–
Expenses										
Personnel expenses	0.026	11.8	2.584	29.4	7.617	28.3	11.213	65.0	6.128	72.4
Other expenses	0.027	12.3	0.790	9.0	2.973	11.0	3.482	20.2	1.959	23.1
Taxes and fees	0.010	4.5	1.201	13.7	6.148	22.8	1.632	9.5	–	0.0
Write-offs	0.005	2.3	0.172	2.0	0.559	2.1	0.271	1.6	0.195	2.3
Profit (retained earnings included)	0.077	35.0	3.525	40.1	9.609	35.7	0.664	3.8	0.182	2.2

Note: Figures for 1925 are converted from schillings to kronen (1 krone = 10,000 schillings).

Source: ÖStA, AdR, Bankkommission, Box 41, File Biedermann Bank, Templates to the ordinary General Assembly of M.L. Biedermann & Co., Bankaktiengesellschaft, 1922, 1923, 1924, and 1925, and Bilanz-Konto per 31. Dezember 1925.

invested remained quite modest and left only minute traces in the balance sheet. Security holdings and syndicate dealings plus capital contributions only amounted to 12.6 percent of the balance sheet total (Table 8.4).

According to the earnings statements, in 1922 interest contributed 1.6 billion, commissions 1.9 billion, and earnings from foreign exchange, securities, and syndicated business 5.2 billion kronen to the gross earnings. Reported net income amounted to only 3.5 billion kronen. To offset the effects of monetary devaluation on the equity capital, which amounted to 0.5 billion kronen by October 1922, profits in the amount of thirtyfold this sum (15 billion kronen) would have been necessary.

In the company report for 1922 the management stated that the bank had obeyed the guidelines for liquidity and avoided hypertrophic exchange transactions "which would have endangered patriotic interests." It was granted that the bank has "remained somewhat behind the success of other financial firms in Austria, but is well prepared to cope with the current status [of the economy after the end of the hyperinflation]."[57]

8.7 Changed business from 1923 onward

The year 1923 brought substantial changes to the direction of business. After hyperinflation ended in autumn 1922, the following period of a strong bull market at the Vienna Stock Exchange allowed for stock issues and diverse kinds of speculative dealings in Vienna. Furthermore, a shift among the groups who influenced the business activities of Biedermann Bank occurred. The most important liaison between Anglobank and Biedermann Bank, Wilhelm Rosenberg, committed suicide on April 3, 1923. This act of desperation seems not to have been triggered by overall business developments but by personal misfortune. Shortly before, his son had ended his life in Paris and his marriage had failed. After these private disasters, Rosenberg had thrown himself into an excess of work.[58]

Furthermore, two other important personalities who had kept up relations between the two banks, namely Max Cavalier de Anhauch and Hugo Schwarz, became alienated from Anglobank due to differences regarding business strategy concepts and difficulties with subsidiary banks and industries. They left the Anglobank and resigned from the board of Biedermann Bank in summer/autumn 1923. Board member Schwarz left the Anglobank in August 1923 to become president of the Internationale Handelsbank.[59] The vacant positions of the three

[57] ÖStA, AdR, BmF, Bankkommission, Box 21, File 7, Templates to the second ordinary General Assembly of M.L. Biedermann & Co., Bankaktiengesellschaft, August 4, 1923, p. 9f.

[58] Detailed obituaries are found in *Neue Freie Presse*, April 3, 1923, pp. 1 and 7; April 4, 1923, p. 5; *Neues Wiener Journal*, April 4, 1923, p. 5; *Die Börse*, April 5, 1923, p. 1f, and April 12, 1923, p. 2.

[59] *Neues Wiener Journal*, August 2, 1923, p. 11; *Reichspost*, August 2, 1923, p. 8.

representatives at Biedermann Bank were not filled by other functionaries of the Anglobank. London had never been very enthusiastic about Rosenberg's Biedermann Bank project and even less so about the relations with the other small subsidiary banks. The British majority owners were aware of the hypertrophy of the Viennese banking sector and regarded the subsidiary banks with suspicion, as they offered the Austrian actors a margin of maneuvering that was difficult to control. Finally, yet importantly, they caused heavy losses, as we will see below. After Rosenberg's death, a final withdrawal from these engagements began.[60]

All in all, it is plausible to assume that the control exercised by the Anglobank over Biedermann Bank relaxed in 1923. Consequently, the groups that were interested more in the "Schumpeterian" kind of banking must have gained leverage against the proponents of conservative "English banking." As mentioned above, around the turn of 1922/3 the president and vice presidents of the board—Schumpeter, Klein, and Kunwald—at least formally also became members of the board of directors, which was responsible for the operational management of the Biedermann Bank. This was partly for tax reasons, as royalties for board members were taxed at 40 percent, while wage payments to employees were subject to substantially more favorable rates, but it may have also increased their direct access to bank business.[61]

In fact, business developed in a very different manner from 1923 onward. Above all, the total balance sum, which in 1922 had shrunk to one-eighth in real terms, grew nominally by a factor of 6.2 during 1923. After a year and a half of overly cautious business policy, a more risk-orientated growth course followed. Adjusted for inflation, this nominal growth of more than 500 percent meant a real increase by some 160 percent, since currency devaluation was curbed but not yet completely halted in 1923. Contemporary commentators noted that in 1923 Biedermann Bank achieved the strongest growth in the balance sheet total of all Viennese banks.[62]

Not just the volume but also the structure of the assets changed significantly. Further investments in bank deposits were almost fully stopped, leading to a decrease in this most liquid asset category from 28.6 to 5.2 percent of the balance sheet total. In contrast, the fastest growing asset categories were debtors and syndicates plus capital contributions. Nominally, investments in debtors rose by a factor of 8.3 and investments in firm equity and syndicated dealings by a factor of seven. The share of these two asset groups rose to 77.1 and 6.3 percent

[60] ÖStA, AdR, BmF, Bankkommission, Box 41, File 9, Biedermann Bank, Report to the parliamentary committee of inquiry concerning Biedermann Bank and Dr Heinrich Mataja, 473rd of the Supplements, National Council, Second Legislative Period, November 27, 1925, p. 64 f, information given by Dr. Hans Simon, General Council of Anglo-Austrian Bank Ltd.

[61] Further directors were Isidor Modern, Paul Halporn, Wilhelm Halporn and Dr Alfred Treichl. Vice directors were Dr Ernst Gibian, Felix Herrnstadt, Josef Schäffel and Oskar Weiner. *Compass*, Vol. 1, 1924, p. 317; ÖStA, Bestand GK, 616–1, Box 757, File 248, Dr D. [Demmer] to M.L. Biedermann & Co., Bankaktiengesellschaft, December 22, 1923.

[62] *Die Bilanzen*, September 27, 1924, p. 401.

of all assets. It is obvious that the bank increased the speculative dealings of customers by a more than proportionate amount, in many cases through types of repo loans. Among the customers who made use of bank loans for speculative dealings were many leading bank functionaries, not least the bank's president Josef Schumpeter. In addition to this, Biedermann Bank continued to supply necessary loans for related group companies and expand its industrial portfolio. The growth of syndicated dealings and securities shows that these firms were accompanied by various types of investment banking services in cases of capital increases.

While the number of small and medium-sized enterprises that were part of the Biedermann group increased slightly, the volume of investments grew substantially. In 1923, Biedermann participated in the capital increases of seven leading Viennese banks and two German banks. The number of non-financial firms in Biedermann's sphere of interest increased to around twenty-five. Important new business cases were: a plaster factory, an electricity plant, and a sawmill in Styria, as well as a factory for scythes in Upper Austria—a business that in retrospect does not seem very innovative, but which gained substantial export successes. The scythe company was converted into a joint-stock company, which yielded sound founders' profits.[63] Other important new clients included a group of lacquer factories in Austria, Hungary, Czechoslovakia, and the Kingdom of Serbs, Croats and Slovenes, as well as the Viennese trading firm Handels Aktien Gesellschaft (Hag) with two subsidiary companies in the new state of the southern Slavs. In this case, the new client company also became an investor in Biedermann Bank itself.

The Biedermann Bank carried out two further substantial capital increases in April and summer 1923, the first by 0.5 billion and the second by 1 billion kronen nominal value, with 1.25 million and 2.5 million new shares, respectively.[64] After these increases, total nominal share capital amounted to 2.5 billion kronen (6.5 million shares). Beyond this, a reserve fund of around 30 billion kronen was reported, which mainly consisted of proceeds in addition to the nominal value achieved in the issues. All in all, the balance sheet for 1923 displayed an equity share of more than 13 percent (after less than 10% in 1922) and, according to the figures, profit nearly tripled nominally compared to 1922.

However, in early 1924 it began to become apparent that, in reality, business had not developed as well as was displayed in the balance sheet for 1923. Once the bull market at the Viennese stock exchange came to an end during the second half of 1923 and many speculators suffered heavy losses through dealings betting on a weakening French franc after March 1924, a severe banking crisis ensued. In

[63] ÖStA, AdR, BmF, Bankkommission, Box 21, File 7, Templates to the third ordinary General Assembly of M.L. Biedermann & Co., Bankaktiengesellschaft, September 27, 1924; *Compass*, Vol. 1, 1925, p. 914, Maria Weinmeister, Sensenwerk A.-G. Biedermann director Alfred Treichl became a board member of this company.

[64] *Compass*, Vol. 1, 1924, p. 317.

this situation, the federal Austrian authorities intensified their bank audits in order to gain a sound understanding of the extent of the problem. Due to the notorious "hypertrophy" of the financial sector, in 1921 the Austrian government had already established a banking commission to oversee the private banks and joint-stock banks.[65]

In this situation, formal negligence on the part of the Biedermann Bank led to the institution also being investigated. In February 1924 state commissioner Juch reported to the Banking Commission that the bank had not held a meeting of the board of directors for several months, although such a meeting was due every month in accordance with the Articles of Association.[66] It is possible that the professional discipline of this body had diminished with the dwindling influence of Anglobank.

8.8 Mounting problems

In May 1924, the Banking Commission carried out a detailed audit of Biedermann Bank, as a result of hints made by state commissioner Juch.[67] In March of that year a special parliamentary committee had already dealt with the acute banking crisis. The deputy chairman of the Banking Commission, Hofrat Georg Stern, then wrote a comprehensive critical report detailing abuses taking place in the Austrian banking system, which included chapters on Biedermann Bank and its associated banks. This secret report was brought to public attention in June 1924.

It contained much relevant criticism. Yet Stern also made some erroneous accusations, for example, in relation to grievances at the Internationale Handelsbank and the Austro-Holländische Bank.[68] Further unfavorable details came to light during a parliamentary inquiry in 1925, which investigated alleged preferential treatment of the Biedermann Bank by the Ministry of Finance.[69] This committee of inquiry was initiated by Social Democrat politicians who primarily wanted to target the Christian Social faction of Mataja, Seipel, and Kunwald.[70] Despite some inaccuracies, all these reports revealed fundamental economic difficulties

[65] This expert commission for banking was active in the Ministry of Finance from 1921 to 1926 based on the Federal Act of October 7, 1921 (BGBl. No 543/1921).

[66] ÖStA, AdR, BmF, Bankkommission, Box 41, Report of State Comissioner Dr Otto Juch to the Banking Commission, February 14, 1924.

[67] ÖStA, AdR, Bmf, Bankkommission, Box 41, Stern's report in the 90th plenary session of the Banking Commission, June 6, 1924.

[68] Georg Stern's report from May 1924 was made public by the newspaper *Die Neue Wirtschaft* on June 4, 1924, pp. 1–6. A typescript of the report, of which the first and last pages are missing, is passed down in ÖStA, AdR, BmF, Bankkommission, Box 17, Quarterly reports, File IX.

[69] ÖStA, AdR, BmF, Bankkommission, Box 41, Report to the parliamentary committee of inquiry concerning Biedermann Bank and Dr Heinrich Mataja, 473rd of the Supplements, National Council, Second Legislative Period, November 27, 1925.

[70] BAK, N1186, 31, Kunwald to Stolper, January 27, 1932.

at Biedermann Bank that were caused by industrial investments, bad debtors (including senior bank officials), corporate governance problems related to the more recent capital increases, and activities of the related banks.

Industrial investments and bad debtors

The industrial investments caused several problems at once. As long as the bull market lasted (until autumn 1923), capital increases brought returns through investment banking services and rising share values, which the Biedermann Bank itself retained. The Viennese stock index stagnated from the second half of 1923 onward and slumped in early 1924. In reality, the situation was even worse because from mid-1923 on prices had already been stabilized through support buying and the market had become tight and illiquid, which meant that the bank had tied up extensive immobilized stock holdings. Since most of the industrial companies performed poorly, they also needed substantial loans, which Biedermann had to procure with expensive refinancing. Finally, as a result of these circumstances, the group companies themselves became bad debtors. Several firms that had been founded during the inflation era or the subsequent stock market boom ultimately turned out not to be viable.[71]

In a commentary on the 1923 balance sheet, a well-informed contemporary wrote that it

> is not known what profit these foundations will bring to the bank. What is certain is that they will tie up the bank's funds in a way that is likely to cause some concern for the management in critical times, both through their shareholdings and the sometimes quite high loans they take out.[72]

Apart from the industrial companies, many speculators whose deals the bank had financed were also affected by the end of the bull market and failed currency speculations. As a result, their solvency became uncertain and the securities deposited as collateral for their debts lost value.

[71] Among the firms who at least survived the following years were the Altesse factories for cigarette paper, Universale Bau (construction company), and Ludwig Marx lacquer factories. The Maria Weinmeister scythe factory was converted into a hydroelectric power plant. Short-lived companies that caused high losses were, for example, Mefra AG (cotton mill), Oscar Schubert (mechanical engineering), Rhombus book publisher, "Riva" perfume and soap company, Gipswerke Admont (plaster production), and the Styrian power plant and sawmill company. *Compass*, Vol. 1, 1928, p. 1314; 1929 pp. 626, 866, 1148f, 1169f, 1218; 1931, pp. 609f, 960, 1221; 1932, pp. 913, 1009; 1937, p. 1033f.

[72] *Die Bilanzen*, September 27, 1924, p. 401.

Capital increases

The situation was further aggravated by a corporate governance problem related to the capital increases which was critically highlighted by the Banking Commission's reports. It seems to have been a common practice for controlling insiders to achieve private gains from capital increases at the expense of the company and small shareholders, thereby reducing the capital injection into the company. At first glance, the three share issues in late 1922 and March and July 1923 seem to have strengthened the equity base of Biedermann Bank in a sound manner. Yet a closer look by the Banking Commission revealed severe deficiencies.[73] While the issues promised enormous revenues for the bank, the sale of stocks was handled in such a way that only a modest proportion of the sales proceeds was channelled into the Biedermann Bank as fresh equity. The new shares were not offered directly to the public. As already mentioned, the existing shareholders and an underwriting syndicate acquired them at a price that was below the actual stock exchange quotation, while the syndicate took orders at the actual market price. Usually, underwriting syndicates serve to ensure the placing of the shares, for which they obtain a somewhat discounted price that they are obliged to pay.

On November 7, 1922, when Biedermann was quoted at the Vienna Stock Exchange, the shares, which had a nominal value of 400 kronen per unit, were listed at a share price of 4,000 kronen. Until June 1923 their stock market price climbed to a peak of 41,000 kronen.

From September 22, 1922 onward, share issue number three was carried out. The existing shareholders could obtain a total number of 625,000 new shares at a price of 1,200 kronen per unit, which meant that they got shares with a total market value of some 2.5 billion kronen for a total payment of some 750 million kronen. An informal underwriting syndicate composed of persons and firms with close ties to Biedermann Bank got the same number of shares at the same price. Among the syndicate members were the biggest shareholders, the owners of the former private Biedermann Bank, and the leading functionaries of the bank. The syndicate was able to market the shares at a price of more than 5,000 kronen. It was therefore sufficient to sell 136,198 on the secondary market to cover the price paid to the bank for the entire share package. In this way, the syndicate *de facto* received the remaining 488,802 shares for free, which had a market value of more than 2.6 billion kronen. The main beneficiaries were the Anglobank with 12.7 percent of the total syndicate volume, vice president Arthur Klein (12.4%), and board member

[73] The details of the share issues numbers three, four, and five are given on the basis of ÖStA, AdR, Bankkommission, Box 21, File 7, Compilation by Georg Stern for the Parliamentary Committee, commissioned on November 6 and 14, 1925, pp. 16–19; and Box 17, Quarterly reports, File IX, Georg Stern's report from May 1924, typescript, pp. 4–6.

Julius Hepner (7.5%), along with president Schumpeter, vice president Kunwald, and board member Max Chevalier de Anhauch (6.2% each).

Share issue number four followed the same pattern. In the same manner as during share issue number three, existing shareholders and a syndicate obtained 625,000 fresh shares far below the actual stock market price. At that time, they were valued at some 9,500 kronen. The existing shareholders had to pay 3,600 kronen per piece and the syndicate 3,850 kronen. Again, this was a risk-free deal, as the syndicate had already gathered substantial advance orders at prices between 8,000 and 18,000 kronen. The advance sales came about thanks to the general bull market mood at the time, which was heated up by additional massive stock orders from Belgium, which were acquired by General Council Schwarz of the Anglobank. In fact, the incumbent major shareholders managed to strengthen their position by issuing new shares, of which they sold a substantial portion on the secondary market at high market prices. In this way, they financed the expansion of their own shareholdings and at the same time diluted the ownership of the new small shareholders. The deputy head of the Banking Commission, Hofrat Georg Stern, estimated the profit margin of the syndicate at some 4.3 billion kronen, while the bank itself only achieved a capital inflow of 2.4 billion kronen.

All in all, out of the third and fourth share issue only 1 billion kronen of new nominal capital and some 5 billion kronen of premiums went to the bank as new equity capital, while the syndicate made a profit of more than 6.9 billion kronen—at least as long as the share price remained stable.

Kunwald defended the practices in December 1925 in a personal, eleven-page letter to then Austrian minister of finance Viktor Kienböck, putting forth arguments that more or less corresponded with the common opinions at the time on the privileges of actual entrepreneurial founders over small shareholders and, in a certain sense, Schumpeter's own arguments about the promoters' or founders' profits from capital gains that are realized by the sale of new shares.[74] These arguments are of general interest because they demonstrate the mix of contemporary prevailing concepts of the role of controlling shareholders within which Schumpeter for his part developed his conception of the promoter's profit in terms of the capital gains from entrepreneurial ventures. Kunwald wrote, with respect to the share issue in March 1923, that Hugo Schwarz had acquired large orders from Belgium at very high prices, to an extent that could not be served by the shares available on the Viennese market. In this situation, it would have been tempting for the syndicate to cash in at high prices (which, by the way, would have been in line with Schumpeter's concept of realizing promoters' profits). Kunwald, however, went so far as to name the founders responsible in that they served the high demand at high prices with a new issue, whereby they themselves merely

[74] See Schumpeter (*GRW*, 1911b) and the corresponding explanations in Chapter 7.

paid the bank the "intrinsic value" of the shares, in part passing these on at the higher market value to the other buyers, and thus financed an increase in their own share ownership. Kunwald took the view that, as long as it remained the controlling shareholder, the founding group had a special responsibility to the stock corporation and committed itself to fulfilling this role by disproportionately expanding its shareholding. On the other hand, he expressed the opinion to Kienböck that the sale of shares at high prices, that is, quick money instead of a sustainable commitment in the company, would not have been responsible. It is obvious that these positions are not in line with today's concepts of the protection of the rights of small shareholders.[75]

Share issue number five caused different problems. At a superficial glance, this share issue, which began in June 1923, had the appearance of an even more successful financial operation than the earlier ones. Until late May 1923 the stock market price for Biedermann shares had risen to some 15,000 kronen. This opportunity was to be used to issue 2.5 million new shares with a total nominal value of 1 billion kronen. The existing shareholders were apportioned 1.25 million shares at a subscription price of 11,275 kronen and this time the underwriting syndicate took 1.25 million shares at 14,300 kronen per unit. Consequently, the entitlement of the bank was 1 billion kronen of fresh nominal share capital and more than 30 billion kronen of equity on the reserve account. This was also reflected in the annual balance for 1923, which displayed total paid-in nominal capital of 2.5 billion kronen and a total capital reserve fund of 33.8 billion kronen.

However, in reality the placement of the fifth share issue proved a failure. Initially, from May to June 1923 the syndicate acquired advance orders for some 500,000 shares and by June the stock price had risen to 41,000 kronen. Yet, soon after this promising start, prices deteriorated and sales began to stagnate. Exactly that kind of situation emerged in which the syndicate would have had to fulfill its duty to purchase the shares at the stipulated price of 14,300 kronen per piece. The informal syndicate lacked binding contracts and failed to fulfill its obligation. The investigations of the Banking Commission found out that Gottfried Kunwald was able to meet his obligations, as they were covered by the Anglobank as a form of remuneration for his legal counselling services, but all in all the syndicate remained in debt for a significant part of share issue number five after June 1923. Kunwald tried to ensure that the other members of the syndicate also complied with their obligations,[76] but the syndicate was so non-committally organized that this was apparently not possible in every case. The outstanding claims at the syndicate were booked among the debtors by Biedermann Bank, while the capital reserve was figured with the complete sum. Furthermore, the bank financed support buyings of Biedermann shares from autumn 1923 on to prevent further price erosion after

[75] ÖStA, Bestand GK, 616–1, Box 758, File 257, Kunwald to Kienböck, posted December 11, 1925.
[76] ÖStA, Bestand GK, 616–1, Box 758, File 257, Kunwald to Kienböck, posted December 11, 1925.

the stock quotation had again gone down from 41,000 to around 20,000 kronen. According to the Banking Commission, from July to December 1923 more than 314,000 shares were bought with the bank's means, which increased the debts of the syndicate. All in all, some 25 to 30 billion kronen out of the means of Biedermann Bank were used for this purpose. In the books, the bank charged interest of around 36 percent per year for these debts. The bank's balance for 1923, which displayed a capital reserve of 32.2 billion kronen, as mentioned above, had receivables of some 30 billion kronen of very dubious collectability on the opposite side. In addition, the unrealistically high interest rates were the reason the bank was able to report any profit at all for the business year.

Subsidiary banks

Another sub-field of the business activities that contributed to the losses were the related smaller banks. Internationale Handelsbank was a problem child from the beginning. Even before Anglobank and Biedermann Bank had become involved, this bank had mounted an industrial group which was too big in relation to its weak capital base. Above all, the branch in Karlovy Vary (Czechoslovakia) served big porcelain companies, oil companies, and other industrial enterprises with weak performance and large capital requirements after the war. Among the biggest firms related to the bank were the "Epiag"—Erste Böhmische Porzellanindustrie AG (First Bohemian Porcelain Company Ltd)—and "Iriag" Internationale Rohölindustriegesellschaft AG (International Crude Oil Industry Company Ltd). In 1921, the speculator Samuel Bronner temporarily showed an interest in the bank. He impressed the previous owners with two personalities bearing great English names. One of his partners was Francis Duncan Heaton-Armstrong, a distant relative of the Armstrong family which was involved in the Armstrong Whitworth Company (later Vickers-Armstrong). The other was Robert Whitehead, a relative of the renowned producers of naval torpedoes. However, neither was in a position to actually raise a significant amount of capital and the group soon left. In this situation, Hugo Schwarz, together with Anglobank, Biedermann Bank, and some industrial colleagues from Bohemia, seized the opportunity to take over the leadership of the Internationale Handelsbank. In the course of a capital increase in 1921 from 80 to 200 million kronen (200,000 to 500,000 shares), he formed a group of investors that finally gained the majority. Anglobank took around 60,000 shares and assumed a leading role, while Biedermann Bank only acquired some 30,000 shares. Hugo Schwarz, Max Chevalier de Anhauch, and Paul Engel from Anglobank along with Arthur Klein and Gottfried Kunwald from

Biedermann Bank became board members. Schwarz's son Georg had already been a director of the bank before the involvement of the two banks.[77]

Yet the problems of weak performing industrial firms and expensive capital needs continued. As a consequence, Internationale Handelsbank decided to sell its branch in Karlovy Vary along with its blocks of Bohemian industrial shares to the "Bohemia" Czechoslovak Foreign Bank. They mainly received payment in "Bohemia" shares. Unfortunately, this bank declared bankruptcy soon afterward. It had suffered heavy losses in speculative foreign commodity transactions due to an increase in the price of the Czechoslovak crowns. Because of the shareholding, the Internationale Handelsbank was also involved in large repo debts to Böhmische Unionbank. Only a painful restructuring move, in which Anglobank, the management, and the shareholders had to make great sacrifices, was able to prevent the Internationale Handelsbank from going bankrupt. This scheme was organized by Gottfried Kunwald on behalf of Anglobank,[78] which alone directly contributed 3.5 million Czechoslovak crowns (around 7.35 billion Austrian kronen based on the exchange rate at the time) to the rescue syndicate. Hofrat Stern found out that, all in all, Anglobank made available 12 billion kronen.[79] This expensive rescue scheme was necessary in order to be able to pass the bank on to new major shareholders. The transaction was carried out in autumn 1923 when Hugo Schwarz left Anglobank and Biedermann Bank to become president of Internationale Handelsbank. While he had already long been alienated from Anglobank, the losses in connection with the Internationale Handelsbank, "Bohemia" Bank, and various Bohemian industrial enterprises also led to a weakening of his standing with his previous employer.

Together with two further board members, Dr Alfred Riesz and Dr Leopold Bestermann, Schwarz managed to find new investors for the Internationale Handelsbank, among others a Dutch company that belonged to the Ofenheim & Co group.[80] Together, they initiated another capital increase. However, they were also unable to find a viable business model and still used considerable funds for supportive purchases of own shares before they decided to liquidate the bank in 1925. Finally, this last phase absorbed much (or maybe all) of the syndicate profits gained from the last capital increase, and the investors who bought the newly issued shares suffered total losses. Hugo Schwarz had to resign as president

[77] *Compass*, Vol. 1, 1923, p. 327; *Die Börse*, September 15, 1921, p. 9, May 25, 1922, p. 6.

[78] ÖStA, Bestand GK, 616–1, Box 763, File 315, Drafts of the rescue agreements; ÖStA, AdR, BmF, Bankkommission, Box 45, File 16, Audit report from January 1925; Causes of the collapse of the Interbank (according to Dr Bestermann); Protocol of the rescue agreement; *Die Börse*, March 22, 1923, p. 7; *Die Stunde*, May 15, 1923, p. 8.

[79] ÖStA, AdR, BmF, Bankkommission, Box 17, File IX, Typescript of Georg Stern's report to the special parliamentary committee dealing with the banking crisis of early 1924 from March 1924, p. 7.

[80] *Die Börse*, September 6, 1923, p. 14; ÖStA, AdR, BmF, Bankkommission, Box 45, File 16, Audit report from January 1925.

in mid-1924.[81] The officials of the Biedermann Bank, Klein and Kunwald, had already *de facto* withdrawn from the Internationale Handelsbank by mid-1923, and did so officially in April 1924.[82]

The other small banks surrounding the Biedermann Bank did not fare better. Austro-Holländische Bank never found a sustainable business model. A later review showed that the small profit reported for 1922 had already been the result of incorrect preparation of the balance sheet. In 1923 a new group, consisting among others of Dr Eduard Prinz von und zu Liechtenstein and the speculators Oskar Poeller and Leo Nowak, organized a capital increase, which meant that Internationale Handelsbank and Biedermann Bank lost their controlling position, and that Schumpeter and Modern left the board. In the era of Poeller, Nowak et al. some capital increases of related firms were carried out, which led to heavy losses for the investors and (possibly ephemeral) gains for the syndicalists.[83] As a last attempt to rescue the bank, in 1924 some small cooperative banks were won as shareholders. However, in 1925 president Prinz Liechtenstein had to liquidate the bank.[84] Since Anglobank and Biedermann Bank had already separated from both the Internationale Handelsbank and the Austro-Dutch Bank by mid-1923, they no longer had anything to do with the subsequent failures.

M.L. Biedermann & Co. Bankkommanditgesellschaft Budapest entered into liquidation in 1926, after several attempts to convert it into a joint-stock bank or rescue it through a merger with another bank had failed.[85] The limited partnership contribution to the Prague bank Fischer, Krasa & Cie. had to be written off in 1924. However, the volume of this investment was very small.[86]

Wiener Handelskreditbank[87] was not mentioned in the company reports of Biedermann Bank as a related firm, but the two companies were closely linked at a personnel level. As already mentioned above, leading Biedermann functionaries such as Schumpeter, Klein, and Kunwald were board members of Wiener Handelskreditbank, and the president of this bank (former count) Dr Josef Ezdorf correspondingly had a seat on the board of Biedermann. The executive board of Wiener Handelskreditbank consisted of Ezdorf, Naftaly Rohatyn, Oscar Rosner,

[81] *Die Börse*, June, 25, 1924, p. 14.

[82] ÖStA, Bestand GK, 616–1, Box 851, File 1274, Kunwald to Dr Alfred Riesz, February 13, 1924.

[83] In this era, Austro-Holländische Bank was involved in capital increases of several firms in the printing, crude oil, and car industry, which all turned out as disasters for the investors. See ÖStA, AdR, BmF, Bankkommission, Box 17, File IX, Typescript of Georg Stern's report to the special parliamentary committee dealing with the banking crisis of early 1924 from March 1924, pp. 8–10; Box 40, File 6, Files on revisions of the Austro-Holländische Bank; *Compass*, Vol. 1, 1924, p. 420.

[84] Compass, Vol. 1, 1924, p. 420.

[85] ÖStA, AdR, BmF, Bankkommission, Box 21, File 7, Templates to the third ordinary General Assembly of M.L. Biedermann & Co., Bankaktiengesellschaft, September 27, 1924, p. 12; Templates to the fourth ordinary General Assembly [...], July 22, 1925, p. 15; Minutes of the 23rd board meeting, October 14, 1926, p. 4.

[86] *Die Bilanzen*, September 27, 1924, p. 401.

[87] See ÖStA, AdR, Bankkommission, Box 34, File 52, Wr. Handelskreditbank, and Box 52, File 33, Audit of Wr. Handelskreditbank; *Compass*, Vol. 1, years 1923 to 1927.

and Schumpeter. The biggest shareholders were Rohatyn, Ezdorf, Rosner, and Heinrich Canetti. Originally, the bank was also closely linked to the Anglobank, but this contract was already terminated in May 1923 when, after Rosenberg's death, the bank began to withdraw holdings from the small bank. However, at this time Sigmund Schwarz, a brother of General Council Hugo Schwarz, moved from Anglobank to Wiener Handelskreditbank as a leading manager (*Generaldirektor*).

The Wiener Handelskreditbank ran into acute economic troubles in early 1924 due to speculative losses and the dubious debts of functionaries and customers, as well as dubious loans to the Braun-Stammfest group (see Chapter 9). As a consequence, a rescue plan was decided in May 1924 which ensured that the senior officials had to make available around 10 billion kronen. Schumpeter had to contribute 1.02 billion kronen.[88] Thereafter, Schumpeter, Klein, and Kunwald resigned their board memberships.[89] The bank continued to find no viable business model. In July 1925 a settlement procedure was initiated and the bank was subsequently closed. No portion of the liquidation proceeds was attributable to the shareholders.[90]

8.9 Acute corporate crisis in 1924

The audit by the Banking Commission in May 1924 revealed a status that was much more alarming than the figures the bank officially presented in September 1924 for the business year 1923. At a meeting of the Banking Commission on June 6, 1924, Hofrat Stern presented an extremely disturbing interim balance sheet of the Biedermann Bank (Table 8.5).

Stern stated that the debts of the syndicate amounted to the complete capital reserves of somewhat over 30 billion kronen. Furthermore, among the debtors with a total volume of more than 110 billion kronen were many clients who had invested in failed speculative dealings and related industrial firms, many of which performed unsatisfactorily. All in all, a substantial share of the debtors had to be regarded as of dubious solvency. Not least, Stern mentioned the worrying indebtedness of Schumpeter. The bank president had a generous credit line with which he financed his entrepreneurial activities, whether they were speculative dealings with securities and the French franc or industrial projects he pursued together with Braun-Stammfest, which will be scrutinized in detail in Chapter 9.

Stern assumed that the losses the Biedermann Bank had accrued during the first months of 1924, due to dubious debtors (besides the syndicate) and the

[88] ÖStA, AdR, Bankkommission, Box 52, File 33, Audit report from December 22–31, 1924, p. 6; Minutes of May 30, 1924, taken at the office of Dr Kunwald.

[89] ÖStA, AdR, Bankkommission, Box 52, File 33, Minutes of the Second Ordinary General Meeting of Wr. Handelskreditbank, July 29, 1924.

[90] *Compass*, Vol. 1, 1927, p. 476.

Table 8.5 Biedermann Bank balance sheet for May 24, 1924 in billion kronen

Assets	Amount	Liabilities	Amount
Cash	3.7	Share capital	2.5
Bills of exchange	2.2	Capital reserves	33.8
Buildings	3.1	Acceptances	3.5
Securities	22.6	Creditors	25.5
Debtors	111.7	Biedermann	9.0
Debtors in foreign currency	132.2	Government deposits and Central bank	98.2
Transitory items	9.2	Diverse creditors	70.7
Loss per 1924	13.5	Daily allowances	34.4
		Transitory items	4.5
		Profit 1923	16.1
Total	298.2	Total	298.2

Source: ÖStA, AdR, BmF, Bankkommission, Box 41, Stern's report in the 90th plenary session of the Banking Commission, June 6, 1924.

depreciation of securities held by the bank, had to be quantified at some 13.5 billion kronen. Given the fictitious character of the reserve, this meant that the bank already had negative equity—in other words, that the bank was broke. The situation was further aggravated by the fact that there were more than 100 billion kronen of diverse creditors and daily allowances on the liabilities side, which constituted a weak and expensive foundation for the loans the bank had conferred.

Stern considered the situation of Biedermann Bank in May 1924 to be untenable and classified the firm as unfit to obtain further deposits from public institutions.[91]

It is obvious that the bank had only been able to survive through the first half of the year 1924 thanks to generous deposits from public institutions and the Austrian Central Bank. After 1923, Gottfried Kunwald and director Alfred Treichl had been successful in requesting substantial deposits from diverse institutions under the direct influence of the government. The Ministry of Finance lodged around 15 billion kronen during 1923, which was much more than any other bank had. By comparison, the second largest deposit was 10 billion kronen at Austria's largest bank Oesterreichische Credit-Anstalt für Handel und Gewerbe, while several other banks obtained between 3 and 5 billion kronen. The nationalized Federal Railways (plus a subsidiary) provided more than 40 billion kronen and the Austrian Central Bank (Oesterreichische Nationalbank, which was not a government institution) allocated more than 36 billion kronen.[92]

[91] Source: ÖStA, AdR, BmF, Bankkommission, Box 41, Stern's report in the 90th plenary session of the Banking Commission, June 6, 1924.

[92] ÖStA, AdR, BmF, Bankkommission, Box 41, Report to the parliamentary committee of inquiry concerning Biedermann Bank and Dr Heinrich Mataja, 473rd of the Supplements, National Council,

In view of the burgeoning restructuring efforts of Biedermann Bank it was extremely inconvenient for the critical report of the Banking Commission to be made public by the sensationalist press. On June 4, 1924 the journal *Die Neue Wirtschaft* published the confidential investigation report on Biedermann Bank and other banks that Stern had written of in March. During the following days, muckraking papers like *Der Abend* and politically motivated papers like the Social Democrat newspaper *Arbeiter-Zeitung* spread further details in a scandalizing manner which was not conducive to the reform approaches of the Biedermann management.[93]

However, aside from its detrimental effects, the scandal seems to have forced the bank's leaders to increase their efforts to resolve the crisis. Around the middle of 1924, a rescue package for Biedermann Bank was put together. It comprised efforts to acquire new shareholders, restructure business activities in accordance with the initial principals of the bank, and cut costs by a significant amount. Last but not least, far-reaching changes in the personnel composition of the management followed.

On June 18, the board of Biedermann Bank, which had not held a meeting since August 1923, convened again, still under the presidency of Schumpeter, but with the course of the meeting being determined by Kunwald. He announced that he would protest in the Federal Chancellery against the allegations of the Banking Commission, and he read out a letter in which he intended to refute all the findings of Hofrat Stern. He asked the assembly to authorize management to initiate further legal steps, and the application was accepted unanimously.[94]

Yet the letter was never sent and any further steps failed to materialize. Kunwald checked the allegations of the Banking Commission internally and, much to his horror, had to acknowledge that the auditors had been right in their diagnosis.[95]

From June 1924 on the board was restructured, and by 1925 the company had succeeded in getting new major shareholders on board. During this period, the Anglobank made a final substantial contribution to the restructuring before quitting its participation. As a kind of farewell, this was of use to the attempted restart of Biedermann Bank in three ways. First, as mentioned above, Anglobank bailed Kunwald out of his obligations as a syndicate member. Second, the Britons supported Biedermann Bank in getting a further emergency loan from the Austrian

Second Legislative Period, November 27, 1925, pp. 3–11; ÖStA, AdR, BmF, Bankkommission, Box 41, Stern's report in the 90th plenary session of the Banking Commission, June 6, 1924, p. 1.

[93] *Die neue Wirtschaft*, June 4, 1924, pp. 1–6; *Arbeiter-Zeitung*, June 6, 1924, p. 4, June 7, 1924, p. 5; *Der Abend*, June 4, 1924, p. 9; *Neue Freie Presse*, June 5, 1924, p. 1.

[94] ÖStA, AdR, BmF, Bankkommission, Box 21, File 7, Minutes of the XVIIth board meeting of M.L. Biedermann & Co., Bankaktiengesellschaft, June 18, [1924].

[95] ÖStA, AdR, BmF, Bankkommission, Box 21, File 7, Zl. 61/1, Compilation of Georg Stern concerning his findings at Biedermann Bank (Zusammenstellung Georg Sterns der bei der M.L. Biedermann & Co., Bankaktiengesellschaft vorgenommenen banktechnischen Feststellungen), Vienna, November 14, 1925, p. 3.

Central Bank. Anglobank granted credit guarantees of up to 45 billion kronen (4.5 million schillings) until the end of 1924, which it replaced with a payment of 20 billion kronen (2 million schillings) around the turn of 1924/5.[96] These interactions were facilitated by the fact that Anglobank was an important shareholder and that the governor of the Bank of England, Norman, had a strong voice in the Austrian Central Bank. On the other hand, the governor of the Austrian Central Bank, Richard Reisch, reminded Norman in a telegram in July 1924 of his "moral obligation" to support Biedermann Bank via Anglobank.[97] The financial means obtained from the central bank were an important prerequisite for the Biedermann Bank to be able to explore new business areas, which are discussed below. Moreover, the public creditors (Ministry of Finance, National Railways, etc.) also undertook to leave their credit balances until the end of the year and only withdraw cautiously thereafter, based on the Biedermann Bank's ability to pay.[98]

Third, the Anglobank granted Biedermann an immediate support payment of 13 billion kronen.[99] All in all, the rescue measures after the crisis of Biedermann Bank in May 1924 cost Anglobank well over 30 billion kronen (3 million schillings).[100]

Changes in the management bodies of Biedermann Bank followed. During the board meeting on June 18, president Schumpeter informed the board members that Dr Rudolf Maria Braun-Stammfest and Dr Josef (Graf) Ezdorf, who also quit his presidency at Wiener Handelskreditbank, had resigned from their board positions "due to present overburdening with other obligations."[101] Finally, in September 1924, Schumpeter himself had to give up his position as bank president.[102] Rumour had it that the Anglobank had asserted its influence on this decision. In 1921, Schumpeter had obtained the position as a brilliant young economist and influential former secretary of state for finance. Now he appeared a heavily indebted bon vivant, who could not be of much further use to the bank. Formally, he remained with Biedermann Bank as an ordinary board member until May 1925. However, he had little to do with the bank's further development. The further fate of Biedermann Bank and Anglobank will therefore only be discussed briefly.

[96] Kernbauer (1991, pp. 256–60).

[97] Bank of England, OV 28–28, Telegrams Reisch to Norman, July 1, 1924; Norman to Reisch, July 2, 1924; Reisch to Norman, July 7, 1924, quoted after Kernbauer (1991, p. 257f).

[98] Kernbauer (1991, p. 258).

[99] *Die Bilanzen*, September 27, 1924, p. 400; ÖStA, Bestand GK, 616–1, Box 758, File 257, Letter Kunwald to Kienböck, Posted December 11, 1925, p. 10.

[100] *Die Börse*, January 13, 1927, p. 5.

[101] ÖStA, AdR, BmF, Bankkommission, Box 21, File 7, Minutes of the XVIIth board meeting of M.L. Biedermann & Co., Bankaktiengesellschaft, June 18, [1924].

[102] *Die Neue Wirtschaft*, September 11, 1924, p. 5, September 18, 1924, p. 5.

8.10 Further developments

While the Anglobank was withdrawing from Biedermann Bank, two new important entrepreneurial personalities gained influence as big shareholders. One was Kiazim Emin, who began purchasing Biedermann Bank stocks in 1923. He was a tobacco tycoon from Galicia who controlled the Bulgarian market for raw tobacco, had acted temporarily as Persian minister of finance, and lived in Saint Moritz, Switzerland. Emin was well positioned as a supplier of the state monopolies for tobacco in France, Italy, Tunisia, Austria, and Czechoslovakia, and he ran the "Turkish-Macedonian Tobacco Company" (Turmac), which had branches in Cairo, Alexandria, the Netherlands, Belgium, and Switzerland. Furthermore, Emin owned about a quarter of the German tobacco industry. However, he got into financial trouble during the late 1920s and withdrew from business toward the end of the decade.[103] Two representatives of Kiazim Emin, Mehmed Emin and judiciary council Otto Kahn (Munich) became board members of Biedermann Bank in 1924.

The other new leading personality was Robert Schoeller, a descendant of a family of Austrian industrialists and bankers. The family group comprised enterprises in the sugar, brewing, and milling industries, iron and steel works, as well as wood, paper, and printing branches in Austria and other successor states of the Habsburg Monarchy.[104] Before joining, Robert Schoeller had been a manager at the Depositenbank,[105] one of the first banks to collapse during the 1924/5 banking crisis,[106] and he also had board memberships at several family firms.

As the new president, from 1925 on Schoeller formed a new Biedermann Bank executive committee, which took responsibility for the restructuring of the firm. Further members were Arthur Klein, who had an interest in the bank and the bank's two experienced directors, Isidor Modern and Alfred Treichl.[107] Kunwald remained associated with the Biedermann Bank as vice president of the general board and advisor of the executive committee.

Schoeller was designated as the new bank president at the nineteenth meeting of the board (Verwaltungsrat) on July 6, 1925.[108] As a new strategic line for the bank, he announced that "the bank is dedicated to the management of external capital and securities depositories."[109] The use of own funds in the sense of "Schumpeterian banking" should therefore be largely reduced.

[103] Rahner and Schumann (2016, p. 138). [104] Falschlehner (s.a., p. 55).

[105] *Compass*, Vol. 1, 1922, p. 307. [106] Weber (2016, p. 112ff).

[107] Schumpeter, Ezdorf, and the Halporn brothers, on the other hand, were eliminated.

[108] This appointment was formally confirmed at the Ordinary General Meeting on July 21, 1925. ÖStA, AdR, BmF, Bankkommission, Box 21, File 7, Templates to the fourth ordinary General Assembly [...], July 22, 1925, p. 9.

[109] ÖStA, AdR, BmF, Bankkommission, Box 21, File 7, Minutes of the 19th board meeting of the M.L. Biedermann & Co., Bankaktiengesellschaft, July 6, 1925, p. 3.

The main method of cost reduction was to cut personnel. The number of employees was reduced from a maximum of around 240 in 1923 to fifty-five in 1925,[110] which was very costly, since bank employees had very strong collective agreements that entitled them to high severance payments.

In July 1925, the management presented the annual accounts for 1924 and a new balance sheet in the new Austrian schilling currency for January 1, 1925. These statements completely confirmed the findings of the Banking Commission from May 1924: most of the equity was lost and, due to write-offs, the total balance was reduced from 300 to less than 140 billion kronen or 14 million Austrian schillings. In the new schilling balance, a share capital of 625,000 schillings and a capital reserve of the same amount were reported. This was only possible because the bank building, which had already been completely written off, was now valued at 800,000 schillings.[111]

During this difficult time, Kiazim Emin saw to it that Biedermann Bank became involved in financing tobacco imports of the Austrian state monopoly. The bank guaranteed voluminous bill credits toward the Austrian Central Bank. These financial operations took on enormous dimensions among all of the business activities. At the end of 1924, tobacco bill credits from the Austrian Central Bank amounted to nearly 30 billion kronen,[112] which accounted for about a quarter of all liabilities in the balance.

Soon after the bank presented these figures, a new problem emerged. In October 1925, several tabloids wrote that Biedermann Bank had obtained inadmissible support from government institutions in the form of the large deposits that had been left from 1923 on.[113] It was implied that federal minister Dr Heinrich Mataja, an old friend of Kunwald's, had been bribed by relinquishing his shares below the market price to ensure the granting of government deposits. The largest monetary deposits of the Ministry of Finance were approved in 1923 by director general Schwarzwald and finance minister Kienböck after interventions by Kunwald.[114] Schwarzwald quit his job at the ministry and became board member of Anglobank in autumn 1923, after Hugo Schwarz and Chevalier de Anhauch left the bank.[115]

110 *Der österreichische Volkswirt*, July 11, 1925, p. 318.

111 *Der österreichische Volkswirt*, July 11, 1925, p. 318; ÖStA, AdR, BmF, Bankkommission, Box 21, File 7, Minutes of the 19th board meeting of the M.L. Biedermann & Co., Bankaktiengesellschaft, July 6, 1925, notes on the preparation of the balance sheet, p. 2.

112 ÖStA, AdR, BmF, Bankkommission, Box 21, File 7, Zl. 61/1, Compilation of Georg Stern concerning his findings at Biedermann Bank (Zusammenstellung Georg Sterns der bei der M.L. Biedermann & Co. Bankaktiengesellschaft vorgenommenen banktechnischen Feststellungen), Vienna, November 14, 1925, p. 8.

113 See for example *Arbeiter-Zeitung*, October 16, 1925, p. 2; *Neue Freie Presse*, October 16, 1925, p. 1; *Der Morgen*, November 9, 1925, p. 1; *Neue Freie Presse*, December 16, 1925, pp. 1–5; *Arbeiter-Zeitung*, December 16, 1925, p. 1f, December 17, 1925, pp. 1–4.

114 ÖStA, AdR, BmF, Bankkommission, Box 41, Report to the parliamentary committee of inquiry concerning Biedermann Bank and Dr Heinrich Mataja, 473rd of the Supplements, National Council, Second Legislative Period, November 27, 1925, pp. 30–3 and 57.

115 *Reichspost*, August 26, 1923 and September 20, 1923.

In earlier years at the start of his career, Kienböck had been sponsored by Kunwald and they had since supported each other where appropriate. However, this affair was the starting point of a bitter estrangement between the two personalities. A parliamentary inquiry commission investigated the deposits and did not find conclusively unlawful behavior.[116] Yet it became publicly known that Biedermann Bank had above all survived the crisis of 1924 thanks to substantial supportive emergency credits from the Austrian Central Bank and unusually large deposits by the Ministry of Finance and state-owned firms. This affair again drew public attention to the economic difficulties of Biedermann Bank, which negatively affected the bank's further development in a number of ways. First, the bank soon thereafter lost its credit business with tobacco bills and Kiazim Emin turned away from the company.

Second, in this negative atmosphere, an intended injection of fresh capital from Austrian, English, and German investors did not materialize.

Third, a final attempt to rescue Biedermann Bank was disturbed by the negative press in 1924 and 1925. Around the turn of 1923/4, Kunwald had met the internationally active financial expert Otto Kahn, who introduced him to his cousin Eugene Kahn, a partner of the private bank Morgan, Livermore & Co. in New York. Kunwald was very impressed with Eugene Kahn, developed full confidence in him, and convinced the partners at Biedermann to cooperate with the New York company in a spirit of trust. They intended to issue Austrian bonds in New York, which would have been very much in line with Biedermann Bank's original concept of bringing foreign capital to Austria. However, Morgan, Livermore & Co. requested a limited partnership contribution of 750,000 US dollars.[117] The cooperation was contractually sealed in May 1924.[118] Initial success seemed to confirm the high expectations. Together with a third firm, J. Lissmann, they prepared a corporate bond of three million US dollars for the Austrian energy supply company Newag Niederösterreichische Elektrizitätswirtschafts AG, which was issued in August 1924. By mid-1924, Biedermann had already put in 475,000 US dollars of the partnership contribution. A value of 200,000 US dollars was disbursed in the form of 800,000 own shares at a price of 25 cents per share, and 275,000 US dollars were raised through the central bank loans, which were

[116] A minority of the commission shared the view that no unlawful behavior had been found, yet the Social Democrat members stated that the issue prices were too low and that the bank had been "improperly favoured by the State money." ÖStA, AdR, BmF, Bankkommission, Box 41, Report to the parliamentary committee of inquiry concerning Biedermann Bank and Dr Heinrich Mataja, 473rd of the Supplements, National Council, Second Legislative Period, November 27, 1925, p. 18ff.

[117] That was more than 50 billion kronen or 5 million schillings. ÖStA, AdR, BmF, Bankkommission, Box 41, Report to the parliamentary committee of inquiry concerning Biedermann Bank and Dr Heinrich Mataja, 473rd of the Supplements, National Council, Second Legislative Period, November 27, 1925, p. 25; *Die Bilanzen*, December 18, 1926, pp. 8 and 142; *Neue Freie Presse*, April 5, 1927.

[118] Kunwald provides a brief overview of the entire business connection from 1924 until 1926 in ÖStA, Bestand GK, 616–1, Box 757, File 250, Kunwald to Kahn, May 25, 1926.

part of the rescue package of Anglobank and the Austrian Central Bank described above.[119] Under normal conditions, Biedermann Bank might have refrained from entering the risky deal with the Americans who were clearly in urgent need of capital. Yet, due to the acute crisis of their own business, the desperate greenhorns at the financial center New York grasped at straws. At the same time, Morgan, Livermore & Co and its (potential) customers and business partners heard about the rumours and negative press regarding Biedermann. This gave them an excuse to refuse to pay the commission for the Newag bond and gradually distance themselves from the partner company in Vienna. In fact, the Americans were affected by a massive loss in value of the Biedermann shares they had accepted as payment. Beyond this, J. Lissmann separated from Morgan, Livermore & Co. and without this partner placed further Austrian bonds, for example a Lower Austrian state bond, after the Newag bond lost value due to negative news about this company.[120] Despite these setbacks, Morgan, Livermore & Co. still lured their Austrian partners with prospects of high future profits, which never materialized. They ultimately demanded the deposit of the last part of the participation sum and a renegotiation of the contracts to their advantage. In September 1924 the well-known business lawyer, Mr Desvernine[121] came to Vienna and urged the Biedermann managers to consent to altered covenants. Biedermann was trapped, since 475,000 US dollars of the capital contribution had already been transferred to New York, and managed to persuade the state-owned Dorotheum Bank to finance the remaining 275,000 US dollars, partly as its own equity investment, partly as a loan. The entire deposits of 750,000 US dollars should have been used to set up an Austria department at Morgan, Livermore & Co., which, however, never commenced its business activities.[122] At the same time, the economic situation of the New York firm deteriorated and it ultimately went into liquidation. Throughout 1925 and 1926, Kunwald desperately tried to negotiate that the limited partnership contribution be considered a loan, which would have provided for better prospects of repayment during the liquidation. He reached an agreement for a long-term instalment, which was, however, never enforced.[123] In the annual balance for 1925, the total assets of Biedermann Bank were valued at less than 12 million schillings. At this time, the claims against Morgan, Livermore & Co., which were in fact already lost, still accounted for the major share of the assets. Even the few

[119] Kernbauer (1991, pp. 258–60); ÖStA, Bestand GK, 616–1, Box 851, File 1271, Kunwald to Schwarzwald, August 12, 1924.

[120] *Die Neue Wirtschaft*, November 19, 1925.

[121] This was possibly the same Raoul Eugene Desvernine, who in the 1930s took a firm stand against the New Deal policy. See Desvernine (1936).

[122] *Die Neue Wirtschaft*, April 7, 1927.

[123] The documents resulting from Kunwald's activities in connection with the Biedermann-Morgan, Livermore & Co. deals, can be found in: ÖStA, Bestand GK, 616–1, Box 757, Files 250, 259, Box 758, Files 253, 255, 260 and Box 767, File 813.

remaining industrial holdings did not make a relevant contribution to improving the situation.[124]

In December 1926, the president of the Biedermann board, Schoeller, and his colleagues finally had to acknowledge that the situation had become untenable and the bank went into liquidation in 1927. The Austrian Central Bank recognized that Biedermann was unable to reimburse the financing of the deal with Morgan, Livermore & Co. and instead accepted the claim against the American bank.[125] This to a certain extent reduced the liability obligations of Biedermann Bank to its creditors. Still, the leading managers had to provide painful contributions to prevent a negligent insolvency proceeding. It was particularly important for the managers to raise the money for a Deutsche Bank deposit of 20,000 marks, since customer securities had been used illegally to cover it.[126] Kunwald, for example, had to make available 50,000 schillings for the liquidation fund[127] and the Austrian banker Heinrich Treichl recalls in his memoirs that his father Alfred Treichl lost the family fortune.[128] Arthur Klein, the former principal owner of the private Biedermann Bank, also suffered heavy losses, since he had left a large part of his assets in the bank. For Schoeller, who had joined the company during its crisis in an attempt at restoration, the final fate of the firm must have been especially frustrating. During liquidation, the smaller creditors obtained a modest sum. Some government firms, such as Dorotheum, tried until 1931 to enforce liability claims, but all in all the federal government had to write off at least 12 billion kronen (1.2 million schillings) and the Austrian Central Bank lost most of its claims against Biedermann Bank and Morgan, Livermore & Co.[129] Finally, M.L. Biedermann & Co., Bankaktiengesellschaft was deleted from the commercial register in December 1931.

In the development of Anglobank, the last restructuring effort and final separation from Biedermann Bank in 1924 can be seen as stages of turning away from Austrian business. At that time, the bank had already begun to reduce its staff and its provision of loans to related industry firms. From autumn 1924 to autumn 1925 alone, about a third of the employees were laid off. The business was further centralized by the establishment of an administrative committee under the leadership of a London representative. In November 1925, Zoltan Hajdu from Budapest advanced to the position of the new general director in Vienna, which

[124] ÖStA, AdR, Bankkommission, Box 21, File 7, Minutes of the board meeting of October 14, 1926 and balance sheet for December 31, 1925.

[125] Kernbauer, 1991, p. 259.

[126] ÖStA, AdR, Bankkommission, Box 21, File 7, Report about the meeting of the Executive Committee and the Board of Directors of December 14, 1926.

[127] Private Archive Ulrich Hedtke, Ottilie Jäckel Letters, Schumpeter to Liebes Gunderl, February 5, 1927. Also published in März (1983/91, p. 173).

[128] Treichl (2003, p. 34ff).

[129] Kernbauer (1991, p. 260); Protokolle des Ministerrates der Ersten Republik (1982, p. 474); Die Bilanzen, December 18, 1926, p 142; *Die Börse*, January 13, 1927, p. 5f.

largely put an end to the previous leadership under General Councils Schwarzwald and Simon. Some time previously, in late 1923, Anglobank had taken over the leadership of an Austro-Russian syndicate which intended to develop this eastern market more effectively. In this context, the appointment of the former Russian finance minister Peter Bark to the management board was also understandable.[130] Hajdu took some further steps to develop Anglobank toward becoming more of a trading bank. Yet all of these activities did not produce sufficiently relevant results, and from 1924 onward exploratory talks took place with potential partners for mergers or sales. Finally, in 1926 the Oesterreichische Credit-Anstalt für Handel und Gewerbe acquired the Austrian business and Anglobank London was merged with the British Trade Corporation into Anglo-International Bank Ltd. In an internal memorandum, the Bank of England noted that the "liquidation would have created a sensation on the Continent, and would inevitably have reacted unfavourably on London credit and prestige."[131] The shareholding in the Anglo-Československá Banka was gradually reduced from 100 to 16.6 percent. In 1944, the year when Montague Norman resigned as governor of the Bank of England, the remainders of the Anglo-International Bank Ltd were transferred to Glyn & Mills, which had been at the origin of Anglobank in 1863.

For Gottfried Kunwald personally, the demise of Biedermann Bank and Anglobank had enduring catastrophic consequences. With the departure of Anglobank from Vienna, he lost his largest individual client. Beyond this, he not only had to make a painful financial contribution to the liquidation of the Biedermann Bank, but the series of failures also seriously damaged his reputation as an infallible financial expert. For example, he had personally advocated for Biedermann Bank to the ministries and Minister Kienböck, and he had advised Biedermann Bank to do business with Morgan, Livermore & Co. Another serious consequence was the alienation of Minister Kienböck. Kunwald had placed him in an unpleasant position as a result of the lost deposits of the Ministry of Finance and the losses that Dorotheum and the Austrian Central Bank suffered through Biedermann. The result of all of these factors was Kunwald's own protracted economic decline. By the 1930s, he notoriously suffered from acute financial worries. He was particularly embittered by the fact that Kienböck, who became president of the Austrian Central Bank in the 1930s, did not keep him on as a consultant to the public authorities. On March 14, 1938, after the "Anschluss" of Austria to Nazi-Germany, Kunwald committed suicide. The National Socialists posed a personal deadly threat in two respects: in their policy of persecuting Jews and their policy of the extermination of physically disabled persons.

[130] *Der Morgen* September 17, 1923, p. 2.

[131] Bank of England, Memorandum Anglo-Austrian Bank & British Trade Corporation, August 10, 1926, quoted after Natmeßnig (1998, p. 264).

During the last two days of his life, Kunwald composed a message to posterity, a will, and a very personal farewell letter. In the first of the three documents, he lamented that 1925 had represented a turning point in his life. During "the high time" of his life from 1915 to 1925 he had been granted the privilege of working for the "highest and dearest earthly," namely for Austria, but "from then on [...] an inconceivable handicap in this work set in." In addition to the general circumstances, he held Kienböck and the Dutch banker Adrianus van Hengel personally responsible for his downfall.

> My pupil Kienböck became President of the National Bank, van Hengel, whom I had introduced to him, General Director of Creditanstalt.[132] But it was him and that one who took me out particularly thoroughly and decisively. Why? Because I would have been called upon to resist that unfortunate policy of liquidation, of desertification, of restriction that had to lead to the end of our fatherland.

In other words, Kunwald was an opponent of Kienböck's policy as president of the Austrian Central Bank during the crisis of the 1930s, which focused on austerity and financial restrictions. He also mentioned Kienböck in his last will and testament: "President Dr. Kienböck, who destroyed my fatherland out of personal vanity, [...] may God forgive him." As executors of his will Kunwald appointed Dr Rudolf Bienenfeld and Dr Karl Schlesinger. We will encounter them again in examining the further fate of Schumpeter.[133]

[132] Austria's largest bank, which had to be rescued in 1931.

[133] According to his nephew, Dr Peter Stadlen, London, Kunwald wrote in his handwritten farewell letter of March 14, 1938: "God forgive my enemy Kienböck, I cannot do it." In 1990, Stadlen sent copies of the message to posterity and the will to Gundl Herrnstadt-Steinmetz, Vienna, as sources for her Kunwald study. Since he could no longer find the handwritten letter, Stadlen transmitted the quote to Kienböck from memory in a letter to Herrnstadt-Steinmetz from October 12, 1990. She has published the documents in Herrnstadt-Steinmetz (1993). The authors wish to thank Georg Herrnstadt for the provision of these materials from his mother's estate. In Enderle-Burcel (2018, p. 78) the last will is quoted from ÖStA, Bestand GK, 616–1, File 1358.

9
The Braun-Stammfest Industrial Group

> There is no doubt that inflation accelerated the impending recovery. At the same time the extent of the inflation and the resulting distortion of the price structure prevented the reconstruction of industry along new lines.
>
> (K.W. Rothschild, 1947, p. 29)

9.1 First industrial investments

Schumpeter's financial ventures were not limited to his banking projects. He also participated in ambitious industrial schemes. His most important partner in these activities was *Rudolf Maria Braun-Stammfest* (1881-1949), a former schoolmate at the prestigious "Theresianum" secondary school, which both of them had attended before their university studies. Braun-Stammfest had inherited a modest bourgeois fortune and become a successful business lawyer.[1] At the beginning of the 1920s, he had intended to invest in a newly founded group of industrial firms to take advantage of business opportunities during the upheaval after the war. At this time, he again contacted Schumpeter, as both of them were participating in projects organized by other Austrian industrialists. They invested in a biscuit company and a factory for caustic soda. The founders of the chemical factory, named Elektrotechnische Werke Aussee AG,[2] were eminent Austrian industrialists and (former) politicians such as Joseph and Victor Ruston, Theodor Dumba, Richard Wustel, Hans Zerdik, and Isidor Pollak, director general of the Skoda Wetzler Works.[3] Some of those mentioned, for example, Zerdik and Wustel, later also participated in the ventures of Schumpeter and Braun-Stammfest. During 1919, Zerdik was also a colleague of Schumpeter's in the Austrian Federal Government in his role as state secretary for trade and industry and building trade. In order to establish the companies mentioned above, the founders applied the method of paying into funds for the start-up companies as a group of investors

[1] WStLA, Lg., Box. 731, VrXXIII, 5603/24, 1. Part, Hearing of the accused Dr Rudolf Maria Braun-Stammfest, 201k and 201kk.

[2] *Zentralblatt* (1922, p. 987f).

[3] Gottfried Kunwald was also a board member of the Skodawerk-Wetzler AG, which had been one of the most important Austrian gunpowder factories during the First World War. *Compass*, Vol. 1, 1925, p. 1010f.

Schumpeter's Venture Money. Michael Peneder and Andreas Resch,
Oxford University Press (2021). © Michael Peneder and Andreas Resch.
DOI: 10.1093/oso/9780198804383.003.0009

even before the planned firms were formally established. This obviously inspired Schumpeter and Braun-Stammfest to set up wholly informal funds for their ventures at the earliest stage of formation.

9.2 The founding of the industrial group

Braun-Stammfest had started his own ventures in 1921. He intended to succeed as a project developer in the fields of technical porcelain, electro-technical components, anti-corrosive paints, and glass production. On the one hand, he bet on the new and fast-growing field of electricity supply and electrical technology, on the other hand on import substitution. To set up the respective factories he chose defunct sites in provincial towns, where building sites were cheap and wages lower than in Vienna. From the beginning, Schumpeter acted as an adviser, investor, and prominent figurehead who helped attract further financiers.

Braun-Stammfest and Schumpeter proved very resourceful at finding ways to finance their ventures. On a larger scale they used the somewhat unorthodox method of raising capital that they had already experienced in the abovementioned ventures. They intended to incorporate the new firms as joint-stock companies. However, to accelerate the cumbersome procedure of founding such a company, they formed investor groups, which were initially designed as completely informal, closed-end investment funds. The investors received an interim-certificate for their payment. The promoters personally guaranteed that the funds gathered would be used for the purposes of the firm under construction, and that the interim certificates would be exchanged for shares of the same nominal value after the formal incorporation of the joint-stock company. The buyers of the interim shares were told that investing the raised money in real assets would help prevent the effects of hyperinflation. Braun-Stammfest on the one hand involved some eminent members of the Viennese political and business elites as figureheads, and on the other hand approached the rural *petite bourgeoisie* as investors. While the founders kept a clear majority of the shares themselves, a substantial chunk of the interim-certificates was sold to lawyers, pharmacists, medical doctors, and small entrepreneurs in provincial towns. Since the shares were issued in small nominal values, thousands of investors could participate in the founding fund.

In retrospect, Schumpeter, who was very aware of conflicts associated with the distribution of founders' profits between entrepreneurs and financial intermediaries, stated in 1925 that he had supported the concept to avoid the use of a bank connection for the foundation of the industries, as was customary in Austria. The reason was that a cooperation with banks would have diverted a relevant share of the means raised to the provider of the financial service. Instead, he preferred a direct approach to the capital market, which he regarded as being more common in England than in Austria.[4]

Factory for technical porcelain

The first project Braun-Stammfest initiated was the construction of a factory for technical porcelain in the provincial town of Wels in Upper Austria. In December 1920, he set up a committee of proponents, who sold interim certificates at a total nominal value of 125 million kronen divided into individual shares of 200 kronen. Consequently, 625,000 certificates were issued. The buyers were assured that the money gathered would be used for the immediate acquisition of a factory site and that they would get shares in the joint-stock company which was to be founded at the same nominal value. Schumpeter was a member of the founders' syndicate and he himself acquired 5,000 certificates.[5] The founder group fulfilled its promises and in March 1921 bought a defunct factory site in Wels for 18 million kronen, and management began to renovate the factory to make it fit for the production of porcelain.

In November 1921 the founders submitted a request for a license to incorporate the Oberösterreichische Porzellanindustrie AG (Upper Austrian Porcelain Joint Stock Company, henceforth Porcelain Company) at the Ministry for the Interior and Education. Despite the site being located in Upper Austria, they listed the office of Braun-Stammfest in Vienna as the official address of the firm. This was also the case with all other firms of the group founded during the following years. The application was signed by two former Austrian government members, Schumpeter and Hans Zerdik. Other applicants were Braun-Stammfest, Julius Hochapfel, the director of the well-established Viennese Mercurbank, and some colleagues from Braun-Stammfest's law firm, including Dr Max Borovy.[6] The applicants advanced two arguments for why their enterprise creation should be authorized by the ministry. First, they mentioned that, due to "politically and economically throttled foreign trade," their strategy of import substitution in the field of technical porcelain would be beneficial for the Austrian economy. Second, they emphasized that, due to a "coal shortage and forced expansion of hydropower for the production of electrical energy," a growing market for technical porcelain was to be expected. As complementary products to the technical porcelain, they

[4] WStLA, Lg., Box 731, VrXXIII, 5603/24, 1. Part, Hearing of the accused Dr Rudolf Maria Braun-Stammfest, p. 511.

[5] WStLA, Lg., Box 731, VrXXIII, 5603/24, 1. Part, Hearing of the accused Dr Josef Schumpeter, p. 511 v.

[6] ÖStA, AdR, BmIuU, Gz. 205,983/21, Letter from Julius Hochapfel and others to the Federal Ministry of the Interior and Education, Notice of receipt November 21, 1921.

also planned to manufacture household porcelain and, in addition to the domestic market, they planned to export the manufactured goods to Italy and the Balkan states. They considered the provincial town of Wels to be a perfect factory location, because kaolin, which was the essential resource for porcelain production, was available from nearby Bavaria and local occurrences in an Upper Austrian region north of the Danube (Mühlviertel). Furthermore, in a provincial region the labor force could be hired and housed at a lower cost than in Vienna.[7]

For legal reasons, all the shares of the new joint-stock company had to be paid in cash. This meant that, formally, the entire share capital had to be financed a second time after the issue of the interim certificates. Braun-Stammfest acquired a bank guarantee for the deposit and he was booked as a debtor for the entire sum. *Pro forma* he provided a list of shareholders who would pay in the capital to the Ministry of the Interior. After that, the shares were exchanged against the interim certificates and the company took over the assets of the founding syndicate. This was a cumbersome procedure, which led to additional financing expenditures.

Among the formal temporary financiers of the joint-stock company, in addition to Braun-Stammfest, were Hochapfel, Schumpeter, Zerdik, and three Romanian financiers as well as two new partners from Bavaria, Prince Oettingen-Wallenstein and engineer Louis Ostertag. All of them officially took share packages of between 18,000 and 45,000 stocks.[8] In reality, the payments were guaranteed by Braun-Stammfest, Schumpeter, and Borovi, and the shares which were to be formally paid in by Ostertag were in reality predominantly guaranteed by Braun-Stammfest, while the shares formally taken by the Romanian financiers were in reality guaranteed by Hochapfel, Braun-Stammfest, and other founders. The additional financiers were mentioned to give a more convincing picture that all of the shares would indeed be paid in in cash.[9]

The Ministry of the Interior approved the foundation of the Porcelain Company around the turn of 1921/2 and the constituting general assembly was held on February 18, 1922. Braun-Stammfest became president of the board, Schumpeter and Borovy vice presidents, and Zerdik, Hochapfel, and others became board members. Further members were investors from provincial regions, such as Dr Franz Czermak and Clemens Walzl, both from Upper Austria, and the engineer Friedrich Jaentsch, who acted as the chief technician in planning the equipment of the new factory, at the same time becoming the engineering manager.[10] Before that, Jaentsch was the chief technical manager at a Kaolin work in Bohemia. At the heart of the factory's design was a modern tunnel kiln, which would

[7] ÖStA, AdR, BmIuU, Gz. 205,983/21, Letter from Julius Hochapfel and others to the Federal Ministry of the Interior and Education, Notice of receipt November 21, 1921.

[8] ÖStA, AdR, BmIuU, Gz. 205,983/21, List of shareholders.

[9] WStLA, Lg., Box 731, VrXXIII, 5603/24, 1. Part, Hearing of the accused Dr Rudolf Maria Braun-Stammfest, p. 201z.

[10] *Compass*, Vol. 1, 1923, p. 597; 1924, p. 676.

allow for flow production at a much lower cost than batch production with a traditional kiln. Later on, Jaentsch also became responsible for the technical design of the other factories of the Braun-Stammfest group.[11] Braun-Stammfest lent the firm considerable private sums at moderate interest rates to enable the necessary construction work at the site, whereby he suffered losses due to hyperinflation.[12]

As early as mid-1921, the founders received very optimistic reports in some newspapers. For example, the local *Tages-Post*, a newspaper which was published in the Upper Austrian provincial capital Linz, reported on June 6, 1921 that the Porcelain Company had been founded in Wels and that it was equipped with an innovative tunnel kiln. The article concluded with the note that share subscription applications were available from the Bank für Oberösterreich und Salzburg (Bank for Upper Austria and Salzburg).[13] On July 29, the same paper cited even more details: the intended capacity of the factory was 250 railroad freight cars per year of insulators and other kinds of technical porcelain, for which several patents from the German Allgemeine Elektrizitätsgesellschaft had been acquired. Three hundred workers would be employed. The tunnel kiln would save 50 percent of coal compared to a traditional kiln, and coal from regional production would be used in a gas generator. On November 12, 1921, *Der österreichische Volkswirt* wrote that the founding committee had announced the start of preliminary production at the porcelain factory, however initially only with a traditional kiln, as the engineers had not yet mastered rational production with the tunnel kiln. Furthermore, the company announced that many orders had already been submitted, which meant that the "utilization of the ovens in the factory was already secured with fixed orders." In the same article, the fact that many shares had been bought by provincial investors was communicated as a good omen for the prospects of the firm: "The lively interest, which was manifested by broad strata of the general public is a sign of the confidence in the prosperity of the business and its further healthy development."[14]

In summer 1922, regular production with the tunnel kiln started. Yet the factory still suffered from "teething pains," since the production flow did not work to the satisfaction of management and the commercial management did not fulfill the expectations of the investors. Technical director Jaentsch had already held out the prospect of profits for the first year of operations of the porcelain factory—a promise on which he was not able to deliver.[15]

[11] WStLA, Lg., Box 731, VrXXIII, 5603/24, 1. Part, Hearing of the accused Franz Haller, p. 545 v.

[12] WStLA, Lg., Box 731, VrXXIII, 5603/24, 1. Part, Hearing of the accused Dr Josef Schumpeter, p. 511 v.

[13] *Tages-Post*, June 6, 1921, p. 6.

[14] *Der österreichische Volkswirt*, November 12, 1921, p. 163.

[15] WStLA, Lg., Box 731, VrXXIII, 5603/24, 1. Part, Hearing of the accused Dr Rudolf Maria Braun-Stammfest, p. 201ff. When Jaentsch was interrogated as a witness he denied that he had made promises he could not keep. He explained that the untrained staff led to faulty burning results. WStLA, Lg., Box 731, VrXXIII, 5603/24, 1. Part, Hearing of witness Fritz Jaentsch, p. 733ff.

After the stabilization of the Austrian currency, on October 17, 1922, an extraordinary general assembly of the joint-stock company determined to redeem the interim certificates as promised. The joint-stock company took over the factory site and debts in connection with construction activities, and the preliminary certificates at a total nominal value of 125 million kronen were exchanged for shares of the company of the same nominal value.[16] In the meantime, due to inflation and initial corporate successes, the market value of the Porcelain Company shares had risen to some 6,000 kronen per 200 kronen nominal value.[17] Consequently, the firm with a nominal capital of 125 million kronen had a market value of some 3.75 billion kronen.

To cover all the costs and debts of the foundation procedures and construction measures, at an extraordinary general meeting in October 1922 it was decided to double the nominal capital from 125 to 250 million kronen. The Ministry of the Interior approved the issue of the new shares at a stock price of 4,000 kronen per piece with 200 kronen nominal value for existing shareholders and an underwriting syndicate. Members of the syndicate were, among others, Braun-Stammfest and Schumpeter. The sale of 625,000 new shares at a price of 4,000 kronen yielded some 2.5 billion kronen of fresh money for the company. This allowed the bearing of the costs of the cumbersome foundation procedures, construction measures, and the first phase of production. The cash injection of the capital increase provided financial breathing space but did not suffice as a sustainable financial basis for the further development of the Porcelain Company (Table 9.1).

Table 9.1 Development of the Braun-Stammfest industrial firms

Company	Founding fund	Purchase of site	Constitution of company	Start of production
Porcelain (Wels, Upper Austria)	December 1920	March 1921	February 18, 1922	Late 1921–2
Glass (Wels, Upper Austria)	February 1922	May 1922	February 22, 1923	–
Electro-technical (Wels, Upper Austria)	March 1922	May 1922	February 28, 1922	December 1923
Metallurgical (Hainfeld, Lower Austria)	Spring 1921	June 1921	March 15, 1922	1922–3*

Note: * In Hainfeld, production of machinery and forgings began at a low level in 1922. The production of anti-corrosive paint started in December 1923.

Source: WStLA, Lg., Box 731, VrXXIII, 5603/24, 1.-3. Part, Lawsuit Braun-Stamfmest, expertise on the firms, interrogations, indictment, and verdict.

[16] ÖStA, AdR, BmIuU, Gz. 205983/21, Minutes of the Extraordinary General Meeting on October 17, 1922; WStLA, Lg., Box 731, VrXXIII, 5603/24, 3. Part, Indictment from March 10, 1928, p. 1451 v.

[17] *Compass*, Vol. 1, 1923, p. 597.

However, seen from the outside, in early 1923 the Porcelain Company made a trustworthy impression. Production was under way with some 300 workers, and the balance sheet for 1922 showed an equity ratio of 55 percent. In addition to the nominal share capital of 250 million kronen, the equity consisted of reserves of 2.15 billion kronen, which originated from the capital increase. Liabilities amounted to 1.95 billion kronen. Among the assets, the factory plus machinery was valued at 557 million kronen and inventories at 1.07 billion kronen, and deposits of 2.39 billion kronen were reported.[18]

Two further factories in Wels

While everything seemed to be going well at the Porcelain Company, Braun-Stammfest and his colleagues set up two further factories in Wels. In February 1922, a founding committee for a glass factory and in March 1922 a further one for the manufacture of electro-technical components were established. In these cases, interim certificates were again issued for the companies at the intended total sum of nominal capital. Again, the founders were eager to immediately invest the gathered capital to avoid the effects of hyperinflation, which was at its maximum from early 1922 until September of that year. Schumpeter took over 250,000 interim shares of the glass factory[19] and 50,000 of the electro-technical venture.[20] In the course of creating the business, the founding committee made an agreement with the owners of a closed briquette factory,[21] which had a site with a railway connection. The real estate belonged to the construction company N. Rella & Neffe, which was represented by the directors Alfred Landesberger and engineer Ludwig Paul Roth during the negotiations. The site was a former cavalry barracks with several stables and riding school buildings. It was agreed that the premises had to be handed over to the founders' consortium by the end of May 1922 and that the founders would be allowed to start with the adaptation measures before this date. As remuneration for the site, the briquette company was to obtain 275,000 shares of the glass factory and 75,000 shares of the planned electro-technical factory. Beyond that, three representatives of the briquette company, or rather the construction company as its owner, were to obtain board memberships.[22]

[18] *Compass*, Vol. 1, 1924, p. 676; WStLA, Lg., Box 731, VrXXIII, 5603/24, 1. Teil, Hearing of the accused Dr Rudolf Maria Braun-Stammfest, p. 201b.

[19] WStLA, Lg., Box 731, VrXXIII, 5603/24, 1. Part, Hearing of the accused Dr Josef Schumpeter, p. 513v.

[20] WStLA, Lg., Box 731, VrXXIII, 5603/24, 1. Part, Hearing of the accused Dr Rudolf Maria Braun-Stammfest, p. 201v.

[21] WStLA, Lg., Box 731, VrXXIII, 5603/24, 1. Part, Hearing of the accused Dr Rudolf Maria Braun-Stammfest, p. 201f v f.

[22] ÖStA, AdR, BmIuU, Gz. 57,903/22, Zl. 2147/23, Richtlinien für die Gründung der Aktiengesellschaften, und zwar (Guidelines for the formation of joint-stock companies, namely): (1)

Yet construction work advanced haltingly, not least because the money that had been gathered by the founding syndicates proved insufficient due to hyperinflation. For the electro-technical factory, the German firm Elektrotechnische Fabrik Offenbach vormals Schröder & Cie was acquired as a technological partner to deliver the technical equipment, innovations, and patents. Furthermore, it was intended that the porcelain factory deliver preliminary materials and parts for production, which would create synergy effects between the two factories of the group. The prospects for market development were viewed in the same manner as for the porcelain factory: due to the expansion of hydroelectrical power plants and the electrification of households and manufacturing, an increased demand for electrical accessories, switches, and so forth could be assumed.

On July 13, 1922, the German firm and Braun-Stammfest together applied at the Ministry of the Interior for the license to found the electro-technical firm, which was to be named Oberösterreichische Elektrotechnische Werke Aktien-Gesellschaft (Upper Austrian Electro-technical Works Joint Stock Company). Formally, the shares again had to be paid in cash to be redeemed for the interim certificates, which had been previously floated. The payments were formally made by Braun-Stammfest (6% of the nominal capital), the German firm (12.5%), and the Oberösterreichische Porzellan Industrie AG (30%), among others. Furthermore, the financial firm Hoerner & Honsell from Trieste, Italy, was named as a substantial investor.

Since the construction work had not yet progressed much, the Ministry of the Interior delayed the founding process. The license was granted shortly before Christmas and the constituting general meeting was held on December 28, 1922. Braun Stammfest became president of the board and Gottfried Kunwald vice president. Ordinary members were, among others, Hochapfel, Jaentsch, and Schumpeter. Members from Germany were Hermann F. Buseck (Frankfurt), Jakob H. Buseck (Frankfurt), and Louis Ostertag (Munich). Landesberger, and Roth from N. Rella & Neffe as well as a further investor from Wels (Josef Waltl) also joined the board.[23]

In October 1922, after the stabilization of the Austrian currency, the consortium also requested a license to found the Glas Industrie Aktien-Gesellschaft "Rudolfshütte" (Glass Industry Joint Stock Company "Rudolf's hut," henceforth referred to as Glass Industry Rudolfshütte or merely Rudolfshütte).[24] Braun-Stammfest, Schumpeter, Hochapfel, and a new member of the syndicate named Friedrich

Glas-Industrie Aktien-Gesellschaft "Rudolfshütte," (2) Oberösterreichische Elektrotechnische Werke Aktien-Gesellschaft, March 3, 1922; WStLA, Lg., Box 731, VrXXIII, 5603/24, Letter from Adolf Schindler to the Vienna Commercial Court on the compensation procedure, November 18, 1924.

[23] ÖStA, AdR, BmIuU, Gz. 40,558/22, Zl. 51061/22, Oberösterreichische Elektrotechnische Werke Aktien-Gesellschaft in Wien. In Errichtung; *Compass*, Vol. 1, 1925, p. 1118.

[24] WStLA, Lg., Box 731, VrXXIII, 5603/24, 1. Part, Hearing of the accused Dr Rudolf Maria Braun-Stammfest, p. 201g.

Mayer-Winterhalde acted as applicants. In the application letter they argued that, during the now disintegrated monarchy, Bohemia had been the center of glass production, a region which was now a foreign country separated by a tariff barrier. Therefore, the applicants expected a "tremendous demand within the national territory for glass products" and they added:

> For the operational management of the glassworks a first-rate glass expert is available. Under his direction the construction works are to be executed. Talented specialised workers, among them glass blowers, are to be employed from Germany. The acquiring of the workers is facilitated by the good relations of the founding consortium to German glass factories.

This time, the total nominal capital was to be 1.6 billion kronen, due to the more advanced inflation. Formally, as shareholders who paid in the capital, some firm-related persons, external investors, and financial firms were named. These were Braun-Stammfest (18,75%), Schumpeter (1.25%), Josef Waltl, an industrialist from Wels (12.5%), Fritz Mayer-Winterhalde (25%), Carl Count Oettingen-Wallerstein from Germany (17.5%), and again Hoerner & Honsell (17.5%)[25]

The founders intended to employ 300 to 400 workers, producing glass bottles and window glass.[26] Unfortunately, just at the time the application to found the glass firm was filed, rumours began circulating that the founding consortia of the Braun-Stammfest firms applied unsound business practices, and this led to a delay in the authorization. The newspaper *Die Börse* had insinuated that the founders sold worthless securities, writing about the development of a flourishing dubious secondary market of interim certificates. Although the paper was infamous for half-truths and untruths, the ministry itself was extremely skeptical of the way in which Braun-Stammfest had managed to initiate the founding procedure of his companies informally several months before officially applying for the license to incorporate the respective firms. The ministry officials noted the informal closed investment fund with strong suspicion, because the official procedure was that a registered firm had to be founded first.

Between December 1, 1922, and January 23, 1923, Braun-Stammfest, his attorney Dr Max Stadlen, and Gottfried Kunwald had several meeting dates at the ministry.[27] They unanimously explained that the founding consortia believed in

[25] ÖStA, AdR, BmIuU, Gz. 57,903/22, Zl. 58,827/22, Schumpeter et al. to Bundesministerium für Inneres und Unterricht, Notice of receipt October 23, 1922.

[26] *Compass*, Vol. 4, 1923, p. 110.

[27] WStLA, Lg., Box 731, VrXXIII, 5603/24, 1. Part, Hearing of the accused Dr Rudolf Maria Braun-Stammfest, p. 201j. When Kunwald was interrogated as a witness in the Braun-Stammfest trial he stated that his role in the industrial group was quite insignificant. He explained that he only had helped Braun-Stammfest with regard to the difficulties with the interim certificates in early 1923 and as a legal adviser in some cases of transfers of real estate. Kunwald emphasized that he was not actively involved in the management of the electro-technical company, where he appeared as vice president. WStLA,

the young enterprises and that they themselves held relevant amounts of the interim certificates, while only some private buyers had sold them on secondary markets, where they had indeed achieved substantial price increases due to inflation. Furthermore, they declared that with the means collected by interim certificates they had made investments which would be brought into the companies at their own cost, through which neither the buyers of the interim certificates nor the company shares would be harmed, whereas all investors would be protected from a fall in value due to inflation. The Viennese police and Wels district administrative authority carried out investigations to determine whether there had been any illegalities in the founding fund. In awkward bureaucratic language, the ministry assessed that the chosen form of financing was "under private law possible yet not entirely harmless from the point of view of the public interest since it opens the door for unprincipled exploitation [of investors]." The approach was not directly considered unlawful and the ministry exhorted the founders that "such papers," since they are not forbidden, should be bought by investors

> in reliance upon the concessionary authority, which implies the duty to closely monitor procedures like this so that no harm is done by the unusual approach which Dr. Braun-Stammfest has chosen, which is to be repelled by the concession regime with its heavy armour.[28]

After the investigation, the license for the incorporation of Glass Industry Rudolfshütte was granted. The company was founded with a share capital of 1.6 billion kronen, divided into eight million shares of 200 kronen each. Again, the founding board represented remarkable social capital. The constituting general assembly on Februray 22, 1923 elected Braun-Stammfest president of the board. Board members became, among others, Borovy, Franz Haller, Hochapfel, Mayer-Winterhalde, Richard Dworczak (authorized signatory of the Biedermann Bank), Karl Krapf (retired senate president in Graz), Siegfried Rebner (authorized signatory of the Anglo-Austrian Bank Ltd), Karl Richter (Mayor of Wels), Josef Waltl (industrialist in Wels), Friedrich Jaentsch, Julian Gečmen (industrialist in Prague), Demetriu Fudulescu (engineer in Bucharest), and Rainer Habsburg

Lg., Box 731, VrXXIII, 5603/24, 3. Part, Hearing of witness Dr Gottfried Kunwald, pp. 1380–1. For statements of Braun-Stammfest concerning this matter, see also ÖStA, AdR, BmF, Bankkommission, Box 52, Protokoll vom 1. Dezember 1922, Polizei-Direktion in Wien, Vereinsbureau, zu Zl. 4489/23; and ÖStA, AdR, BmF, Bankkommission, Box 52, Protokoll vom 1. Dezember 1922, Letter from Braun-Stammfest to Polizeidirektion Wien, Aeusserung betreffend die Ausgabe von Interimsscheinen [...] ad Zl. 1/6.

[28] ÖStA, BmIuU, GZ 57,903/22, Zl. 2147/23, Note in the file from January 12, 1923.

(member of the Habsburg Family, privateer in Vienna).[29] The composition of the board impressively demonstrated the ability of Braun-Stammfest and Schumpeter to match influential public servants, bankers, and industrialists with provincial investors and aristocratic figureheads.

A fourth factory in Hainfeld, Lower Austria

The fourth firm of the Braun-Stammfest group emerged in another provincial town, in Hainfeld, Lower Austria. Here the Metallurgische Werke und Maschinenfabriks Aktien Gesellschaft (Metallurgical Works and Machine Shop Ltd) was to be set up. This establishment was founded in the same way as the three firms in Wels and was financially firmly interwoven with the Braun-Stammfest group. The founders acquired necessary funds by issuing interim certificates, and local investors were also approached. The founding committee acquired the site of a factory that belonged to an engineering firm.[30] On January 4, 1922, the request for the license to found the Hainfeld Joint Stock Company arrived at the Ministry of the Interior. In this case, aside from Braun-Stammfest, the local industrialist Arthur Flusser, Dr Gustav Fall, president of the Südbahn-Gesellschaft,[31] and two representatives of Bulgarian financial firms were among the applicants.

The strategic concept for the Hainfeld factory was similar to the other start-ups. First, the plan was to arrange for the import substitution for goods that had been produced in other regions of the Habsburg Empire and were now outside the customs borders. Second, the factory would produce goods for which a growing sales volume could be expected. In the case of Hainfeld, the entrepreneurs intended

> the production of anti-corrosive paints for iron and masonry, which were to be derived from metals (zinc), the intended use of which can be termed indefinite. This is because almost all machines, iron constructions, railroad cars and the like […] must be provided with such a protective coating.[32]

[29] Zentralblatt 1923, p. 359 f, Wien, I., Renngasse 14, Glasindustrie Aktiengesellschaft "Rudolfshütte," Wien, February 23, 1923; Wiener Zeitung, March 16, 1923, p. 170; *Neues Wiener Journal*, February 24, 1923, p. 11.

[30] Friedländer's und Ferd. Huffel's Nachfolger Ing. J. Schmied in Hainfeld, Lower Austria, owned by engineer Josef Schmidt. See WStLA, Lg., Box 731, VrXXIII, 5603/24, 3. Part, Metallurgische Werke & Maschinenfabriks A.G., Heinfeld Nied.Österr, Gutachten (official expertise), p. 944.

[31] Südbahn-Gesellschaft was a leading railway and tourism company. *Compass*, Vol. 1, 1922, pp. 1058–79.

[32] ÖStA, BmIuU, GZ 993/22, Zl. 3258/22, Application for permission to establish a public limited company under the name "Hainfelder Metallurgische Werke und Maschinenfabriks A. G.," Notice of receipt January 4, 1922.

Other intended products and services were any goods produced with a forging hammer, wind motors, steam boilers, and repair services.[33] In addition to Braun-Stammfest, among the founding shareholders who formally guaranteed to pay in for the new shares were his wife Rose Braun-Stammfest, the local industrialist Oskar Flusser, several representatives from Bulgaria, and Eugen Oettingen-Wallerstein from Bavaria, who had also participated in the foundation of some of the factories in Wels. In this case, neither Schumpeter nor Kunwald appeared as founders.[34] The founding general meeting was held on March 15, 1922, and it immediately decided to take over the assets from the founding committee. Beyond this, expenses of Braun-Stammfest of 119 million kronen were recognized. The share capital amounted to 125 million kronen divided into 625,000 shares at 200 kronen each. Because of the acquisition of the assets of the founding committee and the expenses associated with the foundation, the company was encumbered with debts from the outset. Braun-Stammfest personally suffered losses when he accepted counterfeit interim certificates for new shares.[35]

Braun-Stammfest did not act as president of the board of this company; this was Gustav Fall. In addition to Braun-Stammfest, ordinary board members were Oscar Flusser, Hochapfel (Mercur Bank), Ludwig Ostertag (Munich), Schumpeter, and others. Engineer Richard Heindl was appointed executive director.[36]

The well-established Viennese construction company Redlich & Berger was commissioned with the construction work, and machines were ordered from the company Zahn & Co., Berlin, which also delivered the construction plan. First construction measures were to repair the worn buildings, further expand water power, and build a zinc white hut production plant.[37]

In September 1922, an extraordinary general assembly decided to increase the capital from 125 to 250 million kronen, with a subscription price of 800 kronen for existing shareholders and 850 kronen for the underwriting syndicate. This was at the beginning of the bull market at the Vienna Stock Exchange, so the shares could easily be sold. The issue yielded around 0.5 billion kronen, which allowed a showing of a 432 million kronen premium reserve in the balance sheet for 1922 in addition to the nominal capital of 250 million kronen. The total balance sheet

[33] WStLA, Lg., Box 731, VrXXIII, 5603/24, 3. Part, Metallurgische Werke & Maschinenfabriks A.G., Hainfeld, Official expertise, p. 944.

[34] WStLA, Lg., Box 731, VrXXIII, 5603/24, 3. Part, Metallurgische Werke & Maschinenfabriks A.G., Hainfeld, Official expertise, p. 944.

[35] WStLA, Lg., Box 731, VrXXIII, 5603/24, 1. Part, Hearing of the accused Dr Rudolf Maria Braun-Stammfest, p. 201ll v.

[36] *Compass*, Vol. 1, 1924, p. 829.

[37] WStLA, Lg., Box 731, VrXXIII, 5603/24, 1. Part, Hearing of the accused Dr Max Borovy, p. 521a v; WStLA, Lg., Box 731, VrXXIII, 5603/24, 3. Part, Official expertise Metallurgische Werke, p. 946.

sum was around 1.9 billion kronen and the equity ratio was only about 35 percent, despite the capital increase.[38]

In addition to the four central companies of the Braun-Stammfest group, the founder invested in other ventures where he remained a minority shareholder and did not gain any decisive influence. The most important of these ventures was the Österreichische Holzapfel-Farbenfabriks AG (Austrian Holzapfel Paint Ltd). In this company, which was formed on December 14, 1922, Braun-Stammfest initially served as president and Schumpeter was a member of the board of directors. However, the majority of shares and thus the control lay with the British Holzapfel group, which determined the conduct on this basis. Therefore, this company, which produced anti-rust paints, ship floor paints, and enamel paints in Gutenstein (Lower Austria) cannot be considered an immediate part of the Braun-Stammfest Group.[39] Braun-Stammfest may however, have hoped for some synergies between the company and the factory in Hainfeld, as these sites produced partly similar products.

The actual Braun-Stammfest group presented itself as follows at the turn of 1922/3. The porcelain factory was already producing. It had a financially tense but defensible status. However, the start-up operation was still causing losses and was plagued by technical problems. The construction of the other factories had not yet reached the point of (regular) production. In times of scarce liquidity, this urgently required the provision of financial resources, with the Metallurgical Works in Hainfeld having already repaid expensive debt financing by means of the capital increase in November 1922. During the first months of 1923, as already mentioned, the stock market remained very receptive, so that one could hope for further capital increases.

9.3 The bull market of 1923

At the turn of 1922/3, corporate debts had become a heavy burden in light of the shortage of money and high interest rates in Austria. To escape this cost trap, management aimed to get fresh equity capital via further share issues. At the same time, Braun-Stammfest and his colleagues desperately searched for opportunities to improve the status of the group through cooperation with financially strong partners. Nevertheless, the financial problems became more and more urgent during the year. Braun-Stammfest began to juggle financial means within the

[38] ÖStA, AdR, BmIuU, Gz. 993/22, Zl. 62,261/22, Request for approval of capital increase from 125 million to 250 million kronen, October 24, 1922; *Compass*, Vol. 1, 1924, p. 829.

[39] ÖStA, AdR, BmIuU, Gz. 54,645/22; *Compass*, Vol. 1, 1924, p. 934.

group at the edge of legality in order to bridge the most acute funding shortfalls with short-term shifts between the individual companies.

At the end of 1922, construction work on the glass factory and the electrical engineering work in Wels had to be largely discontinued. Braun-Stammfest instructed the company's management to by all means continue the activities at a very low level, "otherwise it would quickly become known in Vienna that the construction was discontinued. If at least minimal activities continued, he could still claim that there was no question of a complete cessation of building work."[40] The situation in Wels was exacerbated by the fact that the technical director Jaentsch notoriously argued with the construction firm Rella, as he was "always dissatisfied with the work of others."[41] At the time, the two plants had already been burdened with extensive profiteer loans, with weekly interest charges of up to 5 percent, which was more than 1,000 percent per year.

Usurious interest and false promises

In this precarious situation, from mid-1922 onward, Braun-Stammfest clung to the promises of a man who offered to invest in the industries and solve all financial problems. This person, Fritz Mayer-Winterhalde, was introduced to him in May 1922[42] by a certain Colonel Pichler as someone who belonged to a wealthy industrialist family and wanted to participate in emerging Austrian factories. Mayer-Winterhalde's family background gave the impression of utmost respectability. It was said that his mother came from the Mühlig family, one of the most important glass industry dynasties in Bohemia, and his father held a high position (*Sektionschef*) in an Austrian ministry. Mayer-Winterhalde claimed that he owned a quarter of the Mühlig Glass Works in Czechoslowakia, but that he intended to sell his shares to his uncle to invest the proceeds in Austria. He stated that he was particularly interested in the Glass Industry Rudolfshütte and promised enormous sums of money in the medium term, along with as much as 2 billion kronen in the short term in 1922. At the same time, he suggested to Braun-Stammfest, in view of the upcoming business connection, that he not look for contacts with other investors and not search for close ties to a bank, as did most of the Austrian industrial firms.

Yet during the ensuing months he always came up with flimsy excuses when he was supposed to provide larger sums of money. At one point he claimed that a bank had made bad bookings, at other times he pleaded errors and legal problems with

[40] WStLA, Lg., Box 731, VrXXIII, 5603/24, 3. Part, Indictment, June 15, 1929, pp. 1771v–1772.

[41] WStLA, Lg., Box 731, VrXXIII, 5603/24, 1. Part, Hearing of the accused Dr. Schumpeter, p.514g v.

[42] WStLA, Lg., Box 731, VrXXIII, 5603/24, 1. Part, Hearing of the accused Dr Braun-Stammfest, pp. 201c and 201mm v. Mayer-Winterhalde's view is documented in: WStLA, Lg., Box 731, VrXXIII, 5603/24, 2. Part, Hearing of witness Fritz Mayer-Winterhalde, pp. 1304–8.

the transfer of funds from abroad. In the meantime, Braun-Stammfest was stalled and took more and more short-term financing at horrendous weekly interest rates. For several months he hoped to be able to repay this immediately with the expected funds. Mayer-Winterhalde even agreed to a financial plan, which included that he would refund half of the interest costs incurred by the delay. Mayer-Winterhalde convinced Braun-Stammfest to assign him 380,000 shares of the Hainfelder joint-stock company at far below the current price and in October 1922 for the first time provided the modest sum of 200 million kronen. At this time, he again promised to invest between 1 and 2 billion kronen within a month. After a while, he paid in a further small sum of 140 million kronen. Still, he blustered about credits in Munich and brought a check for over 20,000 Swiss francs, which later proved to have been illegally obtained. Braun-Stammfest still relied on Mayer-Winterhalde and left him another 650,000 shares in Glass Industry Rudolfshütte at face value, although the price was four times the nominal value. Meanwhile, Mayer-Winterhalde stalled Braun-Stammfest with ever more unbelievable stories. He told him that a letter from Deutsche Bank to Vereinsbank had been embezzled, but the matter would be cleared up. In early February 1923, he pretended that his uncle Mühlig owed him 2 billion kronen, which he would soon receive in cash. On February 20, 1923 he appeared in the office of Braun-Stammfest with a man whom he introduced as Mühlig. The alleged uncle assured he would immediately send 10 billion kronen to his nephew via the Anglobank. It was not until March 10, 1923, after Mayer-Winterhalde had told him further implausible stories about adversities and repudiations, that Braun-Stammfest contacted the Anglobank directly, only to learn that Mayer-Winterhalde was not known there at all. This was when Braun-Stammfest had to admit to himself that he had been courting an impostor as a potential investor for months.

Desperate moves

In the meantime, the entire group had run into life-threatening debt with short-term money at usurious interest rates. Braun-Stammfest urgently needed to find another, more reliable partner.

Of all the works, the porcelain factory had so far developed best. Although it was still operating at a loss and suffered from quality issues, it had at least taken up regular production. However, the factory's management was not yet successful at producing the appropriate quality with the new tunnel kiln. In this situation, the management of the Braun-Stammfest group decided to enter a far-reaching agreement with a group of Viennese businessmen led by Wilhelm Rasper Sr,[43]

[43] WStLA, Lg., Box 731, VrXXIII, 5603/24, 1. Part, Hearing of the accused Dr Braun-Stammfest, pp. 201c–201f.

who was president of the Wiener Kaufmannsbank (Viennese Merchant Bank) and a well-known porcelain trader. Together they founded the common Porzellan Vertriebsgesellschaft mbH (Porcelain Sales Company Ltd), which was supposed to set up a shop in Vienna in Habsburgergasse. The Wiener Kaufmannsbank provided a loan of 3 billion kronen at an interest rate of some 170 percent per year, which was expensive but still cheaper than the usury loans.[44]

During an extraordinary general assembly on May 9, 1923, several personalities of the Rasper group joined the board of the Porcelain Company, among them Wilhelm Rasper Jr, Dr Franz Quidenus (head of the chamber of trade), and Ferdinand Herzfeld (director of the Wiener Kaufmannsbank). Rasper Sr *de facto* took the lead at the Porcelain Company and his sons formally became directors in Wels, with Wilhelm Rasper Jr responsible for technical management and Robert Rasper for commercial management.[45]

In the course of the organizational changes, Rasper Sr bought 125,000 Porcelain Company shares from Braun-Stammfest. He paid around 3,000 kronen per share while their market value was around 10,000 kronen, and he obtained some 300 million kronen for the renovation of the shop. Ultimately, in the share sale Braun-Stammfest generated fresh cash to the amount of some 375 million kronen and hoped that Rasper would overcome the quality, cost, and marketing problems of the porcelain factory. However, the new strategic orientation of the business required costly investments. Rasper shifted the focus of production from technical porcelain to household porcelain, which required expensive technical renovations in the factory. He ordered a second tunnel kiln for biscuit firing, an expansion of the painting department, and a residential building for workers.[46]

To obtain some financial maneuvering space for the renovation activities, on May 9, 1923 the general assembly of the company decided on a capital increase from 250 to 500 million kronen. Existing shareholders were to get 312,500 fresh shares at a price of 5,600 kronen per piece; an underwriting syndicate would take the remainder of 937,500 shares at 6,000 kronen. The syndicate consisted of new functionaries like Rasper and friends and old ones like Braun-Stammfest, Schumpeter, and friends. At the time of this resolution, the market price for Porcelain Company shares was between 5,000 and 9,000 kronen, which meant that the underwriting syndicate had offered a fair price. The newly raised capital was to be used to pay off loans, finance the reconstruction of the factory, and buy workers' housing. Rasper intended to hire highly skilled workers from Germany to produce high-quality porcelain goods. In June 1923, the capital increase was successfully executed by the Wiener Kaufmannsbank. It gained over 7 billion

[44] WStLA, Lg., Box 731, VrXXIII, 5603/24, 3. Part, Verdict, June 15, 1929, pp. 1775v, 1776.

[45] WStLA, Lg., Box 731, VrXXIII, 5603/24, 1. Part, Hearing of the accused Franz Haller, p. 546.

[46] ÖStA, BmIuU, GZ 205983/21, Zl. 31625/23, Minutes of the first Ordinary Annual General Meeting of the Oberösterreichischen Porzellan-Industrie-Aktien-Gesellschaft, May 9, 1923. A two-page, illustrated report on the factory after this reconstruction was published in Österreichs Industrie (1925, p. 57f).

kronen, of which, however, 250 million had to be paid as fees for the bank. Yet this successful transaction noticeably eased the acute financial pressures.

The factory's previous manager Jaentsch resigned, the adaptation of the porcelain factory immediately set in, and the company bought a residential house for workers at some 3 billion kronen, which absorbed nearly half of the fresh means. This building had been erected between May 1922 and February 1923 by Glass Industry Rudolfshütte. In this firm's accounting records, 950 million kronen in installation costs and substantial fees for financing costs and other expenses were booked on the corresponding account. All in all, the attributed costs amounted to 3 billion kronen.[47] This value was taken as a basis for the sales price. The establishment of the sales business, the reconstruction of the factory, and the acquisition of the house soon depleted the fresh means of the Porcelain Company. Since the revenues of the factory were still not developing well by the summer of 1923, there was again an urgent need for fresh liquidity. Once again, usurous loans had to be taken out. Rasper and his sons failed to overcome quality problems and did not manage to increase production to such an extent that a break-even could be reached. They were not able to realize the cost advantages of mass production in the tunnel kiln. In September 1923, Wilhelm Kostial was hired as a new technical expert for the kiln. He managed to get the production procedures under control and the reject rate was significantly reduced. However, at the end of the year, operational losses amounted to some 100 million kronen in the official balance sheet, while in reality they were much higher. From January 1923 until the shutdown, Kostial served as operations manager of the entire factory.[48]

In the balance sheet for 1923, the Porcelain Company still showed a share capital of 500 million kronen and a reserve fund of 8.2 billion kronen. The level of debt was named at only around 1.9 million kronen. On the asset side, the factory was valued at 6.51 billion kronen and the stock at 2.09 billion. In addition, debtors of 1.23 billion and deposits to the amount of 0.5 billion kronen appeared.[49] Thus, the Porcelain Company still managed to make a solid impression in its balance sheet for 1923. However, the assets were set at a dubiously high value. In autumn 1923, the managers intended to list the Porcelain Company at the Viennese Stock Exchange—a plan that never materialized.[50]

The other establishments in Wels lagged even further behind in their development. As previously mentioned, Glass Industry Rudolfshütte was formally established until February 1923, taking over the founding costs and the assets of the founding committee. Thus, the firm was heavily in debt from the start.

[47] WStLA, Lg., Box. 731, VrXXIII, 5603/24, 3. Part, Indictment, p. 1463f.

[48] WStLA, Lg., Box. 731, VrXXIII, 5603/24, 1. Part, Hearing of the accused Franz Haller, p. 564f; Hearing of the accused Dr Braun-Stammfest, p. 201www v; Hearing of witness Wilhelm Kostial, pp. 748–750; Official expertise Porcelain company, pp. 1027 and 1092.

[49] *Compass*, Vol. 1, 1925, p. 723.

[50] WStLA, Lg., Box. 731, VrXXIII, 5603/24, 1. Part, Hearing of the accused Dr Braun-Stammfest, p. 20mmm v.

Construction work had been delayed due to the devaluation of the Austrian kronen in 1922 and the sellers of the site, the briquette works owners, made additional demands regarding the sales price. To avoid further delays, Schumpeter recommended a settlement, which was finally accepted by Braun-Stammfest.[51] In order to restart the stalled construction activity, substantial additional funds had to be provided. Braun-Stammfest made use of different sources of fresh funds. During March 1923 he, his wife, Schumpeter, and Borovi lent some 300 to 400 million kronen to the company.[52] In April 1923, the private banker Oeller provided 900 million kronen at an interest rate of 84 percent, which had to be secured by mortgage. In October 1923, Braun-Stammfest again procured 200 million kronen. Finally, in December 1923 the firm obtained a loan of 4 billion kronen at 122 percent per year from Wiener Kaufmannsbank. This allowed a roll-over with earlier more expensive financing. At that time, Glass Industry Rudolfshütte also decided to acquire a residential house for workers (after the sale of a house to the Porcelain Company in the middle of the year) at 1.06 billion kronen.[53] At the same time, the company began to prepare a capital increase to pay off the debts. Management hoped to achieve around 20 billion kronen.

However, the construction measures were not finished and Glass Industry Rudolfshütte could still not commence production. In 1924, the construction of the glass trough had only progressed to the point of the excavation of an earth pit, the gas generator was not yet functional, several glass blowing machines had been delivered but not installed, and various construction materials lay around the site. Oddly, only the administration building had been luxuriously completed at an early stage of the construction activities.[54] In contrast to the Porcelain Company, Rudolfshütte refrained from publishing an annual balance for 1923 in the financial yearbook *Compass*. In the edition of the price sheet for exotic securities from September 30, 1923, the share with a nominal value of 200 kronen was quoted at 2,500 kronen.

The electro-technical works also had to take out usury loans, while Braun-Stammfest was being stalled by Mayer-Winterhalde. As in the glass factory, construction work had largely stopped in early 1923.[55] On February 17, the company's management entered a loan agreement with Bankhouse Gerstbauer, which envisaged a credit line of 800 million kronen, though at highly unfavorable conditions.

[51] WStLA, Lg., Box. 731, VrXXIII, 5603/24, 1. Part, Hearing of the accused Dr Schumpeter, pp. 512 v, 513 v.

[52] WStLA, Lg., Box. 731, VrXXIII, 5603/24, 1. Part, Hearing of the accused Dr Braun-Stammfest, p. 201q v.

[53] WStLA, Lg., Box. 731, VrXXIII, 5603/24, 1. Part, Hearing of the accused Dr Braun-Stammfest, p. 201m v.

[54] WStLA, Lg., Box 731, VrXXIII, 5603/24, 1. Part, Letter of Adolf Schindler, November 18, 1924, p. 559f.

[55] WStLA, Lg., Box. 731, VrXXIII, 5603/24, 1. Part, Hearing of the accused Dr Braun-Stammfest, p. 201yy.

By March 1924, the costs for this loan had risen to nearly 940 million kronen. Beyond that, Braun-Stammfest personally provided some means a number of times. All of these measures allowed the resumption of construction activities which were finished by the end of August. Most of the machines had already been ordered and delivered in 1922. Since they were not paid for before 1923, the prices had increased significantly. In September 1923, production started on a trial basis. However, this early stage of production did not yet yield positive returns; it primarily served to coordinate the machines and processes. In the beginning some 80 percent of the goods produced were unusable or inferior. The goods had to be thrown away by the wagonload or sold very cheaply. Directors Tempes and Lederer got into a serious conflict. Lederer claimed that he did not get merchandise of a quality that could be successfully marketed, and Tempes complained about a lack of qualified workers.[56]

In May 1923, the company decided to double the share capital from 200 to 400 million kronen, which meant issuing one million fresh shares at a nominal value of 200 kronen. However, ministerial approval was not granted before October. Bankhaus Gerstbauer was entrusted with the implementation and Braun-Stammfest guaranteed the payment of unsold shares. Only 538,000 shares were absorbed by the market and Braun-Stammfest formally took over the remaining 462,000 shares; allegedly he acquired them directly for third persons in order to spare them the Gerstbauer bank fees. Instead it was more likely that he purchased them himself to uphold the share price and keep up the appearance of a successful share issue. On September 30 in the price sheet for exotic securities the shares were valued at 4,500 kronen. Finally, some shares seem to have been paid for by Schumpeter, Borovi, and others.[57]

At the turn of 1923/4, the electro-technical works could finally take up regular production. However, the products had to be introduced to the market at prices that did not completely cover costs. Moreover, expensive supplies, for example, copper, were a cost burden, and deficient parts delivered by the Porcelain Company caused trouble.[58] The electro-technical works published a balance sheet for 1923 that showed a nominal capital of 400 million kronen, a reserve of 1.835 billion kronen, and a somewhat worrying debt of 5.4 billion kronen. The biggest assets were buildings valued at 3.5 billion kronen, machines and facilities (3.0 billion kronen), and stocks (678 million kronen). Again, as with the porcelain factory, the assets were rated at questionably high values.

[56] WStLA, Lg., Box. 731, VrXXIII, 5603/24, 1. Part, Hearing of the accused Dr Braun-Stammfest, p. 201w v and 201aaa; Hearing of witness Norbert Tempes, pp. 1288–90.

[57] WStLA, Lg., Box 731, VrXXIII, 5603/24, 3. Part, Verdict, June 15, 1929, pp. 1769 v and 1777; 1. Part, Hearing of the accused Dr Braun-Stammfest, p. 201w.

[58] WStLA, Lg., Box. 731, VrXXIII, 5603/24, 1. Part, Hearing of the accused F. Haller, p. 547d; Hearing of the accused Dr. Max Borovy, p. 521.

The factory in Hainfeld developed in a similar manner. Construction activities at the Hainfelder Metallurgical Works dragged on until December 1923. In the beginning the Patak brothers and plant manager Schulz were responsible, and they were replaced in July 1923 by the engineers Förster and Pichler.[59] In Hainfeld as well as in Wels, the fluctuations in managing personnel were an indication of the permanent technical and commercial problems. Above all, the production of anti-corrosive paint was delayed, so that initially only traditional goods produced with a forging hammer could be manufactured. The project of installing wind motors had been completely given up.

During the construction phase, in April 1923 the local Savings Bank in the nearby small town of Mödling provided a loan of 1 billion kronen at an interest rate of 80 percent per year, which was quite favorable at the time. At this time, Schumpeter became actively involved in an attempt to improve the financial situation of the group. Together with Kunwald, he held concrete talks with potential investors who seemed willing to buy the Metallurgical Works in Hainfeld. The sales proceeds would have eased the financial pressures of the other firms of the Braun-Stammfest group. The potential investors were Benjamin Roos from Berlin and a Hungarian group. Yet Braun-Stammfest could not bring himself to agree to the sale of one of his firms. He delayed matters until the opportunity was missed and the interested parties withdrew.[60]

Consequently, there was nothing left to do but develop the company as part of the group. A capital increase, which had been decided at an extraordinary general meeting in May, was not officially approved before December. The ministry had been cautious because of the delays in the completion of the factory. Ultimately, the new capital issue was only a partial success. Of 1.25 million new shares only 340,000 shares were sold at a price of 4,000 kronen, while the rest were taken over by Braun-Stammfest, though he could not pay for them. The entire procedure yielded only 1.36 instead of the hoped for 5 billion kronen and Braun-Stammfest became heavily indebted to the company.

Toward the end of the year, production of the anti-corrosive paint finally began. However, it turned out that the machinery had to be adapted for smooth operations, for which funds were not available. Thus, production at full running costs did not generate any relevant revenue.

In the 1924 edition of the financial yearbook *Compass*, the Hainfeld Metallurgical Company did not yet report a balance sheet; instead, it merely provided outdated information for 1922. However, the company paid out a dividend of 60 kronen for each share with a nominal value of 200 kronen for the business

[59] WStLA, Lg., Box. 731, VrXXIII, 5603/24, 1. Part, Hearing of the accused Franz Haller, p. 547ff.

[60] WStLA, Lg., Box. 731, VrXXIII, 5603/24, 1. Part, Hearing of the accused Dr Schumpeter, p. 514j; ÖStA, Bestand GK, 616-1, Box 850, File 1269, Schumpeter to Kunwald, February 3, 1923 and March 23, 1923.

year 1922. This seems to have supported the share price, as the price sheet for exotic securities from September 30, 1923 reported a market value of 8,000 kronen per share.[61] Yet this publication also seems not to have displayed the values very reliably. It was probably influenced by the interests of market participants, and one must take into account that Vienna had a very tight securities market, which meant that large sales quickly led to price decreases.

The permanent financial distress of all of his start-ups during 1923 forced Braun-Stammfest as well as other managers and investors to seek adventurous redeployments of liquid means. Again and again, they had to withdraw money from one company to sort out urgent financial problems in another. Some examples illustrate this:

- After the Mödling savings bank granted the Hainfeld Metallurgical works a large loan, Braun-Stammfest borrowed a substantial share of this sum in November and lent it to Glass Industry Rudolfshütte, even though the company in Hainfeld had provided mortgage collateral for this money and bore the interests and fees for the loan.
- Braun-Stammfest used the abovementioned sale of the residential house for workers by Glass Industry Rudolfshütte to the Porcelain Company at an overcharged rate of some 3 billion kronen to bolster a separate account, from which he financed the other start-ups as needed. This meant that he withdrew money from the Porcelain Company through the overcharged price and from Glass Industry Rudolfshütte through the establishment of the separate account, although the glass works would have needed the means urgently.
- In May 1923, in agreement with Rasper, Braun-Stammfest handed over 300 to 400 million kronen, which originated from the capital increase of the Porcelain Company, to the glass works.
- In August 1923, Braun-Stammfest borrowed 2 billion kronen from the Hainfeld works to pay the shares he had taken over in the course of the capital increase of the Porcelain Company.[62]

Due to ongoing measures like these, Braun-Stammfest's central office in Vienna became a kind of hub for shifting funds between the group's firms. Since he repeatedly borrowed money from one firm to lend it to another, his positions as both debtor and creditor of the companies took on dramatic new dimensions. The financial situation of the entire group deteriorated during 1923, despite several capital increases, since all of the businesses were not yet manufacturing or were manufacturing at a loss.

[61] *Compass*, Vol. 1, 1924, p. 829f.

[62] WStLA, Lg., Box. 731, VrXXIII, 5603/24, 1. Part, Hearing of the accused Dr Braun-Stammfest, p. 201ac.

9.4 Financial breakdown

As mentioned in the introductory remarks to Chapter 8, the overall economic conditions for companies in Austria were difficult around the turn of 1923/4. The stock market boom was over, major speculation against the French franc had failed in spring, and loans had become even scarcer in the subsequent banking crisis. The entire Austrian economy suffered from an acute shortage of liquidity. In retrospect, Schumpeter[63] considered the crisis of 1924 to be the most serious since the great stock market crash of 1873.[64] Within this economic framework, the Braun-Stammfest group made some final unsuccessful attempts at survival. After the losses of 1923 and due to heavy debt, only desperate financial maneuvers remained, and the group eventually broke down.

Around the end of 1923, Braun-Stammfest acquired 600,000 shares in the Wiener Handelskreditbank. In this bank, which as previously mentioned belonged to the entourage of the Biedermann Bank, Schumpeter held important functions. Braun-Stammfest took over the shares from a syndicate that consisted of the bank's directors Ezdorf, Rohatyn, and Rosner, who together with Schumpeter formed the executive board.[65] Braun-Stammfest paid a portion of the purchase price with shares in his group's companies, while another part he owed the syndicate. As a new major shareholder, he became vice president of the bank and could use his new influence on business conduct to ensure that the Hainfeld Metallurgical works be granted a loan of 2 billion kronen. As in other cases, these means were not exclusively used for the borrower; in this case, some 800 million kronen were transferred to other group companies.[66] The loan was associated with such extremely burdensome conditions that the Braun-Stammfest group had reached the brink of formal insolvency by early 1924. In this situation, directors Rosner and Rohatyn sued for fulfillment of the credit agreement.[67] They sought to exert pressure on Braun-Stammfest, Schumpeter, and the Biedermann Bank to force Braun-Stammfest to mobilize any quiet reserves. Yet this hope proved futile, as he no longer had any reserves at his disposal.[68]

At this time, Schumpeter realized that the three directors who had sold their Handelskreditbank shares to Braun-Stammfest had tried to book the sale as a bank deal and debit the bank with the default after the buyer was unable to pay the full price. Consequently, they had to accept that the deal had been their own personal

[63] WStLA, Lg., Box. 731, VrXXIII, 5603/24, 1. Part, Hearing of the accused Dr Schumpeter, p. 514k.

[64] In this year, the Austrian economy had been lastingly shocked by a severe crash, after which two decades of muted growth followed.

[65] *Compass*, Vol. 1, 1923, p. 1373; WStLA, Lg., Box. 731, VrXXIII, 5603/24, 1. Part, Hearing of the accused Dr Braun-Stammfest, p. 201ad.

[66] WStLA, Lg., Box 731, VrXXIII, 5603/24, 3. Part, Verdict, June 15, 1929, p. 1776v.

[67] *Neue Freie Presse*, August 2, 1924, p. 8.

[68] WStLA, Lg., Box. 731, VrXXIII, 5603/24, 1. Part, Hearing of the accused Dr Schumpeter, p. 514e.

responsibility. Despite this partial success, which Schumpeter had achieved as bank manager, the transactions with Braun-Stammfest, along with failed speculations of bank officials, were the main reasons that the Wiener Handelskreditbank finally liquidated in 1925 after futile and costly rescue attempts.[69]

The Wiener Kaufmannsbank had hesitatingly granted a final loan of 2 billion kronen in March 1924.[70] In this final phase, Braun-Stammfest had to commit to accepting higher and higher fees, which in fact were bribes in the form of shares or cash to some of the directors of the bank.[71] In spring 1924, the Electro-technical Company was debited with 600 million and Glass Industry Rudolfshütte with 1.1 billion kronen out of these agreements.

While in 1923 it had been possible to get rid of expensive debts with capital increases, this way out was blocked by 1924 because of the stock exchange crisis. Two last attempts failed. The Hainfeld Metallurgical Company decided on a capital increase, which was delayed by the responsible ministry. Though the attempt was initiated on April 1, 1924, it was too late. Of 2.5 million new shares only 210,238 were sold, yielding no more than 1.198 billion kronen, whereby 892 million kronen were absorbed as fees for the Wiener Kaufmannsbank. Consequently, in April 1924 the workers of the Hainfeld Metallurgical Company were laid off and the factory was shut down. In September 1924 the company declared insolvency and applied for the settlement procedure.[72]

Even more severe consequences resulted from the last attempt by Glass Industry Rudolfshütte to raise fresh capital. In 1923 this firm had succeeded in rescheduling expensive usury loans through a loan from the Wiener Kaufmannsbank of 4 billion kronen at 122 percent per year. At the end of the year, management intended to pay off this debt through a capital increase. Eight million new shares with a total nominal value of 1.6 billion kronen were to be issued to raise share capital from 1.6 to 3.2 billion kronen. The intention was to sell the shares with a nominal value of 200 kronen at a price of 2,500 kronen, which corresponded to the rating in the price sheet for exotic securities from September 1923.[73] An underwriting syndicate was formed by Braun-Stammfest, Schumpeter, and the bankers Gerstbauer and Meisels, with whom the company was already heavily in debt. The capital increase was again delayed by the Ministry of the Interior, as the plant had

[69] *Compass*, Vol. 1, 1926, p. 482; ÖStA, AdR, BmF, Bankkommission, Box 52, File 33, "Dienstnachricht" (Service Notice) No. 27 regarding the audit of Wiener Handelskreditbank AG, January 23, 1925.

[70] WStLA, Lg., Box 731, VrXXIII, 5603/24, 3. Part, Verdict, June 15, 1929, pp. 1776v, 1777.

[71] WStLA, Lg., Box. 731, VrXXIII, 5603/24, 1. Part, Hearing of the accused Dr Braun-Stammfest, p. 201r.

[72] WStLA, Lg., Box 731, VrXXIII, 5603/24, 3. Part, Verdict, June 15, 1929, p. 1777.

[73] *Compass*, Vol. 1, 1925, p. 723f; ÖStA, BmIuU, GZ 57,903/22, Zl. 22531/24, Glasindustrie-Aktiengesellschaft "Rudolfshütte" in Wien, Capital increase from 1,600 auf 3,200 million kronen, notice of receipt, January 9, 1924; WStLA, Lg., Box. 731, VrXXIII, 5603/24, 1. Part, Hearing of the accused Dr Braun-Stammfest, p. 201s v.

not yet started production. By the time the permit was issued on February 28, 1924, economic conditions had fundamentally worsened. The management tried to adapt the plan to the changed market environment and reduced the issue price from 2,500 to 1,500 kronen. Even on these terms, success was highly uncertain. In this situation, Schumpeter and Meisels declared that they no longer felt bound by the syndicate agreement, as the conditions had fundamentally changed due to the reduction of the issue price. Their retreat was not conducive to the course of the issue, which was launched between March 17 and 28, 1924.[74] Instead of the planned 12 billion kronen, the entire issue only yielded 1.25 billion after deducting 250 million kronen in expenses from the Wiener Kaufmannsbank.

From then on, Braun-Stammfest began to sell off shares in all of his industries in order to yield liquid means, which further accelerated the deterioration of the share prices. In April 1924, construction activities at the glass factory had to be stopped and in summer the company declared insolvency.[75]

Schumpeter himself, after he had retreated from the glass industry syndicate, was still prepared "to do something" for this company. At Braun-Stammfest's request, instead of accepting his obligations from the failed issuing syndicate, he personally assumed a guarantee with the Wiener Kaufmannsbank for a loan of 1.8 billion kronen. He wanted to ensure that the factory could be completed by the start of production.[76] This would later cost him dearly. After the insolvency of Glass Industry Rudolfshütte, he was sued for the amount of the guarantee. At the beginning of July 1924, Schumpeter, the mayor of Wels, Karl Richter, and the industrialist Alois Traut resigned from the board.[77]

As mentioned above, the Electro-technical Company had started regular production at the beginning of 1924. On January 25 this firm also opted for a capital increase, which by this time was, however, completely illusory and failed. Due to acute financial problems, the electro-technical firm stopped production on July 1 and applied for insolvency on July 24, 1924.[78]

In this environment, the porcelain factory was not able to maintain itself much longer. While it had been in full operation with more than 250 workers by the end of 1923, the employees were gradually dismissed between May and June 1924 before the plant was shut down.[79]

[74] WStLA, Lg., Box 731, VrXXIII, 5603/24, 3. Part, Verdict, June 15, 1929, p. 1778.

[75] *Compass*, Vol. 1, 1925, p. 723f; WStLA, Lg., Box 731, VrXXIII, 5603/24, 3. Part, Verdict, June 15, 1929, p. 1770v.

[76] WStLA, Lg., Box. 731, VrXXIII, 5603/24, 1. Part, Hearing of the accused Dr Schumpeter, p. 512v, 514; Hearing of the accused Dr Braun-Stammfest, pp. 201n v, 201o.

[77] Zentralblatt 1924, p. 1138, Wien, I., Renngasee 14, Glasindustrie Aktiengesellschaft "Rudolfshütte," Wien, July 1, 1924.

[78] WStLA, Lg., Box 731, VrXXIII, 5603/24, 3. Part, Verdict, June 15, 1929; *Compass*, Vol. 1, 1925, p. 1118.

[79] *Tages-Post*, August 30, 1924, p. 8; WStLA, Lg., Box. 731, VrXXIII, 5603/24, 1. Part, Hearing of witness Wilhelm Kostial, p. 749v.

While everything was already in the process of collapsing unstoppably, as a last downright crazy move Braun-Stammfest intended to found two more companies around the turn of 1923/4: a wool industry company and a mineral water company. For these start-ups, which stagnated at an early stage, he withdrew another 1.4 billion kronen from the group firms.[80]

The judicial reappraisal of the matters began in August 1924 with the lawsuit filed by the directors of the Wiener Handelskreditbank against Braun-Stammfest at the Public Prosecutor's Office of the Regional Court for Criminal Matters in Vienna.[81] In return, Braun-Stammfest sued the bank,[82] resulting in competition of charges, as noted in a contemporary newspaper.

Toward the end of July 1924 the muckraking newspaper *Der Abend* published a series of articles in which the Braun-Stammfest companies were portrayed as a fraud and Rudolfshütte as a heap of rubble,[83] which further hindered any final restructuring attempts.

After that, in August 1924 a complaint was filed with the police by a newly founded protective association of shareholders of the Braun-Stammfest group. The group, which was represented by attorney Dr J. Tuttman, accused the group's management of investor deception, abusive use of funds, and mismanagement. Above all, the group criticized the aggressive sales methods used in the issue of interim certificates and shares. Tuttman stated that Braun-Stammfest had misled the buyers in several ways. He emphasized three aspects. First, Braun-Stammfest had published prospectuses stating that the companies were being operated properly and prospering. Second, he employed a group of agents at high commissions who gave the public untruthful information about the status of the undertakings. Third, he repeatedly praised his shares using blatant means, concealing the true state of the companies. Tuttmann assumed that the small denomination of the capital into shares with a nominal value of only 200 kronen was already aimed at selling them to small people by a large number of agents. "The inexperienced rural investors were promised great merits and the paper was praised as a safest investment. The agents penetrated the smallest hicksville and praised the shares for sale, because many shares were available for little money," Tuttman explained, stating that he received thousands of applications daily for the shareholder's association, and that the shareholders demanded the immediate

[80] WStLA, Lg., Box 731, VrXXIII, 5603/24, 3. Part, Indictment from March 10, 1928, p. 1465.

[81] *Arbeiter-Zeitung*, August 3, 1924.

[82] The wording of this charge has been handed down in ÖStA, AdR, BmF, Bankkommission, Kart. 52, Klageschrift (bill of complaint) of Braun-Stammfest against Wiener Kaufmannsbank.

[83] WStLA, Lg., Box. 731, VrXXIII, 5603/24, 1. Part, Hearing of the accused Dr Braun-Stammfest, p. 201p.

initiation of criminal proceedings against Braun-Stammfest, his associates, and the sales agents.[84]

After the notices had arrived at the prosecutor's office, extensive investigations began. In addition to Braun-Stammfest, Schumpeter, Borovy, Josef Haller, and Hochapfel, the authorities interrogated Rasper Sr, his sons, and several other functionaries as suspects. Ultimately, on March 10, 1928, only Braun-Stammfest and Franz Haller, who had been director of three of the companies,[85] were formally accused.

The public prosecutor's office conducted extensive interrogations and sworn experts examined the financial management of the group and the development of the single companies. They calculated that, all in all, the firms had caused losses of some 38 billion kronen, while the paid-in capital was only 27.5 billion kronen, which meant that the group was overindebted by more than 10 billion kronen. Furthermore, they showed that the managers themselves were aware of how dubious their actions were. They found an internal comment calling the officially published balance sheets "Poldi Huber Bilanzen," which in very colloquial Viennese means balance sheets for the naïve and clueless.

Schumpeter was interrogated by the Regional Court of Vienna on April 24, 1925, May 2, 1925, and April 8, 1927. Braun-Stammfest, who was interested in emphasizing the responsibility of others as much as possible during his hearing, testified that Schumpeter was always kept informed about all relevant details of business conduct and that he had been in contact with him nearly every day.[86]

The trial concluded on June 15, 1929. That day Braun-Stammfest was found guilty of frivolously causing the insolvency of the Hainfeld Metallurgical Works, Electro-technical Company, and Glass Industry Rudolfshütte during the years 1923 and 1924. Furthermore, he was found guilty of harming the creditors by incurring new debts after November 1923 in ignorance of the insolvency, as well as for not applying for the composition proceedings in time. Finally, he was found guilty of negligently causing his own insolvency as the debtor of several creditors, as well as of recklessly and disproportionately using credit. "He has thereby committed the offence of negligent bankruptcy," it was stated. The verdict was a five-month suspended sentence. Franz Haller was acquitted.[87]

[84] WStLA, Lg., Box. 731, VrXXIII, 5603/24, 2. Part, Criminal complaint by the shareholders of Braun-Stammfest's establishments, represented by Dr J. Tuttmann, filed with the economic crime department, August 19, 1924, pp. 132v–135.

[85] Franz Haller was director (executive manager) of the porcelain factory, the electro-technical factory and the glass factory and board member of the metallurgical works in Hainfeld and the Holzapfel paint company. WStLA, Lg., Box. 731, VrXXIII, 5603/24, 1. Part, Hearing of the accused Franz Haller, p. 542 v.

[86] WStLA, Lg., Box. 731, VrXXIII, 5603/24, 1. Part, Hearing of the accused Dr Braun-Stammfest, p. 201vv.

[87] WStLA, Lg., Box 731, VrXXIII, 5603/24, 3. Part, Verdict, June 15, 1929, pp. 1778v–1780.

9.5 The further fate of firms in the group

All of the firms that had been involved in the development of the Braun-Stammfest group did not last long after the initial insolvencies. The Wiener Kaufmannsbank, which had successfully sued Schumpeter because of the guarantee, was liquidated soon afterward. "Kompaß" Allgemeine Kredit- und Garantie-Bank took over the bank to shut it down. Kompaß assumed direct liability for the depositors and received extensive securities as well as the majority of shares. A regular general assembly on September 21, 1927 determined the liquidation. The shareholders suffered a total loss.[88]

In addition, most of the firms that had directly belonged to the Braun-Stammfest group only existed for a short time. The Hainfeld Metallurgical Works were not able to fulfill the conditions of a settlement procedure. Bankruptcy was declared in 1926, but the settlement was set aside due to a lack of cost coverage. When the firm was liquidated, once again nothing was left for the shareholders.[89]

The fate of the Electro-technical Company was similar. The settlement offer of 25 percent to the creditors could not be met. The firm was liquidated in 1927, whereby the site was acquired by Wiener Kaufmannsbank. The company was deleted from the commercial register on October 25, 1927.[90]

Interestingly, the death throes of the Glass Industry Rudolfshütte lasted somewhat longer, despite this being the only factory that had not yet started production. The settlement procedure of this firm was terminated in May 1925 with a quota of 25 percent payable within two years. In autumn 1925, together with Wiener Kaufmannsbank, the German industrialist family Zaruba began to reconstruct the firm. Share capital was valued at 2,094 billion kronen in accordance with the last capital increase and a reduction was made to one-fifth. Thereafter, the company issued 8.8 million new shares, which resulted in a capital increase to 2.1788 billion kronen (217,880 schillings). Zaruba took three-quarters of the fresh shares, while the old shareholders and Wiener Kaufmannsbank obtained one-quarter. Together they formed a new syndicate, which undertook to complete the factory and invest at least 300,000 schillings. It was agreed that Wiener Kaufmannsbank would waive further claims. When the construction of the factory was finished in April 1926, there emerged so many conflicts between Zaruba and Wiener Kaufmannsbank concerning the settlement of the accounts that the attempt at redevelopment had to be considered a failure. The firm was liquidated and deleted from the commercial register on June 13, 1927.

Another important Braun-Stammfest asset consisted of shares in the Holzapfel-Farbenfabriks AG, where, however, he had never had a decisive influence. This company suffered the same fate. Until 1925, the British principal shareholder

[88] *Compass*, Vol. 1, 1928, p. 463f; 1929, p. 449.
[89] *Compass*, Vol. 1, 1928, p. 900f.
[90] *Compass*, Vol. 1, 1928, p. 117.

provided the firm with floating assets. In light of notorious losses, at a general assembly on June 20, 1926 the owners decided to liquidate the company. In this case, the shareholders were also left with nothing.

Only the porcelain factory was able to survive somewhat longer. Several years of crisis and upheaval followed. In 1925, the Porcelain Company's management succeeded in merging with the world-famous Viennese porcelain factory Augarten AG. Under this constellation, further investments followed. By autumn 1927, the factory was active with three kilns "of the most modern design" and around 300 workers had been employed.[91] However, the cooperation did not prove itself in everyday production and business life. In a general assembly in July 1929, Augarten revoked the merger and the porcelain factory in Wels came under the leadership of an investor from Czechoslovakia who cooperated with the Anglo-Československá Banka and the Viennese private bank Liebieg & Co. The new investors made final efforts to improve the efficiency of the factory but shut down activity in 1930 after the outbreak of the Great Depression.[92] Therefore, from the beginning of the 1930s onward, nothing remained of the Braun-Stammfest group.

Braun-Stammfest lost everything as a result of the bankruptcies. His luxurious villa with its huge plot on Kahlenberg hill—one of the noblest locations in Vienna—was acquired by the Viennese municipality in 1930 in a forced auction.[93] After the court case surrounding fraudulent bankruptcy began in late 1924, the police carried out investigations into his reputation. Particular attention was paid to possible character deficits and a possibly wasteful way of life. The investigators found that Braun-Stammfest suffered from a peculiar form of hypochondria. He spent a lot of money to ensure that doctors were nearby at all times, preferably nerve doctors. As his personal physician he hired the neurologist Dr Karl Noe-Nordberg, who subsequently gave up his position as the director of a Viennese mental institution. The future recipient of the Nobel Prize for Medicine, Dr Julius Wagner-Jauregg, was also among the physicians called upon. Otherwise, he lived rather modestly and was not a gambler, nor did he frequent expensive restaurants and clubs.[94] The police report mentioned that, due to his fanatical will to engage in industrial activity, Braun-Stammfest also repeatedly lost money by financing unsuccessful inventors.[95]

[91] *Compass*, Vol. 1, 1929, p. 668f.

[92] *Compass*, Vol. 1, 1931, p. 644; *Die Bilanzen*, August 10, 1929, p. 522.

[93] *Neues Wiener Tagblatt*, June 14, 1931.

[94] Yet, certain costs resulted from the fact that he had close relations to three women, whom he also supported financially on a modest scale. WStLA, Lg., Box. 731, VrXXIII, 5603/24, 2. Part, Report from Vienna Police Headquarters, Economic Crime Department to Criminal Court, Vienna, October 13, 1924. Braun-Stammfest was divorced from his wife Rose in 1923. Rumours circulated in the press that it had to do with the financial losses, but he explained that they had parted ways by mutual agreement because he "stuck to his bachelor habits." *Die Stunde*, February 20, 1925, p. 5; February 24, 1925, p. 7.

[95] WStLA, Lg., Box. 731, VrXXIII, 5603/24, 2. Part, Report from Vienna Police Headquarters, Economic Crime Department to Criminal Court, Vienna, October 13, 1924.

Since the sentence of 1929 was only fixed at five months of conditional punishment, he was allowed to continue his profession as a lawyer after the verdict, but he does not seem to have acquired any further large cases. In the 1930s, he repeatedly represented members of the right-wing "Heimwehr" group, for example Heimwehr functionary Häger, in a press trial against the Social Democrat newspaper *Arbeiter-Zeitung*. In 1931 he submitted an application to the Ministry of Justice for free escort on his return to Austria in favor of Walter Pfrimer, the leader of a right-wing coup attempt, who had fled abroad, allegedly by his own initiative and without a mandate.[96] In 1940, Braun-Stammfest had to quit his activities as a lawyer pursuant to a decision of the Disciplinary Board of the Lawyers' Chamber (Bar Association),[97] but was again admitted to the bar in 1946.[98] A few final press notes on his work on small cases can be found from the years 1946 to 1948.[99] He passed away on September 14, 1949.[100]

The assurances Schumpeter had given to the merchant bank in favor of Glass Industry Rudolfshütte cost him dearly. After the firm defaulted, the guarantee was invoked. In July 1925, he was sentenced to pay the bank 199,000 schillings (1.99 billion kronen).[101]

Finally, it must be mentioned that not all of Schumpeter's financial ventures failed. There was at least one company with which he was involved that developed relatively well. This was the Aktien-Gesellschaft für Chemische Produkte (Stock Corporation for Chemical Products) in Vienna, which was not part of either the Braun-Stammfest group or the Biedermann group. The firm was incorporated in 1922, with Schumpeter formally officiating as president of the board from 1922 until the late 1930s, and main investors seem to have been members of the German industrialist family Roos. The firm produced chemical substances, mainly for road surfacing.[102] However, it is clear that this single success is only a side note to Schumpeter's failed financial ventures, and that it could not substantially improve his economic situation during the second half of the 1920s.

[96] *Tages-Post*, Oktober 14, 1931. [97] *Amtsblatt zur Wiener Zeitung*, Februry 18, 1940, p. 5.

[98] *Amtsblatt zur Wiener Zeitung*, April 6, 1946, p. 5.

[99] For example, in April 1946 he represented a house owner who sued for outstanding rent payments from the actor Curd Jürgens. *Amtsblatt zur Wiener Zeitung*, April 14, 1946, p. 5.

[100] Information from Dr Andreas Weigl, Municipal and Provincial Archives of Vienna.

[101] *Neue Freie Presse*, June 11, 1925. McCraw erroneously reports that Schumpeter was sentenced to pay "199,000 crowns plus 8 percent interest." He understates the amount by a factor of 10,000. See McCraw (2007, p. 630, Fn. 11).

[102] *Die Börse*, June 8, 1922, p. 13 and August 3, 1922, p. 23; *Reichspost*, July 27, 1922, p. 7 *Compass*, Vol. 1, 1925, p. 996, and 1936, p. 835; Allen (1991, p. 187).

10
Causes and consequences

Fate is having become, or more precisely, irreversibility.

(J.A. Schumpeter)[1]

10.1 Schumpeter's role

When Schumpeter dared to attempt banking and venture investment himself after his activity as secretary of state for finance, he was undoubtedly convinced he was well-equipped for these activities due to his theoretical insights and basic education in business administration. However, as we have seen, nearly all of his practical projects proved failures. The unfavorable economic environment in Austria at the time certainly contributed to a considerable extent. However, it is obvious that each of the ventures also had severe flaws.

The Biedermann Bank suffered from conflicting strategic orientations, never found a sustainable business model, and finally failed due to misguided rescue efforts. Up to 1922 the bank missed speculative business opportunities in times of (hyper-)inflation. From 1923 onward, excessively large capital was immobilized in corporate investments that did not perform well. Beyond this, in spring 1924, the failed speculations on the French franc and a crash on the Vienna Stock Exchange adversely affected the Biedermann Bank, along with its customers.

Schumpeter himself was president of the board from the start, and from late 1922 onward also served as a managing director. Additionally, he acted as a member of the board and the management board of Wiener Handelskreditbank, a board member of Austro-Holländische Bank, and a board member of a few of the industrial firms belonging to the Biedermann Group, for example, "Mefra" Aktiengesellschaft für Garnerzeugung.[2] Numerous meeting minutes of the board of directors and the supervisory board of the Wiener Handelskreditbank, which have been preserved in the Austrian State Archives, reveal that Schumpeter was very conscientious about his participation in the management of this bank.[3]

It is more difficult to say to what extent he was actively involved in the business of the Biedermann Bank as the board meeting minutes of this bank have been passed down incompletely. To determine this, only different information can

[1] "Schicksal ist Gewordensein, genauer gesagt, Irreversibilität" (Undated; HUA, HUGFP-4.3, File "Auto-Biography-start?").

[2] *Compass*, Vol. 1, 1924, passim.

[3] ÖStA, AdR, BmF, Bankkommission, Box 34 and 52.

Schumpeter's Venture Money. Michael Peneder and Andreas Resch,
Oxford University Press (2021). © Michael Peneder and Andreas Resch.
DOI: 10.1093/oso/9780198804383.003.0010

be weighed. The fact that conflicts with other functionaries emerged as early as 1923 and 1924 may be a hint that he was less firmly involved in the business of Biedermann Bank than in the management of Wiener Handelskreditbank. For example, in the letter from June 1924 he mentioned his bank colleague Alfred Treichl, who played a very active role in the rescue attempts from 1924 onward, as "my personal opponent Treichl."[4] In December 1925, Dr Weiss-Wellenstein, a member of the supervisory board of Biedermann Bank gave a report to Werner Sombart on Schumpeter's activities. In evaluating this source, it must be taken into account that Sombart was a determined opponent of Schumpeter in his efforts to obtain a professorship in Germany, which is why he was also interested in negative information on Schumpeter. For his part, Weiss-Wellenstein was probably interested in downplaying Schumpeter's role. Under these circumstances, he wrote that Schumpeter was "not taken seriously in the bank after a short time and was not allowed to participate in business management."[5] Yet this statement may have been somewhat exaggerated in hindsight and probably refers to the conflicts between Schumpeter and director Treichl. While the information provided by Weiss-Wellenstein makes it clear that Schumpeter was not firmly involved in the bank's day-to-day business, the fact that he assiduously fulfilled his duties at Wiener Handelskreditbank makes it plausible that he also took seriously his responsibilities at Biedermann Bank. However, the focus will have been less on routine business. Schumpeter's most important role at Biedermann Bank was probably to act as a resplendent figurehead, to provide for a conducive social environment, to in some cases bring in strategic ideas, and to contribute social capital to the development of the business. As a brilliant economist and former state secretary of finance, he was to attract new business opportunities and take care of business partners. These kinds of duties he seems to have continued to fulfill during the period up to May 1925, after his resignation as president and while he was still a board member. For example, in September 1924, when the American lawyer Mr Desvernine was in Vienna for renegotiations of the deal with Morgan, Livermore & Co., Schumpeter wrote to Kunwald: "Yesterday I took the Desvernines and their offspring for a walk until seven thirty. [...] I understand that for you a ride with D. would still be bearable, but an evening would be unbearable. For such I am therefore available."[6]

To summarize, Schumpeter's responsibility for the bank's various problems was largely strategic. He was undoubtedly in favor of the bank's intensive industrial investments, which later resulted in large losses. The investments corresponded to his understanding of banking as an enabler of industrial innovation. Yet due to

[4] ÖStA, Bestand GK, 616-1, Box 850, File 1269, Schumpeter to Kunwald, June 1924 (The letter is not dated).

[5] GStA, PK, I. HA Rep. 76 VA, Sekt III, Tit. IV, Nr. 55, Vol. 9, sheet 448.

[6] ÖStA, Bestand GK, 616-1, Box 850, File 1269, Schumpeter to Kunwald, September 19, 1924.

his limited influence on day-to-day business, they are not causally attributable to him in any sense of operational management. The same applies all the more to the losses incurred by the Internationale Handelsbank and the Austro-Holländische Bank, where Schumpeter's seats on the boards seem to have been purely formal. Schumpeter personally made a large contribution to the restructuring of Wiener Handelskreditbank. His attitude to the corporate governance problems associated with the capital increases was probably the same as Kunwald's, namely that the founders and managers were morally entitled to draw private profits. Above all, just like all the other managers, he remained helpless in devising a functional business strategy for the given circumstances.

The most important function of the bank for Schumpeter was that it provided a generous line of credit for his personal dealings. The development of his debts will be scrutinized in detail further on. How Schumpeter was drawn into the troubles with Braun-Stammfest can be summarized as follows: it appears that the industrialist impressed Schumpeter with his energetic entrepreneurial approach. Gustav Stolper, a life-long close friend of Schumpeter's,[7] explained in 1931 in a letter to Prof. Heinrich Herkner how Schumpeter's firm business relationship with Braun-Stammfest had transpired. He provided this information when he tried to support Schumpeter in obtaining a professorship in Berlin. While Stolper had regarded Braun-Stammfest as a con man from the start, Schumpeter had seen in him a "highly gifted and imaginative industrial entrepreneur."[8] Schumpeter himself repeatedly explained that he had known Braun-Stammfest as a schoolmate at the Theresianum school and that he had initially been intrigued by his impressive entrepreneurial personality.[9] However, Braun-Stammfest had massively underestimated the difficulties and capital requirements of building up new industrial firms from scratch. During the inflation period, equity was devalued before it could be invested and from 1923 onward no sufficient acquisition of further equity was achieved and the interest costs for borrowed money and operational losses eroded the financial base. All the works suffered from technical problems and mismanagement.

During the Braun-Stammfest trial between 1925 and 1927 Schumpeter was interrogated three times as an accused person. He confirmed that he was

[7] Stolper was editor of *Der österreichische Volkswirt* (*The Austrian Economist*) before he moved to Germany in 1925 to become editor-in-chief of the *Börsenkurier*. In 1926 he founded *Der Deutsche Volkswirt* (*The German Economist*). In addition to his activities in journalism, Stolper temporarily served as a a member of the German Reichstag for a liberal party. His wife Toni Stolper was a close associate. During the Nazi era, they had to leave Germany, and they afterward established themselves in the US as successful journalists. Their eldest son was the famous economist Wolfgang F. Stolper (Holl, 1999, pp. 691–5). Over time, Schumpeter wrote numerous articles for the journals published by Stolper.

[8] BAK, N1186, 31, Stolper to Herkner, April 10, 1931.

[9] See, for example, WStLA, Lg., Box. 731, VrXXIII, 5603/24, 1. Part, Hearing of the accused Dr Josef Schumpeter, p. 511.

continuously involved in the Braun-Stammfest group. Schumpeter stated that he had been a member of the founding syndicates of the porcelain and glass factories and a board member in all of the group's firms. He personally substantially invested in all of the ventures and took part in purchases to support the stock prices. Schumpeter held weekly meetings with Braun-Stammfest to discuss strategy, tax issues, and capital increases.[10] Furthermore, Schumpeter told the investigating authority that he had checked the balance sheets and questioned employees regarding the specification of individual items and the course of business. Thus, he must have been well-informed about the status of all of the companies.

As mentioned above, in 1923 Schumpeter attempted to sell off the factory in Hainfeld to create a sounder financial basis for the other ventures. The divestiture failed due to resistance by Braun-Stammfest. Finally, Schumpeter suffered heavy losses through investments in shares of the Braun-Stammfest companies; even worse, the guarantee that he had provided for a loan to the glass factory subsequently became a particularly burdensome element of his overall debt.

10.2 Personal consequences

Schumpeter's acute financial crisis began after the failure of the speculations against the French franc in March 1924 and the subsequent stock market crisis. Simultaneously, he suffered massive losses from future dealings via telegraph,[11] which became due in May 1924, the crisis of the Braun-Stammfest group, and the rapid devaluation of all the securities he had deposited as collateral for his loans. Therefore, his debts piled up at Biedermann Bank and several other private banks he had hired to carry out his speculative operations. At the same time, also as a consequence of all these factors, his employer and main creditor Biedermann Bank got into acute trouble, which further increased his financial distress. As mentioned above, for the Biedermann Bank it became even more difficult to handle the financial problems, partly because the unfavorable results of the audit by Hofrat Stern had become public by around that time. By July 1924, Biedermann Bank had severe difficulty even paying current wages. Schumpeter was personally *de facto* broke and the president of an insolvent bank. The Biedermann Bank management considered asking Louis Rothschild for an emergency loan and pledged the valuable art collection of Arthur Klein as collateral.[12] Overall, for Schumpeter the situation seemed hopeless. He feared an *éclat* at any time, along

[10] WStLA, Lg., Box. 731, VrXXIII, 5603/24, 1. Part, Hearing of the accused Dr Josef Schumpeter, p. 514f.

[11] In his letters, he called those future dealings via telegraph "Maikabel," because they were due in May 1924. See, for example ÖStA, Bestand GK, 616-1, Box 850, File 1269, Schumpeter to Kunwald, May 20, 1924.

[12] ÖStA, Bestand GK, 616-1, Box 850, File 1269, Schumpeter to Kunwald, July 6, 1924.

with the collapse of his debt scaffolding, which would ruin all his prospects for a further civic existence. For several weeks, Schumpeter tried to survive one day at a time by taking on new debts to meet the most urgent needs.

At this time, the banker Richard Dworzak, who was director of Vereinsbank, a medium-sized Viennese bank, and the private bankers Prym and Gerstbauer, who themselves were affected by the crisis, urged Schumpeter to honor his commitments resulting from future contracts in French franc. In desperate letters to his friend Kunwald, Schumpeter analyzed the situation. In two letters from May 1924, he concluded that he had to repay Prym 490 million kronen by the end of the month and owed Dworzak (respectively Vereinsbank) some 450 million kronen,[13] in addition to owing smaller amounts to other bankers (Wolf, Meisels, Gerstbauer), suppliers, etc. To make matters worse, as mentioned above, in May 1924 his contribution to the restructuring of the Wiener Handelskreditbank, which amounted to more than 1 billion kronen, was due.[14]

We know from the letter from Biedermann supervisory board member Weiss-Wellenstein, already cited above, that at the time Schumpeter owed the Biedermann Bank the immense sum of around 6 billion kronen due to failed speculations and royalties received in advance,[15] which were only partially backed by securities.

In this situation, from May 1924 onward, Schumpeter temporarily even resorted to desperate, illegal means to gain time from one day to the next. For example, he withdrew money from his cousin Carl Schumpeter's Biedermann account without his knowledge and in some cases seems to have sold shares that he was not actually entitled to dispose of, as they were tied up as collateral.[16] Biedermann director Wilhelm Stein assisted Schumpeter in some of his emergency rescue measures at the bank. In return, during the following years, despite his own catastrophic financial situation Schumpeter repeatedly tried to support Stein financially, after he also lost his job and his fortune in the course of the Biedermann crisis.[17]

When nothing seemed to work anymore, Kunwald provided decisive assistance. On May 26, he lent Schumpeter 115 million kronen in cash—a small sum in relation to the total debt, but one that provided valuable marginal room for maneuvering and probably saved him from a public scandal.[18]

[13] ÖStA, Bestand GK, 616-1, Box 850, File 1269, Letters from Schumpeter to Kunwald, May 5, 1924 and May 1924 without exact date.

[14] ÖStA, AdR, BmF, Bankkommission, Box 52, File 33, "Dienstnachricht" (Service Notice) No. 27 regarding the audit of Wiener Handelskreditbank AG, January 23, 1925.

[15] GStA PK I. HA Rep. 76 Va, Sekt III, Tit. IV, Nr. 55, Vol. 9, Letter from Gustav Weiss-Wellenstein to Werner Sombart, December 28, 1925, sheet 447.

[16] ÖStA, Bestand GK, 616-1, Box 850, File 1269, Schumpeter to Kunwald, May 20, June, July 6, 1924; and February 17, 1925.

[17] See for example ÖStA, Bestand GK, 616-1, Box 850, File 1269, Copy of a letter from Wilhelm Stein to Schumpeter, September 6, 1927; Schumpeter to Kunwald, December 31, 1925; February 3, 6, and 16, 1926; September 20, 1927; November 14, 18 and 28, 1927.

[18] ÖStA, Bestand GK, 616-1, Box 850, File 1269, Schumpeter's receipt for the sum received on May 26, 1924.

A substantial part of the debt at Biedermann was based on shares deposited with the bank. Yet those shares rapidly lost their value and Schumpeter had to sell his best stocks in order to achieve some reasonably relevant sales revenues. He himself later quantified his total debt to the Biedermann Bank at 4 billion kronen (400,000 schillings),[19] which was probably the remaining net debt after the sale of marketable securities and included his contribution to the restructuring of Wiener Handelskreditbank.[20] In addition, as mentioned above, he had given a guarantee for a burst loan of about 2 billion kronen from the glass industry company of the Braun-Stammfest group. Thus, it is plausible to estimate Schumpeter's total indebtedness in the second half of 1924 at some 6 billion kronen.[21] According to the Austrian Central Bank's online calculator for historical Austrian currencies, this corresponds to a value of 2.4 million euros in 2018,[22] a disastrous debt burden for a banker who had just lost his job and for some time retired from the academic world.

However, at this low point in his life, Schumpeter managed to make two new starts, as already mentioned in the biographical remarks of the introductory Chapter 1. On the one hand, he reactivated his contacts in the academic world and soon successfully applied for a new job—this time as professor of economics in Bonn, and on the other hand he embarked on a new chapter in his private life with his marriage to Annie Reisinger.

Before Schumpeter was appointed professor in Germany, he had to overcome great academic resistance. One of Schumpeter's leading opponents was the German social scientist Werner Sombart. This story is already well documented in the biographies that have appeared since the 1990s, which is why details can be omitted here.[23] From the correspondence with Kunwald we know that Schumpeter was still very skeptical in September 1925 as to whether he would receive the professorship in Bonn. At the same time, he also applied for a professorship in Tokyo. On September 30, 1925, he wrote: "Bonn does not look good and Tokyo will be difficult."[24] Just a few days later, on October 5, 1925, he was able to report from Berlin: "Fast and red hot the good news that Bonn was officially offered to me."[25] The new job provided a starting point for reducing his mountain of debt, even though income was scarce in relation to total debt. In his research,

[19] BAK, N 1186, 31, Schumpeter to Gustav Stolper, February 22, 1932.

[20] ÖStA, Bestand GK, 616-1, Box 850, File 1269, Schumpeter to Kunwald, October 10, 1924, mentions his contribution to the restructuring fund.

[21] In 1932, Schumpeter wrote in a letter to Werner Richter, the head of the Prussian university administration, that the total sum of his unfunded debts amounted to 300,000 marks, which equalled some 555,000 schillings (5.55 billion kronen). BAK, N/1186/31, Copy of a letter from Schumpeter to Werner Richter, March 26, 1932.

[22] https://www.oenb.at/docroot/inflationscockpit/waehrungsrechner.html (November 20, 2019).

[23] See Allen (1991, pp. 201–7); Swedberg (1991, pp. 69f and 78f); Stolper (1994, pp. 310–20); Hedtke and Swedberg (2000, pp. 12-15); and the relevant letters in this book.

[24] ÖStA, Bestand GK, 616-1, Box 850, File 1269, Schumpeter to Kunwald, September 30, 1925.

[25] ÖStA, Bestand GK, 616-1, Box 850, File 1269, Schumpeter to Kunwald, October 5, 1925.

Ulrich Hedtke has discovered that Schumpeter's earnings before taxes from his professorship were around 20,000 marks in 1926, rose to 24,200 in 1927, and later reached over 30,000 marks. In addition, he obtained a removal allowance of 7,000 marks. Beyond that, he made some 10,000 marks per year through speeches and publications.[26] Overall, his total income before taxes between 1926 and 1931 may have amounted to some 230,000 marks, which was roughly equivalent to 430,000 schillings, while in 1924 his total debt, as mentioned above, amounted to some 600,000 schillings. If we deduct a, for this time, modest tax burden and his cost of living, a disposable income will have remained that represented a small fraction of his debt burden. Schumpeter was offered two visiting professorships at Harvard (autumn 1927 to spring 1928 and autumn 1930), which provided some financial relief, because he could use the ongoing German salary to cover his debts (and pay the rent of his house in Bonn), while covering his living expenses through his American income.[27]

This overview makes it clear that it was impossible for Schumpeter to pay off all of his debts. Nevertheless, he managed to largely overcome his debt burden by the early 1930s. Several friends gave him financial support and he was above all able to repeatedly negotiate highly favorable settlements. The restructuring of his debts at Biedermann Bank in late 1924 already revealed a successful pattern of negotiations, which Schumpeter used to receive substantial debt relief. He pointed out that a formal lawsuit against him or an unacceptable agreement would destroy his social existence as a professor. Thus, he would lose every opportunity to earn any income and, consequently, would not be able to repay anything. In other words, Schumpeter made it clear to his creditors that they would achieve a more favorable pay-off if they were to offer him a bearable compromise. Applying these arguments, in all of the cases, he was able to convince his creditors to renounce large parts of the debts and offer him generous agreements.

In the letter to Sombart, Weiss-Wellenstein mentioned that two persons who were interested in the fate of the bank had supported Schumpeter with private loans.[28] He did not name the supporters, but probably meant Kunwald, who had already helped in May, and Julius Hepner, who had also granted more than 110 million kronen (11,000 schillings) in credit.[29] Further personal friends who notably provided substantial financial aid were Heinrich Höfflinger, Felix Somary, and Karl Schlesinger. Höfflinger (1882-1963) was a former officer in the Habsburg army, who belonged to the conservative Catholic circles with whom Schumpeter

[26] Hedtke and Swedberg (2000, p. 11f).

[27] Letter from Schumpeter to "Liebe Gunde," undated, from late 1927, Private Archive Ulrich Hedtke, Ottilie Jäckel Letters and März (1983/91, p. 177f).

[28] GStA PK I. HA Rep. 76 Va, Sekt III, Tit. IV, Nr. 55, Vol. 9, Gustav Weiss-Wellenstein to Werner Sombart, December 28, 1925, sheet 447 v.

[29] März (1983/91, p. 180f); Private Archive Ulrich Hedtke, Ottilie Jäckel Letters, Letter from Schumpeter to Gunde (Ottilie Jäckel), December 24, 1928.

had maintained close contact during the war. Höfflinger had also temporarily tried his hand as a banker, founded a genealogical journal, and held leading positions in the Order of the Knights of the Holy Sepulchre of Jerusalem. He also employed Ottilie Jäckel, Schumpeter's secretary at the Biedermann Bank, as his private secretary after he had to quit his presidency of the board. Dr Karl Schlesinger was a director of the Anglobank and associate of Schumpeter's at the Austro-Hungarian Trade Chamber, in addition to being an eminent monetary theorist and mutual friend of Schumpeter's, Stolper's, Kunwald's, and Somary's.[30] Felix Somary was a fellow student at the University of Vienna and a very successful banker in Zurich. All of them seem to have contributed a similar amount of support to Schumpeter as Kunwald.

The reduction of Schumpeter's debts at the Biedermann Bank was also further aided by the fact that Schumpeter was probably entitled to a certain severance payment[31] and Anglobank[32] seems to have provided a last contribution. In December 1924, he wrote to Kunwald about a "net debt" of 1,600 [million kronen] which was probably his actual debt at Biedermann Bank. He mentioned that this did not include his indebtedness to Höfflinger, nor did it include his tax debts, lawyer's bills, doctor's bills, and other bills or the guarantee for Braun-Stammfest (Wiener Kaufmannsbank). By the turn of 1924/5 his debt at Biedermann Bank was further reduced to 104,671 schillings (1,046.71 million kronen),[33] for which a payment deferral of three years was granted.

In late 1925, Schumpeter also achieved highly favorable settlements of his other major debts, which allowed him to start a new career in Bonn under the auspices of reasonably orderly financial perspectives. In November/December 1925, with the help of Kunwald, he managed to obtain very favorable restructuring schemes with respect to his remaining outstanding payments to Vereinsbank/Dworzak and his largest single debt toward Wiener Kaufmannsbank. At this time, Schumpeter still owed over 200 million kronen (20,000 schillings) to Vereinsbank, after he had already repaid 200 million kronen (20,000 schillings) and left collateral at a value of 50 million kronen (5,000 schillings). His correspondence with Kunwald suggests that Schumpeter seems to have agreed to cover this remaining debt with a payment of 10,000 schillings, which was not due before November 1928, whereby

[30] For Schlesinger, see *Compass*, Vol. 1, 1925, pp. 335, 1096, 1142; 1925, Separate issue. Directory of board members and directors, p. 1162. ÖStA, Bestand GK, 616-1, Box 850, File 1269, Letters from November 19, December 1, 1925, and January 11, 1926; ÖBL, Vol. 10 (1992, p. 193f).

[31] Although it was part of the rescue package for Biedermann Bank in mid-1924 that the leading functionaries would waive some of their claims of this kind. See ÖStA, Bestand GK, 616-1, Box 758, File 257, Kunwald to Kienböck, December 11, 1925.

[32] Kunwald mentions that the Anglobank was paying Schumpeter an amount in the settlement of his debts in ÖStA, Bestand GK, 616-1, Box 850, File 1269, Kunwald to Schumepter, August 21, 1926.

[33] ÖStA, Bestand GK, 616-1, Box 850, File 1269, Copy of a letter of Biedermann Bank to the Tax Administration for the IX., XVII., XVIII. and XIX. district in Vienna, September 3, 1926.

this extension of the time limit for the reduced residual debt appears to have been partially pre-financed by Dworzak.

The most decisive settlement was reached with Wiener Kaufmannsbank, to which Schumpeter owed 2 billion kronen (200,000 schillings). Thanks to clever negotiations and the active support of Kunwald, the claim holders accepted that Schumpeter only had to pay 5,000 schillings up front and 47,200 schillings by October 1, 1928. Thereafter, only under very vague conditions that were hardly enforceable, a last payment of 30,000 schillings could have become due. With this deal, from a realistic perspective, Schumpeter had rid himself of debts of 200,000 schillings through the payment of 52,200 schillings, most of which was not due for three years.[34]

Yet, to make matters worse, in 1925 the tax office reported tax arrears from 1923, a year in which Schumpeter had still earned well. He took advantage of his relations with the authorities and obtained a deferment of payments and instalments. After 1926 the situation relaxed, since he could now claim losses from the years 1924 and 1925. Biedermann Bank provided a letter confirming that he had not received any severance payment when he quit the board (*Verwaltungsrat*) in May 1925,[35] while such claims had probably arisen at the end of his presidency and his job as director in late 1924 when his debts had been restructured.

Once the biggest debts toward Wiener Kaufmannsbank and Biedermann Bank had been settled, Schumpeter had to cope with short and medium-term payments of around 27,000 schillings, while having some 10,000 schillings at his disposal. In a list from November 1925 Kunwald mentions 10,000 schillings for Wiener Kaufmannsbank (which were not urgent), a partial payment of 5,000 schillings to Vereinsbank (now Verkehrskreditbank[36]), a 4,000-schilling court fee (Kaufmannsbank law suit), and some 6,000 schillings for the lawyers Stadlen, Pressburger, and Blumenthal, who had worked for him in Vienna. Smaller sums were earmarked for financial support, for example, for his mother and Wilhelm Stein. Schumpeter had to cover the gap of some 17,000 schillings (9,000 marks) with savings from his income and/or new private loans. That seemed feasible, even though the money remained scarce. On February 2, 1926, he wrote to Kunwald in a relieved and grateful manner: "[...] I can even report that it works out financially for me, even if it is close [...] needless to say that I sail in much calmer waters than I was entitled to expect a short time ago and that I gratefully remember my patron saint in Schulerstraße" (Kunwald's address in Vienna).[37]

[34] ÖStA, Bestand GK, 616-1, Box 850, File 1269, Draft contracts from November 2 and 5, 1925.

[35] ÖStA, Bestand GK, 616-1, Box 850, File 1269, Copy of a letter of Biedermann Bank to the Tax Administration for the IX., XVII., XVIII., and XIX. district in Vienna, September 3, 1926.

[36] In 1924 Vereinsbank was converted into Österreichische Verkehrskredit-Bank, which was liquidated in 1927.

[37] ÖStA, Bestand GK, 616-1, Box 850, File 1269, Schumpeter to Kunwald, February 3, 1926.

Schumpeter undoubtedly tried to live sparingly during his time in Bonn, but he displayed quite contradictory behavior. On the one hand, he rented a luxurious house—the villa where Crown Prince Wilhelm had lived during his student days, and he repeatedly had expensive holidays, for example, in St Moritz, Switzerland.[38] On the other hand, he seems to have saved on domestic expenses. In 1926, his wife Annie wrote in a letter to her husband, "I spent the whole morning rummaging around again; recalculating how I get by with my monthly money; and what remains; of course exceeded again; it only comforts me that I no longer carry over a deficit."[39]

Since his time in Vienna Schumpeter had held a stake in a real estate property in Berlin. However, in view of the threat of outstanding real estate transfer tax receivables, this asset seems to have limited rather than improved his solvency. Beyond this, in 1925 and 1926, threats of legal action by Schumpeter's first wife Gladys also seem to have caused disconcertment and uncertainty.[40]

In the summer of 1926, Schumpeter's newly founded bourgeois existence was shattered by private catastrophes and soon thereafter new financial challenges emerged. His mother, with whom he had been very close, died on June 22. On August 2, 1926, Schumpeter's young wife Anna passed away during the birth of her son, who also died shortly afterward. Schumpeter was paralyzed with grief and for a long time afterward suffered bouts of depression.

In mid-1927 Schumpeter's secretary Mia Stöckl moved into his home and their working relationship became a private relationship. Schumpeter did not marry her, but he supported her and her family generously after he left Germany in 1932.[41] In addition, he repeatedly sent financial support and Christmas presents to the family of his deceased wife Anna in Vienna.

Toward the end of 1926 it became clear that the situation at Biedermann Bank had become untenable, which would have serious financial consequences for both Kunwald and Schumpeter. With Schumpeter still owing him a loan from 1924, Kunwald found himself in an acute financial crisis, as he had to contribute substantially to enable the liquidation of Biedermann Bank. Consequently, from

[38] März (1983/91, p. 172); Swedberg (1991, p. 73); Allen (1991, p. 209); McCraw (2007, p. 126ff). The fact that Schumpeter was not prepared to seize every opportunity for cost savings and proceeds is also evident from the fact that, after the death of his mother in 1926, he apparently wanted to hold onto her rented apartment in Vienna. After threats of a lawsuit by the landlord, he finally gave the flat up in 1927, but had his mother's household effects and paintings stored in a warehouse instead of being sold. In 1936 he gave the furniture to Mia Stöckl. Private Archive Ulrich Hedtke, Ottilie Jäckel Letters, Schumpeter to Gunde, dated August 5, 1927 by Ulrich Hedtke; Email information from Ulrich Hedtke, November 4, 2019.

[39] HUA, HUGFP—4.4, File "Personal letters—Annie (wife) ca 1923-26," Anna Schumpeter to Schumpeter, 22./VI [1926].

[40] Together with some other investors, Schumpeter seems to have owned a house at the address Lindenstraße 112 in Berlin. See März (1983/91, p. 170ff); Private Archive Ulrich Hedtke, Ottilie Jäckel letters, Schumpeter to Heiner (Höfflinger), 1925 New Year; Schumpeter to Gunde, August 22, 1926.

[41] McCraw (2007, pp. 167, 189ff, 232ff, 282ff); Email information Hedtke, November 4, 2019.

then on he had to apply more pressure to have the debt refunded. To Schumpeter's further detriment, Klein and Treichl demanded the repayment of his Biedermann Bank debt, which had meanwhile climbed to 120,000 schillings due to accruing interests.

Again, Kunwald helped with the negotiations. He achieved a settlement of the claim with a payment of only 25,000 schillings. In a letter from July 25, 1927 addressed to Kunwald, Schumpeter reported with noticeable relief that he had raised the money. While he had had 15,000 schillings at his disposal, he was able to obtain the remaining 10,000 schillings at the last moment thanks to his colleague Prof. Spiethoff in Bonn, though at an interest rate of 20 percent per year. Schumpeter explained:

> That doesn't matter compared to the mountain that's now cleared away. Since the Kaufmanns- and Treuga (Vereins-)bank matters are settled, so the sum of my obligations is reduced to a bearable measure and the prospect of a future is opened, in which I will be free of this cursed writing for money (Lohnschreiberei) and will be able to finally live my science and my grief.[42]

However, after Kunwald more urgently asked for repayment of his personal debts due to his own financial distress, Schumpeter this time responded much less gratefully to his mediation. In a letter to his former secretary and trusted friend Ottilie Jäckel, who lived in Vienna and whom he called "Gunde," he wrote in a pointed tone that Kunwald "apparently seems determined to get every possible penny out of me—and at the same time wants to appear to be a saviour."[43]

The final break in their friendship came in August of 1927 when Kunwald traveled to Berlin to the Hotel Adlon and asked Schumpeter to meet him there, even offering to cover all the costs. Schumpeter refused to comply due to exhaustion and a lack of time—he was in the process of preparing his stay at Harvard. In a handwritten letter draft[44] from the Hotel Adlon, Kunwald vented his disappointment in sarcastic accountant language: "Dear Professor, to be honest, I am more than disappointed, bitter, almost outraged[...]. [That you will not come] means you close the yearlong account. I will simply devalue your moral [account] with loss forever!"[45]

From then on, Kunwald's tone in the written correspondence was emphatically distanced.[46] Nevertheless, in 1932, when rumours of Schumpeter's time as bank

[42] ÖStA, Bestand GK, 616-1, Box 850, File 1269, Schumpeter to Kunwald, July 22, 1927.

[43] Schumpeter to Gunde, May 27, 1927, in März (1983/91, p. 176) and Private Archive Ulrich Hedtke, Ottilie Jäckel Letters.

[44] It is not clear whether this letter was actually sent.

[45] ÖStA, Bestand GK, 616-1, Box 850, File 1269, Kunwald to Schumpeter, August 26, 1927.

[46] For example in a letter from September 6, 1927, which Kunwald sent to Harvard, he addressed Schumpeter as "honoured Mr. Secretary of State!" (Sehr geehrter Herr Staatssekretär!), while before he

president were again used to prevent his appointment to a professorship in Berlin, Kunwald was still prepared to defend his honour in a letter he sent to Gustav Stolper.[47]

After 1927 Schumpeter in fact paid off his debts to Kunwald. He transferred the last instalment of 2,000 schillings on September 11, 1929.[48] His other friendly lenders Somary, Schlesinger, and Höfflinger seem to have been able to be more patient at the time.[49]

One last elementary threat to Schumpeter's bourgeois existence was the trial against Braun-Stammfest for fraudulent bankruptcy, because, as already mentioned, Schumpeter was also questioned three times as a suspect.[50] Thus, it was not clear until 1927 whether formal charges would be brought against him, which would have made it impossible for him to work as a professor. In 1927 good friends advised him to take a star lawyer to extract himself from the matter. Schumpeter wrote to Kunwald and Ottilie Jäckel that, not only did he not have money for a "big animal," but he also feared that such an approach would not make a good impression. For him it was very important not to receive a summons to Bonn, so that the local community would not hear about these events.

The worries and heavy financial consequences of the guarantee prompted Schumpeter to take a more critical view of the role of the group's founder than in his first statements in April and May 1925. In a further letter to Ottilie Jäckel in 1927, he wrote:

> Of course [...] I never knew anything criminal, or I wouldn't have covered for it. Braun always lied to me [...] I'd say that in court. Nothing else. Because more than the examining magistrate said, I don't know today. Braun's tactic [is] to make me an accomplice, a) because he hopes that he too will then be treated mildly, b) because he hopes to force me to answer already in the preliminary investigation in such a way like a defender would answer c) that I necessarily have to exonerate him in the trial. This hope would have to be taken from him. I do not have any

had addressed him as "Dear Friend!" (*Verehrter Freund*). See for example ÖStA, Bestand GK, 616-1, Box 850, File 1269, letters Kunwald to Schumpeter, September 20, 1925, and September 20, 1927.

[47] BAK N/1186/31, Kunwald to Gustav Stolper, January 27, 1932.

[48] ÖStA, Bestand GK, 616-3, Box 887, File 6, Kassaeingänge (cash receipts) from July 1, 1927 to May 5, 1933, Page 15 = sheet 23, Entry from September 11, 1929.

[49] Schumpeter seems to have owed Somary 5,000 marks (some 9,300 schillings). März (1983/91, p 173); Private Archive Ulrich Hedtke, Ottilie Jäckel Letters, Schumpeter to Gunde, January 21, 1927. It is not known whether Schumpeter ever had to repay this sum. No exact data is available on debts and repayments concerning Höfflinger. In a letter from Schumpeter to Höfflinger dated November 28, 1925, it is said that 15 million [kronen] (1,500 schillings) had been made available. In a letter to Ottilie Jäckel dated January 21, 1927, Schumpeter writes, "[...] if Heiner (Höfflinger) curses me because of the 10,000 M (10,000 Marks = 16,600 schillings)[...]." That could mean Schumpeter's debt had grown to that level. But this interpretation is very uncertain. März (1983/91, p. 169) and Private Archive Ulrich Hedtke, Ottilie Jäckel Letters, Copies of letters from November 28, 1925 and January 21, 1927. The repayments to Schlesinger will be mentioned later.

[50] Stolper (1994, pp. 320–5).

> incriminating material unknown to the court. I would say in court, kind to my present conviction, that it was not simply the year 24, as I thought in the past, but him who has ruined the companies, which will probably be followed by a conviction. Even as a witness, I'd have to and would testify like that now.
>
> (Schumpeter to Ottilie Jäckel, 1927)[51]

Only when formal charges were brought against Braun-Stammfest and Director Haller on March 10, 1928, yet not against him, could Schumpeter be sure that this matter would no longer have any legal consequences for him. However, the financial worries were still a heavy burden. On Christmas Day 1928, Schumpeter wrote to Ottilie Jäckel: "Why didn't I write[?] Well, because Kunwald and H[epner] rush me. To the former I gave what I could, but he still wants S 7,900 [...]; the latter wants S 11,550 (which I also owe on bills of exchange)." He concluded the letter remarking that in total he still owed 70,000 marks (around 130,000 schillings, equalling some 460,000 euros in 2018.[52] After all, he had already rid himself of almost four-fifths of his original debts. In 1929 Schumpeter paid off his remaining Austrian tax debts, while still able to delay the payment of the court fee for the law suit with Kaufmannsbank.[53]

It seems that by the early 1930s he had overcome nearly all of his debts. In 1932, in a letter to Werner Richter, head of the Prussian University Administration, Schumpeter wrote that he had covered all debts at Biedermann Bank during a period of time "which I do not wish to live through to any enemy, to which I nevertheless look back in moral relation with complete satisfaction."[54] Among the last repayments seem to have been remittances from Harvard to Schumpeter's old friend Schlesinger.[55] The eminent economist had lost his job at Anglobank in 1925, after which he participated in the business magazine *Der Deutsche Volkswirt* founded by Gustav Stolper, but stayed in Austria. Schlesinger, who came from a Jewish family, took his own life on March 12, 1938, the day of the "Anschluss" of

[51] No exact date, März (1983/91, p. 175f) and Private Archive Ulrich Hedtke, Ottilie Jäckel Letters.

[52] Private Archive Ulrich Hedtke, Ottilie Jäckel Letters, Schumpeter to Gunde, December 24, 1928.

[53] Private Archive Ulrich Hedtke, Ottilie Jäckel Letters, Schumpeter to Gunde, dated October 29, 1929, by Ulrich Hedtke.

[54] BAK, N/1186/31, Copy of a letter from March 23, 1932, which Schumpeter wrote to Werner Richter.

[55] Stolper (1991, p. 309, n. 9). These remittances are mentioned in letters from Mia Stöckl to Schumpeter from February 7, 1933, March 3, 1933, April 23, 1933, and May 4, 1933. On April 23, she wrote: "I can imagine very well and feel with you what relief it means for you to have finished Schlesinger so far. It is enormous what you have achieved in the relatively short time, but at the expense of your health. Because it's been years of hard work and struggle. You know, if the 9,000 are still done, I wouldn't give him a penny more. He's supposed to be glad he got so much. [...]" No currency unit is specified for the monetary amount. It could be schillings, marks, or US dollars. Originally, the loan was probably given in schillings or kronen (1 schilling = 10,000 kronen). The letters of Mia Stöckl are quoted after Private Archive Ulrich Hedtke, Mia Stöckl Letters. The original letters are stored in HUA, HUGFP 4.5.

Austria to Nazi-Germany. When Kunwald appointed him executor of his will on March 14, 1938, he had been dead for two days.[56]

In summary, it can be stated that Schumpeter completely failed in his personal pursuit of promoter's profits on the basis of his banking and industrial ventures. He not only lost all of his fortune, but piled up enormous debts, which repeatedly threatened to destroy his bourgeois existence until the late 1920s. In the literature it is sometimes mentioned that Biedermann Bank went bankrupt under his presidency. This is not correct in the strict sense of the word. Although the bank was *de facto* broke by mid-1924, it was rescued one last time by Anglobank, new investors, and a team of directors before it finally had to be liquidated in 1927, saving Schumpeter from being formally and directly involved in the bankruptcy.

However, these economic problems nevertheless provided fodder for attacks and were misused several times in academic settings in intrigues against him. The subject nearly spoiled his professorship in Bonn in 1925, and it was an important reason why he was not awarded a professorship in Berlin in 1932, much to the advantage of Harvard. Undoubtedly, in addition to his family catastrophes, economic stress massively impaired his ability to carry out academic work for years. Since his "money book" was at the center of his academic interest during these years, this work was probably the most adversely affected by his personal problems.

10.3 Return to academic work

There is no doubt that, from the mid-1920s onward, Schumpeter's ability to carry out academic research was hampered by his financial worries. He himself complained in several letters that the numerous speeches and articles that he had to take over for financial reasons distracted him from his serious scientific work.[57] This must have in particular affected his attempted general treatise on money (*WDG*, 1970). Indeed, this was a kind of *leitmotiv* in his letters to his closest friend Gustav Stolper, in which he mentioned the hard but fruitless work on the book project.

[56] *Zentralblatt* 1925, p. 879f; ÖBL, Vol. 10 (1992, p. 193f); Hedtke and Swedberg (2000, p. 120, n. 1).

[57] On September 21, 1928, Schumpeter wrote to Ottilie Jäckel about his numerous wage jobs, which kept him from his scientific work. This letter was sent from Munich where he had to give a speech. "This prostitution, while I know that it is not a self-deception, that I could achieve some things if I only had the peace to do it, and would not have to steal the hours with a bad conscience. This Bavarian Prime Minister, these Reichsminister, these mayors, these livestock from 'wholesalers' (Viehzeug von 'Großhändlern'). Truly, I often feel sorry for the German fatherland when I look at its politicians and economic leaders. And this slave chain no end—can last 20 years, this forced labour" März (1983/91, p. 179) and Private Archive Ulrich Hedtke, Ottilie Jäckel Letters. Schumpeter liked to complain to his confidante in Vienna, Ottilie Jäckel, about his workload because of the speeches, but at the same time he also coqueted with his rhetorical appearances. For a thorough documentation of Schumpeter's speeches, see Hedtke (March 2013).

His teaching in Bonn, however, proved to be more successful. Among the group of distinguished students were, for instance, *August Lösch* (1906–45), who is famous for his contributions to regional science. Lösch joined a protestant opposition to the Nazi regime and tragically died in hiding shortly before the end of the Second World War. According to his fellow student *Hans Wolfgang Singer* (1910–2006), "August Lösch was recognized by all of us as the most brilliant and promising member of the Schumpeter Seminar."[58] In 1933 Singer had to migrate from Nazi Germany and got the opportunity to study at Kings College in Cambridge after Schumpeter recommended him to Keynes. He later worked at the United Nations and is best known for the *Prebisch-Singer* hypothesis, which predicted a long-term deterioration in the terms of trade for primary goods exporters.[59] Similarly, *Wolfgang F. Stolper* (1912–2002) was an undergraduate student in Bonn, but had to leave Germany before finishing his degree. He followed Schumpeter to Harvard for his PhD studies, where he and Paul A. Samuelson formulated the *Stolper-Samuelson theorem*, which deals with the development of factor prices in the context of international goods markets.[60]

Though Singer and Stolper refer to Schumpeter's theory of economic development as an important inspiration, neither of them seems to have paid particular attention to his basic monetary theory.[61] The financial aspects of Schumpeter's writings may have exerted more influence on *Herbert Zassenhaus* (1910–88), who was another of his students in Bonn. He also emigrated in 1933, first via Bern and London to Harvard, where he was Schumpeter's assistant in 1937/8. After holding several academic positions he joined the International Monetary Fund (IMF) and later became its deputy director from 1969 to 1975. Among further examples, *Sudhir Sen* (1907–89) received his PhD in Bonn under the supervision of Schumpeter and similarly turned to development economics.[62] Finally, *Erich Schneider* (1900–70) wrote his habilitation thesis under the supervision of Schumpeter. He was older and, according to Singer, did not belong to the core of the above group.[63] Later he became president of the Institute of World Economics and director of the university in Kiel.

Remarkably, two of his students, Erich Schneider and Wolfgang Stolper, each authored a biography of Schumpeter, who according to Singer, was the "real center of the Bonn universe"[64] at the time:

[58] Singer (1997, p. 129). [59] Singer (1950).

[60] Samuelson and Stolper (1941). Wolfgang Stolper held several university positions, became director of the Centre for Research in Economic Development in Michigan and worked, for instance, as an adviser to the ministry of economic development in Nigeria. See Stolper (2003).

[61] Singer (1997); Stolper (1997).

[62] After the Second World War Sen headed the Damodar Valley Corporation in India, served as a United Nations Resident in Ghana and Yugoslavia and as a Director in the United Nations Development Program.

[63] Blind and Pyka (2015). [64] Schneider (1970); Stolper (1994); and Singer (1997, p. 131).

> [T]he life of our group gyrated about Schumpeter: he was our idol and mentor. The cliché that a good professor "opens doors" in the minds of his students seemed exactly right in this case. Schumpeter was the very antithesis of the traditional German professor. In every detail—dress, language, lecturing style, relations with students, conduct of examinations, everything—and deliberately so. The doors opened were those to Anglo-Saxons economics, to Walras and Pareto, to inter-disciplinary thinking, to interests in sociology, quantitative methods and econometrics, and to the history of economic thought.
>
> (Singer, 1997, p. 131)

Finally, Singer also offers an explanation for Schumpeter's unusual role as an enabler, emphasizing the "exceptional circumstances" which made him

> much more accessible to a young student than would normally have been the case, especially in the German university system which entirely lacked the touch of college life and the tutorial system. Schumpeter was a lonely man. His adored wife had already died when I came to Bonn. He was a lonely man also because he was out of tune with the stiff university tradition. [Conversely, teaching provided for] contact with a selected group of students in whom he sensed a response and a hope for the future. (Singer, 1997, p. 132)

PART IV
CURRENT LEGACY

11
A legacy lost

> I never wish to say anything conclusive. If I have a function, it is to open doors, not to close them.
>
> (J.A. Schumpeter, 1932, p. 104)

Though Josef Schumpeter certainly was exceptionally ambitious, he never showed much interest in aligning students behind his own ideas. In his farewell speech at the University of Bonn, he directly addressed the unspoken question: "I have never had the ambition to achieve anything like a Schumpeter school. It does not exist, and it should not exist." This assertion is consistent with later reports on his teaching at Harvard University:

> The content of all these courses would be varied from year to year, but they all suffered from one defect: by listening to Schumpeter's lectures and studying his reading assignments and suggestions, students could have never found out that he himself had ever written anything on those subjects. (Haberler, 1950, p. 359)

Gottfried Haberler also offered a very personal explanation:

> The main reason why no Schumpeter school developed is that Schumpeter was neither a reformer nor an enthusiastic partisan of capitalism, socialism, planning, or any other "ism"; he was a scholar and an intellectual. [Furthermore, his] open-mindedness and universality, the lack of fighting spirit for any particular approach, the fact that he found something useful and acceptable in almost every theory and method helped to prevent the development of a Schumpeter school.
>
> (Haberler, 1950, p. 371)

If Schumpeter were alive today, he would not be able to complain about a lack of recognition. However, in the vast majority of references to his work, people tend to only pick out individual popular ideas or notions, such as innovation, entrepreneurship, or "creative destruction." They seldom consider in a thorough manner his overall conception. Conversely, a little reflection on the previous chapters reveals a number of plain reasons for the utterly inferior reception of his monetary theory in particular.

First and foremost, due to his overarching ambition and gross underestimation of the theoretical difficulties he would encounter, Schumpeter never accomplished

Schumpeter's Venture Money. Michael Peneder and Andreas Resch,
Oxford University Press (2021). © Michael Peneder and Andreas Resch.
DOI: 10.1093/oso/9780198804383.003.0011

the attempted consolidation of his monetary ideas into a general treatise on money. In the aftermath of the First World War, the distractions of political office, the failed business ventures, and personal blows of fate had additionally weakened his intellectual and emotional powers. After his move to Harvard, other projects absorbed his attention. His monetary ideas thus remained piecemeal and scattered across various sources, with the consequence that "Schumpeter's work on money and banking is by no means easy to access."[1] Sometimes he presented them unintelligibly, sometimes in an exemplary way, and sometimes only indirectly through the lens of the history of monetary thought. Moreover, they remained in the shadow of other arresting notions of his own, which have become commonplace in economists' habitual language. In addition, he never approved of the unfinished manuscript of his money book. And at the time of its posthumous publication, monetary theory had long moved on to a different agenda.

The second reason is that Schumpeter's disequilibrium view was not palatable to most of the contemporary economists. The controversy with Böhm-Bawerk over interest in a stationary economy is a case in point, which seriously impaired his reputation in monetary matters at the time. Furthermore, his intellectual approach was never well suited to the demand for practical policy advice. During the Great Depression such advice was, however, what was most urgently needed. In contrast, his steadfast adherence to the purity of intellectual arguments meant that he aimed to keep them separate from *a priori* political considerations. It also implied that he denied simplification and instead accepted conditional, seemingly ambiguous conclusions as the appropriate representation of complex realities. Yet this ran against the tide of a growing public anticipation of the practical use of science. Nor could his pragmatic attitude toward policy win him a large following in the raging ideological debates of the post Second World War era.

Finally, Schumpeter's repeated announcements of a forthcoming "money book" must have further dampened the interest in the monetary aspects of his published work. Contemporary economists had ample reason to eschew the effort of compiling it from various sources and instead wait for its heralded comprehensive realization by Schumpeter himself. Other economists, of course, did not even consider waiting for the consolidation of his monetary views. Like the proverbial "caravan," the discipline moved on ahead without him. And while monetary theory made progress in numerous respects, many elements that are important to Schumpeter's dynamic conception were lost from sight:

> In all disciplines theory plays a double role: it is both a lens and a blinder. As a lens, it focuses the mind upon specified problems, enabling conditional statements to be made about causal relations for a well-defined but limited set of phenomena. But as a blinder, theory narrows the field of vision. (Minsky 1986/2008, p. 109)

[1] Festré (2002, p. 221). See also Mann (1958).

This chapter will briefly sketch how Schumpeter's monetary legacy was largely left behind in the theoretical discourse of the subsequent decades. After a brief introductory remark, it will first address the challenge that the success of John M. Keynes presented to Schumpeter's work on money, and then turn to the Neo-Keynesian synthesis, which attracted many of Schumpeter's colleagues and disciples at Harvard. After a brief discussion of monetarism, the attention will focus on the evolution of modern general equilibrium models, beginning with its origin in the Real Business Cycle analysis and moving on to the New Keynesian (NK) models.

11.1 The Keynesian revolution

As previously mentioned, the intrinsic difficulties of an overly ambitious agenda, the First World War and his turbulent personal and professional life during the 1920s had kept Schumpeter from further developing and consolidating his monetary ideas into the general theory to which he aspired. Yet in the 1930s, the success of John M. Keynes also struck a double blow that effectively buried his endeavors. First, in 1930 Keynes' *Treatise on Money* pre-empted the field by advocating some very similar ideas and raising the bar for another like-minded publication. However, Schumpeter could then still consider himself part of the progressive vanguard of monetary theory, which may explain his reportedly positive attitude toward the book.[2] Ironically, the *General Theory* of 1936 was then more detrimental to him, precisely because Keynes had abandoned many of the very elements they had previously held in common. Now Schumpeter's review, like many others, was harsh, finding fault, among other things, with the inappropriate use of "social aggregates."[3] And yet the mainstream of monetary thought, and in particular many of his own students, followed Keynes.

Treatise on Money

In the *Treatise*, Keynes aimed for a comprehensive exposition of the "theory and facts of representative money as it exists in the modern world."[4] While reminiscent in intent of Thornton's *Paper Credit* more than a century earlier, the *Treatise* actually exhibits surprising concurrences with Schumpeter's monetary theory as presented in MSP. Keynes opened with the statement that "money-of-account,

[2] Stolper (1950); *TGE* (1952, p. 277).
[3] "Review of 'The General Theory of Employment, Interest and Money' by John Maynard Keynes" (RGT; 1936, p. 160).
[4] Keynes (1930a, p. vii).

namely that in which debts and prices and general purchasing power are expressed, is the primary concept of a theory of money,"[5] which he explicitly embraced to be endogenous. He considered bank money an "acknowledgement of private debt, expressed in the money-of-account," which constitutes a "serviceable substitute for money-proper in the settlement of transactions,"[6] and which he accordingly counted as part of the total money supply. Unlike Schumpeter and the Austrians more generally, however, Keynes was positively inclined toward the state theory of Knapp, which he invoked to indicate the course of the evolution of money:

> Thus the age of money had succeeded the age of barter as soon as men had adopted a money-of-account. And the age of Chartalist or state money was reached when the state claimed the right to declare what thing should answer as money to the current money-of-account. (Keynes, 1930a, p. 4f)

Similarly to Schumpeter in *WDG*, the *Treatise* engages in a comprehensive discussion of index numbers and the measurement of price levels. Keynes also pointed out that the purchasing power of money does not refer to the subjective utility which one may associate with its command,[7] and elaborated an own version of the "fundamental equation" of exchange. Like Schumpeter, he applied the "pre-classical doctrine that everything is *produced* by *labour*" (including the produced means of production) and emphasized that consumption is "the sole end and object of all economic activity," also substituting total transactions with the flow of current earnings.[8] Though Keynes did not emphasize the overall structure of production in n goods, as Schumpeter had done, he distinguished between consumer goods and investment goods as the two sources of income and further separated consumption and saving as its two alternative uses. He then derived the three "fundamental" equations, which determine the price level of (i) consumption goods, (ii) investment goods, and (iii) total output, respectively.

For our purpose, it is sufficient to illustrate the main idea with respect to the final equation for total output and the aggregate price level. Staying close to his original notation, total output O is comprised of the production of consumer goods R and investment goods C: $O = R + C$. Similarly, aggregate earnings E correspond to total output times the aggregate price index, which is comprised of the respective outputs and prices for consumption and investment goods, that is, $E = P^O O = P^R R + P^C C$. Since the total expenditures on consumption $P^R R = E - S$, and the value of the increment of new investment goods $P^C C = I$, total earnings reduce to $P^O O = E - S + I$. Though Keynes was not explicit about whether the latter variables should be interpreted *ex ante* or *ex post*, we may essentially

[5] Keynes (1930a, p. 3). [6] Keynes (1930a, pp. 6, 5). [7] Keynes (1930a, p. 96).

[8] The quotations are from Keynes (1936, pp. 213, 104) but equally apply to the *Treatise* of 1930. See, for instance, Keynes (1930a, p. 134).

think of them as *planned* saving and investment, which can accordingly differ. If one decomposes the rate of earnings per unit of output $\frac{E}{O}$ into wages W and efficiency e, the aggregate price level amounts to:

$$P^{O} = \frac{E}{O} + \frac{I-S}{O} = \frac{1}{e}W + \frac{I-S}{O} \tag{11.1}$$

Keynes was mainly interested in the second term, which depicts the difference between current investments and savings. This is where he identified the origin of disequlibria that invalidate the quantity theory by affecting general prices, even without a change in the total quantity or velocity of money. It also served to demonstrate his main concerns for monetary policy, in particular his rationale for keeping interest rates low in order to avoid an overhang of savings that would depress consumption and hence income and employment.

In contrast, Keynes paid less attention to the first term of "efficiency-earnings."[9] A joint reading of the impacts and trade-offs of both terms, however, is congruous with basic tenets of Schumpeter's monetary theory. According to him, investments that are not financed by current savings but by an expansion of the monetary circulation (either from new credit or past savings) will leave the price level unaffected only if the growth of output matches the additional expenditures. Likewise, aggregate prices remain stable if the two terms in Keynes' equation cancel out. Of course, in Schumpeter's dynamic perspective such a perfect match would be a rather accidental outcome of aggregation, since it takes time for individual investments to realize productivity gains. New investments first raise the cost of the means of production but generally will not affect efficiency. Only after some time has passed may the efficiency gains counterbalance the initial inflationary impulse, possibly even with a deflationary net effect. In short, the impact on aggregate prices can be positive, negative, or neutral, depending on how productive the additional investments are. Close to full employment, the expansion is more likely to affect prices, while when it is more distant from full employment more opportunities exist to raise production. Either outcome seems to be consistent with the relationships depicted in the above equation.[10]

To conclude, in the *Treatise* one certainly finds striking examples of congruence with Schumpeter's ideas, especially as presented in MSP. Keynes in one instance acknowledged the priority of Mises, Schumpeter, and Hayek with regard to his distinction between savings and investment, but then notoriously asserted that "in

[9] But see also Keynes (1930a, p. 136).

[10] Note that with Schumpeter's dynamic conception full employment is not a binding constraint to the growth of productivity, since endogenous innovation can shift the technological frontier, with creative destruction fostering structural change through the reallocation of resources. As a consequence, the additional financing of investments, if spent productively, can in principle raise output instead of prices, even if the system already operates at full employment. The social surplus will then materialize in higher real per capita incomes rather than an increase in employment.

German I can only clearly understand what I know already!"[11] If we take Keynes at his word and abstain from the occasional mockery the statement has induced, we may recall that at the time both *TED* and MSP were only published in German. In any case, Keynes did not delve very deeply into those areas reminiscent of Schumpeter's conception. Generally, they are to be found at the beginning or in the early parts of the *Treatise*, and they become less relevant as Keynes seems to have found and further developed his original theme. Also, in the preface Keynes admitted that the *Treatise* is not entirely consistent, and that he finished with ideas much different from the beginning: "There are many skins which I have sloughed still littering these pages."[12] Most notably, among the "skins" he had sloughed was the endogeneity of money, thus setting the scene for the central bank to be the only "conductor of the orchestra."[13] As Ingrao and Sardoni observe:

> Keynes's view of banks as firms that are capable to create money *ex novo*, or *ex nihilo*, is not too different from the analyses developed by Schumpeter and Robertson. In some respects, Keynes's analysis is even more detailed and accurate. However, in the subsequent analytical developments in the *Treatise*, Keynes concentrates on the role of banks as creators of "passive" deposits, i.e. those deriving from accepting the public's proper money, so that their lending activity essentially reduces to intermediation. (Ingrao and Sardoni, 2019, p. 94)

As a consequence, the main conclusions of Keynes "can be reached by abstracting from the banking system altogether."[14] He was thus spared many of the complexities that Schumpeter and the Austrians struggled with, and eliminated a potentially disruptive factor in his vision of the effective central management of a currency. Later in the *General Theory*, Keynes consistently ascribed all monetary tasks to the central bank.

The *General Theory*

In the *Treatise*, the difference between investment and savings was based on a peculiar definition of income, in which Keynes had only included "a normal or equilibrium profit; with the result that on this definition saving exceeded investment by the amount of the excess of normal profit over the actual profit."[15] In

[11] Keynes (1930a, pp. 171, 199). With regard to Schumpeter, he referred to the second edition of *TED*.

[12] Keynes (1930a, p. vi). Relatedly, "[a]s I read through the page proofs of this book I am acutely conscious of its defects. It has occupied me for several years, not free from other obligations, during which my ideas have been developing and changing, with the result that its parts are not all entirely harmonious with one another" (Keynes, 1930a, p. v). Despite being aware of such deficiencies, it is striking that Keynes rushed for publication rather than a further revision of his manuscript.

[13] Keynes (1930a, p. 30). [14] Ingrao and Sardoni (2019, p. 98). [15] Keynes (1936, p. 61).

the *General Theory*, Keynes apologized for the confusion and put the actual profit in its proper place. Ignoring both the role of credit and finance and the possibility of temporary differences between planned investments and savings, Keynes turned to embrace "the old-fashioned view that saving always involves investment":[16]

> Whilst, therefore, the amount of saving is an outcome of the collective behaviour of individual consumers and the amount of investment of the collective behaviour of individual entrepreneurs, these two amounts are necessarily equal, since each of them is equal to the excess of income over consumption.
>
> (Keynes, 1936, p. 63)

Differently from the Walrasian attention to the *ex ante* plans of individuals, Keynes thereby followed the Marshallian tradition of denoting observable quantities *ex post*. The consequent identity of investment and saving without a proper distinction between their planned and realized values fared prominently in the academic dispute with Bertil Ohlin (1899–1979) and members of the Stockholm School.[17] But in the *General Theory* Keynes deliberately chose to render his analysis tractable in terms of static equilibrium. Relatedly, he further discarded, for instance, the relevance of cumulative processes, arguing that the "complication" of credit money "also cancels out when we are dealing with aggregate investment."[18] As Greenwald and Stiglitz point out, in the *Treatise* "Keynes had written at length about what he called the Fringe of Unsatisfied Borrowers, and the wider economic significance of credit rationing." In the *General Theory*, however, "[t]hese powerful ideas are almost eclipsed."[19] Relatedly, Keynes renounced the idea of "forced savings" for the difficulties it involved[20] and focused instead on the final static equilibrium as produced by "the logical theory of the multiplier, which holds good continuously, without time-lag, at all moments of time."[21] As Ingrao and Sardoni conclude, "[o]nce Keynes's methodological approach is accepted, it is obviously true that saving and investment are always equal, but it is also evident that the problem of how investment is initially financed becomes irrelevant."[22]

Shifting the attention from wages and resource allocation more generally to the level of aggregate demand, the central concern of the *General Theory* was to demonstrate the possibility of underemployment in a stable equilibrium with

[16] Keynes (1936, p. 83).

[17] See, for instance, the later critique of Leijonhufvud (1981, p. 170f): "If saving and investment are continuously equal, the rate of interest cannot possibly be governed by any difference between them. The possibility of a corresponding excess flow demand for loanable funds has then also been defined away. The loanable funds interest mechanism is gutted. So, the flow part of the Treatise's stock-flow analysis should be erased."

[18] Keynes (1936, p. 75.)

[19] Greenwald and Stiglitz (1987, p. 122).

[20] Keynes (1936, pp. 81, 79).

[21] Keynes (1936, p. 122).

[22] Ingrao and Sardoni (2019, p. 100).

perfect competition.[23] The explanation notably entailed, among others, (i) the diminishing propensity to consume with rising income, (ii) the determination of investment demand by the interaction of the marginal efficiency of capital and the interest rate, which in turn (iii) depended on the interaction of the demand for and given supply of money.

The most distinctive monetary conception of the *General Theory*[24] was Keynes' emphasis on *liquidity preferences*. It meant the economy's propensity to hoard cash, which determines the dichotomous choice between money and interest-bearing securities.[25] Keynes thereby discarded Böhm-Bawerk's explanation of positive time preferences, arguing that they cannot explain the holding of cash which bears no interest. Instead, he pointed at its "transaction"-, "precautionary"-, and "speculative-motives":

> Thus the rate of interest at any time, being the reward for parting with liquidity, is a measure of the unwillingness of those who possess money to part with their liquid control over it. The rate of interest is not the "price" which brings into equilibrium the demand for resources to invest with the readiness to abstain from present consumption. It is the "price" which equilibrates the desire to hold wealth in the form of cash with the available quantity of cash. (Keynes, 1936, p. 167)

Keynes' second and third motives to hold cash invoke the importance of uncertainty about future interest rates. Thereby "animal spirits"[26] and mass psychology determine long-term expectations. This offers opportunities for speculation, which he defined as "the activity of forecasting the psychology of the market."[27] But it also implies the possibility that central banks can actively manage expectations and thus control the interest rate.[28] In a Post-Keynesian interpretation, Tily therefore points out that the theory of liquidity preferences is best interpreted for given quantities of money and income. Consequently, Keynes's "theory of money as a store of value concerns matters that occur after the creation of bank money, and belongs sequentially after that theory."[29]

[23] Schumpeter doubted the need to prove the existence of underemployment for perfect equilibrium: "I have sometimes wondered why Keynes attached so much importance to proving that there may – and under his assumptions generally will – be less than full employment in *perfect equilibrium of perfect competition*. For there is such an ample supply of verifiable explanatory factors to account for the actual unemployment we observe at any time that only the theorist's ambition can induce us to wish for more. [...] But practically, Keynes should have fared equally well with the unemployment that may exist in a permanent state of disequilibrium" (*TGE*, 1952, p. 287).

[24] It already had appeared in rudimentary form in the *Treatise*. See Hicks (1989, p. 61ff) for a critical discussion.

[25] See Keynes (1936, p. 174).

[26] That is, "a spontaneous urge to action rather than inaction, and not as the outcome of a weighted average of quantitative benefits multiplied by quantitative probabilities" (Keynes, 1936, p. 161).

[27] Keynes (1936, p. 158).

[28] See, for example, Chick and Dow (2002); Tily (2006); or Chick and Tily (2014).

[29] Tily (2012, p. 61).

Doubting that the market would lead professional investors and speculators to focus on the creation of long-term values, in the *General Theory* Keynes' emphasis shifted from monetary to fiscal policy:[30]

> For my own part I am now somewhat sceptical of the success of a merely monetary policy directed towards influencing the rate of interest. I expect to see the State, which is in a position to calculate the marginal efficiency of capital-goods on long views and on the basis of the general social advantage, taking an ever greater responsibility for directly organising investment.
>
> (Keynes, 1936, p. 164)

Given the radical change in method and perspective, the *General Theory* naturally met with much criticism. Abandoning his earlier restraint and generally positive attitude toward the *Treatise*,[31] Schumpeter was among the first to write a particularly harsh review of the *General Theory*:

> [Keynes] professes to address it primarily to his fellow economists and seems to invite purely theoretical discussion. But it is not quite easy to accept that invitation, for everywhere he really pleads for a definite policy, and on every page the ghost of that policy looks over the shoulder of the analyst, frames his assumptions, guides his pen. [...] It is, however, vital to renounce communion with any attempt to revive the Ricardian practice of offering, in the garb of general scientific truth, advice which – whether good or bad – carries meaning only with references to the practical exigencies of the unique historical situation of a given time and country. (RGT, p. 160)

Further taking issue with the fact that "Mr. Keynes eliminates the most powerful propeller of investment, the financing of changes in production functions," the only common ground left was "his purely monetary theory of interest which is, as far as I can see, the first to follow upon my own. Unfortunately, I must add that the similarity stops there."[32] In a later obituary on Keynes, Schumpeter strived for a more positive stance, praising in particular his earlier publications. Indirectly, he also pointed at what may have constituted a major difference between the two:

> The first condition for simplicity of a model is, of course, simplicity of the vision which it is to implement. And simplicity of vision is in part a matter of genius and in part a matter of willingness to pay the price in terms of the factors that have to be left out of the picture. (*TGE*, 1952, p. 281)

[30] "For most of these persons are, in fact, largely concerned, not with making superior long-term forecasts of the probable yield of an investment over its whole life, but with foreseeing changes in the conventional basis of valuation a short time ahead of the general public" (Keynes, 1936, p. 154).

[31] See Stolper (1994, p. 47ff) or Schumpeter's letter to Eucken in Dathe and Hedtke (2018, p. 19).

[32] RGT (1936, p. 163).

Schumpeter acknowledged (and maybe envied) that "genius" in Keynes, but probably also meant to explain that he was not willing to pay the same price himself. Among a later generation of monetary economists, Leijonhufvud was more specific about the price of taking "the conceptually trivial option," by which he meant that "Wicksell's rabbit has been stuffed back into Keynes' hat":[33]

> In Wicksell, the excess flow demand for loanable funds governs the interest rate. The *Treatise* has a stock-flow treatment where the interest rate must clear a market that trades not only in new issues but also in outstanding securities. In the *General Theory*, Keynes goes to a pure stock-analysis of interest determination. This last step would be retrogressive in itself. But, on top of that, it is the excess stock demand, not for securities, but for money that – he argues – governs the interest rate. Not an appealing doctrine! (Leijonhufvud, 1981, p. 170)

Of related interest, John Hicks acknowledged that cash may have been a reasonable reserve asset at the time of Keynes, but had lost this function "on the way to a credit economy, in which any money that does not bear interest has become no more than small change."[34] Reinforcing a statement by Dennis H. Robertson (1890–1963),[35] who had accused Keynes of accounting only for the motive to *hold* money, while ignoring the more familiar motive to *use* it, Ingrao and Sardoni conclude that "Keynes's insistence on the demand for idle money as a defence from uncertainty leads him to 'forget' the demand for active money and, hence for loans, which are demand for money to be spent".[36]

11.2 Neo-Keynesian synthesis

Despite much criticism of the above kind, the Keynesian revolution rapidly took root with a younger generation of economists, and Schumpeter's faculty at Harvard was at the forefront of this new development. *Alvin H. Hansen* (1887–1975) had early on converted to the Keynesian paradigm and some of the faculty's brightest disciples, such as Paul Samuelson, James Tobin, and Robert Solow, were among the most renowned proponents. Schumpeter could not fail to notice the change of tide and began his review of the *General Theory* with the following acknowledgement:

[33] Leijonhufvud (1981, p. 172).

[34] Hicks (1989, p. 103) made this comment after a period of high interest rates (also for relatively liquid assets of short maturity).

[35] Robertson was an early proponent of the *loanable funds* doctrine in the tradition of Wicksell. In the *Treatise* Keynes credited him as his main source of monetary ideas. Later, and in particular with respect to the *General Theory*, Robertson became one of his main critics. See Robertson (1922, 1934).

[36] Ingrao and Sardoni (2019, p. 112).

> The book by Mr. Keynes on fundamental questions which are right at the heart of the practical discussions of the day is no doubt an event. Those who had the opportunity to witness the expectations of the best of our students, the impatience they displayed at the delay in getting hold of their copies, the eagerness with which they devoured them [...] must first of all congratulate the author on a signal personal success. (RGT, 1936, p. 160)

The *General Theory* is certainly a much more consistent and concisely written book than the earlier *Treatise*. But apart from such intrinsic qualities, at least two further aspects contributed to its sweeping success. One is historical-demographic. Robert Solow once explained that, growing up in the 1930s, it "was an obvious fact of life to us that our society was malfunctioning politically and economically and that nobody really knew how to explain it or what to do about it."[37] Referring to his studies at the New School for Social Research in 1939, *Franco Modigliani* (1918–2003) similarly explained:

> The *General Theory* of Keynes was the center of discussion, together with the work of Schumpeter on business cycles. We had seminars devoted to them and they were very exciting. Of course at that time we were coming out of the depression. Keynes gave you the feeling that the mysterious disease that produced the depression was something that could be understood and avoided in the future. So there was a lot of excitement associated with that study.
>
> (Modigliani, as reported in Breit and Hirsch, 2009, p. 118).

Put simply, the young generation of economists that embraced the Keynesian revolution had spent their formative years of adolescence in the economic depression, and they were keen to apply their scientific prowess to the concrete problems of their time. This also relates to the second aspect of Keynes' spectacular success: his deliberate simplification of the theoretical frame had indeed opened many "doors" to further refinements and thus absorbed much of the energy and creativity of the younger scholars, who excelled in superior mathematical skills and training.

As early as the 1930s aggregate equilibrium analysis received a big push, when *John R. Hicks* (1904–89) launched the *Neo(classical)-Keynesian synthesis* by introducing the famous IS-LM model. In his later years, Hicks notoriously distanced himself from the IS-LM analysis, agreeing to be an "unwilling hero," who had only tried to summarize Keynes' *General Theory*. After failed attempts to revise it, he got to the point that "[t]he two curves do not belong together. One is a flow equilibrium, the other a stock. They have no business being on the same diagram."[38]

[37] As reported in Breit and Hirsch (2009, p. 154).

[38] Hicks as reported in Klamer (1989, p. 175). On the monetary theory of Hicks, see also Laidler (1994) and Fontana (2004).

At Harvard as well, which was at the forefront of general equilibrium analysis, the assimilation of Keynesian ideas took that route and shunned many of its Marshallian elements. James Tobin pointed out that Schumpeter himself had "fostered this development," consistently with his genuine admiration of Walras "even though his own theory of the dynamics of capitalism was wholly different."[39] Along this path, the caravan of alternating monetary doctrines left behind Schumpeter, whose overriding concern for dynamics and disequilibrium at the time did not accord with the profession's growing demand for mathematical generalizations.[40] Nevertheless, it seems that Schumpeter understood it to be a natural progression which must run its course. Not only did he disapprove, for instance, when Franco Modigliani was discouraged from joining Harvard by the department head, but also he more generally remained supportive of his students.[41] James Tobin provided a lively description of his attitude:

> The faculty adviser for my doctoral dissertation in 1946–47 was, by my choice, Professor Schumpeter, one of the truly great economists, indeed social scientists, of the century. He had no use for Keynes and little for my topic, the consumption function. He read what I wrote and made helpful suggestions, but mostly he kept hands off. When I saw him, we talked of many other things, to my lasting benefit.
> (James Tobin, as reported in: Breit and Hirsch, 2009, p. 100).

At Harvard, Alvin Hansen exerted the most important influence on Tobin. But Schumpeter's attention to monetary economics, and, in particular, his concern for the nexus between finance and aggregate growth, remained a distinctive characteristic of his work to which we will return in Chapter 12.

Initially, Schumpeter also supervised the doctoral thesis of *Hyman P. Minsky* (1919–96), who had studied mathematics at the University of Chicago before turning to economics at Harvard.[42] When Schumpeter died in 1950, Leontief took over as advisor of the thesis. Minsky had little sympathy for the Neo-Keynesian approach and set out to develop his own brand of *Post-Keynesian* analysis. Thereby he also maintained a distinct Schumpeterian flavor (see Section 12.2). Similarly to Goodwin, he acknowledged that "[o]nly complex dynamics can do justice to Schumpeter's vision." However, "[g]iven the command of mathematics that economists of that time possessed, Schumpeter's model was not tractable. As a result his vision was ignored by the candidates striving to be mathematical

[39] James Tobin, in: Breit and Hirsch (2009, p. 101).

[40] The same could be said of the Austrian School, but its more combative attitude and pronounced political agenda granted it further attention and constituency.

[41] Breit and Hirsch (2009, p. 121).

[42] Minsky stressed that he owed his greatest intellectual debts from education to Oscar Lange, Henry Simons, and Josef Schumpeter (Minsky, 1986/2008, p. x).

economists and econometricians."[43] Minsky's personal memories are very critical of his Harvard colleages, but with respect to his conversations with Schumpeter they strike a similar note to those of Tobin:

> By 1948–49 Schumpeter had fallen out of favour with the trend-following and career-oriented graduate students at Harvard. [...] I discovered that Schumpeter would often sit alone, dutifully keeping his promised hours even though few if any students came. I began to join him: he was happy to have company. [...] There was a good deal of tease back and forth, but there also was a great deal of substance. Schumpeter was always involved in the exchanges (taking notes on seemingly random points), encouraging us to develop our own style and to follow our own vision. (Normal science was too easy). (Minsky, 1993, p. 103)

As the "caravan" moved on, economics mainly strived for and evolved on the basis of the growing body and sophistication of aggregate equilibrium models. Arguably, the Neo-Keynesian synthesis reached the pinnacle of its popularity with the notorious *Phillips curve*. Earlier econometric studies by Tinbergen and Klein had included wage equations with a trade-off between inflation and unemployment, which in the mid-1950s also received a detailed discussion by A.J. Brown.[44] It was, however, in 1958 that an influential article by Alban W. Phillips (1914–75) generally established the empirical observation of a negative correlation between the rate of unemployment and wage or price inflation. Despite cautionary remarks about the long-run stability of the resulting negative trade-off, the new equilibrium models suggested a choice between the two evils to policy makers.[45] Though the initial explanation reasoned from unemployment to wages and then prices, the interpretation as a policy trade-off implicitly assumed a strong non-neutrality of money. In contrast, the older disequilibrium views of Schumpeter or Hayek, in which a monetary propagation mechanism with differential effects on prices would produce temporary episodes of rising prices and output to be followed by a period of contraction, apparently had slipped out of perception. The Phillips curve, however, also turned out to be the "Achilles heel" of the Neo-Keynesian approach and ultimately prepared the ground for the subsequent rise of *monetarism*.

11.3 Monetarism

Following the growing prosperity of the post Second World War era and the success of Keynesian employment policies throughout that period, in the 1970s the

[43] Minsky (1993, pp. 114, 104).

[44] The references are to Jan Tinbergen (1903–94), Lawrence Klein (1920–2013), and Arthur J. Brown (1914–2003). See Mitchell (1999) for a comprehensive analysis of the genesis and history of the Phillips curve.

[45] Lipsey (1960, 1978); Samuelson and Solow (1960).

simultaneous rise of unemployment and inflation posed a new problem, which was at odds with the presumed trade-off between the two. One consequence was that the pendulum of professional attention swung back toward the quantity theory of money. In its influential restatement, Milton Friedman replaced total transactions by the payments for final goods and services,[46] similarly to Schumpeter in MSP (Section 6.3). But focusing on the demand for assets rather than income flows, Friedman's analysis was in particular akin to the method of Keynes. The similarities even prompted Don Patinkin to state that Friedman had provided "a most elegant and sophisticated statement of modern Keynesian monetary theory."[47]

Friedman defined the individual demand for money M^d as a function of general prices P, real income y, the fraction w of income derived from property, and a vector of expected nominal returns on money R_M (including liquidity preferences and interest on bank deposits), fixed-value securities R_B, and physical assets R_E plus u other factors:[48]

$$M^D = Pf(y, w; R_M, R_B, R_E; u) \tag{11.2}$$

Reconciliation with the total supply of money M^S required aggregation over the total population N and a vector of interest rates R, further including the change of prices g_P:

$$M^S = h(R, Y, \ldots) = PNf(y, w, R, g_P, u) \tag{11.3}$$

Unlike Schumpeter and the Austrians, but congruently with Keynes' *General Theory*, Friedman considered the money supply exogenous and under the control of the central bank. Unlike either, the velocity of money is assumed to be constant. Consequently, changes in the money supply directly affect nominal income and cannot be absorbed, for instance, by a change in hoarding. Monetarism thus proclaimed that changes in the money supply are the primary cause of fluctuations in economic activity (rather than the changes of effective demand as in the Keynesians framework).

Unlike the orthodox doctrine, the changes in the money supply may in principle affect either prices or production and the neutrality of money becomes foremost an empirical question. Summarizing the empirical evidence, Friedman concluded that "[i]n the short run, which may be as long as three to ten years, monetary changes affect primarily output. Over decades, on the other hand, [...] the rate of monetary growth affects primarily prices."[49] Periods of three to ten years allow for considerable real effects, if one believes, like Schumpeter did, in the continuous endogenous creation of disequilibria. We may therefore speculate that he might have been comfortable with the particular timing of aggregate effects. Still, Schumpeter would certainly have pointed at the irreversible changes of the

[46] Friedman (1959, 1977, 1978).
[47] Patinkin (1969, p. 61).
[48] Friedman (1987, pp. 12, 14).
[49] Friedman (1987, p. 29).

productive structure that must occur and which also constitute significant real effects in the long run. That is, he would have emphasized the difference between mere growth and development.

Returning to the debates about the Phillips curve, in the late 1960s Friedman and Edmund Phelps independently argued that labor will bargain for higher wages, if it expects inflation to increase. *Adaptive expectations*[50] thus shift the Phillips curve outward and thereby cause "stagflation." Though policy may exploit the negative trade-off in the short run by means of unanticipated inflation, labor would adjust expectations and recuperate its loss of real income. In the long-run equilibrium, the "expectations-augmented Phillips Curve" becomes vertical as the economy reaches its "natural rate of unemployment."[51] As a consequence, inflation (deflation) will increase if the unemployment rate stays below (above) its equilibrium level. Since only real factors determine the "natural rate of unemployment," Friedman then also entertained a theoretical explanation for the long-run neutrality of money.[52]

Among recent attempts, Richard G. Lipsey aims to reconcile the Phillips curve with the notion of a *non-accelerating inflation rate of unemployment* (NAIRU). He thereby refers to a deliberate evolutionary and Schumpeterian rationale, which acknowledges uncertainty and endogenous technological change as causes of path dependence and multiple equilibria.[53] In short, Lipsey suggests a "non-accelerating inflation band of unemployment" (NAIBU), where (depending on an economy's specific history and institutions) price stability is consistent with a certain range of different rates of unemployment. Within that "band," the function is about flat and inflation varies within close margins. At the upper and lower bounds of NAIBU, the slope turns negative, depicting the traditional relationship of the Phillips curve, whereby the slope rapidly gets steeper the more the unemployment rate deviates from NAIBU. The vertical slope hence becomes a limiting case, which applies if either very low or very high rates of unemployment exert an accordingly strong inflationary or deflationary impulse on wages.

[50] Mitchell (1999, pp. 29, 35) reports that the forerunners of the Phillips curve had acknowledged the role of expectations, which, however, then got lost in the popular textbook models. He credits Tinbergen and Klein, in particular, for having "estimated 'Phillips curves' with expectations variables included," and A.J. Brown for pointing at the possibility of expectation-led wage-price spirals.

[51] Friedman (1968, p. 8) defined it as "the level that would be grounded out by the Walrasian system of general equilibrium equations, provided there is imbedded in them the actual structural characteristics of the labour and commodity markets, including market imperfections, stochastic variability in demands and supplies, the cost of gathering information about job vacancies and labour availabilities, the costs of mobility, and so on."

[52] According to Friedman, "unanticipated changes in aggregate nominal demand and in inflation will cause systematic errors of perception on the part of employers and employees alike that will initially lead unemployment to deviate in the opposite direction from its natural rate. In this respect, money is not neutral. However, such deviations are transitory"(Friedman, 1977, p. 470).

[53] Lipsey (2016).

11.4 Dynamic general equilibrium models

Neoclassical growth has emerged as a theory of the non-monetary economy. Among the attempts to integrate money in its equilibrium framework, Walsh summarizes three different strands.[54] First, the *money-in-utility* approach directly inserts money-balances into the utility function. Second, the *cash-in-advance* and search cost models assume a positive demand for cash-balances in order to avoid transaction costs in the exchange of assets. And, third, *overlapping generation* models treat money as an asset which facilitates the intertemporal transfer of resources. Either approach establishes a positive demand for money and the interest rate provides for the equilibrating price. Such mechanisms allowed to assimilate Keynesian ideas into the synthesis, whereby money may have (temporary) effects on real production and employment because of rigid wages and/or prices. By ignoring banking and finance, however, the models (implicitly) assume that financing is void of market imperfections and operates efficiently.

The longer we follow the main caravan of equilibrium models in economics, and the closer we get toward contemporary times, the more difficult it becomes to draw sharp boundaries between different strands of monetary thought, and the popular labels appear increasingly clichéd, or even deceptive. While some researchers still group according to political preferences, most of them identify along the technical apparatus they apply and master. For the mainstream of macroeconomic analyses, this implies a certain convergence of accepted methods, championed by the growing body of *dynamic stochastic general equilibrium* (DSGE) models. This section aims to very briefly sketch the route traveled so far, following a common distinction between three successive generations.[55] We begin with the *real business cycle* (RBC) theory that emerged from the so-called New Classical approach to macroeconomics, followed by pre-crisis NK models, and finally turn to the fast-growing variety of post-crisis NK and related models.

New Classical

In the 1970s, financial economics began to thrive on the strength of the *efficient market hypothesis* (EMH). Most notably, Eugene Fama demonstrated that the hypothesis, according to which "security prices at any point in time "fully reflect" *all* available information [...] stands up rather well to the data."[56] Relatedly,

[54] Walsh (2017, p. 42ff). [55] Kehoe et al. (2018).

[56] Fama (1970, p. 388). Among the early origins of the EMH, Goetzmann (2016, p. 275ff) points in particular at the French mathematicians Jules Regnault (1834–94), Henri Lefèfre (1827–85), and Louis Bachelier (1870–1946), who had applied advanced probability theory to the study of asset prices. In the 1960s, the work of Bachelier was rediscovered by Benoit Mandelbrot and Paul Samuelson, who had proved that "properly anticipated prices" must follow a random walk. In contrast with the Chicago

Fisher Black, Myron Scholes, and Robert Merton became known for developing intertemporal asset pricing models for contingent claims with portfolios that can be perfectly hedged within frictionless markets.[57] Such hyperrational market outcomes do not necessarily depend on assuming literally perfect rational behavior by the individual agents. It is sufficient if the irrational choices by noise traders are normally distributed and cancel out on average. Yet, even if irrational choices are not independent, the market can still be efficient as long as smart investors eliminate any mispricing of assets through arbitrage.[58]

Milton Friedman had used to rely on this rationality of market competition, where selection systematically favors the intelligent investors. Conversely, he had discarded the possibility of macroeconomic policy to affect output and employment in the long run. Arguably, however, his analysis had also remained largely within the structure of the Keynesian model. In particular, he had acknowledged disequilibrium during periods of transition and adjustment. In contrast, when exercising his own quantitative models, *Robert Lucas* was puzzled by the fact that Friedman's assumption of adaptive expectations actually did produce a long-term trade-off between inflation and employment.[59] Lucas subsequently turned his attention away from adaptive toward *rational expectations*. This was not meant to represent a realistic behavioral assumption. Rather it defined a property of the economic model: that "the economist cannot claim to possess a particular knowledge that is denied the economic agents whose behavior she is modeling."[60] In practical terms, it means that people make no systematic errors when predicting the future, and that the model can run on accurate expected values. With regard to economic policy, the assumption of rational expectations set a novel pace for the *New Classical* opposition to Keynesian interventions. Most notably, it paved the way toward the *policy irrelevance hypothesis* of Sargent and Wallace[61] as well as the famous *Lucas critique*. Pointing out that in an economic model, policy experiments must be invariant to the experiment itself, it effectively undermined the conventional use of econometric models in simulating the impact of policy changes.[62]

tradition, however, Jung and Shiller (2005) point at "Samuelson's dictum" that stock markets are "micro-efficient" but not "macro-efficient," meaning that the EMH works better for individual stocks than for the aggregate market. See also Lo and Hasanhodzic (2010) and Lo (2017) for critical discussions.

[57] Bailey (2005, p. 480ff), Bernstein (2005, p. 203ff). [58] Alchian (1950).

[59] As reported by Lucas in Breit and Hirsch (2009, p. 288).

[60] Dadkhah (2009, p. 98). The assumption originates with John F. Muth (1930–2005). See also Lucas (1972).

[61] Sargent and Wallace (1975); see also Walsh (2017, p. 195ff) for a discussion in the context of the Lucas model.

[62] "Given that the structure of an econometric model consists of optimal decision rules of economic agents, and that optimal decision rules vary systematically with changes in the structure of series relevant to the decision maker, it follows that any change in policy will systematically alter the structure of econometric models" (Lucas, 1976, p. 41).

A direct descendent of the New Classical approach, the RBC models of Kydland and Prescott[63] had an enormous influence on the further course of macroeconomics by introducing DSGE analysis. Characteristically, this *first generation* of DSGE models assumed perfectly competitive goods, factor, and asset markets with macroeconomic fluctuations being an efficient response to exogenous technology shocks. Consistently with the policy irrelevance theorem, the models show no need for, but only a welfare cost of, public interventions.[64] RBC models exhibit a superficial point of touch with Schumpeter in so far as they consider accumulated technology shocks to be the prime mover of economic fluctuations. But starting from neoclassical production functions, technological change is exogenous and a mechanism of monetary propagation generally missing from the picture. Ingrao and Sardoni therefore consider it "a vision opposite to Schumpeter's."[65]

Yet thinking of Schumpeter's admiration and use of the general equilibrium analysis of Walras as a convenient analytical benchmark, he might actually have rated it more highly. For instance, reminiscent of Schumpeter's attitude toward that "circular flow" (Section 7.5), Woodford acknowledges RBC theory to be an important "building block" of the later generation of models to which he contributed. The reason is that it

> defines not a static "long-run equilibrium" but rather a dynamic path which represents a sort of virtual equiblibrium for the economy at each point in time [...]. The evolution of the virtual equilibrium matters because the gaps between actual quantities and their virtual equilibrium values are important measures of the incentives for wage and price adjustment, and hence determinants of wage and price dynamics. (Woodford, 2003, p. 11)

New Keynesian

In the 1970s and 1980s, the New Classical approach largely dominated the mainstream of our discipline with its advanced formal apparatus and claim of sound micro-foundations. It was based on the assumption of rational expectations among agents who maximize their utility by means of optimal choices in perfect markets. However, as economists increasingly learned to integrate market imperfections in their equilibrium models with optimizing agents, the vanguards of dynamic equilibrium analysis migrated toward a new and *second generation* of models, commonly referred to as *New Keynesian* (NK).[66] The linkage to Keynes, however, is

[63] Kydland and Prescott (1982). *Edward C. Prescott* studied under and collaborated with Robert Lucas at Carnegie Mellon University. Lucas had studied with Friedman in Chicago, among others.

[64] Christiano et al. (2018, p. 115).

[65] Ingrao and Sardoni (2019, p. 206).

[66] Greenwald and Stiglitz (1987).

rather tenuous. Gali describes them as "an effort to combine the methodological tools developed by real business cycle theory with some of the central tenets of Keynesian economics." Similarly, Kehoe et al. conclude that "the New Keynesian models are simply real business cycle models with a few frictions added on."[67]

More specifically, Walsh identifies the NK approach with the integration of price and wage rigidities into the DSGE models, which imply forward-looking rational agents with intertemporal maximization while meeting systematic frictions and market imperfections. Furthermore, he depicts three distinct characteristics of the NK models: First, and differently from the RBC approach, they ignore endogenous variations in the capital stock. Second, firms do not compete for a single final good, but produce a continuum of differentiated goods in imperfect markets of monopolistic competition. Third, a central bank conducts monetary policy by setting the nominal rate of interest, typically as a function of inflation and the output gap ("Taylor rule").[68]

Many models stress the central bank's responsibility to manage the expectations of optimizing households and firms. Consistently with monopolistic competition, the latter face limited flexibility in their adjustment of prices along a downward-sloping demand schedule. Thereby, the combination of rational agents and imperfect markets naturally provides for a strong case in favor of rule-based policies. For example, Woodford explicitly considers such policy rules a substitute to the historical function of gold as the anchor of monetary values.[69] They should target desired economic outcomes, in particular the rate of inflation for the prices of goods but not of assets. It is of interest to note, that Woodford excludes the latter, because of their high volatility and presumed lack of rigidities, as a source of market failure.

A few years later, however, the Great Recession of 2008–9 got the equilibrium models on the wrong foot, precisely because they lacked a meaningful nexus between finance and growth. In the words of Barry Eichengreen:

> Eventually those mathematics took on a life of their own. Latter-day academics embraced models of representative, rational, forward-looking agents in part for their tractability, in part for their elegance. In models of rational agents efficiently maximizing everything, little can go wrong unless government makes it go wrong. (Eichengreen (2015, p. 9)

[67] Gali (2018, p. 88); Kehoe et al. (2018, p. 148). See also Goodfriend and King (1997) and Gali (2008/15). Christiano et al. (2018, p. 116) argue that the typical pre-crisis DSGE models may be equally referred to as "Friedmanite," since monetary policy has only transitory effects. A different strand of research that relates more directly to the latter aligns under the label of *New Monetarist Economics*. It pays particular attention to the microfoundation and explicit characterization of market frictions and institutions in explaining essential functions of money, liquidity, and intermediation in exchange relationships. See Lagos et al. (2017).

[68] Dixit and Stiglitz (1977); Taylor (1993); Walsh (2017, p. 319ff).

[69] Woodford (2003, p. 1f). In 2006 the *Journal of the History of Economic Thought* published a special issue on the connection between Woodford and Wicksell. See, for instance, Boianovsky and Trautwein as well as Laidler (2006).

To this one must add the obvious difficulty of predicting catastrophic events, which occur only at (very) long intervals. In defence of the DSGE approach, its proponents correctly point at the lack of historical data and experience that would have better informed the quantitative models:

> One reason why modelers did not emphasize financial frictions in DSGE models is that until the Great Recession, postwar recessions in the United States and western Europe did not seem closely tied to disturbances in financial markets. [...] At the same time, the financial frictions that were included in dynamic stochastic general equilibrium models did not seem to have very big effects.
>
> (Christiano et al., 2018, p. 125)

While apparently accurate, this explanation is also revelatory about our general inability to predict seemingly random and unexpected shocks. For the same reason, it cannot be an excuse for the recurrent overconfidence of markets and policy in the stability of a monetary system, which has repeatedly failed throughout history.

Post-crisis

The Great Recession did not herald a decline in DSGE modeling, as perhaps some critics have expected. On the contrary, it seems that the crisis has "led macroeconomists to dig more deeply than before into the links between disruptions in the process of financial intermediation and business cycles."[70] A *third generation* of DSGE models has come to the fore, which is equipped with better computers, data, algorithms, and training opportunities. Assimilating a growing variety of frictions and complex settings, it cannot be denied that the DSGE approach demonstrates much flexibility and undiminished vigour. On a cautious note, however, one must also remain alert to the danger of inflated overconfidence.[71]

The new brand of *Heterogeneous Agent New Keynesian* (HANK) models is an encouraging example of the recent progress in broadening the field of vision of the DSGE method. For instance, Kaplan et al. (2018) study the different transmission mechanism of an unexpected reduction in the short-term nominal interest rates. They allow heterogeneous households to be affected by uninsurable income shocks and offer them a choice to save either in a liquid asset with low returns or in an illiquid asset with higher returns. In conventional NK models

[70] Kehoe et al. (2018, p. 142).

[71] For instance, Christiano et al. (2018, published online in 2017) opened with the blunt statement: "People who don't like dynamic stochastic general equilibrium (DSGE) models are dilettantes." This point was later repeated in the same version but removed before its final publication.

with representative agents, the impact of monetary policy depends mainly on direct effects of intertemporal substitution, that is, whether households save more or less in response to the change in the interest rate. In contrast, the HANK model shows the indirect effect from an expansion in labor demand to be more important. One reason is that poor households, whose expenditures are more sensitive to income shocks than to a change in the interest rate, account for a substantial fraction of total consumption. Conversely, wealthy households may adjust their portfolios away from liquid assets toward illiquid assets rather than spend more on consumption. The authors conclude that the interplay of complex institutions (such as labor markets, financial markets, and fiscal policy) makes nominal interest rates less effective in fine-tuning monetary policy.[72] In short, their findings demonstrate that money and the real economy share manifold points of interaction, and that monetary policy shocks can cause a response in consumption and thereby affect output.

The *Financing through Money Creation* (FMC) model of Jakab and Kumhof (2018) is another showcase of the flexibility of DSGE models to assimilate new perspectives. It seems almost a *reincarnation* of some of Schumpeter's ideas, in particular his concern for the banks' ability to create purchasing power *ex nihilo* to be a foremost and constitutive element of monetary theory. Consequently, the conventional reduction of the role of banks to that of mere intermediation between saving and lending is firmly rejected, arguing that the "key mechanism for bank balance sheet growth is that banks fund new loans by creating new ledger-entry deposits for their borrowers, with deposits subsequently circulating as the economy's money."[73] More specifically, the authors point this out with respect to the actual process of lending:

> The bank simultaneously creates a new loan entry, in the name of X, on the asset side of its balance sheet, which represents its right to receive future installments and interest on the loan, and a new and equal-sized deposit entry, also in the name of X, on the liability side of its balance sheet, which represents its obligation to deliver current funds. [In short, this implies, that] banks create their own funding in the act of lending. And because both entries are in the name of the same customer, a new loan involves no intermediation.
>
> (Jakab and Kumhof, 2018, p. 3f)

Though banks face no technical limits to extend their balance sheet, they nevertheless operate within *economic constraints*. Yet in contrast with conventional

[72] Kaplan et al. (2018, p. 700). See also Kaplan and Violante (2018) for a survey. Among other models that can account for some of the classical phenomena observed by Keynes, such as paradox of thrift and paradox of toil, see, for example, Auclert and Rognlie (2020).

[73] Jakab and Kumhof (2018, p. 1). See also Werner (2014) for an empirical validation of money creation *ex nihilo* by the individual banks.

models that are based on the intermediation of loanable funds, here it is neither saving nor the central bank reserves, which determine the volume of credit. The authors deny the practical relevance of the "deposit multiplier," which restricts credit to a multiple of the base money supplied by the central bank. The reason is that under normal conditions central banks typically supply the money which banks demand at a targeted interest rate. Instead the model determines the amount of credit from the simultaneous solution to the maximization problems of banks and their customers. Their expectations about future profits and solvency limit the creation of new money, which is both endogenous and finite. These expectations are volatile and sensitive to financial shocks, which in turn explains the observed volatility of balance sheets in the financial sector, its procyclical leverage, as well as the quantity rationing which occurs during downturns.[74]

To mention a third example, Jorda et al. challenge "the widely accepted benchmark of long-run money neutrality."[75] They begin with an empirical investigation and then build a DSGE model that is meant to assimilate major new findings. In contrast to common empirical approaches that "are designed to maximize short-horizon fit," the focus is on hysteresis effects over extended periods of time. The authors find that, "surprisingly, monetary policy affects TFP, capital accumulation, and the productive capacity of the economy for a very long time." More specifically, if output declines in response to exogenous monetary shocks, it does not return to its previous trend even after twelve years. According to this study, hysteresis affects capital accumulation and TFP, whereas labor volume tends to return rapidly to its initial trend.

To conclude, either of the above examples demonstrates the ability of DSGE models to broaden their reach to a growing number of duly specified mechanisms and effects. If we believe that Schumpeter's comprehensive monetary vision was approximately correct and is still valid, we may also expect that the discipline will eventually progress to recover one of its most prosperous intellectual sources and assimilate a growing number of its core tenets. If that optimism is warranted, the outcome will be a deeper and more detailed understanding of the non-neutrality of money and the according nexus between finance and real production. In other words, though the main "caravan" of monetary macroeconomics definitely moved to places far distant from Schumpeter's own disequilibrium perspective, it is likely to do what caravans usually do: they travel to sell their wares, acquiring new goods on the way, and then come back, possible enriched—in our case, with new experience and techniques.

[74] Jakab and Kumhof (2018, p. 30f). [75] Jorda et al. (2020, p. 32).

12
The vision sustained

> Unlike in business and politics, current success is not what matters in science. [...] For my part, I accept the judgement of future generations.
> (J.A. Schumpeter, 1932, p. 106)

From a Schumpeterian perspective there is always more than one main "caravan" of economic thought to keep an eye on. In this chapter, we will therefore pinpoint some distinctive traces of his vision in the further development of finance and monetary thought up to the present time. Obviously, the economists we will refer to as examples come from a different time, have been shaped by different experiences, perceive different problems, and generally command better methodological tools with which to solve them. As this chapter will demonstrate, it is therefore all the more remarkable that Schumpeter's monetary concept of economic development has stood the test of time in such a lasting way.

To begin with, we will turn to the later monetary theory of John Hicks, which in some respects came surprisingly close to Schumpeter's ideas. The connection is mainly indirect, emphasizing related themes in Keynes' *Treatise on Money*, but also taking into account his attention to the problem of pre-financing investments in innovation. We then turn to further early representatives of the dissenting view that money matters to growth. Among these, Schumpeter's students James Tobin and Hyman Minsky carried important elements of his vision into the emerging Neo-Keynesian and Post-Keynesian strands of economics.

Yet it was only from the 1970s onward that the tides began to turn, slowly and at first rather unnoticed, in favor of a renaissance of Schumpeter's vision. Schumpeter had never believed in perfect competition and fully efficient markets. Now the growing literature on financial frictions substantiated his perspective with exact theoretical explanations. These allowed for the recent integration of finance into Schumpeterian growth models, which have become a forceful strand of the macroeconomic mainstream since the beginning of the 1990s. Similarly, financial frictions provide the theoretical underpinning for scripting the nexus of finance and growth in the more recent ABMs that also bear an explicit Schumpeterian connotation. Finally, these theoretical advances have triggered a growing body of empirical research, to which we will turn at the end of this chapter.

Schumpeter's Venture Money. Michael Peneder and Andreas Resch, Oxford University Press (2021). © Michael Peneder and Andreas Resch.
DOI: 10.1093/oso/9780198804383.003.0012

12.1 Early dissenters

Hicks on money and innovation

In 1936 Schumpeter composed a shortlist of new faculty members that he proposed be hired at Harvard. Among them were John Hicks and his wife Ursula Webb.[1] Despite his early contributions to the Neo-Keynesian synthesis (Section 11.2), Hicks maintained a critical position toward the Walrasian general equilibrium approach. However, the later writings, in particular, reveal a close affinity with Schumpeter's monetary concept. Not only did both share a concern for the nexus between history and monetary theory,[2] but both also sided with a credit theory of money:

> I may pay spot for a newspaper as I walk along the street, but I may also give an order to a newsagent to deliver a copy to my house each morning. I should not then pay for each issue as I received it; I should wait until the end of the month when he sent in his bill. At that time I should have been in debt to him for the papers, I had got from him; the payment I made to him would have been in settlement of a debt. Surely it is the latter which should be taken as the general form of a transaction (of sale or purchase). (Hicks, 1989, p. 41)

Overall, Hicks general monetary concept is strikingly congruent with that of Schumpeter.[3] For example, he pointed out that among the four general functions of money, that of a "store of value" can also be fulfilled by other durable goods, whereas the "standard of deferred payments" is included in the function of a "standard of value," more generally. As was the case with Schumpeter (see Chapter 6), we are thus

> to be left with two distinguishing functions of money: standard of value and medium of payment. Are they independent, or does one imply the other? It is not easy to see that there can be payment of a debt expressed in money, unless money as a standard has already been implied in the debt that is to be paid. So money as means of payment implies money as standard. But could a debt expressed in money be discharged otherwise than in money? Surely it could. It could for instance be set off against another debt. (Hicks, 1989, p. 43)

[1] McCraw (2007, p. 226). Schumpeter further suggested Ragnar Frisch, Nicholas Georgescu-Roegen, Oskar Lange, Joan Robinson, and Arthur Smithies.

[2] "Monetary theory is 'in history'; it is influenced by the course of events in the 'real world'" (John Hicks, 1982, p. xii) as quoted in Fontana (2004, p. 76).

[3] Hicks (1989, p. 41ff).

Similarly, Hicks highlighted the role of money as a unit of account and elaborated the sequential time structure of transactions. Except for simultaneous spot transactions, contracting in the first stage establishes the respective promises of the parties involved to deliver or to pay in either the second or the third stage. Hicks then discussed the relationship between interest and investments, paying particular attention to the case of "innovative investment," where a staged approach reduces the risks, but also lengthens the period of production. This aggravates the problem of pre-financing the innovation effort, and managing liquidity over the entire process becomes a foremost concern. He thus directly addressed Schumpeter's concern about the pre-financing of innovations and elaborated the corresponding investment decisions in terms of the specific sequential structure of finance and production.

Gurley and Shaw on financial diversification

Looking for publications in the core journals of the discipline, only a few economists appear to have realized early on that the main route which the caravan followed might miss some essential facts about the nexus between finance and growth (Table 12.1). Among the earliest authors to voice their dissent in the mid-1950s, Gurley and Shaw stressed that "[d]evelopment involves finance as well as goods."[4] They also pointed at a positive feedback mechanism, since the high income elasticity of demand for financial services implies that a faster growth of income raises the demand for financial intermediation and thereby induces further innovations in the financial sector.[5] Relatedly, they complained about the lack of financial accounts on the accumulation of debt and assets and demanded that a comprehensive system of social accounts must map the flow of loanable funds between different spending units.

Unlike Schumpeter, Gurley and Shaw ignored the *de novo* creation of money through credit. Instead, they emphasized the role of indirect financial intermediation and how it transforms funds to make them available to productive investments. Critical of Keynes' simple dichotomy between money and bonds, they distinguished between (i) self-finance from retained earnings, (ii) direct finance between deficit spending units and surplus spending units, and (iii) indirect finance through intermediation between them.

The latter distinction brings the financial sector back into the picture, which is warranted by its impact on long-term capital accumulation. One important example of this increasing diversification in financial intermediation was the introduction of *open-end mutual funds,* which originated with the launch of

[4] Gurley and Shaw (1955, p. 515). [5] Gurley and Shaw (1955, p. 532).

the Massachusetts Investment Trust in 1924. Offering investors the benefits of a diversified portfolio at comparatively low transaction cost and deeper pools of capital for those seeking funds, the innovation rapidly diffused. Referring also to later waves of related swarms of innovations, such as the introduction of the first institutional indexed funds in the early 1970s, Lerner and Tufano point out that mutual funds have been "one of the most successful financial innovations of the twentieth century" and its initial structure "has been the chassis on which we have seen innovations such as index funds, exchange-traded funds, sector funds, and money market funds."[6]

Furthermore, Gurley and Shaw treated the growing diversification in the supply of financial intermediation as the main characteristic of its development and emphasized that the increasing institutionalisation of saving and investment not only enhances the differentiation of financial products, but thereby also raises the growth rate of debt relative to that of income and wealth. As a consequence, the thicker market for indirect finance absorbs illiquid direct debt, which dampens the upward pressure on interest rates and may thus enhance income growth. They concluded that a "theory of interest and income which allows for accumulation of debt and the growth of non-monetary financial intermediaries is a more useful tool than short-period liquidity-preference theory for analysis of economic development."[7]

Tobin on portfolio choice, inflation, and growth

About the same time, James Tobin took up the Schumpeterian quest for the nexus between money and real production. However, he pursued it from a deliberate Keynesian angle, seeking to extend Keynes' short-run perspective into models that integrate money and long-run growth. Similarly to Gurley and Shaw, he did not consider the choice between cash balances and interest-bearing assets the key monetary variable of interest. In what Tobin later called his favorite piece of work,[8] he had modeled investment as the portfolio choice of the owners of wealth between physical capital and "currency" (including government debt and the gold stock, but not bank deposits) as two alternative stores of value. Price stability depends on the "portfolio balance," which in turn requires equality between the rate of return on capital and the rate of interest for currency (which he assumed to be zero). Tobin further combined such asset preferences with factor substitution, a saving function, and labor-supply restrictions, which jointly produced a "great variety" of growth rates—either steady, in cycles, or stagnating with continuing unemployment.

[6] Lerner and Tufano (2012, p. 556). [7] Gurley and Shaw (1955, p. 528).
[8] Tobin (1955); see also Breit and Hirsch (2009, p. 107).

One key element of the model is that government expenditures must increase the monetary circulation in order to avoid price deflation that would lead to an equilibrium below full employment. The reason are rigidities in the labor market and adjustments in the portfolio balance toward liquid monetary assets at the expense of real capital. In a later paper Tobin dropped the assumption of wage rigidities and focused on the portfolio balance between real and financial assets.[9] But both models point to the need for some inflation, and hence monetary expansion, in order to counter the effect of diminishing returns on physical capital in the growth process.

Considering neither the total quantity of money nor interest rates to be the adequate measure affecting investment decisions, Tobin championed the use of the ratio of the market valuation of capital assets to their replacement costs. Though introduced earlier by Nicholas Kaldor (1908–86),[10] it became generally known as *Tobin's q*.[11]

To summarize, for Tobin "the bottom line of monetary policy is its effect on capital investment." More specifically, he aimed to show "that the stock of capital in a growing economy is positively related to the rates of monetary growth and inflation."[12] Not surprisingly, this contention has remained highly controversial.[13] Recently, it attracted the attention of a new generation of monetary Schumpeterian growth models (Section 12.4). For instance, Chu et al. integrate the cash-in-advance constraint into an endogenous growth model with quality improvements, highlighting an inverted-U-shaped impact of nominal interest rates, and relatedly of inflation, on aggregate growth.[14]

12.2 *Minsky* on financial instability

Hyman Minsky began his doctoral thesis on *Induced Investment and Business Cycles* under the supervision of Schumpeter at Harvard. Arguably, his famous

[9] Tobin (1964). [10] Kaldor (1966).

[11] "[T]he incentive to make new capital investments is high when the securities giving title to their future earnings can be sold for more than the investments cost, i.e., when q exceeds one. We see the reverse in takeovers of companies whose qs are less than one; it is cheaper to buy their productive assets by acquiring their shares than to construct comparable facilities from scratch. That is why in our models q is the link from the central bank and the financial markets to the real economy" Tobin, as reported in: Breit and Hirsch (2009, p. 109).

[12] Tobin, as reported in: Breit and Hirsch (2009, p. 108).

[13] See Dimand and Durlauf (2009, p. 189) for further discussion.

[14] Chu et al. (2017). The non-linear relationship is driven by the negative impact of interest rates on R&D and the arrival rate of inventions, which in turn increases the present value of future profits of an innovation. This induces more entry (because of a lower threshold of quality improvements) in the intermediate goods sector with monopolistic competition, while the resulting lower prices stimulate demand and production throughout the economy. Calibrating their model to US data, they compute a growth-maximizing inflation rate of 2.9 percent. See also Chu et al. (2019) for an open economy model with trade and technology transfer between 'north' and "south."

financial instability hypothesis "was first conceived in his dissertation and developed more fully in later years."[15] Minsky began by discussing a variety of accelerator-multiplier models and the microeconomic foundations of entry, expansion, and survival, as well as their implications for market structure. Then he turned his attention to the problem of funding investments. Thereby, he identified two specific aspects of non-neutrality of money. During the upswing, the main task is to finance investments, while on the downswing concerns about the firms' survival come into focus.[16] The first task, Minsky directly related to Schumpeter's work:

> Just as in Schumpeter's schema development could not take place without a permissive monetary system, so the accelerator process depends upon the existence of a permissive monetary system. [And, a]s a result of the economic system accommodating "itself to the purposes of the entrepreneur" the volume of realized savings differs from the volume of planned savings—savings are "forced". (Minsky, 1954/2004, p. 224)

He then added Keynesian liquidity preferences to the explanation. These must fall during an expansion, because business firms are more willing to go into debt and the owners of liquidity are prepared to spend it. Since the expansion is (at least partly) financed by debt, a corresponding rise in liquidity preferences must occur during the downswing. Relating the two, Minsky argued that due to the accumulation of debt

> the financing of a firm's expansion may result in a deterioration of its survival conditions. Therefore, the liquidity crises of the downswing can be imputed to the development of the expansion. Business cycles are both monetary and real phenomena. (Minsky, 1954/2004, p. 222)

In his thesis, Minsky thus integrated the financing condition of firms with the traditional interaction of income and demand to determine the investment accelerator principle. According to Papadimitriou, "[t]his distinction is undoubtedly the origin of Minsky's *financial fragility hypothesis* for which most of his lifetime intellectual endeavors were devoted."[17]

The thesis at Harvard was only a rudimentary beginning. Minsky later developed the financial instability hypothesis more comprehensively, notably in his books on *John Maynard Keynes* of 1975 and in *Stabilizing an Unstable Economy*

[15] Papadimitriou (2004, p. xv); see also Delli Gatti and Gallegati (1997). Nikolaidi and Stockhammer (2017) offer a comprehensive survey of Post-Keynesian models of the financial instability hypothesis. Davis et al. (2019) or Nishi (2019) are recent empirical studies.

[16] Minsky (1954/2004, p. 220ff); Minsky (1986/2008, p. 160).

[17] Papadimitriou (2004, p. xiii).

of 1986. In the former, Minsky set out to reclaim the Keynesian legacy as opposed to the Neo-Keynesian "aberrations."[18] Consistently with his earlier doctoral thesis, he claimed that "the missing step in the standard Keynesian theory was the explicit consideration of capitalist finance within a cyclical and speculative context."[19] Consequently, Minsky attempted to complement Keynes' investment theory of the business cycle with a financial theory of investment. The latter rests on the interplay of two distinct price systems for (i) current output and (ii) capital assets:

> When the price level of capital assets is high relative to the price level of current output, conditions are favorable for investment; when the price level of capital assets is low relative to the price level of current output, then conditions are not favorable for investment, and a recession—or a depression—is indicated. Business cycles result from a dance of these two price levels.
>
> (Minsky, 1986/2008, p. 160)

Relating the firm's expected cash-flows to the required service of debts, Minsky distinguished three types of increasing financial fragility: First, *hedge*-financing units can reasonably expect to serve interest and principal obligations from their own cash-flow. Second, *speculative*-financing units expect to serve interest payments but must roll over principal on maturing debt. Finally, for "Ponzi"-financing units "the cash payment commitments exceed the expected receipts on account of own assets."[20] As a consequence, they must roll over both interest and principal payments for a growing amount of outstanding debt.

Changes in an economy's overall composition of the different types create an endogenous cycle of financial fragility. If we start from a robust regime, where hedge finance dominates, short-term interest will typically be significantly lower than long-term rates. Minsky emphasized that this creates profit opportunities for more speculative ventures:

> The intrusion of speculative relations into a system of mainly hedge financing of positions increases the demand for assets and therefore raises asset values—that is, it leads to capital gains. A regime in which capital gains are being earned and are expected is a favorable environment for engaging in speculative and Ponzi finance. Profit opportunities within a robust financial structure make the shift from robustness to fragility an endogenous phenomenon.
>
> (Minsky, 1986/2008, p. 234)

[18] In a deliberate *Post-Keynesian* interpretation, Minsky aimed to articulate the distinctly "Keynesian" elements more clearly than the master himself: Because "the General Theory is a very clumsy statement. Much of the old theory is still there, and a great deal of the new is imprecisely stated and poorly explained" (Minsky, 1975/2008, p. 12).

[19] Minsky, 1975/2008, p. 126. See also Knell (2015).

[20] Minsky (1986/2008, p. 231).

In short, as profit incentives induce firms to accumulate debt, their financial positions become increasingly fragile, typically shifting from hedge to speculative finance. Ultimately, their striving for survival may further push them into Ponzi schemes. In the course of time, the accumulation of debt must put an increasing burden on the system, for instance, in terms of inflation, a squeeze of profits after interest payments, or a cascading risk of default. The boom finally breaks when "interest rates rise enough so that attenuations and reversals in present-value relations take place."[21] Whether that break ultimately leads into a mild recession or a deep depression depends on policy and the structural characteristics of an economy. But its further development will also depend on how painful that experience is. Because in "the aftermath of a financial crisis, bankers and businessmen who have been burned shy away from speculative and Ponzi financing." And consequently, the "economy emerges from a recession that follows a financial crisis with a more robust structure than it had when the crisis took place."[22] At this point, Minsky also calls forth the importance of financial innovation, which he considers to arise mainly in times of growing prosperity:[23]

> During periods of tranquil expansion, profit-seeking financial institutions invent and reinvent "new" forms of money, substitutes for money in portfolios, and financing techniques for various types of activity. [...] Each new type of money that is introduced or an old one that is used to a greater extent results in the financing of either some additional demand for capital and financial assets or of more investment. This results in both a higher price of assets, which, in turn, raises the demand prices for current investment, and increases the financing available for investment. Financial innovation therefore tends to induce capital gains, increase investment, and increase profits: the economy will try to expand beyond any tranquil full-employment state. (Minsky, 1986/2008, p. 199)

Minsky famously stressed that *stability itself is destabilizing.* This is because the memory of past crisis erodes over time. Moreover, "success breeds daring" and "a disregard of the possibility of failure." As a consequence, "the successful functioning of an economy within an initially robust financial structure will lead to a structure that becomes more fragile as time elapses."[24] To conclude: in a capitalist system with financial innovations, periods of financial stability must always be transitory, "for within any full-employment situation there are endogenous disequilibrating forces at work that assure the disruption of tranquility."[25] Or, to put it like Robert J. Barbera in his preface to Minsky's book on John Maynard Keynes:

[21] Minsky (1986/2008, p. 245). [22] Minsky (1986/2008, p. 234). [23] Ülgen (2014).
[24] Minsky (1975/2008, pp. 11, 125; 1986/2008, p. 237f). [25] Minsky (1986/2008, p. 199).

> Minsky's greatest insight, in the tradition of his thesis advisor Joseph Schumpeter, is that periodic violent plunges are an inescapable part of the capitalist growth story. Minsky simply expands upon Schumpeter's central observation about creative destruction, linking it to the world of finance. (Barbera, 2008, p. x)

12.3 Financial frictions

Just as innovation and finance are the main drivers of Schumpeterian development, entrepreneurs and investors are its two principal agents. They shape the course of events and are tied to each other by "credit," broadly defined. Schumpeter had already pointed at their mutual dependence and according conflicts of interest. During his time, however, no economic theories existed that would have accounted for its specific mechanism and impacts. Nor were they available to Keynes or to the subsequent efforts of monetary equilibrium models in the post Second World War era.

A meaningful integration of credit markets to monetary macroeconomics had to wait for the rise of a proper *economics of information*. Its main focus and ideas would not have been alien to Schumpeter. Beginning with Carl Menger and leading up to Friedrich Hayek and Fritz Machlup (1902–83), the Austrian School has placed a distinctive emphasis on the system's ability to process information. But Schumpeter and his kinship lacked the modern understanding of market frictions that arise from asymmetric information, and which began to emerge only in the 1970s.[26] For credit and finance, agency models between an investor as "principal" and an entrepreneur as the "agent" have become particularly important. Most notably, Stiglitz and Weiss showed that changes in the interest rate (or other terms of a loan contract, such as collateral) have a non-monotonous impact on the lenders net return, if lenders cannot verify the quality of a financing project or the behavior of a borrower.[27] Expected profits eventually begin to decline with a further rise in rates for two reasons. First, higher rates attract borrowers of lower quality and thus have an *adverse selection* effect on the choice of financing projects. Second, higher rates may create adverse behavioral incentives, called *moral hazards*, for instance, to make riskier choices after the financing was granted.

Problems of asymmetric information similarly affect equity finance and the various intermediate forms of external funding between senior debt and common equity ("mezzanine finance"). Consistently with Schumpeter's broad definition of credit, there is in practice a continuum of options that differ in terms of the priority to redeem and the claims on residual income.[28] Understanding such

[26] Akerlof (1970); Jaffe and Russel (1976). [27] Stiglitz and Weiss (1981).

[28] For instance, Tirole (2006, p. 77) illustrates the priority structure from secured debt to ordinary and subordinated debt, preferred stock, and common stock.

market frictions has re-established the interest in financial structure and largely devalued the practical relevance of the famous *invariance theorem* by Modigliani and Miller.[29]

Of particular importance to the funding of innovation, equity finance by external sources offers the advantage of diversifying and reducing the risks of default. Conversely, entrepreneurs may refrain from it for various reasons. One is the fear to diffuse control rights, and another is to signal that shares are overpriced on the market. Furthermore, shareholders may prefer debt finance in order to impose discipline and keep the management "backs to the wall" or, relatedly, because of simpler state verification.[30] In many instances, therefore, agency problems between entrepreneurs and the investors will determine the particular choice of capital structure, and hence, the according allocation of claims and risks. Furthermore, financing restrictions that are due to problems of asymmetric information may prohibit productive investments, and hence growth and employment. Consistently with Minsky's financial cycle, such funding gaps are more likely to occur during downswings and hence are procyclical. Furthermore, small, young, and innovative firms are generally more exposed to it than others.[31]

To conclude, the possibilities of credit and equity constraints render finance a non-trivial problem of economic development. But along the major tracks which monetary macroeconomic models had followed, the characteristic role of money derived either from the neoclassical interest in facilitating transactions or from the Keynesian emphasis on liquidity preferences and money as a store value. Credit and finance rarely appear to have played a distinct role.

The situation began to change in the 1990s. Different models captured various sources of financial frictions in lending relationships. For example, Dawid and Delle Gatti point at the cost of (i) state verification, (ii) enforcement, or (iii) bankruptcy.[32] Notably, in a series of articles, Greenwald and Stiglitz pursued an "alternative paradigm for monetary economics, based on credit, rather than the transactions demand for money."[33] Largely in accordance with Schumpeter, they adopt a "claim theory" of money (Chapter 6)[34] and emphasize its function as unit of account, while denying that the transactions motive is a satisfactory explanation

[29] Simply put, it states that in perfect capital markets the valuation of a firm is independent of its debt-equity ratio (Modigliani and Miller, 1958). See also Miller and Modigliani (1961).

[30] Stiglitz and Greenwald (2003, p. 35f). See also the pecking order hypothesis by Myers and Majluf (1984) or the discussion in Tirole (2006, p. 246).

[31] The familiar reasons are the lack of collateral and reputation, relatedly, a higher dependence on intangible assets, and the less opaque nature of a business with contingencies that are harder to verify from outside the firm. See, for instance, Peneder (2012).

[32] Dawid and Delle Gatti (2018) refer to the original models of Bernanke and Gertler (1989, 1990), Kiyotaki and Moore (1997), as well as Greenwald and Stiglitz (1993), respectively.

[33] Stiglitz and Greenwald (2003, p. 293).

[34] "The fact that the individual has money ensures that the individual is not attempting to commandeer more resources that his life-time budget constraint allows" (Stiglitz and Greenwald, 2003, p. 293).

of why money matters. Instead, "what is crucial for facilitating economic transactions is not money, but credit,"[35] and in particular the close ties between the two: "Firms do not borrow unless they wish to make a purchase: otherwise, having a credit line will suffice. Thus, the creation of money and the creation of credit occur together." More specifically, Greenwald and Stiglitz point out that "credit is not primarily allocated via an auction market" and, consequently, the "interest rate is not like a conventional price. It is a promise to pay an amount in the future." And "[p]romises are often broken."[36] Therefore,

> [i]t is remarkably difficult to incorporate credit within the standard general equilibrium model. Credit can be created with almost no input of conventional factors, and can just as easily be destroyed. There is no easy way to represent the supply function of credit. The reason for this is simple: credit is based on information. Ascertaining that an individual is credit worthy requires resources; and standing by that judgement, providing or guaranteeing credit entails risk-bearing. There is no simple relationship between these economic costs and the amount of credit extended. (Stiglitz and Greenwald, 2003, p. 26)

Differently from the standard general equilibrium models of anonymous markets where "[n]obody cares who supplies," credit requires specific knowledge that is individual to each case. As a consequence, institutions matter. Banks, in particular, "provide vital certification, monitoring, and enforcement services, ascertaining who is likely to fulfill their promises to repay, ensuring that money lent is spent in the way promised, and collecting money at the due date." In short, they "determine who is likely to default, and in doing so, banks determine the supply of loans."[37] Furthermore, the specific information requirements involve considerable sunk costs, which is why banking is best characterized by models of monopolistic competition. Finally, Greenwald and Stiglitz, among others, emphasize that policy must pay particular attention to the impact of banking regulations on the supply of credit, and on the maintenance of the banking system's informational and organisational capital.

The latter aspect is especially important during times of crisis. For instance, *financial accelerator* models[38] demonstrate how the combination of capital constraints on the side of firms and households lead to a higher premium on external finance, causing a decline in the demand for credit and hence less spending. In turn, this negatively affects money income and asset values. In the presence of financial frictions, the consequent deterioration of net worth on the balance

[35] Stiglitz and Greenwald (2003, p. 293); Moreover, "most transactions do not require money, but can be mediated through credit; and this is increasingly the case" (p. 14ff).

[36] Stiglitz and Greenwald (2003, pp. 295, 27).

[37] Stiglitz and Greenwald (2003, pp. 30, 3, 30f).

[38] Bernanke et al. (1996).

sheets thus propagates a vicious cycle of monetary factors and the decline of real production.

That the credit channel of crisis can also originate with capital constraints on the part of banks, has increasingly attracted scholarly attention after the Great Recession of 2008–9 (Section 13.2). Highlighting the non-linear dynamics of crises, new models demonstrate how the banking sector can absorb minor disturbances, while large shocks generate systemic endogenous risk that can freeze the interbank market for short-term loans.[39] For example, Boissay et al. highlight how the procyclicality of the banks' balance sheets emanates from interbank market funding and thereby "sows the seeds for the next banking crisis," which may be triggered by relatively moderate productivity shock at the end of a prolonged credit boom.

Though the shocks are exogenous and not explained within these models, they apparently associate with Schumpeter's idea of the monetary propagation of a crisis, adding further flesh and specificity to it. While explicit references to Schumpeter are rare, his monetary theory resurfaces more explicitly in a couple of recent articles. The first is by Egger and Keuschnigg, who study how financial frictions affect the distribution of comparative advantages in international trade.[40] The impact originates in financing gaps that lead to the denial of external funding to marginal firms with a positive net value and thus hamper investments and growth of the entrepreneurial sector. In the second model, Kogler and Keuschnigg address "the Schumpeterian role of banks" to allocate credit to its most productive uses, focusing on the liquidation of loans to distressed firms in order to redirect funds to finance the expansion of more successful entrepreneurs. In the model, banks can neither create money *de novo* nor recapitalize from outside investors. Consequently, the liquidation of loans implies a contraction of the balance sheet that corresponds with the realized losses. Since financial frictions render capital buffers expensive, banks are "reluctant to restructure non-performing loans to avoid write-offs" and reallocate too little credit.[41]

12.4 Finance and growth

The early attempts to integrate money and long-run growth by Gurley and Shaw or Tobin made little impact on the tracks the economics profession followed. Instead, the caravan moved to the territories where either the New Classicals came to dominate monetary macroeconomics or the New Keynesians accounted for

[39] Brunnermeier and Sannikov (2014, 2016); Boissay et al. (2016).

[40] Egger and Keuschnigg (2017).

[41] Keuschnigg and Kogler (2020, pp. 14, 2). In contrast, see Dal-Pont Legrand and Hagemann (2017) for a cautionary note on the popular perception of Schumpeter as a "pure liquidationist."

imperfections in the labor and capital markets. Until the 1990s, the relationship of finance and growth thus remained "largely peripheral":

> [T]extbooks on economic development written at the end of the 1980s typically did not discuss the role of finance, and financial economics was largely unconcerned with the impact of finance on long-run economic growth, development, poverty, and the distribution of income. The finance and development literature took off in the 1990s, as researchers [...] started integrating financial frictions into endogenous growth models. (Beck and Levine, 2018, p. ix)

That financial frictions can cause credit constraints was increasingly well understood due to the developments discussed in the previous section. Moreover, financial frictions must generally gain in importance, if the financing is about Schumpeterian ventures to invest in innovation. Not only are uncertainty and risks higher, and intangible assets often sunk and of little use as collateral, but also the fundamental asymmetry of information between investors and the entrepreneur tends to be stronger the more complex and novel the innovations are. There is thus a natural and close complementarity between the two strands of literature.

What in the 1990s decisively changed the situation and increasingly enabled their integration was the emergence of *Schumpeterian growth models* as pioneered by Segerstrom et al., Grossman and Helpman, or Aghion and Howitt.[42] These shifted the focus from the accumulation of physical capital in neoclassical theory to innovation as the principal driver of growth. Merging methods of industrial organization with that of macroeconomic analysis, they managed to implement goods markets with imperfect competition in their aggregate framework. This allowed them to account for the basic Schumpeterian trade-off between innovation and competition (Section 7.3) and thus to provide an endogenous explanation of the incentives to invest resources in R&D. Thereby the Schumpeterian models typically implement a mechanism of creative destruction in the product market: that is, new and better intermediate goods earn a temporary innovation rent by displacing the old variety.

The common label of Schumpeterian "growth" is very accurate, since the models focus on equilibrium steady-state rates of what usually amounts to a balanced growth path. In other words, they sideline the element of structural change in Schumpeter's evolutionary theory of economic development (Chapter 7). This, however, cannot diminish the progress achieved by the Schumpeterian growth models. Not only have they consolidated essential features of his vision of

[42] At the end of the 1980s Paul Romer pioneered endogenous growth theory in a couple of seminal papers. Arguably, the Schumpeter growth models of Segerstrom et al. (1990), Grossman and Helpman (1991), or Aghion and Howitt (1992) helped endogenous growth theory to achieve its breakthrough. For further seminal contributions, see, for instance, Dinopoulos and Thompson (1998) or Chu et al. (2017, 2019), as well as the comprehensive monographs of Aghion and Howitt (1998, 2009).

development into a consistent formal representation, to which Schumpeter himself had much aspired, but they have also provided a productive basis for a variety of additional models that build on the same core assumptions but account for further specific elements.

One such particularly important element is the role of finance for innovation and growth. Schumpeter had understood the mutual dependency and conflicting interest between investors and the entrepreneurs, but he only had a vague idea of the kind of principal-agent problems, we have now become familiar with. In the following paragraphs, we will only very briefly convey the essence of the argument as presented in the Schumpeterian models of finance and growth by Aghion and Howitt.

In short, the model economy knows one final good Y, that is produced at time t under perfect competition with labor L and a continuum of i intermediate inputs x supplied monopolistically at the productivities A_i:[43]

$$Y_t = L^{1-\alpha} \int_0^1 A_{it}^{1-\alpha} x_{it}^{\alpha} di, \qquad 0 < \alpha < 1 \tag{12.1}$$

If μ is the probability of a successful innovation of size $\gamma > 1$, then the average productivity amounts to

$$A_t = \mu\gamma A_{t-1} + (1-\mu)A_{t-1}$$

and its average growth rate is

$$g = \frac{A_t - A_{t-1}}{A_{t-1}} = \mu(\gamma - 1) \tag{12.2}$$

Skipping the details on how the model specifies the innovation technology and the incentive compatibility constraints, or finally resolves the firms' profit-maximization problem, we take a shortcut and simply summarize the three solutions which highlight the difference in average growth rates between economies with financial frictions and without them:

(i) To begin with the case of *unconstrained* credit markets, the equilibrium probability of innovation μ is equal to the ratio of the equilibrium profit from innovation per effective labor supply π and the cost of innovation ψ.

[43] The final good Y is used for consumption and as an input to R&D as well as the production of intermediate goods. L represents a fixed population and is normalized to unity. The intermediate goods x correspond to Schumpeter's notion of the "means of production."

Hence, the average growth rate amounts to

$$g = (\pi/\psi)(\gamma - 1) \tag{12.3}$$

(ii) If problems of *adverse selection* require the further *ex ante* screening of the true quality of a project, profit-maximization additionally requires to account for the screening cost f per unit of output and the probability θ of the venture to be feasible and not failing to repay the credit. The equilibrium growth rate is then:

$$g = \frac{\pi}{(1 + f/\theta)\psi}(\gamma - 1) \tag{12.4}$$

(iii) Finally, if problems of *moral hazard* require the *ex post* monitoring of entrepreneurs, another variant of the basic model introduces a parameter υ, which reflects the cost of defrauding a creditor and the entrepreneur's wage ω (meant to increase the capacity of self-financing an innovation). The equilibrium growth rate becomes:

$$g = (\gamma - 1)\sqrt{2\upsilon\omega/\gamma\psi} \tag{12.5}$$

To conclude, the models show that the average equilibrium growth rates monotonically increase with a lower cost of *ex ante* screening f if adverse selection is present, and with a higher cost of *ex post* defrauding the creditors υ in the case of moral hazard. Both instances indicate the better capability of a financial system to contain problems of asymmetric information in the relationship between investors and entrepreneurs. The models thus relate the degree of financial development with an economy's higher average rate of innovation and growth.

The Schumpeterian growth models have shown to be versatile and to suit a range of further extensions. One of them regards the way financial development enhances the distributive justice of financing entrepreneurs, who lack sufficient initial wealth and according collateral. The better a financial system can deal with asymmetric information, the closer the distribution of funds will match the quality of projects and entrepreneurs instead of their ownership of collateral. It thereby achieves a more equitable distribution of economic opportunities, and hence social mobility, as well as higher aggregate rates of innovation and growth.

Another extension to the basic Schumpeterian growth model accounts for the stylized empirical fact of a negative correlation between the level and volatility of growth rates.[44] Without financial frictions, during recessions the lower opportunities for current sales tend to shift incentives away from investments with a short-term objective toward those with a long-term perspective. In combination with the

[44] Aghion et al. (2010).

greater need of reorganization and innovation, recessions may thus enhance the prospects for long-term growth. In the presence of financial frictions, however, one must additionally factor in the firms' lower earnings, and accordingly their reduced capacity to self-finance the investments, or to borrow. Consequently, this "'Schumpeterian' approach delivers the prediction that the lower the level of financial development, the more negative the correlation between macroeconomic volatility and growth."[45] As a consequence, macroeconomic stabilization policies should generally be more effective in countries with less developed financial markets.

These are only a few examples among a variety of further extensions, which are all based on the same basic Schumpeterian growth model. Others, possibly with less open reference to Schumpeter, will probably follow. Irrespective of the particular labels, however, the caravan of new models on finance and growth will continue to advance.[46]

12.5 "Keynes meets Schumpeter" (ABMs)

Fundamentally opposed to the canonical approach of constrained optimization by representative agents with rational expectations, *agent-based models* (ABMs) originate in the seminal work of Herbert A. Simon (1916–2001), or Richard R. Nelson and Sidney G. Winter, who had early on explored the implications of bounded rationality and behavioral routines.[47] ABMs thus implement a distinct kind of micro-foundations, defining detailed decision rules and protocols for the micro-level interactions between different types of self-contained heterogenous agents. By means of simulations, they compute the values of aggregate variables bottom up as the sum over the individual quantities. The behavioral rules are mostly heuristic and sourced from the stylized facts of empirical and psychological research. The models do not constrain the economy to be in equilibrium, and thus allow for disequilibrium dynamics, structural change, and the emergence of complex systems. The benchmark of validation is the model's ability to reproduce stylized empirical facts with regard to the distributional and time-series properties of the population of agents (possibly at different levels of aggregation).[48]

[45] Aghion and Howitt (2009, p. 320).

[46] For instance, Aghion et al. (2018, p. 25) conclude their survey by stating that "we have only touched upon the issue of finance and innovation-led growth," being confident that "much more work should and will be done in this area." One example is the DSGE model by Moran and Queralto (2018), which demonstrates strong effects of monetary policy on total factor productivity (TFP) growth via its impact on variety enhancing R&D expenditures.

[47] Simon (1959); Nelson and Winter (1982).

[48] Dawid and Delle Gatti (2018) provide a comprehensive survey of the characteristic features and compare them across eight different families of macroeconomic models (MABMs). Dosi and Roventini (2019) discuss the specific advantages of the ABM approach versus DSGE models, whereas Haldane

The agents of a model are typically comprised of households, firms, and banks. Many ABMs are thus capable of simulating interactions between finance and the real sector. Among them, the evolutionary "Keynes meeting Schumpeter" (KS) family of models accords with Minsky's call for an integration of innovation-driven creative destruction with the coordination of effective demand.[49] In the ABM modeling context, Schumpeter and Keynes arguably go well together, since both perceived the economy as a time-dependent process. Furthermore, Minsky clearly followed Schumpeter's trails in emphasizing the sequential structure of (i) finance preceding production and (ii) production preceding exchange.[50]

Scripting the exact time-structure of economic interactions is precisely where ABMs find their natural habitat. For example, the KS models are typically comprised of (i) firms that produce either capital goods or consumer goods under imperfect competition; (ii) households that buy consumer goods and supply labor; (iii) banks that provide credit, gather deposits, and purchase sovereign bonds; (iv) and a government which taxes profits, pays transfers to the unemployed, issues bonds, and bails out banks in default.

Similarly to the aforementioned models of endogenous growth, innovations originate from investments in R&D only in the capital goods sector. In contrast, demand expectations affect investment, competitiveness, and firm dynamics in the consumer goods sector. The Keynesian element is also obvious in the implemented fiscal policies by the government, while the central bank sets the baseline interest rate according to a Taylor rule. Commercial banks then add a risk premium for their loan rate. Regulatory capital requirements restrict their supply of credit, but banks typically maintain an additional buffer, depending on how they assess their financial outlook and fragility. Given their limited supply of credit, banks allocate it according to the creditworthiness of firms proxied by the ratio of past net worth to sales.

Calling their model an "exercise in general disequilibrium analysis,"[51] the various transmission mechanisms operate simultaneously. To begin with, Schumpeterian innovation drives aggregate growth and policies that enhance technological opportunities or the search capabilities of firms also raise the aggregate performance. Second, there is a Keynesian effect of expectations about future demand on investment. Finally, the later generations of the model also account for a Minskian mechanism of financial propagation and instability. During good times, the firms invest more and the growing leverage weakens their balance sheet, causing the number of bankruptcies to rise. Eventually, this leads to the downswing. Banking regulations that tie the banks' lending to their equity provoke a further tightening

and Turrell (2019) tend to emphasize their complementarity. Dawid et al. (2019) point out how to improve the transparency, reproducibility and replication of results.

[49] Dosi et al. (2010, 2017, 2019, 2020).

[50] Sau (2019, p. 8).

[51] Dosi et al. (2010).

of credit and may ultimately lead to a crunch. Against such a scenario, Keynesian fiscal policies are meant to stabilize aggregate demand. To summarize, the

> experiments point to a strong complementarity between Keynesian and Schumpeterian policies. More precisely, when fiscal policies are not in place, the long-run growth of the economy collapses even in the presence of a strong Schumpeterian regime characterized by a high degree of technological opportunities and firms' search capabilities. (Dosi et al., 2017, p. 85)

Furthermore, the authors conclude that

> fiscal policy smoothes out the instability of the matching between demand-driven processes of production and investment, on the one hand, and Schumpeterian processes of technical change, on the author. In turn, the feedbacks between innovation and demand dynamics call for a coordinated set of policies, going against the peculiar schizophrenia between macro policies, if any, for the short-run and "structural" policies for the long-run. (Dosi et al., 2017, p. 86)

12.6 Empirical evidence

The theoretical advances as discussed in the previous sections have triggered a growing volume of empirical studies. In a recent survey, Popov juxtaposes two historical currents of theoretical predictions.[52] Among those who championed the case of non-neutrality, the prime references are Bagehot, Schumpeter, Gerschenkron, and Stiglitz. Conversely, he points at Joan Robinson and Robert Lucas as notable proponents, who explicitly questioned the relevance of monetary matters for the real economy. After the passing of Keynes and Schumpeter, their deliberate lack of interest in the nexus of finance and growth represented the dominant attitude in the economics profession at large. Consequently, only a few empirical studies managed to leave a mark on the literature in the early decades.[53] Since the early 1990s, however, the newly discovered theoretical underpinnings in combination with methodological advances and the growing availability of data initiated a wealth of empirical studies and shaped the further evolution of this strand of literature.

To mention only a few examples, in 1993 King and Levine triggered the first wave of then standard aggregate growth regressions in an article with the self-explanatory title "Finance and Growth: Schumpeter Might Be Right."[54] Further studies confirmed their findings for an increasing variety of measures of financial

[52] Popov (2018). [53] See, for instance, Goldsmith (1969); and McKinnon (1973).
[54] See King and Levine (1993).

development, although the volume of private credit or stock market capitalization (each normalized by GDP) remained the most frequently used indicators. Later, attention increasingly turned to the identification of causal effects by means of instrumental variable regressions, using, for instance, the exogenous variation in a country's legal origin as necessary exclusion restrictions. For example, a recent study has used the composition of the population by religion to identify the impact of financial structure on growth in European regions. It concludes "that financial agglomeration and the development of complex and diversified financial centres are strong engines of economic growth."[55] Further methodological advances were due to the adoption of dynamic panel estimations, which allow he exploitation of time-series variation in conjunction with time-varying exclusion restrictions.[56]

Toward the end of the 1990s, Rajan and Zingales introduced an influential approach to exploit the sectoral variation in the data.[57] Using large listed US companies as a global benchmark, they constructed industry measures of dependence on external finance. The findings demonstrate that industries which typically depend more on external finance grow faster in countries with more developed financial systems. Later studies emulated and extended their approach by applying different industry benchmarks. One example focuses on the function of reallocating capital and takes the actual industry growth in the US as a general proxy of "growth opportunities." The findings again reveal a differential impact of financial development on industry performance, whereby more developed systems tend to favor the expansion of industries with higher growth opportunities.[58] Another example benchmarks industries by their share of small US companies with fewer than twenty employees. It shows that "small-firm industries" benefit disproportionately from higher levels of financial development. The authors emphasize that finance affects growth not only at the level of aggregate economies, but also at that of individual sectors.[59]

Finally, the increasing availability of large firm-level datasets feeds the further exploration of more specific structural characteristics, which associate with financial frictions as well as the micro-level relationship between finance and growth. Among the various findings, further studies have shown, for instance, that small and medium-sized enterprises face more financing constraints, that financial development reduces the sensitivity of investment to own cash-flow, or that it increases the probability of own innovations.[60] Many of these analyses rely on self-reported data from enterprise surveys. Increasingly, authors also gain access to other data. For instance, in a recent study Manaresi and Pierri have used a panel

[55] Rossi and Scalise (2019).
[56] For instance, Beck et al. (2000). [57] Rajan and Zingales (1998).
[58] Fisman and Love (2007). [59] Beck et al. (2008).
[60] Ayyagari et al. (2018); Popov (2018).

Table 12.1 Selected milestones of monetary ideas since the twentieth century

Author (ca.)	**Ideas**
R. Hilferding (1910)	Promoter's profit
I. Fisher (1911/20)	Equation of exchange; debt-deflation theory
J.A. Schumpeter (1911/17)	Monetary theory of economic development
L. Mises (1912/53)	Monetary business cycle (overinvestment)
A.C. Pigou (1917)	Cambridge equation, based on Marshall (1870s)
R.G. Hawtrey (1919)	Cash-balance approach, monetary business cycle
D.H. Robertson (1926/8)	Loanable funds, monetary propagation of cycles
F.A. Hayek (1929/76)	Monetary business cycle; currency competition
J.M. Keynes (1930/6)	Liquidity preferences; IS-LM theory
J. Hicks (1937)	IS-LM model
Gurley/Shaw (1955)	Financial intermediation and growth
J. Tobin (1955/87)	Portfolio selection and growth; deposited currency
Modigliani/Miller (1958)	Capital structure irrelevance theorem
H. Simon (1950s)	Bounded rationality
Phillips/Samuelson/Solow (1958–60)	Phillips curve
N. Kaldor (1966)	Q-ratio ("Tobin's q")
Phelps, Friedman (1967/8)	Expectations-augmented Phillips curve; NAIRU
E. Fama (1970)	Efficient market hypothesis (EMH)
R. Lucas (1972/6)	Rational expectations; Lucas critique
Kahneman/Tversky (1973/9)	Decision heuristics; prospect theory
H. Minsky (1975)	Financial instability hypothesis
Stiglitz/Weiss (1981)	Financial frictions (asymmetric information)
R. Shiller (1981)	Inefficient volatility
Kydland/Prescott (1982)	Real Business Cycles, DSGE modeling
De Long et al. (1991)	Limited arbitrage
J.B. Taylor (1993)	Taylor rule
King and Levine (1993)	Empirical finance and growth (macro)
Bernanke et al. (1996)	Financial accelerator models
Rajan and Zingales (1998)	Empirical finance and growth (sectoral)
Aghion/Howitt (1992/2006)	Schumpeterian growth, w/financial frictions
Woodford, Gali (2003, 2008)	New Keynesian (NK) DSGE models
S. Nakamoto (2008)	Peer-to-peer electronic cash (cryptocurrency)
Dosi et al. (2010)	"Schumpeter+Keynes" (SK) agent-based models (ABMs)
Kaplan et al. (2018)	Heterogenous Agent NK models (HANK)
Kumhof; Brunnermeier et al. (2016, 2019)	Central bank digital currencies (CBDC), etc.
…	…

of bank-firm matched data for Italy, revealing a positive and concave relationship between credit supply and the firms' growth of total factor productivity (TFP). Since negative shocks affect TFP more strongly than positive ones in their model, the stability of banking relationships is a matter of particular importance.[61]

Despite the considerable changes in terms of the methods and data used, the general consensus on the empirical findings has remained surprisingly robust:

[61] Manaresi and Pierri (2018).

> Taken as a whole, the bulk of existing research suggests that (1) countries with better functioning banks and markets grow faster, but the degree to which a country is bank-based or market-based does not matter much, (2) simultaneity bias does not seem to drive these conclusions, and (3) better functioning financial systems ease the external financing constraints that impede firm and industrial expansion, suggesting that this is one mechanism through which financial development matters for growth. (Levine, 2005, p. 865)

Similarly, Allen et al. conclude that "there is a broadly consistent view that overall financial development and legal system efficiency are more important than financial structure in explaining real economic growth." Furthermore, "the existing results indicate that a more balanced structure of the financial system enhances its stability and can significantly buffer shocks from a financial crisis."[62] One important qualification, however, regards the potential differential impact of financial structure on *innovation*. For instance, Hsu et al. find that

> industries that are more dependent on external finance and that are more high-tech intensive exhibit a disproportionally higher innovation level in countries with better developed equity markets. However, the development of credit markets appears to discourage innovation in industries that are more dependent on external finance and that are more high-tech intensive. (Hsu et al., 2014, p. 133)

The authors also point at several likely explanations. Most importantly, equity markets are better positioned than banks to balance the downside risks of failure, since investors also share the positively skewed returns on the upside of a successful innovation. Furthermore, the higher dependence on intangible assets limits the banks' option to use collateral. And while innovation projects are generally difficult to evaluate, equity may be more efficient in processing the information from diverse sources via the price signal from the markets and thus help to mitigate problems of asymmetric information.

Another qualification to the general consensus of a positive relationship between financial development and growth is the increasing evidence of a non-linear relationship, where "too much finance" raises concerns about the negative impacts of *financialization*.[63] Among various explanations, one common worry is that a fast-growing financial industry has attracted too much high-skilled labor away from other sectors. Furthermore, with rising incomes the composition of bank credit may shift from corporate investments toward households and consumption. More generally, for a given pool of projects financing will end up in less productive uses as the available funds increase.

[62] Allen et al. (2018, p. 46f).

[63] Stockhammer (2004); Loayza et al. (2018); Popov (2018); Hein (2019); and Kohler et al. (2019).

Finally, a rapid deepening of financial markets[64] tends to raise overall volatility and risk. Thereby, excessive speculation may inflate the short-term returns of financial assets relative to that of long-term investments in real capital.[65] For instance, in an influential quantitative historical study, Schularick and Taylor show that lagged credit growth is a good predictor of financial crises, indicating "that financial stability risks increase with the size of the financial sector and that boom-and-bust-episodes in stock markets become more problematic in more financialized economies." As the authors emphasize, the results echo "Joseph Schumpeter's diagnosis that 'reckless lending' and financial speculation are closely linked to credit creation as the 'monetary complement of innovation' over the business cycle."[66]

To conclude, the empirical evidence generally confirms the overall benefits of financial development for economic growth. An excessive deepening of financial markets, however, may also create negative externalities by crowding-out skilled labor or productive investment and undermine financial stability. Either mechanism is consistent with Schumpeter's hypothesis of the non-neutrality of money. Taken together, however, they suggest a likely inverted-U shaped relationship between financial development and growth.

[64] That is, a fast-growing volume of financial services relative to total output.

[65] Acknowledging that the direct impact of financial investments by non-financial corporations (NFCs) is a mere transfer of liquidity, Stockhammer (2004) argues that financialization nevertheless affects management priorities in favor of short-term profits at the expense of long-term growth.

[66] Schularick and Taylor (2012, p. 1031f).

13
In the current stream

> A judicious acquaintance of mine, much experienced in the world of affairs, has remarked to me that an inventor is always a ticklish associate—unable to cease experimenting, ever in chase of something new, subject to ill-judged enthusiasms, not content to sit down and develop systematically what is at the stage or near the stage of working success. Certain it is that your inventor is rarely a good manager.
>
> (Taussig, 1915, p. 34)

The "judicious acquaintance" that Harvard economist Frank Taussig referred to in the above epigraph was Josef Schumpeter.[1] Much in accord with his idea of venture finance, Taussig emphasized that an invention "needs to be nursed" and requires funding in advance. In short, both understood that successful innovation depends on the non-trivial task of finding a winning configuration of invention, financing, and business.

While Chapter 12 highlighted the resurgence of Schumpeter's concept of money in economic *theory*, this chapter focuses on three examples from recent *history* in which the interdependence of finance and innovation invokes a Schumpeterian interpretation. The first example is about the striking rise of modern venture capital in his immediate geographical and intellectual environment during his years at Harvard. The second example addresses the recurrent instances of financial crises, in particular the Great Recession of 2008–9. Finally, we turn to the stream of innovations that relate to the increasing digitalization of money.

13.1 Venture finance

At the time Schumpeter moved to Harvard, Boston was already one of the most important financial centers in the US after New York. It had participated in the boom of investment banks, which mainly focused on the issue of public debt, railway bonds, mergers, and the underwriting of large incorporations, and it maintained close ties with commercial banks. Even though the industrial elite had

[1] The two had exchanged correspondence as early as 1912, and during his extensive travel schedule Schumpeter had paid him a visit in 1913. They soon became friends and Taussig ultimately recruited him to the Harvard faculty. See Peneder and Resch (2015).

Schumpeter's Venture Money. Michael Peneder and Andreas Resch, Oxford University Press (2021). © Michael Peneder and Andreas Resch.
DOI: 10.1093/oso/9780198804383.003.0013

played a role in the foundation of many private banks, these primarily served to provide working capital and other short-term commercial credit to established businesses or to underwrite their bond issues. As a consequence, up to the 1920s, personal investments by wealthy individuals tended to be the only source of external venture finance in the US (Section 4.3). These individuals were typically seeking long-term dividend income and not chasing the temporary "promoter's profit," whereas capitalized earnings as practiced by institutional investors were often regarded with suspicion:

> Although venture capitalists today often make their profits by taking firms public and then cashing out their investments, that does not seem to have been the practice in the early twentieth century. To the contrary, investors in start-up enterprises appear to have taken their profits over the long run in the form of dividends on their shareholdings. (Lamoreaux et al., 2007, p. 45f)

The situation changed in the 1920s, when prior institutional reforms of the New York Stock Exchange, the growth of intangible capital, the rising demand for common stock, and the growing interest of a new group of investment bankers had rendered the pursuit of capital gains in place of dividend income increasingly attractive. For a short period, the resulting stock market boom also helped facilitate entry in emerging industries, such as radio or aviation, which were able to capture the public imagination.[2] But the crash of 1929 radically turned the tide. New laws and regulations no longer strove to enable venture finance, but rather to tame and constrain potential sources of financial instability. During the Great Depression of the 1930s "Wall Street's pain was amplified into Main Street's agony."[3] Political concerns about the financing of small and new enterprises were growing, and various committees, proposals, and initiatives were set up, with some promoting public initiatives, while others supported the formation of local capital trusts, an investment corporation under the aegis of the Federal Reserve, or a privately owned national industrial credit corporation.[4]

One particularly influential initiative was the New Products Committee appointed by the New England Council in 1939. According to Ante, it "assembled the brain trust of individuals who would eventually pioneer the venture capital industry," among them MIT's president Karl Compton, industrialist (and later president of the Federal Reserve Bank in Boston) Ralph Flanders, and Georges Doriot from the Harvard Business School (HBS).[5] Doriot headed a subcommittee on Development Procedures and Venture Capital. He also joined Enterprise

[2] Carosso (1970); Baskin and Miranti (1997); Neal and Davis (2007); O'Sullivan (2007), or Nicholas (2003, 2007, 2008).

[3] Hsu and Kenney (2005, p. 581).

[4] Liles (1977); Hsu and Kenney (2005); or Ante (2008).

[5] Ante (2008, p. 76).

Associates Inc., which started as an informal group to get investors involved with scientists. What could have become the birth of modern venture capital, however, was abruptly aborted with the outbreak of the Second World War.

After the war the times were finally favorable, and in 1946 alone three significant venture capital operations were formed. The first was the *J.H. Whitney & Company*, financed by a wealthy family, but not focusing on technology companies in particular. It was the first company to call itself a "venture capital" firm and had early success with the conversion of a surplus war munitions plant into fertilizer production. It is best known for its early venture investment in canned orange juice (Minute Maid) and is still active in private equity, focusing mostly on leveraged buyouts or the recapitalization of mature companies.[6] The second and third venture capital operations formed in that year were *Rockefeller Brothers, Inc.* and the *American Research and Development Corporation (ARD).* Unlike Whitney & Company, the latter two had a deliberate focus on science and technology companies and both also had roots in Schumpeter's proximate intellectual environment at Harvard.

The Rockefeller connection

Rockefeller Brothers, Inc. was owned by the famed siblings and run by Laurance S. Rockefeller. From 1932 to 1934 Laurance had attended Harvard Law School only to decide not to pursue his anticipated career as a lawyer. Instead, his interest had turned to venture capital, for which he had "provided the initial spark in the 1930s."[7] In 1938 and 1939, two spectacular investments in the young aviation industry demonstrated his instinct for long-term capital gains, the first one leading to the foundation of Eastern Airlines and the other enabling "an unknown plane designer, J.S. McDonnell" to found the Aircraft Corporation by the same name.[8] In 1969, the limited partnership changed its name to *Venrock*, conducting early-stage investments in companies such as Intel or Apple, and is still specialized in emerging technologies (e.g., electronics, composite materials, optics, and health care).

We cannot say whether Schumpeter had any opportunity to make a direct or indirect impression on Laurance Rockefeller. Laurance never studied economics, but during his two years at Harvard he apparently acquired an interest in venture finance. Despite his family background, he was not pre-disposed to pursue a similar career in business, first studying philosophy at Princeton and later law. What we can say for certain, however, is that both Schumpeter and his wife Elisabeth entertained a special relationship with the Rockefeller family.

[6] Gupta (2000, p. 95ff). [7] Gupta (2000, p. 107). [8] Time (1959, p. 50).

Schumpeter successfully recommended numerous emigrant scholars for Rockefeller fellowships and helped "persuade the Rockefeller Foundation to fund what became the Center for Research in Entrepreneurial History."[9] The Foundation had also sponsored a book by Elisabeth, who "kept up a lively correspondence with public figures," among them Laurance's younger brother David and their father John D. Rockefeller, Jr.[10] In 1950, David Rockefeller personally ensured that funds were channelled to Elisabeth for the editing of Schumpeter's manuscript of the *History of Economic Analysis*.[11]

David Rockefeller (1915–2017) delivered particular evidence of Schumpeter's lasting impact as a teacher of venture finance. Five years younger than Laurance, David also came to Harvard in 1932 and graduated with a Bachelor of Science in 1936. That same year he reluctantly decided to study economics, first studying one year with Schumpeter, then another year at the London School of Economics, and finally completing his PhD at the University of Chicago. In his memoirs, David Rockefeller recalls: "I was most influenced that year by Joseph A. Schumpeter. In fact, one of the intellectual high points of my graduate work was his basic course in economic theory." Offering another compelling compliment, he writes: "I also discovered that I enjoyed the subject and maybe even had a flair for it."[12] That his praise was not due to mere politeness or political sympathy is evidenced in his less enthusiastic reflections on Friedrich Hayek.[13] Of all the great economists with whom David studied, Schumpeter clearly stands out as the teacher who left the deepest impression on him. David later became head of the Chase Manhattan Bank. Referring to his early promotion of regional development banks in Latin America, Rockefeller recounted: "The 1950 trip was in many ways a watershed event in my life. I saw that banking could be a truly creative enterprise—creative in the sense that my old professor Joseph Schumpeter defined the term."[14]

There is a remarkable correlation between David Rockefeller's attention to development banking and the fact that a significant number of Schumpeter's students in Bonn later became engaged in development economics (see Section 10.3).[15] For instance, after having served for many years at the United

[9] McCraw (2007, p. 471). [10] McCraw (2007, pp. 328, 631).

[11] Harvard University Archive (HUGFP—66.90). [12] Rockefeller (2003, p. 79f).

[13] "Hayek was in his late thirties when I first met him. Indisputably brilliant he lacked Schumpeter's spark and charisma. He was a dull lecturer, very Germanic and methodical. His writings were ponderous and almost impossible to read—or at least stay awake while reading. Nevertheless, I found myself largely in agreement with his basic economic philosophy. Personally, he was a kindly man whom I respected greatly" (Rockefeller, 2003, p. 83).

[14] Rockefeller (2003, p. 133).

[15] All in all, the inclination of the former Schumpeter students from Bonn to engage in development policy activities may have had to do, on the one hand, with the fact that they were sensitized to the issues by their academic teacher. On the other hand, it must also be remembered that just after 1945 many new job opportunities were created in these fields through the expansion of the United Nations and numerous related institutions. International organizations and development banks, more generally, offered good job opportunities.

Nations, Hans W. Singer reflected on Schumpeter's *TED*, stating that he realized "now more clearly than in earlier years how deeply relevant many of its themes are to the development of poor countries." More specifically, he pointed at the key themes of innovation and technology adoption and the implied "disruption of familiar and traditional processes of stationary circulation, arousing resistances and hurting established interests."[16]

In his book on *Creative Management in Banking* David Rockefeller called Schumpeter a "scintillating scholar" under whom he "had the good fortune to study."[17] Furthermore, he situated his discussion firmly within Schumpeter's framework of entrepreneurial growth and took care to cover each of the different types of innovation enumerated in *TED*. Among others, he referred to the evolution of consumer credit (i.e., new markets), credit cards and charge-account banking (new products/services), savings deposits (new resources), computer-aided automation (new processes), or branching and merger policies (new industrial organization). All of these came together in his vision of the "Bank of Tomorrow," which was characterized by many of the now familiar features of electronic banking. But going beyond own innovations, creative banking is ultimately about "spurring the economy by lending to small and medium-sized businesses with growth potential, as well as to such new industries as aerospace and electronics."[18] Industrial ventures are financed by loan instruments as well as direct equity investments through specialized subsidiaries, which also provide technical assistance and know-how. Despite some examples, regulatory restrictions hampered such venture finance by banks in the US. Abroad, however, Rockefeller could promote joint ventures with private development banks and aimed for the promoter's profit of temporary capital gains from founding new businesses: "Once an enterprise is soundly established, our investment subsidiary usually sells out its interest. By rotating the capital, we feel that it can do the most good."[19]

A development bank can be defined as a "national or regional financial institution designed to provide medium- and long-term capital for productive investment, often accompanied by technical assistance, in poor countries."[20] After the Second World War, development banks were a foremost means of overcoming capital shortages in developing economies. After initial successes, the political climate changed during the 1970s and 1980s when concerns about market distortions, the crowding-out of private funds, and general inefficiencies of government enterprises increased. An influential empirical study by La Porta et al. has confirmed that the public ownership of banks, more generally, is associated with slower financial development and productivity growth, presumably because it "politicizes the resource allocation process and reduces efficiency."[21] Recently, a

[16] Singer (1997, p. 131). [17] Rockefeller (1964, p. 33). [18] Rockefeller (1964, p. 37).
[19] Rockefeller (1964, p. 68; italics added).
[20] *Encyclopaedia Britannica*: https://www.britannica.com/topic/development-bank
[21] La Porta et al. (2002, p. 290).

certain disillusionment with the economic policy prescriptions of the "Washington Consensus," together with the growing awareness about the role of financial frictions in development and then the Great Recession of 2008–9, have brought about a renaissance of academic and political interest in development banks. Griffith-Jones and Ocampo emphasize, for instance, their role of counteracting cycles and crisis, to promote innovation and structural change, inclusive finance, or the provision of public goods such as infrastructure or sustainability goals. Against the argument of crowding-out, they point at their capacity to crowd-in private funds for long-term investments by means of private-public partnerships.[22] In contrast, Fernandez-Arias et al. suggest that development banks should address informational problems and "be deployed as an instrument of economic intelligence" that "play an active role in the design, as well as implementation, of productive development policies."[23] Overall, the idea of development banks currently seems to be maturing from the old ideological confrontations to more specific debates on appropriate objectives and governance. We may surmise that these recent trends accord well with Schumpeter's deliberations.

American Research and Development Corporation

Turning to the third significant venture capital operation of 1946, Karl Compton and the "old pals from the New Products Committee"[24] reunited to found ARD, generally credited with being the world's first *institutional venture capital* firm. Unlike operations owned by wealthy families, fundraising from institutional investors (insurance companies, investment trusts, etc.) became a crucial further dimension to manage. In retrospect, given the strong ties with MIT and the initial absence of competition from other venture-investors, the flow of promising new technologies and marketable ideas was probably the smallest difficulty. Managing such start-ups and implementing a business-orientated mindset and attitude might have been the more formidable challenge to which the management know-how of Georges Doriot was equally important. But generating and maintaining the confidence of investors in such a new financial adventure was probably the trickiest challenge. Here, the support from the network of prestigious leaders in the public and business communities was an invaluable asset.

Despite unusually broad political support, financial backing was still precarious in the beginning and only gradually improved when the first and comparatively moderate returns from the first disbursements proved the overall validity of the business model. Furthermore, the portfolio of firms expanded unevenly over time. When in 1957 ARD financed the founding of the Digital Equipment Corporation

[22] Griffith-Jones and Ocampo (2018, p. 6).
[23] Fernandez-Arias et al. (2020, p. 4).
[24] Ante (2008, p. 107).

(DEC), it struck the first big success of the modern venture capital industry. After DEC's initial public offering in 1966, the value of ARD's investment skyrocketed by a factor of 500. The further history of ARD is covered in excellent articles and books.[25] The upshot is that ARD acquired its unique position in financial history by introducing institutional venture capital, rendering it a legitimate and proven investment tool, triggering spin-offs and many imitators in the market. Since then, venture capital has evolved into a highly specialized industry. The success of DEC established a spectacular showcase of what the "promoter's profit" can amount to. In contrast with Hilferding, who had stressed the expropriation of industrial capital and rising power of financial organizations, it highlighted Schumpeter's brighter understanding of venture finance as an enabler of new enterprises and industries.

In contrast with Schumpeter's failed attempts to found technology-orientated start-up companies in the 1920s, ARD is another remarkable example of how creative entrepreneurship offered practical solutions, while economic theory still struggled to understand the problem. In short, Lerner and Tufano summarize the core elements of ARD's new business model as follows:

> The ARD established an approach to addressing these problems that venture capital and private equity groups have followed ever since. First, by intensively scrutinizing companies before providing capital, and only funding a small fraction of those seeking funds, they could alleviate some of the information gaps and reduce capital constraints. Second, they employed a variety of tools that allowed them to monitor and control firms after the transactions. These included the use of convertible securities with powerful control rights, the syndication and staging of investments, the provision of oversight through formal board seats and information rights, the incentivization of management through extensive equity holdings, and informal coaching of management. Finally, there was a real effort to certify the funded entrepreneurs as being different from their peers, which facilitated their ability to enter into alliances, get access to investment bankers, and so forth. (Lerner and Tufano, 2012, p. 541)

While the importance of venture capital certainly varies greatly between countries and industries, there is no doubt that it became a major source of funding for creative entrepreneurs. Lerner and Tufano estimate that companies which at some critical point of their history were backed by venture capital, represent more than

[25] See Lilles (1977); Hsu and Kenney (2005); Ante (2008); or Nicholas and Chen (2012). While ARD was a listed investment company, competitors soon established the limited partnership as a more advantageous corporate form. After Doriot's retirement, ARD was merged with the industrial conglomerate Textron in 1971.

75 percent of total value in the software industry.[26] Relatedly, Akcigit et al. present a Schumpeterian growth model, where venture capitalists select entrepreneurs and support them with finance and complementary expertise. Based on empirical micro-evidence for the US and calibrations of their theoretical macro-model, they conclude that

> despite the fact that VC-backed startups are subject to higher initial selection, failure rates, and dispersion in growth outcomes, they are much more likely than non-VC-backed ones to eventually land in the right tail of the firm size and innovation distributions. In other words, VC appears to contribute disproportionately to the making of large and successful ("superstar") firms.
>
> (Akcigit et al., 2019, p. 2)

Did Schumpeter contribute?

A shared interest in the problem of entrepreneurial finance, together with the close geographical proximity of Schumpeter at Harvard University, Doriot at HBS, and Compton at MIT would suggest some sort of personal interaction. Both Schumpeter's biographer Tom McCraw and Frederic M. Scherer had the same intuition, but did not find any evidence of this.[27] Neither did we, having researched the Schumpeter Archives at Harvard University, the Doriot Archive at HBS, and the comprehensive online documentation of Compton's correspondences.

Given Schumpeter's earlier personal experiences, it is certainly not surprising that he was not directly involved in the process.[28] He had already more than burnt his fingers and was too absorbed in his own theoretical work to take notice or be asked to participate. One must also consider that, even if he had been invited, for example, to lend his academic standing to a supervisory board, his tainted reputation may have backfired with critical investors.

Given their close intellectual and geographical proximity, it is nevertheless likely that there was some sort of interaction, in particular between Schumpeter and Doriot. At least three observations support this conjecture. First, Schumpeter

[26] Lerner and Tufano (2012, p. 544). See also Perez (2002); Gompers and Lerner (2004); or Lerner (2006). Peneder (2012) relates the evidence to Schumpeter's theory of entrepreneurship and innovation.

[27] In an e-mail from July 13, 2009, Tom McCraw replied to our very first inquiry into the matter: "Having researched the entire collection, I am sorry to report that I found no direct correspondence between Schumpeter and Georges Doriot, Karl Compton, or any other figure who pioneered venture capital in Massachusetts. Like you, I was a bit surprised at this." Frederic Scherer, a leading industrial economist and student of Doriot at HBS, confirmed the same intuition in a personal conversation in 2013.

[28] As McCraw explained, "by the time he came to the United States, Schumpeter concentrated strictly on his academic work. He remained in debt from the Vienna crash of 1924 until about 1934 and [...] after that did not even manage his own small amount of capital, delegating the task to his wife, Elizabeth."

frequently visited the Baker Library at HBS, where he took special interest in the collection of business histories. The notorious cultural gap between "pure science" at Harvard University and the applied departments at the Business School was not an obstacle to him.[29] Second, more than a mere professor of manufacturing at HBS, Doriot also took a keen interest in the larger macro-developments of society. Like Schumpeter, he was deeply engrossed in the topic of "Modern Capitalism. Its Origin and Evolution," which is the title of a book by the French historian Henri Sée that Doriot translated into English in 1928.[30] Schumpeter was familiar with the book and refers to both the French edition and its English translation in his "Capitalism" (CAP2; 1946). When discussing the merchants of colonial trade, the translation uses the phrase "venture the capital," which is neither obvious nor necessarily prompted from the French original.[31]

The precise origin of the term venture capital is still obscure. To our knowledge, the earliest use has so far been identified with a quote from a Report of the Industrial Securities Committee of the Investment Bankers Association in 1920, which postulated that the "enlistment of venture capital is necessary for the development and growth of the country."[32] Doriot himself referred to *Ventures Limited*, a Canadian holding company in the mining business and founded in 1928 by the Harvard engineering graduate Thayer Lindslay.[33] Schumpeter frequently used the phrase "industrial venture" in the context of large and long-term investments. In 1943 he used the term "venture capital" in an article on "Capitalism in the Postwar Period," (CAP1) that is, well before it became more widely popular with the foundation and later success of ARD.

In the same article, Schumpeter reprised his optimism about economic opportunities in the post-war reconstruction period, reminiscent of the rationale for his own venture investments after the First World War and certainly reassuring to any aspiring venture capitalist after the Second World War:

> Everybody is afraid of a postwar slump, threatening from a drastic reduction of military expenditure financed by inflationary methods as well as from mere reorientation of production. [...] Viewed as a purely economic problem, that task might well turn out to be much easier than most people believe. [This is because] the wants of impoverished households will be so urgent and so

[29] At a speech in 1947, Doriot introduced himself with the following ironic clue: "I belong to the uneducated part of Harvard—across the river—on the Stadium and playground side" (Georges F. Doriot Collection, Vol. 125, No. 4, p. 9). Conversely, Schumpeter liked to emphasize that business economics "is basic to the work of the economist so soon as he goes beyond the most jejune assumptions about individual behavior, and cooperation between business and general economics is a primary necessity for both" (*HEA*, 1954, p. 944).

[30] The translation was in cooperation with Homer Vanderblu. Originally published in 1926, the French title was *Les origines du capitalisme moderne*.

[31] Sée (1928, p. 56); CAP2 (1946, p. 209). [32] Nicholas and Chen (2012, p.1).

[33] Georges F. Doriot Collection, Vol. 128, No. 2, p. 582.

> calculable that any postwar slump that may be unavoidable would speedily give way to a reconstruction boom. Capitalist methods have proved equal to much more difficult tasks. (CAP1, 1943, p. 182f)

All this suggests that Schumpeter must have been familiar with and most probably was sympathetic to the discourse in New England at the time, and possibly also with the subcommittee on Development Procedures and Venture Capital headed by Doriot.

The third reason to surmise an intellectual influence is the frequent use of vintage Schumpeterian ideas by Doriot and the co-founders of ARD. There are general similarities, for example, with regard to Schumpeter's distinction between statics and dynamics,[34] or his widespread notion of creative destruction,[35] which may not confer too much meaning for our case. But there are at least three further elements, which reflect Schumpeter's theory of venture finance more specifically. The first is Schumpeter's unique concept of the entrepreneur. Up to the present day, there are many competing theories of entrepreneurship (Section 7.4), and especially in the US Frank Knight's emphasis on the risk-bearing function has been very influential. Alternately, one could also adhere to the older tradition and characterize entrepreneurs by the general undertaking of a business. However, Doriot explicitly opted for Schumpeter's concept, repeatedly characterizing the entrepreneur as someone who "makes innovation happen."[36] Further reminiscent of Schumpeter, Doriot stressed that the

> entrepreneur is a man who wants to do something he has never done before and often something that has never been done before. [. . .] The only assets are an idea and a man's ability. This combination will very shortly have to compete with companies having important assets including money—background—experience – trained men—a name and so on. This means that the entrepreneur [. . .] has very little margin of error.
>
> (Georges F. Doriot)

The second such element is Hilferding's idea of a "promoter's profit" in terms of the capital gains realized by the issue of new shares, preferably via an IPO. Nobody

[34] For example, in ARD's mission statement, co-founder Ralph Flanders emphasized that "[t]o be confident that we are in an expanding, instead of a static or frozen economy, we must have a reasonable high birthrate of new undertakings" (Georges F. Doriot Collection, Vol. 114, Confidential Book 2, f.13b).

[35] Georges F. Doriot Collection, Vol. 122, No. 12, p. 81. Even when Doriot disagrees with the term, he reveals himself to be familiar with it: "Let us be careful that this is not an age of destruction instead of an age of building—instead of an age of construction" (Georges F. Doriot Collection, Vol. 127, No. 33, p. 566). Interestingly, in his later work Schumpeter was also careful to avoid the term creative "destruction," replacing it with the less controversial creative "response."

[36] Georges F. Doriot Collection, Vol. 127, No. 33, p. 564.

appears to have used Hilferding's original notion, just as Schumpeter had absorbed it into his more general concept of entrepreneurial profit. But this cannot mask the fact that never before in history had the promoter's profit materialized more convincingly than with the emergence of the new venture capital industry.[37] There, it had indeed turned into a business model *sui generis*. Of course, capital gains were not new. But Doriot understood their elevated significance. In 1961 he resumed that "the most important discovery of the past 15 years is not a technical one nor a new one. It is the rediscovery of capital gains. [. . .] Venture capital has become popular as a method of generating capital gains" (Georges F. Doriot Collection, Vol. 126, No. 3, p. 209).

A final element suggesting an intellectual kinship between Schumpeter and the emerging venture capital industry was their mutual emphasis on the firm's need to match technical expertise and management skills as very distinct personal capabilities. In Doriot's words,

> (t)here have been many fine scientists trying desperately to become poor businessmen. But scientific intelligence, we find, does not always result in business modesty. Success, I feel, would be attained more often if good men would only entrust their ideas to good operating men.[38]
>
> (Georges F. Doriot Collection, Vol. 114 – Confidential Book 2 (f7c–7f and f13i)

Not only could this have been Schumpeter's own resume of his personal history, it also resonated with his general emphasis on the different functions and mindsets of inventors as opposed to entrepreneurs. But Doriot's quotes are even more reminiscent of Schumpeter's mentor at Harvard, Frank W. Taussig. The title of his book *Inventors and Money-makers* reads like a preview of ARD's ground-breaking collaboration between MIT and HBS: "Commonly the inventor is a poor manager. It is when allied with the business man that he is most likely to develop and perfect the usable devices."[39]

If Schumpeter contributed to the rise of venture finance, it was through his ability to identify its essential role in economic development and provide it with a consistent and credible intellectual frame. For example, certain ideas by Schumpeter that reportedly impressed the young David Rockefeller may have also thus affected the business vision of his brother Laurance. Similarly, Schumpeter's mentor and friend Frank Taussig may have diffused ideas that struck a particular

[37] One may doubt whether the promoter's profit was ever that important in the banking operations which Hilferding knew. Although in Austria and Germany the larger universal banks were generally involved in industrial investments, they typically maintained their equity for longer periods, just as individual investors did in the US. The promoter's profit for the most part arose from incorporations, with the issuing banks earning a share from their underwriting. See Section 4.3.

[38] Georges F. Doriot Collection, Vol. 114 – Confidential Book 2 (f7c–7f and f13i).

[39] Taussig (1915, p. 40).

chord within his social networks, possibly reinforced by the experiences and less articulate beliefs of others, which, further diffused, at some point ended as a shared and common truth among people like Compton, Doriot, and other members of the area's business and civic elite. Schumpeter and Doriot both repeatedly emphasized that new and unproven ideas meet with adversities or suspicion and are regularly contested. Any feebleness, such as an inconsistent argument, is thus easily exploited by opponents. Throughout its history, the founders of ARD displayed an astonishing confidence and belief in the social desirability and economic validity of their venture, which they seem to have taken almost for granted. Beyond their immediate reach, the success of ARD also depended crucially on the wider support of investors, the public media, aspiring entrepreneurs, and its own personnel. For all that, a strong and dependable mission must have served as powerful armour, to which—we conclude—Schumpeter's unique theory of venture finance had in some way contributed.

13.2 Recurrent crises

The Great Depression

Our second example for the enduring relevance of the Schumpeterian vision is about the endogenous nature of recurrent crises. For this, we must inevitably invoke Minsky's financial instability hypothesis (Section 12.2). Hyman Minsky had grown up in the era of the Great Depression, which followed the US stock market crash of October 29, 1929, and endured throughout most of the 1930s. His financial instability hypothesis naturally relates to Irving Fisher's *debt-deflation theory,* which aimed to explain it. Clearly akin to Schumpeter's emphasis on innovation-driven cycles and crisis, Fisher started from the observation that

> new opportunities to invest at a big prospective profit, as compared with ordinary profits and interest, such as through new inventions, new industries, development of new resources, opening new lands or new markets [...] was a prime cause leading to the over-indebtedness of 1929. Inventions and technological improvements created wonderful investment opportunities, and so caused big debts. (Fisher, 1933, p. 348)[40]

Similarly to Schumpeter, Fisher believed that crises typically originate with developments on the real side of the economy, but that monetary factors determine

[40] "Other causes were the left-over war debts, whether domestic, foreign, public or private, the reconstruction loans to foreigners, and the low interest policy adopted to help England get back on the gold standard in 1925" (Fisher, 1933, p. 348).

the further course of events.[41] In short, if the above kinds of investments result in a state of overindebtedness, pressure for the liquidation of debt leads to distress sales and deflation, further depressing profits, the net worth of business, output, and employment.

At the time of the Great Depression, monetary policy apparently was not capable of coping with the situation. For instance, Friedman and Schwartz blamed it for having been indecisive and inconsequential. First, US policy "was too easy to break the bull market," and then it was "too tight to permit vigorous business expansion."[42] Bernanke further pointed at flaws of the international monetary system, which had the consequence that "shocks were transmitted around the world primarily through the working of the gold standard."[43] In addition, he highlighted the role of wage rigidities and financial frictions. But either of the major experts considered the Great Depression "curable and preventable," mainly by means of reflation and stabilization as the "scientific medication"—advice which President Roosevelt ultimately followed, on the urging of Irving Fisher.[44]

The Great Moderation

At this point, we run up against another peculiar irony of monetary history. With hindsight, the further developments up to the Great Recession that started in 2008 were remarkably consistent with Minsky's warning about the subversive effect of stability to destabilize the system. It is also true, however, that for the very same reasons it was largely neglected throughout that period. To begin with, the "dominant narrative of the Great Depression, that it was caused by avoidable policy failures, was itself conducive to the belief that those failures could be—and had been—corrected."[45] In many developed economies, the post Second World War era of successful reconstruction and growth further enhanced that confidence. At the same time, the successful advent of general equilibrium analyses simultaneously focused and narrowed the economist's vision. And indeed, as Ng and Wright point out, throughout the 1970s and 1980s recessions in the US were mainly the kind of supply and demand shocks to be explained by fiscal and monetary policies.[46] According to Eichengreen, however, "the longer the period of stability persists, the greater the risks. But this is not the perception while the party is underway." Rather "a long period of stability born of good policy or good luck empowers those inclined to argue that regulation is too strict," and the "heavy hand laid on financial markets in the 1930s could give way to light-touch regulation."[47]

[41] "There is probably always a very real basis for the 'new era' psychology before it runs away with its victims. This was certainly the case before 1929" (Fisher, 1933, p. 349).

[42] Friedman and Schwartz (1963, p. 692).

[43] Bernanke (2000, pp. 6, vii).

[44] Bernanke (2000, p. 24).

[45] Eichengreen (2015, p. 379).

[46] Ng and Wright (2013, p. 1122).

[47] Eichengreen (2015, p. 379f).

But the growing confidence in the stability of the system was not the only force to erode the strict regulations that had emerged in the aftermath of the Great Depression. Financial innovations not only enhance the efficiency of a system by mitigating various kinds of market failure. They also respond to incentives for *regulatory arbitrage*, where financial organizations constantly seek opportunities "to innovate around prohibited or disadvantaged transactions." Thereby "innovations also overcome many of the policy-related regulatory barriers that were put in place as safeguards or for particular policy objectives."[48] In combination with the global competition for financial activities and accordingly deep capital markets, financial innovations are thus also a source of systemic risk, in addition to their apparent benefits: One lesson from history is that finance finds a way. Prohibiting one type of intermediary from engaging in one or more types of growth-enhancing activity promotes the development and entry of new types.[49] One such source of systemic risk has been the growing importance of non-bank financial institutions ("shadow banking"), where market-based intermediaries exploit their greater flexibility relative to the traditional and more strictly regulated banking sector. For instance, *repurchase agreements* (repo) of government securities can substitute for short-term borrowing on the money market. In the US these were first used by the Federal Reserve in 1917, but later diffused to other market participants and expanded rapidly in the 1970s and 1980s.

The growing importance of securitization is another closely related example. In short, by pooling contractual debts of various origin,[50] repackaging the associated cash-flows (interest and principal), and selling them to third parties, a variety of largely illiquid financial claims are bundled and transformed into marketable securities. Among the social benefits, borrowers generally enjoy lower interest rates. Together with better statistical methods and historical data for risk assessment, securitization also extended the reach of "subprime lending" to marginal borrowers who were otherwise credit-constrained.[51]

In the US, securitization was first introduced in the 1920s, but rapidly expanded with the increasing application to home mortgages in the 1970s and 1980s.[52] Thus raising home-ownership rates and generally being more inclusive to marginal borrowers, Lerner and Tufano conclude that "the roughly first three decades of securitization were not likely welfare-reducing. Indeed, having deep pools of capital to fund national mortgage markets was a likely improvement over local mortgage lenders."[53] Beck and Frame point at the apparent incentive problems and conclude that "[s]ubprime lending in general has seemingly been successful at

[48] Knoll (2008, p. 94); see also Levich (1988, p. 247).

[49] Bodenhorn (2018, p. 141.)

[50] Examples are residential and commercial mortgages in the case of "mortgage-backed securities" (MBS), or automobile loans, credit card debts, and other "asset-backed securities" (ABS).

[51] Beck and Frame (2018, p. 372ff).

[52] Lerner and Tufano (2012, pp. 563f, 565).

[53] Lerner and Tufano (2012, p. 567). They also point out that the more recent history before the financial crisis was a different matter.

expanding credit availability to marginal borrowers. However, subprime mortgage lending seems to have been a failed innovation."[54]

It is worth noting that the risks that come with the principle of securitization were not just known in hindsight. As early as the 1980s, for instance, Levich pointed at the according incentive problems:

> Securitization poses another specific example of potential welfare losses associated with financial innovation. Securitization and the increased use of financial intermediaries place the burden of credit evaluation on a larger pool of participants; the increase in market linkages may itself be seen as a source of added risk. To some extent, this may be because the new instruments lack transparency (i.e., they are not well understood), and they have not stood the test of two or three business cycles. (Levich, 1988, p. 217f)

In the meantime, the EMH had also lost its shine. It became the main target of the new branch of *behavioral finance*, which Andrei Shleifer defined as "the study of human fallibility in competitive markets."[55] In the 1950s, Herbert Simon's concept of "bounded rationality" had provided an early lead into behavioral economics. In the 1970s, psychologists like Amos Tversky and Daniel Kahneman began to further undermine the paradigm of rational choice with a series of experimental findings on the use of common heuristics and the resulting systematic distortions in decision making.[56]

The EMH, however, does not require individual agents to be literally perfectly rational (Section 11.4). It rather predicts that arbitrage and market selection will ensure outcomes *as if* their choices were rational and fully informed. But in the 1980s there was growing empirical evidence against such a perfect rationality of the market. Robert Shiller was among the first to point out that the high volatility of the stock markets is inconsistent with the EMH: "If stock prices are supposed to be an optimal predictor of the dividend present value, then they should not jump around erratically when the true fundamental value is growing along a smooth trend."[57] Moreover, according to the EMH only genuinely new information can trigger price changes, which are hence unpredictable and follow a random walk. Further empirical evidence, however, revealed a serial correlation of stock prices—typically being negative in the long run over several years while exhibiting positive momentun in the short run of several months.[58]

In a competitive market, such inefficiencies relate to the fact that the individual deviations from perfect rationality need not be normally distributed and, on

[54] Beck and Frame (2018, p. 374f). [55] Shleifer (2000, p. 23).
[56] Simon (1959); Tversky and Kahneman (1974, 1992); Kahneman and Tversky (1979).
[57] Shiller (1981; 2000, p. 188).
[58] De Bondt and Thaler (1985). See Hirshleifer (2015) for a survey.

balance, cancel each other out, so that arbitrageurs would lean against them. In other words, "[i]nvestor sentiment reflects the common judgement errors made by a substantial number of investors, rather than uncorrelated random mistakes."[59] In addition to the limited opportunities for arbitrage, which can result from fundamental uncertainty and the lack of close substitute assets,[60] smart investors will factor in the "sentiments" which affect the beliefs and valuations of the other traders. In short, when "arbitrageurs trade in anticipation of noise trader demand they move prices away from rather than toward fundamental values."[61] Rational arbitrage may thus reinforce positive feedbacks that create speculative bubbles and destabilize prices.

Some economists were thus less surprised than others by the eventual reappearance of financial instability: first with the US savings-and-loan-crisis of 1990–1, and then the internet bubble of 2001. But as Ng and Wright emphasize, both were relatively "mild and brief."[62] Subsequently, the attention shifted toward the phenomenon of a *Great Moderation* of the business cycle, which presumably began in the mid-1980s.[63] Economists were not short of plausible explanations for the lesser volatility of aggregate production and other macroeconomic variables, pointing, for instance, at the better monetary policy, an improved management of inventories (lean production), structural change from manufacturing toward services (tertiarization), or simply good luck because of less external disturbances. One potential cause was even to be sought in a presumed lesser volatility of residential investment, related to the reduction of volatility of mortgage rates.[64]

The example of the Great Moderation underlines the main conclusion drawn by Reinhart and Rogoff in their comprehensive empirical study of eight centuries of crises. They stress that the general perception of "this time being different" is a recurrent characteristic before booms collapse. People tend to assert that markets and governments have learned their lesson from past failures, and that the current surge of growth "is built on sound fundamentals, structural reforms, technological innovation, and good policy."[65] Inducing growing leverage, their interpretation of the historical record lends much credibility to the kind of balance sheet effects, which Fisher and Minsky had emphasized. Relatedly, it also corresponds to Schumpeter's explanation of the monetary propagation mechanism in his explanation of the business cycle. A case in point is his distinction between primary and secondary waves. Recall that the primary wave reflects the regular clustering

[59] Shleifer (2000, p. 12).

[60] For example, "An arbitrageur who thinks that stocks as a whole are overpriced cannot sell short stocks and buy a substitute portfolio, since such a portfolio does not exist" Shleifer (2000, p. 14).

[61] De Long (1990a,b); Shleifer (2000, p. 27).

[62] Ng and Wright (2013, p. 1122).

[63] Stock and Watson (2002, p. 1) coined the term, observing that the "U.S. economy has entered a period of moderated volatility, or quiescence. The long expansion of the 1990s, the mild 2001 recession, and the current moderate recovery reflect a trend over the past two decades towards moderation of the business cycle and, more generally, reduced volatility in the growth rate of GDP."

[64] Stock and Watson (2002, p. 189).

[65] Reinhart and Rogoff (2009, p. xxxiv).

of entrepreneurial innovations and according profit opportunities, whereas the secondary wave mainly feeds on financial speculation and excess. Though no longer an inevitable part of economic development, it can nevertheless lead into deep recession or depression, if policy fails to intervene (Section 7.7).

Without explicitly saying so, the characterization by Reinhart and Rogoff of the events that led up to the US subprime crisis in 2007 reads very much like a current update of Schumpeter's narration:

> The this-time-is different syndrome has been alive and well in the United States, where it first took the form of a widespread belief that sharp productivity gains stemming from the IT industry justified price-earnings ratios in the equity market that far exceeded any historical norm. That delusion ended with the bursting of the IT bubble in 2001. But the excesses quickly reemerged, morphing into a different shape in a different market. The securitization of subprime mortgages combined with a heavy appetite for these instruments in countries such as Germany, Japan, and major emerging markets like China fueled the perception that housing prices would continue to climb forever. The new delusion was that "this time is different" because there were new markets, new instruments, and new lenders. In particular, financial engineering was thought to have tamed risk by better tailoring exposures to investors' appetites.
>
> (Reinhart and Rogoff, 2009, p. 171f)

The Great Recession of 2008–9

Numerous publications have reviewed the history of the Great Recession of 2008–9. One of the most instructive accounts is by Gertler and Gilchrist, who focus on the interaction of financial factors and real production in bringing about the accelerated deterioration in the balance sheets of households, banks, and non-financial firms. Theoretically, the net worth of assets on the balance sheets of either sector matters only in the presence of financial frictions. Without them, lending should only depend on the merits of the individual financing project, whereas agency problems invoke either a premium to be paid for or restricted access to external finance. By largely ignoring the models of financial acceleration due to market frictions (Section 12.3), the economists' general lack of alertness to the possibility of a major crisis had a profound theoretical reason:

> At the onset of the crisis, the workhorse macroeconomic models assumed frictionless financial markets. These frameworks were thus not able to anticipate the crisis, nor to analyse how the disruption of credit markets changed what initially appeared like a mild downturn into the Great Recession.
>
> (Gertler and Gilchrist, 2018, p. 3)

Real events, however, were characterized by the contagious impact of changes in the balance sheets of borrowers on their access to credit, accordingly affecting aggregate spending and production. In short, the Great Recession of 2008–9 originated in the combination of several factors, which contributed to a pronounced decline in the cost of mortgage finance. Gertler and Gilchrist point at the decline of long-term interest rates, the easing of credit terms, or the growing importance of securitization as well as non-bank financial institutions. Gennaioli et al. further highlight the interplay of financial innovation and fragility. In their model the strong demand by investors for safe assets induces intermediaries to overissue new securities, which seem to be close substitutes but involve low probability risks that investors (and intermediaries) tend to neglect. Their assumptions from behavioral finance thus incorporate a genuine element of surprise when the crisis breaks out.[66]

By means of regulatory arbitrage such financial innovations have raised the competitive pressure on traditional banking organizations. Additionally, induced by the consequent boom in real estate prices, the mortgage-backed leverage of both households and banks surged. When in 2007 house prices started to decline and short-term interest rates rose, mortgage defaults increased. And as the markets for asset-backed securities contracted, funds with high exposure to mortgage risks were the first that fell victim to the change of tides. Lehman Brothers was among those most exposed to the use of mortgage-backed securities as collateral for short-term loans on the repo market. As their value dropped, creditors increasingly refused to accept them as collateral. Unlike the public support which Bear Stearns, Fannie Mae, and Freddie Mac had received before, Lehman Brothers was denied a public bailout. No longer able to raise short-term funds, it defaulted in September 2008. This was the domino that finally triggered the crisis and "freezed" the money market for short-term loans. Arguably, the events amounted to a "bank run" in the "markets for wholesale funding (interbank) as opposed to retail funding."[67] As other investment banks found shelter through merging with commercial banks,

> [t]he financial crisis spread like a cancer from the shadow banking sector, which funded mainly securitized assets, to the commercial banking sector. When commercial banks merged with investment banks, they also absorbed a share of the assets funded by the investment banks. [...] The losses on mortgage-related assets in turn weakened the balance sheets of commercial banks, disrupting the flow of credit through these institutions. Now bank-dependent borrowers, including many nonfinancial firms and households, also faced increasing credit costs. (Gertler and Gilchrist, 2018, p. 14)

[66] Gennaioli et al. (2012). [67] Gertler and Gilchrist (2018, p. 14).

To summarize, the crisis originated from excesses in the interaction of finance and households, which generated a bubble in the markets for real estate and mortgage-backed securities. The consequent decline of net worth in the balance sheets of the banking sector propagated its effects to real production by raising the cost of credit and thereby depressing consumer spending as well as corporate investments. In this process, policy certainly lacked the needed alertness to the possibility of a financial crisis.[68] Moritz Schularick and Alan M. Taylor additionally blame a certain myopia among monetary theorists who had failed to recognize the changing relationship between credit and the monetary base after the Great Depression and the Second World War:

> Our ancestors lived in an Age of Money, where credit was closely tied to money, and formal analysis could use the latter as a proxy for the former. Today, we live in a different world, an Age of Credit, where financial innovation and regulatory ease broke that link, setting in motion an unprecedented expansion of the role of credit in the macroeconomy. [...] It is a mishap of history that just at the time when credit mattered more than ever before, the reigning doctrine had sentenced it to playing no constructive role in monetary policy.
>
> (Schularick and Taylor, 2012, p. 1058)

Among the consequences for monetary policy, they conclude that after the Great Recession of 2008–9 the "influence of the credit view has certainly advanced":[69]

> Specifically, the pre-2008 consensus argued that monetary policy should follow a "rule" based only on output gaps and inflation, but a few dissenters thought that credit deserved to be watched carefully and incorporated into a broader central bank policy framework. (Schularick and Taylor, 2012, p. 1032)

Though policy had failed to prevent and mitigate the crisis in time, the common appraisal is that after its outbreak it reacted decisively with vigorous monetary and fiscal measures. Compared to the Great Depression, policy has thus averted a more severe and prolonged crisis. In conclusion, however, the major historical

[68] For instance, John B. Taylor, famous for the monetary rule named after him, holds policy responsible for a number of mistakes. He poignantly states that "government actions and interventions caused, prolonged, and worsened the financial crisis. They caused it by deviating from historical precedents and principles for setting interest rates, which had worked well for 20 years. They prolonged it by misdiagnosing the problems in the bank credit markets and thereby responding inappropriately by focusing on liquidity rather than risk. They made it worse by providing support for certain financial institutions and their creditors but not others in an ad hoc way without a clear and understandable framework. While other factors were certainly at play, these government actions should be first on the list of answers to the question of what went wrong" (Taylor, 2009, p. 18).

[69] Schularick and Taylor (2012, p. 1032).

assessments after the Great Recession of 2008–9 tend to converge on Minsky's instability hypothesis:

> The lesson of history, then, is that even as institutions and policy makers improve, there will always be a temptation to stretch the limits. Just as an individual can go bankrupt no matter how rich she starts out, a financial system can collapse under the pressure of greed, politics, and profits no matter how well regulated it seems to be. (Reinhart and Rogoff, 2009, p. 291f)

Of particular interest to our concern, Eichengreen takes the opportunity to speculate on what Schumpeter would have thought about the causes and cures:

> No doubt he would have been of the view that the crisis was rooted in earlier excesses. He appreciated the limits of rational decision making and the tendency to engage in herd behavior, and therefore the propensity for markets to boom and bust. He understood these tendencies in terms similar to those of present-day economists specializing in behavioral economics and the economics of information. He understood how easy credit can combine with new technologies to produce an unsustainable boom followed by a disruptive crash.
>
> (Eichengreen, 2010, p. 2)

With regard to policy, Eichengreen points at Schumpeter's stance as a conditional "liquidationist"

> But he did see downturns as correcting earlier mistakes and thus as having a cleansing function. He was conscious that corners had been cut and laws had been broken in the pursuit of quick profits in the 1920s. He thus regarded the decline in stock values and the initial stages of the 1929–30 downturn as "for moral reasons a most sanitary thing," [that is,] until it was allowed to infect the banking system and spawn a full-blown financial crisis.
>
> (Eichengreen, 2010, p. 2)

As Eichengreen points out, Schumpeter would agree to government interventions being needed to prevent the system from further tumbling into depression. However, he would not confide in a mere Keynesian policy to strengthen aggregate demand:

> Were he alive today, I suspect that Schumpeter would argue that we made the wrong choice in the last couple of years by relying so heavily on Keynesian pump priming while not doing enough to fix our broken banking systems, through recapitalization and, where necessary, temporary nationalization. [...] Propping

up demand while leaving the banks weak will make for a credit-less, innovation-poor recovery. (Eichengreen, 2010, p. 2)

13.3 Digital payments and account

The Great Recession of 2008–9 led to a significant loss of public confidence in the monetary system and the political institutions that support it. In addition, the subsequent expansionary monetary and fiscal policies raised the suspicion that governments would spend themselves out of the crisis and depreciate their debts by means of inflation. Having undermined the legitimacy of the established system, the Great Recession of 2008–9 thus gave momentum to the proponents of alternative monetary concepts. In the immediate aftermath of the crisis, one particularly significant development was the introduction of the *Bitcoin* protocol under the pseudonym of Satoshi Nakamoto in 2008. Characteristically, it established the first peer-to-peer system of electronic cash that operates without the intermediation of a financial institution.[70]

The digital revolution

The evolution of digital money, however, goes back further into recent history. New digital technologies had already caused major transformations throughout financial industry for most of the second half of the twentieth century. Schumpeter's former student David Rockefeller was among the early promoters of the widespread use of new information and communication technologies (ICTs) in banking.[71] His memoirs are quite articulate about the importance of their application to the efficiency of the industry's accounting operations: "At the core of any bank's ability to operate effectively and profitably is its back office—the people and technology executing hundreds of thousands of daily customer transactions accurately, expeditiously, and at a reasonable cost."[72] Similarly, his short book on *Creative Management in Banking* is full of optimism about computerization

[70] This section originates in Peneder (2020).

[71] After the Second World War, David Rockefeller had joined the management of the Chase National Bank and became senior vice president in 1952. In 1955 a merger with the Bank of the Manhattan Company formed the Chase Manhattan Bank. From 1969 to 1981 Rockefeller was its chairman of the board and chief executive officer. After another merger in 2000 it has become part of J.P. Morgan Chase & Co.

[72] "In 1954 I had persuaded [the chairman of the Chase National Bank] to commission the Laboratory for Electronics (LFE), a company I had helped start, to study the bank's operations and custom-design a computer to control our operations. The timing was premature and the effort failed, but the LFE's work gave us the courage to pursue a more comprehensive approach to modernizing our operational procedures and staff. In fact, by the early 1960s virtually all of our operations were computerized" (Rockefeller, 2003, p. 213f).

and automation. Rockefeller was convinced that the efficient management and processing of data only created the organizational and technological basis of the benefits, which customers would more directly experience in the future "bank-of-tomorrow." His vision was then strikingly consistent with the current day practice of electronic banking:

> Those of you who have occasionally complained about having to wait in line at the teller's window may see the day when you won't have to go to a bank at all on routine transactions. Your paycheck will be automatically deposited to your account. On your instructions, the computer will deduct a certain amount of savings [...]. If you should want to borrow money, you would simply write a check for the amount up to the limit of a pre-arranged line of credit. [...] On a shopping trip you would present a universal credit card at the department store, the specialty shop, and the supermarket. The bills would be transmitted automatically to your bank and charged to your account. Periodically, the computer would send out a comprehensive statement, recording your checking account transactions, savings deposits, bills paid, personal loan payments deducted, mortgage payments, and the status of any trust investments you might have. (Rockefeller, 1964, p. 13f)

Though in 1964 the vision of the "bank-of-tomorrow" may have sounded "fanciful and far-fetched" to his contemporaries, Rockefeller pointed out that many elements were "already in use on a limited scale," predicting "with confidence that most banks would be offering such services by 1975."[73] In the 1980s James Tobin affirmed the overall macroeconomic significance of the digital revolution in banking, pointing at the fast expansion of consumer credit and other forms of overdraft in the US:

> In the brave new world of electronic payments, all can be linked in a computerized payments network. [...] In this payments system, it will be natural and almost inevitable that banks allow overdrafts up to established credit lines like those now defined by bank credit cards. Extensive use of overdrafts may be the principal monetary innovation of the new system for the United States.
>
> (Tobin, 1985, p. 27)

One of the innovations, which Rockefeller certainly had in mind, was the "quiet revolution" of *payment cards*. Initially targeting restaurants in Manhattan, Diners Club had introduced the first general purpose card in 1950. At the time it was still made of cardboard and each payment consequently implied a trail of traditional paperwork.[74] It was only through the increasing use of computers that they could

[73] Rockefeller (1964, p. 15).

[74] Evans and Schmalensee (2005, pp. xi, 30). Earlier, there had existed special purpose charge cards, such as various "charge-plates" to be used by wholesale merchants, or the Air Travel Card introduced in the US in 1934.

be electronically processed and managed.[75] The earliest systems were simple *charge cards*, which required the full repayment at a due date. Later *credit cards* added the function of revolving credit, meaning that customers can carry over a balance on which they pay interest:

> Over time, entrepreneurs have discovered that they can integrate other products and services into payment cards, thereby making these cards more valuable for consumers and merchants. Combining payment and lending services on the same card was by far the most significant innovation along these lines. It gave consumers a new ability to take out instant loans to make purchases, helped the many merchants who lacked the size or sophistication to extend consumer credit by themselves efficiently, and provided banks with a convenient method for lending money to an ever-expanding set of households and small businesses.
> (Evans and Schmalensee (2005, p. 319)

Meanwhile, *debit cards* (bank cards) gained importance, especially in Europe, by combining many functions of the credit card with that of instant cash withdrawals at automatic teller machines (ATMs). Characteristically, these directly debit the cardholder's bank account. Evans and Schmalensee hence conclude that "[t]oday, people exchange units of account,"[76] and point at two opposing trends of further development. On the one hand, technological advances increase the speed and memory of "smart cards," further enabling them to bundle a growing number of built-in functions. On the other hand, technological progress also facilitates the direct electronic transfer between accounts, and in particular of mobile payments.[77] Thinking of online services, the latter may seem to strengthen the role of banks by reducing their dependence on the providers of card systems. By the same token, however, technological change has enabled an innovation which is deliberately designed to substitute for bank intermediation in payments and brings us to the topic of cryptocurrencies.

Crypto coins

When *Bitcoin* was introduced in 2008 under the pseudonym of *Satoshi Nakamoto*, the opening statement left no doubt about its radical objectives: "A purely

[75] Initially taking off slowly, Diners Club had attracted many competitors by the end of the decade. Among the best-known brands today are American Express, which was founded in 1850 as an express company, successfully introduced traveler's cheques in 1891, and launched its first payment card in 1958. The same year, Bank of America introduced a card system that applied a successful pricing strategy to overcome the chicken-egg problem of winning many customers to attract sufficient merchants who in turn are attracted by many customers. Licensed to other banks as well, it later evolved into Visa. Mastercard originated in a competing card association that was founded in 1966 and later merged with Europay (see Evans and Schmalensee, 2005, 2016).

[76] Evans and Schmalensee (2005, p. 26).

[77] Agarwal et al. (2019).

peer-to-peer version of electronic cash would allow online payments to be sent directly from one party to another without going through a financial institution." Discarding the fundamental premise of money as a social institution, Nakamoto explicitly "proposed a system for electronic transactions without relying on trust."[78] Coming from computer sciences rather than economics or business, the core innovation was to substitute cryptographic proofs that verify the integrity of information about a transaction for that of a trusted third party. Instead, transactions are recorded in *distributed ledgers* (DLTs) of information, where each block of data references the previous one, creating a chain of complex "hash" functions that impede any modification of past entries without the deliberate consensus among the majority of agents ("nodes") in the system.[79] Since each node must maintain and continuously update the records of all historical transactions, DLTs come at a considerable marginal cost of operations and time delay for the verification of transactions, if compared to conventional electronic payments by card or direct electronic transfer between accounts. Given the current state of technology, these pose serious restrictions on the overall scalability of the system:

> Bitcoin's design is built for a world where individuals can trust neither institutions nor each other. Such a world is very costly, because trust in institutions must be substituted by precautionary measures against potential abuse on the individual and systemic level. (Weber, 2018, p. 115)

Overall, the monetary concept behind Bitcoin constitutes a radical departure from the conventional institution of money:

> Bitcoin is a pure asset not related to credit creation processes. There is no central issuing authority behind Bitcoin and it does not represent anybody's liability. This implies that its quantity cannot be adjusted to variations in demand, and it does not come with anybody's promise to convert it into official currency at a certain rate. (Weber, 2018, p. 121)

Absent any central organization, the system is exclusively based on rules, such as those algorithms which define the maximum number of new coins to be issued per period and establish the first transaction of a new block. The "mining" of new coins is competitive and requires verifing transactions in the network by solving computational problems of growing complexity as *proof-of-work*. Successful miners chain their new block to the previous blocks and broadcast it to all other nodes.

[78] Nakamoto (2008, pp. 1, 8).

[79] Tinn (2019), Berg et al. (2019). The term ledger refers to the principal file, or "book," which records and totals economic transactions. Hash functions map keys of variable size to fixed-size values, being very sensitive to minor changes of the former.

These accept it by adding their blocks to the same chain after having verified that the items have not been spent before.

In short, Nakamoto designed electronic coins "as a chain of digital signatures" and solved the double-spending problem by means of "a peer-to-peer distributed timestamp server to generate computational proof of the chronological order of transactions."[80] To be secure, honest nodes must collectively control more computing power than any alliance which aims to hack the system. But even if such an alliance would control more than 50 percent, the idea is that the pay-offs (including transaction fees) must be higher for using that computing power to mine new coins rather than for hacking past transactions.[81] Privacy is imperative, and Bitcoin aims to preserve cash-like anonymity by cryptographic means. Unlike cash, however, blockchains record the historical data of past transactions. This increases the stakes considerably once privacy is lost due to a successful hack of a node's true identity.

Nodes can agree to change the rules. If they disagree on the rules, communities may *fork* into separate blockchains adopting a different set of rules. Forks are significant to the economics of blockchains for at least two reasons. To begin with, they demonstrate that despite their technical origin in the computer sciences peer-to-peer electronic cash remains first and foremost a social institution. Its success depends on the ability to form a consensus about the rules applied, which are then cast into the algorithms of the technical protocols.[82] Second, they induce speciation in terms of functional differentiation, but also competition between a variety of different blockchains.[83] To the extent that one considers them true currencies, blockchains thus offer a technology, which seems particularly congruent with Hayek's idea of a decentralized and competitive monetary system (Section 5.4).

As is the case with conventional fiat currencies, the price of a Bitcoin depends on expectations about its future value. Emulating the nature of gold as an exhaustible resource, the total number of Bitcoins has been restricted to a maximum of 21 million units and the rate at which they can be mined is scheduled to decline by half about every four years.[84] The quantitative restriction promises a steady,

[80] Nakamoto (2008); Double-spending refers to the problem that digital information can be easily copied for multiple uses.

[81] "If a greedy attacker is able to assemble more CPU power than all the honest nodes, he would have to choose between using it to defraud people by stealing back his payments, or using it to generate new coins. He ought to find it more profitable to play by the rules, such rules that favour him with more new coins than everyone else combined, than to undermine the system and the validity of his own wealth" (Nakamoto, 2008, p. 4).

[82] Berg et al. (2019, p. 67) consider blockchains an "institutional technology" for decentralized co-ordination. They emphasize that "the study of ledgers in historical time is the study of how human societies organise and come to consensus around facts; much broader than the study of ledgers as a structured system of accountability over financial information."

[83] Abadi and Brunnermeier (2018); Biais et al. (2019).

[84] According to the established script, about three-quarters had been released already by 2017, whereas 99 percent shall be mined until ca. 2032. The last issue of new coins will be due ca. 2140 (Weber, 2018, p. 109).

non-inflationary supply of coins. However, this does not automatically imply a high stability of its value. What is critically missing is a mechanism to adjust the supply of coins to fluctuations in the demand for Bitcoins. Unlike conventional money, it enjoys neither the elasticity of the endogenous supply of credit, nor the discretionary powers of a central bank to adjust the supply of a currency to changes in demand. As a consequence, the price of Bitcoin has fluctuated strongly over the past years. Its volatility, however, does not merely reflect its early stage of development, as Bitcoin optimists tend to believe. It follows from a fundamental flaw in its design and the simplistic monetary concept behind it. Arguably, the strict supply rules are more reminiscent of Mises's enthusiasm for the pure gold standard, rather than Hayek's acknowledgement of the need to manage a currency in order to reduce its volatility (Section 5.4). Conversely, Hayek would certainly have approved of the competition between alternative blockchains, being confident that the market would ultimately select a better design.

The question of currency competition relates to the proper definition of what constitutes an independent currency. Brunnermeier et al. deliberately link the various payment instruments to the monetary function of a unit of account rather than that of a medium of exchange. They define a collection of payment instruments to form an independent currency, if they are denominated in the same unit of account and fully convertible. Convertibility implies a legally binding peg to the common unit. In contrast, if a payment instrument retains the option to break that peg it also remains an independent currency. Hence, they conclude that Bitcoin and other "[f]iat cryptocurrencies are clearly independent currencies, as they are not convertible into anything and have their own unit of account."[85]

In principle, Bitcoin is also designed to cover all of the three classic functions of money. Not only does it establish an independent unit of value, but it serves as a liquid store of value and facilitates exchange as a convenient means of payment for certain online transactions. In practice, however, these functions are severely hampered by the high volatility of its exchange rate relative to other currencies. As Weber points out, such fluctuations pose considerable risks to sellers who would post the price of goods and services in Bitcoin, thus rendering its use as a unit of account very inconvenient. Similarly, its high volatility makes for an unreliable store of value. Finally, the function of facilitating exchange applies foremost "to transactions where costs and dangers of using official currency are higher, e.g. illicit transactions and small-denomination online payments." As a consequence, many consider it "an object of speculation, instead of functioning money."[86]

Speculation is nourished by the limited quantity of coins and the according expectation of an appreciating exchange rate. To the extent that (against Hayek's

[85] Brunnermeier et al. (2019, p. 5f).

[86] Weber (2018, p. 122ff), Pichler et al. (2018, p. 30f), Summer and Pichler (2018, p. 94); see also Corbet et al. (2020) on price volatility due to cybercrime.

reasoning) Gresham's law also applies in the case of flexible exchange rates, agents then tend to withdraw it from circulation and hoard it, thus further impeding its function as a means of payment. But even the prospects of profitable speculation are clouded by a systemic risk that is likely to undermine its long-term viability. Bitcoin's proof-of-work principle is extremely costly and inefficient in terms of energy use. In addition to the significant constraints on the scalability of DLT systems, the very operation of the blockchain depends on the willingness of nodes to verify transactions, which means that mining plus transaction fees must be profitable. The DLTs may thus imply a significant fragility of the system. If in a scenario of increasing energy costs, falling demand, and, perhaps, additional regulatory hurdles, the cost of energy ever puts sufficient pressure on miners' incomes, the most spectacular financial innovation of the early twenty-first century could end in a burst bubble.[87]

Bitcoin's success and the built-in possibility of forks has induced the creation of numerous other "cryptocurrencies," which are based on blockchains, DLTs, and open source protocols. One example is *Ether*, which runs on the Ethereum platform and was introduced in 2015. It uses a more general scripting language in support of so-called "smart contracts."[88] Ethereum has also become a popular platform for *initial coin offerings* (ICOs), where entrepreneurs raise funds by selling specific crypto tokens to be used as an exclusive means of payment for the services of a newly founded venture (e.g., another digital platform).[89] Though entrepreneurs don't have to issue shares, investors can still extract a "promoter's profit" (Section 7.9) if the coins appreciate in the course of a successful venture.

Stablecoins

The high volatility in the price of Bitcoins has induced the introduction of so-called *stablecoins*. Most are collateralized by various assets held in reserve. Others peg their value by algorithms which adjust the supply of coins to changes in demand. Berentsen and Schär point at numerous problems of the different forms, but also maintain that "blockchain enthusiasts will keep innovating relentlessly until they find a working design."[90] Yet, compared to the wasteful proof-of-work concept, a proper institutional underpinning can contribute much to increase its operational

[87] Das and Dutta (2020).

[88] *Smart contracts* are computer protocols with self-executing and self-enforcing clauses (e.g., executing payments conditional on a specified event).

[89] Catalini and Gans (2018); Fatas and Weder di Mauro (2019).

[90] Berentsen and Schär (2019, p. 69). Similarly, Auer concludes that "Bitcoin's developers have created the backbone of a first-generation decentralised infrastructure that, over the past decade, has survived many attacks. [...] In the long run, the value of cryptocurrencies might be to catalyse our thinking on how society can handle access to data and the right to edit it, a much-needed impulse at a time characterised by loss of privacy and the rise of technology-driven disinformation campaigns" (Auer, 2019a, p. 27).

efficiency. Auer therefore concludes "that in the digital age too, good money is likely to remain a *social* rather than a purely technological construct."[91]

Two notable examples have emerged in 2019. One is the dollar-backed *JPM coin* for interbank payments, which J.P. Morgan Chase offers to its institutional clients. The second example is *Libra*, which was announced with the backing of a most powerful alliance of private businesses and is aimed at a broader retail customer base. Initiated by Facebook, the founding members of the Libra Association included many of the major players in electronic payments (e.g., Mastercard, PayPal, and Visa) and online platforms (e.g., Booking Holdings, eBay, Spotify, and Uber) as well as telecommunications, blockchain technologies, venture capital, and non-profit organizations.[92] Although several founding members soon withdrew from the association due to the bleak prospects of major regulatory obstacles and political headwinds, they reportedly remain in a waiting position to see how the project develops.[93]

The mission statement of Libra emphasizes the objective of financial inclusion, especially for regions that lack efficient financial institutions. Its ambition is none lesser than "to enable a simple global currency and financial infrastructure that empowers billions of people."[94] On the technology side, Libra applies DLTs. But unlike Bitcoin, it opts for a "permissioned" system, where only members of the Libra Association can form nodes that can register transactions. This shall preserve the advantage of higher security and reliability through redundant information being distributed among the different nodes and address concerns expressed by public monetary authorities. At the same time, it significantly improves the scalability of the system. For similar reasons, Libra replaces the conventional blockchain with a structured database. On the economics side, Libra is designed to be a stablecoin—that is, fully backed by liquid assets, such as cash (equivalents) and short-term government securities. Since the weighted average of reserves determines its value, Libra is not independent of the monetary policies of the central banks. This is particularly true if Libra, as announced, supplements its multi–currency coin with coins denominated in a single currency.[95]

As far as monetary policy is concerned, the emergence of a growing variety of cryptocurrencies has given an enormous boost to the idea of currency competition. While "Hayek's proposal languished for decades, more as a curiosity than as a workable idea," technological innovations have made it real. In a recent theoretical model Fernàndez-Villaverde and Sanches (2018) provide for a "partial vindication."[96] Among their main findings, they show that immutable protocols, which enforce an upper bound to the issue of coins, can achieve price stability,

[91] Auer (2019b, p. 44); emphasis added.
[92] Libra Association (2019, p. 4).
[93] Segendorf et al. (2019).
[94] Libra Association (2019, p. 1).
[95] Libra Association (2020).
[96] Fernández-Villaverde and Sanches (2018, pp. 2, 5).

but generally won't be welfare efficient. Furthermore, they report a continuum of equilibrium trajectories, where the value of the private currencies would converge to zero. While private currencies do create problems for monetary policy, central banks can drive them out of the market by pegging the real value of their money and thereby also establish a welfare optimal equilibrium. To conclude, the innovation of crypto coins renders currencies a contestable market. Their main impact is thus to enforce discipline on the issuance of money by the government.

Digital platforms

If we allow ourselves a short digression and speculate on what Schumpeter might have thought, we may first of all assume that he would have doubted Hayek's confidence in an enduring welfare-optimal equilibrium of unfettered competition between currencies. Conversely, he probably would have embraced the idea of contestability and discipline imposed on governments by the ongoing stream of financial innovations. In addition, we may conjecture that Schumpeter would have devoted considerable attention to the industrial organization of the payments market. In modern terminology, *network effects*, which arise from the transaction costs of reporting, searching, and comparing the price of services and goods in different currencies, will favor the emergence of a dominant unit of account. Arguably, such costs have declined with the increasing speed and computational power of new ICTs. Also, the internet has enabled the emergence of global markets for specialized interests and communities that may agree to trade in a particular token. According to Brunnermeier et al., this will lead to an effective *unbundling* of the traditional functions of money:

> When switching costs are low, there is no longer a strong incentive to use one currency as both a store of value, medium of exchange, and unit of account. Instead, users of the network can seamlessly switch among currencies and convert units when needed. (Brunnermeier et al., 2019, p. 11)

Finally, if living today, Schumpeter would probably take additional clues from the literature on the economics of *online platforms*.[97] In the long term, one must expect that a certain degree of consolidation will prevail for at least the most populated virtual market places. Given a tendency of market concentration and winner-take-all dynamics, additional problems can arise if platforms are allowed to bundle their main services with the choice of a preferred own token as means of payment (let's say a Libra, or an "Amazon"). Clearly, the extraordinary economies

[97] Evans and Schmalensee (2016).

of scope of popular online platforms such as Amazon, Google, or Facebook are reminiscent of Schumpeter's late warning and gloomy prediction about the growing trustification in post-capitalist society. In this case, the past decades of ICT-driven entrepreneurship and growth would look like the "another successful run" which he had sardonically conceded to capitalism (Section 1.3).

Following the aforementioned unbundling of the traditional roles of money, Brunnermeier et al. therefore expect a *rebundling of money* with specific functions of the respective digital platforms. It follows that the specific source of competitive advantage, including positive network effects and economies of scope in favor of the largest platforms, may ultimately dominate over individual preferences with regard to the medium of exchange or the associated degree of privacy. However, the rise of digital platforms not only has great potential to affect consumer sovereignty and the industrial organization of markets, but may ultimately have significant macroeconomic implications:

> The most important consequence of a system based on digital platforms may be that agents begin to write contracts in a unit of account specific to a platform rather than the central bank's unit of account. [Consequently, t]he disappearance of the central bank's liabilities as a unit of account would eliminate the monetary authority's ability to reallocate risks among borrowers and lenders. This would also destroy the link between the interest rate set by the central bank and the arbitrage that allows monetary policy to have real effects on the provision of credit. In that case, the power of monetary policy may be severely impaired.
>
> (Brunnermeier et al., 2019, p. 28)

The announcement of Libra certainly added a sense of urgency to such concerns. The worry is that, in collaboration with the big card associations, which are also highly experienced and successful at exploiting the commercial benefits of large networks, powerful online platforms might eventually extend their dominance first to the market for electronic payments and, perhaps ultimately, to the provision of a world currency by controlling the global unit of account. Obviously, such a scenario would severely undermine the existing monetary system and leave the responsibility for its efficiency and the public good of financial stability in the hands of private business—that is, to the rationale of profit maximization.

Central bank digital currencies

The conventional means of policy in responding to the challenges posed by digital platforms and new cryptocurrencies are regulatory rules and restrictions. But the global reach of initiatives such as Libra will make international coordination particularly difficult and regulatory arbitrage very likely. Another policy option is to extend the current activities of the monetary authority and to make greater use of the technological opportunities of digitalization by introducing a *central bank digital currency* (CBDC) itself:

> A central bank digital currency (CBDC), at the most basic level, is simply monetary value stored electronically that represents a liability of the central bank, is available to the general public, and can be used to make payments. Conceptually, this could be considered as an extension of reserves to the general public, which are currently accessible only to certain financial institutions. Alternatively, a central bank could issue a digital currency in a decentralized manner, similar to how physical cash is distributed. (Engert and Fung, p. 57)

Arguably, the term "digital currency" is somewhat misleading, since in the modern economy "the vast majority of money is already electronic."[98] In addition to card payments and the direct transfer between accounts, there is a large digital infrastructure for the clearing of transactions between eligible financial organizations, which the regular users of a payment system never notice. Furthermore, the idea pre-dates the current frenzy toward digitalization. In fact, it goes back to James Tobin, who in the 1980s took issue with the moral hazard that emanates from the public insurance of private bank deposits. His solution was to replace it by "100%-reserve deposits—payable in notes or coin on demand, transferable by order to third parties, secure against loss or theft" and which he considered "a perfect store of value in the unit of account."[99] Tobin envisaged that individuals can hold this *deposit currency* either directly in (branches of) the central bank, or with the commercial banks and other financial organizations. The important point to emphasize was that "[t]he payment system and the integrity of the medium of exchange are public goods. The sovereign monetary fiat, partially delegated to private agents, must be protected" (Tobin, 1987, p. 179). Therefore, "the government should make available to the public a medium with the convenience of deposits and the safety of currency, essentially currency on deposit, transferable in any amount by check or other order" (Tobin, 1987, p. 172).

Tobin aimed at separating deposit money from commercial lending, considering their institutional linkage a mere "accident of history." The proposal, however, differs from the idea that bank money should be fully backed by reserves (the "Chicago Plan"), or initiatives for *sovereign money* ("Vollgeld").[100] In contrast to both, his proposal merely intended to provide safe and liquid deposits directly with a currency from the central bank, whereas commercial banks should continue to

[98] Barrdear and Kumhof (2016, p. 7). [99] Tobin (1985, p. 25).

[100] The Chicago Plan goes back to Irving Fisher in the 1930s and was supported by, among others, Milton Friedman. See also Benes and Kumhof (2012). On "Vollgeld," see Huber (2017).

provide credit by means of fractional reserves.[101] Tobin's deposit currency would therefore not allow for overdrafts and pay only very modest interest, thus leaving higher interest-bearing checking accounts, savings deposits, and time deposits an attractive option for commercial banks to offer: "It is this affiliate that would be subject to fractional reserve requirements and have the privilege of borrowing from the Federal Reserve. As now, these banks would be the major fulcrum of monetary policy" (Tobin, 1987, p. 175). The growing efficiency of new ICTs was already an important argument in Tobin's initial considerations. However, he could not have envisaged anything that comes close to the enormous changes which the digital revolution has since brought about. Barrdear and Kumhof were among the earliest proponents to recognize the potential that modern digitalization offers to Tobin's idea. They assume that CBDCs directly finance government bonds and thus enable lower interest rates and lower distortionary government taxes on top of a general reduction of transaction costs. Building them into a New Keynesian (NK) DSGE model with non-neutral money (Section 11.4), they report a considerable positive impact of a Tobin-like deposited currency on overall GDP.[102]

Despite Tobin's intention of maintaining a viable banking industry that fosters economic development through lending, the risk of crowding out bank deposits and thereby causing a contraction of intermediation and credit remains a major objection to the introduction of CBDCs. The general concern is that depositors internalize the greater stability of CBDCs and hence shift their funds away from commercial banks. As a consequence, "outside money" from government fiat might displace "inside money" that is backed by liabilities on the banks' balance sheet.[103] In addition, many savings of transaction costs will be realized at the expense of banking income. Cukierman therefore expects considerable political resistance to such reforms:

> In the long run issuance of a CBDC is likely to provide immediate clearing of transactions across individuals dramatically reducing the costs of clearing. This may substantially reduce the funding of private banks through checking deposits and open the door for a narrow banking system. Such a radical implementation of a CBDC is likely to encounter political opposition from the financial sector and may take a long time to materialize. (Cukierman, 2019, p. 18)

[101] Tobin (1987, p. 174) explicitly stressed that "[c]ommercial lending is an important economic function. A banker was formerly expected to be an expert in appraising the risks of particular loans, and his continuing relation to borrower-customers served both them and the economy at large."

[102] Barrdear and Kumhof (2016).

[103] *Inside money* is backed by debts from "inside the private sector" circulating as a medium of exchange. It is in zero net supply, because one agent's liability has to be some other agent's asset. Conversely, government fiat or private crypto coins represent examples of *outside money,* which characteristically is not backed by assets in zero net supply.

In contrast, Panetta points at three reasons why the introduction of CBDCs does not have to be disruptive for the banking industry. One is that some deposits may migrate to the central banks. Another is that commercial banks can offer additional lending and payment services. Finally, CBDCs may improve their recourse to wholesale funding.[104] To this one should add that the banking sector may ultimately prefer to maintain a monetary system which is anchored by the central bank and offers recourse to a lender of last resort. This will be the case if it feels threatened otherwise by an anchorless system with many private cryptocurrencies, or one that is dominated by one or a few global online platforms.[105]

During periods of crisis the opportunity to conveniently transfer funds to a CBDC may increase the probability of bank runs.[106] Against such a scenario, Kumhof and Noone develop a number of design principles that aim to prevent the crowding out of bank funding. Conversely, Brunnermeier and Niepelt argue that such a bank run need not undermine financial stability, because funds from the central bank would automatically substitute for the bank deposits held by households and firms. As depositors internalize the greater stability of the banking system, they should be even less likely to run.[107]

If we accept that the above risks can be contained by means of a proper design of the instrument, the literature credits CBDCs with at least three significant economic benefits:

- To begin with, low *transaction costs* fare prominently among the main arguments as many consider CBDCs a "practically costless medium of exchange."[108]
- Another advantage is the higher *contestability* of the market for retail payments, where central banks would force additional discipline upon the industry.[109]
- Finally, the interest paid on CBDCs provides for an additional instrument of *monetary policy*, which strengthens the influence of central banks on the market rate.

Bordo and Levin even argue that a well-designed CBDC could eliminate the need of an inflation buffer and thus allow to target a stable price level with zero inflation. Like others, they refer to the possibility of reducing the interest rate beyond the *effective lower bound* (ELB) at which people would exchange their account balances

[104] Panetta (2018, p. 27).

[105] "If digital currencies succeed in fully exploiting the value underlying the associated networks, the financial system may instead center around the owners of large digital platforms. Payments will not necessarily be linked to the provision of credit by banks" (Brunnermeier et al., 2019, p. 28).

[106] Agur et al (2019); Fernàndez-Villaverde et al. (2020).

[107] Kumhof and Noone (2018); Brunnermeier and Niepelt (2019).

[108] Bordo and Levin (2018, p. 145).

[109] Engert and Fung (2018).

for cash. To remove the ELB, however, implies that CBDCs must largely displace cash from circulation. This would raise at least three other concerns:[110]

- First of all, cash does not require special technical devices and is therefore the most *inclusive* means of payment.
- Second, cash adds variety and thus enhances the *resilience* of the payment system in case of a technical breakdown of the digital infrastructure.
- Finally, cash is the most *anonymous* and untraceable medium of exchange. In contrast with blockchains, it does not (need to) keep any records of who paid, or what for.

Technical devices tend to become ever more convenient to handle and targeted initiatives may help to also educate the marginal users. For the foreseeable future, however, it will still be necessary to maintain a basic infrastructure for the distribution of cash that reaches out to people with difficulties in accessing them. As regards the second problem, keeping sufficient cash in the vaults of the central bank may mitigate the impact of a technical breakdown, but would also reduce the initial cost advantage of a CBDC. Finally, pre-paid cards may offer a good substitute for small amounts of cash in preserving the user's privacy. For larger amounts, however, opinions largely vary about the legitimacy of anonymous transactions. Gnan and Masciandaro therefore consider the valuation of individual privacy versus state control to be the characteristic difference between those parties which are in favor and those which are opposed to CBDCs.[111] On the one hand, anonymous payments facilitate all kinds of illicit transactions, fraud, and tax evasion. On the other hand, if protective measures fail to be effective, a government-controlled payment system is a most powerful means of systematically screening the personal affairs, tastes, and preferences of individual citizens. It could be the ultimate doorway through which a *Leviathan* state can intrude. Hence, a society's overall trust in the political institutions, its democratic maturity, the status of individual liberty, and the rule of law will be important factors in the assessment. Once more, we arrive at the conclusion that, also in the age of digitalization, money at heart remains a social institution.

Problems of privacy particularly affect the *account*-based CBDCs, which follow on Tobin's idea of a "deposited currency." Offering a radically new perspective on monetary policy, these have attracted most of the academic interest. In practice, however, the alternative and less radical concept of a CBDC as non-interest-bearing value *tokens*, which substitute for cash in the payment of small amounts, can better account for privacy concerns. Operating like a private cryptocurrency, it still, however, needs a consistent system of ledgers to prevent double-spending.

[110] Pichler et al. (2019, p. 42f).

[111] Gnan and Masciandaro (2018, p. 21).

For instance, in Sweden, where cash is already on the verge of extinction, the central bank has recently started a test-pilot for the introduction of electronic cash (the *e-krona*).[112] Since Sweden belongs to the most advanced nations in the adoption of new digital technologies, its experiences might more broadly offer a valuable window to future developments. In contrast to most developed economies, where the demand for cash has remained relatively stable or even increased since the Great Recession of 2008–9, the amount of cash in circulation has already dramatically decreased in Sweden (and Norway).[113] The following statement illustrates what is at stake for the central bank:

> Since 1904, the Riksbank has had a monopoly on issuing cash. If the use of cash continues to decline at a rapid pace, Sweden is heading for a situation where the role of the state is changed and all means of payment to which the general public have access are issued and controlled by commercial agents. [...] This would involve a new set of circumstances. Firstly, the general public would no longer have access to what we call central bank money, which has a lower credit and liquidity risk than private bank money. [...] Secondly, the vulnerability of the payment system will increase if the use of cash falls so low that it no longer functions as a practically usable alternative in the event of serious and prolonged disruptions. (Sveriges Riksbank, 2018, p. 9)

Among further examples, in 2014 the *People's Bank of China* (PBOC) has initiated the project "Digital Currency/Electronic Payments" (DC/EP) to prepare the digitization of (part of) its existing monetary base by a renminbi-backed form of electronic payments. Little is yet known about its concrete arrangement, but observers assume that it will be one of the first CBDCs to become operational.[114]

To summarize, the debate about CBDCs is in flux. Most central banks still seem reluctant and cautious, with the first test pilots restricted to experiments with token-based electronic wallets that substitute for cash. The central banks would be responsible for managing a difficult transition. Hence, they must pay close attention to the manifold practical problems (such as privacy, network security, and the fear of crowding out bank deposits) that will come up. Liberated from such practical burdens and political constraints, the academic literature tends to favor

[112] Sveriges Riksbank (2017, 2018, 2020). The technological platform is a DLT with high scaleability, since the participating nodes need to be approved by the Riksbank. End users operate a digital wallet that can be installed via apps (on mobile phones, Smart Watches, etc.), a payment card, or a merchant terminal. Of related interest, see Bergara and Ponce (2018), who report on a pilot-test project of an *e-Peso* in Uruguay.

[113] Survey data for Sweden show that from 2010 to 2018 the share of persons who had paid for their most recent purchase in cash dropped from 39 percent to 13 percent (Sveriges Riksbank, 2019, p. 9). One reason has been the rapid diffusion of its popular mobile app "Swish," which offers instant account-to-account transfers between individual users.

[114] Yang and Lockett (2019).

an account-based CBDC. Three examples may illustrate the prevailing attitude in the present phase of the discourse. To begin with, Eichengreen takes issue with the lacking stability of a system that would depend on the provision of private currencies:

> [T]he only reliable way of creating a stable-value digital currency is for the central bank to issue it. The central bank can issue digital currency by fiat, as it were. It can inject it into circulation by purchasing other financial assets. It can retire it by selling those assets. It can ensure parity between its digital and non-digital liabilities by standing ready to exchange them for one another in unlimited amounts. (Eichengreen, 2019, p. 10)

Cukierman adds a note of urgency and sees benefits for public as well as private actors. On the one hand, a CBDC will be needed to maintain the sovereign capacity to conduct monetary policy. On the other hand, it prevents the alternative need for stricter regulations of private currencies:

> [Central banks] better introduce their own digital currency sooner rather than later in order to provide a dependable currency and preserve the ability to conduct monetary policy. By competing directly with the numerous aspiring private currencies such a move will also potentially reduce the burden of additional regulation of such coins. (Cukierman, 2019, p. 18)

Similarly, Brunnermeier et al. emphasize that CBDCs do not have "to compete other forms of payment out of existence." The reason is that "[t]he unit of account role of money, arguably its most important and basic function, gives the central bank power even when its liabilities are not used as a medium of exchange or a store of value." By fixing the short-term rate on its own liabilities, arbitrage extends its influence to "the whole set of monetary and financial parameters. This will be the case even if no payment was made using central bank money, and if (almost) no value was stored in the central bank balance sheet."[115] Instead, they foresee a functional differentiation. On the one hand, there will be a variety of private cryptocurrencies unbundling the functions of money as a means of exchange or a storage of value according to their specific business opportunities. On the other hand, the system needs a central bank, which provides the monetary anchor and, in cases of emergency, acts as the lender of last resort. Convertibility and interoperability of the private instruments are crucial requirements for such a system. But again, and consistent with Schumpeter's vision, the essential challenge

[115] Brunnermeier et al. (2019, p. 27f).

for the central bank is to maintain its monetary authority by means of a single unit of account:

> For monetary policy to influence credit provision and risk sharing, public money must at least be used as a unit of account. In a digital economy where most activity is conducted through networks with their own monetary instruments, a regime in which all money is convertible to CBDC would uphold the unit of account status of public money. (Brunnermeier et al., 2019, p. 29)

To conclude, the ongoing evolution of money also forces us to rethink its basic phenomenology. The fundamental premises that shaped monetary orthodoxy during the classical and neoclassical periods culminated in Menger's famous explanation of the nature and origin of money by its intrinsic properties to facilitate exchange. In striking accord with the monetary views of Wieser and Schumpeter, however, digitalization brings to the fore the immaterial function of money as a unit of social accounts, increasingly absorbing that of a medium of exchange.

14
Epilogue—a Schumpeterian heritage

> The importance of thinking broadly when engaged in research in the social sciences—to bring to bear on economics elements from sociology, political science, and history—is a hallmark for Schumpeter's work.
>
> (Eichengreen, 2010, p. 1)

The comprehensive scope and structure chosen for this book is based on two assumptions. First, that the long view going back to the history of money and monetary thought provides valuable clues for a thorough understanding of Schumpeter's monetary theory of economic development. Second, that Schumpeter's theory offers an intriguing perspective and a valid intellectual framework for the interpretation of its history and further evolution. We therefore aimed to examine the heterodox sources of Schumpeter's monetary theory and tried to follow selected traces of his concept up to the present.

Thinking of the current stream of financial innovations, one striking observation is how closely the selected topics fit into Schumpeter's perspective and how much the challenges they pose invoke his monetary vision. The final example of CBDCs illustrates this point particularly well. There is little doubt that a comprehensive assessment must take into account the role of technological change, entrepreneurial innovation, and the industrial organization of markets, together with a deep understanding of the essential functions of money and its interaction with the social fabric and political economy of a society.

To summarize, this monograph has highlighted Schumpeter's threefold affair with venture money. Commonly known but underrated is his life-long affection for monetary theory. His striving for a general dynamic theory of money and banking, developed from the singular angle of venture finance and money as the unit of social accounts, was a matter of high-flying and unfulfilled aspirations. Focusing on the venture aspects, however, one finds a fascinating, visionary, and highly original combination of his theory of creative entrepreneurship and neglected heterodox views from the history of monetary thought. To him, all the essentials of the monetary system originated in the creation and allocation of purchasing power to entrepreneurial ventures. As a pre-condition of innovation, venture finance opens new trajectories of industrial activity. Production and the monetary system co-evolve, as difficulties in the financing of innovation also

Schumpeter's Venture Money. Michael Peneder and Andreas Resch,
Oxford University Press (2021).
DOI: 10.1093/oso/9780198804383.003.0014

induce innovations in finance. These fuel economic development, but can also foster instability and recurrent crises due to exuberant expectations. Throughout its long history, money has foremost been a social technology of account rather than a mere commodity, or a legal device. Digitalization and the growing direct exchange of units of account have further exposed this to be its essential function and the ultimate pivot of monetary authority, amidst an increasing variety of private virtual assets, possibly to be used as media of exchange or stores of value.

Little known and incompletely covered has been his personal history as a failed venture investor during his years in Vienna. After abandoning his academic work to engage in a brief and disappointing affair with politics, Schumpeter embarked on serious financial adventures. As a banker and proto-venture capitalist, he co-founded a number of industrial start-ups, also trying to capitalize on his theoretical insights. Significantly, he confined himself to the investor's part, while leaving the role of the entrepreneur to his partners. Unlike others, he was not a wealthy investor by inheritance, but pursued capital gains from entrepreneurial ventures as an opportunity for social advancement. Similarly to modern venture capitalists, he and his partners tried to manage a two-sided market of investor relationships and portfolio companies. The economic rationale seemed sound, but various factors contributed to their spectacular failure. Most striking is the incongruent strategic orientation of his most influential partners, both at the Biedermannbank and in the Braun-Stammfest industrial group. Yet, more generally, one must concede that Schumpeter lacked the advanced knowledge of today's corporate finance, as well as the supportive institutional environment of the modern, highly specialized and differentiated venture capital industry. In short, his vision and confidence had rushed too far ahead of his time and personal abilities.

After the "lost years" of political and financial adventures, Schumpeter returned to his initial interest and devoted his attention to his academic work. In part still unresolved and enigmatic is his impact as a teacher of venture finance. Apparently, his attention to the role of bank credit in economic development has left an enduring impression on several of his students in Bonn who later pursued distinguished careers in development economics. Among his students at Harvard, David Rockefeller later headed the Chase Manhattan Bank, crediting Schumpeter for understanding that "banking could be a truly creative enterprise." Conversely, we do not know for certain whether Schumpeter had any direct impact on the founders of ARD, the world's first institutional venture capital organization, which had emerged in his close environment. Some acquaintanceship, however, is very likely. This especially applies to Georges Doriot, whose speeches and letters display a distinctively Schumpeterian bearing on crucial aspects of entrepreneurship and venture finance. And then, of course, many of his students at Harvard, such as Paul Samuelson, James Tobin, or Hyman Minsky, to name only a few, went on to have exceptional academic careers. Though they primarily aligned themselves with the Keynesian strands of economics, Schumpeter's scholarly mission of "opening doors" and fostering independent and investigative minds apparently fell on fertile ground. Moreover, their Schumpeterian heritage tends to be most evident when it comes to monetary issues.

The fact remains, however, that many of Schumpeter's students felt more attracted by the Keynesian paradigm than Schumpeter's theoretical concept. As Josef Steindl explained with respect to the extraordinary success of Keynes: "[a]n idea can only assert itself when the time is ripe, i.e. it can only win in alliance with powerful social currents or concerns."[1] After the Great Depression, these forces clearly favored the Keynesian agenda. However, the subsequent "arms race" between the various Keynesian and neoclassical strands of the discipline, as well as their various syntheses, continued to dominate the economics discourse throughout the twentieth century. After the spectacular collapse of his financial ventures in the 1920s and his subsequent failure to finish his money book, the consequent marginalization of his monetary ideas marked another profound defeat for Schumpeter. As in any play of lasting interest, the main character of our story was not a radiant hero, but a broken, multi-faceted personality.

Does this imply that Schumpeter's monetary concept of economic development was a blind alley, long since forgotten and thus for good? To be frank, the sophistication and technical levels of analysis have advanced so much that today one can hardly imagine the very same Joseph Schumpeter passing for any assignment to a chair in one of the leading economics departments. But neither would John M. Keynes, nor Karl Marx, nor Adam Smith. Has scientific progress rendered these thinkers obsolete, now only of interest to historians of economic thought? Obviously, this is missing the point. Scientific progress has proved many of the older hypotheses, theorems, and visions wrong, while others have been modified and adapted when absorbed into modern economic models. But only in a naive interpretation of the history of social sciences as a process of continuous progress do the latest models necessarily represent the best of the state-of-the-art or the only models one need know about.

Yet why should one care about older contributions that have since been either forgotten or displaced by newer economic models? Our response lies in the richness of variety. The case of biodiversity may illustrate the argument. Think about apples, for instance: when a few kinds displace a previously wider variety from the store shelves because of the former's superior attributes (let's say, a shinier surface, long storability, or a higher yield), valuable information and choices are lost with the older varieties that are left behind. Some consumers who miss the complex taste of an old type may nevertheless continue to seek them out for the sake of a richer experience, while a few entrepreneurial minds might be smart

[1] Steindl (1987, p. 12).

enough to use those earlier apples' genetic information to breed new types of apple. In short, we believe that the economics profession can gain from a deeper knowledge of the older theories and concepts that have emerged throughout the history of our discipline.

To conclude, Schumpeter's monetary theory of economic development may be considered an old and often unattended variety, but it is still rich in substance. Though lacking the formal resolution and technique of modern theories, its unique and comprehensive vision has endured exceptionally well. Taken as a whole, it offers no less than an endogenous explanation of innovation, growth and development, business cycles, and crises within a monetary economy that deliberately connects finance and real production. Who else can claim to offer anything remotely similar?

Moreover, the further history unfolds, the more it seems to accord with his vision. If so, what is the secret, what is the method that allowed him to connect such different parts into a coherent and undoubtedly analytical approach? We believe that the lasting quality of Schumpeter's vision relates to his profound understanding of science as a truly open system. His insistence on "opening doors" for further doubt and inquiry rather than being "conclusive" (in the sense of closing a model) aligns well with the continuous evolution of money and the corresponding stream of innovation. In other words, Schumpeter lived in the logos of *panta rhei*.

References

Bibliography

Abadi J., Brunnermeier M.K., 2018. Blockchain Economics, Working Paper No. 25407, Cambridge MA: NBER.

Agarwal S., Qian W., Yeung B.Y., Zou X., 2019. Mobile Wallet and Entrepreneurial Growth, *AEA Papers and Proceedings* 109, 48–53.

Aghion P., Howitt P., 1992. A Model of Growth Through Creative Destruction, *Econometrica* 60, 323–51.

Aghion P., Howitt P., 1998. *Endogenous Growth Theory*, Cambridge MA: MIT Press.

Aghion P., Howitt P., 2009. *The Economics of Growth*, Cambridge MA: MIT Press.

Aghion P., Angeletos G.M., Banerjee A., Manova K., 2010. Volatility and Growth: Credit Constraints and the Composition of Investment, *Journal of Monetary Economics* 57 (3), 246–65.

Aghion P., Howitt P., Levine R., 2018. Financial Development and Innovation-led Growth, in: Beck T., Levine R. (eds.), *Handbook of Finance and Development*, Cheltenham: Edward Elgar, 3–30.

Agur I., Ari A., Dell'Ariccia G., 2019. Designing Central Bank Digital Currencies, Working Paper No. 19/252, Washington: IMF.

Akcigit U., Dinlersoz E., Greenwood J., Penciakova V., 2019. Synergizing Ventures, Discussion Paper No. 13932, London: CEPR.

Akerlof G.A., 1970. The Market for Lemons: Quality Uncertainty and the Market Mechanism, *Quarterly Journal of Economics* 84 (3), 488–500.

Alchian A., 1950. Uncertainty, Evolution, and Economic Theory, *Journal of Political Economy* 58, 211–221.

Allen R. L., 1991. *Opening Doors, The Life and Work of Joseph Schumpeter*, 2 Volumes, New Brunswick: Transaction Publishers.

Allen F., Gu X., Kowalewski O., 2018. Financial Structure, Economic Growth and Development, in: Beck T., Levine R. (eds.), *Handbook of Finance and Development*, Cheltenham Edward Elgar, 31–62.

Anderl G., 2012. *"9096 Leben." Der unbekannte Judenretter Berthold Storfer*, Berlin: Rotbuch-Verlag.

Andersen E.S., 2011. *Joseph A. Schumpeter. A Theory of Social and Economic Evolution*, Basingstoke: Palgrave Macmillan.

Ante S., 2008. Creative Capital: *Georges Doriot and the Birth of Venture Capital*, Boston, MA: Harvard Business Press.

Antonelli C., Teubal M., 2008. Knowledge-intensive Property Rights and the Evolution of Venture Capitalism, *Journal of Institutional Economics* 4 (2), 163–82.

Arena R., 2015. On the Intellectual Foundations of Hayek's and Schumpeter's Economics: an Appraisal, *Journal of Evolutionary Economics* 25 (1), 77–90.

Arnon A., 2011. *Monetary Theory and Policy from Hume and Smith to Wicksell*, Cambridge: Cambridge University Press.

Auclert A., Rognlie M., 2020. Inequality and Aggregate Demand, https://web.stanford.edu/~aauclert/inequad.pdf

Auer R., 2019a. Beyond the Doomsday Economics of "Proof-of-Work" in Cryptocurrencies, Discussion Paper DP 13506, London: CEPR.

Auer R., 2019b. The Doomsday Economics of "Proof-of-Work" in Cryptocurrencies, in: Fatás A. (ed.), *The Economics of Fintech and Digital Currencies*, London: CEPR, 39–45.

Ayyagari M., Demirgüc-Kunt A., Maksimovic V., 2018. Financing SMEs and Economic Development, in: Beck T., Levine R. (eds.), *Handbook of Finance and Development*, Cheltenham: Edward Elgar, 503–33.

Ayres R.U., 1994. *Information, Entropy and Progress. A New Evolutionary Paradigm*, New York: AIP Press.

Bachinger K., Matis H., 2009. *Entwicklungsdimensionen des Kapitalismus. Klassische sozioökonomische Konzepte und Analysen*, Vienna: Böhlau Verlag.

Bagehot W., 1873. *Lombard Street. A Description of the Money Market*, New York: Wiley & Sons.

Bailey R.E., 2005. *The Economics of Financial Markets*, Cambridge: Cambridge University Press.

Balabkins N.W., 2003. Adaptation Without Attribution? The Genesis of Schumpeter's Innovator, in Backhaus J. (ed.), *Joseph Alois Schumpeter. Entrepreneurship, Style and Vision*, Boston: Kluwer, 203–20.

Barbera R.J., 2008. Preface to: Minsky (1975/2008), *John Maynard Keynes*, New York: McGraw Hill.

Barrdear J., Kumhof, M., 2016. The Macroeconomics of Central Bank Issued Digital Currencies, Staff Working Paper No. 605, London: Bank of England.

Baskin J.B., Miranti P.J., 1997. *A History of Corporate Finance*, Cambridge: Cambridge University Press.

Battilossi S., 2016. Money Markets, in: Cassis Y., Grossman R., Schenk C.R. (eds.), *The Oxford Handbook of Banking and Financial History*, Oxford: Oxford University Press, 217–39.

Baumol W.J., 2008. Really Thinking Long-Run: Keynes's Other Masterpiece, in: Pecchi L., Piga G. (eds.), 2008. *Revisiting Keynes Economic Possibilities for our Grandchildren*, Cambridge, MA: MIT Press, 199–205.

Beck T., Frame W.S., 2018. Technological Change, Financial Innovation, and Economic Development, in: Beck T., Levine R. (eds.), *Handbook of Finance and Development*, Cheltenham: Edward Elgar, 369–90.

Beck T., Levine R. (eds.), 2018. *Handbook of Finance and Development*, Cheltenham: Edward Elgar, ix–xvi.

Beck T., Demirgüc-Kunt A., Laeven L., Levine R., 2008. Finance, Firm Size and Growth, *Journal of Money, Credit and Banking* 40 (7), 1379–405.

Beck T., Levine R., Loayza N., 2000. Finance and the Sources of Growth, *Journal of Financial Economics* 58 (1), 261–300.

Becker G.S., Baumol W.J., 1952. The Classical Monetary Theory: The Outcome of the Discussion, *Economica* 19 (76), 355–76.

Benes J., Kumhof M., 2012. The Chicago Plan Revisited, Working Paper 12/202, Washington: IMF.

Berentsen A., Schär F., 2019. Stablecoins: The Quest for a Low-Volatility Cryptocurrency, in: Fatás A. (ed.), *The Economics of Fintech and Digital Currencies*, London: CEPR, 65–72.

Berg C., Davidson S., Potts J., 2019. *Understanding the Blockchain Economy. An Introduction to Institutional Cryptoeconomics*, Cheltenham: Edward Elgar.

Bergara M., Ponce J., 2018. Central Bank Digital Currency. The Uruguayan E-Peso Case, in: Gnan E., Masciandaro D. (eds.), Do We Need Central Bank Digital Currency?,

Conference Proceedings 2018/2, Vienna: SUERF – the European Money and Finance Forum, 82–90.

Berger A.N., Roman R.A., 2018. Finance and the Real Economy. Evidence from the US, in: Beck T., Levine R. (eds.), *Handbook of Finance and Development*, Cheltenham, UK: Edward Elgar, 261–88.

Bernanke B., 2000. *Essays on the Great Depression*, Princeton, NJ: Princeton University Press.

Bernanke B., Gertler M., 1989. Agency Costs, Net Worth, and Business Fluctuations, *American Economic Review* 79, 14–31.

Bernanke B., Gertler M., 1990. Financial Fragility and Economic Performance, *Quarterly Journal of Economics* 105, 87–114.

Bernanke, B., Gertler, M., Gilchrist, S., 1996. The Financial Accelerator and the Flight to Quality, *Review of Economics and Statistics* 78 (1): 1–15.

Bernstein P.L., 2005. *Capital Ideas. The Improbable Origins of Modern Wall Street*, Hoboken NJ: Wiley & Sons.

Biais B., Bisière C., Bouvard M., Casamatta C., 2019. Blockchains, Coordination, and Forks, *AEA Papers and Proceedings* 109, 88–92.

Binswanger, M., 2015. *Geld aus dem Nichts – Wie Banken Wachstum ermöglichen und Krisen verursachen*, Weinheim: Wiley-Verlag.

Blanchard O.J., 1990. Why Does Money Affect Output? A Survey, in: Friedman B.M., Hahn F.H. (eds.), *Handbook of Monetary Economics*, Vol 2, 779–835.

Blind G.D., Pyka A., 2015. Erich Schneider. The Admiring Disciple Who Did Not Become a Follower, *Journal of Evolutionary Economics* 25 (1), 239–52.

Block J.H., Fisch, C.O., van Praag M., 2017. The Schumpeterian Entrepreneur. A Review of the Empirical Evidence on the Antecedents, Behaviour and Consequences of Innovative Entrepreneurship, *Industry and Innovation* 24 (1), 61–95.

Bodenhorn H., 2018. Two Centuries of Finance and Growth in the United States, 1790–1980, in: Beck T., Levine R. (eds.), *Handbook of Finance and Development*, Cheltenham: Edward Elgar, 107–44.

Böhm S., 2015. The Best Horse in the Viennese Stables. Gottfried Haberler and Joseph Schumpeter, *Journal of Evolutionary Economics* 25 (1), 107–15.

Böhm-Bawerk E.v., 1884/90. *Kapital und Kapitalzins. Erste Abteilung, Geschichte und Kritik der Kapitalzins-Theorien / Capital and Interest. A Critical History of Economical Theory* (transl. William A. Smart), London: Macmillan.

Böhm-Bawerk E.v., 1889/91. *Kapital und Kapitalzins. Zweite Abteilung, Positive Theorie des Kapitals / The Positive Theory of Capital*, (transl. William A. Smart), New York: Macmillan.

Böhm-Bawerk E.v., 1913a. Eine "dynamische" Theorie des Kapitalzinses, *Zeitschrift für Volkswirtschaft, Socialpolitik und Verwaltung*, Bd. 22, 1–62.

Böhm-Bawerk E.v., 1913b. Eine "dynamische" Theorie des Kapitalzinses, *Schlußbemerkungen, Zeitschrift für Volkswirtschaft, Socialpolitik und Verwaltung*, Bd. 22, 640–56.

Boianovsky M., 1993. Böhm-Bawerk, Irving Fisher, and the Term "Veil of Money": a Note, *History of Political Economy* 725–38.

Boianovsky M., Trautwein H.-M., 2006. Wicksell after Woodford, *Journal of the History of Economic Thought* 28 (2), 171–85.

Boissay F., Collard F., Smets F., 2016. Booms and Banking Crisis, *Journal of Political Economy* 124 (2), 489–538.

Borchardt K., 1961. Zur Frage des Kapitalmangels in der ersten Hälfte des 19. Jahrhunderts in Deutschland, *Jahrbücher für Nationalökonomie und Statistik* 173 (5), 401–21.

Bordo M.D., Cochrane J.H., Seru A. (eds.), 2018. *The Structural Foundation of Monetary Policy*, Stanford: Hoover Institution Press.

Bordo M.D., Levin A.T., 2018. Central Bank Digital Currency and the Future of Monetary Policy, in: Bordo M.D., Cochrane J.H., Seru A. (eds.), *The Structural Foundation of Monetary Policy*, Stanford: Hoover Institution Press, 143–78.

Boyd W., 1796/1811. Report of the Committee, drawn up by Mr. Boyd, and approved by the Meeting of the 5th April; reprinted in Boyd W. (1811), *A Letter to the Right Honourable William Pitt*, 2nd edition, Ridgway, London.

Boyd W., 1800/11. A Letter to the Right Honourable William Pitt, on the Influence of the Stoppage of Issues in Specie at the Bank of England: on the Prices of Provisions, and other Commodities, reprinted in Boyd W. (1811), *A Letter to the Right Honourable William Pitt*, 2nd edition, Ridgway, London.

Braunberger G., 2016. Joseph A. Schumpeter. Ein Pionier der Makrofinanz, Schumpeter Discussion Paper: Bergische Universität Wuppertal.

Breit W., Hirsch B.T., 2009. *Lives of the Laureates. Twenty-three Nobel Economists*, 5th edition, Cambridge MA: MIT Press.

Brunnermeier M.K., Niepelt D., 2019. On the Equivalence of Private and Public Money, *Journal of Monetary Economics* 106, 27–41.

Brunnermeier M.K., Sannikov Y., 2014. A Macroeconomic Model with a Financial Sector, *American Economic Review* 104 (2), 379–421.

Brunnermeier M.K., Sannikov Y., 2016. The I Theory of Money, Discussion Paper No. 11444, London: CEPR.

Brunnermeier M.K., James H., Landau J.-P., 2019. The Digitalization of Money, Working Paper No. 26300, Cambridge, MA: NBER.

Budischowsky J., 2014. Vom Ehehindernis des (noch) bestehenden Ehebandes. Zur Zweiten Ehe Joseph Alois Schumpeters, in: *Adler. Zeitschrift für Genealogie* 26 (6–7), 65–72.

Burgelman R.A., 1983a. Corporate Entrepreneurship and Strategic Management: Insights from a Process Study, *Management Science* 29, 1349–64.

Burgelman R.A., 1983b. A Model of Interaction of Strategic Behavior, Corporate Context, and the Concept of Strategy, *Academy of Management Review* 8, 61–70.

Burhop C., Guinnane T.W., Tilly R., 2019. The Financial System in Germany, 1800–1914, in: Beck T., Levine R. (eds.), *Handbook of Finance and Development*, Cheltenham: Elgar, 148–72.

Butschek F., 2011. *Österreichische Wirtschaftsgeschichte. Von der Antike bis zur Gegenwart*, Vienna: Böhlau.

Cantner U., Dopfer K., 2015. Schumpeter and His Contemporaries – Précis and Road Marks, *Journal of Evolutionary Economics* 25 (1), 1–19.

Capie F.H., Wood G.E. (eds.), 1990. *Unregulated Banking Chaos or Order?* London: Macmillan.

Carosso V.P., 1970. *Investment Banking in America*, Cambridge, MA: Harvard University Press.

Carruthers B.G., Ariovich L., 2010. *Money and Credit. A Sociological Approach*, Cambridge: Polity Press.

Cassis Y., Cottrell P.L., 2015. *Private Banking in Europe. Rise, Retreat and Resurgence*, Oxford: Oxford University Press.

Cassis Y., Grossman R., Schenk C.R., 2016. *The Oxford Handbook of Banking and Financial History*, Oxford: Oxford University Press.

Casson M., Godley A., 2010. Entrepreneurship in Britain, 1830–1900, in: Landes D.S., Mokyr J., Baumol W. J. (eds.), *The Invention of the Enterprise. Entrepreneurship from Ancient Mesopotamia to Modern Times*, Princeton: Princeton University Press, 211–42.

Catalini C., Gans J.S., 2018. Initial Coin Offerings and the Value of Crypto Tokens, Working Paper No. 24418, Cambridge, MA: NBER.
Cesarano F., 2014. The Puzzle of Metallism. Searching for the Nature of Money, *History of Political Economy* 46 (2), 177–210.
Chaloupek G., 2010. "Neutrality of Money' versus 'Stability of the Price Level' – Issues of Monetary Theory within the Austrian School of Economics, paper presented at the 14th ESHET conference, Amsterdam, March 25–7.
Chandler A.D. Jr., 1977. *The Visible Hand. The Managerial Revolution in American Business*, Cambridge, MA: Harvard University Press.
Chick V., Dow S., 2002. Monetary Policy with Endogenous Money and Liquidity Preference: A Nondualistic Treatment, *Journal of Post Keynesian Economics* 24 (4), 5587–607.
Chick V., Tily G., 2014. Whatever Happened to Keynes's Monetary Theory, *Cambridge Journal of Economics* 38, 681–99.
Christiakis N.A., Fowler J.H., 2009. *Connected. How Your Friends' Friends' Friends Affect Everything You Feel, Think and Do*, New York: Little, Brown & Co.
Christiano L.J., Eichenbaum M.S., Trabandt M., 2018. On DSGE Models, *Journal of Economic Perspectives* 32 (5), 113–40.
Chu A., Cozzi G., Furukawa Y., Liao C.-H., 2017. Inflation and Economic Growth in a Schumpeterian Model With Endogenous Entry of Heterogenous Firms, *European Economic Review* 98, 392–409.
Chu A., Cozzi G., Furukawa Y., Liao C.-H., 2019. Inflation and Innovation in a Schumpeterian Economy with North-South Technology Transfer, *Journal of Money, Credit and Banking* 51 (2–3).
Clemence R.V., Doody F.S., 1950. The Schumpeterian System, Cambridge MA: Addison-Wesley.
Collins M., 2012. *Money and Banking in the UK. A History*, 2nd edition, London: Routledge.
Compass, Financial Yearbook, Vienna: Compassverlag.
Corbet S., Cumming D.J., Lucey B.M., Peat M., Vigne S.A., 2020. The Destabilising Effects of Cryptocurrency Cybercriminality, *Economic Letters* 191, 1–8.
Cottrell P.L., 1994. The Historical Development of Modern Banking within the United Kingdom, in: Manfred Pohl, Sabine Freitag (eds.), *Handbook on the History of European Banks*, Cheltenham: Edward Elgar, 1137–61.
Crum W.L., Schumpeter J.A., 1947. Rudimentary Mathematics for Economics and Statisticians, New York: McGraw-Hill.
Cukierman A., 2019. Welfare and Political Economy Aspects of a Central Bank Digital Currency, Discussion Paper No. 13728, London: CEPR.
Cull R., Morduch J., 2018. Microfinance and Economic Development, in: Beck T., Levine R. (eds.), *Handbook of Finance and Development*, Cheltenham: Edward Elgar, 550–71.
Cumming D. (ed.), 2012. *The Oxford Handbook of Entrepreneurial Finance*, Oxford: Oxford University Press.
Dadkhah K., 2009. *The Evolution of Macroeconomic Theory and Policy*, Springer: Berlin.
Dal-Pont Legrand M., Hagemann H., 2017. Business Cycles, Growth and Economic Policy. Schumpeter and the Great Depression, *Journal of the History of Economic Thought*, 39 (1), 19–33.
Das D., Dutta, A., 2020. Bitcoin's Energy Consumption. Is it the Achilles Heel to Miner's Revenue? *Economics Letters* 186, 1–6.
Dathe U., Hedtke U. (eds.), 2018. Habent sua Fata Professores. Joseph A. Schumpeter an Walter Eucken, Schumpeter-Archiv herausgegeben von Ulrich Hedtke.
Davis L.E., de Souza J.P.A., Hernandez G., 2019. An Empirical Analysis of Minsky Regimes in the US Economcy, *Cambridge Journal of Economics* 43, 541–84.

Dawid H., Delli Gatti D., 2018. Agent-based Macroeconomics, in: Homme C., LeBaron B. (eds.), *Handbook of Computational Economics*, Vol. IV: *Heterogeneous Agent Modeling*, Amsterdam: Elsevier, 63–156.

Dawid H., Harting P., van der Hoog S., Neugart M., 2019. Macroeconomics with Heterogenous Agent Models. Fostering Transparency, Reproducibility and Replication, *Journal of Evolutionary Economics* 29, 467–538.

De Bondt W.F.M., Thaler R.H., 1985. Does the Stock Market Overreact? *Journal of Finance* 40 (3), 793–805.

Delli Gatti D., Gallegati M., 1997. At the Root of the Financial Instability Hypothesis: "Induced Investment and Business Cycles," *Journal of Economic Issues* 31 (2), 527–34.

De Long J.B., Shleifer A., Summers L., Waldmann R., 1990a. Noise Trade Risk in Financial Markets, *Journal of Political Economy* 98, 703–38.

De Long J.B., Shleifer A., Summers L., Waldmann R., 1990b. Positive Feedback Investment Strategies and Destabilizing Rational Speculation, *Journal of Finance* 45 (2), 374–97.

Denzel M.A., 2008. The European Bill of Exchange. Its Development from the Middle Ages to 1914, in: Chaudhuri S., Denzel M.A. (eds.), *Cashless Payments and Transactions from the Antiquity to 1914*, Stuttgart: Steiner, 153–94 (quotations are from the same paper as presented at the IEHC 2006 in Helsinki).

de Roover R., 1963. *The Rise and Decline of the Medici Bank 1397–1494*, Cambridge, MA: Harvard University Press.

de Soto J.H., 2002. *Money, Bank Credit, and Economic Cycles*, 2nd edition, Auburn, AL: Ludwig von Mises Institute (English translation from 2006).

Desvernine R.E., 1936. *Democratic Despotism*, New York: Dodd, Mead & Co.

Diewert W.E., 1993. The Early History of Price Index Research, in: Diewert W.E., Nakamura A.O. (eds.), Essays in Index Number Theory, Volume 1, Amsterdam: Elsevier, 33–71.

Dimand R.W., Durlauf S.N., 2009. James Tobin and Growth Theory. Financial Factors and Long-Run Growth, *History of Political Economy* 41 (annual suppl.), 182–99.

Dinopoulos E., Thompson P., 1998. Schumpeterian Growth Without Scale Effects, *Journal of Economic Growth* 3, 313–35.

Dixit A.K., Stiglitz J.E., 1977. Monopolistic Competition and Optimum Product Diversity, *American Economic Review* 67(3), 297–308.

Dosi G., Roventini A., 2019. More is Different... and Complex! The Case for Agent-based Macroeconomics, *Journal of Evolutionary Economics* 29, 1–37.

Dosi G., Fagiolo G., Roventini A., 2010. Schumpeter Meeting Keynes: A Policy Friendly Model of Endogenous Growth and Business Cycles, *Journal of Economic Dynamics and Control* 34 (9), 1748–67.

Dosi G., Napoletano M., Roventini A., Treibich T., 2017. Micro and Macro Policies in Keynes+Schumpeter Evolutionary Models, *Journal of Evolutionary Economics* 27, 63–90.

Dosi G., Napoletano M., Roventini A., Treibich T., 2019. Debunking the Granular Origins of Aggregate Fluctuations. From Real Business Cycles Back to Keynes, *Journal of Evolutionary Economics* 29, 67–90.

Dosi G., Napoletano M., Roventini A., Stiglitz J., Treibich T., 2020. Rational Heuristics? Expectations and Behaviors in Evolving Economies with Heterogeneous Interacting Agents, Working Paper No. 26922, Cambridge, MA: NBER.

Downing N.W., 2005. Transatlantic Paper and the Emergence of the American Capital Market, in: Goetzmann W.N., Rouwenhorst K.G. (eds.), *The Origins of Value*, Oxford: Oxford University Press, 271–98.

Drake W.F., 2018a. Entropy, in: *Encyclopedia Britannica* (https://www.britannica.com/science/entropy, last updated: April 13, 2018).

Drake W.F., 2018b. Thermodynamics, in: *Encyclopedia Britannica* https://www.britannica.com/science/thermodynamics (last updated: March 23, 2018).

Edgeworth F.Y., 1888. The Mathematical Theory of Banking, *Journal of the Royal Statistical Society* 51, 113–26.

Eichengreen B., 2010. The Crisis in Financial Innovation, remarks on the occasion of the award of the Schumpeter Prize, Vienna, January 20, 2010.

Eichengreen B., 2015. *Hall of Mirrors. The Great Depression, the Great Recession, and the Uses – and Misuses – of History*, Oxford: Oxford University Press.

Eichengreen B., 2019a. *Globalizing Capital. A History of International Monetary Systems*, 3rd edition, Princeton, NJ: Princeton University Press.

Eichengreen B., 2019b. From Commodity to Fiat and Now to Crypto: What Does History Tell Us?, Working Paper No. 25426, Cambridge, MA: NBER.

Enderle-Burcel G., 2018. *Berta Zuckerkandl – Gottfried Kunwald*. Briefwechsel 1928–1938, Vienna: Böhlau.

Engert W., Fung B.S.C., 2018. Motivations and Implications of a Central Bank Digital Currency, in: Gnan E., Masciandaro B.D. (eds.), Do We Need Central Bank Digital Currency?, Conference Proceedings 2018/2, Vienna: SUERF – the European Money and Finance Forum, 56–71.

Evans D.S., Schmalensee R., 2005. *Paying with Plastic. The Digital Revolution in Buying and Borrowing*, 2nd edition, Cambridge, MA: MIT Press.

Evans D.S., Schmalensee R., 2016. *Matchmakers. The New Economics of Multisided Platforms*, Boston, MA: Harvard University Press.

Falschlehner H., s.a. 175 Jahre Schoellerbank, Vienna: Schoellerbank Aktiengesellschaft.

Fama E., 1970. Efficient Capital Markets. A Review of Theory and Empirical Work, *Journal of Finance* 25 (2), 383–417.

Fatás A. (ed.), 2019. *The Economics of Fintech and Digital Currencies*, London: CEPR.

Fatás A., Weder di Mauro B., 2019. Initial Coin Offerings. Fundamentally Different but Highly Correlated, in: Fatás A. (ed.), *The Economics of Fintech and Digital Currencies*, London: CEPR, 75–82.

Ferguson N., 2008. *The Ascent of Money. A Financial History of the World*, New York: Penguin Press.

Fernandez-Arias E., Hausmann R., Panizza U., 2020. Smart Development Banks, *Journal of Industry, Competition and Trade* 20 (2), 395–420.

Fernàndez-Villaverde J., Sanches D., 2018. On the Economics of Digital Currencies, Working Paper WP 18-07, Philadelphia: Federal Reserve Bank of Philadelphia.

Fernàndez-Villaverde J., Sanches D., Schilling L., Uhlig H., 2020. Central Bank Digital Currency. Central Banking for All?, Working Paper No. 26753, Cambridge, MA: NBER.

Festré A., 2002. Money, Banking and Dynamics: Schumpeter vs. Hayek, in: Arena R., Dangel-Hagnauer C. (eds.), *The Contribution of Joseph Schumpeter to Economics: Economic Development and Institutional Change*, London: Routledge.

Festré A., 2003. Money, Banking and Dynamics. Two Wicksellian Routes from Mises to Hayek and Schumpeter, *American Journal of Economics and Sociology* 61 (2), 439–80.

Festré A., 2006. Knut Wicksell and Ludwig von Mises on Money, Interest and Price Dynamics, *Journal of the History of Economic Thought* 28 (3), 333–57.

Festré A., Nasica E., 2009. Schumpeter on Money, Banking and Finance: An Institutionalist Perspective, *European Journal of the History of Economic Thought* 16 (2), 325–56.

Fetter F.W., 1965. *Development of British Monetary Orthodoxy*, Cambridge MA: Harvard University Press.

Fiebiger B. (ed.), 2012. Modern Monetary Theory. A Debate, PERI Working Paper No. 279, University of Massachusetts Amherst.

Fisher I., 1911/20. *The Purchasing Power of Money*, revised edition, New York: Macmillan.

Fisher I., 1930. *The Theory of Interest. As Determined by Impatience to Spend Income and Opportunity to Invest It*, New York: Macmillan.

Fisher I., 1933. The Debt-deflation Theory of Great Depressions, *Econometrica* 1, 337–57.

Fisman R., Love I., 2007. Financial Dependence and Growth Revisited, *Journal of the European Economic Association* 5 (2–3), 470–9.

Fohlin C., 2007. The History of Corporate Ownership and Control in Germany, in: Morck R.K. (ed.), *A History of Corporate Governance in the World. Family Business Groups to Professional Managers*, Chicago: University of Chicago Press, 223–82.

Fohlin C., 2016. A Brief History of Investment Banking from Medieval Times to the Present, in: Cassis Y., Grossman R., Schenk C.R. (eds.), *The Oxford Handbook of Banking and Financial History*, Oxford: Oxford University Press, 133–62.

Fontana G., 2004. Hicks on Monetary Theory and History: Money as Endogenous Money, *Cambridge Journal of Economics* 28, 73–88.

Freeman C., Soete L., 1997. *The Economics of Industrial Innovation*, 3rd edition, Cambridge MA: MIT Press.

Freudenberger H., 1996. The Schwarzenberg Bank: A Forgotten Contributor to Austrian Economic Development, 1788–1830, *Austrian History Yearbook* 27.

Frieden J.A., 2015. Currency Politics. *The Political Economy of Exchange Rate Policy*, Princeton, NJ: Princeton University Press.

Friedman M., 1959. The Demand for Money. Some Theoretical and Empirical Results, *Journal of Political Economy* 67 (4), 327–51.

Friedman M., 1968. The Role of Monetary Policy, *American Economic Review* 58 (1), 1–17.

Friedman M., 1977. Nobel Lecture: Inflation and Unemployment, *Journal of Political Economy* 85 (39), 451–72.

Friedman M., 1987. Quantity Theory of Money, in: Eatwell J., Milgate M., Newman P. (eds.), *The New Palgrave. A Dictionary of Economics*, London: Palgrave, Vol. 4, 3–20.

Friedman M., Schwartz A.J., 1963. *A Monetary History of the United States 1867–1960*, New York: NBER and Princeton: Princeton University Press.

Friedman M., 1992. Money Mischief. Episodes in Monetary History, San Diego: Harcourt Press.

Frost R., 1954. The Macmillan Gap 1931–53, *Oxford Economic Papers* 6 (2), 181–201.

Fulford S.L., 2015. How Important Are Banks for Development? Natinal Banks in the United States, 1870–1900, *Review of Economics and Statistics* 97 (5), 921–38.

Fullarton J., 1844. *On the Regulation of Currencies*, London: John Murry.

Gali J., 2008/15. *Monetary Policy, Inflation, and the Business Cycle. An Introduction to the New Keynesian Framework*, 2nd edition, Princeton, NJ: Princeton University Press.

Gali J., 2018. The State of New Keynesian Economics: A Partial Assessment, *Journal of Economic Perspectives* 32 (3), 87–112.

Gelderblom O., Jonker J., 2005. Amsterdam as the Cradle of Modern Futures and Options Trading, 1550–1650, in: Goetzmann W.N., Rouwenhorst K.G. (eds.), *The Origins of Value*, Oxford: Oxford University Press, 189–205.

Gennaioli N., Shleifer A., Vishny R., 2012. Neglected Risk, Financial Innovation, and Financial Fragility, *Journal of Financial Economics* 104, 452–68.

Georgescu-Roegen N., 1971. *The Entropy Law and the Economic Process*, Cambridge, MA: Harvard University Press.

Georgescu-Roegen N., 1992. Nicholas Georgescu-Roegen about Himself, in: Szenberg M. (ed.), *Eminent Economists. Their Life Philosophies*, Cambridge: Cambridge University Press, 128–59.

Georgescu-Roegen N., 1994. Time in Economics, in: Hagemann H. and Hamouda O.F. (eds.), *The Legacy of Hicks. His Contribution to Economic Analysis*, London: Routledge, 235–52.

Gerschenkron A., 1962. *Economic Backwardness in Historical Perspective*, Cambridge MA: Belknap.

Gertler M., Gilchrist S., 2018. What Happened: Financial Factors in the Great Recession, *Journal of Economic Perspectives* 32 (3), 3–30.

Gesell S., 1919/49. *Die Natürliche Wirtschaftsordnung*, 9th edition, Lauf: Rudolf Zitzmann Verlag.

Gnan E., Masciandaro D. (eds.), 2018. Do We Need Central Bank Digital Currency? Conference Proceedings 2018/2, Vienna: SUERF – the European Money and Finance Forum.

Goetzmann W.N., 2016. *Money Changes Everything. How Finance Made Civilization Possible*, Princeton: Princeton University Press.

Goetzmann W.N., Rouwenhorst K.G., 2005. *The Origins of Value*, Oxford: Oxford University Press.

Goldsmith R., 1969. *Financial Structure and Development*, New Haven, CT: Yale University Press.

Gompers P., Lerner J., 2004. *The Venture Capital Cycle*, 2nd edition, Cambridge, MA: MIT Press.

Goodacre A., Tonks I., 1995. Finance and Technological Change, in: Stoneman P. (ed.), *Handbook of the Economics of Innovation and Technological Change*, Oxford: Blackwell.

Goodfriend M., King R.G., 1997. The New Neoclassical Synthesis and the Role of Monetary Policy, NBER Macroeconomics Annual 12, Cambridge, MA: MIT Press, 231–96.

Goodhart C., Jensen M., 2015. Currency School versus Banking School: an Ongoing Confrontation, *Economic Thought* 4 (2), 20–31.

Goodwin R.M., 1990. Walras and Schumpeter: The Vision Reaffirmed, in: Heertje A., Perlman M. (eds.), *Evolving Technology and Market Structure. Studies in Schumpeterian Economics*, Ann Arbor, MI: University of Michigan Press, 39–49.

Grebel T., 2007. Neo-Schumpeterian Perspectives in Entrepreneurial Research, in: Hanusch H., Pyka A. (eds.), *Elgar Companion to Neo-Schumpeterian Economics*, Cheltenham: Edward Elgar, 147–58.

Green D., 1894. Pain-Cost and Opportunity-Cost, *Quarterly Journal of Economics* 8 (2), 218–29.

Greenwald B.C., Stiglitz J.E., 1987. Keynesian, New Keynesian and New Classical Economics, *Oxford Economic Papers* 39, 119–32.

Greenwald B.C., Stiglitz J.E., 1993. Financial Market Imperfections and Business Cycles, *Quarterly Journal of Economics* 108 (1), 77–114.

Greitens J., 2012. *Finanzkapital und Finanzysteme. "Das Finanzkapital" von Rudolf Hilferding*, Marburg: Metropolis.

Griffith-Jones S., Ocampo J.A, 2018. *The Future of National Development Banks*, Oxford: Oxford University Press.

Grossman G., Helpman E., 1991. *Innovation and Growth in the Global Economy*, Cambridge, MA: MIT Press.

Grubb F., 2018. Colonial American Paper Money and the Quantity Theory of Money. An Extension, *Social Science History* 43 (1), 1–23.

Guinnane T.W., 2010. Financing Technological Innovation in the Kaiserreich. Some Remarks on the Theory, Institutions, and State of the Literature, in: Kollmer-von Oheim-Loup G., Streb J. (eds.), *Finanzierung von Innovationen*, Ostfildern: Thorbecke, 169–82.

Gupta U., 2000. *Done Deals. Venture Capitalists Tell Their Stories*, Cambridge, MA: Harvard Business School Press.

Gurley J.G., Shaw E.S., 1955. Financial Aspects of Economic Development, *American Economic Review* 45 (4), 515–28.

Haberler G., 1950. Joseph Alois Schumpeter 1883–1950, *Quarterly Journal of Economics* 64 (3), 333–72.

Hagemann H., 2003. Schumpeter's Early Contribution on Crises Theory and Business-Cycle Theory, *History of Economic Ideas* 11 (1), 47–67.

Hagemann H., 2010. L. Albert Hahn's Economic Theory of Bank Credit, Working Paper No. 134, Wirtschaftsuniversität Wien, Vienna.

Hahn L.A., 1924. *Volkswirtschaftliche Theorie des Bankkredits*, 2nd edition, Tübingen: Mohr.

Haldane A.G., Turrell A.E., 2019. Drawing on Different Disciplines. Macroeconomic Agent-based Models, *Journal of Evolutionary Economics* 29, 39–66.

Hall P.A., Soskice D., 2001. *Varieties of Capitalism. The Institutional Foundations of Comparative Advantage*, Oxford: Oxford University Press.

Hanappi H., 2015. Schumpeter and Goodwin, *Journal of Evolutionary Economics* 25 (1), 277–92.

Hanusch H., 1999. Schumpeter's Life, Work and Legacy, in: Hanusch H. (ed.), *The Legacy of Joseph A. Schumpeter*, 2 Vols, Cheltenham: Edward Elgar, xi–lxiv.

Hanusch H., Pyka A. 2007. Schumpeter, Joseph Alois (1883–1950), in: Hanusch H., Pyka A. (eds.), *Elgar Companion to Neo-Schumpeterian Economics*, Cheltenham: Edward Elgar, 19–26.

Hawtrey R.G., 1919. *Currency and Credit*, London: Longmans, Green and Co.

Hayek F.A., 1929/33. Geldtheorie und Konjunkturtheorie, Beiträge zur Konjunkturforschung No. 1, Österreichisches Institut für Konjunkturforschung, Vienna (English translation: Monetary Theory and the Trade Cycle, London: Jonathan Cape).

Hayek F.A., 1931/5. *Prices and Production*, 2nd edition, New York: Kelly.

Hayek F.A., 1932. A Note on the Development of the Doctrine of "Forced Saving," *Quarterly Journal of Economics* 47 (1), 123–33.

Hayek F.A., 1939. Introduction to: Thornton H., *An Enquiry into the Nature and Effects of the Paper Credit of Great Britain, 1802*, New York: Kelly.

Hayek F.A., 1941. *The Pure Theory of Capital*, Norwich: Jarrold.

Hayek F.A., 1945. The Use of Knowledge in Society, *American Economic Review* 35 (4), 519–30.

Hayek F.A., 1976/90. *Denationalisation of Money. The Argument Refined. An Analysis of the Theory and Practice of Concurrent Currencies*, 3rd edition, London: Institute of Economic Affairs.

Heblich S., Trew A., 2019. Banking and Industrialization, *Journal of the European Economic Association* 17 (6), 1753–96.

Hedtke U., 2004a. Forschungsbericht zu Schumpeters friedenspolitischen Initiativen in den Jahren 1916–1918, Vortrag zur Schumpeter-Konferenz der Polytechnischen Hochschule Jihlava, https://schumpeter.info/schriften/Hedtke-Friedenspolitik.pdf

Hedtke U. (ed.), 2004b. Josef Alois Schumpeter. Politische Memoranden 1916–1918, Berlin, https://schumpeter.info/schriften/Memoranden.pdf

Hedtke U. (ed.), 2013. Josef Alois Schumpeter, Vorträge in der Bonner Zeit, https://schumpeter.info/schriften/Bonner-Vortraege.pdf

Hedtke U., Swedberg R. (eds.), 2000. *Joseph Alois Schumpeter, Briefe*, Tübingen: J.C.B. Mohr – Paul Siebeck.

Hein E., 2019. Financialisation and Tendencies Towards Stagnation: The Role of Macroeconomic Regime Changes in the Course of and after the Financial Economic Crisis 2007–09, *Cambridge Journal of Economics* 43, 975–99.

Heinzel C., 2013. Schumpeter and Georgescu-Roegen on the Foundations of an Evolutionary Analysis, *Cambridge Journal of Economics* 37, 251–71.

Hendrickson J.R., 2018. The Bullionist Controversy: Theory and New Evidence, *Journal of Money, Credit and Banking* 50 (1), 203–41.

Herger N., 2017. An Empirical Assessment of the Swedish Bullionist Controversy, Working Paper 17.01, Gerzensee: Study Center Gerzensee.

Herrendorf B., Rogerson R., Valentinyi A., 2013. Two Perspectives on Preferences and Structural Transformation, *American Economic Review* 103, 2752–89.

Herrnstadt-Steinmetz G., 1993. Dr. Gottfried Kunwald (Typoscript. A copy of this manuscript is available in the library of the Documentation Centre of Austrian Resistance (DÖW) in Vienna).

Hicks J. (ed.), 1982. *Money, Interest and Wages, Collected Essays on Economic Theory*, Vol. 2, Oxford: Basil Blackwell.

Hicks J., 1989. *A Market Theory of Money*, Oxford: Oxford University Press.

Hilferding R., 1910/81. *Finance Capital. A Study of the Latest Phase of Capitalist Development* [English translation from 1981], London: Routledge.

Hippel E., 1986. Lead Users: A Source of Novel Product Concepts, *Management Science* 32 (7), 791–805.

Hirshleifer D., 2015. Behavioral Finance. *Annual Review of Financial Economics* 7, 1333–59.

Holl K., 1999. Stolper, Gustav, in: Hagemann H., Krohn C.-D. (eds.), *Biographisches Handbuch der deutschsprachigen wirtschaftswissenschaftlichen Emigration nach 1933*, Vol. 2, Leichter-Zweig, Munich: Saur, 691–5.

Huber J., 2017. *Sovereign Money. Beyond Reserve Banking*, London: Palgrave Macmillan.

Hume D., 1752. Political Discourses, London: Scott.

Humphrey T.M., 1986. Cumulative Process Models from Thornton to Wicksell, Federal Reserve Bank of Richmond *Economic Review* (May/June), 18–25.

Humphrey T.M., 1991. Nonneutrality of Money in Classical Monetary Thought, Federal Reserve Bank of Richmond, *Economic Review* (May/June), 3–15.

Humphrey T.M., 2004. Classical Deflation Theory, Federal Reserve Bank of Richmond *Economic Quarterly* 90 (1), 11–32.

Hoshi T., Kashyap A., 2001. *Corporate Financing and Governance in Japan*, Cambridge, MA: MIT Press.

Hsu D.H., Kenney M., 2005. Organizing Venture Capital. The Rise and Demise of American Research & Development Corporation, 1946–1973, *Industrial and Corporate Change* 14 (4), 579–616.

Hsu P.H., Tian X., Xu Y., 2014. Financial Development and Innovation: Cross-Country Evidence, *Journal of Financial Economics* 112, 116–135.

Ingham G., 2018. A Critique of Lawson's "Social Positioning and the Nature of Money," *Cambridge Journal of Economics* 42 (3), 837–50.

Ingrao B., Sardoni C., 2019. *Banks and Finance in Modern Macroeconomics. A Historical Perspective*, Cheltenham: Edward Elgar.

Jaffe D., Russel T., 1976. Imperfect Information, Uncertainty, and Credit Rationing, *Quarterly Journal of Economics* 90 (4), 651–66.

Jakab Z., Kumhof M., 2018. Banks Are Not Intermediaries of Loanable Funds – Facts, Theory and Evidence, Staff Working Paper No. 761, London: Bank of England.

Jevons W.S., 1865. Variations of Prices and the Value of Currency since 1782, *Journal of the Royal Statistical Society* 28, 294–325.

Jevons W.S., 1875. *Money and the Mechanism of Exchange*, New York: Appleton (reprint of 1896).

Jobst C., Kernbauer H., 2016. *Die Bank. Das Geld. Der Staat. Nationalbank und Währungspolitik in Österreich 1816–2016*, Frankfurt am Main: Campus.

Jones C.I., Klenow P.J., 2016. Beyond GDP? Welfare across Countries and Time, *American Economic Review* 106 (9), 2426–57.

Jordà O., Singh S.R., Taylor A.M., 2020. The Long-Run Effects of Monetary Policy, Working Paper No. 26666, Cambridge, MA: NBER.

Jung J., Shiller, R.J., 2005. Samuelson's Dictum and the Stock Market, *Economic Inquiry* 43 (2), 221–8.

Kahneman D., Tversky A., 1979. Prospect Theory: An Analysis of Decision Under Risk, *Econometrica* 47 (2), 263–91.

Kaldor N.C., 1966. Marginal Productivity and the Macro-Economic Theories of Distribution: Comment on Samuelson and Modigliani, *Review of Economic Studies* 33 (4), 309–19.

Kaplan G., Violante G.L., 2018. Microeconomic Heterogeneity and Macroeconomic Shocks, *Journal of Economic Perspectives* 32 (3), 167–94.

Kaplan G., Moll B., Violante G.L., 2018. Monetary Policy According to HANK, *American Economic Review* 108 (3), 697–743.

Karayiannis A.D. (2005). The American Apogee of Contributions on Entrepreneurship (1880s–1920s), *American Review of Political Economy* 3 (2), 72–96.

Kehoe P.J., Midrigan V., Pastorino E., 2018. *Journal of Economic Perspectives* 32 (3), 141–66.

Keister L.A., 1997. Insider Lending and Economic Transition. The Structure, Function, and Performance Impact of Finance Companies in Chinese Business Groups, William Davidson Institute Working Paper 195, University of Michigan Business School.

Kenney M., 2014. Financiers of Innovation. The History of the Venture Capital Industry in the U.S., unpublished manuscript.

Kernbauer H., 1991. *Währungspolitik in der Zwischenkriegszeit. Geschichte der Oesterreichischen Nationalbank von 1923 bis 1938*, Vienna: Oesterreichische Nationalbank.

Keuschnigg C., Kogler M., 2020. The Schumpeterian Role of Banks: Credit Reallocation and Capital Structure, *European Economic Review* 121(C).

Keynes J.M., 1923. *A Tract on Monetary Reform*, London: Macmillan.

Keynes J.M., 1930a. *A Treatise on Money* (2 Volumes), Cambridge: Cambridge University Press.

Keynes J.M., 1930b. *Economic Possibilities for our Grandchildren*, reprinted in: Pecchi L., Piga G. (eds.), 2008. *Revisiting Keynes Economic Possibilities for our Grandchildren*, Cambridge, MA: MIT Press, 17–26.

Keynes J.M., 1936. *The General Theory of Employment, Interest and Money*, London: Palgrave Macmillan.

Kindleberger C.P., 1975. Commercial Expansion and the Industrial Revolution, MIT Working Paper No. 154, Cambridge, MA.

Kindleberger C.P., 1984. *A Financial History of Western Europe*, London: Allen & Unwin.

Kindleberger C.P., Aliber R.Z., 2005. *Manias, Panics, and Crashes. A History of Financial Crises*, 5th edition, Hoboken NJ: Wiley & Sons.

King R.G., Levine R., 1993. Finance and Growth. Schumpeter Might Be Right, *Quarterly Journal of Economics* 108 (3), 717–37.

Kirzner I.M., 1997. Entrepreneurial Discovery and the Competitive Market Process: An Austrian Approach, *Journal of Economic Literature* 35, 60–85.

Kiyotaki N., Moore J., 1997. Credit Cycles, *Journal of Political Economy* 105, 211–48.

Klamer A., 1989. An Accountant Among Economists: Conversations with Sir John R. Hicks, *Journal of Economic Perspectives* 3(4), 167–180.

Klausinger H., 1990. The Early Use of the Term "Veil of Money" in Schumpeter's Monetary Writings – A Comment, *Scandinavian Journal of Economics* 92 (4), 617–21.

Klausinger H., 1991. *Theorien der Geldwirtschaft. Von Hayek und Keynes zu neueren Ansätzen*, Berlin: Duncker & Humblot.

Klausinger H., 2008. Hayek's Monetary and Capital Theories. Puzzles and Controversies, paper presented to the HOPE workshop at Duke University, Durham, NC, December 5.

Klein B., 1974. The Competitive Supply of Money, *Journal of Money, Credit and Banking* 6 (4), 423–53.

Knapp GF., 1905/24. *The State Theory of Money*, London: Macmillan.

Knell M., 2015. Schumpeter, Minsky and the Financial Instability Hypothesis, *Journal of Evolutionary Economics* 25 (1), 293–310.

Knoll M.S., 2008. The Ancient Roots of Modern Financial Innovation. The Early History of Regulatory Arbitrage, *Oregon Law Review* 87, 93–116.

Köhler I., 2008. *Die "Arisierung" der Privatbanken im Dritten Reich*, 2nd edition, Munich: Beck.

Kohler K., Guschanski A., Stockhammer E., 2019. The Impact of Financialisation on the Wage Share: A Theoretical Clarification and Empirical test, *Cambridge Journal of Economics* 43, 937–974.

Kumhof M., Noone C., 2018. Central Bank Digital Currencies – Design Principles and Balance Sheet Implications, Staff Working Paper No. 725, London: Bank of England.

Kunwald G., 1934. *Das Leben der Erwartungs- und Kreditwirtschaft*, Jena: Gustav Fischer.

Kurz H.D., 2011. Einhundert Jahre Rudolf Hilferdings Das Finanzkapital, in: Chaloupek et al. (eds.), *Rudolf Hilferding. Finanzkapital und organisierter Kapitalismus*, Graz: Leykam.

Kurz H.D., 2012. Schumpeter's New Combinations. Revisiting his Theorie der wirtschaftlichen Entwicklung on the Occasion of its Centenary, *Journal of Evolutionary Economics* 22, 871–99.

Kurz H.D., 2015. The Beat of the Economic Heart – Joseph Schumpeter and Arthur Spiethoff on Business Cycles, *Journal of Evolutionary Economics* 25 (1), 147–62.

Kurz H.D., 2016. *Economic Thought. A Brief History*, New York: Columbia University Press.

Kuznets S., 1940. Schumpeter's Business Cycles, *American Economic Review* 30 (2), 257–71.

Kydland F.E., Prescott E.C., 1982. Time to Build and Aggregate Fluctuations, *Econometrica* 50 (6), 1345–70.

Lagos R., Rocheteau G., Wright R., 2017. Liquidity: A New Monetarist Perspective, *Journal of Economic Literature* 55 (2), 371–440.

Laidler D.E.W., 1991. *The Golden Age of the Quantity Theory*, Princeton: Princeton University Press NJ.

Laidler D.E.W., 1994. Hicks's Later Monetary Thought, in: Hagemann H. and Hamouda O.F. (eds.), *The Legacy of Hicks. His Contribution to Economic Analysis*, London: Routledge, 159–70.

Laidler D.E.W., 2000. Highlights of the Bullionist Controversy, Research Report No. 2000–2, London (Ontario): The University of Western Ontario, Department of Economics.

Laidler D.E.W., 2006. Woodford and Wicksell on Interest and Prices. The Place of the Pure Credit Economy in the Theory of Monetary Policy, *Journal of the History of Economic Thought* 28 (2), 151–9.

Lamoreaux N.R., 1996. *Insider Lending. Banks, Personal Connections, and Economic Development in Industrial New England*, Cambridge: Cambridge University Press.

Lamoreaux N.R., Sokoloff K., 2007. Introduction: The Organization and Finance of Innovation in American History, in: Lamoreaux N.R. and Sokoloff K., *Financing Innovation in the United States 1870 to the Present*, Cambridge, MA: MIT Press, 39–84.

Lamoreaux N.R., Levenstein M., Sokoloff K., 2007. Financing Invention During the Second Industrial Revolution. Cleveland, Ohio, 1870–1920, in: Lamoreaux N.R., Sokoloff K., *Financing Innovation in the United States 1870 to the Present*, Cambridge, MA: MIT Press, 39–84.

Lange O., 1941. Business Cycles. A Theoretical, Historical and Statistical Analysis of the Capitalist Process by Joseph A. Schumpeter, *Review of Economics and Statistics* 23 (4), 190–3.

La Porta R., Lopez-de-Silanes F., Shleifer A., 2002. Government Ownership of Banks, *Journal of Finance* 57 (1), 265–301.

Laski H.J., 1917. The Early History of Corporation in England, *Harvard Law Review* 30 (6), 561–88.

Law J., 1705. Money and Trade Considered. With a Proposal for Supplying the Nation with Money, London: Anderson.

Lawson T., 2016. Social Positioning and the Nature of Money, *Cambridge Journal of Economics* 40 (4), 961–96.

Lawson T., 2018. The Constitution and Nature of Money, *Cambridge Journal of Economics* 42 (3), 851–73.

Lazear E.P., 2004. Balanced Skills and Entrepreneurship, *American Economic Review* 94, 208–11.

Le Bris D., Goetzmann W.N., Pouget S., 2019. Testing Asset Pricing Theory on Six Hundred Years of Stock Returns: Prices and Dividends for the Bazacle Company from 1372 to 1946, *Journal of Financial Economics* 132 (1), 248–65.

Lehman-Hasemeyer S., Wahl F., 2017. Savings Banks and the Industrial Revolution in Prussia Supporting Regional Development with Public Financial Institutions, CEPR Discussion Paper No. DP12500, available at SSRN: https://ssrn.com/abstract=3089756

Leijonhufvud A., 1981. The Wicksell Connection. Variations on a Theme, in: *Information and Coordination. Essays in Macroeconomic Theory*, Oxford: Oxford University Press, 131–202.

Le Maux L., 2012. The Banking School and the Law of Reflux in General, *History of Political Economy* 44 (4), 595–618.

Lerner J., 2006. The New New Financial Thing: The Origins of Financial Innovations, *Journal of Financial Economics* 79, 233–55.

Lerner J., Tufano P., 2012. The Consequences of Financial Innovation: A Counterfactual Research Agenda, in: Lerner J., Stern S. (eds.), *The Rate and Direction of Inventive Activity Revisited*, Chicago: University of Chicago Press.

Levich R.M., 1988. Financial Innovations in International Financial Markets, in: Feldstein M. (ed.), *The United States in the World Economy*, Chicago: University of Chicago Press, 215–257.

Levine R., 2005. Finance and Growth: Theory and Evidence, in: Aghion P., Durlauf S. (eds.), *Handbook of Economic Growth*, Vol. 1, Amsterdam: North Holland, 865–934.

Libra Association, 2019. An Introduction to Libra. White Paper, Geneva: Libra Association.

Libra Association, 2020. An Introdution to Libra. White Paper 2.0, Geneva: Libra Association.

Liles P., 1977. Sustaining the Venture Capital Firm, Unpublished PhD Thesis, Harvard Business School (HBS Archives, Baker Business Historical Collections, Baker Business Stacks - LC Books HD69.N3L542).

Lipsey R., 1960. The Relation Bewteen Unemployment and the Rate of Change of Money Wage Rates in the United Kingdom, 1862–1957: A Further Analysis, *Economica* 27 (105), 1–31.

Lipsey R., 1978. The Place of the Phillips Curve in Macroeconomic Models, in: Bergstrom A.R., Catt A.J.L., Silverstone B.D.J. (eds.), *Stability and Inflation. A Volume of Essays to Honour the Memory of A. W.H. Phillips*, Chichester: Wiley and Sons.

Lipsey R., 2016. The Phillips Curve and an Assumed Unique Macroeconomic Equilibrium in Historical Context, *History of Political Economy* 38 (4), 415–29.

Lo A.W., 2017. *Adaptive Markets. Financial Evolution at the Speed of Thought*, Princeton: Princeton University Press NJ.

Lo A.W., Hasanhodzic J., 2010. *The Evolution of Technical Analysis. Financial Prediction from Babylonian Tablets to Bloomberg Terminals*, Hoboken NJ: Wiley & Sons.

Loayza N., Ouazad A., Ranière R., Financial Development, Growth and Crisis: Is There a Trade-Off? in: Beck T., Levine R. (eds.), *Handbook of Finance and Development*, Cheltenham: Edward Elgar, 289–311.

Lodewijk P., 2014. *The World's First Stock Exchange*, New York: Columbia University Press.

Louca F., 2015. The Improbable Econometric Connection - Schumpeter and Frisch at the Midnight of the Century, *Journal of Evolutionary Economics* 25 (1), 173–84.

Louca F., 2007. Long Waves, the Pulsation of Modern Capitalism, in: Hanusch H., Pyka A. (eds.), *Elgar Companion to Neo-Schumpeterian Economics*, Cheltenham: Edward Elgar, 766–74.

Lucas R., 1972. Expectations and the Neutrality of Money, *Journal of Economic Theory* 4 (2), 103–24.

Lucas R., 1976. Econometric Policy Evaluation: A Critique, in: Brunner K., Meltzer A. (eds.), *The Phillips Curve and Labor Markets*, New York: American Elsevier, 19–46.

Macleod H.D., 1866. *The Theory and Practice of Banking*, 2 volumes, 2nd edition, London: Longman et al.

Macleod H.D., 1893. *The Theory of Credit*, 2 volumes, 2nd edition, London: Longman et al.

Malmendier U., 2005. Roman Shares, in: Goetzmann and Rouwenhorst (eds.), *The Origins of Value*, Oxford: Oxford University Press, 31–42.

Malmendier U., 2009. Law and Finance "at the Origin." *Journal of Economic Literature* 47 (4), 1076–108.

Manaresi F., Pierri N., 2018. Credit Supply and Productivity Growth, Working Paper No. 711, Basel: BIS.

Mankiw G., 2020. A Skeptic's Guide to Modern Monetary Theory, *AEA Papers and Proceedings* 110, 141–4.

Mann F.K., 1958. Bemerkungen über Schumpeters Einfluß auf die amerikanische Wirtschaftstheorie, *Weltwirtschaftliches Archiv* 81, 149–75.

Marget A.W., 1951. The Monetary Aspects of the Schumpeterian System, *The Review of Economics and Statistics* 33 (2), 112–21.

Marshak J., 1940. Business Cycles: A Theoretical, Historical, and Statistical Analysis of the Capitalist Process by Joseph A. Schumpeter, *Journal of Political Economy* 48 (6), 889–94.

Marshall A., 1871. Money, in: Whittaker (ed.) (1975) *The Early Economic Writings of Alfred Marshall*, 2 Vols. Macmillan, London.

März E., 1983/91. *Joseph Alois Schumpeter – Forscher, Lehrer und Politiker*, Vienna: Verlag f. Geschichte u. Politik (English translation: *Joseph Schumpeter. Scholar, Teacher and Politician*, New Haven: Yale University Press).

Matis H., 2005. *Die Schwarzenberg-Bank. Kapitalbildung und Industriefinanzierung in den habsburgischen Erblanden 1787–1830*, Wien: Verlag der Österr. Akademie der Wissenschaften.

McCaffrey M., 2014. *Mises and Schumpeter: Friendly Rivals?* Mises Institute (https://mises.org/library/mises-and-schumpeter-friendly-rivals).

McCraw T., 2006. Schumpeter's Business Cycles as Business History, *Business History Review* 80 (2), 231–61.

McCraw T., 2007. *Prophet of Innovation – Joseph Schumpeter and Creative Destruction*, Cambridge MA: Belknap.

McCraw T., 2012. *The Founders and Finance. How Hamilton, Gallatin, and Other Immigrants Forged a New Economy*, Cambridge MA: Harvard University Press.

McKinnon R., 1973. *Money and Capital in Economic Development*, Washington, DC: Brookings Institution.

Menger C., 1871. *Grundsätze der Volkswirtschaftslehre*, Vienna: Braumüller.

Menger C., 1892. On the Origin of Money, *The Economic Journal* 2 (6), 239–55.

Menger C., 1909/1936. Geld, in: *Handwörterbuch der Staatswissenschaften*, 3rd edition, Volume IV (1st edition 1892; reprinted in: *The Collected Works of Carl Menger*, Volume IV, Vienna: Hölder-Pichler-Tempsky).

Mensik J., 2014. The Origins of the Income Theory of Money, *Review of Economic Perspectives* 14 (4), 373–91.

Messori M., 1997. The Trials and Misadventures of Schumpeter's Treatise on Money, *History of Political Economy* 29, 639–73.

Messori M., 2003. Credit and Money in Schumpeter's Theory, in: Arena R. and Salvadori N. (eds.), *Money, Credit and the Role of the State. Essays in Honour of Augusto Graziani*, Aldershot: Ashgate, 175–200.

Messori M., 2014. A Schumpeterian Analysis of the Credit Market, *Structural Change and Economic Dynamics* 28 (C), 43–59.

Metcalfe J.S., 1998. *Evolutionary Economics and Creative Destruction*. The Graz Schumpeter Lectures, London: Routledge.

Michaelides P., Milios J., 2005. Did Hilferding Influence Schumpeter?, *History of Economics Review* 41, 98–125.

Michaelides P., Milios J., 2015. The Schumpeter-Hilferding Nexus, *Journal of Evolutionary Economics* 25 (1), 133–46.

Michie R., 2016. *British Banking. Continuity and Change from 1694 to the Present*, Oxford: Oxford University Press.

Micklethwait J., Wooldridge A., 2003. *The Company. A Short Story of a Revoluionary Idea*, London: Weidenfeld & Nicolson.

Mill J.S., 1848/71. *The Principles of Political Economy with Some of Their Applications to Social Philosophy*, 7th edition, London: Longmans, Green and Co. (http://oll.libertyfund.org/title/101).

Miller M., Modigliani F., 1961. Dividend Policy, Growth and the Valuation of Shares, *Journal of Business* 43, 411–33.

Minsky H.P., 1954/2004. *Induced Investments and Business Cycles*, Cheltenham: Edward Elgar.

Minsky H.P., 1975/2008. *John Maynard Keynes*, New York: McGraw Hill.

Minsky H.P., 1986/2008. *Stabilizing an Unstable Economy*, New York: McGraw Hill.

Minsky H.P., 1990. Schumpeter: Finance and Evolution, in: Heertje, A., Perlman, M. (eds.), *Evolving Technology and Market Structure*, Ann Arbor, MI: University of Michigan Press, 51–74.

Minsky H.P., 1993. Schumpeter and Finance, in: Biasco S., Roncaglia A., Salvai M. (eds.), *Market and Institutions in Economic Development. Essays in Honour of Paulo Sylos Labini*, New York: St. Martin's Press, 103–15.

Mises L., 1912/53. *Theorie des Geldes und der Umlaufsmittel*, Berlin: Duncker & Humblot [quoted from the English translation (with Part IV added), *The Theory of Money and Credit*, New Haven: Yale University Press].

Mises M., 1976. *My Years with Ludwig von Mises*, New Rochelle, NY: Arlington House.

Mitchell W.F., 1999. The Origins of the Phillips Curve, University of Newcastle Working Paper No. 99–02, Callaghan, Australia: Coffee.

Modigliani F., Miller M., 1958. The Cost of Capital, Corporate Finance, and the Theory of Investment, *American Economic Review* 48, 261–97.

Mokyr J., 1998. *The British Industrial Revolution. An Economic Perspective*, 2nd edition, London: Westview Press.

Moran P., Queralto A., 2018. Innovation, Productivity, and Monetary Policy, *Journal of Monetary Economics* 93, 24–41.

Murphy A.E., 1997. *John Law. Economic Theorist and Policy Maker*, Oxford: Oxford University Press.

Murphy A.E., 2000. Canons of Monetary Orthodoxy and John Law, in: Murphy A.E., Prendergast R. (eds.), 2000. *Contributions to the History of Economic Thought*, London: Routledge, 294–317.

Murphy A.E., 2009. *The Genesis of Macroeconomics. New Ideas from Sir William Petty to Henry Thornton*, Oxford: Oxford University Press.

Naderer B., 1990. *Die Entwicklung der Geldtheorie Joseph A. Schumpeters. Statische und dynamische Theorie des Geldes im kapitalistischen Marktsystem*, Berlin: Duncker & Humblot.

Nakamoto S., 2008. Bitcoin: A Peer-to-Peer Electronic Cash System, https://bitcoin.org/bitcoin.pdf.

Natmeßnig C., 1998. *Britische Finanzinteressen in Österreich. Die Anglo-Oesterreichische Bank*, Vienna: Böhlau.

Neal L., Davis L.E., 2007. Why Did Finance Capitalism and the Second Industrial Revolution Arise in the 1890s?, in: Lamoreaux N.R. and Sokoloff K (eds.), *Financing Innovation in the United States 1870 to the Present*, Cambridge MA: MIT Press, 129–61.

Nelson R.R., Winter S.G., 1982. *An Evolutionary Theory of Economic Change*, Cambridge, MA: Belknap Press.

Ng S., Wright J.H., 2013. Facts and Challenges from the Great Recession for Forecasting and Macroeconomic Modeling, *Journal of Economic Literature* 51 (4), 1120–54.

Nicholas T., 2003. Why Schumpeter was Right: Innovation, Market Power and Creative Destruction in 1920s America, *Journal of Economic History* 63, 1023–57.

Nicholas T., 2007. Stock Market Swings and the Value of Innovation, 1908–1929 in: Lamoreaux N.R., Sokoloff K (eds.), *Financing Innovation in the United States 1870 to the Present*, Cambridge, MA: MIT Press, 217–245.

Nicholas T., 2008. Does Innovation Cause Stock-Market Runups? Evidence from the Great Crash, *American Economic Review* 98, 1370–96.

Nicholas T., Chen D., 2012. Georges Doriot and American Venture Capital, product no. 812 110 - HCB - ENG (see hbsp.harvard.edu/product/cases).

Nicolaidi M., Stockhammer E., 2017. Minsky Models: A Structured Survey, *Journal of Economic Surveys* 31 (5), 1304–31.

Nicolis G., Prigogine I., 1989. Exploring Complexity. An Introduction, New York: W.H. Freeman.

Nishi H., 2019. An Empirical Contribution to Minsky's Financial Fragility. Evidence from Non-financial Sectors in Japan, *Cambridge Journal of Economics* 43, 585–622.

Nye J., 2014. Boom, Crisis, Bust, in: Schifferes S., Roberts R. (eds.), *The Media and Financial Crises. Comparative and Historical Perspectives*, Routledge, New York.

ÖBL – *Österreichisches Biographisches Lexikon 1815–1950* (*Austrian Biographical Encyclopedia, 1815–1950*), Vienna: Österreichische Akademie der Wissenschaften.

Orrell D., Chlupaty R., 2016. *The Evolution of Money*, New York: Columbia University Press.

O'Sullivan M.A., 2007. Funding New Industries. A Historical Perspective on the Financing Role of the U.S. Stock Market in the Twentieth Century, in: Lamoreaux N.R. and Sokoloff K (eds.), *Financing Innovation in the United States 1870 to the Present*, Cambridge, MA: MIT Press, 163–216.

Österreichs Industrie, 1925. I. Band: Oberösterreich, Linz a. d. Donau, Bergland-Verlag.

Panetta F., 2018. 21st Century Cash. Central Banking, Technological Innovation and Digital Currencies, in: Gnan E., Masciandaro D. (eds.), Do We Need Central Bank Digital Currency? Conference Proceedings 2018/2, Vienna: SUERF. The European Money and Finance Forum, 23–32.

Papadimitriou D.B., 2004. Introduction: The Financial Fragility Hypothesis: the Offspring of "Induced Investment and Business Cycles," in Minsky H.P., 1954/2004. *Induced Investment and Business Cycles*, Cheltenham: Edward Elgar.

Patinkin D., 1956/89. *Money, Interest, and Prices. An Integration of Monetary and Value Theory* (abridged of 1965 2nd edition], Cambridge, MA: MIT Press.

Patinkin D., 1969. The Chicago Tradition, the Quantity Theory and Friedman, *Journal of Money, Credit and Banking* 1 (1), 46–70.

Pecchi L., Piga G. (eds.), 2008. *Revisiting Keynes Economic Possibilities for Our Grandchildren*, Cambridge, MA: MIT Press, 135–41.

Peneder M., 2001. *Entrepreneurial Competition and Industrial Location*, Cheltenham: Edward Elgar.

Peneder M., 2009. The Meaning of Entrepreneurship: A Modular Concept, *Journal of Industry, Competition and Trade* 9 (2), 77–99.

Peneder M., 2012. Firm Growth, Schumpeterian Entrepreneurship and Venture Capital, in Cumming, D.J. (ed.), *Oxford Handbook of Entrepreneurial Finance*, Oxford: Oxford University Press, 424–66.

Peneder M., 2017. Competitiveness and Industrial Policy. From Rationalities of Failure Towards the Ability to Evolve, *Cambridge Journal of Economics* 41, 829–58.

Peneder M., 2020. Digitization and the Evolution of Money as a Social Technology of Account (mimeo).

Peneder M., Resch A., 2015. Schumpeter and Venture Finance. Radical Theorist, Broke Investor and Enigmatic Teacher, *Industrial and Corporate Change* 24 (6), 1315–52.

Peneder M., Streicher G., 2018. De-industrialization and Comparative Advantage in the Global Value Chain, *Economic Systems Research* 30 (1), 85–104.

Peng Xinwei, 1994. *A Monetary History of China* (translated by Edward H. Kaplan), Bellingham, WA: Western Washington University.

Perez C., 2002. *Technological Revolutions and Financial Capital. The Dynamics of Bubbles and Golden Ages*, Cheltenham: Edward Elgar.

Pezzolo L. 2005. Bonds and Government Debt in Italian City-States, 1250–1650, in: Goetzmann and Rouwenhorst (eds.), *The Origins of Value*, Oxford: Oxford University Press, 145–63.

Phillips A.W., 1958. The Relation Between Unemplyoment and the Rate of Change of Money Wage Rates in the United Kingdom, 1861–1957, *Economica* 45, 283–99.

Pichler P., Schierlinger-Brandmayer A., Summer M., 2018. Digital Money, *OeNB Monetary Policy & The Economy* Q3/18, 87–99.

Pichler P., Summer M., Weber B., 2019. Does Digitalization Require Central Bank Digital Currencies for the General Public?, *OeNB Monetary Policy & The Economy* Q4/19, 40–56.

Pierenkemper T., 1990. Zur Finanzierung von industriellen Unternehmensgründungen im 19. Jahrhundert – mit einigen Bemerkungen über die Bedeutung der Familie, in: Petzina (ed.), *Zur Geschichte der Unternehmensfinanzierung*, Berlin: Duncker & Humblot, 69–98.

Pigou A.C., 1917. The Value of Money, *Quarterly Journal of Economics* 32 (1), 38–65.

Polanyi K., 1944. *The Great Transformation. The Political and Economic Origins of Our Time* (reprint of 1957), Boston: Beacon Press.

Polo M., Rustichello of Pisa, 1920. *The Travels of Marco Polo* (translation by Henry Yule, revised by Henri Cordier for the 1920 edition), London: John Murray (quotation from wikisource, book 2, chapter 24).

Popov A., 2018. Evidence on Finance and Economic Growth, in: Beck T., Levine R. (eds.), *Handbook of Finance and Development*, Cheltenham: Edward Elgar, 63–106.

Poterba J.M., 2005. Annuities in Early Modern Europe, in: Goetzmann and Rouwenhorst (eds.), *The Origins of Value*, Oxford: Oxford University Press, 207–24.

Potter W., 1650. *The Key of Wealth. Or a New Way for Improving of Trade*, London.

Protokolle des Ministerrates der Ersten Republik (Minutes of the Council of Ministers of the First Republic), 1982, Abteilung VIII, 20. Mai 1932 bis 25. Juli 1934, Vol. 2, Kabinett Dr. Engelbert Dollfuß, Vienna, Verlag der Österreichischen Staatsdruckerei.

The Prudential Insurance Company of America, 1915. *The Documentary History of Insurance 1000 B.C. – 1875 A.D.*, Newark, NJ: Prudential Press.

Rahner St., Schumann S., 2016. Die "deutsche Orientzigarette," in: Yavuz Köse (ed.), *Osmanen in Hamburg – eine Beziehungsgeschichte zur Zeit des Ersten Weltkrieges*, Hamburg: Hamburg University Press, 135–154.

Rajan R., Zingales L., 1998. Financial Dependence and Growth, *American Economic Review* 88, 559–86.

Rayo L., Becker G.S., 2007a. Evolutionary Efficiency and Happiness, *Journal of Political Economy* 115 (2), 302–37.

Rayo L., Becker G.S., 2007b. Habits, Peers, and Happiness. An Evolutionary Perspective, *American Economic Review: Papers and Proceedings* 97 (2), 487–91.

Redish A., 2016. Monetary Systems, in: Cassis Y., Grossman R., Schenk C.R. (eds.), *The Oxford Handbook of Banking and Financial History*, Oxford: Oxford University Press, 321–341.

Reiner M., 1989. The Transformation of Venture Capital. A History of the Venture Capital Organizations in the United States, PhD dissertation in Business Administration, Berkeley, CA: University of California.

Reinhart C.M., Rogoff, K.S., 2009. *This Time is Different. Eight Centuries of Financial Folly*, Princeton: Princeton University Press.

Resch A., 1997. Die M.L. Biedermann & Co. Bankaktiengesellschaft (1921–1927/31), in: H. Matis (ed.), *Historische Betriebsanalyse und Unternehmer*, Vienna: ÖGU, 71–99.

Resch A., 2010. Under Pressure to Adapt: Corporate Business and New Order in Post-1918 Central Europe, in: G. Bischof, F. Plasser, P. Berger (eds.), *From Empire to Republic. Post-World War I in Austria, Contemporary Austrian Studies*, Vol. XIX, New Orleans, Innsbruck: uno press, iup, 336–69.

Resch A., 2013. "Selbstverständlich...habe ich niemals etwas kriminell Belastendes gewusst." Josef Schumpeter und die Industriegruppe von Rudolf M. Braun-Stammfest nach dem Ersten Weltkrieg, in: Eigner P., Matis H., Resch A. (eds.), *Entrepreneurship in schwierigen Zeiten*, Vienna: LIT, 165–200.

Resch A., 2018. Österreichische Privatbanken von 1919 bis 1945, in: Eigner P., Falschlehner H., Resch A. (eds.), *Geschichte der österreichischen Privatbanken. Von Rothschild bis Spängler*, Wiesbaden, Springer VS, 81–211.

Resch A., Stiefel D., 2011. Vienna: The Eventful History of a Financial Center, in: Günter Bischof et al. (eds.), *Global Austria. Austria's Place in Europe and the Word*, Contemporary Austrian Studies, Vol. 20, Innsbruck: uno press, iup, 117–46.

Reserve Bank of India, 1998. Payment Systems in India, Mumbai (available at: https://m.rbi.org.in//scripts/OccasionalPublications.aspx).

Ricardo D., 1811. *The High Price of Bullion. A Proof of the Depcreciation of Bank Notes*, 4th edition, London: John Murray [quotations from Sraffa P. and Dobb M.H. (eds.), 1951. *The Works and Correspondence of David Ricardo*, Volume III, Cambridge: Cambridge University Press / reprint by the London: Liberty Fund, 47–128].

Ricardo D., 1816. *Proposals for an Economical and Secure Currency*, London: John Murray [quotations from Sraffa P. and Dobb M.H. (eds.), 1951. *The Works and Correspondence of David Ricardo*, Volume IV, Cambridge: Cambridge University Press / reprint by the London: Liberty Fund, 43–142].

Ricardo D., 1824. *Plan for the Establishment of a National Bank*, London: John Murray [quotations from Sraffa P. and Dobb M.H. (eds.), 1951. *The Works and Correspondence of David Ricardo*, Volume IV, Cambridge: Cambridge University Press / reprint by the London: Liberty Fund, 273–302].

Robertson D.H. 1922. *Money*, Cambridge: Cambridge University Press.

Robertson D.H. 1934. Industrial Fluctuation and the Natural Rate of Interest, *Economic Journal* 44 (176), 650–6.

Rockefeller D., 1964. *Creative Management in Banking*, New York: McGraw-Hill.

Rockefeller D., 2003. *Memoirs*, New York: Random House.

Rossi P., Scalise D., 2019. Financial Development and Growth in European Regions, Working Paper No. 1246, Milan: Banca D'Italia.

Rothschild K. W., 1947. *Austria's Economic Development Between the Two Wars*, London: Frederick Muller Ltd.

Rothschild K.W., 1973. Buchbesprechung zu: Schumpeter J.A., *Wesen des Geldes*, in: *Weltwirtschaftliches Archiv* 109, 140–1.

Rothschild K.W., 2015. Eduard März and Joseph Schumpeter, *Journal of Evolutionary Economics* 25 (1), 229–38.

Rouwenhorst K.G., 2005. The Origins of Mutual Funds, in: Goetzmann W.N., Rouwenhorst K.G. (eds.), *The Origins of Value*, Oxford: Oxford University Press, 249–69.

Samuelson P.A., 1943. Dynamics, Statics, and the Stationary State, *Review of Economics and Statistics* 25 (1), p. 58–68.

Samuelson P.A., 1966. Foreword by Paul A. Samuelson, in Georgescu-Roegen N., *Analytical Economics. Issues and Problems*, Cambridge, MA: Harvard University Press, vii–ix.

Samuelson P.A., 1971. Paradoxes of Schumpeter's Zero Interest Rate, *Review of Economics and Statistics*, 53 (4), 391–2.

Samuelson P.A., Solow R., 1960. Analytical Aspects of Anti-Inflation Policy, *American Economic Review* 50 (2), 177–94.

Samuelson P.A., Stolper W.F., 1941. Protection and Real Wages, *Review of Economic Studies* 9 (1): 58–73.

Sandgruber R., 1995. *Ökonomie und Politik. Österreichische Wirtschaftsgeschichte vom Mittelalter bis zur Gegenwart*, Vienna: Ueberreuter.
Sargent T.J., Wallace N., 1975. "Rational" Expectations, the Optimal Monetary Instrument, and the Optimal Money Supply Rule, *Journal of Political Economy* 83 (2), 241–54.
Sau L., 2019. Schumpeter vs. Minsky on the Evolution of Capitalism and Entrepreneurship, Working Paper 23/19, Torino: Department of Economics and Statistics, Università degli Studi di Torino.
Schlegel H. (ed.), 1987. *Das Zürich Kosmos Haus, ehemals Palais Ofenheim* (*The Zürich-Kosmos Building, formerly Palais Ofenheim*), Vienna: Zürich Kosmos Versicherungen AG.
Schlesinger K., 1914. *Theorie der Geld- und Kreditwirtschaft*, Berlin: Duncker & Humblot.
Schmandt-Besserat D., 1992. From Counting to Cuneiform, Vol. 1, Austin: University of Texas Press.
Schneider E., 1970. Joseph A. Schumpeter, Tübingen: J.C.B. Mohr.
Schularick M., Taylor A.M., 2012. Credit Booms Gone Bust: Monetary Policy, Leverage Cycles, and Financial Crises, 1870–2008, *American Economic Review* 102 (2), 1029–1061.
Schumpeter J.A. [*WHN*] 1908. *Das Wesen und der Hauptinhalt der theoretischen Nationalökonomie*, Berlin: Duncker & Humblot.
Schumpeter J.A. [CSV] 1909. On the Concept of Social Value, *Quarterly Journal of Economics* (Feb.), 213–32.
Schumpeter J.A. [GRW] 1911. Gründungsgewinn in Recht und Wirtschaft, *Zeitschrift für Notariat und freiwillige Gerichtsbarkeit in Österreich* No. 4, 25. Jänner (as reported by "Dr. M."; and reprinted in Seidl and Stolper, 1993, 123–5).
Schumpeter J.A. [*TED*] 1911/34. *Theorie der wirtschaftlichen Entwicklung*, Berlin: Duncker & Humblot [quoted from the English translation of the 3rd edition, New Brunswick: Transaction Publishers].
Schumpeter J.A. [INT] 1913. Eine "dynamische" Theorie des Kapitalzinses, *Zeitschrift für Volkswirtschaft, Socialpolitik und Verwaltung*, Bd. 22, 599–639.
Schumpeter J.A. [*EMD*] 1914/24 *Epochen der Dogmen- und Methodengeschichte*, 2nd edition 1924, Tübingen: Mohr (English translation as *Economic Doctrine and Method*, London: Allen & Unwin, 1954).
Schumpeter J.A. [BRS] 1915. Book Review of Schlesinger Karl, Theorie der Geld- und Kreditwirtschaft, *Archiv für Sozialwissenschaft und Sozialpolitik* 41 (1), 239–42.
Schumpeter J.A. [MSP] 1917–18/56. Das Sozialprodukt und die Rechenpfennige. Glossen und Beiträge zur Geldtheorie von Heute, in *Archiv für Sozialwissenschaft und Sozialpolitik* 44, 627–715 (quoted from the English translation by A.W. Marget "Money and the Social Product," *International Economic Papers* 6, 148–211).
Schumpeter J.A. [RGU] 1924. Geldwerttheorie und Währungspraxis. Einige Bemerkungen zur 2. Auflage der "Theorie des Geldes und der Umlaufmittel" von Ludwig Mises, *Die Neue Wirtschaft* 2 (5), December 12 (downloaded from Ulrich Hedtke's Schumpeter Archiv at: https://schumpeter.info/schriften/Zu-Mises.pdf).
Schumpeter J.A. [WWW] 1932. Das Woher und Wohin unserer Wissenschaft, in: Hedtke U. (2013), Josef Alois Schumpeter. Vorträge in der Bonner Zeit, Schumpeter-Archiv (www.Schumpeter.info), 102–110.
Schumpeter J.A. [RGT] 1936. Review of "The General Theory of Employment, Interest and Money" by John Maynard Keynes, *Journal of the American Statistical Association*; reprinted in Clemence, R.V. (ed.) 1989. *Joseph A. Schumpeter. Essays on Entrepreneurs, Innovations, Business Cycles, and the Evolution of Capitalism*, New Brunswick: Transaction Pub., 160–4.

Schumpeter J.A. [*BC*] 1939. *Business Cycles: A Theoretical, Historical, and Statistical Analysis of the Capitalist Process*, New York: McGraw Hill.

Schumpeter J.A. [GOL] 1941. The Future of Gold, Address to the Economic Club of Detroit, Book-Cadillac Hotel, April 14 (Harvard University Archives – Schumpeter collection: HUGFP 4.50 "Speeches, Lectures and Misc. Writings").

Schumpeter J.A. [*CSD*] 1942/50. *Capitalism, Socialism and Democracy*, 3rd edition, New York: Harper & Row.

Schumpeter J.A. [CAP1] 1943. Capitalism in the Postwar Period, in: Clemence, R.V. (ed.) (1989), *Joseph A. Schumpeter. Essays on Entrepreneurs, Innovations, Business Cycles, and the Evolution of Capitalism*, New Brunswick: Transaction Pub., 175–88.

Schumpeter J.A. [CAP2] 1946. Capitalism, in: *Encyclopedia Britannica*, Vol. IV; reprinted in Clemence, R.V. (ed.) (1989), *Joseph A. Schumpeter. Essays on Entrepreneurs, Innovations, Business Cycles, and the Evolution of Capitalism*, New Brunswick: Transaction Pub., 189–210.

Schumpeter J.A. [CRH] 1947. The Creative Response in Economic History, *Journal of Economic History* 7 (2), 149–59.

Schumpeter J.A. [INF] 1948. There is Still Time to Stop Inflation, *Nation's Business* (June), 33–5.

Schumpeter J.A. [*TGE*] 1952. *Ten Great Economists: From Marx to Keynes*, London: Routledge.

Schumpeter J.A. [*HEA*] 1954. *History of Economic Analysis*, Oxford: Oxford University Press.

Schumpeter J.A. [WDG] 1970. *Wesen des Geldes*, Göttingen: Vandenhoeck & Ruprecht.

Sée H.E., 1928. *Modern Capitalism, its Origin and Evolution* [translated by Homer B. Vanderblue and Georges F. Doriot], London: N. Douglas.

Segendorf B., Eklööf H., Gustafsson P., Landelius A., Cicovic S., 2019. What is Libra? *Economic Commentaries* No. 9, October 29, Stockholm: Sveriges Riksbank.

Segerstrom P.S., Anant T., Dinopoulos E., 1990. A Schumpeterian Model of the Product Life Cycle, *American Economic Review* 80, 1077–92.

Seidl C., Stolper W.F., 1993. *Joseph A. Schumpeter. Aufsätze zur Tagespolitik*, Tübingen: Mohr Siebeck.

Shiller R.J., 1981. Do Stock Prices Move Too Much to Be Justified by Subsequent Movements in Dividends? *American Economic Review* 71 (3), 421–36.

Shiller R.J., 2000. *Irrational Exuberance*, Princeton: Princeton University Press.

Shionoya Y., 1997. *Schumpeter and the Idea of Social Science*, Cambridge: Cambridge University Press.

Shleifer A., 2000. *Inefficient Markets. An Introduction to Behavioral Finance*, Oxford: Oxford University Press.

Sicard G., 1953. *Aux Origines des Sociétés Anonymes. Les Moulins de Toulouse au Moyen Age*, Paris: Armand Colin.

Silverberg G., 2007. Long Waves. Conceptual, Empirical and Modelling Issues, in: Hanusch H., Pyka A. (eds.), *Elgar Companion to Neo-Schumpeterian Economics*, Cheltenham: Edward Elgar, 800–19.

Simon H., 1959. Theories of Decision-making in Economics and Behavioral Science, *American Economic Review* 49, 253–83.

Singer H.W., 1950. Gains and Losses from Trade and Investment in Under-Developed Countries, *American Economic Review* 40, 473–85.

Singer H.W., 1997. The Influence of Schumpeter and Keynes on the Development of a Development Economist, in: Hagemann H. (ed.), *Zur deutschsprachigen wirtschaftswissenschaftlichen Emigration nach 1933*, Marbug: Metropolis Velag, 127–50.

Skaggs N.T., 1995. Henry Thornton and the Development of Classical Monetary Economics, *Canadian Journal of Economics* 28, 1212–27.

Skaggs N.T., 1998. Debt as the Basis of Currency. The Monetary Economics of Trust, *American Journal of Economics and Sociology* 57 (4), 453–67.

Smith A., 1776. An Inquiry into the Nature and Causes of the Wealth of Nations, Lon-don: Strahan and Caddel, Vol. 1&2 (reprint by Liberty Press).

Sobel R., 1965. *The Big Board. A History of the New York Stock Exchange*, New York: Free Press.

Sraffa P., 1951. Note on "Plan for a National Bank," in: Sraffa P. and Dobb M.H. (eds.), 1951. *The Works and Correspondence of David Ricardo*, Volume IV, Cambridge University Press/reprint by the Liberty Fund, 272–5.

Steindl J., 1987. Keynes' "General Theory" nach 50 Jahren, *Wirtschaft und Gesellschaft*, 13 (1), 11–18.

Stiefel, D., 1993. Österreich, in; H. Pohl (ed.), *Europäische Bankengeschichte*, Frankfurt/Main: Knapp.

Stiglitz J.E., Greenwald B., 2003. *Towards a New Paradigm in Monetary Economics*, Cambridge: Cambridge University Press.

Stiglitz J.E., Weiss A., 1981. Credit Rationing in Markets with Imperfect Information, *American Economic Review* 71 (3), 393–410.

Stiglitz J.E., Fitoussi J-P., Durand M., 2018, *Beyond GDP. Measuring What Counts for Economic and Social Performance*, Paris: OECD.

Stock J., Watson M., 2002. Has the Business Cycle Changed and Why? *NBER Macroeconomics Annual* 17, 159–218.

Stockhammer E., 2004. Financialisation and the Slowdown of Accumulation, *Cambridge Journal of Economics* 28, 719–41.

Stolper T., 1950. Letter to Gottfried Haberler, New York, January 17.

Stolper W.F., 1994. *Alois Schumpeter, The Public Life of a Private Man*, Princeton: Princeton University Press.

Stolper W.F., 1997. Facts without Planning, in: Hagemann H. (ed.), *Zur deutschsprachigen wirtschaftswissenschaftlichen Emigration nach 1933*, Marbug: Metropolis Velag, 95–126.

Stolper W.F., 2003. *Inside Independent Nigeria. Diaries of Wolfgang Stolper, 1960–1962*, Aldershot: Ashgate.

Streissler E., 1973. Menger's Theory of Money and Uncertainty – a Modern Interpretation, in: Hicks J.R., Weber W., *Carl Menger and the Austrian School of Economics*, Oxford: Clarendon Press, 164–189.

Streissler E., 1982. Schumpeter's Vienna and the Role of Credit in Innovation, in: Frisch H., *Schumpeterian Economics*, Eastbourne: Praeger, 60–83.

Streissler E., 1983. Schumpeter and Hayek: on Some Similarities in Their Thought, in: Machlup F., Fels G., Müller-Groeling H. (eds.), *Reflections on a Troubled World Economy*, New York: Macmillan.

Streissler E., 1994. The Influence of German and Austrian Economics on Joseph A. Schumpeter, in: Shionoya, Y., Perlman, M., *Schumpeter in the History of Ideas*, Ann Arbor: University of Michigan Press, 13–38.

Sturn R., 2016. Joseph Alois Schumpeter (1883–1950), in: Faccarello G. and Kurz H.D. (eds.), *Handbook on the History of Economic Analysis*, Volume 1. Great Economists since Petty and Boisguilbert, Cheltenham: Edward Elgar, 484–97.

Summer M., Pichler P., 2018. Digital Money, Cryptocurrencies and Central Banks, in: Gnan E., Masciandaro D. (eds.), Do We Need Central Bank Digital Currency? Conference Proceedings 2018/2, Vienna: SUERF – the European Money and Finance Forum, 91–8.

Sveriges Riksbank, 2017. The Riksbank's e-krona Projekt. Report 1, Stockholm: Sveriges Riksbank.

Sveriges Riksbank, 2018. The Riksbank's e-krona Projekt. Report 2, Stockholm: Sveriges Riksbank.

Sveriges Riksbank, 2019. Payments in Sweden 2019, Stockholm: Sveriges Riksbank.

Sveriges Riksbank, 2020. The Riksbank's e-krona Pilot. Stockholm: Sveriges Riksbank.

Swedberg R., 1991. *Joseph A. Schumpeter. His Life and Work*, Princeton: Princeton University Press.

Sylla R., 2005. Origins of the New York Stock Exchange, in: Goetzmann W.N., Rouwenhorst K.G. (eds.), *The Origins of Value*, Oxford: Oxford University Press, 299–312.

Taussig F.W., 1915. *Inventors and Money-Makers*, New York: Macmillan.

Taylor J.B., 1993. Discretion versus Policy Rules in Practice, *Carnegie-Rochester Conference Series on Public Policy* 39, 195–214.

Taylor J.B., 2009. The Financial Crisis and the Policy Response. An Empirical Analysis of What Went Wrong, in: Bank of Canada Staff (ed.), Festschrift in honour of David Dodge's contributions to Canadian public policy. Proceedings of a conference held by the Bank of Canada, November 2008, Ottawa: Bank of Canada, 1–18.

Tedlow R.S., 2001. Giants of Enterprise. Seven Business Innovators and the Empires They Built, New York: HarperCollins.

Teles P., Uhlig H., Valle e Azevedo J., 2015. Is Quantity Theory Still Alive? *Economic Journal* 126 (March), 442–64.

Thornton H., 1802/1939. *An Enquiry into the Nature and Effects of the Paper Credit of Great Britain* [edition of 1939 with an Introduction by F.A. v. Hayek], New York: Kelley.

Tichy G., 1984. Schumpeter's Monetary Theory – An Unjustly Neglected Part of his Work, in: Seidl C. (ed.), *Lectures on Schumpeterian Economics*, Berlin: Springer.

Tily G., 2012. Keynes's Monetary Theory of Interest, *BIS Papers* 65, 52–81.

Tily G., 2006. Keynes's Theory of Liquidity Preference and his Debt Management and Monetary Policies, *Cambridge Journal of Economics* 30 (5), 657–70.

TIME, 1959. Laurance Rockefeller: Space-Age Risk Capitalist, August 24, p. 50.

Tinn K., 2019. Distributed Ledger Technologies and Start-up Financing, in: Fatás A. (ed.), *The Economics of Fintech and Digital Currencies*, London: CEPR., 15–20.

Tirole J., 2006. *The Theory of Corporate Finance*, Princeton: Princeton University Press.

Tobin J., 1955. A Dynamic Aggregative Model. *Journal of Political Economy* 63, 103–15.

Tobin J., 1965. Money and Economic Growth, *Econometrica* 33, 671–84.

Tobin J., 1985. Financial Innovation and Deregulation in Perspective, *Bank of Japan Monetary and Economic Studies* 3 (2), 19–29.

Tobin J., 1987. The Case for Preserving Regulatory Distinctions, Proceedings of the Economic Policy Symposium, Jackon Hole, Federal Reserve Bank of Kansas City, 167–83.

Tooke T., 1844. An Inquiry into the Currency Principle, London: Longman.

Treichl H., 2003. *Fast ein Jahrhundert. Erinnerungen*, Vienna: Zsolnay.

Tversky A., Kahneman D., 1974. Judgment Under Uncertainty: Heuristics and Biases, *Science* 185 (4157), 1124–31.

Tversky A., Kahneman D., 1992. Advances in Prospect Theory. Cumulative Representation of Uncertainty, *Journal of Risk and Uncertainty* 5 (4), 297–323.

Ülgen F., 2014. Schumpeterian Economic Development and Financial Innovations. A Conflicting Evolution, *Journal of Institutional Economics* 10 (2), 257–77.

Usher A.P., 1934. The Origins of Banking. The Primitive Bank of Deposit, 1200–1600, *The Economic History Review* 4 (4), 399–428.

Usher A.P., 1943. *The Early History of Deposit Banking in Mediterranean Europe*, Cambridge MA: Harvard University Press.

Vanberg V., 2015. Schumpeter and Mises as "Austrian Economists," *Journal of Evolutionary Economics* 25 (1), 91–105.

van de Mierop M., 2005. The Invention of Interest. Sumerian Loans, in: Goetzmann and Rouwenhorst (eds.), *The Origins of Value*, Oxford: Oxford University Press, 17–30.

Viner J., 1937. *Studies in the Theory of International Trade*, New York: Harper.

Von Glahn R., 2005. The Origins of Paper Money in China, in: Goetzmann and Rouwenhorst (eds.), *The Origins of Value*, Oxford: Oxford University Press, 65–90.

Voth H.-J., 2018. Finance and Growth in the United Kingdom, in: Beck T., Levine R. (eds.), *Handbook of Finance and Development*, Cheltenham: Edward Elgar, 173–193.

Walras L., 1886. *Théorie de la Monnaie*, Lausanne: Corbaz.

Walsh C.E., 2017. *Monetary Theory and Policy*, 4th edition, Cambridge, MA: MIT Press.

Wasserman J., 2019. *The Marginal Revolutionaries. How Austrian Economists Fought the War of Ideas*, New Haven: Yale University Press.

Weber B., 2018. *Democratizing Money? Debating Legitimacy in Monetary Reform Proposals*, Cambridge: Cambridge University Press.

Weber F., 2016. *Vor dem großen Krach. Österreichs Bankwesen der Zwischenkriegszeit am Beispiel der Credit-Anstalt für Handel und Gewerbe*, Vienna: Böhlau.

Weissensteiner F., 2004. Dr. Gottfried Kunwald. Bundeskanzler Seipels Finanzberater und Freund, *Österreich in Geschichte und Literatur*, Vol. 48, No. 3–4, 208–226.

Werner R.A., 2014. Can Banks Individually Create Money Out of Nothing? – The Theories and the Empirical Evidence, *International Review of Financial Analysis* 36, 1–19.

Westerhuis G., 2016. Commercial Banking. Changing Interactions between Banks, Markets, Industry, and State, in: Cassis Y., Grossman R., Schenk C.R. (eds.), *The Oxford Handbook of Banking and Financial History*, Oxford: Oxford University Press, 110–132.

White L., 1984. *Free Banking in Britain*, Cambridge: Cambridge University Press.

Wicksell K., 1898/1936. *Interest and Prices. A Study of the Causes Regulating the Value of Money*, London: Macmillan.

Wieser F., 1889/93. *Der natürliche Werth*, Vienna (English translation as *Natural Value*), London: Macmillan.

Wieser F., 1891. The Austrian School and the Theory of Value, *The Economic Journal* 1, 108–121.

Wieser F., 1893. Resumption of Specie Payments in Austria-Hungary, *Journal of Political Economy* 1, 380–405.

Wieser F., 1904. Der Geldwert und seine geschichtlichen Veränderungen, *Zeitschrift für Volkswirtschaft, Sozialpolitik und Verwaltung*, XIII, Wien.

Wieser F., 1909. Der Geldwert und seine Veränderungen, *Schriften des Vereins für Socialpolitik* Vol. 132, quotation from reprint in: Hayek F.A. (ed.), *Friedrich von Wieser. Gesammelte Abhandlungen*, Saarbrücken: VDM Verlag Dr. Müller, 193–242.

Wieser F., 1914/27. *Theorie der gesellschaftlichen Wirtschaft*, Mohr: J.C.B. Tübingen (2nd edition 1924; English translation as *Social Economics*, New York: Adelphi).

Wieser F., 1927. "Geld," in: *Handwörterbuch der Staatswissenschaften*, 4th edition, Vol. IV, Jena.

Witt U., 1998. Imagination and Leadership. The Neglected Dimension of an Evolutionary Theory of the Firm, *Journal of Economic Behaviour and Organisation* 35, 161–77.

Woodford M., 2003. *Interest and Prices. Foundations of a Theory of Monetary Policy*, Princeton, NJ: Princeton University Press.

Wray R.L., 2000. The Neo-Chartalist Approach to Money, Working Paper (available at: SSRN: https://ssrn.com/abstract=1010334).

Yang Y., Lockett H., 2019. What is China's digital currency plan?, *Financial Times*, November 25 2019 (available at: https://www.ft.com/content/e3f9c3c2-0aaf-11ea-bb52-34c8d9dc6d84).

Contemporary newspapers and journals

Amtsblatt zur Wiener Zeitung
Arbeiter-Zeitung
Der Abend
Der Montag
Der Morgen
Der österreichische Volkswirt
Die Bilanzen. Beilage zum Österreichischen Volkswirt
Die Börse
Die neue Wirtschaft
Die Stunde
Neue Freie Presse
Neues Wiener Journal
Neues Wiener Tagblatt
Österreichischer Zentralkataster
Reichspost
Tages-Post
Wiener Völker Echo
Wiener Zeitung
Zentralblatt (= *Zentralblatt für Eintragungen in das Handelsregister in Österreich*).

Correspondences and gathered materials of the authors quoted in the text

Hedtke U., 2019. Correspondence by e-mail to Andreas Resch dated November 4.

Materials from the estate of Gundl Herrnstadt-Steinmetz, Vienna, provided by Georg Herrnstadt:

- Letter from Dr. Georg Stadlen, London to Gundl-Herrnstadt-Steinmetz, October 12, 1990
- Copies of the last will and a message to the posterity from Gottfried Kunwald
- Typescript of Gundl Herrnstadt-Steinmetz's article on Kunwald (see bibliography)

McCraw T., 2009. Correspondence by e-mail to Michael Peneder dated July 13.

Stolper W.F., 1999, Letter from Wolfgang F. Stolper to Andreas Resch, July 21, Ann Arbor.

Archival sources

Abbreviations and translations of archival denominations

AdR – Archiv der Republik (Archive of the Republic)
BAK – Bundesarchiv Koblenz (Federal Archives Koblenz)
Bankkommission – Banc Commission (Federal supervisory board for Austrian banks, which existed from 1921 to 1926)
Bestand GK – Bestand Gottfried Kunwald (Estate Gottfried Kunwald)
BmF – Bundesministerium für Finanzen (Federal Ministry for Finance)
BmIuU – Bundesministerium für Inneres und Unterricht (Federal Ministry of the Interior and Education)
GSTA, PK – Geheimes Staatsarchiv, Preußischer Kulturbesitz (Secret State Archives, Prussian Cultural Heritage Foundation)
Gz. – Geschäftszahl (case number)
HUA – Harvard University Archives
Lg. – Landesgericht für Strafsachen (Regional criminal court)
ÖStA – Österreichisches Staatsarchiv (Austrian State Archives)
WStLA – Wiener Stadt- und Landesarchiv (Municipal and Provincial Archives of Vienna)
Zl. – Zahl (number)

Archival materials

Archive of the Vienna University of Economics and Business

- Report cards of Josef Schumpeter, 1902/3 to 1904/5
- First Main Catalogue, First Volume, Colloquia (from 1901 to 1908/9)

Austrian State Archive

- ÖStA, AdR, BmIuU, Gz. 205,983/21
- ÖStA, AdR, BmIuU, Gz. 993/22
- ÖStA, AdR, BmIuU, Gz. 40,558/22
- ÖStA, AdR, BmIuU, Gz. 54,645/22
- ÖStA, AdR, BmIuU, Gz. 57,903/22
- ÖStA, AdR, BmF, Zl. 16,038/21
- ÖStA, AdR, BmF, Bankkommission, Boxes 17, 21, 34, 41, 45, 52
- ÖStA, Bestand GK, 616, Series 1, Boxes 198, 199, 205, 236, 240, 241, 247, 248, 249, 250, 253, 259, 757, 758, 766, 850, 851; Series 3, 887

Federal Archives Koblenz

- BAK N/1186/31 Correspondence of Gustav Stolper with Schumpeter

Harvard University Archives

- HUA, HUGFP 4.3 Beginnings of an autobiography and source material
- HUA, HUGFP 4.4 Personal letters, miscellany
- HUA, HUGFP 4.5 Mia (Maria Stöckl Bicanska)
- HUA, HUGFP 4.7, Box 4 Correspondence and other papers (Contains folder "Gundl").
- HUA, HUGFP 4.7.5 Miscellaneous correspondence
- HUA, HUGFP 66.55 Original manuscript of *Money*, in German and English, Chapt. 1–2

Municipal and Provincial Archives of Vienna

- WStLA, Lg., Box 731, VrXXIII, 5603/24, 1. – 3. Part (3 boxes)

Private Archive Ulrich Hedtke, Berlin

- *Ottilie Jäckel Letters.* Letters written by Schumpeter and mainly addressed to his former secretary at Biedermann Bank Ottilie Jäckel ("Gunde," "Gundel," or "Gunderl") in Vienna. These documents are not preserved as originals. Gottfried Haberler made xerox copies in 1971 and returned the letters to Ottilie Jäckel. During the early 1980s he made the copies available to Eduard März and Wolfgang Stolper. März's copies seem to be lost. In 1995 Stolper sent copies to Hedtke to be used for the letter edition (Hedtke and Swedberg, 2000). A few letters are published in this volume and several excerpts in März, 1983/91, (Information by email from Ulrich Hedtke, October 22, 2019)
- *Mia Stöckl Letters.* Letters written from Maria (Mia) Stöckl to Schumpeter. The original letters are preserved in the Harvard University Archives (HUGFP 4.5). Copies are stored in Ulrich Hedtke's private archive

Secret State Archives, Prussian Cultural Heritage Foundation

- GSTA, PK, I. HA Rep. 76 VA, Sekt III, Tit. IV, Nr. 55, Vol. 9, Letter from Weiss-Wellenstein to Sombart, December 28, 1925

Index